CALENDAR OF THE COURT BOOKS
OF THE BOROUGH OF NEW WOODSTOCK
1607-1622

Cover illustration: Copy of minutes of Portmoot court meeting of 24th April 1609, (B78/2) f.79.

(The illustration is reproduced by kind permission of Oxfordshire Record Office)

The Oxfordshire Record Society

CALENDAR OF THE COURT BOOKS OF THE BOROUGH OF NEW WOODSTOCK 1607-1622

(WBM B78/2 & WBM B78/3)

WBM B78/2 Edited by Royston Taylor
WBM B78/3 Edited by Mary Hodges, Pat Crutch
Mollie Moisley and Mary Hallissey

VOLUME No. 65

2007

ISBN 0 902509 53 5

Produced for the Society by
Past Historic, Kings Stanley, Gloucestershire
Printed in Great Britain

TABLE OF CONTENTS

page

FOREWORD vi

EDITORS' PREFACE vii

LIST OF ABBREVIATIONS viii

CONTENTS OF INTRODUCTION xii

INTRODUCTION xiii

EDITORIAL NOTE xlii

GLOSSARY xliii

CALENDAR OF WOODSTOCK BOROUGH COURT BOOKS 1

WBM B78/2 December 1607 – January 1614 1

WBM B78/3 January 1614 – March 1622 189

APPENDIX 1: List of Portmoot and Frankpledge Court officers 367

APPENDIX 2: Portmoot actions unresolved at March 1622 372

INDEX OF PERSONS 373

INDEX OF PLACES 405

INDEX OF SUBJECTS 411

Figure 1. Distribution of Portmoot outsider litigants 1607 – 14 xxiv

FOREWORD

This is the second edition of Woodstock Borough Court Books to be prepared by the Woodstock Society's Local History Group, as outlined in the Editors' Preface. The two volumes represent a remarkable achievement, well deserving of the Oxfordshire Record Society's warm gratitude. We hope that the example contained here will inspire others to undertake similar projects.

The Society's thanks are due first and above all to the editors. The Society would like also to express thanks to Miss Mary Hodges and to Dr Paul Brand, FBA, for their sustained encouragement of the project and for their expert advice. The Society is again grateful to Woodstock Borough Council for allowing access to the records that form this latest volume. Following on from the *Woodstock Chamberlains' Accounts, 1609*-50 (ORS vol. 58) and *The Calendar of the Court Books, 1588*-95 (ORS vol. 63), this latest edition means that Woodstock is now better served than many small towns in terms of the availability in print of its early modern records.

Oxford, October 2007

Christopher Day
General Editor, O.R.S.

EDITORS' PREFACE

The calendar of WBM B78/2 was embarked upon in 1990 as a project of a local history class, organised by the Oxford University Department for Continuing Education, under the guidance of its tutor Miss Mary Hodges.

The following members in particular partook in preparing transcripts of the English texts dealing with criminal proceedings and corporation business: Pat Crutch, Mary Hallissey, Mollie Moisley, Mary Hodges, Jack Shipp, Joan Richards, Audrey Percival, Elizabeth Woodward, Elizabeth Wood, Heather Steven, Teresa Coates, Margaret Poskitt and Violet Organ.

Subsequently, the present editors and Jack Shipp formed the Local History Group of The Woodstock Society, working on these court books and associated sources.

We acknowledge here the work done as one of the editors by Mollie Moisley, who died in June, 2006

WBM B78/2 calendar in draft served as guide for the collaborative work interpreting and structuring that for WBM B78/3.

By courtesy of the Mayor and Council, the honorary archivist for Woodstock, Dr. Molly Barratt, provided the copies of the documents essential for undertaking this work, together with continuing advice. Mr. Alan Crossley of the Victoria County History team injected vital encouragement at the start of the projects.

We are greatly indebted to Dr. Paul Brand of All Souls College, Oxford, for refereeing these texts and for the substantial improvements his advice has brought to them; and to Mr. Christopher Day as supervising editor and for seeing the volume through the press.

LIST OF ABBREVIATIONS

Common abbreviations are used for months, towns, counties and personal names

B78/1 Cal.	*Calendar of Woodstock Borough Court Book 1588-95* ed. RF Taylor (2002), *O.R.S.* 63
Baker (1977)	JH Baker, *Reports of Sir John Spelman* (Selden Soc. 94, 1977)
Baker	JH Baker, *Introduction to English Legal History*, 3rd edn. (Butterworth 1990)
Bateson	M Bateson ed. *Records of Leicester Borough III* (Cambridge, 1905)
Beier	AL Beier, *Masterless Men* (London 1987)
Bellamy	JG Bellamy, *Criminal Law & Society in Late Medieval & Tudor England* (Gloucester, 1984)
Beresford	MW Beresford, *The Common Informer* Econ. Hist. Rev. 10 (1957/8)
Bettey	JH Bettey ed. *The Casebook of Sir Francis Ashley JP, Recorder of Dorchester 1614-35* (Dorset Record Society, DRS No.7, 1981)
Bolton & Maslen	JL Bolton & M Maslen, *Calendar of Witney Court Books 1538-1610.* (*O.R.S.* 54, 1985)
Bowden	P Bowden, *Agrarian History of England & Wales IV* 1500-1640 (1967)
Briquet	C-M Briquet, *Les Filigranes*, ed. A. Stevenson (Amsterdam, 1968)
Brooks	CW Brooks, *Pettyfoggers & Vipers of the Commonwealth: Lower Branch of Legal Profession in Early Modern England* (Cambridge, 1986)
Brown	NP Brown, *Paperchase: The Dissemination of Catholic Texts in Elizabethan England,* in "English Manuscript Studies 1100 – 1700", Vol. 1, ed. P Beal & J Griffiths, (Oxford 1989).
Chambers's	*Twentieth century Dictionary,* (Edinburgh, 1952)
Cheney	CH Cheney, *Handbook of Dates* (Royal Historical Society, 1991)
Connor	RD Connor, *The Weights and Measures of England* (HMSO, 1987)
Cox	J&N Cox, "*Probate 1500 –1800*" in T.Arkell, N.Evans & N.Goose, eds. *When Death Do Us Part* (Oxford 2000)

Dalton	Michael Dalton, *The Countrey Justice* (London, 1622)
Davies	G Davies, *The Early Stuarts 1603-1660* (Oxford, 1959)
Evans	HA Evans, *Highways and Byways in Oxford and the Cotswolds* (London, 1905: Hereford, 1994)
Galloway & Murphy	JA Galloway & M Murphy, British Association of Local History, News Letter 51 (1999)
Gaskell	P Gaskell, *A New Introduction to Bibliography* (Winchester, 1995)
Gelling	M Gelling, *The Place-Names of Oxfordshire* (Cambridge, 1954)
Gilmore	GD Gilmore, unpublished commentaries on the Bedford Court of Pleas, Bedford Borough Records (1984)
Gleason	JH Gleason, *The JPs in England 1588-1640* (Oxford 1969)
Gretton	M Gretton, *Oxfordshire JPs in the 17th Century O.R.S.* 16 (1934)
Gretton R	RH Gretton, *Burford Records* (Oxford, 1920)
Hallissey & Shipp	M Hallissey & J Shipp *Inhabitants of Early 17th cent. Woodstock O.L.H.*, 3, 240, (1991)
Havinden	MA Havinden, ed., *Household and Farm Inventories in Oxfordshire 1550-1590* (London, 1965)
Herrup	CB Herrup, *The Common Peace* (Cambridge, 1987)
Hoskins	WG Hoskins, *Agricultural History Review*, XII (1964)
Ivamy	ERH Ivamy, *Law Dictionary*, 10th edn. (Butterworth 1988)
Jones	N Jones, *God and the Moneylenders* (Oxford, 1989)
Lambarde	W Lambarde, *Eirenarcha* (London 1591)
Langbein	JH Langbein, *Prosecuting Crime in the Renaissance* (Cambridge, Mass. 1974)
Latham	RE Latham, *Revised Medieval Latin Word-list* (London, 1979)
Maitland	FW Maitland, *The Forms of Action at Common Law* (Cambridge, 1962)
Milward	R Milward, *Glossary of Household, Farming & Trade Terms from Probate Inventories*, 3rd edn. (Derbyshire Record Society, 1986)
MSS Wills Oxon.	Wills & inventories of the Oxford diocese (in O.R.O.)
Muldrew	C Muldrew, *The Economy of Obligation* (Basingstoke, 1998)
Nicolson	N Nicolson, The Counties of Britain – a Tudor Atlas by John Speed (London 1988)
Notestein	W Notestein, *The House of Commons 1604-1610* (New Haven & London 1971)

O.E.D.	*Oxford English Dictionary*, 2nd edn. (Oxford 1933)
O.L.H.	*Oxfordshire Local History*
O.R.O.	Oxfordshire Record Office
O.R.S.	*Oxfordshire Record Society*
Porter	S Porter, *The Local Historian*, 23 (1993)
P.R.O.	Public Record Office – Wills proved in Prerogative Court of Canterbury (PCC)
Rep.Com.Mun.Corpns.	*Report of the Commissioners on Municipal Corporations* (1835)
Sainty	JC Sainty, *Parliamentary Functions of the Sovereign Since 1509* House of Lords, 1980
Sharpe (1984)	JA Sharpe, '*Crime in Early Modern England 1550-1750*' (London, 1984)
Sharpe (1988)	JA Sharpe, *Early Modern England – a Social History* 1550-1760) (London, 1988)
Slack	P Slack, *Trans. Royal Historical Society*, 5th series 30 (1990)
S.T.C.	WA Jackson & FS Ferguson, *A Short-title Catalogue of Books Printed in England 1475-1640* (London 1976-)
Stevenson	A Stevenson, see Briquet
Tate	WE Tate, *The Parish Chest* (Cambridge, 1983)
Taylor (1991)	RF Taylor *O.L.H.* 3 (6), (1991)
Taylor (1992)	RF Taylor *O.L.H.* 3 (8), (1992)
Trice-Martin	C Trice-Martin, *The Record Interpreter* 2nd edn. (Chichester 1982)
V.C.H.	*Victoria County History*
WBM	Woodstock Borough Muniments
WBM B82	Woodstock Borough Council Orders & Constitution 1580
WBM B83/4	Woodstock Borough Documents, miscellaneous 16/17th centuries
W.C.A.	M Maslen, *Woodstock Chamberlains' Accounts 1609-50*, *O.R.S.* 58 (1993)
Webster	CD Webster, *The Local Historian*, 24 (3), 177/8
Wills P.C.C.	Copies of Prerogative Court of Canterbury Wills, PROB 11; Public Record Office, London
Wrightson	K Wrightson, *English Society 1580-1680* (London, 1982).
Wrigley	EA Wrigley, RS Davies et. al. *English Population History from Family Reconstruction 1580-1837* (London 1997)
Youings	J Youings, *Sixteenth-Century England* (Harmondsworth, 1984)

Additional sources used in confirming Portmoot suitors and their provenance:

Barratt	DM Barratt, *Diocese & Archdeaconry of Oxford Probate Records 1516–1732*, British Record Society (1981)

Bladon Parish Registers 1545–1700

Howard-Drake	JH Drake, *Calendar of Oxford Church Court Depositions 1581-1596* (Oxford 1991-98)

International Genealogical Index, Oxfordshire & Berkshire, 1992

Oxfordshire Marriage Index 1538-1837 (in O.R.O.)

Wootton Parish Registers 1564-1700

CONTENTS OF INTRODUCTION

page

COURT OFFICERS ... xiv

PORTMOOT COURT ... xvi

USAGE & OUTCOME OF PORTMOOT ACTIONS ... xviii

PROVENANCE OF PORTMOOT LITIGANTS ... xx

CENTRAL COURTS AT WESTMINSTER ... xxiii

SOME FORMS OF ACTION ... xxv

Actions of Debt & Trespass on the case ... xxv

Action of Account ... xxv

Action of Detinue ... xxvi

Conveyance, Dower, Ejectment & Collusive Common Recovery ... xxvi

Qui Tam Actions ... xxviii

GUARDIANSHIP ... xxix

WAGER OF LAW ... xxix

USAGE OF ATTORNEYS ... xxx

APPRENTICESHIPS ... xxxi

VIEW OF FRANKPLEDGE ... xxxi

CORONER ... xxxi

SESSIONS OF THE PEACE ... xxxii

TRAVELLERS' EXAMINATIONS ... xxxv

VICTUAL LICENSING ... xxxvii

FLESH IN LENT ... xxxvii

WEIGHTS & MEASURES ... xxxviii

DEARTH SURVEY ... xxxix

ASSIZE OF BREAD & ALE ... xxxix

CORPORATION BUSINESS ... xl

WBM B78/3 ENDPAPERS ... xli

INTRODUCTION

The borough of Woodstock is fortunate in possessing some record of its court proceedings stretching from the 13th century to recent times. More particularly over the period 1581 to 1847 there are court books of various dates for the portmoot and frankpledge courts and the borough sessions court.

The present two manuscripts, WBM B78/2 and WBM B78/3, are in the care of Oxfordshire Record Office, through whom they may be inspected. They are two successive court minute books, the first from December 1607 to January 1614, the second from January 1614 to March 1622 (historical years). Each is written on paper of uniform size, 20cm by 14cm for B78/2 and 20 cm by 15cm for B78/3, enclosed in parchment wraps; is about 5cm thick and is in good condition. In B78/2 the folios are numbered 1-287, and the cover bears the inscription 'Woodstock Boock for the Portmouth Courte, beginninge 21 December..' with two more lines which are illegible. Written at the top is 'First Booke of Edm. Hiorne clarke'. In B78/3 the folios are numbered 1-261, with the cover inscribed 'Woodstock Court Booke beginning in January 1613 ...', with two more illegible lines perhaps referring to the time of Edmund Hiorne.[1]

Both are quarto books made up of eight-page sheets cut in half before folding: in the first the leaves are gathered in 16s, in the second gathered in 8s. The leaves have horizontal chain-lines, with watermarks running across the middle of half the spine-folds and with no countermarks. These are Norman papers, commonly used in English books in the 16th and 17th centuries; the two sets of similar Normandy-pot watermarks, are shown in the Calendar of B78/1 Figures 1D and 1E, and are seen to be two members of a closely related family. In B78/2 the belly of the pot carries a top band containing the letter 'P' above a central band with the initials 'DB', (Figure 1D). It has been suggested that these initials are likely to be those of Phillipe de Bosy, a paper maker of Troyes, and supplier of paper to the University of Caen in 1592. The book used for B78/3 seems to have been purchased by Hiorne for 3 shillings in Oxford in July 1614. If so, the court minutes for January to July that year were entered retrospectively from draft notes – perhaps a not uncommon practice.[2]

The two volumes contain records of the proceedings of the Portmoot court, the court leet (frankpledge), and the borough sessions court, together with aspects

[1] Hiorne and subsequent townclerks used the dialect form 'Portmouth'; those from 1584-95, and their copyists used 'Portmoth' and 'Portmothe'. The more common form in modern English is 'portmoot', and this is the style used here : as it is in the pertinent references *VCH Oxon* xii, and the Chamberlains' Accounts calendar O.R.S. 58.

[2] Gaskell (1995), 83,106; Briquet *IV*, 'pot' Figs.12740-12801; Stevenson, 34; *WCA*, 52; Brown, 129-39.

of corporation business. However, whereas B78/2 has extensive accounts of many criminal examinations these are completely absent from B78/3. Portmoot proceedings are recorded almost entirely in abbreviated law-Latin; frankpledge and the sessions court matters are largely in English but with occasional Latin in headings, recognisances, etc.; borough administration and regulatory matters are given mainly in English but again sometimes with Latin headings.

The two documents are almost entirely in the hand of the town clerk Edmund Hiorne and the first opens with his first court in that post. They are minute books providing, in places, rather full accounts of the progress of various aspects of the borough's courts and law-control; but in other places only abbreviated summaries. These minutes are broadly comparable, in their information, with those extant for the Portmoot and the court leet in the preceding years 1581 (B77/1), and 1588-1607 (B77/1, 78/1, 80). The falling away of the accounts of criminal examinations, at least, in B78/3 and B77/2 (covering the period 1622-35) perhaps reflects an intention of Hiorne to use the present compilations as aides memoire for later reference.

Thus the scope of the accounts given in these minute books is quite variable, so that for example:

> on the one hand they record many signatures and marks of litigants and witnesses including that of the recorder (**439**), examples of elaborate titling and calligraphy, and repetitive details in land conveyances which suggest their potential use as authoritative legal documents, for some matters on certain occasions;
>
> yet elsewhere the progress of Portmoot actions is recorded in minimum detail, with no information on the substance of the actions and money sums usually omitted;
>
> minutes of the borough sessions vary from extensive accounts in 1608 (**38-45**, **98-105**), to no items recorded in March 1613 and barely any misdemeanours between April 1616 and April 1619.

Court officers

A list of court officers over this period (1607-1622) is given in Appendix 1.

Edmund Hiorne was the town clerk from 10 December 1607 until his dismissal in a Civil War purge of 1645, then restored to office in 1662 until his retirement in 1663. He first took the post from his father-in-law Thomas Rawlins and finally handed over to George Ryves, his granddaughter's husband. He played a central role in much of the borough's business over this extended period and a large part of the borough's records, such as the court books and the chamberlains' accounts, are in his hand.

Though we have no reference to Hiorne's education in law, his duties and record as clerk of the borough's courts, and as deputy steward of Woodstock manor, suggest that like similar office-holders elsewhere he may have trained at an Inn of Chancery. In 1625 he was made a JP of the borough and sat in the courts. On matters of dispute, or of an exceptional nature, expert legal advice came from the recorder of the borough.[3]

Hiorne was paid 26s8d a year for life as town clerk and the chamberlains' accounts show that he also received 13s4d for attendance at the assizes in Oxford twice a year, when he reported on the borough sessions court, and 5s for writing and casting up the chamberlains' accounts; a total of 45s a year. In addition there would be certain fees received in the courts.

The recorder, a lawyer responsible for providing expert legal advice to the borough courts, was Sir James Whitelocke up to 1620, succeeded by William Lenthall for the rest of the period. Whitelocke also represented the town in parliament (see **125**), and his role as MP has been accounted important in establishing the bounds of the Stuart constitution in his argument that taxation was vested in the sovereign authority, which was neither king nor parliament alone but king-in-parliament together. In the mayoral elections taking place after death in office his advice, together with that of his predecessor Sir Lawrence Tanfield, was called upon (**13**, **302**).[4]

Whitelocke is recorded in the minutes on nine other occasions, ranging from attendance at borough sessions and frankpledge (**146**), ruling on distraint of charity land (**71**), to examination of horse-theft (**175**). Lenthall's presence as recorder is noted on just one occasion, in December 1621; he succeeded Whitelocke as the borough's MP in 1624.

The recorder was included in the commission of the peace for the borough, and he or his deputy was supposed to attend the court of sessions and the leet and to form a quorum with the mayor for the court of record.[5]

Presence of the high steward in court proceedings is not recorded here, but Walter Culpeper of the county commission of the peace administered the oath of mayoralty in 1608 (**90**). Sir Thomas Spencer is named as holder in the list of 11 November 1616 (B78/3 end-papers iii).

The borough commonalty comprised a common council of twenty councillors and five aldermen including the mayor, and in this period about forty or so other freemen (**86**; B78/3 end-papers ii & iii). This council, governing the borough, largely came from leading businessmen and other notables. Mayor and aldermen were the king's justices of the peace within the borough by virtue of their office and were regularly so acknowledged in the full titlings of entries in the original minutes. Thus their courts, criminal examinations and other legal functions were recognised as courts of record and were

3 *VCH Oxon,* xii, 434n; Dr Paul Brand, private communication (1998); Brooks, 151-165

4 Notestein, 326, 375-81, 561; Sainty, 211.

5 WBM B83/4; *Rep.Com.Mun.Corps.*, (1835) 141.

usually held before the mayor. In 1612 two of these men were included in a commission of the peace.[6] Under the 1580 constitution (WBM B82) aldermen were limited to six and were elected from the common council or must have served as chamberlain. The mayor must have experience as chamberlain and he was elected annually from the aldermen, but was usually re-elected for a second year.

These elections were on the Monday before St.Matthew's Day (21 Sept.) and office was assumed at Michaelmas (29 Sept.). The procedure on death of the mayor in office, as advised by consulting with the recorder, is invoked both for William Meatcalfe in January 1608 (**13**) and for John Raunson in January 1611 (**302**).

Raunson made his mark in place of signature not only when close to death (**290/1**, **297**) but also in borough orders of 1589 (WBM B82). As a presiding JP he presumably relied upon support from his fellow JPs and the town clerk in dealing with written work.

The sergeant-at-the-mace kept his office for life, although he was elected annually in September at the same time as the mayor. In the Portmoot he dealt with the execution of writs and regularly acted as attorney. His duties included charge of the town prison used for detention in both civil and criminal cases. Henry Rudgate was holder up to November 1611 when he was succeeded by his son, Edmund (**491**), followed by Jerome White from October 1617, and Thomas Heathen from February 1618.

In this period Edward Longe was confirmed as holding the posts of clerk of the church and court crier for his life-span (**91**).

Elections to the role of freeman-burgess are recorded in April 1608 for an outsider, fine 40s (**48**), and in January 1609 presumably for an inhabitant, fine 30s (**129**). The freeman's oath of Woodstock is set out on *f.256* of B78/3. The election of recorder James Whitelock as the borough member of parliament in place of the deceased Sir Richard Lee also took place in January 1609.

Election to the borough common council of schoolmaster Simon Jeames is noted in October 1608 (**91**) and of mercer William Bradshewe in February 1611 (**314**).

Of the other officers of the Portmoot and frankpledge courts the aldermen, five in number, were elected for life; the two chamberlains were elected at their annual audit, and the rest, constables, tithingmen and ale-tasters, were elected at view of frankpledge.

Portmoot court

New Woodstock, founded in the 12th century, by the 13th century had a borough court or portmoot, meeting on Mondays, frequently recorded. The

6 Gleason, 256; Dalton, 6; *VCH,Oxon,* xii, 393.

town was taxed as a borough in the early 14th century and from 1338 onwards the office of mayor was regularly noted. Criminal jurisdiction seems to have been exercised by 1402. In 1453 the borough's charter, based closely on that of New Windsor, granted wide jurisdiction to the mayor and commonalty thereby confirming much that had been long enjoyed. About this time the term Portmoot was applied more specifically to the regular sessions of the borough court, held fortnightly on Mondays. Most recorded business before the 1580's dealt with land transfers and by that date the document was usually called a final concord.[7]

Actions initiated by writ of right were explicitly recorded from the early 16th century though they had long been in use, and by charter the court had return of writs. In 1580 it was agreed that actions between freemen for less than 5s should be settled out of court by the mayor or any alderman (WBM B82). Also freemen were given two court session days longer than any foreigner to answer an action in the Portmoot. These regulations also formalised the money to be paid to the mayor's private profit: he would no longer handle profits from all the courts in the borough; instead he would receive an annual fee of £10 and retain fees from the Portmoot and from licences, recognisances, and warrants granted by him, but would still pay the fee farm together with charges for sessions and lawday dinners.[8]

Sittings of both the Portmoot and the Sessions of the peace courts seem to have been held regularly in the Guildhall and this location is occasionally identified in the court headings.

In general the Portmoot was called quite regularly at fortnightly intervals over the fourteen years: in this period there were fifteen occasions when it sat after one week's interval, and conversely on fourteen occasions after three week's break; in 1619 it did not meet between 24 May and 2 August. Changes in sequence arose particularly at the end of December.

There were twelve instances where the date recorded for the court does not correspond to a Monday; these were:

Tuesday: 7 & 21 February; 7 & 21 March 1615
Wednesday: 13 July 1608; 20 September 1615; 10 January 1621
Friday: 22 January 1613
Sunday: 10 May 1612;16 April 1615; 3 March 1616; 23 November 1617.

There are no textual clues to doubt these dates, apart from a minor uncertainty concerning the month of the Friday meeting. Similarly there is no indication of the reason for the run of Tuesday meetings. Sunday sittings of the Portmoot may be unexpected but with four occurences here and one in 1590 (B78/1 Cal.)

7 *VCH Oxon*, xii, 326, 372, 391.

8 WBM B82, clause 48.

perhaps the court followed the example of criminal examinations, recorder's rulings, and recognisances, which were undertaken on that day when required (see **24**, **53**:5/5, **71-2**, **163**, **547**, **597-9**).

As a borough court of record the Portmoot employed common law process: actions generally started with a plaint entered in a court book (see B78/1 Calendar, xxi & Appendix 2), rather than by writ; followed the usual methods for obtaining attendance of the defendant in court, and then the formal stages of pleading to achieve agreement on the point at issue. This agreement was commonly reached without pleading beyond the third, replication, stage.[9]

In 78/3 there are nine occasions when the Portmoot mistakenly includes (court) Baron in the title (*ff.17, 19, 38v, 45, 70v, 83, 154, 158v, 159v*); in five cases the error is crossed through. On *f45* the title includes 'Hundred of Wootton with---' crossed through. At this time Hordley and Old Woodstock shared a single court with Wootton, and Edmund Hiorne, as town clerk, held and recorded all the courts, including those of the attached Wootton hundred; for each town the courts baron were called as required.[10]

Usage and outcome of Portmoot actions

Over the fourteen years covered by the minutes of B78/2 & 78/3 a total of 922 Portmoot actions were recorded, giving an average of 65 suits per year. But the rate of litigation was peaking over the last decades of the 16th and the early decades of the 17th centuries. Thus over the seven years covered by minute-book B78/1 (1588-95) the average annual rate was 70 suits; over the six years of B78/2 (1607-14) it was 73 suits/year; and over the eight years of B78/3 (1614-22) down to 58 suits/year. This maximum in the high levels of civil litigation in this era has been noted countrywide, both by reviewers of Tudor times and observers of the credit economy. Its underlying cause was the massive recourse to the courts for settling financial quarrels, eased in later times by the introduction of forms of contract such as bonds and credit notes to deal with these needs (see below).[11]

During the period of these two court-books the proportions of the various forms of action used were as follows:

debts rose slightly from 55 to 60% of the total;
trespass-on-case ran at around 22%;
trespass, including with assault, 10-11%;
account at 2-3%;
detinue at 1½%;
Qui tam rose from 1% to 4%; all from a cluster of cases in 1614;

[9] Gilmore, *passim*; Muldrew, 205.

[10] *VCH,Oxon,* xii, 434ii.

[11] WBM.B78/1 Calendar; Youings, 225; Muldrew, 236.

actions for land transfer, such as conveyance, ejectment, dower, and common recovery fell from 7% to 1%;

in B78/2 between 1-2% of actions were not specified.

The average number of entries on the progress of each case is about 5, with nearly a third having just a single entry and three-quarters not more than 6. Many single entries record an immediate discharge (e.g. actions **16**, **18**, **19**, **23**), and in those where the recorded finish is the plaintiff's declaration some at least may have been settled out of court directly after having been registered there. In contrast to this brevity a few actions (e.g. **240**, **259**, **303**, **312**, **444**) may proceed for twenty, or even fifty, entries with apparently no resolution and a final entry given as "continues".

For 1607-14 about half (48%) of all actions were eventually discharged, with the proportion falling to 40% for trespass, but rising to 60% for the category "other" actions. However over 1614-22 the proportion of all actions resolved rose to 67%. In the first period, for all those cases not discharged their final entries fall into the following categories of progress:

Progress; final entry	Proportion of all actions
Plaintiff declares	13%
Plaintiff/defendant defaults	2%
Arbitration	1%
Referred to Westminster Courts	4%
Imparlance	2%
Continues	18%
Jury called	1%
Judgment passed	2%
Execution issued	5%
Scire facias & renewals issued	4%
	52%

Thus 13% of actions do not proceed beyond plaintiff's declaration and 18% "continue" unresolved; 9% end on default or arbitration/imparlance or reference to the Westminster Courts; while the residual 12% remain at a stage beyond calling a jury, up to the issue of renewals of *scire facias* on the execution of judgment.

Over the fourteen years 16 actions went to arbitration, typically before the mayor or an alderman, but not all these were resolved by this procedure, though some pairs of litigants put themselves under penalty of a bond to settle. Six of the cases fell into two sets of collective actions (**501**, **503-4**, **559**, **561-2**). In one Sessions action on breaking the peace an order was set by the recorder but arbitration was still unsuccessful (**279**).

Imparlance was invoked on some nineteen occasions, but notably thirteen of these suits were contemporaneous (**525-37**, **540-2**). Certain other legal procedures also seem to have periods of greater and lesser popularity; as indicated by the clustering of the references to these procedures in the Index. Litigants presumably tended to follow those processes recently successful in the court, some of which may have been introduced by the attorneys.

In three actions, **55** and the counter-actions **285** & **287,** writ of execution is given against Edmund Hiorne as clerk of the court and commonalty: these awards may reflect errors by the court in their conduct of the suits, but no details are given. Action **287** is notable for Robert Payne of Cassington's claim for 100 marks damages for the capture and imprisonment of his wife by John Charles, in a suit presumably based on a plaint of abduction and loss of service of the wife.[12]

Provenance of Portmoot litigants

Comparing the records in B78/1 (1588-95), B78/2 (1607-14) and B78/3 (1614-22), there is found a significant decline in the recording of the residence of Portmoot litigants with the passing of time. A similar decline from the 1570s to the early 17th century has been noted in the rolls of the Court of Common Pleas. Thus the analysis of provenance of Portmoot litigants in these minute books is most thorough for B78/1, less so for B78/2, and least for B78/3.[13]

In B78/2, two-thirds of the borough's eighty-five freemen (59) appeared in litigation in this court with an average three actions per suitor. Overall they appeared as plaintiff only slightly more often than as defendant. They constituted just over 10% of suitors and partook in one-fifth of its business; combined with the other listed 90 Woodstock househeads, they made up 16% of suitors engaged in a quarter of actions. In B78/3 the freeman usage rose as a proportion of the court's total business to 32%, still a little more often as plaintiff than defendant.

As a body the freemen were obliged to use this court for actions against one another (WBM B83, p111), and they no doubt found it convenient and reasonably placed for local business compared with more central courts. In B78/2 about half of the freemen litigants engaged against fellow freemen in some 6% of all suits; over the years of B78/3 this proportion had risen to 9% of all suits. These changes resulted from disproportionately large losses of outsiders' custom, as they progressively found declining need for Portmoot settlement of their transactions.

For the above reasons this present survey, except where indicated otherwise, is based largely on data from B78/2 (1607-14).

Those freemen most using the court were, in descending order:

Alderman Thomas Browne, plaintiff in 15 debt suits to 1614; then 8 more until his death in 1620;

William Raunson, 12 suits to 1614; then 8 more to 1622;

[12] Baker, 518/9.

[13] Galloway & Murphy, 4.

- John Heath, 12 suits, defendant in 9;
- Thomas Painter, 10 suits, debt defendant in 9, 7 together;
- Randall Richards, 9 suits, debt defendant in 6;
- Thomas Meatcalfe, 7 suits to 1614; then 8 more to 1622;
- Alderman William Rayer, 7 suits; debt plaintiff in 5, including £134 & £14;
- Thomas Screevin, 7 suits to 1614; then 16 more to 1622;
- Town clerk, Edmund Hiorne, plaintiff in 6 debt suits to 1614; then 6 more to 1622;
- Andrew Jarnes, 6 suits, plaintiff in 2; debtor for £48;
- John Batt (senior & junior), 5 suits to 1614; then 11 more to 1622;
- Francis Collingwood, 5 suits, plaintiff in 2; defendant for £20 damages;
- John Stone, 5 suits to 1614; then 8 more to 1622;
- In the period 1614-22 butcher Richard Reade was involved in 11 actions sometimes with his wife Katherine.

Many freemen, including senior members, featured in only one or two or no actions at this time. Simon James, for example, though regularly acting as attorney for others in the court, engaged in just two actions: as plaintiff in suits of land recovery.

Twenty-nine of the non-freemen househeads (32%) partook in a total of fifty-one actions, so their individual usage was notably less than that of the freemen. Only five of them were involved in 3 or more suits, and these were:

- John Symons, 5 suits, plaintiff in 3;
- Richard Coles, 3 suits;
- Saloman Flye, 3 suits; plaintiff for £20 in one; & 2 conveyances;
- Widow Ann Leake, plaintiff in 3 suits, one for £21 debt;
- William Raunson, defendant in 3 suits.

There were comparatively few suits (10) between freemen and non-freemen househeads, and in these freemen were plaintiff in seven. Non-free househeads engaged in a total of 34 suits with outsiders, as plaintiff in 19 cases.

Some regular court users were clearly resident in the borough though not listed as freemen or househeads, and these included:

- Richard Heath, glover; defendant in 9 debt suits;
- Jerome Kyte, lawyer and JP; plaintiff in 4 debt suits to 1614, 1 for £40 against the sergeant; and in another 10 to 1622;
- Widow Elizabeth Ryly, plaintiff in 3 out of 4 suits;
- Widow Merriall Taylor, defendant in 3 debt suits, including £20 and £134 as administratrix for her late freeman husband.

Since no indication of the provenance of suitors is given in the Portmoot minutes it is not possible to distinguish in all cases between unidentified residents of the borough and outsiders. If, for the moment, the Woodstock residents' list is augmented with people who can be so identified with some assurance from evidence elsewhere in the minute book, or the chamberlains' accounts etc., then that body constitutes:

- 30% of all suitors;
- one third of both plaintiffs and defendants in debt actions;
- nearly one third of plaintiffs, but only one eighth of defendants, in trespass actions.

Alternatively, by classing more clearly suitors who are neither freemen nor househeads as "outsiders" (but thereby not distinguishing between certain Woodstock common sort or impermanent residents and true outsiders) then the following proportions hold:

- outsiders are suitors against freemen/househeads in 27% of suits;
- and against outsiders in 58% of suits.

Outsider suitors most using the court were:

- William Harris, plaintiff in 10 out of 14 suits; notably brings 5 *Qui Tam* actions (also 7 in 1592-95); plaintiff for £10 debt & 2 ejectment suits; In 1615 John Taylor, yeoman of Leafield, seems to have succeeded as local informer and brought 19 *Qui Tam* actions; 5 were against borough freemen and in 3 cases fines were imposed;
- Richard Stutter of Hanborough, defendant in two sets of 13 overlapping debt suits including £24 to John Gregory, £6 to Edmund Hiorne, and £12, £8 & £7.
- John Cooke of Begbroke, plaintiff in 5 out 11 suits;
- Ralph Shurly, plaintiff in 2 out of 11 suits;
- Robert Payne of Cassington, plaintiff in 5 out of 8 suits, one claiming damages for capture and imprisonment of his wife;
- John Gregory of Hordley in Wootton, plaintiff in 7 suits, including debts of £24 and 4 cows;
- John Fawler of Hanborough, plaintiff in 6 out of 7 suits;
- William Abbott, of Bladon, plaintiff in 2 out of 7 suits;
- Henry Alberte, defendant in 7 suits, one for 4 cows, one for £21;
- Humfrey Hamond (?Wootton), plaintiff in 6 debt suits;
- Thomas Basly, butcher of Deddington, debt defendant in 5 out of 6 suits;
- Christopher East of Bletchingdon, defendant in 4 out of 5 suits;
- Robert Bincks of Bladon, plaintiff in 3 out of 5 suits;
- Edward Roberts, defendant in 4 out of 5 suits;
- Richard Whinge, plaintiff in 5 debt suits.

There were nine suitors with 4 actions each, including:

- Edmund Hiorne senior, father of town clerk, plaintiff in all;
- Humfrey Fitzharbert of Begbroke, plaintiff in all, including 2 for 'waste';
- Richard Manning of Begbroke, defendant in all, 3 against Fitzharbert;
- William Wise (?Eynsham), plaintiff in all.

There were 19 suitors with 3 actions each, including:

Robert Cherry of Cassington, defendant in all;
Edward Browne, baker of Eynsham, in counter-cases against John Doa;
Francis Gregory of Hordley, Wootton, plaintiff in all;
Widow Margaret Hatten, defendant in all;
William Jeffes of Bladon, defendant in 2;
Robert Symons of Hensington, defendant in 3;
John Whitton als. Darlinge of Hensington, plaintiff in 3; plus 4 conveyances.

Stephen Medhopp was defendant in an extraordinary action (**422**) in which he confessed to damages of £1,000 to the mayor and commonalty of the borough for arresting William Raunson on a plea of trespass under a warrant the county sheriff had directed to the bailiff of Wootton Hundred. But Medhopp acted without agreement of the mayor - the circumstances of the original plea are not known. The heavy penalty presumably reflects the offence taken at Medhopp's apparent challenge to the mayor's jurisdiction within the borough.[14]

In August 1621 six actions of debt and trespass **(1240-5)** were brought against William Cotes by Rowland, Bishop of Bristol, and William Bostock. They ran concurrently for debts recorded up to £300 and damage claims to £600; in the September they were referred by *habeas corpus* to a Westminster court.

Central courts at Westminster

In overall terms the referral rate to the Westminster courts from the Portmoot was rather steady over these fourteen years: averaging 3½ transfers per year at the equivalent of 5-6% of all actions. In practice numbers of these actions were related and tended to cluster together on occasion as noted above. A total of 22 actions was removed to Westminster over 1607-14; the total for 1614-22 was 28, and these constituent numbers are added in brackets.

12 by *habeas corpus*: (15 in 1614-22)
 9 of these to King's Bench (**214**, **285**, **286**, **361** & **368**, **443**, **582**, **338,** and **228** which presumably determined the outcome of eleven debt suits against Richard Stutter);
 3 to courts not specified (**252**, **254**, **377**);
1 by *corpus cum causa* presumably to Common Pleas (**209**); (1 in 1614-22);
4 by writ of error to King's Bench (**6**, **261** twice, **433**);

[14] See **422**, note 73.

Fig.1 Distribution of Portmoot Outsider Litigants (1607-1614)

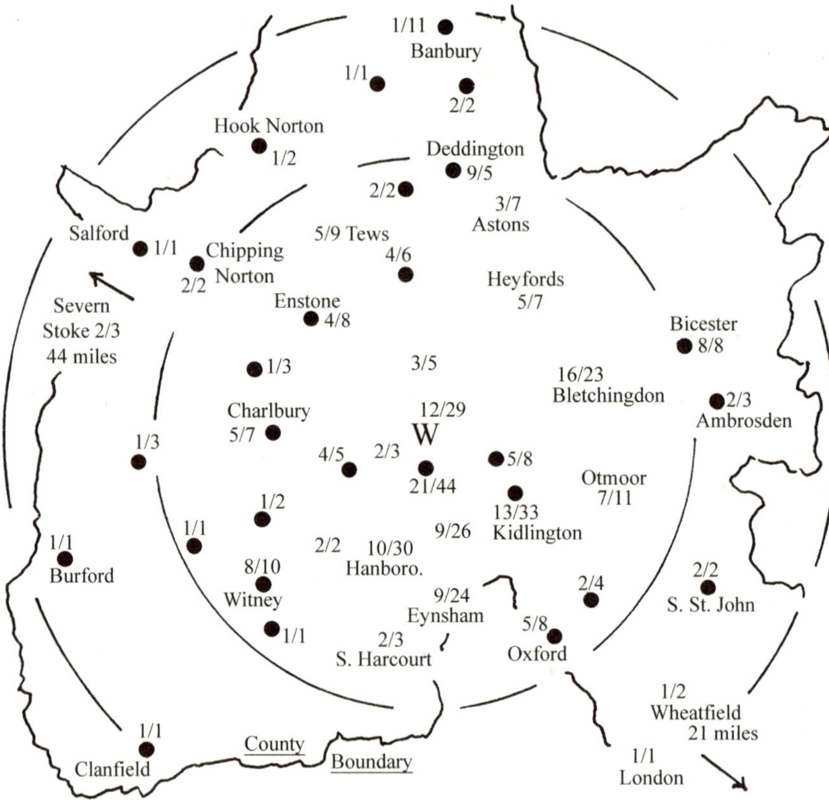

Each location gives: Number of litigants/Number of actions.
Black dots • denote individual towns and villages; Names/Numbers alone denote aggregate numbers from areas comparable in size with that covered by those Names/Numbers.
The circles are of 10 and 15 miles radius from Woodstock. Many locations are derived from sources listed in Abbreviations pt.2. To avoid local overcrowding of data some neighbouring places have been aggregated, for example: Bladon & Hensington; and Kirtlington and Weston-on-the-Green with Bletchindon.
Of these outsider litigants with reasonably established provenance:

nearly all come from within 15 miles of Woodstock;

four-fifths come from within 10 miles, and these are engaged in five-sixths of the actions plotted here.

The absence of locations in the nearer parts of the adjoining counties may be due in part to lack of search in the corresponding records for these counties, where they exist.

2 writs of privilege were used (6 in 1614-22), one by Ralph Saunders to Common Pleas, the other by John Cronye; (**144**, **353**);

a pair of defendants to trespass/assault used *certiorari* to transfer to Chancery (**473** & **474**); (2 in 1614-22);

one debt action (**205**:5/5) was sent to King's Bench subsequent to execution being granted, seemingly with no writ raised.

In a trespass for assault plaint against William Ratlife of the university of Oxford, he produced the university's half-seals to remove the suit to the vice-chancellor's court in Oxford (**484**).[15]

Some forms of action

Actions of Debt & Trespass-on-case

At this time the major part of the country's litigation was taking place in borough courts and most cases dealt with unpaid debts or broken contracts covered by the actions of debt, trespass-on-case, and *assumpsit*. In the Portmoot the proportion of such cases in 1588-95 amounted to 66% of the total, and by 1607-14 had risen to 77%, and by 1614-22 to 83%. Most of the underlying business transactions were generated by oral agreements on unpaid sales credits and reckonings on consumer goods.[16] Written transactions and bonds are recorded in only 12 cases over the 1590s period and just 15 in the 1610s book. Such meagre growth in reliable documentation of business could relate to the persistance of wager trial at the Portmoot (see **Wager of Law**)

Action of Account

This type of action continued to be used at this time against bailiffs, common receivers, or other agents where debt was precluded because of the uncertainty as to the balance between the parties.[17]

Six such suits took place in 1607-14:

one by freeman John Batt against non-freeman Anthony Noble clerk who was attached by body (**54**), a day was granted for rejoinder though no replication was recorded;

one by Thomas Penn against Richard Ockly who won £27 trespass damages in a counter-action (**138, 120**);

two were brought against the *Qui tam* informer William Harris, but ended unresolved (**503, 504**);

the suit against freeman Randall Richards (**521**) was discharged;

[15] See **484** note 88.

[16] Muldrew, 204; B78/1, Cal. xxiv; B78/2; B78/3, Cal.

[17] Baker, 411-3.

whilst execution of the plaint was granted for Thomas Basly, butcher of Deddington, against Daniel Witham (**616**).

Numbers increased to fourteen over 1614-22, but a fifth of these actions were inconclusive; Gray Bridges, Lord Chandos, entered as plaintiff in one (**1164**).

Action of Detinue

Over the fourteen years 1607-22 the proportion of detinue cases was steady at around 1½% of the total. Of the seven actions in 1614-22 one concerned a horse (**659**) and another a parcel of chattels (**1173**).

The absence of actions of trover at this time, where there had been some in 1588-95, appears a change counter to that from detinue to trover taking place in the central courts and elsewhere over these decades (see also Wager of Law).[18]

Conveyance , Dower, Ejectment, & Collusive Common Recovery

Conveyance by proclamation was customary with the claim made in open court asking that the grant be recorded and proclaimed on three, usually successive, court days. The earlier actions (**14**, **22**, **27** & **46**) have entries for just these three proclamations, but the following ones commence with a summary of the original writ of covenant which initiates the fictitious litigation. Over 1607-14 twenty one conveyances are recorded; and one claim to land by virtue of succession (**475**). This latter claim appears to be based on the rules of intestate succession.[19]

In the 21 conveyances by proclamation:

borough freemen were:

querents in 9 cases (**22**, **27**, **46**, **69**, **210**, **333**, **461**, **481**, **593**), with William Rayer and Edmund Hiorne each involved twice;

deforciants in 6 cases (**27**, **289**, **291**, **418**, **425**, **487**), with Thomas and Mary Painter involved three times. In **289** and **291** Mary Painter was privately questioned on her consent, and since the warranties were against cognisors and heirs of both husband and wife it signified the purpose of the fine was to dispose of the married woman's freeholds.[20]

borough non-freemen were:

querents in 3 cases (**14**, **297**, **418**); in **297** George Noble obtained the Chantry House; in **418** Salloman Flye obtained four messuages from his parents;

[18] B78/1 Cal.; Maitland, 71; Gilmore, 87.

[19] Baker, 436.

[20] Gilmore, 'Fine (3)'.

deforciants in 2 cases (**333**, widow Elizabeth Fleming and children sold to Edmund Hiorne; **420** Salloman Flye sold two messuages).

Seventeen of these conveyances involved parties not included in the 1608 borough census but these people, by definition, had owned property there and they or their kin had often taken part in borough affairs. The Whittons (**14, 60, 210, 271**) were resident in Hensington, while the Damerys (**289, 400**) and Warrens (**291, 419**) were masons in Bladon. Humphrey Silver became a freeman in 1618 and John Kerby (**400, 419, 425**) made regular entries in the chamberlains' accounts. Joan Collingwood (**586, 617**) widow of Francis, sold some seven messuages; Joan Daunter (**461**) was widow of Abraham, a weaver in the borough. William Dunforde (**420**) was a non-freeman in the borough in 1617. Henry Barneshawe sold two properties in the Holloway (**22, 46**) within a year, yet his children may have been receiving charity at that time (**21**).

A number of these conveyances described given areas of land used for different purposes (e.g. **379**): the suggestion has been made that since the final concord was really a quit claim to deal with all sorts of development a statement of '50a of arable land, 50a of pasture', may have meant a total of 50a used either as land or pasture, rather than a total of 100a.[21]

Only six conveyances took place in the eight years 1614-22. Alderman Thomas Browne purchased two properties involving three messuages (**650, 842**), while the Collingwood family (**650, 889**) and John Whitton (**842, 848**) each appeared in two transfers.

Three actions for ejectment took place in 1607-14, two brought by the penal-statute informer William Harris (**240, 319**); none arose in 1614-22.

There was a single action of dower in the first period (**320**) in which Mary Phillips of the borough successfully recovered seisin of her widow's third of her late husband's messuage (**320**:20&21/21).[22] None arose in the second period.

Collusive Common Recovery: there were 4 examples over the years 1607-22 of this collusive conveyancing device for freeing land from entails and other encumbrances to allow selling it or revesting it in the owner. In the first Thomas Grove and Thomas Samwell recovered seisin of five messuages, five gardens and some five acres of land within the borough (**10**). In the other three Simon Jeames made common recovery of significant properties:

one of 6 acres with messuage, featured in a recent transfer (**51**);
another of 3 acres with two messuages, barns & gardens (**379**);
and a third of 2 acres with five messuages and gardens from William Meatcalfe (**665**).

[21] See Webster.

[22] Ivamy, 150.

Qui tam Actions

A total of twenty-four *Qui tam* actions were brought in two bursts of litigation. The first set of five within the span March 1608 to December 1609 were all brought by William Harris, who had previously brought seven such suits in the period 1592-95.[23] In the second set, nineteen in number, the charges were all brought between July and November 1614 by John Taylor of Leafield.

These two surges reflect, to a degree, the numbers of informations in the Court of the Exchequer, where in 1608 there was a peak of activity in that year of dearth, with many actions on engrossing of grain and illegal sale of animals. In this court 1613 was another peak year with these two types of offence at twice the high levels of 1608.[24]

At this time, of the 115 penal statutes still in force, 23 came from Henry VIII's reign, 11 from Edward VI, 30 from Elizabeth and 19 from James I. From 1616/17 however, several classes of information were stayed, by 1619 Exchequer informations had fallen to a sixth of those in 1613, and a bill of 1621 with three reforming statutes of 1624 (21 Jas.I c.2, 3, 24, 28) formally closed this court to such actions. Common informers' powers to prosecute on others' breaking of penal statutes was finally abolished only in 1951 (14 & 15 Geo.VI, c.39).[25]

Although Beresford classes the penal statutes as a chief instrument for enforcement of economic legislation and indirect taxation, he discounts their efficiency as such and sees them more as a political irritant. Nevertheless during the 1608 dearth, for example, those Woodstock worthies engrossing barley futures at half the market price may well have tempered their speculations in view of Harris's current informations.[26]

Unlike some cases in B78/1, no information is provided on the particular penal statutes invoked in the actions of B78/2 & 78/3; but the procedure was confined in the main to economic regulation, when it could be foreseen that the offender would be able to pay a fine in which the prosecutor would share.[27] Thus in two of the B78/2 actions against borough freemen they both compounded, with George Noble (**213**) paying 2s6d and William Kinge (**219**) paying 2s to the chamberlains.[28]

And in the three other Harris actions, against foreigners, they each requested to imparl (**25**, **134**, **168**). The occupation of Harris may be reflected in the two

[23] See B78/1 Cal..

[24] Beresford, 231.

[25] Beresford 221, 237.

[26] Beresford 221,237; B78/2, **112**; Taylor 357.

[27] Langbein, 44.

[28] *WCA*, 2,7.

actions for ejectment (out of a total of three in this period) he brought (**240** & **319**) and in his defending an action of account (**504**).

Of the nineteen defendants in B78/3 seven are known Woodstock inhabitants (**676** the sergeant, **677**, **678**, **679**, **680**, **697**, **719**); half of the actions reached no stated conclusion and the rest compounded to pay the fine which in one case was resolved as nil (**697**).

Guardianship

Two cases of the appointment of guardians are recorded: the sergeant-at-mace, Edmund Rudgate, to have care of John Robins (**785**), and Ralph Bradshewe, aged seven, chose Ralph Clements of Bicester for his custodian (**1021**). Some boroughs had special customs as to guardianships of this type, and reference is made to Woodstock borough custom in the second case though the details are not given. Moreover the law made specific provision for children aged seven or over to choose their guardians, and this sitting seems timed to allow use of this power.[29]

Wager of Law

Use of wager of law *(vadiatio legis)*: (whereby a defendant could discharge himself from a claim of debt or detinue on his own oath augmented by the sworn belief of a number of his neighbours in his denial) was in marked decline at this time in the central courts.[30] In the Portmoot its usage and rate of success was different in the two books, not in the way to be expected.

In B78/2 (1607-14) there were seven cases:

in two suits (**239**, **415**) four hands gave their oaths, and in the second one at least were true (Otmoor) neighbours;

in the other five suits (**124**, **441**, **531**, **548**, **577**) six hands were claimed but four actions did not follow full process.

Over 1614-22 (B.78/3) usage increased to twelve actions, only one of which was unsuccessful in that it transferred to Westminster under writ of privilege (**1229**).

Slade's Case in 1602 is said to have resulted in the complete replacement of wager trial by jury trial at Westminster and the central courts; to have similarly displaced actions of detinue with those of trover, and greatly increased the use of actions of assumpsit. Woodstock, however, moved in the opposite direction:

from a single wager in the 1590s, to 7 in 1607-14, and 12 in 1614-22;

29 Ivamy, 209; Cox,17,21.

30 Baker, 88, 396.

from 5 detinue and 3 trover in 1590s, to 13 detinue and no trover in 1607-22;

and from 6% assumpsit actions in 1590s, to none in 1607-22.

These Woodstock procedures were all dependent upon retaining wager trial.

Recorder Whitelocke and town clerk Hiorne, with charge of the borough courts no doubt had good reasons for allowing this counter-reformation in procedure. Whereas the central courts dealt largely with written bonds, the corresponding Woodstock cases were based mostly on oral contracts and therefore spoken evidence of neighbours. Illiteracy in the borough was still significant around 1610-12: for example, neither mayor John Raunson, nor sergeant/attorney Henry Redgate, nor half the coroner's jury (**460**), could sign their names; and such inability must have influenced modes of bargaining and choice of trial procedure (see *Actions of Debt*, above). At a time of sharply declining custom in other local courts such as Witney, Banbury and Burford, these measures may have delayed the loss of custom for a few years (see above 'Usage' & Fig.1). Although some third of wager trials were called by outsiders (**415, 548, 577, 819, 886** & **922**) who formed the bulk of the individual users of the court, they seem to have moved away over time to avoid this tilt in justice towards locals who had borough neighbours always to hand.[31] Over these fourteen years there were twice as many trials by jury as by wager, and litigants put themselves 'on the country' nearly two times for every jury actually sitting.

Usage of Attorneys

Parties in 447 civil actions of B78/2 were represented by attorney 101 times, in 48 cases acting for the defendant alone, and in 18 cases for both parties. By 1621 nearly 90% of cases had them acting for both parties, in a few cases for plaintiff only, and in even fewer for neither party. The sergeant-at-mace commonly appeared for defendants, and schoolmaster Simon Jeames, who was registered as a professional attorney by 1617, was virtually the only other attorney operating, usually for plaintiffs.[32]

In B78/2 three actions, together in time (**535, 537, 540**), noted that the defendant did not appear or instruct his attorney (*non sum informatus*) so that the case went by default; in B78/3 the number of these defaults increased to thirteen.

Town court attorneys often trained by serving as clerks to town clerks or recorders and some had contact with Inns of Chancery. During 1588-95 two of the Woodstock attorneys also served as town clerk and may well have benefited from such training. Schoolmaster Simon Jeames as professional attorney must

[31] Baker,88,396; Muldrew,63,96,204; Bolton, xviii; Gretton 53ff; *VCH Oxon*, x 77

[32] *VCH, Oxon*, xii,392; B78/3, Feb.1617

also have been well qualified, yet Henry Rudgate appeared unable to sign his name even though he also coped with the duties of sergeant-at-mace and the execution of writs.[33]

Apprenticeships

Indentures of apprenticeship were enrolled in the Portmoot court books as decreed in the borough orders of 1580, with a payment of 12d to the town clerk.[34] Twenty-eight such enrolments are given over these fourteen years: including six to tailors, four to bakers, three to shoemakers, and two each to joiners, smiths and butchers. Most of these lads appear to have come from the borough or near at hand; two came from Otmoor, two from Milton, one each from Steeple Aston and Cleveley, and two further afield from London. Rules for bakers' apprentices are included in the assize of bread and ale regulations of 1608 (**88**).

View of Frankpledge

The view of frankpledge, sometimes called a court leet, was held from the 16th century onwards twice yearly shortly after Lady Day and Michaelmas, usually combined with the general sessions of the peace. On two occasions when it is recorded separately, October 1609 and October 1611, the mayor alone presided and election of constables, tithingmen and tasters took place before a jury of homage. Bylaws were issued and presentments made by the homage of offences such as nuisances and encroachments (**325**). Appointment of Surveyors is occasionally recorded (**324**, **753** & **981**), as is the handing over of estreats to the constables and chamberlains (**41**, **105**, **485**:7/7). Each parish was required to have two surveyors to plan and supervise work on its highways according to the 1555 Act of Phillip & Mary.[35]

Coroner

The mayor acted as coroner within the borough, as exemplified by the inquest in 1612 on the death of John Brooman of Littlemore allegedly from an assault (**460**). This sitting seems to have provoked a challenge to the mayor's right to the office in the following year, which, in view of the inquest's conduct, is perhaps not surprising. Porter has established that in then current practice such an inquest was generally convened soon after death, and that the process caused just a few days delay before burial could take place. Here, though the inquest opened within a day or so of death and witnesses then bound themselves to give

[33] Brooks, 41; WBM. B82, 23

[34] WBM.82, clause 11.

[35] 2 & 3.Phil. & Mary. c.8 (1555); Dalton,60; Tate,234,304.

further evidence, they were not recalled, and proceedings were immediately postponed for seven weeks. A jury was then sworn in, but there is little reason to suppose their verdict drew upon direct examination of the body while it lay in Woodstock.[36]

Sessions of the Peace

The general sessions of the peace were usually held together with frankpledge; but on two occasions when it was recorded separately (October 1609 & October 1611) it sat before the mayor with three other justices.

Business included nominating a jury for the crown, and appointing innholders and victuallers for the town. Recognisances were dealt with, including many concerning misbehaviour at the fairs and markets.

An example of a full heading for the court is given for October 1609. The borough justices exercised criminal jurisdiction by virtue of their privileges set out in the charters of 1453 and 1565 which were confirmed, along with details of long-established practice, in the charter of 1664: their powers being those of county justices except for the prosecution of felonies involving loss of life or limb.[37] At this time they operated through the two annual general sessions and occasional summary examinations or petty sessions. Because these criminal examinations are so numerous and extensive in B78/2 (1607-14) and yet completely absent from B78/3 (1614-22), the two periods are dealt with quite separately in this section.

Up to 1614 much of the magistrates' work, as described here, was carried out by the mayor and alderman Thomas Browne. In the only case concerning a death, when alderman Thomas Bradshewe was on his final sick-bed, four days before his death, his daughter accused Joyce Coles in court of exercising witchcraft upon him (**583**). Although an examination of the accused seems to have been planned no findings are recorded. Subsequently Coles was in prison and died within half a year. This single example of a witchcraft charge was notably brought just following the notorious series of trials of Lancashire witches in London; and jurors, magistrates and coroners typically exercised particular caution over accusations that could lead to capital punishment.[38]

Major crimes were referred to the county courts after depositions of the examinations had been taken in the borough. Although the mayor was expected to attend the Lent and Summer assizes in Oxford, in this period he appears to have been represented by the town clerk.[39] The accounts of informations and examinations given here in Hiorne's minutes presumably

36 *WCA*. 47; Porter, 202

37 *VCH Oxon* xii 393; Dalton, *passim*.

38 *WCA*, 46,47; Herrup, 199. Sharpe (1988), 314

39 *WCA*, xv, 6,45.

served as the basis of the legal depositions for the actions he took forward to Oxford.

Numbers of the accused came from distant parts and their evidence was sometimes checked with magistrates in their home counties: for example Nottingham (**50**:5/6), Kent (**175**), Buckinghamshire (**229**), Staffordshire (**349**) and Herefordshire (**421**).

Out of a total of 90 criminal cases up to 1614 thirteen (and possibly horse-theft **436** and deer-theft **547**) were referred onwards to the Oxford assizes or sessions, with the suspects usually transferred to Oxford gaol awaiting the next general gaol delivery.

In only two of these cases were the suspects, or their accusers, Woodstock inhabitants. In the first (**348**) William Butterfeild was accused of assaulting an Eynsham man so severely that he was in danger of death. The second (**437**) was exceptional in that John Barnes repeatedly stole haberdashery from the shop of mercer William Bradshewe and implicated some twenty persons locally as receivers. As well as Barnes, four others, including Butterfeild again, were sent to the Oxford courts.

The rest of the actions involved thefts typically of such items as horses, cattle, sheep, deer, money and clothing, with suspects coming from up to 100 miles away or more. At this time, as up to the 19th century, prosecution of crime remained a primarily private responsiblity of the victims; and as they often came from distant places such people needed to be well-endowed to pursue such long-range justice.[40] In one case (**163**) a paid informer, John George reimbursed by Edmund Hiorne, seems to have been used to help catch two inveterate horse-thieves, one of whom was subsequently executed.

The 90 criminal cases divide approximately into 40% each for assault (38 cases) and theft (35 cases) and 20% miscellaneous other misdemeanours (17 cases). To contemporary reporters the country's main problem with crime, at a time when felony was at peak level, was seen to be theft rather than violence. Indictments at assizes and quarter sessions consisted largely of property offences: larceny, burglary, house-breaking, highway robbery, robbery and pickpocketing, and these typically made up two-thirds to three-quarters of all offences.[41]

In the assault actions some 60% of both plaintiffs and defendants were from the town, but the number of individual plaintiffs from outside were notably less than the number of defendants. Most of these offences were breaches of the peace taking place in or around the borough's inns and alehouses or at the markets or fairs. Heavy drinking was usually involved and often enough several

[40] Herrup, 26,32,86,88.

[41] Wrightson, 162; Sharpe (1984) 55,57-9; Herrup, 38-9.

defendants and plaintiffs were engaged. Typically offenders were bound over and fined, with weapons sometimes confiscated.

In the theft actions well over twice as many defendants were outsiders as were borough inhabitants. Moreover the outsider plaintiffs outnumber the townspeople by half. Thus a preponderance of the thefts involved outsiders and, as with the Oxford court referrals above, a significant proportion of all cases dealt with items stolen well away from the town. In this function, at least, the Woodstock courts were exercising some aspects of justice over appreciable areas: largely due to the customers drawn to its fairs and markets as these records show.

Two of the local thefts, about a year apart, involved repetitive pilfering of goods and money from the mercer's shop of William Bradshewe. The thieving by his assistant Walter Hollis (**334**) took place over a period of a year up to early 1611 including items worth about £10; with some seven receivers implicated. Hollis and his girl-friend and the key receiver, Anne Barnes, were punished by whipping and sitting in the stocks. Hollis incriminated his girl-friend as receiver when examined under oath (**334**:4/14), which appears to conflict with the Marian statute that suspects should not be put under oath to avoid them indicting themselves.[42] In the following year Anne Barnes' son, John, carried out more extensive pilfering from this source culminating in four miscreants being sent to Oxford assizes (see above).

The 20% other crimes (neither assault nor theft) were 17 in number and were largely civil misdemeanours associated with the townsfolk. Four related to family matters: 2 cases concerning reputed fathers, 1 of child maintenance (2 in 1614-22), and 1 case concerning unlawful copulation. Three cases arose from neglect of duty by junior officers such as the sergeant, constables and watchmen plus a similar one in which a prisoner escaped from custody.

Individual cases concerning outsiders were a runaway apprentice, a counterfeiter of letters, and slander between two Bladon men. Six cases cannot be classified because of lack of information.

As mentioned above, B78/3 covering the years 1614-22 contains no account of criminal examinations, moreover recording of the sessions of the peace appears less regular with only one offence noted between May 1616 and December 1618. As in the previous period the main magistrates were the sitting mayors and alderman Thomas Browne but here assisted by the non-freeman lawyer Jerome Kyte JP. In April and in May 1621 Kyte refused to sit with mayor John Glover at the Sessions so that the Recorder signed the licensing of victuallers with the mayor on this occasion. At the following sessions alderman Joseph Harris sat in addition to the mayor and Kyte, no doubt as potential

[42] Dalton, 273; Beier, 157.

replacement. In these eight years 24 individual actions of breach of the peace were dealt with, wrongdoers mostly under recognisance to appear at the next sessions.

Travellers' examinations

Very few depositions from Assizes of this time have survived since they were informal documents; those that have are largely from the North of England. The bare outcomes of several hundred examinations and trials at the East Sussex Quarter Sessions over the early 17th century have been reviewed. Earliest surviving Oxford Quarter Sessions records date only from 1687. More directly comparable in content to the present examinations are those heard before Sir Francis Ashley, recorder and borough magistrate for Dorchester, for committals to the Dorset Quarter Sessions and Assizes over the years 1614-35.[43]

Of the Woodstock court records B78/2 is noteworthy for the accounts of criminal examinations. Many of these are of suspects travelling through the town, some vagrants and some in trade or looking for employment. The testimonies provide quite extensive information on the life-styles, travels, acquaintances and contacts, and transactions of money and goods of those involved

Thus James and Isabel Smith of London gave accounts (**50**) of their marriage arrangements two years previously and their travels since, both together and separately, through Oxford to York and back, and their jobs, horse-dealings, and purse-thefts.

Horse-thief Francis Withe of Essex described in some detail (**53**) his activities over three months concerning picking-up acquaintances in London, their detention in Oxford, rural horse-bartering sessions and contacts on their route to Evesham, where the theft took place. This account reveals the extensive planning over time and distance for his exploits and the key roles a number of women played in their achievement, from the traveller Mary Bishop of Oxford, to his accomplice's wife accompanying him from Broadway, the lodging-keeper at Evesham and alehouse keeper at Offenham, and his wife and mother-in-law receiving him at Woodstock. He was committed to the next general gaol delivery in Oxford and was probably there sentenced to the death penalty.

Thomas Bradforde (**132**) of Ludlow set out his methods for stealing money from the travelling Lord Chandos players he was serving and for escaping their company.

[43] Herrup, 67; Gretton, M, xciii; Bettey, *passim*

William Hickes of Standlake confessed (**140**) to a whole series of sheep slaughterings in the Eynsham and Enstone areas so as to sell the skins to Woodstock and Oxford glovers.

Robert Debanck and Walter Howells of Winchcombe appeared a formidable pair of horse-dealers and thieves (**163**) who had trade contacts from Derbyshire, London, South Wales and the Midlands. Debanck carried sets of horse-theft tools, weapons including a charged pistol, and a bible; both men were forwarded to Oxford gaol where Debanck was subsequently executed.[44]

Thomas Jarratt from Warwickshire confessed (**179**) to writing and delivering a series of counterfeit letters supposedly between various members of the Phipps family who lived in places scattered across North Oxfordshire and thereby extorting payments from them.

Thomas Phillippson of Buckingham described (**229**) having his cloak stolen by 'hooking', that is by removing through a window on an extended hook (see Glossary).

Humphrey More, sheep-dealer from North Staffordshire, set out in detail his travels and transactions over a month (**349**). He brought a flock down to the Cotswold area, then spent 27 days travelling 200 miles around markets from Worcester to Bicester buying and selling some 155 sheep for £60. This sum of money was equivalent to that for the Borough annual acount of the time. He gave extensive information on sale prices and sizes, names of dealers, details of stopping places such as inns and alehouses, and a money deposit at an inn.[45]

George and Alice Bennett of Worcestershire gave accounts (**407**) of their travels and mishaps in the Midlands since leaving home a fortnight before; ending in their arrest at Deddington fair.

Jasper Taper, horse-dealer of Hertfordshire, gave details of how he travelled with fellow dealers (**436**) to Woodstock fair and his methods of bartering at Islip and the fair.

In two cases of killing deer in Woodstock Park it is noticeable that both Robert Dimock of Ditchley (**534**) and Ellis Olliver of Hook Norton (**547**) came from away. Methods of hunting with greyhounds and disposing of the bodies were outlined, together with procedures for catching the poachers. Dimock and his men came from the household of Sir Henry Lee who had charge of the deer; so that the raid falls in with the observation that much poaching of the period was by gangs organized by the gentry and wealthy farmers.[46]

Thomas Basly, butcher of Deddington, set out details (**538**) of rural cattle and

[44] *WCA*, 5,6,8

[45] *WCA*, *passim*.

[46] VCH Oxon xii 444 Sharpe (1984) 129-30

sheep-trading at Deddington bridge and on the downs nearby, using animals brought over from Northamptonshire commons.

Victual licensing

The magistrates commonly licensed five inn-keepers and some sixteen or more alehouse-keepers twice yearly at the borough sessions. This is recorded on twenty-two occasions during the fourteen years, missing Easter 1610, '13, & '17; and Michaelmas 1612 '15, '17, '18 and '21. Though this duty was often part of the borough sessions, it took place separately on occasion (see **83**, **142**). Licencees were commonly bound over in £10 with two sureties of £5, but in one year this doubled (**280**) and in March 1609 the recognisance rose to £100 and the sureties to £30. In April and September 1608 (**44**, **83**) examples are given of the fees actually paid for licences, and their loans. These records, together with the activities of the licencees and their customers, have been reviewed.[47]

A full record of a licensing session, including a copy of the national covenant and an exemplary licence is given in September 1608 (**83-4**): presumably consequent to the publication in June 1608 of the Privy Council Order 'Articles of Direction touching Alehouses'.[48] A similar exemplary licence is recorded in May 1621 (**1225**), in another time of grain shortage. In October 1609 all victuallers within the town were discharged, apparently by means of a jury largely chosen from offenders attending the borough sessions (**194**:2/2, **197**). A comparable contemporary example of drafting court customers to duty as petty jurors in criminal cases at county Assizes has been noted.[49] The cause of this overall dismissal is not known, and completely stopping their trade for any appreciable time seems hardly practicable. It may be relevant that though the dearth survey of barley and malt took place in November 1608 (**112**) the national peak in barley prices was reached in this year 1609.[50]

Although the magistrates discharged victuallers of their licences on occasion for a variety of misdemeanours, in the April 1608 session alderman Thomas Bradshewe defiantly declared in open court that he would keep piping and dancing in his inn at 10 and one o'clock in the night hereafter.

Flesh in Lent

A court sitting on this matter is recorded for the years 1608-1612 and 1620-2, in fulfilment of the statute of 1603 requiring them to pass judgment on those who had transgressed the law concerning the killing, dressing or eating of

[47] Taylor (1991), 251-65

[48] S.T.C., 92, 94-6.

[49] Herrup, 136.

[50] Bowden, 820.

flesh in Lent.[51] The last three sittings quote the king's proclamation at Royston the previous November for 1620, at Westminster the previous month for 1621, and at Newmarket a month before for 1622. Generally a few people were found guilty; ranging from none in 1610, to four including the mayor in 1609, and to seven including an alderman in 1611. Offenders were commonly inn or alehousekeepers, perhaps involved by their trades; a few cases of butchers killing animals also arose (e.g. **238**, **432**, **1125**, **1208**); all occupations specified in the recognisance of March 1622.

The extent of 'Puritan' influence in Woodstock at this time is unclear. On the one hand the council promoted notable series of church sermons; the purge of women victuallers in 1607 and withdrawal of all licences in 1609 (see above) suggest moral crusades quite beyond any necessary measures. Moreover the single court case of unlawful copulation and just three cases of base-child charity over a period of 14 years, compared with an expected some ten such births at the national illegitimacy rate, all point to a relatively sober community. Yet these Lenten courts derived directly from the 1603 statute and James's re-issues of it as in the proclamations 1620,1621 & 1622; during 1588-95 there was just a single sitting in 1591 following augmentation (33 Eliz.c.7) of the original penal statute. Thus these courts might be seen as features of political Lent rather than religious observance. As for victualling, from 1604 to 1614 the number of sellers increased by half and the women returned, and alderman Thomas Bradshewe openly challenged social restrictions on his inn (see above).[52]

Weights and measures

On four occasions in this period a survey of the bushels, weights and measures allowed in the borough was made by jury under the mayor as clerk of the market. Three of these surveys accompanied assize surveys in September 1608, November 1609 and July 1616 with one done alone in August 1611. As with the commodity assizes no mention is made to the royal clerk of market, in contrast to an inference drawn from the chamberlains' accounts.[53]

Individual holdings of these measures changed significantly from one survey to the next, though whether this reflected changes in the distribution of trading is not known. One intriguing detail is that Mr Fly owned not only two stones of seven pounds each, but also another at a weight of five pounds (**378**). The major survey and directive of September 1608 included definitions of bushel and gallon and of the difference between troy and avoirdupois weights (**88**:2/5).

[51] Statute 1 Jac.29.P.7; Dalton, 48.

[52] *WCA, passim*; Taylor (1991), 262/3; Wrigley, 224; WBM B78/1.

[53] *WCA*,8, n24.

Dearth survey

Hiorne's records were fuller in the early period of his office, as in B78/2, and generally diminished with time, with increasing omissions in successive books. Over this present period re-issues by the government of the 1586 Book of Dearth Orders, with only minor alterations, were made in the years of scarcity in 1608 and just after the end of B78/3 at the harvest of 1622.[54]

The 1608 issue, in addition to the grain survey itself (**112**), no doubt gave rise to several other special entries that year:

(a) an account of the general covenant on granting alehouse licences (**83**), directed by the separate publication of 'Articles of Direction touching Alehouses' (London 1608-9);
(b) census of freemen and inhabitants of the borough (**86**);
(c) setting out conditions of trading and marketing within the borough (**88**).

The survey of grain dearth provided details of the numbers of inhabitants in 29 important houses in the borough, together with the stocks of grain held by the various heads. In addition the rates of bread-baking and of brewing were registered, thus providing direct information on some rates of food consumption within the town. From these production rates it appears that a significant fraction of the borough's total calorie intake was taken in the form of the ale being brewed.[55]

Assize of bread and ale

On twelve occasions over the (1607-22) period the mayor called a court of assize, with himself as clerk of the market under the sovereign's patent, to price commodities on sale in the town. Sometimes two other JPs sat with the mayor, sometimes not. The jury of between 12 and 17 freemen presented to the court, upon their oaths, the prices that wheat and malts were fetching in Woodstock on the previous market day. Following these current free-market prices for best-, second-, and up to 1609 for third-wheats, and for best- and second-malts, the mayor set the assize prices for various commodities on all bakers, brewers, innholders, and victuallers in the borough.

Assizes were held in both May and September 1608, just prior to the dearth survey in that November, and in November 1609; none are recorded for 1610 & 1611, but an assize on best-wheat was made in 1612 at a time of increasing national price. In September 1608 the assize jury were given detailed direction on various aspects of bread and ale production (**88**). This set of assize prices for the period have been analysed and a possible system for the grading and pricing

54 Slack, 3,6.

55 Slack, 3; Taylor (1992), 345.

of loaves has been suggested.[56] From 1614 assizes were held in July 1616, and, under increasing prices, in August & December 1621 and March 1622.

Hoskins summarized the countrywide harvests for this period as follows:[57]

> 1607 average to poor; and 1608 bad;
> The decade from 1610-19 about average as a whole: two deficient harvests (1613, 1617), but nothing disastrous; and two good harvests to end the decade (1618, 1619)
> The next really bad harvest came in 1622.

A 'deficient' harvest is here defined as existing where the price of wheat is 10-25% above the long-term average; 'bad' where it is 25-50% above that average; and 'dearth' at over 75% above. On this basis the Woodstock prices confirm:

> September 1608 as dearth conditions;
> May 1608 and July 1616 as approaching 'bad';
> and March 1622 as 'deficient'.

For given grain cost the later bread prices were much higher than earlier ones: thus in March 1622, at similar wheat prices, the penny white loaf was 50% dearer than in May 1608; and the penny household loaf was 25% dearer in the later years, admittedly when third-wheat prices were no longer quoted.

In August and December 1621 the penny white loaf is described as 'drawn from fine Cockett'; denoting a quality just below that of top-class wastel flour and bread.[58]

No mention is made of the presence or influence of the clerk of the market of the royal household at these assizes, whereas the presence of this official, Mr Mosse, in Woodstock is noted in each of the years 1608-12. In some years his presence followed a week or two later than the assize, but in 1612 a specific note is made of the money 'payed for diet for Mr Mosse when he last sate as clark of the markett'.[59]

Corporation business

Occasional reference was made to corporation properties in leet business (**325**) and their rental at special meetings (**79**, **342**, **439**); memoranda dealt with ready moneys (**539**), an incidental purchase of nails (**247**), and Doleman's charity payments (**78**). Donation to an external charity cause was noted in July 1608 (**69**).

[56] Taylor (1992), 345.

[57] Hoskins, 29, 32.

[58] *O.E.D.*, 'cocket', 'boultel'.

[59] *WCA*, 5, 8, 13-15, 20, 26.

B78/3 Endpapers

At the back of volume B78/3 there are six folio pages bearing material different in nature to the rest of the contents. The items consist of:

the borough freeman's oath (**1287**)

names of the mayor, aldermen, common council, and non-councillor freemen for August 1619 (**1288**); and for November 1616 (**1289**) including non-freemen. These lists may be compared with the census list of 1608 (**86**) and the tithing lists of Hallisey and Shipp.

Copies, apparently in Hiorne's hand, of three feoffments:

one of 4 June 1302 for houses on the Oxford Road (**1290**);

one for a plot 'on the king's highway' dated 10 August 1469 (**1291**);

and the third dated 26 May 1409 for a local plot (**1292**).

Though Edmund Hiorne was granted three houses by the corporation in 1618 and he became a substantial property owner, a personal link between him and these properties has not been established.[60] These copies were perhaps made as of interest to the local Dennett, Jeffes and Taylor families of his day.

[60] *VCH Oxon* xii, 383,386.

EDITORIAL NOTE

The individual civil actions, criminal cases and corporation businesses are each given an entry number in bold type; successive appearances of each action etc. are then numbered consecutively out of the total number of appearances, e.g. **59**:7/14.

For those actions under way prior to the beginning of WBM B78/2 the appearance number is in brackets, e.g. **6**:(1/16); though the number of previous stages is not known. For those Portmoot actions continuing beyond that minute book the last appearance includes the run into WBM B78/3, e.g. **620**:4/7; in two cases the end of the action has not been found - to give, for example: **535**:29/52+.

Editorial additions are put in brackets. Years and dates have been put into historical years, beginning on 1st January.

Minutes of the Portmoot proceedings are in abbreviated law-Latin and these have been calendared in modern English. Headings have been abbreviated, but examples of full headings for Portmoot courts are given on the first page of each book, and for sessions of the peace in October 1609. Court business has sometimes been rearranged for ease of calendaring, but only within a particular recto or verso. The court officers are listed in Appendix 1.

Criminal examinations have been abbreviated, particularly with regard to repetitive informations; nevertheless the aim has been to retain the tone and scope of these contributions, as Hiorne himself seems to have done.

The original spelling of surnames has been retained; Christian names have been put into a standard modern form except in cases of doubt. Place names are given their modern spelling, together with the original spelling in brackets.

The counties are those before the local government reorganization of 1974.

GLOSSARY

The definitions are taken from : *The Oxford English Dictionary*; JH Baker; AL Beier; PA Brand; RD Connor; Michael Dalton; GD Gilmore; ERH Ivamy; W Lambarde and R Milward (see List of Abbreviations)

account, action of (*computo*):	to compel a bailiff, receiver or guardian to yield up his accounts
administrator, administratrix:	man (or woman) appointed to administer an intestate estate
affeerers:	jury to assess amercements
ale-draper:	alehousekeeper
alias (als.):	alternative surname indicated in brackets ( )
andirons:	metal fire-irons to support logs on open fires
appurtenance:	that which belongs, or relates to, other property
assumpsit:	a voluntary promise, for a consideration, to perform for another
attachment:	primarily, finding of sureties for the appearance of an individual
base-child:	an illegitimate child. By Acts of 1575/6 justices were empowered to charge either the mother or the putative father with the cost of the child's upkeep
bay:	mill-dam or sluice
blown:	stale, tainted
capias, writ of:	writ to arrest defendant to compel him to appear before court
certiorari, writ of :	writ commanding proceedings to be removed into a superior court for review
chafing-dish:	small portable vessel to hold live coals, used for keeping food hot; sometimes for cooking in
chandler:	merchant or dealer, especially in candles
cheat:	a lower grade of wheaten loaf
chirurgion:	surgeon
close:	a piece of ground surrounded by e.g. hedges, walls, buildings
closh ('cloche'):	a game like nine-pins or skittles

cockett:	bread of a lesser quality than best wastel (i.e.white) bread
common recovery:	here, a conveying device freeing land from entails and other encumbrances and selling it or revesting it in the owner
computo:	see account, action of
compounding:	arranging, coming to terms
compurgator:	those called, in wager of law, to swear belief in the truth of the defendant's denial
contra formam statuti:	against the form of the law
convented:	in breach of a covenant
coram nobis:	before King's Bench
coram justiciarii Domini Regis:	before the Court of Common Pleas
corpus cum causa:	a writ to produce someone under arrest or detention with a justification for their arrest
country (put him/themselves on the):	to submit to decision of jury (see *ponit se super patriam*)
court baron:	a manorial court which enforced the customs of the manor
cowle:	a large, two handled, cooling vessel used in brewing
curtilage:	the yard, garden or enclosure of a dwelling-house included within a fence
deforciant:	person transferring land by conveyance device known as a fine
demurrer :	objection, in an action, to a pleading on ground that it is insufficient in point of law
detinue:	an action to recover a moveable item of property unlawfully detained
dwt.:	pennyweight; 20 dwt. = 1 ounce troy
ejectment *(ejectione firme):*	an action to recover damages for ejection from land as lessee, or to try the title of land
ell:	a measure of cloth of 45 inches
enjoin:	prohibit, enforce or restrain by injunction
error, writ of:	writ raised in Chancery to obtain an annulment of proceedings on grounds of an error. For local courts of record, as here, error went to the King's Bench
estreat:	a copy of a court record, here of obligations
execution, writ of:	writ to put in force the sentence of a judicial proceeding; the final process (e.g. *fieri facias*)

fairing:	a present from a fair
felony:	a capital offence
feoffment:	a mode of transferring estates of freehold in possession (B78/3 Endpapers)
fiat executio:	an order for execution of an order or judgment whose execution has not yet been carried out
fieri facias:	a writ of execution to levy debt or damages from a party against whom judgment has been awarded or given
foot-clothes:	a pack-horse cloth reaching to the horse's feet
foreign plea:	plaint outside the court's jurisdiction
furlong:	(B 78/2, *f 70v*) the headland of a ploughed field
furnace kettle:	a cauldron
galloon (lace):	narrow ribbon or braid
garbell (garbol): avoirdupois, all of	a wide range of materials weighed in which give rise to refuse or waste (Dalton, 129)
gawne:	a gallon vessel
gridiron:	a grated iron utensil for broiling meat or fish
gurgeons ('gurgins'):	coarse meal
habeas corpora (juratorum):	a writ to summon a jury
habeas corpus:	here a writ to remove an action to the central courts at Westminster
habere facias seisinam:	a writ of execution to recover possession of seisin
hay-mow:	place for storing hay in a barn
hoggerel ('hoggerill'):	a young sheep of the second year
holland ('hallan'):	a linen fabric
homage:	in service to the King
hooking:	stealing by removing through a window on an extended hook (included in burglary in 1584; Baker, 605, Dalton, 231)
horseloaves:	bread made of bran or beans, for horses
horse-scorcer:	a jobbing dealer in horses
imparl:	discuss
information:	of several kinds, including two used here:- 1) an information on a penal statute, giving the informer a right to share in the penalty. See below '*Qui Tam*'

information (cont.):	2) a statement by which a JP is informed of a criminal offence for which a summons or warrant is required
inquiry, writ of:	inquiry, by oaths of a 12-man jury, into amount of damages to be awarded
ipse in m(isericord)ia:	he is in mercy, i.e. he is spared the fine or punishment
jakes:	privy
keever:	a tub or vat used in brewing
kilderkin (kinderkin):	a barrell of 16 or 18 gallons
lawn ('lane, laune'):	linen
leet:	view of frankpledge
levy:	seize goods by a writ; raise money by legal execution
liege:	loyal (subject of the King)
lockram:	coarse linen
logetts:	a game where pieces of wood are thrown at a stake
Martlemas:	Martinmas
maslin:	mixed grain, especially rye and wheat
medley ('medly'):	cloth woven of wool of different colours
messuage:	a dwellinghouse with its adjacent buildings and land for the use of the household
modo et forma:	defendant pleads denying the thing 'in the manner and form' as in the declaration
mound(s):	hedges or fences to delineate property
mozled:	muzzled; speckled with white or grey ('mezled' – Lambarde, *Eirenarche*)
neat:	any animal of the ox kind
nihil dicit (nil dicit):	failure on the part of the defendant to put in his defence
non assumpsit: *assumpsit*, that the	plea to the general issue in action of defendant did not promise as alleged in plaintiff's declaration
non-culpabilis (non-cul):	plea of not guilty
non debet (modo et forma):	a submission that no debt exists in the manner and form presented by plaintiff
non est factum:	plea by defendant that the writing is not his deed
non est informatus (*ad respondendum*):	attorney has no information on which to base a response to the plaint

non retinuisset:	he did not retain (him)
obligation:	a promise (usually written) to pay a debt
Osnaburg ('Osenbrigge'):	a coarse linen originally made in Osnabruck
overplus (*nimia, nirmia)*:	surplus
oyer of condition:	hearing of a document read in court (cf. *oyer et terminer*)
pallett:	a straw mattress
passport:	official licence that convicted vagrants carried home
peremptory day:	a final date determined by court for response to the point at issue
per minas:	contract made under duress
placito terre super recupero:	fine of land recovery; common recovery ('recov')
platter:	large flat dish, usually of wood
ponit se super patriam:	submission to trial by jury after issue had been joined on the pleadings
posnett:	small saucepan with three 'feet' for sauces etc.
precluded:	not allowed in law
privilege day:	the two extra days allowed a Woodstock freeman to answer Portmoot actions. (WBM B82, clause 40, 1580)
privilege, writ of :	plea intended to oust jurisdiction of the court on grounds that the defendant is privileged (a form of *habeas corpus*)
procedendo, writ of :	a Chancery writ commanding the judge of an inferior court to proceed without delay to a judgment
proclamation:	a form of conveyance of land by claim made in open court on three (usually successive) occasions
prosequendo, writ of :	writ of prosecution
putgally:	sweep-well; a long pole fixed on a high fulcrum having a counterpoise on the handle to lift water from a well or put
querent:	purchaser of land by conveyance
Qui Tam action:	a species of action of debt, where a statute forbade something under penalty to be paid, half to the King and half to anyone who sued for it

quitclaim:	formal renunciation of a claim, especially as part of the process of conveying land
racking:	describing a horse's gait
rash ('rashe'):	a smooth fabric of silk or worsted
rebuttal:	defendant's answer to plaintiff's surrejoinder, eighth stage in pleading
recognisance:	a legal obligation to do some particular act, or refrain from doing some particular unlawful act; the sum pledged as security that this obligation will be observed
recovery (of land):	a conveyancing device for freeing land from entails and other encumbrances in order to allow a sale
recusant:	one who refuses to acknowledge ecclesiastical authority; especially a Roman Catholic not attending Church of England services
rejoinder:	defendant's answer to plaintiff's reply; therefore the fourth stage in pleading
release (*relaxacio*):	release from a deed
remise:	resignation of a claim by deed
replevin:	a redelivery to the owner of his cattle or goods distrained on any cause upon surety that he will prosecute the action of replevin against the person who distrained
replication:	plaintiff's reply to defendant's plea; third stage in pleading
rescue ('rescussus'):	illegal recovery of goods or persons from custody when taken in distraint or arrested
ribanding:	ribboning
rogue(s):	for definition of them and their treatment *see* Dalton, 108-16; and Beier on vagrancy
safeguard ('savegard'):	woman's outer skirt for protection when riding
say:	fine silk cloth
scire facias:	a judicial writ equivalent to a summons to show cause why execution of action/ judgment should not take place; (also *alias scire facias* - renewal of above; and *sicut alias scire facias* - further renewal of above)
scorce:	to bargain for (a horse)
seizure:	legal possession

settlement deed:	a deed whereby property is settled, i.e. subjected to limitations; e.g. marriage and family settlements
shop-board:	counter division in a shop
sine die:	lit. 'without a day' i.e. discharge
skiving ('sciving'):	cutting skin with a knife
small drink:	weak beer
special verdict:	jury state the facts of the case, as they find proven, leaving the court to draw the proper legal inferences therefrom
surety:	one jointly bound with another; one bound to answer for another's appearance in court, payment of debt etc.; a guarantor
tallet:	a hay-loft over a stable
tallow:	melted fat of oxen and sheep used for making candles
tammy (?'tamey'):	a fine worsted cloth
tenement:	dwellinghouse; house, shop, land etc. held by a tenant
theve:	ewe of one or two years that has not had a lamb
thirdendall:	a standard measure of ale for victuallers; one and one third quarts
tippler:	an alehouse keeper, victualler
tipplinge-house:	an ale-house or tavern
toft:	homestead
tun-dish:	a dish of stated dimensions for measuring the toll of grain at a mill
utter:	offer for sale
venire facias (juratores):	a writ commanding, when issue was joined in an action, the summoning of a jury
wager of law ('*vadiatio legis*'):	procedure whereby defendant discharges himself from a claim on his own oath, bringing with him a declared number of his neighbours to swear their belief in his denial
wake:	feast day of a patron saint
waste, action of ('*vasti*'):	a tenant was liable for waste, spoil and destruction to houses, lands etc., during his estate in them
wrought, wrote:	worked, work
yeelvat:	a brewing vessel

CALENDAR OF WOODSTOCK BOROUGH MUNIMENT WBM 78/2

Minute book of New Woodstock Borough courts December 1607 to January 1614

[f1v]

1: 10 January 1608. The first court that Edmund Hiorne town clerk kept after he was elected, in the time of alderman William Meatcalfe mayor.

[f2]

Portmoot court of our lord king held in the borough of New Woodstock on the 21 December, in the fifth year of the reign of James by the grace of god king of England, France and Ireland, defender of the faith, and in the forty-first year of his reign of Scotland. Before William Meatcalfe mayor.[1]

Actions of debt:

2:(1/25) Hiorne vs Wierman - case continues.

3:(1/1) Gregory vs Batt - *alias scire facias* granted.

4:(1/5) (Richard) Whinge vs (Anthony) Maunde - *venire facias* granted.

5:(1/5) Seare vs Ashpole - copy of declaration granted.

Actions of trespass:

6:(1/16)(William) Todman vs (John) Batt - as before.

7:(1/15) Painter vs Forest - peremptory day to respond.

[f2v]

Action of debt:

8:(1/3) Thomas Browne, alderman vs Thomas Ayleworth, gent - continues.

Action of trespass on case:

9:1/1 Drewe vs Batt - Henry Rudgate undertakes for plaintiff to pay defendant's amercement and costs in next court as ruled.

Action of common recovery:

10:1/1 Thomas Grove and Thomas Samwell, gent, claim against William Meatcalfe senior for five messuages, one barn, five gardens, four acres of land and one acre of woodland with appurtenances in the borough of New Woodstock aforesaid, for which William Meatcalfe senior vouches to warranty his own elder son Thomas Meatcalfe, who willingly appears and warrants and vouches his younger brother William Meatcalfe who similarly warrants and vouches Henry Rudgate who warrants and then joins issue with the claimants by denying the assertion to the effect that William Meatcalfe senior has disseised them; afterwards in the same court on the demand of three calls he did not appear. Judgment is given by the court that the aforesaid Thomas Grove and Thomas Samwell should recover their seisin against William

[1] Following this example of a full heading to a Portmoot court, the rest are abbreviated to the date. Details of the court officers are given in Appendix 1.

Meatcalfe senior of the messuages, barn, gardens, four acres of land and one acre of woodland with appurtenances. The writ of *habere facias seisinam* was granted on this and was returned by the sergeant-at-mace[2] as executed while the court was still sitting.

[f3]

Portmoot court held 4 January 1608...

Actions of debt:

4:(2/5) Richard Whinge vs Anthony Mawnde - *venire facias* executed and returned, writ of *habeas corpora* granted.

5:(2/5) Seare vs Ashpole - plaintiff and defendant put themselves on the country, writ of *venire facias* granted.

Actions continuing: **2**:(2/25); **6**:(2/16).

[f3 v]

Action of trespass:

7:(2/15) Painter vs Forest - defendant responds by putting himself on the country; writ of *venire facias* granted.

Actions of debt:

11:1/9 Thomas Needler vs Andrew Jarnes for £48 - plaintiff puts declaration through his attorney; defendant, in prison, appears in person and asks for first privilege day: he remains in custody of the sergeant-at-mace.

12:1/2 William Rayer vs George Deye, administrator of the goods and chattels of his father John Deye who died intestate, on a plea of debt on demand for twenty marks. Plaintiff through his attorney states his case and George Deye comes in person and declares he cannot deny proof of the bequest so he himself owes the said William Rayer the debt of twenty marks in the manner and form aforesaid. Judgment by the court is that William Rayer should recover against the said George Deye both the debt of twenty marks and 7s for amercement and his costs. Also the court assesses damages at five shillings for detinue of his debt. Judgment to follow.

Action continuing: **8**:(2/3).

[f4]

Portmoot court held 18 January 1608...

Action of debt:

5:(3/5) Seare vs Ashpole - *venire facias* executed and returned; *habeas corpora* granted.

Actions continuing: **2**:(3/25); **6**:(3/16).

[f4 v]

Action of trespass:

7:(3/15) Painter vs Forest - *venire facias* executed and returned; *habeas corpora* granted for return in next court.

2 Sergeant Rudgate is here acting as the equivalent of the common vouchee in the similar Common Pleas collusive common recovery (See Baker (1977), 204-5).

Actions of debt:
8:(3/3) Browne vs Aylesworth - debt discharged.
11:2/9 Needler vs Jarnes - sergeant returns sureties, namely John Heath and Alexander Hed; second privilege day granted defendant to respond.
4:(3/5) Richard Whinge vs Anthony Maunde, clerk - the jury between parties namely

Richard Meades,	Jerome White,	Robert Bignill,
Joseph Harris,	John Heath,	William Edwards,
Edmund Rudgate,	Roger Sturgis,	William Bradshewe,
Robert Seare,	John Dissell,	John Wilkinson

on oath declare that the aforesaid bond has been made by the defendant, and assess damages at 2s, amercement ld and costs ld. Judgment in next court.
13:1/3 **Memorandum**. The end of William Meatcalfe's time as mayor of the borough.

[f5]

13:2/3 **Memorandum. Friday 22 January 1608.**
William Meatcalfe died in the time of his mayoralty and, since no record could be found of any man so doing heretofore, it was considered by the common council that the opinion of the borough recorder should be taken. Whereupon Edmund Hiorne, town clerk, took the opinion of the recorder James Whitlock

[f5v]

esquire, who had advice from Sir Lawrence Tanfield, lord chief baron of the exchequer and lately recorder of the borough. It was ordered and agreed that the commonalty of the borough should meet at the guildhall and there elect and choose one of the aldermen to be mayor and govern for the residue of the present year. The said election to be in such sort as used to elect the mayor at any time heretofore, with the like oath to be given to the new mayor as to any other. Testified by Edmund Hiorne.

[f6]

13:3/3 **Memorandum**. Alderman Thomas Browne was elected mayor for the residue of the year.

[f6v] (Blank)

[f7]

Portmoot court held 1 February 1608...
Action of trespass:
6:(4/16) Todman vs Batt - plaintiff produces and renders a writ of *procedendo* dated 23 January this year, and writ of *habeas corpus* is granted for return in next court.
Action continuing: **2**:(4/25).

[f7v]

Actions of debt:
11:3/9 Needler vs Jarnes - last privilege day granted to defendant.

4:(4/5) Whinge vs Maunde - court gives judgment that plaintiff should recover [blank] debt and [blank] for amercement and costs, *scire facias* granted.
12:2/2 William Rayer vs George Deye - plaintiff through his attorney Simon James comes and acknowledges himself to be satisfied of the debt between parties. Therefore George Deye goes quit.
Actions continuing: **5**:(4/5); **7**:(4/15).

[f8]

Portmoot court held 15 February 1608...

Conveyance:
14:1/3 First proclamation between William Porter querent and John Whitton alias Darlinge gentleman deforciant concerning one burgage messuage or tenement with appurtenances now held by William Porter or his assignees; situate, lying and existing in the borough in Hogmarket Street between the tenement of a certain Henry Whitton gent on the east now occupied by widow Amye Powell, with Petty John's Lane on the east and abutting on the north, and the lane leading to the Common Green on the south. Which the said William Porter has recently purchased and the aforesaid John Whitton alias Darlinge has handed over.[3]

[f8v]

Actions of debt:
4:(5/5) Whinge vs Mawnde - *alias scire facias* granted.
5:(5/5) Seare vs Ashpole - case discharged by agreement.
Actions continuing: **2**:(5/25); **6**:(5/16); **7**:(5/15); **11**:4/9.

[f9]

15. Flesh in Lent, 16 February 1608...

The persons here under written were sworn to enquire what disorders were committed within this borough concerning the killing, dressing or eating of flesh in the time of Lent.

Jury: Thomas Blith,	Francis Garter,	William Hickes junior,
Richard Hawkins,	Richard Jarnes,	Robert Bignill,
Thomas Godfrey,	Hugh Hamond,	John Ackley,
Thomas Abbott,	John Munck,	John Dissell.

They declare on oath that Thomas Screevin (2s) and Hugh Hamond (6d) have dressed flesh in their houses in the time of Lent contrary to the statute, and that Richard Coles (3s4d) has killed flesh and sold it to divers persons unknown. Therefore each of them is in mercy and must present themselves on the first day of the month.

[f9v] (Blank)

[3] See also *WCA*, 39.

[f10]

Portmoot court held 29 February 1608...

Conveyance:

14:2/3 Second proclamation between William Porter querent and John Whitton alias Darlinge deforciant concerning one burgage messuage or tenement with appurtenances in Hogmarket Street . . .

[f10v]

Actions of trespass:

6:(6/16) Todman vs Batt - provided that plaintiff does not begin case in next court, then defendant wins by default.

16:1/1 Henry Price vs Thomas Screevin - trespass and battery; action discharged.

11:5/9 Needler vs Jarnes - defendant did not appear on three occasions to answer. Therefore etc.

Action of trespass on case:

17:1/2 Henry Triplett vs Richard Taylor - day for declaration granted.

Actions of debt:

18:1/1 John Ryly vs Thomas Painter - action discharged.

19:1/1 Francis Garter vs Thomas Martyn - action discharged.

Actions continuing: **2**:(6/25); **7**:(6/15).

[f11]

20. Examinations before Thomas Browne mayor and Thomas Bradshewe JP, 9 March 1608 . .

John Lowe binds himself in £10 of his goods and chattels that John Symons carpenter will appear in person before the justices at the next borough sessions of the peace to receive judgment and will keep the king's peace towards all people. No surety needed, therefore discharged. John Symons pays 3s fine for breaking peace to William Rayer chamberlain. For breaking the peace William Edwards of the borough binds himself in £10, with Richard Hawkins weaver of the borough going surety on £5 of his goods and chattels, that Edwards will appear in person before the justices at the next borough sessions to receive judgment and meanwhile keep the peace towards all.

The justices commit Robert Addison and Robert Symons to the custody of Edward Rudgate constable and Richard Hawkins. John Symons and Robert Symons, junior, claim that Christopher Henworth, in service to John Throckmorton esquire, has broken the peace upon them.

[f11v]

John Symons and Robert Symons swear that great disorder was committed in William Edwards' house, with themselves, Edwards, Robert Addison butcher, and Christopher Henworth breaking the peace. Blood was drawn upon most of them, and Addison and Henworth had drawn their daggers and struck them.

All discharged after Addison paid 16d, John Symons 3s, John Lowe surety for John Symons 22d on 25 March 1608, and Henworth 20d.

21. Charity.

These moneys, total 7s10d, were delivered to Mr Rayer chamberlain to be bestowed on the Widow Towe for a gown and the making thereof; together with 7s for Barneshewe's children.

[f12]

Portmoot court held 14 March 1608...

Conveyances:

14:3/3 Third proclamation between William Porter querent and John Whitton alias Darlinge gent deforciant.

22:1/3 First proclamation between Robert Seare querent and Henry Barneshewe deforciant concerning one burgage messuage or tenement with appurtances now held by Seare or his assignees, situate, lying and existing in the borough between the tenement of Robert Chamberlain on the east side, and the tenement of the said Henry Barneshewe on the west side and abutting the Holloway on the south side. Which messuage[4] Seare has recently purchased and Barneshewe has handed over.

[f12v]

Actions of debt:

11:6/9 Needler vs Jarnes - judgment given for recovery of £48 for debt, and 18s6d for fines and costs; and a writ of *scire facias* against defendant's surety.

23:1/1 William Loggon vs William Nurth - represented by attorneys; plaintiff declares, with copy granted. Action discharged by agreement of plaintiff.

24:1/3 John Rylye vs Robert Winter - it is reckoned by the court held in the guildhall before Thomas Bradshewe, then mayor, on 24 June 1605 that the plaintiff should recover £3 for debt and 11s3d amercement and costs. Judgment of *scire facias* against defendant's surety and a further execution of action against Robert Winter.

Action of trespass:

6:(7/16) Todman vs Batt- *habeas corpus* taken for both defendant and plaintiff.

Action of trespass on case:

17:2/2 Triplett vs Taylor - action discharged.

Actions continuing: **2**:(7/25); **7**:(7/15).

[f13]

Portmoot court held 21 March 1608...

Conveyance:

22:2/3 Second proclamation between Robert Seare querent and Henry Barneshewe deforciant...

[4] See also *WCA*, 39.

Action of trespass on case:
6:(8/16) William Todman vs John Batt - the jury of

Robert Bignill,	Jerome White,	Nicholas Taylor,
Francis Garter,	John Ackly,	Ralph Durbridge,
William Edwards,	Thomas Screevin,	Richard Hawkins,
Robert Seare,	Thomas Martyn,	Thomas Williams

declare on oath that the claim of John Batt previously offered in reply to the allegation had been void. They assess damages at 13s4d, amercement and costs 2d, with judgment adjourned to next court.

[f13v]

Action of Qui Tam:
25:1/2 William Harris vs Thomas Bellingham - plaintiff lays an information on behalf of the king and of himself on a contravention of the statutes; defendant seeks licence to imparl.
Actions continuing: **2**:(8/25); **7**:(8/15); **11**:7/9; **24**:2/3.

[f14]

26. Examination before Thomas Browne, mayor, 24 March 1608...
Isabel Catesby, servant to William Edwards, confessed that she went to the house of John Gadbury gent in Woodstock on 22 March and stole a linen apron worth 6d which she delivered the same day to John Hinnett of Tew to deliver to her mother widow Margaret Catesby of Tew Magna. William Edwards charged her with taking 10s of gold from the purse of one Rowland of Gloucester coming lying in his alehouse about Shrovetide last. Catesby confessed to having the money but says she found it in the chimney ashes in the house and gave it to a stranger William Hastey, for but 4s, when he lodged at the alehouse. (Mark of) Isabel Catesby.

[f14v]

Portmoot court held 4 April 1608...
Conveyances:
22:3/3 Third proclamation between Robert Seare querent and Henry Barneshewe deforciant...
27:1/3 First proclamation between William Rayer alderman and his son Thomas Rayer querents and John Taylor clerk, Robert Heath and Frances his wife, and John Taylor woolman and Merriall his wife deforciants: concerning one burgage messuage or tenement with appurtenances now held by John Taylor woolman; situate, lying and existing in the borough in Oxford Street between the tenement of Robert Symons now occupied by Andrew Jarnes on the north side and the tenement of Nicholas Glover on the south side. Which property William and Thomas Rayer have purchased and John Taylor[5] clerk, Robert Heath, and John Taylor woolman have handed over.

[5] See also *WCA*, 38.

[f15]

Action of debt:
28:1/4 Justinian Redhead vs Richard Heath - plaintiff produces declaration through attorney, defendant's attorney requests copy.
Actions of trespass:
29:1/7 John Batt vs William Todman - plaintiff produces declaration and defendant's attorney requests copy.
31:1/4 Leonard Masse vs Richard Busbye - plaintiff's attorney produces declaration and defendant's attorney requests copy.
Action of trespass on case:
30:1/4 William Buller vs Richard Busbye - as above.
Action of Qui Tam:
25:2/2 William Harris vs Thomas Bellingham - action discharged.
Actions continuing: **2**:(9/25); **6**:(9/16); **7**:(9/15); **11**:8/9; **24**:3/3.

[f15v]

Actions of debt:
32:1/1 William Brotherton, plaintiff vs John Parsons.
33:1/7 Thomas Screevin vs Edward Prince - plaintiff produces declaration, defendant's attorney requests copy.
34:1/4 Roger Shirte vs Henry Rudgate - plaintiff produces declaration and defendant in person requests privilege day in next court.
Action of trespass:
35:1/1 John Heath plaintiff vs William Springall.

[f16]

36. Examination before Thomas Browne mayor, 7 April 1608...
William Godwine yeoman, late of Wookey, Somerset, being demanded how he came by a pair of worsted stockings taken upon him, said he had bought them for 6s8d on 21 March in 'Loudon'[6] in Cornwall from a man whose name he did not know but who dwelt at the sign of the Red Cock. He went from the house of his father Mr Anthony Godwine at Wookey about 12 March, taking with him 3s in money and a cloak which he sold to Richard Parker keeper of the Three Horseloaves in Wells for 10s. Upon his first apprehension he told the constable that he dwelt in Chipping Norton, being a tapster at the Swan there, and had bought the stockings from a traveller in victuals.

(Signed) William Godwin.

37. Charity. The stockings are delivered to Mr Rayer chamberlain who gave to Mr Mayor by his appointment 18d.

[f16v]

38. Sessions of the Peace and View of Frankpledge held 13 April 1608 before Thomas Browne esquire mayor and Thomas Bradshewe gent alderman JPs

6 ? Lewdon, Devon.

with many others there from the community, by me Edmund Hiorne clerk of the commonalty there.

Court officers as before except that John Bradshewe replaces John Lowe as tithingman.

Jury of homage:

Michael Nursse, Francis Collingwood, John Lowe, Edward Rudgate, John Bradshewe, John Dubber, John Heath, Thomas Screevin, Jerome White, Alexander Head, Richard Meades, Robert Bignill, Thomas Williams, William Meatcalfe, Roger Sturgis, Bennet Painter: sworn.

[f17]

10 December 1607. (Presumably antedated)

39:1/2 *Maintenance order*. Nicholas Glover binds himself in £20, with Richard Hawkins and Richard Shad each giving £10 surety, that Glover will attend this court day in person to answer.

The court orders that Nicholas Glover, the supposed father, shall pay towards the maintenance of John Turtle alias Glover, base son of Margaret Turtle, six pence a week, to begin this day. The child is to remain with Ellen Hinnye the wife of Thomas Hinny of Begbroke. Nicholas Glover and William Raunson as his surety in £10 are required to arrange the aforesaid in person and to appear at the next borough sessions of the peace. This order to continue during the justices' pleasure.[7]

40. *Recognisance*. Phillip Collier binds himself in £20 and Simon Collier gives surety in £10 that the said Phillip will appear in person at this court day, with recognisances continuing until the next sessions of the peace.

(see **100** and **147**)

(Apparently relating to sessions and frankpledge 13 April 1608).

41. *Estreats*. The presentments of the jury appear on the file and the estreats thereof were delivered to the constables aforesaid, amounting to the sum of £6.17s.10d .

42. *Recognisance*. William Edwards binds himself in £10 with Richard Hawkins his surety in £5 that he will present himself at court this day. The court gives judgment that on paying 5s fine to the mayor and commonalty he is exonerated and continues his victualling license.

The sessions of the peace is adjourned until 9 May next;

adjourned until 30 May

Affeerers: John Dubber, John Lowe, Michael Nursse: sworn in.

Robert Bignill and Thomas Williams: deleted.

[7] See also references in *WCA*, 251, index under: Glover alias Turtle, John. See Glossary: base child.

[f17v]

39:2/2 *Maintenance order* before Thomas Browne mayor, 17 April 1608. Margaret Turtle, spinster of Woodstock, binds herself in £10, with Jerome White shoemaker as her surety in £10, on the conditions following: that she, the mother of John Turtle alias Glover a base child of herself and Nicholas Glover born in Woodstock, shall pay or cause to be paid to the chamberlains of Woodstock for the time being towards the maintenance of the child 4d weekly for the full time of two years; the first payment to begin on Wednesday next. Also she assigns a debt of 12s due to her from Drewe Gregory, which he has undertaken to pay by 6d per week to be employed towards the maintenance of the child. (see also **99**)

43. Examination before mayor, 18 April 1608.... Runaway apprentice. William Humphries, son of Thomas Humphries of Farmington in Gloucestershire, was bound apprentice to John Merrall baker of Cheltenham, Gloucestershire, for 7 years and stayed with him about 4 years. At Michaelmas last he ran away and came to John Glover baker of Woodstock and served him as covenanted servant for one year at 30s per annum, as he confesses.

[f18]

44. Victualling licences: The names of those victuallers that are appointed to continue victualling in the borough and are appointed to have 10s a piece ready at such time as they shall be appointed by the mayor and justice aforesaid, by virtue of the king's majesty and orders thereunto annexed.

Innholders:

Thomas Bradshewe, alderman	William Rayer, alderman
John Glover,	Richard Meade,
Thomas Williams,	John Dissell.

Memo: Mr Bradshewe did say in open court that he would keep piping and dancing in his house at 10 and one a clock in the night hereafter.

Victuallers:

Henry Rudgate,	William Edwards,	Jerome White,
Hugh Hamond,	John Acklye,	Nicholas Taylor,
Ralph Durbridge,	Thomas Godferye,	John Taylor,
William Hickes,	Thomas Screevin,	Nicholas Glover,
Bennett Painter.		

Thomas Abbott was licensed by Mr mayor only, and Mr Thomas Bradshewe did deign to give his consent thereunto. (Deleted: Bennett Painter was discharged from his victualling for he did not desire to continue it - discharged.
Sessions of the peace: discharged). (signed) Edmund Hiorne.

[f18v]

45. *Property dispute*: The jury (**38**) upon view of a mound between Alderman Ryly and John Glover, did agree that Ryly shall set the mound upright by

Michaelmas Day next. And also find that the apple tree that Mr Ryly cut there belongs to Glover. Ryly under a penalty of £10.

[f19]

Portmoot court held 18 April 1608...

Conveyances:

27:2/3 Second proclamation between William Rayer and son querents and John Taylor clerk and others deforciants.

46:1/3 First proclamation between Thomas Painter querent and Henry Barneshewe deforciant concerning one burgage messuage or tenement with appurtenances now occupied by the said Thomas Painter or his assignees, situate, lying and existing in the borough between the tenement of Robert Seare on the east side, and the clerk of a certain Jerome Nash gent occupied by the said Thomas Painter on the west side, and abutting the Holloway. Which Painter has purchased and Barneshewe has handed over.

[f19v]

Actions of debt:

11:9/9 Needler vs Jarnes - executed *sicut alias scire facias* returned, defendant appears in person and is committed by court to sergeant.

28:2/4 Redhead vs Heath - peremptory day to respond granted.

33:2/7 Screevin vs Prince - similarly.

47:1/12 John Greene vs Timothy Walker - plaintiff declares, with copy to defendant whose attorney requests privilege day.

Actions of trespass:

6:(10/16) Todman vs Batt - the court adjudges for plaintiff 13s.4d damages and £3:12s amercement and costs; *scire facias* granted.

29:2/7 Batt vs Todman, - day to respond granted; not peremptory.

31:2/4 Masse vs Busbye - peremptory day to respond granted.

Action of trespass on case:

30:2/4 Buller vs Busby - similarly.

Actions continuing: **2**:(10/25); **7**:(10/15); **34**:2/4.

[f20]

48. Election. 23 April 1608.

Memorandum. These persons were present at the admission of William Kinge shoemaker to be a freeman burgess of this borough, namely:

Thomas Browne, mayor, Edmund Hiorne, clerk of the council,
Henry Rudgate, sergeant, John Glover, chamberlain,

Richard Meade,	John Dubber (deleted),	Nicholas Taylor,
Richard Wrighte,	John Heath,	John Lowe,
Joseph Harris,	Thomas Screevin,	Robert Bignill,
Thomas Williams,	John Raunson,	Jerome White.

He was elected by the consent of the 12 (sic) persons above who all, but those persons underlined, consented that he pay to the town but 40s, namely: 10s presently and 30s at 8 December: Thomas Kinge of Hayford ad pontem (i.e. Lower Heyford) in county Oxon., husbandman to be bound for it - sworn. A bond delivered to chamberlains Mr Rayer and John Glover for the 30s and also 10s in money. (signed) Edmund Hiorne.

[f20v]

49. Information: given 24 April 1608 before Thomas Browne mayor and Thomas Bradshewe gent JPs.

Anthony Hunslowe shepherd of Thrupp declares on oath that on Friday last 22 April he was at Campsfield looking after his master's sheep when he saw a carter coming along the highway take a bottle of his master's hay from his rick and being followed left it by the highway. Presently Richard Heath glover of Woodstock came on horse and would have taken the hay though told it belonged to his master, Mr Gregory. When Hunslowe tried to recover the hay Heath would have tripped up his heels, and after foul speech between them, drew his sword and struck Hunslowe's back with it.

[f21]

50:1/6 **Examination 24 April 1608.**

James Smith late of the Strand in London, glover journeyman to Mr Edward Hayward, is examined on when and where he married Isabel his wife. He says he married her by the name of Isabel Savidge at St. Giles-without, Cripplegate, London on 5 August two years past by licence from the Arches[8] procured by Mr Andrew Billins who serves the clerk of the council table with pen, ink and paper. The bay trotting stone horse (stallion) he now has at Woodstock, he bought about Christmas last at John Jepson's inn at Warsop, Notts. He knows no horse scorcer dwelling in Kent through the innkeeper, and he paid for the horse £6 in gold without tolling. He and his wife came from London together last Thursday intending to ride to York and lay the first night at Wycombe ('Wyckham') at a place not known. Next day they came and lay that night at Thomas Williams innkeeper of the Rose until today. He had brought with him about £5; he did not know that his wife continued at Oxford since their marriage. There was in his purse £3:3:4d in gold and 12s2d in silver, which gold is left in the hands of Thomas Williams constable.

(mark of) James Smith.

[f21v]

50:2/6 *Re-examination of James Smith*, 26 April 1608, before Thomas Browne and Thomas Bradshewe.

[8] Court of Arches of the Archbishop of Canterbury.

Smith says they came to Oxford on way to York since his wife was owed 20s for a gold ring, pillion and savegard she had in Oxford. He did not know who owed the money nor where they were, nor the times his wife was in Oxford. She left him in London about three-quarters of a year after their marriage and he did not know where she had lived until about the first week in Lent last. He then met her in Drury ('Drewery') Lane, London, since when they have lived together. During her absence he thinks she lived with Sir Thomas Mettam's lady. He bought his horse from Thomas Beecham horsescorcer of Bromley, Kent and kept it until Easter term at his father's house on Peeter Smith's dwelling in Holden ('Howden'), twelve miles from York. From there it was sent to him in London by Richard Barraclewe carrier of Wainegate, York. He left his father about Candlemas last with this carrier and went on horse and foot to his master in London. He kept his horse at the Three Cups in Holborn ('Howborne') at 6d/day and night till last Thursday. Note: He gave me for my pains for writing letters and other things of his own accord: 2s. (*mark of*) James Smith (?)

[f22]

50:3/6 *Examination of Isabel Smith*, 26 April 1608.
She says that two years ago she was going from York to London when, in an alehouse at Deddington, Oxon, in the company of seven other men and women, she was apprehended on suspicion of felony for the cutting of purses. For one of her company was suspected of that crime and all of them were sent to the gaol where she lay fifteen weeks until the assizes. At mid-Lent last she hired a horse of a carrier at Clifford, Leicestershire, for 1s. to bring her to Oxford, where she left her pillion and savegard at the alehouse of one Harris in Saint Thomas parish. She then went to renew an acquaintance at Oxford gaol but a prisoner there in familiar sort pulled from her finger her gold ring worth 20s. Mr Bagwell, now the gaoler, promised to deliver the ring to her or pay her 20s for it. When she came from London on Thursday last she had 10s in her purse which her husband did not know of, this she gave to him.
50:4/6 *Memorandum*, 26 April 1608.
On this day James Smith was given liberty to go abroad in the town until the return of the messenger who was travelling to the justice of the peace in Nottingham concerning the trial. Smith came to the mayor Thomas Browne in the market and in the middle of the market claimed the mayor had wronged him and he, Smith, would call him in question before the Lords of the Council for his injustice and for the charge putting him on trial.

[f22v]

50:5/6 *Re-examination of James Smith*, 4 May 1608.
James Smith says that a week before Christmas last he came alone from London to Kegworth, Leicestershire, by Nottingham, where he met his mother's sister and went together to Warsop. He had ridden from London upon a brown

trotting mare, bought from a stranger in Smithfield for 26s8d and noted by Mr Russell the toll-keeper. He left the mare, without any consideration, with a labourer at 'Baseforth' (? Basford) two miles from Nottingham and from there 'Basenworth' he and his aunt went to Nottingham, she riding a bay nag. There he bought his horse from one Beecham at Mr Littleford's house the Bull's Head. Upon Christmas Eve last at the same inn he, perceiving a stranger bidding 20 nobles for the said horse (one Henry Nolton of Lenton by Nottingham, horsescorcer), asked Beacham a stranger, to let him try the horse to Warsop. The three of them rode the horse there in turns and he bought it for £7, but did not toll. (Margin note: Sir Henry Parryn, JP in Nottingham refused to break up a writ). He further said he will buy another horse as unlawfully if he can come by it. He denies that he or his wife, to his knowledge, did use any trade or sell any small wares up and down the country around Warsop, or that his wife was with him at Warsop at Christmas last, or at York, or that he married her as a widow. Beacham and himself and his aunt parted at Warsop town's end on St. Stephen's day when Beacham intended to go by foot to Rotherham, about 12 miles off.
50:6/6 On being told by the mayor that he had uttered threatening speeches to the mayor in the market place on Tuesday last, Smith said he was then in his drink and had drunk too much. (mark of) James Smith.

[f23]

Portmoot court held at the Guildhall 2 May 1608.[9]

Conveyances:

27:3/3 Third proclamation between William Rayer with son querents and John Taylor clerk with others deforciants.

[f23v]

46:2/3 Second proclamation between Thomas Painter querent and Henry Barneshewe deforciant.

Action of common recovery:

51: Simon Jeames gent claims against William Rayer alderman and Thomas Rayer his son, one messuage, one barn, two gardens, three acres of land, two acres of pasture, and one acre of woodland, with appurtenances in the borough of New Woodstock. For which William and Thomas Rayer vouch to warranty John Taylor, clerk, Robert Heath and John Taylor woolman who warrant to vouch Henry Rudgate sergeant who warrants and joins issue with the claimants by denying the assertion that the two John's have disseised the said Simon Jeames. And afterwards Henry Rudgate solemnly demanded on three calls in the court did not appear, but in contempt of court withdrew and made default. Judgment is given that Simon Jeames recovers his seisin of the property against William and Thomas Rayer, and a writ of *habere facias seisinam* was granted

[9] The Guildhall meeting place is recorded occasionally.

on this and returned by the sergeant as executed while the court was still sitting, which was executed according to the law of this kingdom of England. (see also **27**).

[f24]

Actions of debt:
28:3/4 Redhead vs Heath - defendant does not appear after three calls, therefore in default.
33:3/7 Screevin vs Prince - similarly.
34:3/4 Shirte vs Rudgate - defendant in person acknowledges his debt of £16, which judgment grants with amercement and costs to be executed at next court.
47:2/12 Greene vs Walker - peremptory day to respond granted.
Actions of trespass:
6:(11/16) Todman vs Batt - sergeant has returned executed *scire facias*, and renewal is granted against defendant's surety.
31:3/4 Masse vs Busbye - since defendant does not appear after three summonses, judgment is given for a writ of inquiry on damages.
Action of trespass on case:
30:3/4 Buller vs Busbye - similarly
Actions continuing: **2**:(11/25); **7**:(11/15); **29**:3/7.

[f24v]

52: Assize of Bread and Ale. The court of Thomas Browne mayor and clerk of the market held 2 May 1608 by virtue of the king's majesty's letters patents granted by him and his highness's progenitors.
Jury for the king:

John Raunson,	John Dubber,	Thomas Screevin,
Joseph Harris,	Alexander Head,	Roger Sturgis,
Francis Garter,	John Bruce,	Robert Seare,
James Dissell,	William Hickes junior,	Richard Jarnes: sworn in

The jury present on their oaths that last market day the best wheat was sold for 41s4d the quarter, second for 37s4d, and third for 33s2d. Best malt for 21s4d. The mayor commands all bakers, brewers, innholders and tipplers to keep the assize according to the rates aforesaid, namely: the baker to make his penny white loaf to weigh 10 ounces and a half, the penny wheaten loaf to weigh 15 ounces and a half, and the penny household loaf to weigh 21 ounces and a half. And the innkeeper to sell a quart of the best beer and ale within and without their houses for a penny, and 2 quarts of small drink within and without their houses for a penny.

[ff25 and 25v] (Blank).

[f26]

53:1/5 Examination before Thomas Browne mayor and Thomas Bradshewe gent JPs, 7 May 1608.

Examination of Francis Withe, gent, late servant to John Smith gent of London late dwelling at Leyton, Essex, touching the stealing of a brown bay trotting mare from Christopher Newinton gent of Offenham, Worcs., on Monday night last 2 May from his grounds at Offenham. He says on Monday 27 April he and one George Ayngell were at his mother-in-law's, widow Smith, in Woodstock. He first met Ayngell, a joiner from Evesham, Worcs., in mid-Lent last at the Old Bailey, London, when he was at the Roebuck, and they rode from London to Broadway, Worcs., he on a bay gelding and Ayngell on a grey, trotting gelding.

On coming to Oxford they were attached by the bailiffs on suspicion of felony, and bound to appear at the town sessions. Discharged by proclamation on Thursday sennight after Easter,[10] they proceeded towards Ayngell's mother's house in Evesham; taking a maid Mary Bishop and a young man from Oxford who they left in Enstone after one night in Woodstock. He and Ayngell rode a bay ambling mare which he bought for 7 nobles, without tolling, since Easter last from a stranger in Wanstead, Essex.

[f26v]

53:2/5 After 3 weeks he scorced the mare on Broadway Hill with a tanner, of unknown name, of Saintbury ('Sayntbury'), Glos., whose father dwells in Cleeve (i.e. Cleeve Prior), Worcs., for a little black trotting nag plus 10s, without tolling. He sold the black nag to a stranger dwelling in Chipping Norton on Wednesday sennight last 27 April for 30s without tolling, but William Dolefyn of Adlestrop by Chipping Norton would give his word for the sale.

He and Ayngell rode from Chipping Norton towards Evesham on a little bay trotting nag carrying his saddle and bridle; that night he stopped at Bourton-on-the-hill while Ayngell went on to Evesham. After two nights he went by foot on Friday to stay the night at Anthony Brod's Green Dragon at Broadway and met Ayngell and his wife. Next day Ayngell rode to Evesham while he and Ayngell's wife went by foot; he spent the night at Widow Decon's house and dined there on Sunday (he was there to collect 30s Ayngell owed from a loan during their troubles at Oxford).

53:3/5 After dinner he went alone to Offenham to see Mrs. Watson at the alehouse and met by appointment Ayngell, who promised to pay the 30s loan, and George Jeames of Evesham.

[10] At the end of sessions any prisoners not indicted were discharged, if the proclamation for evidence against them was made with no response. Baker, 581.

[f27]

About half an hour after sunset the three of them returned together to Evesham, and he denies that he was in any grounds near the Offenham alehouse that day. All three were in Evesham by nine o'clock and he slept in the same bed as Ayngell in his house. On Monday 2 May he came afoot alone to Woodstock, leaving his bridle and saddle with Ayngell, and lay all day and night on Tuesday and Wednesday with his wife at Woodstock. On Thursday he walked to the 'Tabut' (?Talbot/Tabard) at Enstone to meet Roger Legge, butcher, but missed him and stayed two or three hours with Giles Parker, butcher of Great Tew, and 3 or 4 men of Enstone without private conference. He then went to the Swan at Chipping Norton but was unable to collect 5s owing him from the sale of a horse there on 27 April, and he stayed the night without company. On Friday morning he came afoot to Woodstock. Concerning the stealing of the aforesaid brown bay trotting mare from the grounds of Christopher Newington of Offenham on Monday night last, he says he did not steal her or know or is acquainted with the stealing of her.

Francis Withe's mark.

[f27v]

53:4/5 *Committal.* Before the aforesaid justices 7 May 1608. Christopher Newington, gent, of Offenham, Worcestershire, and Thomas Hewbande alias Hibbotts gent of Inkberrow ('Inckbourough'), Worcestershire, bind themselves on £40 each under condition that Newington provides evidence according to the terms of the statutes against Francis Withe on suspicion of felony at the next general gaol delivery held in the county of Oxon.

53:5/5 *Re-examination of Francis Withe* before the mayor and aforesaid justice, 8 May 1608.

Re-examined touching the colour of his saddle and when he did bait on Monday last when he came afoot from Evesham to Woodstock, Withe says he did not stay or drink in any place but at the Chapel-of-the-Heath by Chipping Norton.[11]

The colour of his saddle is red and it is left in Evesham.

He was married about two years since at Welford, Warwickshire, by one Sir Rogers without a licence, being not asked according to the law; there were half a dozen men in his company, namely one Parker and Smith and others.

[f28]

Portmoot court held 9 May 1608...

Conveyance:

46:3/3 Third proclamation between Thomas Painter querent and Henry Barneshewe deforciant. None come for it to be refused. Judgment given......

[11] The Chapel-on-the-Heath on John Speed's 1605 Oxfordshire map (Nicholson,146). Originally a chapel of the priory of Cold Norton, becoming an inn by the end of the 17th C. (Evans. 382/3)

[f28v]

Actions of debt:
28:4/4 Redhead vs Heath - surety accepted, action discharged.
33:4/7 Screevin vs Prince - court judges plaintiff should receive £3:19s for debt, [blank] amercement, and 2d damages and detinue; *scire facias* granted against surety.
34:4/4 Shirt vs Rudgate - defendant's arrears to be executed and plaintiff's attorney Simon Jeames acknowledges satisfaction with £16 for debt, 14s2d amercement and 2s damages. Therefore defendant goes quit.
47:3/12 Greene vs Walker - defendant does not appear after three summonses; therefore default granted.
Actions of trespass:
31:4/4 Masse vs Busby - action discharged.
6:(12/16) Todman vs Batt, - sergeant returns writ, defendant does not appear; therefore execution of sentence granted against defendant and surety.
29:4/7 Batt vs Todman - defendant puts response of a foreign plea, and swears in person that his own action is the true one.
Action of trespass on case:
30:4/4 Buller vs Busby - action discharged.
*Actions continuing: **2**:(12/25); **7**:(12/15).*

[f29]

Portmoot court held 23 May 1608...
Actions of trespass:
6:(13/16) Todman vs Batt - sergeant returns that he has received in custody the goods of John Bradshewe as surety for the defendant by effect of a royal writ of *fieri facias*: three and a half pieces of sackcloth and one piece of tufted fustian valued at 47s. The defendant produces in this court a royal *writ of error* to be returned on the octave of Trinity next, bearing the date 21 May instant. Wherefore the court will advise at the next sitting. Aforesaid goods appraised at [blank].
29:5/7 Batt vs Todman - court will advise.
Actions continuing: **2**:(13/25); **7**:(13/15).

[f29v]

Actions of debt:
33:5/7 Screevin vs Prince - the executed *scire facias* is returned and renewed.
47:4/12 Greene vs Walker - court adjudges plaintiff should recover 48s for debt, 16s6d amercement and costs, and 7s damages for detaining the debt; *scire facias* granted against the surety.

[f30]

Portmoot court held 30 May 1608...

Actions of debt:

33:6/7 Screevin vs Prince, - the renewed *scire facias* is returned executed, and defendant does not appear. Writ of execution is granted against defendant and his surety.

47:5/12 Greene vs Walker - the executed *scire facias* is returned and renewed.

Actions continuing: **2**:(14/25); **6**:(14/16); **7**:(14/15); **29**:6/7.

[f30v]

Portmoot court held 13 June 1608...

Actions of trespass:

7:(15/15) Paynter vs Forrest - action fails by default of plaintiff.

6:(15/16) Todman vs Batt - plaintiff's attorney Henry Rudgate produces royal writ of execution, directing judgment by mayor and commonalty of the borough, dated 8 June, to be proclaimed in open court.

Actions of debt:

33:7/7 Screevin vs Prince - action discharged by assent of plaintiff.

47:6/12 Greene vs Walker - sergeant returns executed writ of *alias scire facias*, defendant does not appear; execution of action against defendant and his surety.

Actions continuing: **2**:(15/25); **29**:7/7.

[f31]

Action of account:

54:1/5 John Batt vs Anthony Noble, clerk - defendant attached by his body and his attorney appears; plaintiff's attorney puts declaration, with copy to defendant.

Actions of debt:

55:1/6 Richard Wright vs William Porter - defendant appears and plaintiff requests day to put declaration at next court.

56:1/4 Richard Whinge vs Thomas Smith - defendant appears by attorney and plaintiff puts declaration with copy granted.

57:1/3 John Bradshewe vs William Hickes jun. - defendant appears by attorney; plaintiff requests day to declare at next court.

Action of trespass:

58:1/4 John Hasle vs Thomas Skey - defendant appears by attorney; plaintiff puts declaration with copy granted.

Action of trespass on case:

59:1/14 Edward Carpenter vs Andrew Jarnes - defendant appears by attorney and plaintiff requests day to put declaration at next court.

[f31v]

Conveyance:

60:1/4 before mayor Thomas Browne 17 June 1608.

Order: John Whitton gent that justly he keep the agreement with William Rayer concerning one messuage or tenement and its backside with appurtenances in the said borough, now in the occupation of the said William. And if he does not do so etc....

And the concord is as follows: that the said John Whitton acknowledges the said tenement with appurtenances to be the right of the said William which he has as the gift of the said John, and he remits and quitclaims them for the said John Whitton and his heirs to the said William Rayer and his heirs in perpetuity. And in addition the same John Whitton concedes for himself and his heirs that he will warrant the said tenements with appurtenances to the said William Rayer and his heirs against all his heirs and against the heirs of his deceased father George Whitton in perpetuity. And for this fine etc...

Signatures of John Whitton, mayor, and town clerk.

[f32]

Portmoot court held 27 June 1608...

Conveyance:

60:2/4 First proclamation between William Rayer querent and John Whitton alias Darling deforciant concerning one messuage or tenement with garden with appurtenances now occupied by William Rayer or his assignees, situate lying and existing in the borough between the tenement of William Porter now occupied by John Symons on the east side and the tenement of the said John Whitton now occupied by widow Eadie Hollis on the west side and lying on the north on Petty John's Lane. Which William Rayer has purchased and John Whitton has handed over.[12]

Actions continuing: **2**:(16/25); **47**:7/12.

[f32v]

Action of account:

54:2/5 John Batt vs Anthony Noble - peremptory day granted to answer in next court.

Actions of debt:

55:2/6 Richard Wright vs William Porter - because plaintiff does not appear to bring suit, therefore etc.

56:2/4 Richard Whinge vs Thomas Smith - peremptory day to respond granted in next court.

57:2/3 John Bradshewe vs William Hickes - plaintiff puts declaration and defendant requests privilege day in court.

[12] See also *WCA*, 40.

61:1/2 John Bradshewe vs William Heath - plaintiff puts declaration and defendant in person acknowledges his debt of 15s1d. Judgment given with committal to sergeant.
Action of trespass:
58:2/4 John Hasle vs Thomas Skeye - peremptory day to respond granted in next court.
Action of trespass on case:
59:2/14 Edward Carpenter vs Andrew Jarnes - plaintiff puts declaration and defendant's attorney requests privilege day in court.

[f33]

Action of trespass:
6:(16/16*)* Todman vs Batt - sergeant returns that he takes the bodies of John Bradshewe and Alexander Head as sureties for John Batt to cover 13s4d damages and £3:12:2d amercement and costs. The said John Bradshewe and Alexander Head have handed over in court one silver and gilt salt-cellar with cover and a silver spoon gilt, both weighing 16¼ ounces valued at £4:16s. These remain with Henry Rudgate sergeant. The goods aforesaid, namely 3½ pieces of sackcloth and a piece of tufted fustian, have been handed to the court by John Bradshewe. And on this the court will advise.

[f33v]

Portmoot court held 13 July 1608...
Conveyance:
60:3/4 Second proclamation between William Rayer querent and John Whitton alias Darling deforciant.
Action of account:
54:3/5 Batt vs Noble - defendant responds with copy to plaintiff.
Actions continuing: **2**:(17/25); **47**:8/12.

[f34]

Actions of debt:
55:3/6 Write vs Porter - judgment that defendant should recover 17s10d for amercement and costs, and *scire facias* granted.
56:3/4 Whing vs Smith - defendant responds, copy granted.
57:3/3 Bradshewe vs Hickes - action discharged.
61:2/2 Bradshewe vs Heath - action discharged.
62:1/1 Elizabeth Harper executrix of the last testament of Thomas Harper vs Robert Maye - action discharged.
63:1/1 Richard Whinge vs Thomas Gibson - action discharged.
Action of trespass:
58:3/4 Hasle vs Skey - day for response granted in next court.
Actions of trespass on case:
59:3/14 Carpenter vs Jarnes - second privilege day granted.

64:1/6 Bennett Roberts vs William Baker - plaintiff puts declaration and requests day for amendment in next court; attorney appears for defendant.

[f34v]

65. Examination before Thomas Browne mayor and Thomas Bradshewe gent, 15 July 1608.

Richard Coles of the borough complained on oath that Phillip Harton chapman of Bredstreet, London, late servant to John Danniell a tallow chandler there, today struck him at the Bull inn in Woodstock. Harton broke the king's peace on him and drew blood. Harton confessed to this and paid his fine of 2s to Mr Rayer. Harton said he had bought from Mr Peat and Mr Olylverte at the Cross Keys in Ludgate Hill linen drapes, diapers and damask amounting to £50. This they trusted him with, without bill or bond, only setting his hand to their book. He came out of London about the 3rd of July. (see **67**).

Phillip Harton binds himself in £40, and William Porter and Henry Price of Woodstock chapmen each go surety for £20, that Harton shall appear in person at the next borough sessions of the peace to make his case and receive the court's charge. He promised to save Porter harmless before the law.

66. Examination, 23 July 1608.

Clement Jordon of Banbury swore that Griffin Williams ostler of Banbury broke the peace upon him and gave him a box of the ears. Williams fined 12d, paid to Mr Rayer.

[f35]

Portmoot court held 25 July 1608...

Conveyance:

60:4/4 Third proclamation between William Rayer querent and John Whitton alias Darlinge deforciant.

[f35v]

Action of account:

54:4/5 Batt vs Noble - peremptory day granted for rejoinder.

Actions of debt:

55:4/6 Write vs Porter - *alias scire facias* granted for return in next court.

56:4/4 Whing vs Smith - peremptory day granted for response. Action discharged.

Actions of trespass:

58:4/4 Hasle vs Skey - action discharged.

67:1/1 Richard Coles vs Phillip Harton - plaintiff defaults on three summonses and does not present case. Default etc. (see **65**).

Actions of trespass on case:

59:4/14 Carpenter vs Jarnes - final privilege day granted in next court.

64:2/6 Roberts vs Baker - copy of declaration to defendant.

68:1/1 John Harris vs William Plot - day to declare granted in next court.

Actions continuing: **2**(18/25); **47**:9/12.

[f36]

69. Charity. 31 July 1608.

Mr mayor appointed Mr Rayer chamberlain to give Mr William Hobson, minister of Wootton Underwood, Bucks., who has preached here at Woodstock, 6s8d and to discharge his charge at his inn. For his house was burned down and all his goods with it, as appeared by a certificate under the hands of Sir Francis Goodwin, John Crok, John Doren, Christopher Piggott and George Throckmorton knights and JPs in Co. Bucks.[13]

70:1/2 Examination, 5 August 1608.

Thomas Williams constable charged the underwritten to watch in service of the king in this borough on the last Thursday night of July, namely: Thomas Gee, John Gyles, William Mawkins and Michael White. They all affirm they found Phillip Hawthorne, Edward Barnes and John Vardam drinking at victualler's Nicholas Glover between the hours of 11 and 12. Michael White on oath says while drinking there he saw Hawthorne privily take his bill outside and when he called for it Hawthorne claimed he could not be watchman since he had no bill; and he has detained it until now.

[f36v]

Thomas Gee on oath says that he and the other watchmen met Hawthorne in the street and demanded the bill off him and told him he could not depart without delivering it up. They were taking him towards the stocks when he bit Gee's hand and tore his neckband, scratched Mawkins' face and struck White. Mawkins on oath said Hawthorne tried to break his arm, and after he laid in the stocks struck his face. John Gyles affirmed this on oath.

Recorder's ruling 7 August 1608: By Mr Recorder's opinion Hawthorne is to be committed to prison and bound to good behaviour for disorder in the house of Nicholas Glover on the night of 28 July last and for refusing to go home, taking the watchman's weapon, tearing his band and biting his fingers.

[f37]

71. Charity, 7 August 1608.

Mr Recorder Whitlock's opinion is that we should distrain upon the land of Mr Doleman that was in his hands at the time of the grant, or of the land or goods of his tenants granted since the time of the granting of the annuity.[14] (*see* also **78**)

70:2/2 *Recognisance*: before Thomas Browne mayor and Thomas Bradshewe JP, 7 August 1608.

Phillip Hawthorne, labourer of Woodstock, binds himself in £20, with Joseph Harris and Thomas Screevin of Woodstock each surety in £10, to appear in person before next borough sessions to hold, do and receive that which the

[13] Sir Jn Croke, Sir Fras. Goodwyn and Sir Geo. Throckmorton, Bucks Commission of Peace 1609; JH Gleason 247.

[14] See *WCA*, xxii, xxvii, 249; *VCH Oxon* xii, 416.

court imposes; and to keep the king's peace towards all and bear himself well. (see **101**)

[f37v]

Portmoot court held 8 August 1608...

Action of account:

54:5/5 Batt vs Noble - because the plaintiff does not appear on three occasions to prosecute etc. therefore etc. default etc. Action discharged.

Action of debt:

55:5/6 Write vs Porter - executed *alias scire facias* returned, and execution of action granted.

Action of trespass on case:

64:3/6 Roberts vs Baker, - defendant responds by putting himself on the country; *venire facias* granted.

Actions continuing: **2**:(19/25); **47**:10/12; **59**:5/14.

The court adjourns to 29 August.

[f38]

Examinations before Thomas Browne mayor and Thomas Bradshewe JPs 23 August 1608.

72. George Beedle, shoemaker, servant to Robert Brewce, says on oath that Paul Pearce, shoemaker, servant to John Bruce, this day assaulted and broke the peace upon him; and he was thereupon committed to the constables.

73. John Archer, servant to John Glover of Woodstock, says on oath that yesternight he found Donhowe Dennis in a chamber of one of the king's grooms about 10 o'clock stealing a cloak, stockings, bands and other things. Whereupon he was committed to prison and enjoined to a whipping

74:1/2 John Baker, clothier of Witney, charged Edward Clark glover of Bicester, Oxon, upon suspicion of felony: for unlawfully coming by one ambling and racking mare with a brand mark on the near shoulder. This mare he had bought from Clark about 3 years since at Thomas Godfery's house on a market day for 44s but did not toll for her.

Recognisance/Committal: John Baker binds himself in £40 to testify in person according to the terms of the statutes against Clark at the next sessions of the peace and gaol delivery in Oxon, to hold the aforesaid.

And Edward Clark binds himself in £100, with George Maunde yeoman of Bicester and Arthur Jeames yeoman of Wootton each binding himself in £40, that Clark will appear in person at the assizes at the next general gaol delivery to make his case and receive the court's imposition.

Memorandum: 6 January 1609: It was examined by the consent of the justices before Mr Browne, (signed) Thomas Browne and Edmund Hiorne.

[f38v]

74:2/2 Edward Clark says that about 4 years since he bought the mare from one Fowck (?i.e. Fulk/Fowke) Parrishe, carrier of Bicester, at the stable of

John Pearte for 26s, 2 calf-skins, and 2 pairs of gloves, but did not toll for her. After three-quarters of a year he sold her to Baker for 44s as said but did not toll for her.

75. *Recognisance*: William Turner, one of the queen's grooms, testifies that John Knapp, saddler of Oxford, broke the peace upon him and one of the king's porters by giving them bad speeches and by fighting with them. Whereupon Knapp was committed to prison and Mr Bradshewe undertook his appearance at the next sessions at Woodstock, and for his contempt in selling his wares in the Bull backside without licence.

Memorandum. 19 August before the mayor and the same justice.

76. *Recognisance*: John Ashpole binds himself in £20, with surety of £10 from Simon Collier, to keep the peace towards all and especially John Heath, and to appear in person at the next borough sessions of the peace to make his case and receive judgment. (see **103**).

Council business:

77. *Goldsmith*: Mr Write, the goldsmith of Oxford, requested permission to sell his wares in the borough during the king's abode, which was granted by the mayor and common council; whereupon he promised to give something to the borough's poor people.

78. *Mr Doleman's money*. Given to William Rayer, chamberlain, the money that came trom Mr Doleman's £12 for one and a half year's annuity ending at Lady Day last, and also 15s for the arrearage thereof.

79. *Taylor's fine*. Also given to him the £7 fine for a lease to be granted to one Taylor of the yards in Hampton Meade at Michaelmas next for 10 years.[15]

[f39]

Portmoot court held 29 August 1608...

Action of debt:

55:6/6 Write vs Porter - Edmund Hiorne clerk of court paid defendant 17s10d amercement and costs in execution of writ; and he goes quit.

Action of trespass on case:

64:4/6 Roberts vs Baker, *venire facias* returned; *habeas corpora* granted for jury in next court.

Actions continuing: **2**:(20/25); **47**:11/12; **59**:6/14.

[f39v]

Examinations before Thomas Browne mayor 6 September 1608.

80. John Powell did depose that he stood in dread of his life from William Inglishe, shoemaker of the borough, who had threatened to beat him and cut his hose from his breeches and whereupon was apprehended. Edward Rudgate and William Kinge, shoemakers of the borough, each assigned £10 and Inglishe £20 that he would keep the peace against all the king's leige people and especially

[15] See also *WCA*, 31, 41.

Powell, and would appear. at the next borough sessions of the peace to answer there.
Addendum: By John Powell's agreement Inglishe was discharged before the mayor.
81. Richard Hawkins swore that Richard Peton has broken the peace upon him, and that Francis Garter witnessed the throwing of two pots at him. Whereupon Peton was committed to the constables.

[f40]

Portmoot court held 12 September 1608...
Action of debt:
82:1/5 Thomas Penn vs John Davies alias Butcher, - defendant appears and plaintiff requests day to declare in court.
Action of trespass on case:
64:5/6 Bennett Roberts vs William Baker. Jury of

John Raunson,	Michael Nursse,	Francis Collingwood,
Jerome White,	Joseph Harris,	John Lowe,
Thomas Williams,	William Edwards,	Edward Rudgate,
John Bradshewe,	Robert Seare,	Ralph Durbridge

find for the plaintiff and assess damages at 20s with amercement and costs 2d. Judgment adjourned to next court.
Actions continuing: **2**:(21/25); **59**:7/14.

[f40v]

83:1/3 General covenant on granting of alehouse licences, 17 September 1608.
Covenant of the justices of the peace of the borough Thomas Browne mayor and Thomas Bradshewe gentleman both by effect of the royal charters and formerly of the advisory articles given by the statutes and provisions of the king's privy council. For the covenant, with the full agreement of the justices, it is ordered that each and every burgess and inhabitant of the borough and its liberties to whom any licence or licences is granted to keep an alehouse or alehouses within the borough or its precincts will be bound by the royal statute with two sureties, namely:- for every alehousekeeper in £10 with each of his sureties in £5 of legal English money, by way of recognisances of his goods and chattels to the right of possession of the king holding under the following conditions, namely:-

[f41]

83:2/3 *Conditions of licence.* The condition of this recognisance is such that, during the time you shall keep alehouse or tippling-house within the borough or its liberties, you do not permit or suffer any unlawful play at tables, dice or cards, or any other unlawful game within your house, orchards or backsides; Nor dress, cause, or suffer to be dressed, any flesh to be eaten on any forbidden day unless in licenced case of sickness; Nor suffer any person to drink or tipple in your house or rooms but only such and at such times and such order as you may lawfully justify; Always uttering and selling your best ale and beer at prices and measures as limited by the laws and statutes of the realm; And specially not allowing tippling at the time of divine service or sermon on the sabbath or holy-days, unless for wayfarers in travel: Otherwise your recognisance to be void, or else to stand and remain in full force and virtue.

Thus for the same covenant of the said justices held at that day and place for each and every burgess and other inhabitant of the borough and its liberties: those whose names follow have been individually licensed to keep his own alehouse and each bound by royal declaration in his person with two sureties under the conditions given above; and as follows:

[f41v]

83:3/3 *Form of licence:* Example licence under the general covenant, 17 September 1608.

A licence is granted to Henry Rudgate to keep an alehouse in his present home at his dwelling-house in the aforesaid borough (and no other) for one full year from now; according to the form. regulation, statutes and articles as are enacted and provided for in this case. He binds himself to the king in £10 and each of his sureties for £5 of their respective goods and chattels in way of recognisance for the benefit of the royal declaration, levied under the stated conditions, as is manifest from the record. Providing always that at the next general covenant of the borough justices, next Easter-tide, Henry Rudgate brings his licence here before the mayor and justice and there it is allowed for the future or not according to inspection. Otherwise it will be annulled.

Note:	Mr mayor and Michael Nursse 10s for Godfery
	William Hickes senior 8s for Durbridge
	Joseph Harris 8s for Hamond
	Thomas Screevin 8s for himself
	John Glover debt 8s for Nicholas Taylor.

[f42]

84:1/2 List of those licensed according to the procedure given above; with each licencee bound in £10 and each of his sureties in £5:

Thomas Abbott:	sureties Robert Bignill & John Ackley
John Ackly:	sureties Thomas Abbott & John Heath
Nicholas Taylor:	sureties John Glover & Thomas Screevin
William Edwards:	sureties Robert Bignill & Edward Long
Henry Rudgate:	sureties Michael Nursse & Edward Rudgate
Thomas Screevin:	sureties Nicholas Taylor & John Heath
Edward Rudgate:	sureties Henry Rudgate & Joseph Harris
William Hickes senior:	sureties Joseph Harris & Robert Bignill

Ralph Durbridge:	sureties William Hickes senior & Edward Longe;

not allowed for present, he has not paid 8s to the king's majesty

Hugh Hamond:	sureties Joseph Harris & John Heathe
John Taylor:	sureties Nicholas Taylor & John Glover
Nicholas Glover:	sureties Nicholas Taylor & William Hickes
Thomas Godfery:	sureties Michael Nurrse & Edward Rudgate

(signed by) Thomas Browne, mayor, and Thomas Bradshewe.

[f42v]

84:2/2 Certificate of alehouse licences, 10 November 1608. A true certificate of all those that are licensed to keep any alehouse within the borough, to continue their licences until Trinity term next, namely:

Thomas Abbott,	John Ackly,	Nicholas Taylor,
William Edwards,	Henry Rudgate,	Thomas Screevin,
Edward Rudgate,	William Hickes the elder,	Hugh Hamond,
John Taylor,	Nicholas Glover,	Thomas Godfery

In witness whereof Thomas Bradshewe mayor, Thomas Browne JP together with the town clerk have set our hands hereunto and on the seals of the licences, signed this day.

[f43] (Blank)

[f43v]

Portmoot court held 19 September 1608...

Action of trespass on case:

64:6/6 Bennett Roberts vs William Baker - judgment that plaintiff should recover both 20s damages and 40s1d for amercement and his costs; *scire facias* granted.

Actions continuing: **2**:(22/25); **59**:8/14; **82**:2/5.

85. Examination. 22 September 1608.

John Price a sivier (sieve-maker) dwelling at Cumnor, with his boy Barnaby Price aged 21 born at Stow-on-the-Wold, came to Woodstock in the company of Joan Griffine a widow aged 50 of Britwell, Oxon. Barnaby, a very little boy, would have married Griffine and took a ring from her and would have sold it in Woodstock. As for the two double gilt rings they had, she said that Mr Write of Oxford did gild the bigger and the other she bought from him about a fortnight since.

[f44]

86:1/3 **The names of all the freemen and all the Inhabitants of the borough of New Woodstock, taken 19 September 1608.**[16]

Freemen of the Common Council:

Thomas Browne alderman, mayor; William Rylye alderman; (del.);

[16] ' Inhabitants' are probably heads of households, see Hallissey & Shipp, *OLH,* 3(6), 245; some name deletions (del.) at least, date from later times, e.g. ald. John Raunson died Jan. 1611. Several series of markings against many names have been omitted.

Thomas Bradshewe alderman;		William Rayer alderman;
William Flye alderman;		Thomas Rawlins gent;
Edmund Hiorne, town clerk;		Simon Jeames gent;
John Glover chamberlain;	John Dubber;	John Raunson (del);
John Taylor;	Michael Nursse (del);	Nicholas Taylor;
Richard Meades;	Francis Collingwood;	Thomas Blith;
William Ball;	Richard Wrighte (del);	Jerome White;
Henry Rudgate sergeant;	Joseph Harris;	Robert Bignill;
John Lowe;	Thomas Screevin;	John Heath;
Thomas Williams;	John Bradshewe;	Thomas Meatcalfe;
William Bradshewe.		

[f44v]

86:2/3 Freemen namely:

John Dissell;	Thomas Meatcalfe (del);	Timothy Walker (del);
John Rylye (del);	Robert Bruce (del);	William Kinge (del);
Thomas Abbott;	Edward Longe;	John Wilkinson;
William Wells;	Richard Lowe;	Robert Seare (del);
Simon Jeames gent (del);	William Edwards;	Francis Garter;
Thomas Godferye;	Edward Barnes (del);	Andrew Jarnes;
Thomas Martyn (del);	Thomas Gee;	John Batt;
Alexander Headd;	William Meatcalfe;	Phillip Jeames;
Richard Hawkins;	Robert Winter;	John Bradshewe (del);
Richard Shadd;		

[f45]

Thomas Painter;	Bennett Painter;	Drewe Gregory;
Roger Sturgis;	John Powell;	William Bradshewe (del)
Hugh Hamond;	John Acklye;	William Hickes sen.;
William Hickes jun.;	Ralph Durbridge;	John Bruce;
James Dissell;	Edward Rudgate;	Richard Jarnes (del);
William Richards (del);	Henry Ledbroke(del.);	Thomas Gee (del);
William Raunson;	Richard Wrighte;	John Doe;
Randall Richards;	Thomas Bruce;	George Noble;
Robert Ducock;	Bryan Steephens;	William Butterfeild;
William Archer;	Thomas Rayer;	John Stone; Thomas Joyner.

[f45v]

86:3/3 Inhabitants being not freemen:

widow Leake;	Richard Pryvate;	widow Maynard;
Ralph Hull;	widow Hollis;	William Rayer;
John Symons;	William Porter;	ohn Combes;
John Gadbury gent;	William Raunson (del);	John Mason;
John Seelye;	Richard ?Weswod (del);	Henry Johnson (del);
Anthony Noble clerk.;	widow Tanner;	William Homes;

Thomas Norwood; widow Smith; Christopher Bowman; John Norman; widow More; Benedict Norwood; Nicholas Glover; widow Jarnes; John Tomlyns; widow Munck;

[f46]

Phillip Hawthorne; William Heath (del); William Gilkes (del); Simon Collyer; Thomas Smith; Felix Holloway (del); widow Bowland; William Phillips (del); John Browne; Gyles Coles; Richard Dee (del); John Ashpole; Michael Pullcrowe; widow Phillipps; John Hamond; widow Fletcher; John Abbott; John Boddye (del); John Price; John Taylor; Thomas Jackson; Henry Price; John Robinson (del); widow Meadowes; William Holloway; John Archer; widow Fleminge; John Gilberd; Anthony Shadd;

[f46v]

John Lucas; Nicholas Ludnam; Nicholas Stayner; Robert Spitle; widow Nursse; widow Lynn; Thomas Bellsire; Richard Coles; John Daysey; Bartholomew Edging; George Heath. Robert March; Richard Barnes; Richard Peeters; William Hitch; widow Bradshewe; John Cooper (del); Walter Parker; John Woodroofe; Thomas Judge; Salloman Flye; [...]Heynes; John Vardam; widow Spitle; widow Rathbone; John Gibbs; Richard Newall (del); John Parker; John Bennett; Guy Becklye; George Noble;

[f47]

Review: Assize of Bread, Ale and other commodities; and of Trading and Marketing within the borough.

87:1/2 Assize of Bread and Ale. Monday 26 September 1608.

The court of Thomas Browne mayor and clerk of the market held by virtue of the king's majesty's letters patents, by him and his highness's progenitors granted.[17]

The jury: John Raunson, Jerome White, William Edwards, Francis Garter, James Dissell, Hugh Hamond, John Dubber, John Lowe, William Bradshewe. Alexander Head, William Hickes junior, Richard Wrighte sworn in. Michael Nursse, John Heath, Richard Hawkins, Richard Shadd, John Bradshewe,

[17] See Introduction '*Dearth Survey*'.

The jury present that the best wheat on the last market day was worth £3 the quarter; second wheat was worth 46s the quarter, and third wheat 36s. And the best malt was worth 28s the quarter.

[f47v]

87:2/2 *The Assize.* The mayor straightly charges and commands all the bakers within this borough to bake good and wholesome bread fit for men's bodies. And to keep the assize following: Every penny white loaf to weigh 6oz; Every penny wheaten loaf to weigh 13oz; Every penny household loaf to weigh 18oz; The (?half) penny cheate to weigh 8oz.

The brewers and victuallers are to brew good and wholesome ale and beer, and to sell a thirdendell for a penny forth of the doors, and within doors a quart for a penny. And they are to keep that assize upon pain and peril that shall fall thereon.

The mayor gives assize to the butchers to sell their tallow at 3s the stone, and to the chandlers to sell their candles at 4s the pound. and both are subpoena to keep the assize.

Review of Trading and Marketing conditions within the borough.

88:1/5 A note of the principal points delivered to the jury in charge to inquire of, namely:

1 Bakers' apprentices. Whether any person has kept any common bakehouse in this borough who have not been apprenticed or brought up therein for 7 year

2 Lawful bread to be made. Whether any baker or any other person do make, bake, utter and sell any other bread than simnel bread, wastel, white, wheaten, household and horse bread.

[f48]

3 What sorts of bread to be made to be sold. Whether any baker or other person, but at time of Christmas, makes any other sort of bread than farthing, white bread, halfpenny white, penny white. halfpenny wheaten, penny wheaten bread, penny household and twopenny household loaves: if they do it is forfeit to the poor.

4 Bakers not to sell above 13d loaves for 12d. Whether they sell to any innholder or victualler either in man's bread or horse bread (which shall retail the same) above 13 pennies worth of bread for 12d, without any poundage or other advantage. And whether they sell to them above 3 horseloaves for a penny, and 13d worth for 12d any loaf weighing a penny white loaf, whether wheat be good cheap or dear.

5 Unlawful bread forbidden. Whether any baker or other person makes, utters or sells by retail to any of his King's majesty's subjects any spice cakes, buns, biscuits, or other spice breads (except at burials, or on Good Friday or Christmas): if they do it is forfeit to the poor.

6 Foreign bakers to keep greater assize than the townsmen. Whether the foreign bakers keep the assize or not, namely: that their one penny white loaf do weigh one ounce more than the bakers' of the borough, their penny wheaten loaf 2 ounces more. and their penny household loaf two ounces more: otherwise a fine.

88:2/5

7 The market bushel to be placed in a convenient place. There shall be a market bushel provided for this borough placed to serve the king's majesty's subjects that come to buy or sell at this market or not; and if the measure be wanting the town forfeits to the king's majesty's penalties.

[f48v]

8 No person or persons within this borough to use to buy or sell with any weights or measures but such as are sealed by the mayor as clerk of the market here: if not, a penalty.

9 The measure of the bushel and the difference between troy weight and avoirdupois. You are to make every bushel to be used within this borough after this rate, namely: every pound avoirdupois contains 16oz. and serves to weigh butter, cheese, flesh, tallow, wax and every other thing that bears the name garbell and whereof issues refuse or waste. The difference between troy and avoirdupois is that 14½ oz troy weigh 16oz avoirdupois at this day. And according to the rate 7 pounds avoirdupois make the gallon in measure, 14 pounds the peck, 28 pounds the half bushel, and 56 pounds make the bushel; which bushel agrees with the 64 pounds troy weight.

88:3/5

10 Unwholesome ale or beer. Whether the innholders or victuallers within this borough brew their ale or beer with any musty malt, or eaten with vermin, or put it to sale in any musty or corrupt vessels; if so, fine.

11 Assize of victuallers. Whether the innholders and victuallers have kept the assize as last set forth and appointed by the mayor or not, on pain of a fine.

[f49]

12 Quart and pint pots and thirdendells ('thurdendalls'). Whether the innholders sell and retail their ale and beer with any measure other than a quart and pint pot after the rate of 4d the gallon; or the victualler with any other measure, than with a thirdendell and half-thirdendell after the rate of 3d the gallon, on pain of a fine.

13 Unwholesome victuals. Whether any innholder or victualler bakes, seeths, or roasts any fish or flesh twice, or sells or utters to the king's subjects any manner of corruptible victuals which may hurt or infect man's body.

False Measures. Or utters or sells their ale or beer within or without their houses by retail or otherwise to the king's subjects with any false or unsealed measures less then the standard; or utter or sell their provender within their ostleries with any false or unsealed measures repugnant to the standards of the Exchequer.

14 Innholders for their rates of hay, litter and provender. Whether any innholder or victualler within this borough have taken for hay above 6d for one day and night for one horse, or above a halfpenny profit on a bushel of oats, or anything for his litter; or have sold any penny bottles of hay weighing less than four pounds: on pain of a fine.

88:4/5

15 Artificers conspiring. Whether any butchers, bakers, brewers. innholders or victuallers or any other of any other mystery have conspired, or taken any oath or promise, not to sell but at certain prices agreed between them: if so, pain of a fine.

[f49v]

16 Butchers dressing corrupt victuals. If any butcher has sold or offered to sell mozled (?mezled) swine's flesh or any flesh that died of the murrain; or killed and sold any unbaited bulls, or any cow or kine great with calf or near calving, any ewe with lamb or taken the ram, or any sow great with pig or taken the boar; or have blown the flesh they sell, or geld the kidneys of their muttons, veals or lambs taking away the fat thereof, or deceitfully raise the same kidneys with any stopping or underputting them to deceive the ignorant buyers thereof: on penalty of a fine.

17 Chandlers. Whether any chandler shall sell his candles for above three farthings in a pound dearer than he paid the butcher for his rough tallow: penalty a fine.

18 Toll dish. Any miller taking toll by heaped measure: penalty.

19 Gashed and watered hides. If any butcher has gashed or cut the hide of any ox, bull. steer or cow whereby it is impaired; or has watered any hide (except in June, July and August) or has put to sale any putrified or rotten hide: penalty a fine.

20 Tanner. If any tanner has put to sale any leather insufficiently or not thoroughly tanned or not well and thoroughly dried: he shall forfeit.

21 Currier, If any currier has curried any leather, except in his own house, within this borough etc.,

[f50]

22 Currier. If any currier has, during the time he has used currying, used the feat of a tanner, cordwainer, shoemaker, butcher or other artificer using the cutting of leather: then etc.

23 Shoemaker. If any shoemaker has made any boots, shoes, buskins. start-ups (i.e. gaitered boots), slippers or pantofles ('pantifles') or any part of

them of English leather wet, curried (other than deer, calf or goatskin dressed like Spanish leather) but of leather well tanned, and curried if required, and well sewn with threads well twisted, waxed and rosined, with the stitches hard drawn with hand leathers, and without mixing neat's and calve's leather with the other leathers: If so, you shall fine.

88:5/5

24 Weights and measures. If any person has bought or sold using any unlawful weights or measures, or bought or sold in this borough or in any city or market with any weight or measure that is not lawfully marked or signed; or has bought corn by heaped measure in any place (except within shipboard); or has used double measures, the one to buy with and the other to sell with: if so you shall fine.

25 Assize. Lastly you are to enquire what price the best, second and third wheats, and the best and second malts did bear here within this market on the last market day. That by your presentment Mr mayor, as clerk of the market of this borough, may give and set down an assize: at what rate the bakers shall bake and sell their bread, and the innholders and victuallers shall brew and sell their ale and beer unto the king's majesty's subjects. Finish.

[f50v]

89. Weights and measures in use. A note of all such weights and measures found by the said jury to agree with the standard of the exchequer within this borough and sealed with the seal of James now king and that of the said borough. As follows:-

Firstly one market bushel sealed with the crown and 'F' and 'M'

William Rayer alderman 2 bushels; John Glover 2 bushels.

Each with one bushel:

Michael Nurse; Nicholas Glover; Thomas Godferye; Robert Bignill; Henry Rudgate; Thomas Williams; Jerome White; William Edwards; Richard Meades; Thomas Browne alderman; John Raunson; Simon Colliar; Thomas Bradshewe alderman; Edmund Hiorne; John Taylor; John Lowe; Anthony Noble clerk; John Dubber; William Ball.

[f51]

Each with one peck:

William Edwards; Thomas Bradshewe alderman; John Dissell; Mr Noble; William Ball; Edmund Hiorne; John Lowe; William Bradshewe; Thomas Browne.

Each with one half-peck:

Richard Meades; Thomas Bradshewe alderman; Edmund Hiorne.

Each with one ell and one yard: William Bradshewe; John Bradshewe.

Also the jury did present that either of Thomas Browne alderman and Francis Collingwood kept a bushel that was too little which they had defaced by consent. And remaining in the hall not sealed is a bushel of Thomas Painter that is too little.

90. Oath of mayoralty and mending of measure - 3 October 1608.

90:1/2 Mr Walter Culpepper esquire comes to Woodstock to administer the oath of mayoralty to Mr Thomas Bradshewe, there being present: Alderman Rayer, Thomas Raulins gent, myself (Edmund Hiorne), John Glover, Nicholas Taylor, Simon Jeames, Michael Nursse, Henry Rudgate, Ralph Durbridge and Richard Shadd.

90:2/2 The defaced bushel of Alderman Browne was mended with leather and measured against the standard brass measures, and 2 quarts being added to it, it was found good and allowable and somewhat with the biggest. And on trial it was found to be as good as Mr Rayer's bushel which was newly sealed, within half a handful of corn.

[f51v and f52] (Blank.)

[f52v]

Portmoot court held 26 September 1608...

Actions continuing: **2**:(23/25); **47**:12/12; **59**:9/14; **82**:3/5.

[f53]

91. Council elections. At a council held at the guildhall before mayor Thomas Browne, aldermen Thomas Bradshewe, William Rayer and William Flye, town clerk Edmund Hiorne, chamberlain John Glover, and John Dubber, John Raunson, Michael Nursse. Jerome White, sergeant Henry Rudgate, John Lowe, John Heath, Thomas Williams, Francis Collingwood and Robert Bignill all of the common council of this borough: That Simon Jeames now schoolmaster shall hereafter be of the common council of this borough during his life. And that Edward Longe shall be clerk of the church and court crier during his life and shall have such fees and duties as he now does.

92. Here ends the time of Thomas Browne's mayoralty.

[f53v] (Blank.)

[f54]

Portmoot court held 3 October 1608 before Thomas Bradshewe mayor.

Action of debt:

93:1/2 Henry Tyms vs Thomas Iveto - plaintiff puts declaration and defendant requests copy in court.

Actions continuing: **2**:(24/25); **59**:10/14; **82**:4/5.

[f54v]

94. Custody. 3 October 1608 before Thomas Bradshewe mayor and Thomas Browne JP.

Thomas Durran of Stratton Audley, Oxon, swears that William Heath had threatened him to the danger of his life, whereupon Heath was committed to the constables.

[f55]

Portmoot court held 17 October 1608...

Actions of debt:

2:(25/25) Hiorne vs Wierman - action discharged.

82:5/5 Penn vs Davis - action discharged.

93:2/2 Tyms vs Iveto - action discharged by plaintiff's attorney Simon Jeames.

96:1/1 Thomas Browne alderman vs William Richardson, defendant in arrearage - plaintiff puts declaration and defendant appears in person as a prisoner and acknowledges the action: namely, that he is in debt for a bill of £6. Judgment given for recovery of said bill with 8s amercement and 2d damages.

97:1/1 Henry Price vs William Richardson, defendant in arrearage - plaintiff declares and defendant appears in person and acknowledges his debt of £4:7:6d and is committed to the custody of the sergeant. Therefore judgment given for recovery of said debt with 8s amercement and 4s8d damages.

Actions of trespass on case:

59:11/14 Carpenter vs Jarnes - continues by agreement.

95:1/1 John Collingwood vs William Richardson - action discharged.

[f55v]

98. Sessions of the Peace with View of Frankpledge, held 20 October 1608, before Thomas Bradshewe mayor and Thomas Browne gent JPs, with court officers as previously.

Crown jury of homage:

John Raunson,	John Dubber,	Michael Nursse,
Francis Collingwood,	John Lowe,	John Heath,
Thomas Blith,	Francis Garter,	ohn Bruce,
Robert Bruce,	William Bradshewe,	Bennett Paynter,
Alexander Head,	William Meatcalfe,	William Edwards sworn.

[f56]

Recognisances:

99. *Maintenance order*. Nicholas Glover, on his own recognisance of £10 and William Raunson's surety of £10 from the last sessions, does not appear to receive judgment: recognisance forfeited. (see **39**).

100. *Base-child*: Phillip Colliar, on his own recognisance of £20 and Simon Colliar's surety of £10 from the last sessions, appears in person to make his case and receive process. Memorandum: Priscilla Barnaby swears that the said Phillip Colliar is the true father of the child that she now goes with. (see **40** and **147**).

101. *Assault*: (see **70**). Phillip Hawthorne, on his own recognisance of £20 and the sureties of £10 each of Joseph Harris and Thomes Screevin since 7 August last, appears in person to make his case and receive process. He was discharged, paying his fees which Mr mayor has promised he shall pay to the town clerk.

[f56v]

102. *Assault*: (see **75**). John Knapp appears in person on the surety of Thomas Bradshewe as mayor, and makes his case and is discharged without fee.

103. *Assault*: (see **76**). John Ashpoole, on his own recognisance of £20 and £10 surety of Simon Colliar since 19 August last, appears in person and makes his case: discharged without fee.

Affeerers:John Raunson, John Dubber, Michael Nursse,
William Edwards (deleted)

104. *Elections*: Joseph Harris, Robert Seare (deleted), Francis Garter, Richard Hawkins, Thomas Martyn and William King are elected tithingmen.

105. *Constables' money*: 12d given to constables for breach of peace by John Ashpoole, and 12d by Phillip Hawthorne. Estreats: I delivered to constables Edward Rudgate and Thomas Williams the estreats of this leet and sessions, amounting to £9:8:10d. (signed) Edmund Hiorne.

[f57]

106. Examination. 31 October 1608 before Thomas Bradshewe mayor.

The examination of James Mason, shoemaker, servant to William King of this borough, concerning a cloak that Richard Meades, innholder, lost out of his house last night. He confessed nothing and thereupon was discharged but he and one Richard Newall were both committed to prison until 12 o'clock today.

[f57v]

Portmoot court held 31 October 1608...

Action of debt:

107:1/5 Andrew Jarnes vs John Woodrough - plaintiff puts declaration and defendant's attorney requests copy in court.

Action continuing: **59**:12/14.

[f58]

Portmoot court, held 14 November 1608...

Actions of debt:

107:2/5 Jarnes vs Woodrough - defendant puts himself on the country, and *venire facias* granted.

108:1/1 John Sanson vs William Bradborne - plaintiff puts declaration and defendant requests copy in court.

Actions of trespass on case:

109:1/11 John Symons vs Humphrey Bennett - similarly.

110:1/2 John Symons vs William Jeffes - plaintiff requests day to declare in court.

111:1/1 Phillip Hawthorne vs William Raunson.

Action continuing: **59**:13/14.

[f58v]

112. Survey of grain dearth. 9 November 1608.

Thomas Bradshewe mayor did appoint these jurors hereunder written to enquire upon the proclamation and articles touching the prevention and remedy of the dearth of grain and other victuals.

Jury: Jerome White,	Joseph Harris,	John Lowe,
John Heath,	Robert Bruce,	Robert Seare,
William Edwards,	Alexander Head,	Richard Shadd,
William Meatcalfe,	Richard Hawkins,	Bennett Painter,
Hugh Hamond,	John Ackly,	William Hickes senior,
John Bruce: sworn.		

The Jury presents in the form following:

Anthony Noble clerk has 4 persons in his house, and has bought not yet delivered barley: from William Castell 4 quarters for £3; from Mr Newberrye 8 quarters for £6; from John Kent 2 quarters for 30s; from William Tutchine 1 quarter for 15s; from Richard Mowlden 1 quarter for 14s; and he has 14 bushels of green malt and 1 quarter of dry malt in his house.

John Glover, baker and innholder, has 9 persons in his house, and bakes weekly 2 quarters of meal.

Robert Bignill baker, has 11 persons in his house and does the like (bakes weekly 2 quarters of meal).

Thomas Williams, baker and innholder, has 7 persons in his house and bakes weekly 6 bushels of flour.

Mr Browne has 12 persons in his house and has 20 quarters of barley and malt in his house, and has bought the following barley not yet delivered: from Mr Whitton 10 quarters for £10, from John Barrett 20 quarters for £24, and from Mr Kerke 40 quarters for £48.

[f59]

Mr Rayer has 6 persons in his house, and brews weekly 4 bushels of malt and has about 12 quarters of dry malt.

Nicholas Taylor has 4 persons in his house and brews weekly 2 bushels of malt.

Edward Rudgate has 7 persons in his house and brews weekly 2 bushels of malt.

Thomas Abbott has 7 persons in his house and brews weekly 2 bushels of malt.

Mistress Leake widow has 3 persons in her house and has 3 loads of maslin and 3 quarters of green malt at John Dubber's, and has 18 bushels of green malt and 3 quarters of barley bought from Mr Nashe beforehand.

Hugh Hamond has 7 persons and brews 2 bushels a week.

William Meatcalfe has 3 persons and has bought undelivered from Richard

Laude 3 quarters of barley for 40s and from William Woodbridge 2 quarters for 25s.
William Hickes senior has 7 persons and brews weekly 3 bushels malt.
Jerome White has 8 persons and brews weekly 2 bushels of malt.
Ralph Durbridge has 8 persons and brews weekly 3 bushels of malt.
William Edwards has 3 persons and brews weekly 2 bushels of malt.
Michael Nursse has 11 persons in his house and has a stack of barley of about 4 quarters by estimation.
Thomas Godferye has 8 persons and brews weekly 3 bushels of malt.
Nicholas Glover has 5 persons and brews weekly 3 bushels of malt.
John Ackleye has 4 persons and brews weekly 2 bushels of malt.
John Taylor has 3 persons and brews weekly 2 bushels of malt.
Thomas Screevin has 8 persons and brews weekly 3 bushels of malt.
Henry Rudgate has 8 persons and brews weekly 3 bushels of malt.
William Bradshewe has 6 persons and has bought from John Kent 3 quarters of barley at 14s a quarter and from Edward Warre of Tackley so much barley upon the ground as he paid £5:10s for it.
John Raunson has 3 persons in his house and 10 bushels of green malt.
William Ball has 4 persons and 6½ quarters of green and dry malts.
Francis Collingwood has 3 quarters of malt.
Mr Gadbury has 7 quarters of barley and malt.
Edmund Hiorne bought from John Hiat of Hordley Mill 22 bushels of barley for 22s.

[f59v]

113. *Information*. 14 November 1608 before Thomas Bradshewe mayor. Phillip Hawthorne took his oath that John Taylor woolman of Woodstock did strike and break the peace upon him, in his own house this day.

[f60]

Portmoot court held 28 November 1608…

Actions of debt:

107:3/5 Jarnes vs Woodrough - *habeas corpora* for jury granted.
114:1/12 William Wise vs John Heath - plaintiff declares with copy to defendant, first privilege day granted.
115:1/1 Thomas Browne alderman vs Hugh Hamond - action discharged

Action of trespass:

116:1/1 Edward Harris vs Simon Blackman - day to declare granted in next court. Action discharged.

Actions of trespass on case:

59:14/14 Carpenter vs Jarnes - action continued then discharged.
109:2/11 Symons vs Bennett - peremptory day for response granted.
110:2/2 Symons vs Jeffes - action discharged.

[f60v]

Portmoot court held 12 December 1608... [18]

Actions of debt:

114:2/12 Wise vs Heath - second privilege day granted to defendant.

117:1/6 Joan White vs William Hearne - plaintiff puts declaration and requests day to amend it.

Actions of trespass on case:

109:3/11 Symons vs Bennett - defendant responds and puts himself on the country; *venire facias* granted.

118:1/1 William Loggon vs Richard Cherry - action discharged.

Action continuing: **107**:4/5.

[f61]

Action of debt:

119:1/1 Richard Ockly vs Thomas Penn - defendant in person acknowledges his debt of the £40 on the declaration. Therefore payment of the debt and amercement in court is entrusted to the sergeant. Action discharged.

Actions of trespass on case:

120:1/10 Richard Ockly vs Thomas Penn - plaintiff puts declaration with request to amend it in next court.

121:1/4 Richard Ingrome vs John Tyms - peremptory day to declare granted in next court.

122:1/2 Thomas Cornishe vs Anthony Russell - similarly.

Action of trespass:

123:1/9 Henry Tyms vs Robert Silverside - plaintiff puts declaration with copy to defendant.

[f61v]

Portmoot court held 19 December 1608...

Actions of debt:

114:3/12 Wise vs Heath - final privilege day granted defendant.

107:5/5 Jarnes vs Woodroofe - action discharged.

117:2/6 White vs Hearne - peremptory day to complete declaration granted at next court.

Action of trespass:

123:2/9 Tyms vs Silverside - defendant makes response and grants a copy.

Actions of trespass on case:

109:4/11 Symons vs Bennett - executed *venire facias* returned and *habeas corpora* granted.

120:2/10 Ockly vs Penn - plaintiff completes declaration and grants copy to defendant.

121:2/4 Ingrome vs Tyms - declaration made with peremptory day granted to correct in next court.

[18] Neither mayor nor presiding JP recorded.

122:2/2 Cornishe vs Russell - action discharged.

[f62]

Portmoot court held 9 January 1609...

Actions of debt:

114:4/12 Wise vs Heath - peremptory day for response granted.

117:3/6 White vs Hearne - declaration completed, copy granted.

Actions of trespass on case:

120:3/10 Ockly vs Penn - peremptory day for response granted.

109:5/11 John Symons vs Humphrey Bennett; the jury between parties of

Michael. Nursse,	Jerome White,	Joseph Harris,
Thomas Screevin,	John Heath,	Thomas Williams,
William Edwards,	Francis Garter,	Alexander Head,
William Meatcalfe,	Richard Shad,	Edward Rudgate

find for the defendant with judgment adjourned until next court.

[f62v]

Action of debt:

124:1/5 Henry Nasshe vs John Woodroofe - plaintiff requests day to declare in next court.

Action of trespass:

123:3/9 Tyms vs Silverside - peremptory day for replication granted to plaintiff in next court.

Action of trespass on case:

121:3/4 Ingrome vs Tyms - plaintiff defaults and does not make his case.

[f63]

125. Election of Recorder as Burgess for Parliament, 16 Jan. 1609.

By the consent of Thomas Bradshewe mayor, Thomas Browne and William Rayer aldermen, Edmund Hiorne town clerk, John Glover and Richard Meades chamberlains, Simon Jeames gent, John Raunson, Michael Nursse, Jerome White, John Dubber, Henry Rudgate, John Heath, Joseph Harris, Nicholas Taylor, Robert Bignill, Thomas Williams and John Lowe of the common council of borough, that James Whittlock esq. shall be Burgess of said borough in place of Sir Richard Lee knight late deceased late Burgess of the borough for the parliament.[19] (signed) Edmund Hiorne.

[f63v]

Portmoot court held 23 January 1609...

Actions of debt:

114:5/12 Wise vs Heath - defendant responds and puts himself on the country, as does the plaintiff.

117:4/6 White vs Hearne - peremptory day granted next court.

[19] See also *WCA*, 6, 8; *VCH Oxon* xii, 400 n.90.

Actions of trespass on case:
109:6/11 Symons vs Bennett - judgment adjourned to next court.
121:4/4 Ingrome vs Tyms - judgment against plaintiff for 9s7d amercement and costs to be paid into court, which will consider allowance for damages; and he goes quit.

[f64]

121a:1/5 Richard Ingrome vs John Tyms - attorney Simon Jeames for plaintiff declares with day for amendment in next court.
120:4/10 Ockly vs Penn - defendant pleads *non-assumpsit* to the form of the action and puts himself on the country.
126:1/3 James Waste vs Francis Wood - attorney appears for defendant and plaintiff does not prosecute as defendant pays 5s3d amercement into court. Defendant goes quit.
Action of debt:
124:2/5 Nasshe vs Woodroofe - plaintiff puts declaration, with day for correction granted in next court.
Actions of trespass:
123:4/9 Tyms vs Silverside – plaintiff's attorney enters a demurrer on defendant's response.
127:1/2 William Ball & Dorothy his wife vs Isabel Huniborne - defendant appears in person in custody of sergeant and plaintiffs declare with copy granted.

[f64v]

Action of debt:
128:1/5 Robert Beck vs Francis Collingwood - defendant appears and plaintiff's attorney requests day for declaration in next court.
Action of trespass on case:
126:2/3 Christian Waste widow vs Francis Wood - plaintiff puts declaration with day for correction granted in next court.

[f65]

129. Election of freeman-burgess.
Memorandum. By consent of Thomas Bradshewe mayor; Thomas Browne, William Rayer and William Flye aldermen; Edmund Hiorne town clerk; Simon Jeames gent, John Glover and Richard Meades chamberlains; John Raunson, Henry Rudgate, Jerome White, Nicholas Taylor, Thomas Blith, Joseph Harris, Robert Bignill, Thomas Screevin, John Lowe, John Heath and Thomas Williams of the common council: Henry Ledbrock currier was elected and sworn a freeman burgess of this borough; Fine 30s.[20]
130:1/2 *Recognisance*, 23 Jan. 1609 before Thomas Bradshewe mayor. William Edwards binds himself on £10, with Thomas Screevin and Edward

[20] See also *WCA*, 1.

Longe each surety on £5, that he will appear in person at the next borough sessions of the peace to make his case and accept the court's judgment then imposed.

[f65v]

131. Examination, 3 February 1609 before Thomas Bradshewe mayor and Thomas Browne JP.

William Bridges labourer, late of the city of Oxford, servant of Mr John Farrer of the New Inn, says he departed from there on Monday 23 January by his master's consent. On the Thursday he went to Mr Needler of Farthingstone in his master's name without appointment for a black cloak with velvet cape faced with black rash ('rashe'). He was not at home but his wife not knowing this examinant gave the cloak next day to a stranger of her acquaintance, a Mr Hastings mercer of Towcester, to deliver to Bridges which he did at home. Bridges tarried next day at Mr Hastings and on Sunday came to Helmdon ('Helmeden') and lay there at an alehouse. (signed) William Brigis.[21]

This cloak had hanging sleeves, but altered at Helmdon the tailor had the sleeves for his pains; given to John Glover chamberlain.

Passport: date and place as above.

Richard Rogers, apprentice to John Rowden silkweaver of Woodstock, was taken in the company of William Bridges, punished as a rogue, and sent to his master by a passport.

[f66]

132. Examination, 4 February 1609 before the said justices.

Thomas Bradforde, late sawyer of Ludlow, Salop, confessed that on 26 January last he, as servant to certain Lord Chandos players coming to Buckingham town, found a little key in the parlour of Mr Porter innkeeper of The Bell. Wherewith he there opened the desk of one of the players, Richard Durand, and took about 10s in silver from a purse and locked the desk again. He opened two other desks of the players with the key but found no money. About a week later when driving the horses of the players from Woodstock to Eynsham he left them on the highway and departing from the players returned to Woodstock. As for the five pounds in gold stolen about a week before from Durand's doublet and charged against this examinant, he denies that he had it. Thomas Bradforde's mark.

Recognisance; date as above. Richard Durrand, London player, binds himself on £40 that he will himself present evidence according to the statutes against Thomas Bradforde at next county general gaol delivery to make his case.[22]

[21] See also *WCA*, 3. Indicted and sent as prisoner to Oxford.

[22] See also *WCA*, 1, 3.

[f66v]

22 Portmoot court held 2 February 1609...[23]

Actions of debt:

114:6/12 Wise vs Heath - sergeant returns executed *venire facias*, writ of *habeas corpora* for jury granted.

117:5/6 White vs Hearne - defendant responds, day to amend granted in next court.

Action of trespass:

123:5/9 Tyms vs Silverside - defendant puts demurrer, plaintiff requests copy in court.

Actions of trespass on case:

109:7/11 Symons vs Bennett - judgment that Bennett should recover 17s4d for his amercement and costs, and *scire facias* granted.

120:5/10 Ockly vs Penn - sergeant returns executed *venire facias*; *habeas corpora* granted.

[f67]

Actions of debt:

124:3/5 Nasshe vs Woodroofe - plaintiff completes declaration with copy granted.

128:2/5 Beck vs Collingwood - plaintiff declares with day for amendment; defendant's attorney requests privilege day.

133:1/2 John Newman vs Richard Knevett alias Horsman - plaintiff declares with copy granted.

Actions of trespass on case:

121a:2/5 Ingraham vs Tymes - similarly.

127:2/2 Ball vs Hunniborne - action discharged.

126:3/3 Waste vs Woodd - plaintiff completes declaration; copy for Simon Jeames for defendant. Action discharged.

Action of Qui Tam:

134:1/4 William Harris for his lord the King and for himself vs Robert Parran - plaintiff lays information on contravention of the statutes and Simon Jeames for defendant requests copy in court.

[f67v]

Actions of debt:

135:1/4 Edward Roberts vs John Heath - plaintiff puts declaration with copy granted, first privilege day granted to defendant.

136:1/1 William Dunforde vs Christopher Easte - action discharged..

Action of trespass on case:

137:1/8 William Borman vs Tustian Humphries - plaintiff declares with day for amendment granted in next court.

[23] Neither mayor nor presiding JP recorded.

[f68]

Portmoot court held 20 February 1609...

Action of debt:

114:7/12 William Wise vs John Heath - the jury between parties of

John Raunson,	Jerome White,	Joseph Harris,
Robert Bignill,	John Lowe,	Thomas Williams,
William Edwards,	Alexander Head,	William Meatcalfe,
Richard Shadd,	Roger Sturgis,	William Hickes, senior

find that the bond was made by the defendant and assess damages at 4d with amercement and costs at 2d. Judgment adjourned to next court.

Action of trespass on case:

120: 6/10 Richard Ockly vs Thomas Penn - the jury between parties of

Michael Nursse,	Thomas Blith,	Robert Bignill,
Thomas Screevin,	Thomas Williams,	William Meatcalfe,
Francis Garter,	Thomas Martyn,	William Bradshewe,
John Bradshewe,	William Hickes, junior,	James Dissell

find for the plaintiff and assess damages at £25:12d with amercement and costs at 2d. Judgment in next court,

[f68v]

Actions of debt:

117:6/6 White vs Hearne - action continues by agreement.

124:4/5 Nasshe vs Woodrooffe - defendant responds by wager of law with six hands at next court.

128:3/5 Beck vs Collingwood - plaintiff completes declaration and defendant granted second privilege day.

133:2/2 Newman vs Knevett - action discharged.

Action of trespass:

123:6/9 Tyms vs Silverside - demurrer enjoined to trial in next court.

Actions of trespass on case:

121a:3/5 Ingram vs Tyms - peremptory day for response granted in next court.

137:2/8 Borman vs Humphries - plaintiff completes declaration with copy granted to defendant.

Action of Qui Tam:

134:2/4 Harris on behalf of crown vs Parran - defendant responds, with day for amendment in next court.

Action continuing: **109**:8/11.

[f69]

Action of account:

138:1/2 Thomas Penn vs Richard Ockly - plaintiff declares, day for amendment granted in next court.

Action continuing: **135**:2/4.

[f69v]

Portmoot court held 6 March 1609...

Action of debt:

114:8/12 Wise vs Heath - judgment that plaintiff should recover [blank] for debt, [blank] amercement and 4d damages; *scire facias* granted.

Action of trespass:

123:7/9 Tyms vs Silverside - continues until 3 April for trial on demurrer.

Action of trespass on case:

120:7/10 Ockly vs Penn - judgment that plaintiff should recover £25:12d for damages, and 36s7d amercement and costs; *scire facias* granted for next court.

Actions continuing: **109**:9/11; **121a**:4/5.

[f70]

Actions of debt:

124:5/5 Nasshe vs Woodrooffe - defendant responds and presents six hands: John Glover, Thomas Williams, Thomas Screevin, Ralph Durbridge, Edward Longe and Francis Garter who swear and declare Woodroofe swears truly. Therefore defendant goes quit.

128:4/5 Beck vs Collingwood - final privilege day granted.

139:1/8 Thomas Browne vs Robert Bignill - plaintiff puts declaration with copy granted to defendant.

Action of trespass on case:

137:3/8 Borman vs Humphries - peremptory day to respond granted in next court.

Action of Qui Tam:

134:3/4 Harris and crown vs Parran - defendant granted leave to imparl.

Action of account:

138.2/2 Penn vs Ockly - since plaintiff does not prosecute judgment is postponed. Action discharged.

Action continuing: **135**:3/4.

[f70v]

140:1/3 **Examination. 7 March 1609 before Thomas Bradshewe mayor**. William Hickes of Standlake, Oxon, labourer is examined where he obtained the sheepskin worth 2s4d which he sold this day to Thomas Godfery of this borough for 14d. He says that about Allhallowstide last he and one John Hickes bought from a stranger at Burford market 10 white wether sheep for £3:13:4d and did not toll for them.

And bringing them all to Eynsham about a sennight ago he killed three poor ones unable to travel with the rest, and gave the flesh to his dog. Upon Tuesday last he brought to Godfery two of the skins for 2s4d, and on Friday he sold the third skin with another skin for 13d a piece to one Bartholomew Edginge, glover of Woodstock. The flesh of the fourth he gave to the dog and yesterday left the flesh in a common close in Eynsham called Broadclose. He killed the sixth in daytime and left the flesh in a furlong near the tower called Dedbone.

[f71]

The skin he sold to a glover in Oxford for 12d in the market about a sennight since. The other four remain at Eynsham with nine more which he bred and bought about 12 months since; seven remain with the brand as for the skin he sold he sold to Godfery. Being demanded how he spent his time this last sennight, he said on Wednesday and Thursday last he was sick, on Friday he wrought (i.e. worked) with one Quench of Standlake at threshing for 6d and find for himself. Last Saturday, Sunday and Monday he was also sick and did not work. He denied to set his hand to his examination.

140:2/3. He confessed that this morning he killed a ewe sheep of Mistress Hampshire's of Eynsham and sold the skin in Woodstock market to Thomas Godfery for 14d, and the flesh he flung into a ditch near the sheep-house in Broad close in Eynsham. A sennight ago in the morning he killed at the folds three sheep of William Brokes of Eynsham and brought the skins to Woodstock market and sold them for 13d a piece to Thomas Godfery. And the Wednesday before he likewise killed another of William Brockes' sheep and sold the skin in Oxford market for 12d, and the flesh he laid near the jakes where he killed them. He also confessed that on Friday night last he lay at his mother's house at Clifly[24] and in the morning went into the Clifly field and there killed 2 sheep of Abraham Millens, his uncle, leaving the flesh and selling the skins for 14d a piece to Bartholomew Edging. He denied to set his hand to the confession.

[f71v]

Being re-examined before the said justice, Hickes confessed that about 10 o'clock on Friday night last he came into West Mead[25] in Cassington fields and there killed and flayed a white wether and a white ewe of Richard Cherry. He left the carcases under the hedge and next day sold the skins for 2s4d in Woodstock to Bartholomew Edging, glover. Hickes, his mark.

Recognisance:

140:3/3 Richard Cherry of Cassington, Oxon. yeoman binds himself on £40 that he will give evidence hereupon at next county gaol delivery against William Hickes acccording to the provisions of the statutes.

[f72]

141. Flesh in Lent. The names of the jury appointed for the inquiry into the eating and dressing of flesh in the time of Lent, according to the statute. Appointed and sworn before Thomas Bradshewe mayor and Thomas Browne JP; 9 March 1609:

[24] Cleveley, near Enstone; M.Gelling, Pt II, 348.

[25] *VCH Oxon*. xii, 38.

Jerome White, Nicholas Taylor, Francis Garter, Andrew Jarnes, Thomas Martyn, Thomas Gee, Richard Hawkins, William Hickes junior, Ralph Durbridge, John Wilkinson, Thomas Godferye, Hugo Hamond, William Edwards and John Acklye: sworn in.
Who make presentment that Jerome White dressed flesh in his house twice. Therefore he is in mercy.

[f72v]

142. List of licensed victuallers. (Each victualler has £100 recognisance against his name, with two sureties each at £30; the exception is Thomas Bradshewe who has one surety named, without money.)
Thomas Bradshewe mayor £100: Jerome White - no recognisance;

Richard Meade:	Jerome White &. William Edwards;
John Glover:	Thomas Williams & Edward Rudgate;
Thomas Williams:	Edward Rudgate & William Hickes senior;
William Rayer:	Henry Rudgate & John Glover;
John Dissell:	William Edwards & John Ackly;
John Ackly:	John Dissell & William Hickes senior;
Nicholas Taylor	Jerome White & Henry Rudgate;
William Edwards:	Richard Meades & John Dissell;
Henry Rudgate:	John Glover & Nicholas Taylor;
Edward Rudgate:	Henry Rudgate & Thomas Williams;
	[f73]
William Hickes senior:	Andrew Jarnes & John Ackly;
Hugh Hamond:	William Hickes & Francis Garter;
Thomas Godfery:	Edward Rudgate & Andrew Jarnes;
Thomas Abbott:	John Abbott & John Ryly.

Michael Nursse, butcher £100; Jerome White & John Ackly £30 each.

[f73v]

Portmoot court held 20 March 1609...

Actions of debt:
114:9/12 Wise vs Heath - *alias scire facias* granted.
128:5/5 Beck vs Collingwood - peremptory day for response granted. Action discharged.
135:4/4 Roberts vs Heath - action discharged by agreement of plaintiff.
139:2/8 Browne vs Bignill - second privilege day granted to defendant.
Actions of trespass on case:
120:8/10 Ockly vs Penn - *alias scire facias* granted.
121a:5/5 Ingrome vs Tyms - action discharged by agreement of plaintiff.
137:4/8 Borman vs Humphries - defendant responds, and copy granted.
Actions continuing: **123**:8/9; **134**:4/4.

[f74]

Portmoot court held 3 April 1609...

Actions of debt:

114:10/12 Wise vs Heath - sergeant executed writ of *sicut alias scire facias*, defendant does not appear. Therefore execution granted against defendant and surety.

139:3/8 Browne vs Bignill - defendant's attorney Henry Rudgate acknowledges said debt, judgment in next court.

Action of trespass:

123:9/9 Tyme vs Silverside - judgment that defendant's demurrer bars the action therefore he goes quit.

Actions of trespass on case:

120:9/10 Ockly vs Penn - sergeant returns executed *sicut alias scire facias;* defendant appears in person and is committed to custody of sergeant, and sureties go quit.

137:5/8 Borman vs Humphries - both parties put themselves on the country, therefore *venire facias* issued for jury.

[f74v]

Actions of debt:

143:1/2 Edward White vs Richard Russell - plaintiff declares, copy granted.

144:1/19 William Bickerstaffe vs Ralph Saunders - similarly.

Actions of trespass on case: (see **109**:7/11, f66v)

109:10/11 Release by John Symons - Memorandum. In open court John Symons of Bladon, through attorney Henry Rudgate, discharges and releases Humphrey Bennett of Bladon from his action of trespass on the case for the slander proclaimed by the said Humphrey. Therefore Humphrey goes quit.

109:11/11 Release by Humphrey Bennett. Memorandum. In open court Humphrey Bennett, through attorney Simon Jeames, releases John Symons concerning the action of trespass on the case in which Symons was found against; therefore he goes quit.

[f75]

Portmoot court held 10 April 1609...

Actions of debt:

139:4/8 Browne vs Bignill - judgment for plaintiff to recover [blank] debt, amercement and costs at [blank] and damages for detinue at [blank]; *scire facias* granted.

143:2/2 White vs Russell - action discharged.

144:2/19 Bickerstaffe vs Saunders - peremptory day granted for response.

145:1/17 Thomas Meatcalfe vs Richard Heath - plaintiff's attorney Simon Jeames puts declaration and defendant's attorney Henry Rudgate requests copy in court.

Actions of trespass on case:
137:6/8 Borman vs Humphries - executed *venire facias* returned by sergeant and *habeas corpora* granted for return in next court.
120:10/10. Ockly vs Penn - defendant handed to custody of sergeant.
Action continuing: **114**:11/12.

[f75v] (Blank).

[f76]

146. Sessions of the Peace with View of Frankpledge held 12 April 1609, before Thomas Bradshewe mayor, James Whitlock knight and recorder of the borough, and Thomas Browne JP, by me Edmund Hiorne clerk of the mayor and the commonalty of the borough. (Edmund Rudgate constable is the same person as Edward 'Ned' Rudgate).
Jury of homage for the Crown:

John Raunson,	Michael Nursse,	Nicholas Taylor,
Francis Collingwood,	Thomas Blith,	William Ball,
Jerome White,	John Lowe,	Thomas Screevin,
John Heath,	Thomas Williams,	William Meatcalfe,
William Bradshewe,	John Bradshewe,	William Edwards,
Francis Garter,	Thomas Martyn,	Richard Shadd,
Roger Sturgis,	Hugo Hamond: sworn in.	

147(see **40** and **100**) Phillip Collier appears in person and discharges his recognisance.
130:2/2 William Edwards appears in person and discharges his recognisance.

[ff76v to f78v] (Blank).

[f79]

Portmoot court held 24 April 1609…
Actions of debt:
114:12/12 Wise vs Heath - action discharged.
139:5/8 Browne vs Bignill - *alias scire facias* granted.
144:3/19 Bickerstaffe vs Saunders - defendant in response proffers document showing this to be a foreign plea; the next court will advise on acceptance of this.
Action of trespass on case:
137:7/8 William Borman vs Tustian Humphries - jury between parties:

John Raunson,	Michael Nursse,	Joseph Harris,
Robert Bignill,	John Lowe,	Thomas Screevin,
Thomas Meatcalfe,	William Edwards,	Thomas Martyn,
Alexander Head,	Ralph Durbridge	

find for the plaintiff and assess damages at 41s with amercement 2d; judgment in court.
Action continuing: **145**:2/17.

[f79v]

Conveyance:

148:1/4 before Thomas Bradshewe mayor. 24 April 1609.

Order: Order Robert Chamberlain and Helen his wife that justly they keep agreement with Nathaniel Noble concerning two burgage messuages or tenements with appurtenances in the borough now in separate tenure or occupation by Thomas Jackson and Elizabeth Fleminge widow. And if they do not do so etc..

And the concord is as follows: that the said Robert and Helen acknowledge the said tenements with appurtenances to be the right of the same Nathaniel which he has of the gift of the said Robert and Helen. And remit and quitclaim them for the said Robert and Helen and their heirs in perpetuity to the said Nathaniel Noble and his heirs in perpetuity. And in addition the said Robert and Helen concede for themselves and their heirs that they will warrant the said tenements with appurtenances to the said Nathaniel Noble and his heirs against themselves and their heirs, etc.[26] (signed) Robert Chamberlain, Thomas Bradshewe and Edmund Hiorne; (mark of) Helen Chamberlain.

[f80]

Portmoot court held 8 May 1609...

Conveyance:

148:2/4 First proclamation between Nathaniel Noble querent and Robert Chamberlain and Helen his wife deforciants concerning two burgage messuages or tenements with appurtenances now in separate tenancy or occupation by Thomas Jackson and Elizabeth Fleming widow: one of them next to the Holloway and the other in Blackhall Lane below the said burgage. Which the same Nathaniel recently purchased and Robert Chamberlayne and Helen have handed over.

Actions of debt:

139:6/8 Browne vs Bignill - *alias scire facias* executed, and execution of action granted against defendant and surety.

149:1/15 Ann Leake widow vs Henry Alberte - day to declare granted in next court.

Action of trespass on case:

137:8/8 Borman vs Humphries - action discharged by agreement.

Action continuing: **145**:3/17.

[f80v]

Actions of debt:

144:4/19 Bickerstaffe vs Saunders - day to respond in next court, but jury to advise on the other plea.

[26] See also *WCA*, 1, 38.

150:1/2 Robert Bignill vs Bennett Painter - plaintiff declares and grants a copy.

151. Recognisance to keep peace; 9 May 1609 before Thomas Bradshewe mayor and Thomas Browne JP.

Edmund Hiorne of Great Tew, yeoman, JP against John Hasle - John Hasle binds himself in £20, with John Heath and Richard Hawkins each surety in £10, that he keeps the peace towards the said Edmund and all others, and appears in person at the next borough sessions of the peace to make his case and receive judgment. Discharged.

[f81]

Portmoot court held 22 May 1609...

Conveyance:

148:3/4 Second proclamation between Nathaniel Noble querent and Robert & Helen Chamberlayne deforciants.

Actions of debt:

149:2/5 Leake vs Alberte - plaintiff declares and grants copy to defendant.

150:2/2 Bignill vs Paynter - second privilege day granted defendant in next court. Action discharged.

Actions continuing: **139**:7/8; **145**:4/17.

[f81v]

Actions of debt:

144:5/19 Bickerstaffe vs Saunders - defendant denies the deed in full and puts himself on the country; *venire facias* for jury.

152:1/6 William Raunson vs Andrew Jarnes - plaintiff puts declaration, defendant requests copy and first privilege day.

153:1/1 William Meatcalfe vs William Richardes - plaintiff requests day to declare in next court, and defendant appears through attorney Henry Rudgate.

154:1/2 Edmund Hiorne senior vs John Hasle - plaintiff declares, with day to amend granted in next court.

155:1/2 Edmund Hiorne senior vs Joan Hasle widow, executrix of the last testament of her husband John Hasle - similarly.

Actions of trespass on case:

156:1/2 Edmund Hiorne senior vs John Hasle - similarly.

157:1/2 Edmund Hiorne senior vs Joan Hasle widow and executrix, similarly.

Court adjourned for three weeks.

[f82]

Portmoot court held 12 June 1609...

Conveyance:

148:4/4 Third proclamation between Nathaniel Noble querent and Robert & Helen Chamberlaine deforciants.

Actions of debt:

139:8/8 Browne vs Bignill - action as previously. Discharged.

144:6/19 Bickerstaff vs Saunders - executed *venire facias* returned and *habeas corpora* for jury granted.
149:3/15 Leake vs Alberte - peremptory day granted for response.
Actions of debt:
154:2/2 Hiorne vs Hasle - plaintiff completes declaration; copy granted to defendant; peremptory day to respond granted.
*Action continuing: **145**:5/17.*

[f82v]

155:2/2 Hiorne vs Hasle widow - similarly.
Actions of trespass on case:
156:2/2 Hiorne vs Hasle - similarly.
157:2/2 Hiorne vs Hasle widow - similarly.
Actions of debt:
152:2/6 Raunson vs Jarnes - second privilege day granted defendant in next court.
158:1/1 Humphrey Hamond vs John Kente - plaintiff puts declaration; copy to defendant.
159:1/1 Matthew Parrett vs Robert Butcher - day to declare granted in next court.
160:1/2 **Recognisance. 18 June 1609 before Thomas Bradshewe mayor and Thomas Browne JP.**
Robert Bruce junior binds himself in £20, with Edward Rudgate and John Bradshewe sureties each in £10, that he will keep the peace towards William Kinge and all others and will appear at the next borough sessions of the peace to make his case and receive justice. (see *f98*).

[f83]

Portmoot court held 26 June 1609…
Actions of debt:
144:7/19 William Bickerstaffe vs Ralph Saunders; the jury between parties of

John Raunson,	Michael Nursse,	Jerome White,
William Meatcalfe,	William Edwards,	Alexander Head,
John Bradshewe,	Edward Rudgate,	John Dissell,
William Hickes senior,	Francis Garter,	John Wilkinson

declares that the bond was made by the defendant, and assess damages at 4d, with amercement at 2d. Judgment adjourned to next court.
149:4/15 Leake vs Alberte - since defendant does not appear after three summonses judgment is prevented.
152:3/6 Raunson vs Jarnes - final privilege day to respond granted.
161:1/12 Thomas Browne vs Richard Jarnes and John Heath - plantiff declares, defendants request first privilege day in next court.
Action continuing: **145**:6/17.

[f83v]

Portmoot court held 10 July 1609...

Actions of debt:

144:8/19 William Bickerstaffe vs Ralph Saunders - judgment adjourned to next court which will consider the advice of the borough recorder.

149:5/15 Leake vs Alberte - judgment given that plaintiff should recover £20 debt with 20s8d for her amercement and costs; *scire facias* granted.

152:4/6 Raunson vs Jarnes - peremptory day granted.

161:2/12 Browne vs Jarnes and Heath - second privilege day granted in next court.

Action of trespass:

162:1/3 Richard Browne vs Richard Reade - plaintiff declares, defendant requests copy in court.

Action continuing: **145**:7/17.

[f84]

163:1/6 **Examination before Thomas Bradshewe mayor and Thomas Browne JP. 23 July 1609.**

Examination of Walter Howell, butcher of Winchcombe, Gloucestershire, who says he bought a grey trotting mare from one Robert Pore of Derbyshire on the downs highway between Stow and Winchcombe about 6 weeks since for 4 marks 3s4d, and did not toll for her. Previously he had only met Pore once at London, once at the Bell in Carter Lane and other places there. The two came from the downs to the alehouse of Richard Bicks in Great Tew and lay there three days.

[f84v]

After a fortnight he rode the mare to Staunton, Gloucestershire, with an alehousekeeper Price of Pye Corner, Smithfield, London, to collect a debt and then on to his wife at Winchcombe for a fortnight (this paragraph deleted). Bicke would not buy the mare so he sent Pore to fetch John George, smith, of

[f85]

Ledwell, with his father and friend, and he bought her for £3, with 20s in hand and the rest to be paid at Bick's house 3 weeks later. He had met George through John Cherry of Ledwell and a fortnight before had offered George a grey trotting mare he had bought from his uncle Lewis Pritchett of Llantilio Crossenny ('Landilo Cresselle') near Abergavenny, a quarter of a year since

[f85v]

with money owed. This is the mare now in Woodstock town. He went from his uncle to his brother's, one Davy Howell embroiderer ('imbroder') of King's Street, Westminster, from there to Ledwell and on to Winchcombe where he kept the mare a fortnight.

163:2/6 In the last week Howell said he lay up and down the country but could not say where until upon Friday last he came to Ledwell to demand his 40s which George the smith owed him,

[f86]

and he lay at an alehouse at Sandford (St. Martin). George denied to pay the remaining 40s without vouchers for the sale, according to the law, but agreed to meet at Woodstock fair on Mary Magdalen day 22nd. of this month to enter sale in the toll-book and pay the 40s. After they met and came to the toll-book he was apprehended since he could not give warranties according to

[f86v]

the law, and had only one voucher, Robert Debanck, calling himself Robert Johnson. He met Debanck on Thursday last and came with him to Woodstock, staying at Sandford on the way. Howell had 3¾ yards of russett fustian, 3 dozen green silk buttons and 3 skeins of green silk which he bought for 8s from a mercer in Tanworth ('Tannworth'), Warwickshire, whose name he did not know. Also a broadsword with basket hilt and a pair of shoes:

(signed) Walter Howell.

[f87]

163:3/6 *Examination* of Robert Debanck, same day before said JPs. Being examined how he came by a brown bay ambling gelding here in town, Debanck said that in easter term last he bought him from a Mr Dod lying at the sign of the Plover in Holborn, London, for which he paid but did not toll for her. He was in Woodstock because he was to have gone to Virginia[27] and about a month since came into the country to his sister near Kettering,

[f87v]

Northamptonshire, now married to one William Richardson. He had no argument with him until lately at London. Debanck said he met Howell on Friday last upon the downs by Duns Tew and they lay the night at an alehouse at Sandford. Being demanded how he came by a hammer, horselock, and certain keys and picklock found on him, he said that he found them whilst alone last Friday morning in a bag upon the highway near Aynho-on-the-hill. These were: 5 horselock keys; 5 picklock keys, 2 of them hollow; 3 instruments of wire crooked; 3 small keys for cupboards or coffers.[28]

He also brought to Woodstock a charged pistol, one bible in quarto, a pair of shoes, a sword with case and a bodkin, and a halter.

(signed): by me Robert debanke.

[f88]

163:4/6 *Examination* of Henry Debanck of Droitwich, Worcestershire, brother of Robert Debanck. taken the same day.

[27] Emigration to Virginia, and transportation there from 1607; Davies, 327; Beier, 162/3.

[28] Beier, 130.

He says that on Thursday last he visited his father who sent him this morning to Woodstock to see the occasion of Robert's stay here, and he came for no other purpose. He brought with him a sorrell bay mare which was sent to Oxford by the justice to carry the prisoners to the gaol.
The marks of the horses:-
Debanck's: one bay ambling and trotting nag, with a white spot under the saddle, a slit on the near ear and a fire brand on the near buttock.
Howell's: two grey trotting mares, the lesser with a firebrand on the near shoulder and a white nose; the other slit down under both ears and cut off, without any other mark.

[f88v]

163:5/6 *Information*. 1 August 1609 before the same justices. John Battman of Clifton-upon-Dunsmore, Warwickshire, says that on Thursday 20 July last he tied with a rope and a lock his bay ambling and trotting gelding which had a slit in the near ear and a firebrand on the near buttock, and left it at about six o'clock in the evening in a meadow belonging to Clifton. That night it was stolen but was seen at Clifton with Debanck and another man, and it is the gelding he found here in Woodstock.
163:6/6 *Recognisances*: John and Richard Battman each binds himself in £40 that John Battman will appear in person to present and give evidence according to the statutes against Robert Johnson alias Debanck and Walter Howell at the next sessions and gaol delivery in county Oxon.
Recognisance: 23 July 1609.
John George of Ledwell, smith, binds himself in £40 to present a case against Debanck and Howell at the general gaol delivery in county Oxon.[29]

[f89]

Portmoot court held 24 July 1609...
Actions of debt:
149:6/15 Leake vs Alberte - sergeant returns executed *scire facias; alias scire facias* granted.
161:3/12 Browne vs Jarnes and Heath - final privilege day granted.
Action of trespass:
162:2/3 Browne vs Reade - defendant's attorney Henry Rudgate admits the action; writ of inquiry for damages granted for return in next court.
Actions continuing: **144**:9/19; **145**:8/17.

[f89v]

Actions of debt:
152:5/6 Raunson vs Jarnes - defendant responds and puts himself on the country; *venire facias* granted.

[29] *WCA*, 1, 2, 5, 6. Eight entries: from selling Howell's possessions, sending messengers to Clifton and Winchcombe, indictments at Oxford and Debanck's execution, to George's payments.

164:1/1 William Bradshewe vs John Kente senior - plaintiff declares and defendant's attorney requests copy.
165:1/1 Thomas Rowden vs Richard Anstell alias Austen - similarly.

[f90]

Portmoot court held 7 August 1609...

Actions of debt:
149:7/15 Leake vs Alberte - sergeant returns executed *sicut alias scire facias*: defendant does not appear, therefore execution granted against defendant and surety.
152:6/6 Raunson vs Jarnes - executed *venire facias* returned and *habeas corpora* granted.
161:4/12 Browne vs Jarnes - peremptory day granted for response.
166:1/1 Humphrey Hamond vs Richard Manning - plaintiff declares, with copy to defendant's attorney.
167:1/11 John Bradshewe vs Richard Jarnes - similarly; and privilege day granted to defendant.
Action of trespass:
162:3/3 Browne vs Reade - continues. Discharged.
Actions continuing: **144**:10/19; **145**:9/17.

[f90v]

Portmoot court held 21 August 1609...

Action of debt:
161:5/12 Browne vs Jarnes – defendants' attorney Henry Rudgate admits their debt, judgment adjourned to next court
Action of Qui Tam:
168:1/1 William Harris on behalf of the lord king and himself vs William Minchine, lays information on contravention of the statutes - defendant's attorney Simon James requests copy of the information in court. Permission to imparl granted. And thereafter action discharged.
Actions continuing: **144**:11/19; **145**:10/17; **149**:8/15; **167**:2/11.

[f91]

Portmoot court held 4 September 1609...

Actions of debt:
161:6/12 Browne vs Jarnes - judgment for [blank] debt [blank] for amercement and costs, *scire facias* granted against surety.
169:1/1 Thomas Harris gent vs William Hickes, senior, plaintiff's attorney requests day to declare in next court. Discharged.
170:1/1 Richard Grigson, clerk vs George Robinson - defendant in person asks to reply with silence,[30] and after three solemn summonses does not reply. Judgment given.

[30] 'reply with silence', a tactful response possibly related to both suitors being clergy (see Oxon probates)?

171:1/1 Richard Grigson clerk vs George Robinson - similarly.
Actions continuing: **144**:12/19; **145**:11/17; **149**:9/15; **167**:3/11.

[f91v]

172:1/3 **Base-child recognisance**, before Thomas Bradshewe mayor. Richard Browne binds himself in £20, with Thomas Williams and Ralph Durbridge sureties in £10 each, that he will appear in person at the next borough sessions of the peace to make his case and accept the judgment imposed. For that he is reputed by Ursula to be the father of the child she now goes with.

173. Examination. 6 September 1609.

Francis Vahan (i.e Vaughan) of Presteigne, ('Presteene') Radnorshire ('com. Ladnock'). sold to Francis Collingwood a hat, a pair of shoes and a shirt for 6s. The hat he had from Joan Swaffame of Greenwich ('Greenewich') about a fortnight since, to be given to Francis Bown's sister at Presteigne He was committed to be punished as a rogue; 2s given to Edward Rudgate constable.[31]

[f92]

Portmoot court held 18 September 1609…

Actions of debt:

161:7/12 Browne vs Jarnes - executed *scire facias* returned and renewed.
167:4/11 Bradshewe vs Jarnes - second privilege day granted.
174:1/4 William Whitfeild vs Thomas Kent - plaintiff declares and defendant requests copy.
Actions continuing: **144**:13/19; **145**:12/17; **149**:10/15.

[f92v]

175. Examination for horse-theft, before Thomas Bradshewe mayor and James Whitlock esquire borough recorder. 22 September 1609.

Edmund Evans of Edenbridge ('Eatonbridge') Kent, gardener, says he came from there on Tuesday last intending to go to William his brother at Allym (?Lymm), Cheshire, for maintenance, and lay at the Hartshorn at Stowe, Buckinghamshire. On Wednesday he came to Bicester, Oxon, and on the morrow to Woodstock. He bought his mare, which he is now charged with, from one Thomas Cashworth a tanner at Edenbridge on Wednesday sennight for 30s and did not toll for her. Edward Evans (his mark)

A mare, saddle, bridle, cloak, sword, £2 in money given to Rudgate.

Isack Potter knight and Nicholas Silliard esq. Justices of Kent near Edenbridge.

176. Recognisance. Escapes from custody. Robert Huet, Edmund Browne and Walter Adams escaped from Edmund Rudgate constable. Edmund Butler gent binds himself in £10, and Browne in £5, that Browne will appear at the next borough sessions of the peace. (see **195**, **196**)

[31] See also *WCA*, 2.

177. Examination on possession of sheep, 29 September 1609.
John Minchine of Lambeth by London, servant to Mr Nicholas Kinget attorney,says he bought from Richard Fowler of Great Barrington, Gloucestershire, 3 score and 4 ewes and rams for 16 nobles a score. And he bought from James Harris his neighbour 20 wethers for £6:6s, and he had mind to drive them to Lambarte (?Lambeth) in Surrey.
Minchine was born at Churchill - he also bought 7 ewes from Hugh Mathews of the same town for 4s apiece.

[f93]

178. Examination for theft, 26 September 1609, before Thomas Bradshewe mayor and Thomas Browne JP.
Bartholomew Hodges of the Leafield ('le Feild') Oxon, labourer, being here yesterday in the market was arrested upon suspicion for the stealing of two ewes and two lambs which he sold here to one George Stowt for 16s. He says that about midsummer last in Burford market he bought two couples of ewes and lambs from a stranger for 16s, and one other theve for 6s8d from another stranger. He lost one couple in the woods but has kept the rest in the common of the Feild. They are all cropped on the far ('furr') ear.

Bartholomew Hodge (his mark).

Recognisance. 29 September 1609, before the mayor.
Bartholomew Hodges binds himself in £40, with William Hodges labourer and Thomas Riste each of Leafield and each bound in £20, that Bartholomew will appear in person at the next county general gaol delivery to make his case and receive judgment.

[f93v]

179:1/2 **Examination on forging letters, 30 September 1609**, before Thomas Bradshewe mayor and Thomas Browne JP.
Thomas Jarratt of Cherrington, Warwickshire, labourer, being here at Woodstock stayed upon suspicion of going with counterfeit messages and writing counterfeit letters. He confesses that he wrote a letter to Robert Phipps' son dwelling at Aynho-on-the-hill ('Aynow upon the hill') that he should come to his father in Oxford and give Jarratt 2s4d for his pains, which he did. Also a letter to John Phipps of Ledwell to come to William Phipps his brother at Oxford and pay Jarratt 12d for his pains, which he received. And a letter to Richard Rowland of Hanborough to come to John Phipps his father-in-law at Ledwell and give Jarratt 20d, which he did.
Also another letter to John Mayne of South Leigh to come to John Phipps of Ledwell his father-in-law and he should have paid Jarratt 20d for his pains, but as he was not at home Jarratt had nothing.[32] (signed) Thomas Jarrard.

[32] 33 Henry *VIII, c. 1* dealt with counterfeiting letters for obtaining money. Bellamy, 37.

[f94]

Portmoot court held 2 October 1609...

Actions of debt:

144:14/19 William Bickerstaffe vs Ralph Saunders - defendant's attorney Henry Rudgate produces here in court a royal writ of privilege for return before the king's justices at Westminster on the morrow of All Souls' Day; and. dated 5 July 1609. This writ is issued and approved, and judgment is therefore adjourned: plaintiff granted copy of writ.

161:8/12 Browne vs Jarnes and Heath - executed *alias scire facias* returned; execution granted against defendants and sureties.

Actions continuing: **145**:13/17; **149**:11/15.

[f94v]

Actions of debt:

167:5/11 Bradshewe vs Jarnes - final privilege day granted to defendant.

174:2/4 Whittfeild vs Kente - peremptory day to respond granted defendant in next court.

180:1/1 Francis Townsend vs Francis Collingwood - action discharged.

181:1/9 William Dunforde vs William Austine - plaintiff's attorney puts declaration, copy to defendant.

182:1/9 John Gregorie vs Richard Stutter - plaintiff declares with copy to defendant.

183:1/5 William Loggon vs Richard Stutter - similarly.

184:1/7 John Cobbett vs Richard Stutter - similarly.

185:1/5 Edmund Hiorne vs Richard Stutter - similarly.

Action of trespass on case:

186:1/1 Nicholas George vs [blank] - action discharged.

[f95]

Portmoot court held 16 October 1609...

Actions of debt:

167:6/11 Bradshewe vs Jarnes - peremptory day to respond.

174:3/4 Whitfeild vs Kente - defendant does not appear after three summonses. Therefore etc.

181:2/9 Dunford vs Austen - defendant responds, copy granted.

182:2/9 Gregorie vs Stutter - peremptory day to respond.

Actions continuing: **144**:15/19; **145**:14/17; **149**:12/15; **161**:9/12.

[f95v]

Actions of debt:

183:2/5 Loggon vs Stutter - peremptory day to respond.

184:2/7 Cobbett vs Stutter - similarly.

185:2/5 Hiorne vs Stutter - similarly.

187:1/1 John Gregorie vs Richard Stutter - action discharged.

188:1/2 Humphrey Hamond vs Thomas Rooke - plaintiff declares with copy to defendant.
189:1/6 William Bradborne vs Richard Heath - similarly.
Actions of trespass on case:
190:1/8 William Harris vs Richard Horskins - similarly.
191:1/5 Robert Annison vs John Annison - plaintiff declares with day for correction in next court.

[f96]

192:1/2 **Examination, 18 October 1609** before Thomas Bradshewe mayor and Thomas Browne JP.
Examination of John Polly of the city of Oxford, musician. Sergeant Henry Rudgate on oath says that yesterday Polly took him by the throat and held him in his own house. Whereby Richard Stutter, a prisoner arrested on the execution on several debt actions by divers men, and then in his charge, broke from within his hands in his hall and escaped. But by chance he was taken running away by William Bradshewe.
John Bradshewe, mercer, confirms this on oath the same day.
John Polly binds himself in £40, with John Dubber and John Glover each sureties in £20, that he will appear at the next borough sessions of the peace.

[f96v]

193. View of Frankpledge, held at the guildhall 19 October 1609 before Thomas Bradshewe gent mayor, by Edmund Hiorne clerk to the mayor and the commonalty of the borough.
Changes in officers:
Constables : Thomas Williams and Edward Rudgate discharged; Joseph Harris and Thomas Meatcalfe elected and sworn in.
Tithingmen : addition of Robert Spitle, John Norman and William Bradshewe; 3s4d against Thomas Martyn.
Aletasters : addition of William Kinge and Richard Shadd;
Edward Rudgate (deleted).

Crown jury of homage:

Michael Nursse,	John Raunson,	Thomas Blith,
Jerome White,	Thomas Screevin,	John Heath,
Thomas Meatcalfe,	William Bradshewe,	John Bradshewe,
Francis Garter,	Hugh Hamond,	William Hickes, sen. ,
John Dubber,	Richard Wright,	Robert Bignill: sworn in.

Affeerers: William Bradshewe, John Heath, Thomas Blith: sworn in.

[f97 & f97v] (Blank)

[f98]

194:1/2 **Sessions of the Peace held at the guild hall, 19 October 1609, before Thomas Bradshewe gent mayor and Thomas Browne gent JPs** to conserve the King's peace, and to hear and determine the various felonies, trespasses and other misdemeamours perpetrated within the said borough as assigned, according to the custom of the borough used and approved from time immemorial; by Edmund Hiorne clerk to the mayor and commonalty of the borough.

[f98v]

Recognisances:

160:2/2 Robert Bruce junior binds himself in £20, with Edward Rudgate and John Bradshewe each surety in £10, that Robert appears in person at the sessions of the peace. He appears and is discharged by the court.

172:2/3 Base-child surety. Richard Browne binds himself in £20, with Thomas Williams and Ralph Durbridge each surety in £10, that Richard continues to appear in person at the sessions of the peace. Recognisances on Richard and the sureties until next sessions. Discharged. (but see *f118v*).

195:1/2 Escape from custody. Edmund Browne binds himself in £20, with Edmund Butler gent surety in £10, that Browne appears in person at this sessions. He does not appear; therefore forfeits recognisance. Discharged (see *f118v*).

196: Edmund Rudgate did suffer Robert Huett to escape from him. Therefore etc.

[f99]

179:2/2 Thomas Jarrett bound in £20; with Robert Bignill surety in £10, appears in person and is discharged.

192:2/2 John Polly bound in £20, with John Glover and John Dubber each surety in £10, appears in person and is discharged by court.

194:2/2 Jury to the assize:

Robert Bruce,	Richard Browne,	William Walford,
John Polly,	John Doe,	Randall Richards,
George Bruce.		

197: **Memorandum**: in this Sessions all victuallers within this borough were discharged.

[f99v, f100 & 100v] (Blank)

[f101]

Portmoot court held 30 October 1609...

Actions of debt:

167:7/11 Bradshewe vs Jarnes - defendant's attorney Henry Rudgate acknowledges the debt of £3:4:8d, day in next court.

174:4/4 Whittfeild vs Kente - judgment for [blank] debt and [blank] amercement, *scire facias* granted.

181:3/9 Dunford vs Austine - defendant responds and puts himself on country, plaintiff similarly; therefore *venire facias* granted.

Actions of debt:
198:1/3 John Gregory vs Richard Stutter - defendant appears by attorney, plaintiff declares, copy granted.
182:3/9 Gregory vs Stutter - defendant does not appear after three summonses, therefore judgment adjourned to next court.
Actions continuing: **144**:16/19; **145**:15/17; **149**:13/15; **161**:10/12.

[f101v]

183:3/5 Loggon vs Stutter - similarly.
184:3/7 Cobbett vs Stutter - similarly.
185:3/5 Hiorne vs Stutter - similarly.
188:2/2 Humphrey Hamond vs Rooke - action discharged.
199:1/1 Thomas Browne vs William Altoffe - defendant appears through attorney Henry Rudgate, plaintiff declares, copy granted.
200:1/4 Richard Busby vs Nicholas Morton alias Hassam - similarly.
201:1/12 Richard Whinge vs Robert Payne - similarly.
202:1/10 William Bradshewe vs John Heath - defendant appears by attorney, day for plaintiff to declare in next court.
Actions of trespass on case:
190:2/8 Harris vs Horskins - peremptory day to respond granted.
191:2/5 Annison vs Annison - similarly.
Action continuing: **189:**2/6.

[f102]

203. Assize of Bread and Ale... 6 November 1609...

The court of Thomas Bradshewe mayor and before Thomas Browne JP assisting the mayor as clerk of the market within this borough. The jury of

John Raunson,	John Dubber,	John Lowe,
John Heath,	William Bradshewe,	William Edwards,
John Ackly,	Alexander Headd,	Richar Shadd,
James Dissell,	John Bradshewe,	Edward Rudgate,
Thomas Martyn,	Francis Garter,	Michael Nursse,

William Meatcalfe and William Hickes junior: sworn in.
The jury present that:
best wheat last market day was worth 32s the quarter, second wheat was worth 24s (?) the quarter, and third wheat worth 24s: best malt in the same market was worth 20s the quarter.

[f102v]

Within this borough the bakers to bake good and wholesome bread fit for men's bodies and to keep the following assize: every penny white loaf to weigh 13 ounces, every penny wheaten loaf to weigh 18 ounces, and every penny household loaf to weigh 23 ounces.
And the brewers and victuallers to brew good and wholesome ale and beer,

and to sell a thirdendell for a penny worth outdoors, and a quart for a penny indoors.
The butchers to sell their tallow at 3s4d the stone, and the chandlers their candles at [blank] the pound.
And all to keep the assize upon pain and peril that shall fall thereon.

(signed) Edmund Hiorne.

[f103]

204. Weights and measures sealed and allowed at this meeting.
One bushel each of Thomas Browne alderman, Joseph Harris, Francis Collingwood, Thomas Painter, Widow Spitle, John Ryly and William Ball;
One peck each of Robert Bignill, Thomas Meatcalfe and William Rayer;
One half-peck each of Thomas Meatcalfe, Robert Bignill, John Lowe and Joseph Harris.

[f103v] (Blank)

[f104]

Portmoot court held 13 November 1609...

Actions of debt:

167:8/11 Bradshewe vs Jarnes - judgment that plaintiff should recover [blank] for debt, [blank] amercement; *scire facias* against surety.
181:4/9 Dunforde vs Austine - sergeant returns executed *venire facias*. and *habeas corpora* granted.
Actions continuing: **144**:17/19; **145**:16/17; **149**:14/15; **161**:11/12.

[f104v]

Actions of debt:

182:4/9 Gregory vs Stutter - judgment of £24 for debt, [blank] amercement and costs, 12d damages for detinue; execution granted against defendant.
183:4/5 Loggon vs Stutter - similarly, with £12 for the debt.
184:4/7 Cobbett vs Stutter - similarly, with £8 for the debt.
185:4/5 Hiorne vs Stutter - similarly, with £6 for the debt.
198:2/3 Gregory vs Stutter - peremptory day for response.
189:3/6 Bradborne vs Heath - defendant granted peremptory day to respond in next court.
200:2/4 Busby vs Morton alias Hassam - similarly.

Actions of trespass on case:

190:3/8 Harris vs Horskins - defendant responds and puts himself on the country; therefore *venire facias* granted.
191:3/5 Annison vs Annison - similarly.

[f105]

Actions of debt:

201:2/12 Whinge vs Payne - defendant granted peremptory day to respond in next court.

202:2/10 Bradshewe vs Heath - plaintiff declares, defendant granted first privilege day in next court.

[f105v]

Portmoot court held 27 November 1609...

Actions of debt:

145:17/17 Meatcalfe vs Heath - action discharged.

149:15/15 Leake vs Albett - sergeant returns execution of judgment against body of Albott and continues it against body of surety.

161:12/12 Browne vs Heath and Jarnes - sergeant returns execution of judgment against body of Heath, and continues execution against Jarnes and surety.

Action continuing: **144**:18/19.

Actions of debt:

182:5/9 Gregory vs Stutter - sergeant returns execution of judgment on body of defendant who remains in his custody.

[f106]

198:3/3 Gregorie vs Stutter - since defendant does not appear after three summonses judgment adjourned to next court.

183:5/5 Loggon vs Stutter - sergeant returns execution of judgment on body of defendant who remains in custody.

184:5/7 Cobbett vs Stutter - similarly.

185:5/5 Hiorne vs Stutter - similarly.

200:3/4 Busby vs Morton alias Hassam - defendant pleads that bond is not his deed, and puts himself on the country as does plaintiff; *venire facias* for jury.

201:3/12 Whinge vs Payne - since defendant does not appear after 3 summonses judgment adjourned to next court.

167:9/11 Bradshewe vs Jarnes - sergeant returns executed *scire facias*, but defendant does not appear; *alias scire facias* granted against surety.

Actions of trespass on case:

190:4/8 Harris vs Horskins - sergeant returns executed *venire facias*; *habeas corpora* for jury granted in next court.

191:4/5 Annison vs Annison - similarly.

Action continuing: **189**:4/6.

[f106v]

Actions of debt:

181:5/9 William Dunford vs William Austine; the jury of

Michael Nursse,	Francis Collingwood,	Joseph Harris,
Robert Bignill,	Thomas Screevin,	Thomas Williams,
Thomas Meatcalfe,	William Meatcalfe,	Alexander Head,
Richard Hawkins,	Thomas Martyn,	John Bradshewe;

finds plaintiff makes default. Therefore etc.

205:1/5 Humphrey Hamond vs Henry Albott - plaintiff puts declaration, copy to defendant.
206:1/5 Henry Rowleright vs Richard Stutter - similarly.
207:1/14 William Dunford vs Troylus Butcher - defendant appears in person, plaintiff declares and copy to defendant.
Actions of trespass on case:
208:1/4 Brian Bradforth vs John Payne - plaintiff declares and requests day to amend in next court.
209:1/5 Richard Heynes vs Francis Brangwin - similarly.
Action continuing: **202**:3/10.

[f107]

Conveyance:
210:1/4 11 Dec. 1609 before Thomas Bradshewe mayor.
Order: Order John Whitton alias Darlinge that justly he keep the agreement with William Meatcalfe concerning five burgage messuages or tenements with appurtenances in the borough now in tenure or occupation by Thomas Belcher, James Dissell, John Lowe, John Bruce and widow Dorothy Whorde. And if he does not do so etc..
And the concord is as follows: that the said John Whitton alias Darlinge acknowledges the said tenements with appurtenances to be the right of the said William Meatcalfe of the gift of the said John, and remits and quitclaims them for the said John and his heirs to the said William and his heirs in perpetuity. And in addition the said John concedes for himself and his heirs that he will warrant the said tenements with appurtenances to the said William Meatcalfe and his heirs against himself and his heirs and against all heirs having or claiming a right on, through, or under his father George Whitton esquire deceased, in perpetuity. And for this fine etc..

(signed by) John Whitton and the mayor and town clerk.

[f107v]

Portmoot court held 11 December 1609...
Actions of debt:
182:6/9 Gregorye vs Stutter - judgment that plaintiff should recover the £20 debt with 13s1d amercement and costs, and execution granted against defendant now in custody of sergeant.
189:5/6 Bradborne vs Heath - defendant does not appear; therefore judgment adjourned to next court.
200:4/4 Busby vs Morton alias Hassam - sergeant returns executed *venire facias; habeas corpora* granted. Action discharged by assent of plaintiff.
201:4/12 Whinge vs Payne - judgment that plaintiff should recover [blank] debt, and [blank] amercement and costs, with *scire facias* against surety.
Actions continuing: **144**:19/19; **202**:4/10.

[f108]

Actions of debt:

167:10/11 Bradshewe vs Jarnes - sergeant returns executed *sicut alias scire facias*; execution granted against defendant and surety.

181:6/9 Dunford vs Austine - judgment that defendant recovers [blank] debt and [blank] amercement; *scire facias* granted.

205:2/5 Hamond vs Albott - peremptory day to respond.

206:2/5 Rowlewright vs Stutter - similarly.

207:2/14 Dunford vs Butcher - copy and peremptory day in next court; sureties Robert Bignill and William Kinge hand over defendant in court and he is committed to custody of sergeant.

211:1/4 Thomas Dey vs Henry Albott - plaintiff declares, with copy.

212:1/2 Robert Laughton vs Henry Boutcher - similarly.

Action of trespass on case:

209:2/5 Richard Heynes vs Francis Brangwin - day to respond in next court.

Action continuing: **208**:2/4.

[f108v]

Action of Qui Tam:

213:1/1 William Harris on behalf of the lord king and himself vs George Noble - plaintiff lays information on contravention of the statutes; defendant requests copy and permission of court granted. Action discharged by assent of borough chamberlains. To the chamberlains 2s6d.[33]

Actions of debt:

214:1/4 John Birde vs Henry Albott - plaintiff declares, with copy to defendant.

215:1/9 Edmund Hiorne vs Geoffrey Crutchly - similarly.

Action of trespass on case:

190:5/8 William Harris vs Richard Horskins - the jury of

John Raunson,	Joseph Harris,	Robert Bignill,
Thomas Screevin,	John Heath,	Thomas Williams,
Thomas Meatcalfe,	William Meatcalfe,	John Bradshewe,
William Edwards,	Alexander Hedd,	Roger Sturgis

finds for plaintiff for debt of £10; judgment in next court.

Conveyance:

210:2/4 First proclamation between William Meatcalfe querent and John Whitton alias Darlinge deforciant concerning five burgage messuages or tenements with appurtenances lying and existing in the borough in Coopyeware Street now in separate tenure or occupation by Thomas Belcher, James Dissell, John Lowe, John Bruce and widow Dorothy Whorde. Which the said William has lately purchased and John Whitton has handed over.

[33] See also *WCA*, 2, 7; but note this was a penal action with Noble as discharged defendant paying the penalty of 2s6d.

[f109]

Action of debt:

216:1/3 Alexander Houlebrock gent vs Richard Stutter - plaintiff declares, with copy granted.

Actions of trespass on case:

191:5/5 Robert Annison vs John Annison - Jury between parties of

Francis Collingwood,	Thomas Blith,	John Acklye,
William Hickes senior,	William Hickes junior,	Richard Shadd,
William Raunson,	John Powell,	Randall Richards,
James Dissell,	Richard Jarnes,	Andrew Jarnes

finds for plaintiff and assesses damages at 20s. amercement and costs 2d. Judgment adjourned to next court.

217:1/1 John Annison vs Robert Annison - plaintiff declares. with copy granted.

218:1/2 Edward Hall vs Henry Francklyn - similarly, with day for amendment; and defendant pays £3:10s into court.

[f109v]

Portmoot court held 18 December 1609...

Actions of debt:

167:11/11 Bradshewe vs Jarnes - action discharged.

182:7/19 Gregory vs Stutter - continues with order for execution of the writ held in abeyance.[34]

189:6/6 Bradborne vs Heath - action discharged by assent.

205:3/5 Hamond vs Albott - defendant does not appear after three summonses, therefore judgment adjourned until he does.

206:3/5 Rowleright vs Stutter - defendant requests extension. both parties put themselves on country; *venire facias* granted.

Action of trespass on case:

209:3/5 Heynes vs Brangwin - defendant produces writ of *corpus cum causa* returnable at Westminster on the Tuesday next after the quindene of Hilary; dated 28 November 1609.

Actions continuing: **201**:5/12; **202**:5/10; **208**:3/4.

[f110]

Actions of debt:

181:7/9 Dunford vs Austine - plaintiff offers in court to make a release of the deed, bearing date 15 December instant, and his plaint thereon; defendant granted *scire facias*.

207:3/14 Dunford vs Boutcher - copy granted defendant who responds.

211:2/4 Dey vs Albott - peremptory day to respond granted.

212:2/2 Laughton vs Boutcher - similarly. Action discharged.

214:2/4 Bird vs Albott - peremptory day to respond in next court.

[34] 'fiat exec(utio)'; GD Gilmore – Glossary L.1/13.3.

215:2/9 Hiorne vs Crutchly - similarly.
216:2/3 Howlebrock vs Stutter - similarly.
Actions of trespass on case:
190:6/8 Harris vs Horskins - judgment that plaintiff should recover £10 debt, with [blank] damages, amercement and costs; *scire facias* granted against surety in next court.
218:2/2 Hall vs Francklyn - action discharged.
Conveyance:
210:3/4 Second proclamation between William Meatcalfe querent and John Whitton alias Darlinge deforciant

[f110v]

Action of debt:
184*:6/7 John Cobbett vs Richard Stutter - plaintiff declares, copy to defendent. (Note: a new action).
Action of Qui Tam:
219:1/1 William Harris on behalf of the lord king and himself vs William Kinge, lays information on contravention of the statutes - defendant appears and requests authority of the court to compound and for copy of information.[35]

[f111]

Portmoot court held 8 January 1610...
Actions of debt:
182:8/9 Gregory vs Stutter - execution of action returned and body of defendant remains in hands of sergeant.
201:6/12 Whinge vs Payne - executed *scire facias* returned and renewed.
205:4/5 Hamond vs Albott - judgment that plaintiff should recover [blank] debt, [blank] amercement and costs, and execution against defendant.
Action of trespass on case:
208:4/4 Bradford vs Payne - action discharged.
Actions continuing: **202**:6/10; **209**:4/5.

[f111v]

Actions of debt:
207:4/14 Dunford vs Butcher - both parties put themselves on the country.
211:3/4 Dey vs Albott - defendant does not appear after three summonses, therefore judgment given.
214:3/4 Bird vs Albott - similarly.
184*:7/7 John Cobbett vs Richard Stutter - similarly. (2nd action).
216:3/3 Howlebrock vs Stutter - similarly.
Actions of trespass on case:
190:7/8 Harris vs Horskins - executed *scire facias* returned and renewed.

[35] See also *WCA,* 2,7; but note this was a penal action with Kinge as defendant, perhaps compounded, paying the penalty of 2s.

220:1/1 Thomas Meatcalfe vs William Abbott - action discharged.
Actions continuing: **181**:8/9; **206**:4/5; **215**:3/9.

[f112]

Action of trespass:
221:1/1 Thomas Meatcalfe vs William Abott - action discharged.
Actions of debt:
222:1/2 John Gregory vs Richard Stutter - plaintiff declares; defendant does not appear after three summonses therefore etc.
223:1/2 Robert Bincks vs Richard Stutter - similarly.
224:1/2 Robert Belcher vs Henry Albott - similarly, with judgment in next court.
225:1/6 John Warren vs John Cooke - day to declare in next court.
Action of trespass on case:
226:1/9 William Gadbury gent vs Richard Jarnes - plaintiff declares and defendant granted first privilege day.
Conveyance:
210:4/4 Third proclamation between William Meatcalfe querent and John Whitton alias Darlinge deforciant.

[f112v]

Actions of debt:
227:1/2 Nathaniel Noble vs Edward Stacy - plaintiff puts declaration, with copy granted to defendant.
228: Richard Stutter produces a royal writ of *habeas corpus* for his return before the lord king at Westminster on the Tuesday next after the octave of Hilary; dated 28 November last. (see *Actions* **182-185**, **192**, **198**, **206**, **216**, **222**, **223** and **232**).
229:1/7 **Information. 16 January 1610 before Thomas Bradshewe mayor and Thomas Browne JP.**
Thomas Phillippson of Akeley ('Ackly') by Buckingham says on oath that on the Friday night a week before Christmas day last his cloak of medley cloth, having a russett coloured velvet ('vellett') cape with buttons and loops, was hooked out of a hall window in the house of Mr Doctor Smith, commissary of the county of Bucks.[36] He found this cloak, which was his proper goods at the time of the loss, in the hands and possession of one Thomas Joyner, baker, of Woodstock.
Thomas Joyner says that a week ago on Saturday he bought the cloak for 23s from one Francis Moslye, a cutler, in the presence of Henry Price and Drewe Gregory.

[36] A common form of theft/burglary; see JH Baker, 605; AL Beier, 130.

[f113]

Recognisances: Thomas Phillippson binds himself in £20 that he will proceed against Thomas Joyner at the next borough sessions of the peace.
Thomas Joyner binds himself in £40, with Joseph Harris of Woodstock surety in £20, that he will appear at the next borough sessions.
229:2/7 *Examination* before the said commissioners 9 March 1610. Francis Moslye, cutler, of Attercliffe ('Aterclife') in the parish of Sheffield county York, says that on Saturday 6 January last in Richard Meade's George Inn, Woodstock, he bought the said cloak for 20s from one Robert Meares, pedlar, who dwelt between Warwick and Coventry. He presently sold it to Thomas Joyner for 23s, after which he was arrested by Thomas Phillippson of Buckingham upon felony for hooking the same cloak from Doctor Smith's house. (Mark of) Francis Moslye.
229:3/7 Francis Moslye also says that upon Monday the last day of February he bought a roan racking and trotting nag, with a white star on the forehead and cropped on both ears, for 26s from a priste (i.e. priest) in Birmingham market and entered him in the toll book. Which horse, with packsaddle, surcingle and bridle, is given to Joseph Harris of Woodstock, constable.
229:4/7 *Recognisances* same day. Francis Moslye binds himself in £40, with Thomas Perkins, upholsterer, of Dunstable, Bedfordshire, surety in £20 and Henry Price, chapman of Woodstock, surety in £20, that he will appear at the next borough sessions to make his case and receive judgment imposed by the court.

[f113v]

Portmoot court held 22 January 1610...
Actions of debt:
182:9/9 Gregory vs Stutter - remains on royal writ of *habeas corpus*.
201:7/12 Whing vs Payne - sergeant returns executed *sicut alias scire facias*; defendant does not appear, therefore execution of writ in abeyance ordered against defendant and surety.
205:5/5 Hamond vs Albott - as previously. Sent to King's Bench.
207:5/14 Dunford vs Butcher - executed *venire facias* returned and *habeas corpora* granted for return in next court.
211:4/4 Dey vs Albott - remains on royal writ of *habeas corpus*.
214:4/4 Bird vs Albott - similarly, which defendant produces in this court for return before the lord king on the Tuesday next after the octave of Hilary; bearing date 28 November 1609.
Actions continuing: **181**:9/9; **202**:7/10; **206**:5/5; **209**:5/5.

[f114]

Actions of debt:
222:2/2 Gregory vs Stutter - remains on writ of *habeas corpus*.
223:2/2 Bincks vs Stutter - similarly.

224:2/2 Belcher vs Albott - similarly.
225:2/6 Warren vs Cooke - peremptory day to respond.
227:2/2 Noble vs Stacy - action discharged.
231:1/1 John Cobbett vs William Edwards - plaintiff declares with copy to defendant. Action discharged.
232:1/1 Ann Nursse widow, administratrix of goods and chattels of her husband Michael Nursse recently deceased, vs Richard Stutter - plaintiff declares and remains on writ of *habeas corpus*.
Action of detinue:
233:1/1 John Gregory vs Henry Albott - for four cows; plaintiff declares, return on writ of *habeas corpus*.
Action of trespass:
234:1/1 William Harris vs Thomas Screevin - plaintiff declares, copy granted
Actions of trespass on case:
190:8/8 Harris vs Horskins - executed *sicut alias scire facias* returned; defendant does not appear therefore order to execute writ in abeyance against defendant and surety. Action discharged.
226:2/9 Gadbury vs Jarnes - second privilege day granted in next court.
Action continuing: **215**:4/9.

[f114v]

Portmoot court held 5 February 1610...
Actions of debt:
201:8/12 Whinge vs Payne - execution continues.
225:3/6 Warren vs Cooke - no plea issued, judgment adjourned.
235:1/25 Edmund Hiorne vs John Cooke - day to declare granted in next court.
Actions of trespass on case:
226:3/9 Gadbury vs Jarnes - final privilege day granted.
236:1/1 Christopher Weedon vs Thomas Townsend - discharged.
Actions continuing: **202**:8/10; **207**:6/14; **215**:5/9.

[f115]

Portmoot court held 19 February 1610...
Actions of debt:
225:4/6 Warren vs Cooke - judgment that plaintiff should recover 40s for debt, [blank] amercement and costs; *scire facias* granted.
235:2/25 Hiorne vs Cooke - defendant does not appear after three summonses. Therefore etc.
237:1/1 Ralph Longworth vs William Colegrove - plaintiff declares and defendant in person acknowledges debt of £32 and is committed to custody of sergeant.
Action of trespass on case:
226:4/9 Gadbury vs Jarnes - peremptory day to respond granted.

Actions continuing: **201**:9/12; **202**:9/10; **207**:7/14; **215**:6/9.

[f115v]

238 Flesh In Lent. 6 March 1610. The jury to inquire of the eating and dressing of flesh in the time of Lent, sworn before Thomas Bradshewe mayor and Thomas Browne JP.

The jury for the crown:

William Edwards,	Francis Garter,	John Acklye,
Hugh Hamond,	John Powell,	William Hickes senior,
Thomas Abbott,	Thomas Gee,	John Tomlins(deleted),
Nicholas Glover,	John Abbott,	Benedict Norwood,
John Wilkinson,	Richard Hawkins	

presents that: Jerome White dressed a rabbit; Mr mayor dressed a loin ('lyne') of veal; Richard Coles and Edward Barnes killed flesh to sell. Therefore etc.

[f116]

Portmoot court held 5 March 1610...[37]

Actions of debt:

202:10/10 Bradshewe vs Heath - discharged.

225:5/6 Warren vs Cooke - *alias scire facias* granted.

235:3/25 Hiorne vs Cooke - judgment that plaintiff should recover [blank] for debt, and [blank] amercement; *scire facias* against surety.

239:1/3 Thomas Butcher vs Robert Bincks - plaintiff declares with day to amend in next court, defendant appears by attorney.

Action of trespass and ejectment:

240:1/29 William Harris vs John Abbott - similarly.

Action of trespass on case

226:5/9 Gadbury vs Jarnes - defendant does not appear after three summonses; writ of inquiry into damages granted.

Actions continuing: **201**:10/12; **207**:8/14; **215**:7/9.

[f116v]

Portmoot court held 19 March 1610...

225:6/6 Warren vs Cooke - executed *alias scire facias* returned, execution granted against defendant and surety. Discharged.

235:4/25 Hiorne vs Cooke - executed *scire facias* returned and renewed.

239:2/3 Butcher vs Bincks - defendant wages law with four hands in next court.

Action of ejectment:

240:2/29 Harris vs Albott - copy of declaration granted to defendant.

Actions continuing: **201**:11/12; **207**:9/14; **215**:8/9; **226**:6/9.

[37] Neither mayor nor presiding JP recorded.

[f117]

Portmoot court held 2 April 1610...

Actions of debt:

207:10/14 William Dunford vs Troylus Butcher - the jury of

John Raunson,	Thomas Blith,	Jerome White,
John Heath,	Roger Sturgis,	William Bradshewe,
Richard Shad,	John Powell,	William Hickes, senior,
Edward Rudgate,	Richard Write and	James Dissell

finds for the plaintiff and assesses damages at 4d and amercement at 2d; judgment adjourned to next court.

235:5/25 Hiorne vs Cooke - executed *alias scire facias* returned and execution granted against defendant and surety.

239:3/3 Butcher vs Bincks - defendant in person wages law with four hands, namely Simon Jeames, John Glover, William Bradshewe and Edward Rudgate; therefore he goes quit.

201:12/12 Whing vs Payne - continues on execution.

Actions of trespass on case:

241:1/3 Richard Steere vs [blank] Sansom, chapman - plaintiff declares, with day to amend granted in next court.

242:1/3 John Steere vs the same Sansom - similarly.

243:1/9 Richard Coles vs Simon Meacock - day to declare granted in next court.

Action of ejectment:

240:3/29 Harris vs Abbott - peremptory day to respond granted.

Actions continuing: **215**:9/9; **226**:7/9.

[f117v]

Actions of debt:

244:1/4 Robert Maulthouse vs Francis Garter - plaintiff declares, with copy granted.

245:1/16 Humphrey Hamond vs Robert Mudd - similarly.

[f118]

246 Sessions of the Peace with View of Frankpledge. 5 April 1610, before Thomas Bradshewe mayor and Thomas Browne JP.

Crown jury of homage:

John Raunson,	Nicholas Taylor,	Francis Collingwood,
Thomas Blith,	Jerome White,	John Lowe,
Thomas Screevin,	John Heath,	Thomas Williams,
Robert Bignill,	William Bradshewe,	John Bradshewe,
William Edwards,	Francis Garter,	Richard Shadd,
Hugh Hamond,	Edmund Rudgate,	John Ryly - sworn in.

Affeerers: Nicholas Taylor, Jerome White, Thomas Screevin and Richard Shadd - sworn in.

[f118v]

Recognisances:

172:3/3 Base-child. Richard Browne bound in his own £20, with sureties of Thomas Williams and Ralph Durbridge in £10 each, that he presents himself at these sessions.

195:2/2 Escape from custody. Edmund Browne bound in his own £20, with surety of Edmund Butler gent in £10, that he appear at the last sessions which he did not do; surety forfeited (see **176** and **195**:1/2)

229:5/7 Cloak theft: Thomas Phillipson gent of Akeley, Bucks., bound himself in £20 to give evidence at this sessions against Thomas Joyner. Presents evidence - discharged.

229:6/7 Thomas Joyner, baker of Woodstock, bound in £40, with Joseph Harris of Woodstock surety in £20, to attend this sessions which he does; discharged as innocent.

229:7/7 Francis Moslye cutler of Attercliffe, Yorkshire, bound in £40, with Thomas Perkins of Dunstable and Henry Price chapman of Woodstock each surety in £20, that he will appear at this sessions, which he does not do. The sureties are forfeited.

247 Corporation purchase: given to the chamberlains 22d for the nails bought for the town from the sale of pewter goods to Thomas Screevin.[38]

[f119 to f120v] (Blank)

[f121]

Portmoot court held 16 April 1610...

Actions of debt:

207:11/14 Dunford vs Butcher - judgment that plaintiff should recover [blank] debt and [blank] amercement; *scire facias* against surety.

244:2/4 Maulthouse vs Garter - second privilege day granted defendant to respond.

245:2/16 Hamond vs Mudd - defendant responds, copy granted.

Actions of trespass on case:

241:2/3 Steere vs Sansome - copy of declaration to defendant.

242:2/3 Steere vs Sansome - similarly.

243:2/9 Coles vs Meacock - similarly.

Action of ejectment:

240:4/29 Harris vs Abbott - defendant responds, copy to plaintiff.

Actions continuing: **226**:8/9; **235**:6/25.

[38] See also *WCA*, 9.

[f121v]

Portmoot court held 30 April 1610...

Actions of debt:

207:12/14 Dunford vs Butcher - *alias scire facias* granted for return in next court.

245:3/16 Hamond vs Mudd - peremptory day for replication in next court.

Actions of trespass on case:

243:3/9 Coles vs Meacock - peremptory day to respond in next court.

241:3/3 Steere vs Sansome - similarly: } Both cases discharged
242:3/3 Steere vs Sansome - similarly: } by assent of plaintiff.

226:9/9 Gadbury vs Jarnes - discharged.

248:1/9 William Durbridge vs Robert Payne - plaintiff declares, day for correction granted in next court.

Actions continuing: **235**:7/25; **240**:5/29; **244**:3/4.

[f122]

249:1/2 **Examination 2 May 1610 before Thomas Bradshewe mayor.**

James Marshowe of the city of Oxford, aqua-vitae man in the parish of Holywell, says that on Sunday night last he lay at Hugh Busbye's alehouse at Sandford before going to Charlbury on the Monday. Returning to bed that night at Nicholas Taylor's, Woodstock, bringing with him two bottles of aqua-vitae. His brother, Robert Marshowe, was in his company at Deddington on Thursday last and did not leave him until 9 or 10 o'clock on Monday at Kiddington. and yesterday met again in Woodstock market. He confesses that his brother brought him two and a half hundred cabbage plants better than Mistress Crosly had.

249:2/2 Examination of Robert Marshowe on the same day.

He says that he lay at Sandford on Sunday night, as aforesaid, and then went directly to his mother's in Oxford on Monday where he lay the night. On Tuesday he brought to his brother at Woodstock half a hundred cabbage plants, which he had bought from Mistress Crosly at the Bell for 5d yesterday morning, together with two hundred which his brother had previously bought from her.

[f122v]

Portmoot court held 14 May 1610...

Actions of debt:

207:13/14 Dunford vs Butcher - defendant does not appear therefore execution granted against defendant and surety.

245:4/16 Hamond vs Mudd - plaintiff puts replication, with copy.

Actions of trespass on case:

243:4/9 Coles vs Meacock - defendant by attorney responds *non-assumpsit* to manner and form of the action, and puts himself on the country; therefore *venire facias* granted.

248:2/9 William Durbridge vs Robert Payne - copy of declaration granted.
Actions continuing: **235**:8/25; **240**:6/29; **244**:4/4.

[f123]

Recognisances 15 May 1610 before Thomas Bradshewe mayor and Thomas Browne JP.

250:1/6 John Charman to keep the peace against Nicholas Raynolds and bound in £20 to prosecute his case against said Nicholas at next sessions of peace. Discharged (in margin).
250:2/6 Nicholas Reynolds bound in £20, with John Hiorne and Humphrey Hedges each surety in £10, that he will appear in person at next sessions of peace and make his case. Discharged (in margin).
250:3/6 Nicholas Raynolds to keep the peace against John Charman. and bound in £20 to prosecute at next sessions against Charman. Discharged (in margin).
250:4/6 John Charman bound in £20, with John Bradshewe and John Heath each surety in £10, that he will appear in court to defend himself. Discharged (in margin).
250:5/6 John Hasle to keep the peace against Nicholas Reynolds, and bound in £20 to prosecute at next sessions. Discharged (in margin).
250:6/6 Nicholas Reynolds bound in £20, with John Hiorne and Humphrey Hedges each surety in £10, that he will appear and prosecute at next sessions. Discharged (in margin).

[f123v]

Portmoot court held 21 May 1610...

Action of debt:
245:5/16 Hamond vs Mudd - peremptory day for rejoinder granted.
Actions of trespass on case:
243:5/9 Coles vs Meacock - sergeant returns executed *venire facias* and *habeas corpora* for jury granted.
248:3/9 Burbridge vs Payne - defendant responds and puts himself on country, therefore *venire facias* granted.
Actions continuing: **207**:14/14; **235**:9/25; **240**:7/29.

[f124]

Portmoot court held 4 June 1610...

Actions of debt:
251:1/4 William Abbott vs John Heynes - plaintiff declares, copy for defendant.
252:1/3 William Meatcalfe vs Salloman Flye - similarly.
Actions of trespass on case:
243:6/9 Richard Coles vs Simon Meacock - the jury of

John Raunson,	Nicholas Taylor,	Robert Bignill,
Jerome White,	John Lowe,	John Rylye,

Roger Sturgis,	Francis Garter,	Richard Shadd,
William Hickes senior,	William Raunson,	William Hickes junior

finds for plaintiff and assesses damages at 26s8d and amercement at 2d; judgment adjourned to next court.
248:4/9 Durbridge vs Payne - executed *venire facias* returned and *habeas corpora* granted in next court.
Actions continuing: **235**:10/25; **240**:8/29; **245**:6/16.

[f124v]

Portmoot court held 18 June 1610...
Actions of debt:
252:2/3 Meatcalfe vs Flye - peremptory day to respond in next court.
253:1/1 William Wise vs Richard Heath - plaintiff declares, copy to defendant.
Actions of trespass:
254:1/4 Thomas Heathen vs John Symons - similarly.
255:1/2 John Whitton vs Henry Triplett - similarly
256:1/2 John Whitton vs Bartholomew Edginge alias Love - similarly.
Actions of trespass on case:
243:7/9 Coles vs Meacock - judgment that plaintiff should recover 26s8d for damages and 40s3d amercement; *scire facias* granted.
257:1/10 Thomas Meatcalfe vs John Hadden - plaintiff declares, copy for defendant.
258:1/1 William Harris vs William Bradborne - plaint entered.
Action of ejectment:
240:9/29 Harris vs Abbott - plaintiff produces replication with copy granted.
Actions continuing: ***235**:11/25; **245**:7/16; **248**:5/9; **251**:2/4.*

[f125]

Portmoot court held 2 July 1610...
Actions of debt:
252:3/3 Meatcalfe vs Flye - defendant's attorney Henry Rudgate produces royal writ of *habeas corpus*, dated 26 June this year, for return on the Tuesday next after the octave of Michaelmas, and approved.
259:1/26 Richard Harris clerk vs William Raunson - plaintiff declares, copy for defendant.
260:1/1 John Cooke vs John Payne - plaint entered.
Actions of trespass:
254:2/4 Heathen vs Symons - peremptory day for response.
255:2/2 Whitton vs Triplett } defendants through their attorney
256:2/2 Whitton vs Edgkins } Henry Rudgate acknowledge their trespass;
writ of inquiry into damages granted plaintiff for return in next court.
261:1/39 John Heath vs Christopher Forty - plaintiff declares with copy for defendant.

Action of trespass on case:
243:8/9 Coles vs Meacock - executed *scire facias* returned and renewed for return in next court.
Action of detinue:
262:1/4 Robert Payne vs William Durbridge - day given plaintiff to declare in next court.
Actions continuing: **235**:12/25; **240**:10/29; **245**:8/16; **248**:6/9; **251**:3/4; **257**:2/10.

[f125v]

Portmoot court held 16 July 1610…
Actions of debt:
251:4/4 Abbott vs Heynes - discharged.
259:2/26 Harris vs Raunson - second privilege day granted.
Actions of trespass:
243:9/9 Coles vs Meacock - execution granted.
254:3/4 Heathen vs Symons - defendant responds, copy granted.
261:2/39 Heath vs Forty - peremptory day for response.
Action of ejectment:
240:11/29 Harris vs Abbott - they put themselves on the country, therefore *venire facias* granted.
Actions unspecified:
263:1/1 (blank) Brangwine vs (blank) Woodbridge, plaintiff declares. Discharged.
264:1/1 William Wise vs William Abbott - similarly.
*Actions continuing: **235**:13/25; **245**:9/16; **248**:7/9; **257**:3/10; **262**:2/4.*

[f126]

Portmoot court held 30 July 1610…
Actions of debt:
245:10/16 Hamond vs Mudd - day for rejoinder in next court.
259:3/26 Harris vs Raunson - last privilege day granted defendant.
265:1/4 John Cobbett vs Richard Stutter - plaintiff declares, with copy.
Actions of trespass:
254:4/4 Heathen vs Symons - defendant produces a royal writ of *habeas corpus* for return on the Saturday next after the quindene of Michaelmas; dated 27 June this year.
261:3/39 Heath vs Forty - defendant responds, with day for completion in next court.
266:1/12 Christopher Easte vs Humphrey Silver - plaintiff declares, copy for defendant.
Action of trespass on case:
248:8/9 Durbridge vs Payne - continues under a compromise between parties.

Action of detinue:
262:3/4 Payne vs Durbridge - similarly.
Action of ejectment:
240:12/29 Harris vs Abbott - executed *venire facias* returned and *habeas corpora* granted for next court.
Actions continuing: **235**:14/25; **257**:4/10.

[f126v]

Portmoot court held 13 August 1610...
Actions of debt:
245:11/16 Hamond vs Mudd - defendant brings plea of demurrer without the signature of counsel; therefore peremptory day given defendant for rejoinder.
259:4/26 Harris vs Raunson - peremptory day to respond next court.
265:2/4 Cobbett vs Stutter - similarly.
Actions of trespass:
261:4/39 Heath vs Forty - defendant pleads that the action concerning the wool and yarn is a foreign plea, outside the court's jurisdiction, and so swears according to the custom of the court. Therefore defendant goes quit with regard to the wool and yarn and the plaint for that is abandoned. Copy granted for plaintiff.
266:2/12 Easte vs Silver - plaintiff completes declaration, copy for defendant.
Action of trespass on case:
248:9/9 Durbridge vs Payne - continues under compromise between parties
Action of detinue:
262:4/4 Payne vs Durbridge - compromise between parties as in **248**
Action of trespass on case:
257:5/10 Meatcalfe vs Hadden - peremptory day to respond.
Action of ejectment:
240:13/29 Harris vs Abbott - *h*abeas corpora granted.
Action continuing: **235:**15/25.

[f127]

Portmoot court held 27 August 1610...
Actions of debt:
245:12/16 Hamond vs Mudd - defendant does not plead in terms ordered by the previous court, therefore judgment adjourned to next court.
265:3/4 Cobbett vs Stutter - judgment that plaintiff should recover [blank] for debt and [blank] amercement.
Action of trespass:
266:3/12 Easte vs Silver - peremptory day to respond granted.
Action of trespass on case:
257:6/10 Meatcalfe vs Haden - defendant does not plead; therefore writ of inquiry into damages granted for return in next court.
Actions continuing: **235**:16/25; **240**:14/29; **259**:5/26; **261**:5/39.

[f127v]

Portmoot court held 10 September 1610...

Actions of debt:

245:13/16 Hamond vs Mudd - judgment of 50s granted for an ignorance of procedure and executed.

267:1/7 Richard Writon vs Thomas Basly - plaintiff declares; copy for defendant.

268:1/3 Joseph Harris vs Anthony Maunde - plaintiff given day to declare in next court.

Actions of trespass:

261:6/39 Heath vs Forty - copy of sworn statement granted to plaintiff.

266:4/12 Easte vs Silver - defendant pleads not guilty and puts himself on the country; therefore *venire facias*.

Actions continuing: **235:**17/25; **240**:15/29; **257**:7/10; **259**:6/26; **265**:4/4.

[f128]

Portmoot court held 24 September 1610...

Actions of debt:

267:2/7 Writon vs Baslie - copy of declaration granted to defendant.

268:2/3 Harris vs Maunde - plaintiff declares, copy to defendant.

Action of trespass:

261:7/39 Heath vs Forty - plaintiff brings plaint of demurrer, with copy for defendant.

Action of trespass on case:

269:1/9 Thomas Pearson vs Richard Horskins - day for declaration granted in next court.

Actions continuing: **235**:18/25; **240**:16/29; **245**:14/16; **257**:8/10; **259**:7/26; **266**:5/12.

270 *Apprenticeship*: Same day. Robert Belcher son of Alice Belcher swears and binds himself apprentice to Brian Steephens, tailor. for the term of seven years from Michaelmas next.

[f128v]

Conveyance:

271:1/4 28 Sept. 1610 before Thomas Bradshewe, mayor.

Order: Order Henry Whitton gent that justly he keep the agreement with John Whitton gent concerning the burgage messuage or tenement with a garden and close with appurtenances in the borough in the tenure or occupation of John Gadbury gent, William Raunson, Richard Wrighte, John Mason and John Coombs. And if he does not do so etc.

And the concord is such, namely that the said Henry Whitton acknowledges the said messuage, garden and close with appurtenances to be the right of the said John which he has of the gift of the said Henry and remits and quitclaims them for the said Henry and his heirs to the said John Whitton and his heirs in perpetuity. And in addition the same Henry concedes for himself and his heirs that he will warrant the said tenement and appurtenances to the said John Whitton his heirs against all his heirs and against all having or claiming a right on, through, or under him and his heirs in perpetuity. And for this fine etc... (Signed by) Henry Whitton, the mayor and the town clerk.[39]

[f129]

Portmoot court held 1 October 1610...

Actions of debt:

267:3/7 Writon vs Baslie - day to respond in next court.

268:3/3 Harris vs Maunde - continues. Discharged.

272:1/4 John Hewett vs Thomas Aynger - defendant surrendered to hands of the sergeant; plaintiff declares, copy granted.

Actions of trespass:

261:8/39 Heath vs Forty - day to enjoin a demurrer granted.

266:6/12 Easte vs Silver - executed *venire facias* returned and *habeas corpora* granted.

Action of trespass on case:

269:2/9 Pearson vs Horskins - plaintiff declares; day to amend granted.

Actions continuing: ***235**:19/25; **240**:17/29; **245**:15/16; **257**:9/10; **259**:8/26.*

Conveyance:

271:2/4 First proclamation between John Whitton gent querent and Henry Whitton gent deforciant concerning one messuage or tenement situated in the borough between Coopyeware Street and Horsemarket Street now in the separate tenure of John Gadbury gent, William Raunson, Richard Right and John Mason, and one garden called the Pigeon-House garden, and a close called Mr Whitton's close, with their appurtenances. Which John Whitton lately has purchased and Henry Whitton has handed over.

273 Election: John Raunson is elected mayor.[40]

274 Swearing in for the oath of Allegiance.

[f129v]

The names of those taking the oath of Allegiance at this court:
Thomas Bradshewe-mayor;
Thomas Browne, William Rayer, William Flye and John Raunson-aldermen;
Edmund Hiorne, town clerk; Henry Rudgate, sergeant;
Richard Meades, chamberlain; Joseph Harris, constable;
Edward Longe, court crier.

[39] See also *WCA*, 34, 35.
[40] See also *WCA*, 12.

[f130]

Portmoot court held 15 October 1610...

Conveyance:

271:3/4 Second proclamation between John Whitton gent querent and Henry Whitton gent deforciant.

Actions of debt:

245:16/16 Hamond vs Mudd - execution of judgment continues.

267:4/7 Writon vs Baslie - renewed day to respond in next court by assent of plaintiff.

272:2/4 Hewett vs Ainger - peremptory day to respond granted.

275:1/1 Abraham Millen vs William Pangborne - plaintiff declares, and defendant, in hands of sergeant, requests a copy.

276:1/1 Justin Goode vs William Pangborne - similarly.

277:1/4 William Wise vs Richard Heath - plaintiff declares, with copy granted to defendant.

Action of trespass:

261:9/39 Heath vs Fortye - further day to enjoin demurrer granted.

Actions of trespass on case:

257:10/10 Meatcalfe vs Hadden - discharged.

269:3/9 Pearson vs Horskins - declaration copy granted defendant.

Actions continuing: **235**:20/25; **240**:18/29; **259**:9/26; **266**:7/12.

[f130v]

278. Sessions of the Peace and View of Frankpledge held 17 October 1610 before John Raunson mayor and Thomas Browne and Thomas Bradshewe JPs.

Jury for the crown:

John Dubber,	Nicholas Taylor,	Thomas Blith,
Jerome White,	Robert Bignill,	John Lowe,
John Heath,	Thomas Williams,	John Bradshewe,
William Bradshewe,	William Edwards,	Richard Shadd,
Roger Sturgis,	Hugh Hamond,	Richard Write

and Edward Rudgate:

These persons of the jury were sworn in and sworn to the oath of allegiance.

Affeerers: William Bradshewe, John Bradshewe, Richard Write: sworn.

[f131]

Court officer replacements:

Constables: William Meatcalfe and William Bradshewe elected and sworn.

Tithingmen: John Norman, George Noble and Robert Ducock elected and sworn (names of Hugh Hamond and John Ackly deleted).

Tasters: Richard Shad and John Doe.

This Sessions of the borough is remained until the Monday sennight after All Hallows Day next.

279:1/3 Thomas Screevin delivers on bail to keep peace and to appear at this sessions which he does. By order from Mr Justice Crooke this matter is referred to Mr Recorder.

280 *Victualler licensing*: At this sessions of the peace, by agreement of the mayor and justices aforesaid, the parties below are licensed to keep an alehouse or alehouses within the borough:

1. John Ackly bound in £20; sureties William Hickes & Hugh Hamond in £10 each.
2. Nicholas Taylor; sureties Richard Meades & Jerome White similarly.
3. William Edwards; sureties Robert Bignill & Edward Longe; similarly.

[f131v]

4. Henry Rudgate; sureties William Bradshewe and John Bradshewe; similarly.
5. Thomas Screevin; sureties William Bradshewe and John Lowe; similarly.
6. Edward Rudgate; sureties Thomas Williams and John Bradshewe similarly.
7. William Hickes senior; sureties John Bradshewe and John Ackly; similarly.
8. Hugh Hamond; sureties John Heath and John Ackly; similarly.
9. Thomas Godfery; sureties William Bradshewe and John Bradshewe; similarly.
10. Jerome White; sureties Thomas Williams and Roger Sturgis; similarly.
11. Thomas Paynter; sureties Robert Bignill and Edward Longe; similarly.
12. Bennett Paynter; sureties John Heath and John Doe; similarly.
13. Ralph Durbridge; sureties Robert Bignill and Richard Shadd; similarly.
14. Nicholas Glover; he is to enter recognisance and was allowed.

(signed) Edmund Hiorne clerk to the mayor and commonalty of the borough.

John Taylor was allowed by Mr mayor and Mr Browne, but denied to be allowed by Mr Bradshewe.

William Wells was allowed to victual in regards of his poverty, but was not allowed to enter recognisance.

Thomas Abbott was discharged from his victualling in open sessions.

[f132 &132v] (Blank)

[f133]

Portmoot court held 29 October 1610...

Conveyance:

271:4/4 Third proclamation between John Whitton gent querent and Henry Whitton gent deforciant.

Actions of debt:

267:5/7 Writon vs Baslie - peremptory day to respond granted.

272:3/4 Huet vs Ainger - judgment and execution granted against defendant who is surrendered to hands of sergeant.
277:2/4 Wise vs Heath - peremptory day to respond granted.
Action of trespass:
261:10/39 Heath vs Fortie - defendant produces plea, with copy for plaintiff.
Actions of trespass on case:
269:4/9 Pearson vs Horskins - peremptory day to respond granted.
281:1/6 Humphrey Fitzharbert gent vs Thomas Norwood - plaintiff declares. with copy to defendant.
Actions continuing: **253**:21/25; **240**:19/29; **259**:10/26; **266**:8/12.

[f133v]

Portmoot court held 12 November 1610...

Actions of debt:
267:6/7 Writon vs Baslie - defendant responds and puts himself on the country; therefore *venire facias*.
272:4/4 Hewett vs Aynger - execution of judgment executed and returned; defendant surrendered to hands of sergeant.
277:3/4 Wise vs Heath - defendant does not appear after three summonses, therefore *nihil dicit.*
Action of trespass:
261:11/39 Heath vs Fortie - day for replication granted.
Actions of trespass on case:
269:5/9 Pearson vs Horskins - defendant responds and puts himself on country; therefore *venire facias* granted.
281:2/6 Fitzharbert vs Norwood, peremptory day to respond granted.
Actions continuing: **235**:22/25; **240**:20/29; **259**:11/26; **266**:9/12.

[f134]

Portmoot court held 26 November 1610...

Actions of debt:
267:7/7 Writon vs Baslie - discharged by assent of plaintiff and defendant; therefore defendant goes quit.
282:1/2 Humphrey Hamond vs Richard Baylies - plaintiff declares, with copy for defendant.
Action of trespass:
261:12/39 Heath vs Fortie – plaintiff enters a demurrer on the rejoinder, with copy to defendant.[41]
Action of trespass on case:
281:3/6 Fitzharbert vs Norwood - defendant responds and enters a demurrer.
Actions continuing: **235**:23/25; **240**:21/29; **259**:12/26; **266**:10/12; **269**:6/9; **277**:4/4.

[41] Receipt of plaintiff's replication and of defendant's rejoinder to it seem to be implied here, without specific statements.

[f134v]

Actions of debt:

283:1/1 John Craker vs Richard Baylies - discharged by assent of plaintiff. therefore defendant goes quit.

284:1/3 John Hodges vs Robert Payne - plaintiff declares, with copy to defendant who is surrendered to hands of sergeant.

285:1/5 John Charles vs Robert Payne - plaintiff declares, copy to defendant.

286:1/4 Thomas Raulins gent vs Robert Payne - similarly.

Action of trespass on case:

287: 1/5 Robert Payne vs John Charles - for arresting and imprisoning Payne's wife at harvest was 12 months, to the damage of 100 marks; day given in next court.

Action of dower:

288:1/1 To this court came Mary Phillipps widow through her attorney Simon Jeames and made claim in the following form etc. ----. Plaintiff at court held 1 April 1611 before Mr Rayer mayor. (see **320**:1/20, *f146*).

[f135] (Blank)

[f135v]

Conveyance:

289:1/4 27 November 1610 before John Raunson mayor.

Order: Order Thomas Painter and Mary his wife that justly they keep agreement with Anthony Damery concerning one messuage or tenement with appurtenances in the borough now in the occupation of John Parker. And if they do not do so etc.

And the concord is as follows: that the said Thomas & Mary Painter, she privately examined by the mayor, acknowledge the said tenement and appurtenances to be the right of the said Anthony Damerye, and as that which he has of the gift of the said Thomas & Mary and they remit and quitclaim them for the said Thomas & Mary and their heirs to the said Anthony and his heirs in perpetuity. And in addition Thomas & Mary concede for themselves and their heirs that they will warrant the said tenement with appurtenances to the said Anthony and his heirs against all their heirs in perpetuity.

And for this fine etc.[42] (signed) Mary Painter, (mark of) Thomas Painter.

290 Settlement deed, date as above:

Thomas Paynter did promise to give his house which he now dwells in and all his goods to his wife during her widowhood.

(marks of) Thomas Painter and John Raunson mayor;

(signed by) Edmund Hiorne, Thomas Brown and William Rayer.

[42] Wife's private examination; see JH Baker, 552; See also *WCA*, 15.

[f136]

Conveyance:

291:1/4 27 November 1610 before John Raunson mayor.

Order: Order Thomas Painter & Mary his wife that justly they keep agreement with Richard Warren concerning one messuage or tenement with appurtenances in the borough in the occupation of Bennett Paynter. And if they do not do so etc.

And the concord is that the said Thomas & Mary Painter, she privately examined by the mayor, acknowledge the said tenement with appurtenances to be the right of Richard Warren and as that which he has of the gift of the said Thomas & Mary and they remit and quitclaim them for the said Richard and his heirs in perpetuity. And in addition the same Thomas & Mary concede for themselves and their heirs that they will warrant the said tenement with appurtenances to the said Richard Warren and his heirs against all their heirs in perpetuity.[43] And for this fine… (signed by) Mary Painter and Edmund Hiorne, (marks of) Thomas Painter and John Raunson, mayor;

[f136v]

292:1/2 **Information:** 6 December 1610 before John Raunson mayor. William Boddely swears on the breaking of the peace by Robert Rose, ironmonger, of Deddington.

Recognisance: Robert Rose bound in £40, Robert Bignill and Richard Shadd sureties in £20 each, he to keep peace towards all, particularly Boddely, and appear at next borough sessions to make his case and receive judgment.

[f137]

Portmoot court held 10 December 1610…

Actions of debt:

282:2/2 Hamond vs Baylies - discharged.

285:2/5 Charles vs Paine - peremptory day to respond granted in next court.

286:2/4 Raulins vs Payne - similarly.

Action of trespass:

261:13/39 Heath vs Fortie - day in next court for plaintiff to impose his demurrer.

Action of trespass on case:

281:4/6 Fitzharbert vs Norwood - similarly.

Actions continuing: **235**:24/25; **240**:22/29; **259**:13/26; **266**:11/12; **269**:7/9; **284**:2/3.

[f137v]

Action of debt:

293:1/19 William Rayer alderman vs John and Richard Heath - plaintiff declares, with copy for defendants.

[43] Wife's private examination, see JH Baker, 552; See also *WCA*, 15.

Actions of trespass:
294:1/3 William Boddely vs Robert Rose - similarly. (see also **292**).
295:1/3 William Boddely vs Robert Rose - day for plaintiff to declare in next court. (see also **292**).
Action of trespass on case:
287:2/5 Payne vs Charles - plaintiff declares by presenting a plaint of non-payment, with copy for defendant.
Conveyances:
289:2/4 First proclamation between Anthony Damerye querent and Thomas & Mary Paynter deforciants, concerning one messuage or tenement with appurtenances in the borough now in the occupation of John Parker. Which Anthony Damery has lately purchased and Thomas & Mary Painter have handed over.
291:2/4 First proclamation between Richard Warren querent and Thomas & Mary Painter deforciants concerning one messuage or tenement in the borough now in the occupation of Bennett Painter son of Thomas. Which the said Anthony Damery (sic. Richard Warren) has lately purchased and Thomas & Mary Painter have handed over.

[f138]

Portmoot court held 17 December 1610...
Conveyances:
289:3/4 Second proclamation between Anthony Damery querent and Thomas Paynter and Mary his wife deforciants.
291:3/4 Second proclamation between Richard Warren querent and Thomas Paynter and Mary his wife deforciants.
Action of trespass:
266:12/12 Easte vs Silver - discharged.
Actions continuing: **235**:25/25; **240**:23/29; **259**:14/26.

[f138v]

Actions of debt:
284:3/3 Hodges vs Payne - alderman William Rayer arbitrating between them has this day awarded that Payne shall pay to Hodges 8s before 20 January next, and either to release all actions until this day to the other and to become lovers and friends.
285:3/5 Charles vs Payne - defendant through his attorney denies the said bond and puts himself on the country, therefore *venire facias* granted.
286:3/4 Raulins vs Payne - similarly.
293:2/19 Rayer vs Heath & Heath - peremptory day to respond.
296:1/7 Henry Triplett vs John Heath - plaintiff declares; with copy for defendant.

Actions of trespass:
261:14/39 Heath vs Forty - it is ordered by the court that the plea of demurrer on the response is imposed and also on proving a special title to taking and carrying off the wool and yarn; and to refer to judgment of the borough recorder.
294:2/3 Boddely vs Rose - peremptory day to respond.
295:2/3 Boddely vs Rose - copy of declaration to defendant.
Action of trespass on case:
287:3/5 Payne vs Charles - since plaintiff does not prosecute he is in default.
Actions continuing: **269**:8/9; **281**:5/6.

[f139]

Conveyance:
297:1/4 5 January 1611 before John Ranson mayor.
Order: Order Abner Walker that justly etc. he keep the agreement with George Noble concerning one burgage messuage or tenement with appurtenances in the borough called the Chantry House lately in the occupation of Robert Walker father of the said Abner and recently deceased. etc.
And the concord is such that Abner Walker acknowledges the said tenement with appurtenances to be the right of said George Noble as those which George has of the gift of said Abner remits and quitclaims them for said Abner and his heirs to the said George Noble and his heirs in perpetuity. And in addition the said Abner concedes for himself and his heirs that he will warrant the said tenement with appurtenances to the said George Noble and his heirs against all his heirs and against the heirs of Robert Walker deceased and against Thomas Walker his brother and his heirs, and against all having or claiming a right on, through, or under the said Abner, Robert and Thomas Walker and their heirs in perpetuity. And for this fine etc.
(marks of) Abner Walker & John Raunson mayor, (signed) Edmund Hiorne

[f139v]

Portmoot court held 7 January 1611...
(Officers: no presiding mayor or JP recorded; new chamberlains: Joseph Harris and Thomas Meatcalfe).
Conveyances:
289:4/4 Third proclamation between Anthony Damerye querent and Thomas & Mary Paynter deforciants.
291:4/4 Third proclamation between Richard Warren querent and Thomas & Mary Paynter deforciants.
297:2/4 First proclamation between George Noble querent and Abner Walker deforciant concerning one messuage or tenement with appurtenances called the Chantry House next to the Church lately in the occupation of Robert Walker

father of the said Abner; which George Noble has recently purchased from the said Abner.[44]

Actions of debt:

286:4/4 Raulins vs Payne - Defendant's attorney, Henry Rudgate, produces in this court a royal writ of *habeas corpus* for return before lord king at Westminster on Wednesday next after octave of Hilary, dated 28 November 1610.

285:4/5 Charles vs Payne - defendant's attorney Henry Rudgate produces in this court a royal writ of *habeas corpus* for return before lord king at Westminster on Wednesday next after octave of Hilary; dated 28 November 1610.

[f140]

Actions of debt:

293:3/19 Rayer vs Heath - after three summonses defendants do not appear, therefore etc.

298:1/4 Thomas Browne alderman vs Richard Heath - plaintiff granted day to declare in next court.

Actions of trespass:

287:4/5 Payne vs Charles - since plaintiff has not paid amercement, judgment granted for 13s10d amercement and 2d damages.

299:1/3 William Jeffes vs Robert Symons - plaintiff declares with copy for defendant.

Action of trespass on case:

300:1/1 Humphrey Bennett & his wife vs William Jeffes - plaintiffs declare, day for amendment.

Actions continuing: **240**:24/29; **259**:15/26; **261**:15/39; **269**:9/9; **281**:6/6; **294**:3/3; **295**:3/3; **296**:2/7.

[f140v]

Portmoot court held 21 January 1611 before John Raunson mayor:

Conveyance:

297:3/4 Second proclamation between George Noble querent and Abner Walker deforciant.

Action of debt:

293:4/19 Rayer vs Heath - judgment that plaintiff should recover [blank] for debt and [blank] amercement; *scire facias* granted.

Action of trespass on case:

287:5/5 Payne vs Charles - execution is granted against Edmund Hiorne, clerk to the mayor and commonalty, for amercement.

[44] See also *WCA*, 15, 34 and *VCH Oxon,* xii, 353ii.

Action of ejectment:
240:25/29 Harris vs Abbott, plaintiff does not prosecute his plaint, therefore non-suit.
Actions continuing: ***259**:16/26; **261**:16/39; **296**:3/7; **298**:2/4; **299**:2/3.*
301. The end of the time of John Raunson as mayor of the borough; noted by me Edmund Hiorne clerk to the mayor and commonalty of the borough.[45]

[f141]

Death of mayor in office. Memorandum 30 January 1611.
John Raunson died in the time of his mayoralty and since James Whitlock esquire recorder of the borough, with the advice of Sir Lawrence Tenfield lord chief baron of the exchequer, had willed and appointed the procedure to adopt upon the death of mayor William Meatcalfe in office this was now followed.[46] That the senior alderman should call those together that give voices in the borough and proceed to election of a mayor then, as is used when his year expires. And as the custom is to choose one of the aldermen there is no necessity to tie the commonalty to choose the ancient alderman but him that has most voices for it. As may appear by a letter from Mr Whitlock to the worshipful Mr Thomas Browne and Mr Thomas Bradshewe gents aldermen and Justices of the peace in the said borough. Whereupon now Thomas Browne senior alderman with the consent

[f141v]

of the rest of the aldermen did will and command Henry Rudgate sergeant-at-mace that he should warn all the aldermen, common council and freeburgesses that they and any of them shall personally appear at the guildhall on Saturday 2 February next by 8 o'clock in the morning, there to elect and choose one of the aldermen to be mayor and to govern the said borough for the residue of the present year.
At which said election William Rayer alderman was elected mayor for the residue of this present (mayoral) year.

[f142]

Portmoot court held 4 February 1611 before William Rayer mayor:
Conveyance:
297:4/4 Third proclamation between George Noble querent and Abner Walker deforciant.
Actions of debt:
285:5/5 Charles vs Payne - renewed writ of execution against clerk of court for the order of amercement against Payne. (see **287**:5/5).
303:1/53 Richard Ingram vs Richard Tyms - day to declare in next court.

[45] See also *WCA*, 17.
[46] See **13**, *f5*.

304:1/2 Edmund Hiorne vs Edward Stacy - plaintiff declares, copy for defendant.
Action of trespass:
299:3/3 Jeffes vs Symons - discharged.
Action of ejectment:
240:26/29 Harris vs Abbott - judgment that defendant should recover [blank] amercement; *scire facias* granted.
Actions continuing: **259**:17/26; **261**:17/39; **293**:5/19; **296**:4/7; **298**:3/4.

[f142v]

305. Examinations held 8 February 1611 before Willian Rayer mayor and Thomas Browne JP.

306:1/4 *Unlawful copulation.* Lettice Gibbs, widow, confessed that William Wheeler, carpenter, has promised her marriage and that she has suffered him to have carnal copulation with her divers times yet she does not know whether she is with child or not.
306:2/4 William Wheeler confessed that on St. Clement's Day last he contracted himself in matrimony with Lettice Gibbs and since then has continued in her house both for his diet and lodging and confessed that he has had carnal copulation with her, and that he will presently marry her.[47]

(marks of) Lettice Gibbs and William Wheeler.

307: *Sergeant's dereliction*: Henry Rudgate sergeant confessed that he being required to go to Mr Bradshewe to meet Mr mayor and Mr Browne for the examination of certain parties concerning business of the king, he answered that he would not come to the town clerk's house nor any place where he had to do.

[f143]

306:3/4 *Recognisance*: William Wheeler binds in £40. with sureties of William Edwards and William Hickes each in £20, that he will appear in person at the next borough sessions of the peace to answer the charge.

[f143v]

Portmoot court held 18 February 1611...

Actions of debt:
298:4/4 Browne vs Heath - discharged.
304:2/2 Hiorne vs Stacye - peremptory day to respond. Discharged.
308:1/1 Nicholas Elliott vs Christopher Toms - plaintiff declares, copy for defendant; writ of *habeas corpus* proffered in this court for return before Sir John Crooke knight. Surety of William Fryer at the assizes at Oxford, and it has been executed.
309:1/1 John Hall vs Thomas Baslie - plaintiff declares, copy for defendant.
310:1/1 Thomas Baslie vs William Bradborne - discharged.

[47] See *WCA*, 32.

311:1/4 Robert James vs John Lyllie - plaintiff granted day to declare in next court.
Action of trespass on case:
312:1/23 Francis Rose vs John Mincham - plaintiff declares, copy for defendant.
Action of ejectment:
240:27/29 Harris vs Abbott - *sicut alias scire facias* for defendant.
Actions continuing: **259**:18/26; **261**:18/39; **293**:6/19; **296**:5/7; **303**:2/53.

[f144]

313. Flesh in Lent. 18 February 1611.
The following jury were sworn before William Rayer mayor and Thomas Browne alderman, assistant, for the killing, dressing, and eating of flesh in the time of Lent within the borough, according to the statute in the case made and provided. Jury for the lord king:[48]

[f144v]

314. Election. 18 February 1611.
William Bradshewe was chosen of the common council.
315. Information, 21 February 1611, before William Rayer mayor and Thomas Browne JP.
William Edwards, servant to Edward Painter keeper of Hensgrove in Woodstock Park, says on oath that widow Ashpole of Woodstock maintains a boy in her house to steal wood and thorns out of the king's park. This day he took the boy with the maund (i.e. basket), and she said to him that if he should see her boy then he should take no notice of him.[49] (mark of) William Edwards

[f145]

Portmoot court held 4 March 1611...
Action of debt:
311:2/4 Robert James vs Lyllie - plaintiff declares, with copy to defendant.
Action of trespass on case:
316:1/2 Richard Colesborne vs William Butterfeild - plaintiff declares, with copy; defendant granted first privilege day.
Action of ejectment:
240:28/29 Harris vs Abbott - *sicut alias scire facias* for defendant continues.
Actions continuing: **259**:19/26; **261**:19/39; **293**:7/19; **296**:6/7; **303**:3/53; **312**:2/23.
317. *Fine at fair.* Mr Knotsford, brother-in-law of Mr Whitton, for breach of the peace upon William Boddely cutler, paid 18d which was given to Mr mayor who gave it to three watchmen for watching at the fair.[50]

[48] See *WCA*, 15.
[49] See *VCH Oxon*, xii, 447.
[50] See also *WCA*, 15.

[f145v]

Portmoot court held 18 March 1611...

Actions of debt:

296:7/7 Triplett vs Heath - action discharged.

318:1/7 Thomas Harris gent vs William Fly alderman - plaintiff declares, defendant's attorney requests first privilege day.

Action of trespass on case:

316:2/2 Colesborne vs Butterfeild - action discharged.

Actions of ejectment:

240:29/29 William Harris vs John Abbott - as previously. (With non-suit against plaintiff, and defendant granted *sicut alias scire facias*).

319:1/13 William Harris vs John Abbott - plaintiff declares; copy granted.

Actions continuing: **259**:20/26; **261**:20/39; **293**:8/19; **303**:4/53; **311**:3/4; **312**:3/23.

[f146]

Portmoot court held 1 April 1611...

Actions of debt:

311:4/4 Jeams vs Lyllie - discharged.

318:2/7 Harris vs Flye - second privilege day granted.

Action of ejectment:

319:2/13 Harris vs Abbott - peremptory day to respond.

Action of dower:

320:1/21 Mary Phillipps widow, who was wife of John Phillipps lately of this borough, glover, deceased, through her attorney Simon Jeames makes claim against Robert Symons for the third part of one messuage or tenement with appurtenances in the borough now in the tenure of Walter Parker; that given as the dower of the said Mary by the endowment of the said John her late husband.[51]

Actions continuing: **259**:21/26; **261**:21/39; **293**:9/19; **303**:5/53; **312**:4/23.

[f146v]

Portmoot court held 15 April 1611...

Actions of debt:

318:3/7 Harris vs Flye - final privilege day granted defendant.

321:1/1 Henry Tredwell vs Thomas Basly.

Action of trespass:

322:1/1 Humphrey Fitzharbert gent vs Richard Maning - in August last.

Action of ejectment:

319:3/13 Harris vs Abbott - defendant responds and puts himself on country, and *venire facias* granted.

[51] See also *WCA*, 38; and MS Wills Oxon 299/4/26.

Action of dower:
320:2/21 Mary Phillipps vs Robert Symons on an action of tenure - defendant appears through attorney Henry Rudgate and in person, and requests copy from plaintiff which is granted.
Actions continuing: **259**:22/26; **261**:22/39; **293**:10/19; **303**:6/53; **312**:5/23.

[f147]

323. Sessions of the Peace with View of Frankpledge held 17 April 1611 before Willian Rayer mayor and Thomas Browne and Thomas Bradshewe aldermen JPs.
Jury for the crown:

John Dubber,	Nicholas Taylor,	Jerome White,
John Lowe,	Thomas Screevin,	Thomas Williams,
John Bradshewe,	William Edwards,	John Norman,
Roger Sturgis,	Hugh Hamond,	John Acklie,
Edmund Rudgate,	Alexander Head and Robert Ducock: sworn in.	

324. Surveyors: Thomas Williams and William Edwards are elected surveyors.

[f147v]

Recognisances:
292:2/2 For breaking peace on William Bodely; Robert Rose of Deddington bound in £40, with Robert Bignill and Richard Shad sureties in £20 each, that he appears at this sessions to receive judgment, which he does and is discharged.
279:2/3 For breaking peace on Ralph Durbridge; Thomas Screevin is bound in £40, with Thomas Raulins and James Chesterman sureties in £20 each, on condition that etc.
306:4/4 Unlawful copulation. William Wheeler bound in £40, with William Edwards and William Hickes junior sureties in £20 each, could not prove sureties according to the law to appear at the next sessions, therefore he is committed to prison.
Leet Presentment:
325. Notice of inspection - The aforesaid jurors make presentment that William Rayer and Richard Privat broke ground and dug upon the waste ground near Jerome Kyte's malthouse belonging to the mayor and commonalty of the borough, whereby the water from the bays was hindered in its passage.[52]
Also they present that Mr Jerome Kyte has built two walls on the same ground and set a wooden frame thereupon without consent of the mayor and commonalty. Judgment on both to pay in amercement 5s.

[52] See *WCA*, 30.

Notice of inspection.[53] It was ordered and agreed by the mayor and jury of homage that Jerome Kyte shall remove the two walls and timber frame from the ground before the 24 June next under the pain of 40s.

[f148]

326. The names of the victuallers allowed at the last sessions.

Innholders:

1. William Rayer ald.;	2. Thomas Bradshewe ald.;	3. John Glover ald.;
4. Richard Meades;	5. Thomas Williams;	6. John Dissell.

Victuallers allowed 14:

1. John Ackly;	2. Nicholas Taylor;	3. William Edwards;
4. Henry Rudgate;	5. Thomas Screevin;	6. Edward Rudgate;
7. William Hickes senior;	8. Hugh Hamond;	9. Thomas Godfery;
10. Jerome White;	11. Thomas Paynter;	12. Bennett Paynter;
13. Ralph Durbridge;	14. Nicholas Glover.	

At the last sessions suffered to victual but not licensed by way of recognisance at sessions, 3: John Taylor, William Wells and Thomas Abbott.

[f148v]

Victualler recognisances:

327 In this sessions John Taylor binds himself in £20, with Nicholas Taylor and Nicholas Glover sureties in £10 each, that he is licensed to sell ale according to the statutes.

328 Nicholas Glover binds himself in £20, with John Taylor and William Hickes Jun. sureties in £10 each, under the conditions aforesaid.

Arbitration.

279:3/3. Mr Recorder of this borough has ordered that if the matter in controversy between Ralph Durbridge and Thomas Screevin concerning the peace could not be ended by the mayor and Mr Bradshewe before this sessions, then the parties should attend here to expect justice to be done as the cause should require. Since the matter was not ended they have submitted themselves to stand to the order and award of the mayor and Thomas Bradshewe alderman concerning the said cause; it to be ended before midsummer day next, giving one another 6d upon the pain of a further 20d apiece to stand to and perform the said order herein. Likewise all other matters between them to this day be ended or Mr recorder's order to stand in effect.

329. Jury are appointed to attend to finish the sessions and leet on Monday sennight next.

[f149]

330. *Market stalls*. Said jury agreed, with consent of the mayor, that whosoever within this borough shall hereafter set any stalls in the market shall every

[53] 'bill a veva', Latham, 510.

Tuesday night take them in and close the place where they stand, upon pain of 3s4d for every default.

331. *Victualler dismissal.* It is ordered that widow Ashpole be dismissed from victualling and finds sureties that she will not victual again without licence; otherwise she is to be attached by the constables and sent to gaol.

332. *Fine.* Henry Price was bound over to this sessions for striking John Norman, tithingman, and on his submission he was discharged and paid to the use of the town 2s4d which was given to Joseph Harris chamberlain.[54]

[f149v] (Blank)

[f150]

Conveyance:

333:1/4 15 April 1611, before William Rayer mayor.

Order: Order Elizabeth Flemminge widow, John Flemminge and George Flemminge that justly they keep the agreement with Edmund Hiorne concerning the one burgage messuage or tenement with curtilages and garden with appurtenances in the borough now in the occupation of William Holloway gent. and if they do not do so etc.[55]

And the concord is such that Elizabeth, John and George Flemminge acknowledge the said tenement with appurtenances to be the right of the said Edmund Hiorne as those he has of the gift of the said Elizabeth, John & George and remit and quitclaim them for the said Elizabeth, John & George and their heirs to the said Edmund Hiorne and his heirs in perpetuity. And in addition the same Elizabeth, John & George concede for themselves and their heirs that they will warrant the said tenement with appurtenances to the said Edmund Hiorne and his heirs against the said Elizabeth, John & George Flemminge and their heirs in perpetuity. And for this fine etc.

(Mark of) George Flemminge; (Signatures) Elizabeth and John Flemminge, William Rayer mayor, and Edmund Hiorne.

[f150v]

334:1/14. **Information and Examinations, 18 April 1611, before William Rayer mayor and Thomas Browne JP.**

The information of William Bradshewe, mercer of Woodstock, who says he has lost two and one quarter ells of flaxen cloth at 18½ pence an ell and about 3 ells of other cloth at 15 pence an ell and divers other things. These he found in his hay tallet and suspected his servant Hollis who kept keys of his shopdoor and of his hay and other keys of his house.

334:2/14 *Examination of Walter Hollis*, same day.

Walter Hollis, his servant, says that a fortnight ago in the daytime he took the said cloth out of his master's shop and laid it in the hay-mow, between the wall

[54] See also *WCA*, 16.

[55] See also *WCA*, 16 and *VCH Oxon*, xii, 350.

and the hay, with purpose to steal it and run away from his master and to make himself two shirts with it. He also confesses that twelve months ago he stole a blue leather purse priced 2d and had often stolen 2d or 3d a time from his master's shop box (i.e. shop-till) and spent it in company.

334:3/14 *Examination of Ann Cooper*, servant of John Bradshewe of Woodstock, same day.

She says that before Easter last Hollis gave her 6d to buy a cake, and at Bicester fair on St John's day last he gave her a leather purse with 3d for a fairing. Around Christmas he gave her 12d as a token of their love, and after she came to her master a pair of gloves and bought himself a pair at Randall's.

[f151]

He also bought her a pair of gloves, price 18d, with tyings and facing of red suter (i.e. suture or stitching) before Easter last at Oxford; and a dark-coloured silk girdle, price 2s6d, about Christmas last, and a ring of silver and gilt for a New Year's gift. All of which she left at her mother's house at Barton so as not to be found on her, telling her mother they were from Hollis. Every week since before Christmas he gave her twopenny cakes likely bought from Thomas Williams and she had given him two or three of them eaten together at her master's house. She confesses she bought two handkerchieves and a band of lawn ('laune') price 2s8d in the market and gave them to Hollis. He had given her some sweet powder and in whole he had given her at sundry times about five shillings, as she thinks in love to her. (Mark of) Ann Cooper.

334:4/14 *Re-examination of said Hollis*, same day.

Hollis first answers that he has not given Ann Cooper any money or goods since Michaelmas last, but then confesses to giving her the leather purse at Bicester, to her account of the several pairs of gloves, and to stealing the girdle from his master's shop. He bought the ring of silver and gilt from Margaret Rathbone

[f151v]

of Woodstock with sundry payments amounting to 4 or 5 shillings from money stolen from the shop on several occasions. He had often taken money from the shop, amounting in all to 3s, to buy cakes from the Woodstock baker; various sums amounting to 4s which he had given Ann Cooper since Allhallowtide last; and money from his master's packsaddle with which he bought a pudding from widow Munck. (signed) Walter Hollis.

334:5/14 *Examination of John Barnes*, apprentice with William Butterfeild of Woodstock, tailor, taken 19 April 1611 before the aforesaid JPs.

He says he has no acquaintance with the dealings of the two earlier examinations neither does he know of the conveyance of any of William Bradshewe's goods by the said Hollis.

[f152]

335:1/1 **Information and Fine, 19 April 1611, before the aforesaid mayor and justice.**

John Norman and John Doa, tithingmen, swear that yesterday night between the hours of nine and ten, one Edward Browne baker of Eynsham ('Ensham') was in a quarrel with Richard Collingwood and Robert Bruce within this borough. He had his dagger drawn and struck Bruce with it and then struck Doa with his fist, as he came to preserve the peace.

Edward Browne confessed that he, being drunk, did shrike Bruce with his dagger; and he paid 2s 4d for his abuses.[56]

334:6/14 *Re-examination of Walter Hollis*, 20 April 1611, before said mayor and justice.

He confesses that the lawn band aforesaid he gave to Thomas Webb servant to Edward Rudgate and the wrought (i.e.worked) handkerchief he gave to Mr Thomas Abram's present maid and the other he has lost.

334:7/14 *Examination of Katherine Fox*, servant to Mr Thomas Metcalf, taken the same day.

She says that about a month since Ralph Symons, servant to Thomas Metcalf, gave her a handkerchief, wrought with blue silk, to wash and return to him.

[f152v]

334:8/14 *Examination of Ralph Symons*, servant to Thomas Metcalfe, date and court as above.

He confesses to receiving the new wrought handkerchief from Walter Hollis to deliver to Mr Abram's maid as a token that she should receive for Communion that day. This he did but denies giving her any other sort that she has confessed to. A fortnight since he and Hollis going craw (i.e.cray) fishing went to Bennett Painter's house and ate a 2d cake with 2 pots of ale also paid for by Hollis. And they have often drunk at the bottle makers in Bicester at 2d or 3d a time paid by Hollis and none by himself. Hollis also paid for 18d of ale for him spent together at sundry times which he is to repay. Also Hollis used to buy apples which this examinant helped him to eat. (mark of) Ralph Symons.

Hollis confessed this same to be true.

[f153]

334:9/14 *Re-examination of Walter Hollis*, 23 April 1611, before the said mayor and justice.

He confesses that about Christmas last he delivered to Richard Barnes' wife of Woodstock 30s at two times which he stole from his master's shop at divers times and laid it in his master's stables at Richard Bradshewe's house. He entreated her to keep it until he demanded it and to keep his counsel and tell no one. Questioned on whether he stole from the shop 38s which widow

[56] See also *WCA*, 16.

Bradshawe, mother of William, had in a paper behind the smallwares[57] a year and a half since, he confessed that about that time he took from that place a piece of paper containing 33s in silver. He kept it in the stable until before Christmas last when he delivered 30s to Anne, wife of Richard Barnes, alone at her house for keeping until he required it. As for the other 5s he does not know what became of it, otherwise he will not confess. (signed) Walter Hollis.

[f153v]

334:10/14 *Examination of Anne Barnes*, date and court as above. She denies Walter Hollis ever delivered any money or goods to her at any time before this day, to keep for him or otherwise.

334:11/14 *Re-examination of Walter Hollis*, date and court as above. He says that about a fortnight ago he demanded of Ann Barnes at her house the 30s he had delivered to her at Christmas. She told him he should have it, but had lent it to her brother in Buckinghamshire who needed the money to buy sheep from Mr Nash's shepherd. She would go over to her brother for the money and deliver it to Hollis. This examinant upon his oath[58] said the foresaid 30s was the money he stole from his master and that he delivered to Ann Barnes as he had confessed. (signed) Hollis.

[f154]

334:12/14 *Re-examination of Ann Cooper,* same day.

She confesses that at MidLent Sunday last she told Hercules Judge her father-in-law that Hollis had told her he had £10 at use in his uncle's hands at his dwelling at Stonesfield ('Stonsfeild'). He said this at her master's house and that he would marry her if she would tarry till his apprenticeship ended in about four year's time. (mark of) Ann Cooper.

334:13/14 *Sentences*. It was ordered by the mayor and justice aforesaid that this Tuesday the said Hollis and Cooper should sit in the stocks at the high cross with the stolen cloth to be hung before them. And afterwards both of them to be openly whipped at the new building before one o'clock on the same day: which was effected by the officers accordingly.

[f154v]

334:14/14 *Re-examination and sentencing of Ann Barnes*, before the mayor 24 April 1611.

She confessed that a week or so before Christmas last she received 25s from Walter Hollis and 5s later to keep until he required it, of which nobody was acquainted. Of this, 2s she laid out in corn, the other 28s she lost at the brook in her purse. She says she never acquainted her husband or sister, or anybody else, of these matters. She now thinks Hollis stole the money from his master but

[57] Small-wares: small textile articles of the tape kind; also buttons, hooks & eyes, etc..

[58] See Introduction footnote 42, and associated text.

denies receiving any other money or goods from Hollis or any other servants whatsoever. (mark of) Ann Barnes.
She was appointed to be openly whipped at the post; which was effected.
Settlement. Richard Barnes, husband of Ann, has promised that William Bradshewe shall have his sow and other goods of his (a pair of sheets) till Michaelmas next, as payment of the 30s.

[f155]

Portmoot court held 29 April 1611...

Actions of debt:
259:23/26 Harris vs Raunson - defendant does not appear after three solemn summonses, therefore 'no plea' issued.
318:4/7 Harris vs Fly - peremptory day to respond next court.
336:1/4 Thomas Wise vs Richard Streete - plaintiff declares, copy granted.
Actions of trespass on case:
337:1/2 William Hickes senior vs Richard Oram - day to declare granted in next court.
338:1/4 William Hickes junior vs Richard Oram - plaintiff declares, day to amend in next court.
Action of ejectment:
319:4/13 Harris vs Abbott - executed *venire facias* returned, and writ of *habeas corpora* granted.
Action of dower:
320:3/21 Mary Phillipps vs Robert Symons - peremptory day to respond in next court.
Actions continuing: **261**:23/39; **293**:11/19; **303**:7/53; **312**:6/23.

[f155v]

Portmoot court held 6 May 1611...

Actions of debt:
259:24/26 Harris vs Raunson - judgment that plaintiff should recover £5 for debt, [blank] damages, [blank] amercement and costs; *scire facias* granted.
318:5/7 Harris vs Flye - defendant responds and puts himself on the country; *venire facias* for jury.
Actions of trespass on case:
337:2/2 Hickes senior vs Orame - plaintiff does not prosecute his action; therefore...
338:2/4 Hickes junior vs Orame - copy of declaration granted.
Actions continuing: **261**:24/39; **293**:12/19; **303**:8/53; **312**:7/23; **319**:5/13; **320**:4/21.

[f156]

Actions of debt:
339:1/3 Thomas Maurice vs Ambrose Saunders - plaintiff declares, copy to defendant.

340:1/2 William Austen vs John Cleevely - similarly.
341:1/3 William Belcher vs Dorothy Holloway - similarly.
Conveyance:
333:2/4 First proclamation between Edmund Hiorne gent querent and Elizabeth, John & George Fleminge deforciants concerning one burgage messuage or tenement, curtilages and garden with appurtenances in the borough now in the occupation of William Holloway gent. Which Edmund Hiorne has lately purchased and Elizabeth, John & George Fleminge have handed over.
Action continuing: **336**:2/4.

[f156v]

342. Corporation property. At a meeting at the guildhall before William Rayer mayor; Thomas Bradshewe and John Glover aldermen; Edmund Hiorne town clerk; and of the common council Simon Jeames gent, Henry Rudgate sergeant, Joseph Harris chamberlain, Nicholas Taylor, Robert Bignill, Francis Collingwood, Thomas Blith, John Lowe, John Heath, Thomas Williams, Thomas Screevin, William Bradshewe and John Bradshewe: a lease shall be made to Simon Collier of a garden at the end of his house and the piece of ground before his house for 20 years from Lady Day last, reserving (i.e. preserving) the trees and mounds, at 4s per annum at Michaelmas and Lady Day.[59]

[f157]

Portmoot court held 20 May 1611…
Actions of debt:
259:25/26 Harris vs Raunson - *alias scire facias* granted. Discharged.
318:6/7 Harris vs Flye - executed *scire facias* returned; *habeas corpora* granted for return in next court.
339:2/3 Maurice vs Saunders - peremptory day to respond.
340:2/2 Austen vs Cleevely - similarly.
341:2//3 Belcher vs Holloway - similarly.
343:1/2 Thomas Maurice vs John Heath - day to declare granted.
344:1/5 Thomas Browne alderman vs Richard Hawkins - plaintiff declares, with copy to defendant.
Action of trespass:
345:1/6 John Doe vs Edward Browne - similarly.
Actions of trespass on case:
338:3/4 Hickes junior vs Oram - peremptory day to respond in next court.
346:1/3 John Vardam vs Thomas Kerkwood - plaintiff declares, with day to amend in next court.
Actions continuing: **261**:25/39; **293**:13/19; **303**:9/53; **336**:3/4.

[59] See *WCA*, 35.

[f157v]

Conveyance:
333:3/4 Second proclamation between Edmund Hiorne querent and Elizabeth, John & George Fleminge deforciants.
Action of debt:
347:1/5 Francis Collingwood vs John Ascole - plaintiff declares, with copy granted.
Action of ejectment:
319:6/13 William Harris vs John Abbott. - the jury between parties:

Jerome White,	John Lowe,	Thomas Screevin,
Thomas Williams,	John Heath,	Robert Bignill,
William Edwards,	John Norman,	John Ackly,
Alexander Head,	Robert Ducock and	Richard Shadd.

Action continuing: **320**:5/21.

[f158]

348. Information. 22 May 1611, before William Rayer mayor and Thomas Bradshewe JP.

Richard Martyn gent of Eynsham ('Ensham') came and charged William Butterfeild tailor of Woodstock upon suspicion of felony for the hurting of James Arthure yeoman of Eynsham who lies in great danger of death and is now in the surgeon's hands.
Committal. Richard Martyn binds himself in £40 to prosecute against William Butterfeild concerning the said hurt at the next assizes and gaol delivery to be held at Oxford.

[f158v]

349:1/3 **Examination of Humphrey More, husbandman of Beamhurst, Staffordshire, 22 May 1611, before William Rayer mayor and Thomas Browne JP.**

More says that about a month past he came from the house of his mother, Margaret More at Beamhurst ('Beamehurst'), with 8 or 9s in his purse and bringing 44 wethers, bearing no pitch-marks[60] but reddled, which had wintered there. The first night he lay at the Hart, Lichfield ('Litchfeild'); the next day he came with them to Birmingham ('Broomecham') and on the third night to the new inn at Warwick at the end of town. On the fourth day at Alcester ('Auster') market he sold 24 sheep for 19 groats and 2d a piece to an unknown man dwelling near to Avon bridge, but did not toll for them. After first not agreeing on a price he lay overnight at the man's house before settling the deal. Next day, Wednesday, he drove the other 20 sheep to Stratford-upon-Avon, laying at the Swan, then sold them untolled next day at the market to an unknown young man for £6:3:4d; and lay there the night.

60 A brand mark with pitch.

(Margin note): Mr Walter Bagott esquire of Blithfield ('Blifild'). Staffordshire; Sir William Chettwine.[61]

[f159]

349:2/3 From Stratford he went to Shipston-on-Stour ('Shipson') and lay at the Swan of Robert Danforde's till Monday, then on to Evesham ('Eysham') market where he bought 20 hoggerills and Mr Sambridge's ram for £7:5s and another hoggerill for 17 groats. He also bought 9 wethers for 7s4d a piece, entered in the tollbook, then lay the night there at the Hart. On Tuesday he lay at Mr Smithe's at Morton Hinmost (i.e. Moreton-in-Marsh) and next day brought the sheep to Chipping Norton market and there sold his 21 hoggerills for £7:13:4d to a stranger and the 9 wethers at 7s6d a piece to another stranger, without tolling them. After laying there at the Hart he went next day to the Bull at Pershore ('Parshewe') and on the Friday to Worcester, where next day he bought at the market 40 welch wethers from two strangers for £12 without tolling them. On Sunday night he returned to Pershore, and next day came to Evesham market with the wethers without selling; then after staying the night at a village near Stratford he brought them into the town on Tuesday and lay there two nights.

[f159v]

349:3/3 In the market on Thursday he sold them all to a stranger for £12:13:4d without tolling, and lay there till Sunday night when he came to Evesham to bed. Next day at the market there he bought 24 wethers and 4 theves from two strangers, without tolling, at 7s6d a piece for twenty of them and 7s a piece for the other eight. He came to Morton Hinmost with the sheep next day and lay at Mr Smithe's. On Wednesday he sold 8 sheep for 8s a piece, untolled, to a stranger at Chipping Norton market then went with the rest to an alehouse at Hook Norton. He did not sell at Banbury ('Bandbury') market next day and went to bed that night at Deddington. On Friday last he went with the 20 sheep to Bicester ('Bister') market where he sold them to a stranger for £7:5s. He then came to an inn at Heyford ('Hayford') and on the Saturday came to Shipston ('Shipson') market where he bought 13 wethers, 10 from one Warde of Tysoe ('Ticoe') at 8s6d a sheep and 10d over, and the other 3 from a gentleman near Shipston at 11s a sheep, all untolled. Those two nights he lay there at the Swan of Robert Danforde.

[f160]

349:3/3 On Monday night he came with the 13 sheep to an innkeeper's at Enstone and the next day to Woodstock market but did not sell; the three sheep of higher price he sent to a backside. He says he left with his host Robert Danforde of Shipston £7 on Saturday last. (Signed): Humpfry Moore.

[61] Walter Bagot and William Chetwind, Staffordshire Commission of Peace 1609; Gleason, 257.

[f160v]

Portmoot court held 3 June 1611…

Actions of debt:

318:7/7 Harris vs Flye - discharged.

336:4/4 Wise vs Streete - discharged.

339:3/3 and **343**:2/2 Maurice vs Saunders and Heath - John Glover alderman paid 12s7d surety; discharged.

341:3/3 Belcher vs Holloway - defendant makes plea for pity; and 8s5d allowed to defendant for amercement. Discharged.[62]

Action of trespass:

345:2/6 Doe vs Browne - peremptory day to respond.

Action of trespass on case:

338:4/4 Hickes junior vs Oram - writ of *habeas corpus* produced, dated at Westminster 28 May 1611, for return *coram nobis* Westminster on the Tuesday next after Trinity three weeks.

Actions continuing: **259**:26/26; **261**:26/39; **293**:14/19; **303**:10/53; **320**:6/21; **346**:2/3.

[f161]

Actions of debt:

344:2/5 Browne vs Hawkins - second privilege day granted in next court.

347:2/5 Collingwood vs Ashcole - peremptory day to respond.

Actions of trespass on case:

350:1/1 Edward Bagge vs Walter Pettybone - plaintiff declares, with day to amend. Discharged.

351:1/1 John Wiggins vs John Powlton - Discharged.

Action of ejectment:

319:7/13 Harris vs Abbott - court will advise on a special verdict.

Conveyance:

333:4/4 Third proclamation between Edmund Hiorne querent and Elizabeth, John & George Fleming deforciants concerning one messuage.

[f161v]

352 Information, 6 June 1611, before William Rayer mayor and Thomas Browne JP.

James Collier shoemaker of Harborough ('Harborowe'), Leicestershire, came and said that 15s6d was taken from his purse during the night at Bennett Painter's house in Woodstock. Simon Addams and Christopher Newton two journeymen shoemakers and Abel Robinson the manservant were lying in the house but he will not charge any of them with the theft and they deny it. They

[62] In action of debt, in which judgment might be given on default without a verdict, costs varying from 4s. to 9s. were awarded as amercement (1621) and costs awarded to defendant were also known by that name. Gilmore, 52

confessed that yesterday they spent 13d in money for ale at widow Ashpole's alehouse.

[f162]

Portmoot court held 17 June 1611...

Actions of debt:

344:3/5 Browne vs Hawkins - final privilege day granted.

353:1/8 Thomas Meatcalfe vs John Cronye - plaintiff declares. with copy to court.

354:1/4 Thomas Harris, administrator of the goods and chattels. of John Sheppard deceased, plaintiff vs Margaret Harris widow, executrix of the last will of Thomas Harris senior of Charlbury, her late husband - plaintiff declares, with copy to defendant.

Actions of trespass:

345:3/6 Doe vs Browne - defendant responds and plaintiff replicates and puts himself on country; *venire facias* granted.

355:1/2 Michael George vs Henry Parsons - plaintiff declares and defendant through attorney Henry Rudgate confesses the action. Writ of inquiry into damages granted.

Actions of trespass on case:

346:3/3 Vardam vs Kerkwood - Discharged.

356:1/2 John Eglesbee vs Bryan Steephens - day to declare in next court.

Action of ejectment:

319:8/13 Harris vs Abbott - the court will advise at next sitting.

Actions continuing: **261**:27/39; **293**:15/19; **303**:11/53; **312**:8/23; **320**:7/21; **347**:3/5.

[f162v]

Portmoot court held 1 July 1611...

Actions of debt:

344:4/5 Browne vs Hawkins - peremptory day to respond next court.

353:2/8 Meatcalfe vs Cronye - similarly.

Actions of trespass:

261:28/39 Heath vs Fortie - day given defendant to hear judgment in next court.

345:4/6 Doa vs Browne - executed *venire facias* returned, with *habeas corpora* granted for next court.

Actions continuing: **293**:16/19; **303**:12/53; **319**:9/13; **320**:8/21; **347**:4/5.

[f163]

Action of trespass:

355:2/2 George vs Parsons - Discharged.

Action of trespass on case:

356:2/2 Eglesbee vs Steephens - Discharged.

Actions continuing: **312**:9/23; **354**:2/4.

[f163v]

357. Sentence, 2 July 1611, before William Rayer mayor.

Ralph Durbridge comes to swear to keep the peace towards Simon Addams, shoemaker of the borough; and is committed to the custody of the constables.

358. Sentence, 15 July 1611, before William Rayer mayor.

Walter Hollis, Simon Rayer, John Barnes and Giles Mason being watchmen last night, were committed to the stocks by the constables for not preventing the disorder at Ned Rudgate's house at one o'clock at night. Knowing of the disorder by William Browne, Thomas Joyner, Robert Bruce, John Vardam, Richard Nickoles, Richard Reade and two shoemakers, they did not punish it nor make it known to the constables.

Richard Reade and a shoemaker broke the peace upon one another there in the house and Reade broke the shoemaker's head with a stone pot. The same night Pulchoe's wife complained that George the winder[63] would have murdered her.

[f164]

Portmoot court held 15 July 1611…

Actions of trespass:

261:29/39 Heath vs Forty - judgment granted against defendant for default of plea; writ of inquiry granted.

345:5/6 Doa vs Browne - Jury between parties:

William Meatcalfe,	Jerome White,	William Edwards,
Alexander Headd,	John Bradshewe,	William Bradshewe,
Richard Shad,	Roger Sturgis,	Hugh Hamond,
John Ackly,	William Hickes senior	Ralph Durbridge sworn.

Actions continuing: **293**:17/19; **303**:13/53.

[f164v]

Actions of debt:

344:5/5 Browne vs Hawkins - Discharged.

347:5/5 Collingwood vs Ascole - Discharged.

353:3/8 Meatcalfe vs Cronye - writ of privilege dated 12 June 1611 for return at Westminster on the Wednesday next after the octave of Michaelmas.

354:3/4 Harris vs Harris widow - peremptory day for defendant to plead in next court.

359:1/1 Thomas Wellman vs Edward Roberts - Discharged.

360:1/1 Thomas Saunders and Grace his wife vs Edward Roberts. Discharged.

Action of trespass on case:

361:1/6 Thomas Everie vs Edward Roberts - day to declare in next court.

Action of trespass:

362:1/2 Edward Browne vs John Doa and Mary his wife - plaintiff declares, day to amend in next court.

63 A winder is a workman employed in winding wool, etc..

Actions continuing: **312**:10/23; **319**:10/13; **320**:9/21.

[f165]

Actions of debt:

363:1/6 Elizabeth Harper widow, executrix of the last will of her husband Thomas Harper, vs Robert Maye - plaintiff declares with copy for defendant.

364:1/1 John Shawe vs Jerome White - Discharged.

365:1/1 Thomas Carter vs Charles Ovmine clerk - Discharged.

366:1/1 William Mattyn vs Edward Roberts - Discharged.

Action of trespass:

367:1/1 Miles Haddon vs Thomas Leighe - Discharged.

Action of trespass on case:

368:1/7 William Dewe vs William Roberts - day to declare in next court.

[f165v]

369:1/2 **Examination, 23 July 1611, before William Rayer mayor and Thomas Browne JP.**

John Mosley of Broad Campden ('Broade Camden'), Gloucestershire. confessed that in the fair yesterday he drew his sword and dagger and hurt one Mr Smith's horse in two places; and offered to strike divers other persons, not having any quarrel with them being, as he thinks, drunk. The bald, trotting and ambling stone (i.e. stallion) colt he had here to sell he bought from one Austen Jarratt his neighbour in Campden for 13 nobles but did not toll for it.

(Mark of) John Mosley.

Recognisance. John Mosley £40 recognisance, with Robert and William Dison yeomen of Inkberrow ('Inckborrough'), Worcestershire, each surety in £20, that he will appear at the next borough sessions of the peace and make his case.

Upon delivery of 4d to Mosley by Robert Dison he affirmed on the pain of. £80 to save them harmless for this recognisance so entered.[64] (see *f176v*).

[f166]

Portmoot court held 29 July 1611…

Action of debt:

370:1/1 Thomas Turton vs John Cartright - William Ball undertakes to pay Thomas Turton £4:4s by 29 September next, or judgment and levy up till then; by agreement of Simon James plaintiff's attorney.[65]

Actions of trespass:

261:30/39 Heath vs Fortie - defendant produces a *writ of error* dated at Westminster 17 July aforesaid, for return on Michaelmas three weeks next.

345:6/6 Doa vs Browne - Discharged.

Actions continuing: **293**:18/19; **303**:14/53; **319**:11/13; **320**:10/21.

[64] See also *WCA*, 16.

[65] Levy on a third party in settlement of debt agreed upon.

[f166v]

This leaf was mistaken. (The court record on *f166* continues directly on *f167v*).

[f167] (Blank)

[f167v]

Actions of debt:
354:4/4 Harris vs Harris - Discharged.
363:2/6 Harper vs Maye - peremptory day to respond next court.
371:1/2 Walter Callcott vs William Pufford - plaintiff granted day to declare in next court.
372:1/1 Edward Fidler vs John Heath - Discharged.
373:1/5 Francis Rose vs John Shaylord - plaintiff declares, with day to amend in next court.
Actions of trespass:
362:2/2 Browne vs Doa - Discharged.
374:1/28 William Ball vs Thomas Verny - declaration, with copy.
Actions of trespass on case:
361:2/6 Eaverie vs Roberts - similarly.
368:2/7 Dewe vs Roberts - plaintiff puts declaration with day to amend its terms in next court.
Actions continuing: **312**:11/23; **353**:4/8.

[f168]

Portmoot court held 12 August 1611...
Action of trespass:
261:31/39 Heath vs Fortie - action remains on writ of error.
Actions of trespass on case:
361:3/6 Every vs Roberts - peremptory day to respond.
368:3/7 Dewe vs Roberts plaintiff declares, copy to defendant.
Actions continuing: **293**:19/19; **303**:15/53; **312**:12/23; **319**:12/13; **320**:11/21; **353**:5/8; **363**:3/6.

[f168v]

Actions of debt:
371:2/2 Calcott vs Pufford - Discharged.
373:2/5 Rose vs Shaylorde - plaintiff declares, with day for correction in next court.
375:1/1 John Edgkins vs Ralph Shurly - Discharged.
376:1/1 Henry Stiles vs John Doa - Discharged.
Action of trespass:
374:2/28 Ball vs Varnye - peremptory day to respond in next court.
Action of trespass on case:
377:1/8 Andrew Jarnes vs Thomas Chamberlain - plaintiff requests day to declare in next court.

[f169]

378. Court of Clerk of the Market, 16 August 1611. Before William Rayer mayor, held by the assistance of Thomas Browne alderman, by virtue of the king's majesty's letters patents granted by him and by his highness's progenitors.

Jury: John Dubber, Jerome White, Thomas Screevin, John Bradshewe, William Edwards, Robert Ducock, Richard Shadd, Hugh Hamond, George Noble, Edward Rudgate, John Acklie, Randall Richards, John Doa, sworn in.

A note of bushels and weights and measures allowed by the said clerk of the market:

Each one bushel: John Taylor, alderman Thomas Bradshewe, Thomas Williams, Jerome White, Robert Bignill, alderman John Glover,

[f169v]

Edmund Rudgate, Randall Richards, John Norman, John Lowe, Thomas Painter, William Meatcalfe. (Two names deleted: Jerome Kite and Thomas Godferie).

Each one bushel and one peck: William Edwards 3d, John Dissell, Anthony Noble clerk.

Henry Rudgate one bushel and half a peck; alderman Thomas Browne 2 bushels and one peck; Thomas Meatcalfe 1 bushel, l peck and half peck; mayor William Rayer 2 bushels, l peck and half peck. Also the jury finds the bushel of Thomas Browne which was defaced with John Bradshewe two years since, and now mended with leather, is agreeable with the standard yet it is not appointed to be sealed. Item: one market bushel and one peck sealed for the Town. William Ball: 1 bushel, l peck and half peck - 4d.

Walter Parker: allowed 3 pound, 2 half-pounds, and 2 pound weights -3d.

Joseph Harris: 2 ells -2d; John Bradshewe:2 yards and 1 ell.

William Porter: 1 yard -1d; Mr Fly: 2 seven pounds and 1 five pound stone - 3d.

[f170]

Each one bushel: Bridget Spittle, Mistress Leake, Mistress Raunson and Francis Collingwood.

[f170v] (Blank)

[f171]

Portmoot court held 26 August 1611… (No presiding JP recorded).

Action of common recovery:

379:1/1 Simon Jeames gent claims against Francis Collingwood two messuages, two barns, two gardens, one acre of land, one acre of pasture, and one acre of woodland, with appurtenances situate in Crowe's Lane. Which Collingwood also vouches to warranty John Ascole of Hanborough ('Handborowe') who willingly appears and warrants etc., and vouches Henry Rudgate who appears etc., and afterwards withdraws and makes default. Therefore etc.[66] The whole form remains upon the file.

Action of ejectment:

319:13/13 Harris vs Abbott - discharged by agreement of both parties.

Actions continuing: **261**:32/39; **303**:16/53; **320**:12/21.

[f171v]

Actions of debt:

380:1/2 Thomas Gearing vs Roger Powell - plaintiff requests day to declare in next court.

381:1/9 Thomas Meatcalfe vs Thomas Painter - plaintiff declares and copy granted to defendant.

Actions of trespass:

374:3/28 Ball vs Varnye - defendant pleads not guilty; therefore puts himself on country; *venire facias* granted.

382:1/3 Thomas Bedall vs Thomas White - plaintiff declares. with day to amend in next court.

Actions of trespass on case:

361:4/6 and **368**:4/7 (Edward Roberts and William Roberts now treated as identical). Everie and Dewe vs Roberts - defendant produces royal writ of *habeas corpus* for return *coram nobis* at Westminster on the Wednesday next after Michaelmas three weeks; dated at Westminster 12 June 1611.

377:2/8 Jarnes vs Chamberlaine - plaintiff declares, with day to amend in next court.

383:1/2 Vincent Barrie vs Ralph Shurlie - similarly.

Actions continuing: **312**:13/23; **353**:6/8; **363**:4/6; **373**:3/5.

[f172]

384. Examination, 2 September 1611, before William Rayer mayor and Thomas Browne and Thomas Bradshewe JPs.

Thomas Williamson yeoman of Clandon, Surrey, says he dwelt with Mr Morcam of Allerton, Nottinghamshire, and left him 20 weeks since, when he was imprisoned for going with the lady Arabella. Since then he made hay with Mr Write of 'The Castle' at Smithfeild bar until Saturday last, and was there taken by the officers for selling a bridle and two halters to a Kirtlington butcher for 12d. He also had about him to sell three women's brass stirrups and a male pillion; and he resisted constable William Bradshewe searching him. He also confessed selling a pair of boots at Oxford to goodman Triplett for 8d, and said he had the three stirrups of Mistress Morcambe. He had in his purse 25d.

66 See Introduction, Common recovery; and also *WCA*, 16.

[f172v]

Portmoot court held 9 September 1611…

Action of debt:

363:5/6 Harper vs Maye - defendant denies the deed to be his, therefore *venire facias* granted.

Action of trespass on case:

377:3/8 Jarnes vs Chamberlaine - plaintiff completes declaration with copy; day to imparl granted defendant.

Actions continuing: **261**:33/39; **303**:17/53; **312**:14/23; **320**:13/21;**353**:7/8; **361**:5/6 and **368**:5/7; **373**:4/5; **374**:4/28; **383**:2/2.

[f173]

Actions of debt:

380:2/2 Gearing vs Powell - since plaintiff does not declare.therefore etc..

381:2/9 Meatcalfe vs Painter - second privilege day granted defendant in next court.

385:1/2 Henry Sims vs Michael Stocklie - plaintiff declares and since defendant does not appear after three summonses, therefore etc..

Action continuing: **382**:2/3.

Apprenticeship:

386. Clement Archer applies to apprentice himself by indenture dated 30 July 1611 to Drewe Gregory cutler for the term of seven years from the feast of the Annunciation last.

[f173v]

387: *Information,* 19 September 1611, before William Rayer mayor. Information of Edward Clark of Bicester, Oxon, glover: (deleted).

388:1/2 *Recognisance* same day before William Rayer mayor, Jerome Kyte esquire and Thomas Bradshewe gent.

Richard Nicholes, smith of the borough, comes and binds himself in £40, with Robert Spitle and Robert Ducock each surety in £20, that he will appear in person at the next borough sessions of the peace to make his case and receive judgment.

[f174]

Portmoot court held 23 September 1611…

Action of debt:

363:6/6 Harper vs Maye - sergeant returns executed *venire facias*, and *habeas corpora* granted for return in next court. Discharged.

Action of trespass:

374:5/28 Ball vs Varnie - sergeant returns executed *venire facias*, and *habeas corpora* granted for return in next court.

Action of trespass on case:
361:6/6 and **368**:6/7 Every and Dewe vs Roberts - action remains on writ of *habeas corpus*. (see *f192v*).
Actions continuing: **261**:34/39; **303**:18/53; **312**:15/23; **320**:14/21; **353**:8/8.

[f174v]

Actions of debt:
373:5/5 Rose vs Shaylord - discharged.
381:3/9 Meatcalfe vs Painter - final privilege day for defendant to plead in next court.
385:2/2 Sims vs Stocklie - judgment that plaintiff should recover 16s for debt, [blank] amercement and costs, and [blank] damages for detention of the debt; *scire facias* granted against defendant and his surety.
Actions of trespass:
389:1/2 John Dalbye vs Hugh Carter - defendant requests copy of declaration.
390:1/1 John Hiorne vs Nicholas Raynolds - Discharged.
Actions of trespass on case:
377:4/8 Jarnes vs Chamberlaine - peremptory day to plead granted defendant in next court.
391:1/6 Thomas Guye vs Thomas Rooke - plaintiff declares through his attorney Simon Jeames, with copy to defendant.
392:1/6 Robert Hiate and Elizabeth his wife vs Edward Camden - request day to declare.
Action continuing: **382**:3/3.

[f175]

Actions of debt:
393:1/1 Robert Allen vs Edmund Crosshewe gent.
394:1/8 William Whitfeild vs Edward Caple - plaintiff declares, with copy.
Apprenticeship:
395. William Clark applies to apprentice himself to Randall Richards for the term of 7 years from the date of the indenture 16 July 1611.

[f175v]

396. Sessions of the Peace, held 5 October 1611 before Willian Rayer mayor, and Jerome Kite esq., Thomas Browne and Thomas Bradshewe esq., JPs.
Jury for the crown:

John Dubber,	Nicholas Taylor,	Jerome White,
John Lowe,	Thomas Screevin,	Thomas Williams,
John Bradshewe,	William Edwards,	Alexander Head,
Richard Shad,	Thomas Paynter,	Hugh Hamond,
John Acklie,	Edward Rudgate,	Randall Richards,

Robert Ducock: sworn in.

[f176]

397: *Innholders and victuallers.*
Innholders: William Rayer, Thomas Bradshewe, John Glover, Richard Meades, Thomas Williams, John Dissell.
Victuallers: John Ackly, Nicholas Taylor, William Edwards, Henry Rudgate, Thomas Screevin, Edward Rudgate, William Hickes sen., Hugh Hamond, Thomas Godfery, Jerome White, Thomas Painter, Ralph Durbridge, Nicholas Glover, John Taylor.

[f176v]

Recognisances:
369:2/2 It is considered by the court that John Moslie who had misbehaved himself in the fair on Magdalen Day shall pay to the use of the mayor and commonalty 6s8d and to be discharged of his recognisance, paying his fees. 5s given to Joseph Harris, chamberlain.
388:2/2 Richard Nickoles, Robert Spittle's man, was discharged of his recognisance, paying his fees.

[fl77 and 177v] (Blank)

[f178]

Portmoot court held 7 October 1611…

Actions of debt:
381:4/9 Meatcalfe vs Painter - peremptory day to respond granted to defendant.
394:2/8 Whitfeild vs Caple - similarly.
398:1/2 Dorothy Gaskine vs Roger Legg - plaintiff declares; copy granted.
Action of trespass:
389:2/2 Dalby vs Hugh Carter - defendant responds, with copy to plaintiff; the parties put themselves under the arbitration of William Rayer mayor and Thomas Browne alderman in accordance with their action to be settled in the next court, under penalty of £10 each on a bond of 6d.
Actions of trespass on case:
377:5/8 Jarnes vs Chamberlaine - defendant enters a demurrer; copy granted to plaintiff..
391:2/6 Guye vs Rooke - peremptory day to respond for defendant in next court.
392:2/6 Hiate vs Camden - plaintiffs declare, with day to correct in next court.
Actions continuing: **261**:35/39; **303**:19/53; **312**:16/23; **320**:15/21.

[f178v]

Action of trespass:
374:6/28 William Ball vs Thomas Varney - Trial; Jury between parties:

Jerome White,	John Lowe,	Thomas Screevin,
John Bradshewe,	William Bradshewe,	William Meatcalfe,
William Edwards,	Alexander Head,	Hugh Hamond,

William Hickes junior,	George Noble,	Robert Ducock:

A special verdict in writing remaining upon the file.

[f179]

399. View of Frankpledge, held on Thursday 17 October 1611 before William Rayer mayor.

Jury of homage:

John Dubber,	Nicholas Taylor,	Jerome White,
Thomas Williams,	John Bradshewe,	William Edwards,
John Norman,	Richard Shadd,	Hugh Hamond,
Edmund Rudgate,	Robert Ducock,	George Noble,
Alexander Head,	Randall Richards,	William Archer:

sworn in.

Affeerers: Jerome White, John Bradshewe, John Norman: sworn in.

[f179v]

Elections:

Constables: John Bradshewe and John Norman: sworn in.

Tithingmen: Robert Ducock, Geo. Noble, Randal Richards and Richard Reade.

Tasters: Richard Shad and Edward Longe. (William Edwards deleted).

[f180 and 180v] (Blank)

[f181]

Conveyance:

400:1/4 18 October 1611 before William Rayer mayor.

Order: Anthony Damerie and Alice his wife that justly etc. they keep agreement with John Kerbie concerning one burgage messuage or tenement with appurtenances in the borough now in the tenure or occupation of John Parker. And if they do not do so etc.

And the concord is such that Anthony & Alice Damerie acknowledge the said tenement with appurtenances to be the right of the said John Kerbie as those which John has of the gift of said Anthony & Alice and remit and quitclaim them for said Anthony & Alice and their heirs to the said John Kerbie and his heirs in perpetuity. And in addition the same Anthony & Alice concede for themselves and their heirs that they will warrant the said tenement with appurtenances to the said John Kerbie and his heirs against the said Anthony & Alice and all their heirs in perpetuity. And for this fine etc.[67]

(Marks of) Anthony & Alice Damery; (Signatures of)William Rayer and Edmund Hiorne. The first proclamation passed to the court 23 December 1611.

[f181v] (Blank)

[67] See also *WCA*, 33, 44.

[f182]

Portmoot court held 21 October 1611…

Actions of debt:

381:5/9 Meatcalfe vs Painter - defendant pleads in the form stipulated, and plaintiff makes replication and puts himself on country; *venire facias* granted.

394:3/8 Whitfeild vs Caple - defendant denies deed to be his and puts himself on country; *venire facias* granted.

Action of trespass:

261:36/39 Heath vs Fortie - carried over.

Actions of trespass on case:

377:6/8 Jarnes vs Chamberlaine - demurrer imposed, day next court.

391:3/6 Guy vs Rooke - renewed peremptory day to plead granted by agreement of plaintiff.

392:3/6 Hiate vs Camden - plaintiffs declare, copy granted.

Actions continuing: **303**:20/53; **312**:17/23; **320**:16/21.

[f182v]

Actions of debt:

398:2/2 Gaskine vs Legg - discharged.

402:1/1 John Hursle vs William Austen. - 10s8d.

Action of trespass:

374:7/28 Ball vs Varny - continues on special verdict.

Action of waste:

401:1/1 John Rayer vs Tustian Humphries - plaintiff declares, with day to amend in next court.

[f183]

Portmoot court held 4 November 1611…

Action of trespass:

261:37/39 Heath vs Forty - since defendant brought a writ of error before the writ to inquire of damages was executed, and judgment thereupon given, therefore the Recorder was certified (i.e. notified). Mr Whittlock esq. borough Recorder has appointed the writ to inquire of damages to be executed and judgment thereupon given and so proceed unless the defendant brings a new writ of error after judgment because the first writ was brought before the judgment was perfect. Therefore writ of inquiry into damages is granted to plaintiff for return in next court.

Action of trespass on case:

312:18/23 Rose vs Minchine - defendant pleads to set right his wording; given day in next court to amend and complete.

Actions continuing: **303**:21/53; **320**:17/21.

[f183v]

Actions of debt:
381:6/9 Meatcalfe vs Paynter - sergeant returns executed *venire facias*, and *habeas corpora* granted for return next court.
394:4/8 Whitfeild vs Caple - similarly.
Actions of trespass:
374:8/28 Ball vs Varnye - day given in next court to hear judgment of court on special verdict aforesaid.
403:1/2 Edward Browne vs John Meade - plaintiff requests day to declare in next court.
Actions of trespass on case:
377:7/8 Jarnes vs Chamberlaine - day given in next court for hearing.
391:4/6 Guye vs Rooke - defendant pleads not guilty and puts himself on the country.
392:4/6 Hiate vs Camden - defendant pleads and copy granted to plaintiffs.
404:1/2 Thomas Meatcalfe vs William Abbott - day given plaintiff to declare in next court.

[f184]

Portmoot court held 18 November 1611...
Action of trespass:
261:38/39 Heath vs Forty - sergeant returns that the inquiry on oath assesses for the plaintiff 23s4d damages and amercement; judgment adjourned to next court.
Action of trespass on case:
312:19/23 Rose vs Minchine - copy of plea granted to plaintiff.
Action of dower:
320:18/21 Phillipps vs Symons - defendant pleads through Henry Rudgate his attorney as before, and plaintiff replicates as before. Therefore they put themselves upon the country; *venire facias* granted.
Action continuing: **303**:22/53.

[f184v]

Actions of trespass:
374:9/28 Ball vs Varnye - day in next court for hearing.
403:2/2 Browne vs Meade - since plaintiff does not appear to declare, the court finds defendant should recover [blank] amercement and grants *scire facias* against plaintiff's surety.
Actions of trespass on case:
377:8/8 Jarnes vs Chamberlaine - defendant through his attorney produces a royal writ of *habeas corpus* dated 13 Nov. 1611 for return on the Saturday next after the octave of Hilary.
391:5/6 Guy vs Rooke - sergeant returns executed *venire facias*, and *habeas corpora* granted for return in next court.

392:5/6 Hiate vs Camden - day for replication granted plaintiffs.
404:2/2 Meatcalfe vs Abbott - discharged by agreement.
Action of waste:
405:1/2 Humphrey Fitzharbert gent vs Richard Manninge - plaintiff granted day to declare in next court.
Action of debt:
406:1/2 Humphrey Fitzharbert gent vs Richard Manninge - similarly.

[f185]

Actions of debt:
381:7/9 Meatcalfe vs Painter - the jury between parties, namely:

Francis Collingwood,	Nicholas Taylor,	Jerome White,
Robert Bignill,	Thomas Williams,	John Bradshewe,
William Bradshewe,	William Edwards,	Alexander Head,
William Hickes junior,	Ralph Durbridge and	Randall Richards

finds that the defendant has not paid the debt under the conditions of the bond and assesses damages at 2d and amercement at 2d; with judgment in next court.
394:5/8 William Whitfeild vs John Caple - jury between parties, namely:

Nicholas Taylor,	Thomas Blith,	John Lowe,
John Heath,	William Bradshewe,	John Bradshewe,
William Meatcalfe,	William Edwards,	Alexander Head,
Richard Hawkins,	Hugh Hamond and	Edmund Rudgate

finds that the deed was made by the said John Caple and assesses damages at 2d and amercement at 2d; judgment in next court.

[f185v] (Blank)

[f186]

407. Examinations, 18 November 1611, before William Rayer mayor and Jerome Kyte, Thomas Browne and Thomas Bradshewe JPs

George Bennett, labourer of Hanlinge,[68] Worcestershire, under examination says he and his wife Alice came from there on Saturday a fortnight ago. They travelled up and down the country having no business, nor above the 10s10d he brought forth with him, until he came to Deddington fair on Monday 11 November. Having no business there and with about 7s in his purse, he was there stayed by the constable upon suspicion of felony for the stealing of 8 ells of hempen cloth of John Elliott of Deddington, 2 pairs of new shoes of Thomas Trenton shoemaker of Deddington, one new brass gallon ('gawne') kettle of one Hall, brazier of Bicester ('Bissiter'), and one new bolster tick of one Wells of Farthinghoe ('Farthingoe') upholsterer, all found in a sack in his possession. He says that the 10s he brought from Hanling he got by his labour

68 ?Hanley or Hanbury, Worcestershire or Hawling, Gloucestershire.

but he spent most of it before he came to his sister-in-law (i.e. step-sister), wife of John Williams dwelling at Markett Harborowe, Warwickshire (i.e.Market Harborough, Leicestershire), three days before coming to Deddington. Yet there was about him at Woodstock 7s3d: he says his sister gave him 8s6d and 2 and one half ells of Scotch holland ('hallan') since she had no more money to give him.

[f186v]

As for the rest of things in the sack he says that a stranger delivered it to him in Deddington fair, at the entry door of alehousekeeper Anthony Mercer, only to carry it to Adderbury nor was promised reward except for supper. As for the platter found upon his wife, stolen from Anthony Mercer, this was given to him by the said stranger and he gave it to his wife. (Mark of) George Bennett.

Examination of Alice Bennett before the same court.

She denies ever seeing the aforesaid piece of Scotch hallan until she was taken here at Woodstock and denies she knew what money her husband brought forth with him or had from his sister. She says that her husband gave her the brass platter at Deddington only to keep for him without her knowing how he came by it. She knew not how he came by the sack and goods until the constable of Deddington had stayed him.

Recognisance/Committal: 6 December 1611 before William Rayer mayor.

Edward Hall brazier of Bicester Oxon, and Thomas Wells upholsterer of Farthinghoe Northants, each give surety in £40 to show evidence according to the statutes against the said George Bennett at the next county gaol delivery.

Reward to constable. Given to John Bradshewe, constable, 7s3d and one piece of Scotch holland of about two and a half ells.[69]

[f187]

408:1/2 **Examinations, 18 November 1611, before William Rayer mayor**.

Henry Flexon of Stanton Harcourt ('Stannton Harecout') Oxon confessed that in defence of himself he grappled with William Castell of Wootton and struck him. And on oath he said Castell struck him this day without any cause offered. Therefore etc... William Castell confessed on oath that Henry Flexny struck him this day and broke the peace upon him in Woodstock without any occasion being offered.

Recognisances: Henry Flexny and Walter Steephenson of Stanton Harcourt each binds himself in £10 that Henry will appear at the next borough sessions of the peace to make his case. William Castell and Richard Horne each binds himself in £20 that William Castell will appear in person at the next borough sessions to make his case and receive justice.

[69] See also *WCA*, 16.

[f187v]

409. Recognisance: 7 November 1611 before William Rayer mayor and Thomas Bradshewe JP.

Robert Bignill gives recognisance in £10, with John Bradshewe and Robert Ducock each sureties in £5, that Robert & Elizabeth his wife appear in person at the next borough sessions to make their case and receive justice.

410. *Recognisance*: Thomas Durdon and Thomas Saunders each binds himself in £5 to prosecute against their etc,.

[f188]

411. Information, 28 November 1611 before William Rayer mayor and Thomas Browne and Thomas Bradshewe gent JPs.

Richard Meades, innholder of Woodstock, says on oath that yesterday night between the hours of nine and ten (blank) Lylly and (blank) Munck gent came into his house with one Thomas Gee carrying a light for them and a noise of musicians following them: a Walter Parker and his company. Lylly and Munck broke into his chamber and beat back his lock and threw open his chamber door where he and his wife were in bed and asleep together, and a young child with them. The light-bearer and the musicians followed into the room.

Munck sat upon his bed then lay upon him and did blow and sputter upon his face. Lillie took the informant's sword and flourished it in the chamber and, when Meades said he would send for the constables, said he would set back any knave of them if they came. Munck did bid him cry 'Murder, Murder' and complain if he would, saying that Meades was in great fear of them, and they both called him boar, knave and hog and delivered other speeches of disgrace. (signed) Richard Meades.

[f188v] (Blank)

[f189]

Portmoot court held 2 December 1611...

Actions of trespass:

261:39/39 Heath vs Fortie - defendant's attorney produces royal writ of *habeas corpus* dated 8 November 1611; for return at Westminster *coram nobis* on the Wednesday next after the quindene of Hilary.

374:10/28 Ball vs Varny - day in next court for hearing.

Actions of trespass on case:

312:20/23 Rose vs Minchine - day for replication in next court.

391:6/6 Guy vs Rooke - continues. Discharged.

392:6/6 Hiate vs Camden - under surrender of 6d each parties go to arbitration by Joseph Harris and Edmund Rudgate. Discharged.

Action of dower:

320:19/21 Phillipps vs Symons - sergeant returns executed *venire facias, habeas corpora* for next court.

Action continuing: **303**:23/53.

[f189v]

Actions of debt:

381:8/9 Meatcalfe vs Painter - court rules that plaintiff should recover [blank] debt, [blank] amercement and costs, and [blank] damages that he maintained; *scire facias* granted against the surety.

394:6/8 Whitfeild vs Caple - similarly.

412:1/1 Robert Maye vs Henry Howlton - discharged.

406:2/2 Fitzharbert vs Manninge - plaintiff declares, with day to amend in next court. Discharged.

Action of waste:

405:2/2 Fitzharbert vs Manninge - discharged.

Apprenticeships:

413. Richard Hearles, son of Michael Hearles deceased of New Woodstock, puts himself apprentice to John Norman, butcher of this borough, for the period of eight years from Easter Day last, dated 22 July 1611.

414. Jerome Longe, son of Edward Longe, shoemaker of the borough, puts himself apprentice to the said John Norman for the period of seven years from 1 May 1610, dated 31 March 1611.

[f190]

Portmoot court held 16 December 1611…

Actions of debt:

303:24/53 Ingrome vs Tims, discharged. - (case continues to *f249*)

381:9/9 Meatcalfe vs Painter - sergeant returns executed *scire facias*; *alias scire facias* granted.

394:7/8 Whitfeild vs Caple - similarly.

415:1/5 Francis Silverside vs Thomas Blake - plaintiff declares, copy granted to defendant.

416:1/2 Edmund Abbott vs Richard Heath - plaintiff requests day to declare.

Action of trespass:

374:11/28 Ball vs Varny - hearing next court.

Actions of trespass on case:

312:21/23 Rose vs Minchin - parties put themselves on country.

417:1/5 William Symons vs Henry Howlton - plaintiff declares with copy granted.

[f190v]

Action of dower:

320:20/21 Mary Phillipps widow vs Robert Symons in a plea of dower - The jury between parties:

Jerome White,	Nicholas Taylor,	Robert Bignill,
John Lowe,	Thomas Screevin,	John Bradshewe,
John Heath,	William Meatcalfe,	William Edwards,
Alexander Head,	Richard Shadd and	Robert Ducock.

The jury on oath find that the aforesaid John Phillipps had been seised of the said messuage with appurtenances, in his demesne as of fee, during the marriage between himself and Mary. So that it can thereby be dowered to the aforesaid Mary - and they assess damages at 2d. Therefore judgment is that the said Mary Phillipps should recover her own seisin against Robert Symons of the said third part of the messuage or tenement with appurtenances.

Conveyance:

418:1/4 21 December 1611 before William Rayer mayor.

Order: William Fly and wife Ann that justly etc. they keep the agreement with Salloman Fly their son concerning four messuages or tenements, one shop, a third holding of an orchard, and one garden, with appurtenances in the borough now in the separate tenures or occupation of the said William Fly, William Holloway, the said Salloman Fly, Edmund Rudgate, Drewe Gregory and Hugh Hamond. And if they do not do so etc.

And the concord is such that the said William & Anne acknowledge the said tenements with appurtenances to be the right of the said Salloman Fly as those which Salloman has of the gift of the said William & Ann and remit and quitclaim them for the same William and Ann and their heirs to the said Salloman Flye and his heirs in perpetuity. And in addition the same William and Ann concede for themselves and their heirs that they will warrant the said tenements with appurtenances against the said William and Ann and their heirs in perpetuity. And for this fine etc.[70]

(marks of) William and Anne Fly; (signed by) mayor and town clerk.

[f191]

Conveyance:

419:1/4 21 December 1611 before William Rayer mayor.

Order: Richard Warren and wife Ursula that justly etc. they keep the agreement with John Kerbie concerning one messuage or tenement with appurtenances in the borough now in the tenure or occupation of Bennett Painter. And if they do not do so etc.

And the concord is such that the said Richard and Ursula acknowledge the tenement with appurtenances to be the right of the said John as those which John has of the gift of the said Richard and Ursula and remit and quitclaim them for the said Richard and Ursula and their heirs to the said John Kerbie and his heirs in perpetuity. And in addition the same Richard & Ursula concede for themselves and their heirs that they will warrant the said tenements with appurtenances to the said John Kerbie and his heirs against all their heirs in perpetuity. And for this fine etc.[71] (Signatures of) mayor and town clerk.

[70] See also *WCA*, 29, 42.

[71] See also *WCA*, 44.

[f191v]

Portmoot court held 23 December 1611...

Actions of debt:

394:8/8 Whitfeild vs Caple - writ of *sicut alias scire facias* returned, and execution granted against surety and defendant. Discharged.

415:2/5 Silverside vs Blake - peremptory day to respond.

416:2/2 Abbott vs Heath - Discharged.

Action of trespass:

374:12/28 Ball vs Varny - day in next court for hearing.

Actions of trespass on case:

312:22/23 Rose vs Minchine - executed *venire facias* returned. and *habeas corpora* granted for return in next court.

417:2/5 Symons vs Howlton - since defendant does not appear therefore writ of inquiry etc.

Action continuing: **303**:25/53.

[f192]

Action of dower:

320:21/21 Phillipps vs Symons - sergeant returns executed writ of *habere facias seisinam* directed to himself, namely: that the third part set out by a jury, which the plaintiff made choice of, was the kitchen and the chamber over it, with the entry on the north side of the tenement, also the stable adjoining and the barn standing in the backside and part of the backside as it is bounded out by the jury. Also the plaintiff is to have ingress, egress and regress into and from the same premises so divided without interruption; she to be at the charge of making the mound between the tenant and herself.

Also Mr Martyn was content that the jury should appoint the place where the writings should be kept and the time when they should be delivered to the said Symons. The jury have appointed them to be kept in the town office with the town clerk of the borough for the space of two years and then to be delivered to Robert Symons or his heirs or assignees; and in the meantime either of them which shall have need of them to have copies thereof at their own charges. (signed) Edmund Hiorne.

Conveyances:

400:2/4 First proclamation between John Kerbie querent and Anthony Damery deforciant concerning one burgage messuage or tenement with appurtenances within the borough now in the occupation of John Parker. Which the same John Kerby has recently purchased and was handed over by the said Anthony Damery.

[f192v]

419:2/4 First proclamation between John Kerby querent and Richard Warren deforciant concerning one messuage or tenement with appurtenances within the borough now in the occupation of Bennett Painter. Which the same

John Kerby has recently purchased and was handed over by the said Richard Warren.

Action of trespass on case:

368:7/7 William Dewe vs T. Roberts, plaintiff produces a crown writ of *procedendo*, dated 18 November 1611.

Conveyance:

420:1/3 23 December 1611 before William Rayer mayor.

Order: Salloman Flye that justly etc. he keep the agreement with William Dunford concerning two messuages or tenements, a third holding of one orchard and one garden, with appurtenances in the borough with their parts now in the separate tenure or occupation of the said Salloman Flye, William Flye, Edmund Rudgate, Drewe Gregory and William Holloway. And if he does not do so etc.

And the concord is such that the said Salloman (and Mary - deleted) acknowledges the said tenements with appurtenances to be the right of the said William Dunford as those which William has of the gift of the said Salloman & Mary and remit and quitclaim them for the said Salloman & Mary and their heirs to the said William Dunford and his heirs in perpetuity. And in addition the same Salloman & Mary concede for themselves and their heirs that they will warrant the said tenements with appurtenances to the said William Dunford and his heirs against Salloman and his heirs in perpetuity. And for this fine etc.[72]

[f193]

421:1/2 Examination, 24 December 1611 before William Rayer mayor and Thomas Browne JP.

James Wilse, butcher of Much Marcle ('Mitch Markle') Herefordshire, son of Anne Wilse, widow, says he came to Woodstock on 5 December. being a bachelor who had wrote (i.e. worked) as a partner with the butcher Edward Saunders at Much Marcle until a month since. He came to Clapton[73] near Stratford and lay at the house of Mr Richard Wright his kinsman for three days. The cause of his coming from his country was that he had hurt one Henry Sheppard of Sutton, Herefordshire, and was afraid a suit would be brought against him. He had struck Sheppard whilst on the highway at the Hind near Much Marcle, being informed of his coming by one Heming a cornbuyer, about six weeks since on a Friday. 42s2d of his was taken upon him.

John Kerle esq and Mr Wallwine esq both justices of Much Marcle.[74]

72 See also *WCA*, 37, 44.

73 ?Clapton-on-the-hill, Gloucestershire.

74 John Curle & Elias Walwin, Herefordshire Commission of Peace1609; Gleason, 251/2.

421:2/2 *Re-examination of James Wilse* before said JPs 31December 1611. The mayor and justice have received a letter from one Mr John Kerld JP of Much Marcle that the examinant had departed his country for stealing certain sheep from one Mr Caple of Caple, as he was credibly informed, which Wilse being charged has denied. (mark of) James Wilse.

[f193v] (Blank)

[f194]

Portmoot court held 13 January 1612...

Action of debt:

415:3/5 Silverside vs Blake - defendant responds, copy to plaintiff; also court will advise.

Action of trespass:

422:1/1 The Mayor and Commonalty vs Stephen Medhopp - for damages to the plaintiffs of £1,000, why he arrested one William Raunson at the suit of Richard Stockman on a plea of trespass by virtue of a warrant under the seal of the sheriff of the county of Oxfordshire directed to the bailiff of the hundred of Wootton in the county of Oxfordshire. The said Stephen Medhopp in person confesses that he arrested the said William Raunson without the agreement of the mayor of the said borough. Therefore it is adjudged that he is to be amerced.[75]

Actions continuing: **303**:26/53; **312**:23/23; **374**:13/28; **417**:3/5.

[f194v]

Actions of debt:

423:1/5 Margaret Raunson, executrix of the will of her husband John Raunson, vs John Heath - plaintiff declares, copy to defendant.

424:1/1 Margaret Raunson vs Andrew Jarnes; - Henry Rudgate sergeant swears on oath that he arrested Jarnes in suit of Margaret Raunson. Since said Andrew illegally recovered goods from custody ('*fecit recussus*'), therefore Andrew is himself in mercy.

Conveyances:

400:3/4 Second proclamation between John Kerbie querent and Anthony Damery & Alice his wife deforciants.

419:3/4 Second proclamation between John Kerbie querent and Richard Warren & Ursula his wife deforciants.

[f195]

Conveyance:

425:1/4 25 January 1612 before William Rayer mayor.

Order: Thomas Painter and wife Mary that justly etc. they keep the agreement with John Kerbie concerning one messuage or tenement with appurtenances

[75] A Stephen Medhopp, son of Roger Medhopp of Cote (d. 1605), was named as Roger's heir (aged 20y11m. in March 1608) in his inquisition post mortem (PRO, C.142/410, no 49).Also see Introduction, note 14 and text.

in the borough now separately in the tenure or occupation of Henry Price and widow Gyles. And if they do not do so etc.
And the concord is such that the said Thomas & Mary acknowledge the tenement with appurtenances to be the right of the said John Kerbie and as those which John has of the gift of the said Thomas & Mary remit and quitclaim them for the said Thomas & Mary and their heirs to the said John Kerbie and his heirs in perpetuity. And in addition the same Thomas & Mary concede for themselves and their heirs that they will warrant the said tenements with appurtenances to the said John Kerbie and his heirs against the said Thomas & Mary and their heirs in perpetuity. And for this fine etc.[76]
(Mark of) Thomas Painter, Signatures of Mary Painter, mayor and town clerk.

[f195v]

Portmoot court held 27 January 1612...
Actions of debt:
415:4/5 Silverside vs Blake - day in next court to wage law with four hands.
423:2/5 Raunson vs Heath - second privilege day granted defendant.
426:1/2 Richard Houlton vs Simon Collier - day granted in next court to declare.
427:1/8 John Bradshewe vs Randall Richards - similarly.
428:1/2 Magdalen Cole vs Humphrey Davis - plaintiff declares.
Actions of trespass:
429:1/5 Richard Busby vs Robert Cherry - plaintiff declares, with day to amend in next court.
430:1/5 John Drinkwater vs same Robert Cherry - similarly.
Actions continuing: **303**:27/53; **374**:14/28; **417**:4/5.

[f196]

Conveyances:
418:2/4 First proclamation between Salloman Flye querent and alderman William Flye and Anne his wife deforciants concerning four messuages or tenements, one shop, a third part holding of one orchard, and one garden, with their appurtenances in the borough now in the separate tenure or occupation of the said William Fly, William Holloway gent, the said Salloman Flye, Edmund Rudgate, Drewe Gregory and Hugh Hamond. Which Salloman Flye has recently purchased and was handed over by the said William & Anne Flye.
400:4/4 Third proclamation between John Kerby querent and Anthony Damery & Alice his wife deforciants.
419:4/4 Third proclamation between John Kerbie querent and Richard Warren & Ursula his wife deforciants.

[76] See also *WCA*, 44.

[f196v]

Portmoot court held 10 February 1612...

Actions of debt:

415:5/5 Silverside vs Blake - defendant wages law in person with four hands, namely: Thomes Priste senior of Fencott, Clive Pangborne of Charlton ('Charleton'), Christopher Sharpe of Murcott and Edward Shurte of Charlton, yeomen of county Oxon'. And the said defendant goes quit.

423:3/5 Raunson vs Heath - final privilege day granted defendant.

426:2/2 Howlton vs Collier - discharged.

Actions of trespass:

429:2/5 Busbye vs Cherry - copy granted to defendant.

430:2/5. Drinkwater vs Cherry - similarly.

Actions continuing: **303**:28/53; **374**:15/28; **417**:5/5.

[f197]

Actions of debt:

427:2/8 Bradshewe vs Richards - plaintiff declares, with copy and second privilege day to defendant.

428:2/2 Magdalen Cole vs Humphrey Davis - peremptory day to respond granted defendant.

Conveyances:

418:3/4 Second proclamation between Salloman Fly querent and alderman William Fly & Ann his wife deforciants.

425:2/4 First proclamation between John Kerbye querent and Thomas Painter & Mary his wife deforciants concerning one messuage or tenement with appurtenances in the borough now in the separate tenure or occupation of Henry Price and widow Giles. Which same John Kerbye has recently purchased and was handed over by the said Thomas & Mary Paynter.

[f197v]

Portmoot court held 24 February 1612...

Actions of debt:

423:4/5 Raunson vs Heath - peremptory day to respond.

427:3/8 Bradshewe vs Richards - final privilege day granted to defendant.

Actions of trespass:

429:3/5 Busby vs Cherry } defendant puts himself on country;
430:3/5 Drinkwater vs Cherry } and *venire facias* granted.

431:1/2 William Walle vs Edward Kempe & Bridget his wife - day to declare in next court.

Actions continuing: **303**:29/53; **374**:16/28.

Conveyances:

418:4/4 Third proclamation between Salloman Fly querent and alderman William Flye & Ann his wife deforciants.

425:3/4 Second proclamation between John Kerby querent and Thomas Painter & Mary his wife deforciants.

[f198]

432. Flesh In Lent. The jury sworn to search and inquire what flesh shall be killed, dressed or eaten in the time of Lent within this borough, deposed before William Rayer mayor 27 February 1612:

Hugh Hamond,	John Acklye,	John Dissell,
Thomas Gee,	Richard Hawkins,	Thomas Bruce,
Randall Richards,	Bryan Steephens,	William Butterfeild,
William Archer,	William Hickes junior,	John Archer,
Thomas Abbott - sworn in		

Who present in the form signed, namely:
That Richard Coles has killed and dressed meat in this time of lent and sold it to divers persons contrary to the statute.
That Mr alderman Glover has dressed a pig's head and that it was eaten in his house.
That a pig was dressed at Richard Meades' house.
That Jerome White dressed a loin ('lyne') of veal in his house.
That Edmund Rudgate dressed a calf's head in his house.
That William Archer dressed a shoulder of veal in his house.
That Thomas Abbott dressed a piece of pork in his house.

[f198v] (Blank)

[f199]

Portmoot court held 9 March 1612...

Actions of debt:
423:5/5 Raunson vs Heath. continues - Discharged.
427:4/8 Bradshewe vs Richards - peremptory day to respond.
429:4/5 Busby vs Cherry) executed *venire facias* returned,
430:4/5 Drinkwater vs Cherry) writ of *habeas corpora* granted.
Action of trespass:
431:2/2 Wall vs Kempe - discharged.
Actions of trespass on case:
433:1/10 Salloman Flye vs Francis Collingwood - plaintiff declares, with day to amend; first privilege day granted to defendant.
434:1/5 Edmund Fidler vs Richard Streete - plaintiff granted day to declare.
Actions continuing: **303**:30/53; **374**:17/28.
Conveyances:
425:4/4 Third proclamation between John Kerby querent and Thomas & Mary Painter deforciants.

[f199v]

420:2/3 First proclamation between William Dunford querent and Salloman Flye deforciant concerning two messuages, a third part holding of an orchard with garden with their appurtenances in the borough now separately in the tenure or occupation of the said Salloman Fly, Edmund Rudgate, Drewe Gregory and William Holloway gent. Which same William Dunford has recently purchased and was handed over by the said Salloman Fly.

[f200]

Portmoot court held 23 March 1612...

Action of debt:

427:5/8 Bradshewe vs Richards - defendant through his attorney acknowledges his debt of £6:12d and court rules that plaintiff should recover the debt.

Action of trespass on case:

433:2/10 Flye vs Collingwood - copy of declaration granted.

434:2/5 Fidler vs Streett - plaintiff declares, with day to amend in next court.

Conveyance:

420:3/4 Second proclamation between William Dunford querent and Salloman Flye deforciant.

Actions continuing: **303**:31/53; **374**:18/28.

[f200v]

Actions of trespass:

429:5/5 Richard Busby vs Robert Cherrie - the jury between parties:

Jerome White,	William Meatcalfe,	Robert Bignill,
William Edwards,	Hugh Hamond,	Ralph Durbridge,
William Hickes junior,	Robert Ducock,	George Noble,
Edmund Rudgate,	Alexander Head and	Roger Sturgis:-

430:5/5 John Drinkwater vs Robert Cherry - the jury between parties:

John Lowe,	Francis Collingwood,	Thomas Screevin,
Thomas Williams,	William Bradshewe,	John Ackly,
John Dissell,	Richard Hawkins,	Drewe Gregory,
Thomas Bruce,	William Archer and	William. Hickes senior:-

Action of trespass and assault:

435:1/1 John Drinkwater vs Robert Cherrye & Alice his wife - plaintiff declares, with day to amend granted in next court.

[f201]

All matters between the said parties are referred to Mr Browne and Mr Bradshewe to be ended before Easter day next; if they cannot, then to Mr mayor for one month after the umpirage thereof; upon the delivery of 6d, sub pena £40 each. (Presumably referring to actions **430**, **429** and **435**).

[f201v]

436:1/2 Examination 26 March 1612 before William Rayer mayor, and Thomas Browne and Thomas Bradshewe JPs.

Jasper Taper of Aldenham, Hertfordshire ('Alnam in Com. Hatford') says that on Monday last by the persuasion of Nicholas Stanhopp of Aldenham and Jonas Chaundler of Watford ('Wattford') parish, horse scorcers, he came to

this Woodstock fair. Here he prised a grey ambling nag of one James Right of Bledington, Gloucestershire, at 58s. He confessed to riding the horse two miles from Woodstock and meant never to pay for it but to market it with the other parties at Enstone that night. But he was overtaken by one Horne and brought back to Woodstock. He went in boots and the other two in shoes and they went abroad only to buy horses although he himself had none. They come forth with a little ambling nag and sold him at Banbury ('Bandbury').
Recognisance: James Write gives recognisance in £20 to present the case.
436:2/2 *Re-examination of Jasper Taper* 31 March 1612. Taper says that on the sennight before last Monday he and John Issard of Gloucester with Nicholas Stannhopp horsescorcer and Jonas Chaundler came from Stannhopp's house at Aldenham. He came in boots and Issard brought a poor horse worth 5s which he sold at Kitt Mauds in Islip ('Islipp'), and they all came to Woodstock together. Stanhopp procured him to go with him from fair to fair and he heard Issard say he would get a horse at Woodstock fair although Taper could not perceive that he had money to buy one. Stanhopp had willed him to ride the horse away saying he would pay for it and that they should meet again at Islip. (mark of) Jasper Taper.

[f202]

437 Examinations of John Barnes 31 March 1612 before William Rayer mayor, and Thomas Browne and Thomas Bradshewe JPs.

437:1/20 John Barnes, a tailor, of Woodstock says that since Christmas last he came to buy half a quarter of black thread at William Bradshewe's shop where he found a card of silk and silver buttons, being three dozen, lying upon the table. And he stole it and carried it away and never intended to pay for it. He offered the buttons to be sold to Ralph Tame, Robert Spittle's man, about Candlemas last and sold them to him for 12d.

[f202v]

437:2/20 *Re-examination of John Barnes* 2 April 1612 before the same Justices.
The examinant confessed that since Christmas last he came into William Bradshewe's shop to buy wares and, having bought them, Bradshewe's wife set before him two boxes of ribanding and then looked down on the ground for something fallen behind the board. He then stole two bundles of ribanding: one carnation and white @ 3d/yard which Bradshewe says was about 36 yards but he thinks was about 8 yards. The other bundle of yellow silk @ 6d/yard contained a dozen yards. He confesses he paid Roger Sturgis, the barber of Woodstock, 3d to make the carnation and white into 22 poynts (i.e points).[77]

[77] Points- ribboning made into laces for fastening clothing.

He delivered the points to his mother Ann Barnes for safe keeping saying he had found them. He sold 4 yards of the yellow ribanding to Thomas Screevin's wife of Woodstock for 12d, two yards to Richard Shadd's wife of Woodstock for 6d, and two yards to Richard Meades' maid of Woodstock for 6d, and four yards to John Abbotts wife but she did not pay him. Further, he gave two yards to John Ackly the younger, he telling them all that he had it for his master's journeyman.

[f203]

He further confessed that about a fortnight after, he came into the shop to buy wares and, while Bradshewe's wife was looking for wares to serve him, he reached over the shop board and took out of a box, a bundle of thirty yards of black silk ribanding @ 6d/yard. Of this he sold 18 yards to widow Elizabeth Ryly of Woodstock @ 2d/yard; 4 yards @2d/yard to Ann Taylor daughter of Nicholas Taylor of Woodstock; and the other 8 yards to Nicholas Taylor for 16d. He told them all he sold it for a journeyman tailor who was a traveller and who lay at Hugh Hamond's although there was no such man.

At the same time he also stole from the box 8 yards of carnation and white silk ribanding @ 4½d/yard sold to Ann Taylor @ 2d/yard and a total of 10 yards of silk russet lace @ 4d/yard, with 6 yards sold to Elizabeth Ryly @ 2d/yard and the rest to Ann Taylor @ 1½d/yard. Also stolen were 10 yards of carnation @ 4d/yard with

[f203v]

4 yards sold to Ann Taylor and the rest to Elizabeth Ryly, all at 2d/yard. He also took 4 yards of blue silk ribanding @ 6d/yard sold to Ursula Poole, servant to Elizabeth Ryly, for 9d. Since last Lent he stole from the same box 10 yards of green silk ribanding @ 6d/yard:4 yards sold to Elizabeth Ryly for 8d; 4 yards to Ann Taylor for 8d; and the rest he gave to John Abbott of Woodstock. Also 6 yards of white and red carnation silk ribanding at10d/yard sold to Thomas Screevin's wife of Woodstock for 9d, together with 16 yards of carnation silk ribanding sold to Elizabeth Ryly for 1½d/yard, and 2 yards of green silk ribanding @ 6d/yard which he sold in his master's shop to Bentlie's man of Cutteslowe ('Custislow') mill for 4d.

[f204]

Four yards of say green silk ribanding @ 4d/yard he sold to Robert Archer's man, a tailor, for 6d and gave him 2 yards of the green silk ribanding worth 6d/yard. He also confesses that at the several times aforesaid he stole from the same box 1 yard of matched silk ribanding @ 6d/yard given to Mr Bradshewe's ostler, another yard given to Thomas Screevin's journeyman; and 2 yards of carnation and white ribanding @ 6d/yard also given to the ostler, and 1 yard of 6d brode (?broider) carnation and white ribanding given to John Flye.

Two times he came to William Bradshewe's wife in the shop and stole 7 cards of silk and silver buttons of value about 20s, of which he sold to Robert Spitle's man 1 card for 12d, and to Daniel Mr Pore's man a card for 12d. Three dozen he left with his aunt Elizabeth Scasborowe of Woodstock only to keep for him; four cards wanting two buttons he delivered to John Abbott only to keep for him, saying to them he found them.

[f204v]

On the last times he stole out of two papers from the table 12 skeins of green stitching silk worth 12d sold to widow Ryly for 6d, and 16 skeins of black sowing silk worth 16d sold to her for 8d. Also 6 skeins of tawny silk and 5 skeins of green silk worth 9d which he gave to John Abbott. And three yards of silk binding lace for a gown worth 6d/yard, half of which he sold to widow Ryly for 4d and the rest to William Wheeler's wife of Woodstock for the same. Five yards of red and green silk lace @ 3d/yard he sold to the said Archer's man for 10d; fourteen and a half yards of red and blue silk lace @ 3d/yard he left only to keep with Ann Taylor; and 4 skeins of black silk sold to Elizabeth Ryly for 2d. He denies that his master was never acquainted with any of these particulars. (mark of) John Barnes

[f205]

Also he confesses that about Christmas last he came into the shop to fetch his iron (i.e.flat-iron) and stole about 3 yards of Osenbrigge (i.e. Osnaburg) worth 2s which he gave to his aunt Scasborowe only to keep for him, saying he found it on the highway. Another time he stole a little over 3 ells of holland in one piece @ 2s4d/ell which he sold to John Abbott's wife for 4s in lieu of 4s which he had lost of hers.

437:3/20 *Re-examination of John Barnes,* 3 April 1612 before the same justices and Jerome Kyte esq JP.

The examinant denies that he stole from William Bradshewe two pairs of stockings now found in his mother's keeping yet confesses that Walter Hollis, sometime servant of Bradshewe, about 12 months since brought them and 1½ ells of brown canvas for a doublet cloth and a silken girdle and a pair of caddow (woven tape) garters to his mother only to keep for Hollis. These Hollis had stolen from Bradshewe and had been punished for taking other wares; he then demanded the stockings, doublet cloth and girdle and garters, which he had stolen and not confessed to, from this examinant and his mother knowing them to be stolen.

[f 205v]

Barnes denied to deliver them to Hollis and had kept them to the present without revealing this to any JP or other officer. He further confesses that at the aforesaid times he stole more lace, namely 2yards of silk russet ribanding @ 6d/yard sold to Randall Richards' wife for 5d; 1 yard of yellow ribanding @ 6d/yard given to Elizabeth Cundall of Woodstock only in love; one and a half yards of the same ribanding sold to John Cooke's wife of Begbroke

('Begbrock') along with ½ yard of carnation and white ribanding @ 3d given her.
He sold ½ ell of holland to Elizabeth Ryly for 8d and the same to Richard Shadd's wife, and to Winifred Lowe daughter of Richard Lowe of Woodstock, telling them all he had saved the material out of certain boothose (over-stocking) made at his master's shop. He also stole 12 skeins of stitching silk sold to Elizabeth Ryly for 5d, and more than ½ yard of 6d white and carnation ribanding which he gave to Muckell, slatter of Woodstock.

[f206]

He further stole 1 yard of lockram ('Lockerom') worth 12d sold to Abbott's wife for 8d, and claimed that John Abbott and his wife Isabel knew he had stolen all the aforesaid ribanding delivered to them by him from William Bradshewe.
(Mark of) John Barnes; (signature of) Edmund Hiorne.
437:4/20 *Examination of Anne Barnes*, wife of Richard Barnes and mother of the aforesald John Barnes, 3 April 1612.
She confesses that their said son John Barnes about a year and a half since brought her one and a half ells of brown canvas for a doublet cloth, which he told her he had from Walter Hollis then servant of William Bradshewe. Also she confessed that a day or two after John brought her a pair of green stockings, now found in her keeping, which he said he had received from Hollis. She confessed that she then thought and was always persuaded in her conscience that Hollis or her son had stolen the goods from William Bradshewe and that she concealed it and had not made it known to any person.

[f206v]

About three weeks since her son brought her 3 yards of Osenbrigge and 22 poynts of carnation and white 3d ribanding now found upon her, only to keep, desiring her to keep his counsel saying it should be the last he would steal and that he would become a new man.
About a year and a half since Hollis brought a pair of women's stockings, two silk girdles for women and two pairs of worsted garters now found with her and not demanded from her by Hollis. Yet at their delivery she thought that either Hollis or her son had stolen them from Bradshewe and, since she mistrusted her house should be searched since the apprehension of her son, she conveyed and hid them in the thatch of her pigstye. But she denies knowing of or receiving any other goods which her son or any other person had stolen from William Bradshewe or anyone else. (mark of) Ann Barnes.

[f207]

437:5/20 *Examination of Walter Hollis*, 3 April 1612. Hollis confesses that he left the woman's stockings, two silk girdles and a pair of worsted garters with Ann Barnes, and for that he had been punished for the like before. He never since demanded them of Ann Barnes nor confessed he had stolen them from

Bradshewe for he feared being further punished and he says he is heartily sorry for the same. (signature of) Walter Hollis.

437:6/20 *Examination of Elizabeth Skasborowe,* sister of said Ann Barnes, 3 April 1612.

She confesses that about Michaelmas last John Barnes brought her a doublet cloth of brown canvas, one pair of green stockings, 10 yards of red and black galloon lace, 1 dozen silk poynts, two silk girdles and one pair of worsted garters at two times, only to keep for him; and recently he brought a card of silk and silver buttons similarly. But thinking they were stolen and understanding John Barnes was in trouble and fearing their houses should be searched for these goods she and her sister Ann Barnes hid them in the thatch of the pigstye and burned the buttons. (mark of) Elizabeth Skasborowe.

[f207v]

437:7/20 *Examination of John Abbott*, sawyer, of Woodstock, 3 April 1612. The examinant denies knowing at any time that the said John Barnes had stolen anything from William Bradshewe; yet he confesses that about a week since Barnes gave and delivered him a yard or so of galloon silk ribanding worth 6d/yard, he not knowing it was stolen from anybody. (signature of) John Abbott.

437:8/20 *Examination of Elizabeth Cundall*, of Woodstock, spinster 3 April 1612.

She confesses that about Christmas last John Barnes gave her a poynt of yellow silk ribanding, only in kindness, but she denies knowing he had stolen it or any other things at any time. She also confesses she has stolen at two times from her master's William Bradshewe cellar about six pounds of prunes ('prewans') but never stole any other thing from her master or any other.

(mark of) Elizabeth Cundall.

Sentence: She is enjoined to be whipped at the post at the cross.

(signature of) Edmund Hiorne.

[f208]

437:9/20 *Examination of Isabel Abbott*, wife of John Abbott of Woodstock, 3 April 1612.

The examinant confesses that about three weeks since the said John Barnes brought her a whole piece of holland of about nine or ten ells, of which he delivered to her five ells in lieu of 4s which he had received before from her husband. The rest he carried away saying Bradshewe's wife had given it to him for herself to cut out so much as she needed and return the rest to her. After she received it she feared Barnes had stolen it but never made it known to any officers of the law. Further she confessed that since Christmas last Barnes gave her: a little piece of coarse canvas to line the bodice of her gown, and a pair of silk garters and two cards of buttons of silk, gold and silver. At other times he gave her and her children many pieces of ribanding but she never gave him any money for the same. She says when she told her husband that Barnes had delivered her the holland he told her they should be undone by it, but neither of them made it known to any officers. (mark of) Isabel Abbott.

[f208v]

437:10/20 *Examination of widow Elizabeth Ryly*, before the mayor and foresaid justices. 4 April 1612.

The examinant confesses that about Christmas last the said John Barnes and a journeyman tailor, Nicholas Taylor's man, brought her a little piece of (?)Tamey for which she gave them 4d. A little after Christmas Barnes brought to her house ½ ell of holland for which she gave him 8d, but she denied he ever sold her any other lawn ('lane') or holland.

She further confesses that at sundry times since Christmas last Barnes brought her several things mentioned in his examination for which she paid him the several prices mentioned therein. She says she did not know he had stolen them for he told her he had them from a journeyman tailor. At his first coming she said if he would bring her any more such things she would give him money for them, and would dress herself in a gown with part of the ribanding only to see if he were willing to have it worn openly. He said he did not care, it would do well, yet she did not dress her gown with it. And she denies she ever received any other goods or wares from Barnes. (signed) Elizabeth Rili.

[f209]

437:11/20 *Re-examination of Isabel Abbott*, 4 April 1612.

She says about a week since John Barnes told her that Richard Shadd's wife owed him 4s, and that if her husband had not fallen out with him he would have given her 18 yards of ribanding to dress her gown, but instead he had sold it for 2s but to whom she did not know. She denies receiving from Barnes more than she confessed before, but claims Barnes said he had lent 16d to Ann daughter of Nicholas Taylor. (mark).

437:12/20 *Examination of Ursula Poole*, servant to Elizabeth Ryly of Woodstock, 4 April 1612.

She confesses that she bought four and a quarter yards of sea-water ribanding for 9d or 10d from Barnes about Shrovetide last, when he said he sold it for the aforesaid journeyman tailor. She denies ever buying or receiving any other wares from Barnes. (mark).

[f209v]

437:13/20 *Re-examination of the said John Barnes*, 6 March (sic) 1612.

He further confesses that about two years since he sold to Thomas Screevin's wife 3 yards of velvet lace worth 4d/yard for 9d, which lace he sold for Thomas Debanck a journeyman tailor. Also he sold a pair of stockings to Mr Stevenson for 8d about a year and a half since for Debanck at his request. He says he delivered 2s6d to Ned Rudgate only to buy a pair of shears.

Item, a little before Christmas last he and his master William Butterfeild went three times to Campsfield in the night to steal hay at Mr Gregorie's rick there and the two of them brought 3 horse loads over these times. And Butterfeild went 3 or 4 times before this alone and did the like himself. Nobody knew of the two of them going, but when his master went alone Mr Gregorie's shepherd made delivery of the hay to him.

437:14/20 7 April 1612. Also he and his master went into Munck's mead about midsummer last in the night time and stole two sacks of hay each time; and his master sent him to Robert Spitle's man in the evening three times to fetch about ½ peck of oats each time. He thinks they were stolen from Spitle for his own master. Sometimes he received the oats immediately, at other times by appointment later. (mark of) John Barnes.

[f210]

437:15/20 *Examination of William Butterfeild,* tailor, 6 April 1612 before the aforesaid court.

The examinant confesses that about Christmas last he went twice in the evening to Campsfield to Mr John Gregorie's rick to steal hay. He thinks he had in whole about 3 loads ('lodes'), but he denies Mr Gregorie's man was acquainted therewith only that he begged a little from the shepherd.

Another time he and Barnes went in the evening to the rick and stole a horse load of hay and brought it to the house of Thomas Abbott of Woodstock, where his horse stood, but he denies that either Abbott or his wife at any time was acqainted therewith. (mark of) William Butterfeild.

Committals to Quarter Sessions and Assizes:

Recognisance:

437:16/20 Before the said justices, 7 April 1612. William Bradshewe binds himself in £40 to give evidence according to the statutes against John Barnes, Ann Barnes, John Abbott and Isabel Abbott his wife at the next sessions and gaol delivery.

Recognisance:

437:17/20 Before the said justices 6 April 1612. John Abbott binds himself and his wife in £40 that they will present themselves and appear before the justices at the assizes at the next gaol delivery to make their case and receive the court's judgment. Thomas Abbott gives surety in £40 for the said John and Isabel under the conditions aforesaid.

[f210v]

437:18/20 *Re-examination of William Butterfeild*, 7 April 1612 before the aforesaid mayor and justices.

He confesses that about midsummer last in the evening he stole two sacks of hay out of Widow Munck's mead in the Le Poole.[78] Mr Gregorie's shepherd

[78] See *WCA*, 28.

Francis was acquainted with him taking the hay from Gregorie's rick but was never with him at the time. Also Robert Spitle's man had done him a little wrought (i.e. work) and in recompense thereof he would give him some oats if they agreed that Spitle's man should take oats from his master and send it to this examinant. Spitle's man once brought him a little oats in a bag and about three times he sent his apprentice to Spitle's for about ½ peck of oats each time. (mark of) Butterfeild

437:19/20 **Assizes committal** 9Apr. 1612 before William Rayer mayor.

Recognisance:

William Butterfeild binds himself. in £40, and William Todman of Woodstock park-keeper and Drewe Gregory of Woodstock cutler each go surety in £20, that Butterfeild will present himself before the justices at the assizes at the next county gaol delivery to make his case and receive etc.

[f211]

437:20/20 *Re-examination of the said John Barnes* 7 April 1612.

He says that at one of the former times in that same shop he had also stolen 18 yards of russet silk ribanding worth 6d/yard which he delivered to Richard Shadd's wife only for her to sell for him @ 2d/yard, and the overplus to take herself, which lace she sold and paid him 3s. He also stole 16 yards of broad carnation ribanding and 16 yards of say green ribanding which he gave to goodwife Shadd which he denies telling her he stole it but that he sold it for the foresaid overplus ('nirmia').[79]

He likewise stole there another 4 yards of 6d laying lace which he delivered to his aunt Scasborowe only to keep for him. He also stole 4 yards of 3d laying lace and sold it for 6d to Daniel, Mr Pour's cadman (assistant), who said if he had any such commodities to sell he would give him money for it. In addition he gave to the said John Ackly 3 yards of 6d lace which he stole out of the same shop. (mark of) John Barnes.

[f211v]

438. Examination of Ralph Lucas, 8 April 1612 before said justices

Ralph Lucas, servant to Robert Bignill baker of Woodstock, confesses that yesterday he stole from his master's pastery[80] one peck of wheaten gurgeons ('gurgins') worth 9d which he sold to Jerome Smith's wife of Hanborough for 8d. At three or four other sundry times he likewise stole 4 pecks of the like gurgins which he sold to her for 4d/peck, but does not confess that she was privy to the stealing thereof but that he sold it only for his own maintenance to spend without his master's privity. About three times of late he stole a half

[79] 'nirmia'= nimia = overplus.

[80] pastery = place where pastry is made.

peck of wheaten flour which he gave to Mary Abbott, wife of Thomas, who counselled and persuaded him to steal it, telling him it should make fritters of which he should have part.
Within this twelve months he has spent two to four pence a time at several alehouses in Woodstock, especially at Abbott's; the money he made from meal stolen from his master.

[f212]

At other times he has stolen one peck of fair wheaten flour given to John Abbott's wife to make into puddings for himself and John Barnes who brought currants for the puddings, and he and Barnes then spent 2d a piece. John Abbott and his wife at divers times before persuaded him to steal meal and money from his master. Another half bushel of gurgins he sold to Walker's wife of Wootton at several times for 8d.
Also he thinks he has spent at Thomas Abbott's house about 10s within this 12 months stolen from his master at several times. He has spent about 8d a week at that house over this last two years, all of which he stole from his master, together with about 3s lost on skittles and other sports. He says Thomas Abbott and William Butterfeild have provoked him to do this.

(mark) Ralph Lucas.

[f212v] (Blank)

[f213]

439. Corporation Order. 6 April 1612 before William Rayer mayor, James Whitlock esquire, recorder of the borough, and the other justices.
439:1/4 First Mr Kite is content to pay his 18d per annum for his quit rent for his house; for his putgally rent he is content to pay per annum for 21 years from henceforth by composition 6d.[81]
439:2/4 Mr Kyte shall use a common brewhouse, but it shall be at the neighbours' and victuallers' choice to take their beer and ale from him at their pleasure.
439:3/4 It is fit that the articles set down by the justices of the assise concerning victualling and alehouses shall be put in operation by the magistrates of this borough.
439:4/4 This is a true copy of an order set down in the form aforesaid by William Rayer mayor, James Whitlock esq., recorder, Jerome Kite esq., Thomas Bradshewe and Thomas Browne gents, JPs of the said borough: which order under their hands is remaining upon a file here.

(signed) Edmund Hiorne, town clerk.

[81] See Glossary & also *WCA*, 35, 42.

[f213v]

440. *Victualler dismissal*: 6 April 1612 before William Rayer mayor and James Whitlock recorder.

It is ordered by the mayor, recorder and justices here that, since Thomas Paynter has disobeyed the mayor and beaten the constables at the setting up of his signpost, he shall be suppressed from his victualling. (signed by) mayor, recorder, Jerome Keyte, Thomas Brown and Thomas Bradshewe.

[f214]

Portmoot court held 6 April 1612...[82]

Action of debt:

441:1/2 John Warren vs John Prydy - defendant responds and wages law with six hands in the next court.

Actions of trespass on case:

433:3/10 Flye vs Collingwood - final privilege day granted.

434:3/5 Fidler vs Streete - peremptory day to respond granted.

442:1/8 Fidler vs Streete - plaintiff declares, copy granted.

443:1/7 John Tyms vs John Newman - day granted for declaration.

Actions continuing: **303**:32/53; **374**:19/28; **427**:6/8.

[f214v]

Portmoot court held 20 April 1612...

Actions of trespass on case:

433:4/10 Fly vs Collingwood - peremptory day to respond granted.

443:2/7 Tyms vs Newman - plaintiff declares and copy granted.

444:1/21 Richard Wright vs Ralph Shurly - plaintiff declares, with copy granted defendant.

Actions continuing: **303**:33/53; **374**:20/28; **427**:7/8; **434**:4/5; **441**:2/2; **442**:2/8.

[f215]

Portmoot court held 4 May 1612...

Actions of trespass on case:

433:5/10 Flye vs Collingwood - defendant responds and puts himself on the country.

434:5/5 Fidler vs Streete - discharged.

443:3/7 Tyms vs Newman - peremptory day to respond in next court.

444:2/21 Wrighte vs Shurlie - similarly.

Actions continuing: **303**:34/53; **374**:21/28; **427**: 8/8; **442**:3/8.

[f215v]

Actions of debt:

445:1/1 Thomas Willis vs John Cooke - plaintiff declares, with copy. Discharged.

[82] No officers other than mayor given.

446:1/15 Humphrey Hamond vs Roger Sturgis - plaintiff declares, and defendant surrendered to hands of sergeant.
447:1/1 Henry Browne knight vs Anthony Damery - plaintiff declares with day to amend; discharged on payment of £4:15s for debt and 6s ld amercement.
448:1/2 George Carter vs William Haynchoe - plaintiff declares and copy granted.
Action of trespass:
449:1/1 John Harris vs William Porter - discharged.
Action of trespass on case:
450:1/4 Anthony Damery vs Richard Temple - day to declare granted.

[f216]

Portmoot court held 10 May 1612 ...[83]
Action of debt:
446:2/15 Hamond vs Sturgis - defendant granted second privilege day.
Actions of trespass on case:
433:6/10 Fly vs Collingwood - *venire facias* granted.
442:4/8 Fidler vs Streete - recovered for plaintiff 31s8d for debt and 6s9d amercement; action continues.
443:4/7 Tyms vs Newman - defendant responds *non-assumpsit* to manner and form of action; the parties put themselves on country.
444:3/21 Wright vs Shurly - defendant responds not guilty to manner and form of action and puts himself on the country.
450:2/4 Damery vs Temple - plaintiff declares, day to amend.
Actions continuing: **303**:35/53; **374**:22/28.

[f216v]

Actions of debt:
448:2/2 Carter vs Haynchoe - peremptory day to respond.
451:1/3 Edmund Hiorne vs Thomas Rooke - plaintiff declares, copy to defendant.
452:1/1 John Hunte vs Christopher Weedon - since plaintiff does not wish to prosecute plaint defendant goes quit.
453:1/1 Robert Bincks vs Randell Richards - plaintiff declares, defendant granted first privilege day. (date in margin) 2 June 1612.
Action of trespass:
454:1/5 Hugh Hamond vs William Symonds "arr"[84]

[f217]

455. Assize of Bread and Ale set down in open sessions. 8 April 1612..
The best wheat at the quarter 40s.

83 Date is a Sunday. Mayor but no other officers listed.
84 ?arrearage; apparently related to assault in **454**:2/5.

The penny white loaf to weigh 8oz.
The penny wheaten loaf to weigh 12oz.
The penny household loaf to weigh 17oz.
A quart of ale within doors for a penny; and a thirdendall of wholesome drink without doors for a penny. (signed) Town clerk.

[f217v]

456. View of Frankpledge and Sessions of the Peace, held 8 April 1612; before William Rayer mayor, and Jerome Kite esq., Thomas Bradshewe and Thomas Browne esq., justices of the peace of the said borough.

(Officers as previously).

Jury for the crown:

John Dubber,	Nicholas Taylor,	Jerome White,
John Lowe,	Thomas Screevin,	Thomas Williams,
William Bradshewe,	John Bradshewe,	William Meatcalfe,
William Edwards,	Phillip James,	Hugh Hamond,
William Hickes senior,	Edmund Rudgate,	George Noble and

Randall Richards: sworn in.

[f218]

457. The names of Innholders and victuallers licensed to brew and utter ale and beer in their houses within this borough:

Innholders: Thomas Bradshewe gent, John Glover alderman,Richard Meades.
Victuallers: William Rayer
(Nominee victuallers appointed by all the justices except where noted otherwise).

Nominees, bound in £10	Sureties, each bound in £5
Thomas Williams	Robert Bignill, Francis Collingwood, appointed by mayor and Mr Browne.
John Dissell	John Heath, Francis Garter.
John Ackleye	Robert Bignill, Thomas Abbott.
Nicholas Taylor	William Edwards, Thomas Screevin.
	[f218v]
William Edwards	Thomas Screevin, Nicholas Taylor, appointed by mayor and Mr Browne.
Henry Rudgate	William Bradshewe, John Bradshewe.
Thomas Screevine	Jerome White, Richard Shad.
Edward Rudgate	Thomas Williams, Thomas Screevin.
William Hickes, senior	William Bradshewe, John Ackley.
Hugh Hamond	Richard Shad, Randall Richards.
Thomas Godferie	Edward Rudgate, Nicholas Glover.
	[f219]
Jerome White	Thomas Screevin, Ralph Durbridge.

Thomas Painter	Jerome White, John Bradshewe, appointed by mayor and Mr Bradshewe.
Bennett Painter	
Ralph Durbridge	Thomas Screevin, Jerome White.
Nicholas Glover	Nicholas Taylor, Edward Longe, appointed by mayor and Mr Browne.
John Taylor (no monies)	appointed by all the justices to be licensed at his cousin's home.

[f219v]

408:2/2 The jury presents on oath that William Castell and Henry Flexnie have broken the peace and both are judged in mercy for 2s6d. Paid into court - 5s. It is ruled by the court that both parties go quit and are discharged.
459:1/2 The court of the borough sessions of the peace is adjourned until 8 June next. (signed by) town clerk.
459:2/2 The court of the sessions of the peace is further adjourned after the custom of the borough until a Monday, namely 6 July next.

(signed by) mayor and town clerk.

[f220]

460:1/6 **Coroner's court. 23 April 1612 before William Rayer mayor and coroner of the borongh.**[85]
Martin Blay, yeoman of Littlemore ('Litlemore'), Oxon, says on oath that last Monday 20 April, he being in the company of John Brooman of Littlemore, at a court leet held in Cowley, he heard him complain of his head and often laid his hands upon it. On the morrow, after breakfast at his house in Littlemore, the two walked in the street and Blay said he thought all was not well with Brooman since he held his head and Brooman answered that he had a booming ('stooming') in his head and that the blow he had received on his head would be the death of him. (mark of) Martin Blay.

[f220v]

460:2/6 *Deposition of William Knott,* 23 April 1612 before William Rayer.
William Knott, yeoman of Littlemore, says that on Thursday 26 March coming towards Oxford he met Brooman and three of his neighbours going homewards towards Littlemore. Parting after private conversation between them he looked back and perceived two scholars and a (?)husbandman about twelve score (paces) from him and saw Brooman upon the ground. He went back to understand the cause and before reaching Brooman he met the two scholars; the one went by him and said nothing. The other who had struck Brooman, (as he has heard), said it were good you make haste for there was a simple country man so drunk that he had fallen down and broken his head (being in a

[85] In Michaelmas term 1613 Mr James Chesterman of Oxford challenged the mayor's right to act as coroner: *WCA*, 47, 49; *VCH*, *Oxon* xii, 393.

meadow ground). This deponent told him he was astonished ('marvaile'), for he then presently met him and then he was (?)enough. The said neighbours of Brooman, being John Frewen and William Benwell, went back after the scholars and told the scholar a Mr Morgan that he had slain Brooman. Morgan struck at the neighbours and broke his staff upon Benwell's shoulder and then

[f221]

presently ran away and could not after be taken. (mark of) William Knott.

460:3/6 *Deposition* same day, by William Brooman, brother of the said John Brooman.

Deponent says that about a fortnight since, he and his brother walking in the fields near Cowley, his brother told him that he had received a hurt in his head by one Mr Morgan which would be the death of him.

(mark of) William Brooman.

460:4/6 *Recognisances*: Martin Blay, William Knott and William Brooman yeomen of Littlemore each bind themselves in £40 to present ("at the next assises"- crossed through) and give evidence against Mr Thomas Morgan of Martyn (i.e. Merton) College according to the form of the statutes.

(signed by) town clerk.

460:5/6 The verdict to be taken the Monday sennight after Whitsunday next.

[f221v]

Portmoot court held 25 May 1612...

Actions of debt:

446:3/15 Hamond vs Sturgis - final privilege day granted defendant.

451:2/3 Hiorne vs Rooke - peremptory day to respond.

Action of trespass on case:

433:7/10 Flye vs Collingwood - executed *venire facias* returned and *habeas corpora* granted.

Actions continuing: **303**:36/53; **374**:23/28; **442**:5/8; **443**:5/7; **444**:4/21; **450**:3/4.

[f222]

454:2/5 **Examination. 2 June 1612 before William Rayer mayor**. William Symons confessed that this present day he broke the peace and drew blood upon Hugh Hamond, having no quarrel with him but upon a rash hand, here in Woodstock. (signed by) William Symons.

Recognisance: William Symons bound in £40, with Joseph Harris surety in £20, to appear at the next sessions in Woodstock.[86]

[f222v]

Conveyance:

461:1/4 5 June 1612 before William Rayer mayor.

Order: Joan Daunter that justly etc. she keep the agreement with Richard Hawkins and wife Ann concerning one burgage messuage or tenement with

[86] See also *WCA*, 23.

appurtenances in the borough now in the tenure of the said Richard Hawkins. And if she does not do so etc.
And the concord is such that the said Joan acknowledges the said tenement with appurtenances to be the right of the same Richard & Ann as those they have of the gift of the said Joan and remits and quitclaims them for the said Joan and her heirs to the said Richard & Ann and their heirs in perpetuity. And in addition the same Joan concedes for herself and her heirs that she will warrant the said tenement with appurtenances to the said Richard & Ann and their heirs against the said Joan and her heirs in perpetuity. And for this fine etc.[87]

(mark of) Joan Daunter; (signed by) mayor and town clerk.

[f223]

Portmoot court held 8 June 1612...

Actions of debt:
446:4/15 Hamond vs Sturgis - peremptory day to respond.
451:3/3 Hiorne vs Rooke - discharged.
Actions of trespass on case:
442:6/8 Fidler vs Streete - peremptory day to respond.
443:6/7 Tyms vs Newman - executed *venire facias* returned, *habeas corpora* granted.
450:4/4 Damery vs Temple - discharged.
462:1/7 Ann Leake vs William Abbott - declaration with copy.
Actions continuing: **303**:37/53; **374**:24/28; **444**:5/21.

[f223v]

Actions of debt:
463:1/2 Thomas Browne alderman vs Elizabeth Ryly - declaration with copy.
464:1/17 Thomas Browne alderman vs Ralph Shurley - similarly.
465:1/12 William Raunson vs Randall Richards and Thomas Screevin - similarly.
Action of trespass:
454:3/5 Hugh Hamond vs William Symons - similarly.
Actions of trespass on case:
433:8/10 Salloman Flye vs Francis Collingwood - jury between parties:

Nicholas Taylor,	Jerome White,	ohn Lowe,
William Bradshewe,	William Edwards,	William Hickes senior,
Ralph Durbridge,	Francis Garter,	Randall Richards,
Robert Ducock,	John Ackley,	John Bradshewe

on oath find for plaintiff and assess damages at £20:5d and for amercement and costs 2d. Judgment adjourned to next court.
466:1/3 Richard Streete vs Francis Fidler - day to declare in next court.
467:1/2 Edmund Hiorne vs Thomas Blith.

[87] See also *WCA*, 32.

Conveyance:
461:2/4 First proclamation between Richard Hawkins and Ann his wife querents and Joan Daunter deforciant concerning one messuage or tenement with appurtenances in Woodstock.

[f224]

460:6/6 **Coroner's court held 8 June 1612 before William Rayer mayor and coroner of this borough.**
The names of the jury sworn to enquire how one John Brooman of Littlemore who late died in this borough came to his death, namely:

Jerome White,	Edmund Rudgate,	Richard Shad,
Robert Bignell,	William Edwards,	George Noble,
Thomas Gee,	Francis Garter,	John Ackly,
William Butterfeild,	William Hickes senior and Henry Price	

who say upon their oaths that they find that the said John Brooman died of the visitation of almighty god, and not of any wound or hurt to their knowledges. (Signed by) William Rayer, Edmund Hiorne, Jerome White, Edmund Rudgate, Robert Bignell, Richard Shadd, William Edwards and George Noble; (Marks of) Francis Garter, John Ackly, Henry Price, Thomas Gee, William Hickes senior and William Butterfeild.

[f224v]

Recognisances. 20 June 1612 before William Rayer mayor.
468:1/2 William Jencks gent of Yarnton ('Yearneton') binds himself in £40 and Simon James gent goes surety in £20 that said William shall personally appear at the next sessions of the peace here.
468:2/2 Thomas Rea gent of Severn ('Seaverne') Stoke, Worcs., and John Underill yeoman of the same place each binds himself in £20 and John Gadbury gent goes surety for each of them in £20 on the conditions aforesaid.[88] (Added note): Discharged in sessions of the peace.

[f225]

Portmoot court held 22 June 1612...
Action of debt:
446:5/15 Hamond vs Sturgis - defendant through his attorney acknowledges the debt; day in next court for payment and judgment.
Action of trespass:
454:4/5 Hamond vs Symons - peremptory day to respond in next court.
Actions of trespass on case:
443:7/7 Tyms vs Newman - defendant brings writ of *habeas corpus* dated the 16 June aforesaid for return *coram nobis* at Westminster on the Monday next after Trinity three weeks.

[88] See actions **473** & **474**; and also *WCA*, 22.

462:2/7 Leake vs William Abbott - peremptory day to respond in next court.
Actions continuing: **303**:38/53; **374**:25/28; **442**:7/8; **444**:6/21; **466**:2/3.

[f225v]

Actions of debt:
463:2/2 Browne vs Ryly - second privilege day to defendant.
464:2/17 Browne vs Shurley - peremptory day to respond next court.
465:2/12 Raunson vs Randall (Richards) - second privilege day granted in next court.
470:1/3 William Rayer vs Randall Richards - day to declare granted in next court.
Actions of trespass on case:
433:9/10 Flye vs Collingwood - court rules plaintiff to recover £20:6d for damages and [blank] amercement; *scire facias* granted.
467:2/2 Hiorne vs Blith - defendant personally acknowledges action, therefore writ of inquiry granted.
Actions of trespass and assault:
471:1/8 William May vs Nicholas Yonge - day to declare next court.
472:1/3 John Gadbury gent vs Richard Trubshawe - plaintiff declares, with copy to defendant.
473:1/12 William Jencks vs Thomas Rea gent - similarly } see
474:1/12 William Jencks vs John Underill - similarly } **468.**
Conveyance:
461:3/4 Second proclamation between Richard and Ann Hawkins and Joan Daunter.
Land claim for wife:
475. To this court comes John Jarrett of Weston-on-the-Green in county Oxon yeoman, in right of his wife Jellian, the daughter of one John Barrett, yeoman of the said Weston, lately deceased, and made claim to two messuages or tenements with appurtenances within this borough now in separate tenure or occupation by William Hitch and John Ackley, as the nearest heir of one Owen Barrett of Weston deceased and the said John Barrett.
(Marginal note): The will of the said Owen dated 15 August 1558.

[f226]

Portmoot court held 6 July 1612...
Actions of debt:
446:6/15 Hamond vs Sturgis - court rules plaintiff should recover £4 for debts and [blank] amercement; *scire facias* granted against defendant's surety.
464:3/17 Browne vs Shurly - defendant responds that he has paid the debt according to the conditions of the bond; *venire facias* granted.
470:2/3 Rayer vs Randall Richards - plaintiff declares, with copy; second privilege day for defendant.

Action of trespass:
454:5/5 Hamond vs Symons - continues under specific agreement. Discharged.
Actions of trespass on case:
442:8/8 Fidler vs Streete - discharged by assent.
433:10/10 Fly vs Collingwood - defendant brings writ of error, dated 23 June 1612, for return on the octave of Michaelmas: approved.
462:3/7 Leake vs Abbott - defendant responds not guilty.
466:3/3 Streete vs Fidler - Discharged.
Actions continuing: **303**:39/53; **374**:26/28; **444**:7/21.

[f226v]

Actions of debt:
465:3/12 William Raunson vs Thomas Screevin and Randall Richards - plaintiff declares, and first privilege day granted.
476:1/4 Thomas Meatcalfe vs Richard Hawkins and Robert Bignill - plaintiff declares, with copy; first privilege day.
Actions of trespass and assault:
471:2/8 Maye vs Yonge - declaration, day to amend next court.
472:2/3 Gadbury vs Trubshawe - peremptory day to respond in next court.
473:2/12 Jencks vs Rea - peremptory day to respond.
474:2/12 Jencks vs Underill - peremptory day to respond.
Conveyance:
461:4/4 Third proclamation between Richard Hawkins and Ann his wife querents and Joan Daunter deforciant concerning one messuage.

[f227]

477:1/3 **Examination 4 July 1612 before Willian Rayer mayor and Thomas Bradshewe JP., of William Stockdall yeoman of Ashby-de-la-Zouch ('Asbie de la zouch'), Leicestershire.**

477:2/3 Information of William Edwards, of Woodstock on oath. About two o'clock upon Thursday night last Stockdall came to his house with the watchmen of the town and called for beer and wanted lodgings. Edwards would not be troubled at that time in his house, whereupon Stockdall called him a tapsterly fellow, ale-draping knave, and that if he had him out of the house he would pull him by the ears and beat him. On the morrow about one o'clock in the afternoon Stockdall came to his house and there railed upon him and threatened to beat him if he could get him out of his house, or else would set twenty boys to beat him. And further said that there was never a Scotchman in England, the king's grace and progeny excepted, but was a base fellow and gross companions; and he has seen some of them to beg at the table for gross swines flesh and roast meat; and he has since met them in London riding with their foot-clothes. And today Stockdall returned to his (ale)house and called for a pot of beer and presently did cast (i.e.vomit) in the house in an unmanlike fashion; he also confessed to walking that night in Woodstock park on unknown purpose. (signed by) William Edwards.

[f227v]

477:3/3 *Examination of the said Stockdall*, same day.
William Stockdall says that he lately served Sir William Feilding at Newnham ('Newnam'), Warwickshire, and departed from him in Lent last only in discontent because he was in love with one of his lady's gentlewomen. From there he went to London, then on to the Bath ('Bathe') and Bristol ('Bristowe'), going only to associate Sir William Turpin's eldest son. Sir William Feilding upon his departure gave him £30 in money and sealed him a bond for the pay of £20. Of this, £20 he set to use and the other £10 he has spent in his journeys. This master gave him a grey ambling gelding which he kept eight weeks and then sold him to the ostler of the White Hart in the Strand for 45s at Whitsuntide last and tolled for him in Smithfield by the name of William Stockdall. Within a fortnight after he bought a grey fleabitten working nag in Smithfield from a stranger for 40s and tolled for him, and kept it until Saturday last when he broke his leg near Oxford. He says he brought to this borough a suit of apparel consisting of a cloak, doublet, jerkin and hose; the cloak being of sheep's russett with lace at 2d a yard. The doublet of white fustian with silver lace, the jerkin and hose of a sky-coloured cloth with silver lace; one rapier sanguined, with divers other goods remaining in a bag at Mr Bradshewe's house, namely: 3 shirts, 4 pairs of silver stockings which he has pawned to Mr Bradshewe for 40s to be redeemed in three weeks upon payment of the said 40s.[89]
(signed by) William Stockdall and town clerk.
[Oxon assizes was the 14 July 1612.]

[f228]

Portmoot court held 20 July 1612...
Actions of debt:
446:7/15 Hamond vs Sturgis - sergeant returns executed writ of *scire facias,* and *alias scire facias* granted.
470:3/3 Rayer vs Richards - discharged by plaintiff's assent.
Action of trespass on case:
462:4/7 Leake vs Abbott - the parties put themselves on the country, therefore *venire facias*.
Actions continuing: **303**:40/53; **374**:27/28; **444**:8/21; **464**:4/17.

[89] The amount of interest is presumably hidden. In 1601 de Malyne noted the most favourable extortion by usury inflicted by pawnbrokers was 6d on the pound for a standard month of 28 days, amounting to a rate of 30%. Jones, 161.

[f228v]

Actions of debt:
476:2/4 Meatcalfe vs Hawkins and Bignill - second privilege day granted to defendants.
478:1/14 Ann Leake widow vs Margaret Hatten, widow - plaintiff declares and day to amend.
479:1/14 Francis Collingwood vs Margaret Hatten, widow - similarly.
480:1/2 William Abbott vs Margaret Hatten, widow - plaintiff requests day to declare in next court.
481:1/2 Richard Reade vs – Scott - Discharged.
Actions of trespass and assault:
471:3/8 Maye vs Yonge - plaintiff declares, with copy.
472:3/3 Gadbury vs Trubshawe - they released each other of all actions and quarrels till this day, and doth promise this Trubshawe his servant shall also release all actions, trespasses and quarrels to Mr Gadbury till this day. Discharged by assent of both parties.
Actions continuing: **465**:4/12; **473** and **474**:3/12.

[f229]

Portmoot court held 3 August 1612...
Actions of debt:
446:8/15 Hamond vs Sturgis - defendant does not appear on writ of *alias scire facias*; therefore execution of action granted against defendant and his surety.
465:5/12 Raunson vs Screevin and Richards - final privilege day for defendants.
476:3/4 Meatcalfe vs Hawkins and Bignill - similarly.
478:2/14 Leake vs Hatten) plaintiff completes
479:2/14 Collingwood vs Hatten) declaration, copy granted.
Action of trespass on case:
462:5/7 Leake vs Abbott - *venire facias* returned and writ of *habeas corpora* granted.
Actions of trespass and assault:
471:4/8 Maye vs Yonge - peremptory day to respond.
473:4/12 Jencks vs Read) defendants respond to defend
474:4/12 Jencks vs Underill) themselves, copies granted.
Actions continuing: **303**:41/53; **374**:28/28; **444**:9/21; **464**:5/17.

[f229v]

Actions of debt:
480:2/2 Abbott vs Hatten - since plaintiff does not prosecute, judgment given against him for amercement.
481:2/2 Reade vs Scott - Discharged.
482:1/2 Ralph Shurly vs John Symons - plaintiff declares and copy granted.
483:1/13 Michael Dennett vs Ralph Shurly - similarly.

Action of trespass:
484:1/2 John Coles vs William Ratlife gent - plaintiff declares and copy granted; and said defendant produces in court the half-seals from the vice-chancellor of the university of Oxon'.[90]

[f230]

Portmoot court held 17 August 1612
Actions of debt:
465:6/12 Raunson vs Richards and Screevin - peremptory day to respond granted.
476:4/4 Meatcalfe vs Hawkins - similarly. Discharged.
Actions of trespass and assault:
471:5/8 Maye vs Yonge - defendant responds *non-assumpsit* to the manner and form of the action; therefore *venire facias* granted.
473 and **474**:5/12 Jencks vs Rea and Underill - plaintiff responds and puts himself on country; therefore *venire facias* granted.
Actions continuing: **303**:42/53; **444**:10/21; **446**:9/15; **462**:6/7; **464**:6/17.

[f230v]

Actions of debt:
478:3/14 Leake vs Hatten - peremptory day to respond in next court.
479:3/14 Collingwood vs Hatten - similarly.
482:2/2 Shurly vs Symons - similarly. Discharged.
483:2/13 Dennett vs Shurley - peremptory day to respond.
Action of trespass:
485:1/7 Alice Belcher vs Thomas Hanwell - plaintiff declares and defendant through attorney requests copy.
Action of replevin:
486:1/6 Phillip James vs Thomas Bradshewe alderman - complains of the taking and unjust detention of one gelding. Said plaintiff declares through his attorney and defendant does not appear, to respond. Therefore *writ of capias* granted against defendant according to custom of this borough.

[f231]

Conveyance:
487:1/4 20 August 1612.
Order: Richard Hawkins and wife Ann that justly etc. they keep the agreement with Edmund Hiorne gent concerning one messuage or tenement with appurtenances in the borough now in the tenure or occupation of the said Richard Hawkins. And if they do not do so etc.
And the concord is such that the said Richard & Ann acknowledge the aforesaid

[90] Actions involving university members could be removed to the vice-chancellor's court in Oxford by the 'half-seal' of the university. *VCH, Oxon* iv, passim; xii, 392; M Underwood, *Journal of Soc. of Archivists*, vi, 18-27. But see *f238v*.

tenement with appurtenances to be the right of the same Edmund as those which Edmund has of the gift of the said Richard & Ann and remit and quitclaim for the same Richard & Ann and their heirs to the said Edmund Hiorne and his heirs in perpetuity. And in addition the same Richard & Ann concede for themselves and their heirs that they will warrant the said tenement with appurtenances to the said Edmund Hiorne and his heirs against themselves and their heirs in perpetuity. And for this fine etc.[91]

(Marks of) Richard & Ann Hawkins, (Signed by) mayor and town clerk.

[f231v]

Portmoot court held 31 August 1612...

Actions of debt:

465:7/12 Raunson vs Richards and Screevin - since defendants do not appear, therefore judgment upon them.

478:4/14 Leake vs Hatten - defendant responds, and copies granted.

479:4/14 Collingwood vs Hatten - similarly.

483:3/13 Dennett vs Shurly - defendant pleads *non est factum*; therefore *venire facias*.

Actions continuing: **303**:43/53; **444**:11/21; **446**:10/15; **462**:7/7; **464**:7/17; **471**:6/8; **473**:6/12; **474**:6/12.

[f232]

Action of debt:

488:1/2 John Charman vs John Archer - plaintiff declares, and copy granted.

Actions of trespass:

485:2/7 Belcher vs Hanwell - peremptory day to respond.

489:1/4 Hugh Fawdery vs James - declaration with copy.

Action of replevin:

486:2/6 James vs Bradshewe - *writ of capias* granted in next court.

Conveyance:

487:2/4 First proclamation between Edmund Hiorne querent and Richard Hawkins & Ann his wife deforciants concerning one messuage with appurtenances.

[f232v]

Portmoot court held 14 September 1612, before William Rayer mayor.

Actions of debt:

465:8/12 Raunson vs Richards and Screevin - court judges plaintiff should recover [blank] for debt, and [blank] amercement; *scire facias* granted.

478:5/14 Leake vs Hatten - peremptory day for replication.

479:5/14 Collingwood vs Hatten - similarly.

488:2/2 Charman vs Archer - peremptory day to respond in next court. Discharged.

[91] See also *WCA*, 32, 44.

490:1/3 Richard Collett vs Edmund Paxton - plaintiff declares and defendant does not appear, therefore no defence offered; judgment in next court.
Actions of trespass:
485:3/7 Belcher vs Hanwell - since defendant does not respond writ of inquiry granted for return in next court.
489:2/4 Fawdery vs James - peremptory day to respond.
Actions continuing: **303**:44/53; **444**:12/21; **446**:11/15; **464**:8/17; **471**:7/8; **473**:7/12; **474**:7/12; **483**:4/13; **486**:3/6.
Conveyance:
487:3/4 Second proclamation between Edmund Hiorne and Richard Hawkins and his wife.

[f233]

491. Election of mayor, 14 September 1612, being the Monday before St. Matthew's day.
John Glover alderman was elected mayor for the year following. And likewise Edmund Rudgate was elected sergeant for the said borough for the year now following.

[f233v]

492:1/2 **Examination 25 September 1612 before William Rayer mayor.** Anthony Meades sawyer late servant to John Tompson sawyer of St. Giles, London, says he came from London on Sunday last intending to go to Swerford ('Swarford') where he was born; and confesses he came yesterday afternoon to Old Woodstock where he stole a sheet and a smock, the goods of Jerome Nash gent, from his bushes in his close near his dwelling house.
(mark of) Anthony Meades.
492:2/2 *Sentence.* It is ordered that the constables do whip Meades at the high cross this day; and that he may be sent to Swerford as a vagrant.
(signed by) mayor and town clerk.

[f234]

Portmoot court held 28 September 1612...
Actions of debt:
465:9/12 Raunson vs Richards and Screevin - sergeant returns executed writ of *scire facias* against surety, and *sicut alias scire facias* granted.
478:6/14 Leake vs Hatten - plaintiff puts replication and puts herself on country. Defendant likewise; *venire facias* granted.
479:6/14 Collingwood vs Hatten - similarly.
483:5/13 Dennett vs Shurley - sergeant returns executed *venire facias*; *habeas corpora* granted.

Action of trespass:
489:3/4 Fawdery vs James - defendant enters a plea in abatement because his surname is not known, court adjourns to advise.[92]
Actions of trespass and assault:
471:8/8 Maye vs Yonge - sergeant returns *venire facias*, and *habeas corpora* granted.
473:8/12 Jencks vs Rea - similarly, for return in next court.
474:8/12 Jencks vs Underill - similarly.
Actions continuing: **303**:45/53; **444**:13/21; **446**:12/15; **464**:9/17; **486**:4/6.

[f234v]

Actions of debt:
490:2/3 Richard Collett vs Edmund Paxton - court rules that plaintiff should recover £40 for debt and 2s amercement and costs on the opposing party. Therefore *scire facias* against defendant's surety.
493:1/9 John Fawler vs Ralph Shurley - plaintiff declares and copy to defendant.
494:1/1 Hugh Turferie vs Edward Busby - plaintiff declares and defendant does not appear. Therefore court rules plaintiff should recover [blank] debt and [blank] amercement.
Action of trespass:
485:4/7 Alice Belcher vs Thomas Hanwell - sergeant returns writ of inquiry to himself which he implements by putting on oath:

Jerome White,	Thomas Screevin,	Robert Bignill,
Thomas Williams,	John Bradshewe,	William Edwards,
Francis Garter,	Phillip Jeames,	Ralph Durbridge,
William Hickes senior,	William Butterfeild and	Randall Richards.

Which jury assess damages for the plaintiff at 12d over amercement and costs at [blank]. The court rules plaintiff should recover 12d for damages and [blank] amercement and costs as regards her suit on the opposing party.
Actions of trespass on case:
495:1/1 John Saunders vs Thomas Sutton - Discharged.
496:1/3 John Archer vs Thomas Turner - plaintiff declares and copy granted.

[f235]

Action of debt:
497:1/6 William Gadbury gent vs William Raunson - similarly.
Action of trespass on case:
498:1/1 Roger Sturgis vs Roger Bowman - Discharged.

[92] Misnaming or misdescription of parties, along with other errors unconnected with the merits of the case, could provide grounds for quashing the proceedings; unless remedied. Ivamy, 2; Gilmore, 21.

Conveyance:
487:4/4 Third proclamation between Edmund Hiorne querent and Richard Hawkins and Ann his wife. And since none comes to object etc. Therefore etc.[93]

[f235v]

Portmoot court held 5 October 1612...
Actions of debt:
465:10/12 Raunson vs Richards and Screevin - *sicut alias scire facias* executed, and writ of execution granted.
478:7/14 Leake vs Hatten - *venire facias* returned and *habeas corpora* granted
479:7/14 Collingwood vs Hatten - similarly.
490:3/3 Collett vs Paxton - *scire facias* returned and *sicut alias scire facias* granted.
493:2/9 Fawler vs Shurley - peremptory day to respond.
497:2/6 Gadbury vs Raunson - second privilege day granted.
Action of trespass:
485:5/7 Belcher vs Hanwell - *scire facias* returned and *sicut alias scire facias* granted.
Action of trespass on case:
496:2/3 Archer vs Turner - peremptory day to respond.
Actions continuing: **303**:46/53; **444**:14/21; **446**:13/15; **464**:10/17; **473**:9/12; **474**:9/12; **483**:6/13; **486**:5/6; **489**:4/4.

[f236]

Action of trespass on case:
499:1/6 Thomas Screevin vs William Harris - plaintiff declares with day to amend the form thereof; defendant surrendered to hands of sergeant of borough.

[f236v]

Portmoot court held 19 October 1612 before John Glover mayor.
Actions of debt:
465:11/12 Raunson vs Richards and Screevin - execution granted.
493:3/9 Fawler vs Shurley - defendant responds not guilty, therefore *venire facias* granted.
497:3/6 Gadbury vs Raunson - final privilege day granted.
Action of trespass:
485:6/7 Belcher vs Hanwell - executed *alias scire facias* returned and defendant does not appear; therefore writ of execution granted against defendant and surety.

[93] The only example of this provision in a *Conveyance*: in WBM B78/2.

Action of trespass on case:
499:2/6 Thomas Screevin vs William Harris - plaintiff completes declaration, copy to defendant.
Actions continuing: **303**:47/53; **444**:15/21; **446**:14/15; **464**:11/17; **478**:8/14; **479**:8/14; **483**:7/13; **486**:6/6; **496**:3/3.

[f237]

Actions of debt:
500:1/1 Robert Tredwell vs Merrial Taylor widow; administratrix of the goods and chattels of her husband John Taylor deceased - day to declare granted.
501:1/7 John Fawler vs William Harris - plaintiff declares, day to amend in next court.
502:1/10 John Jarvis vs John Stone - plaintiff declares and copy to defendant.
Actions of account:
503:1/7 John Fawler vs William Harris - plaintiff declares, day to amend in next court.
504:1/7 John Cooke vs William Harris - similarly.
Actions of trespass on case:
505:1/2 Thomas Bincks vs John Woollam - plaintiff declares and copy to defendant.
506:1/1 Thomas Abbott & Mary his wife vs William Rayer.

[f237v]

Actions of trespass and assault:
473:10/12 William Jencks vs Thomas Rea - the jury between parties:

John Lowe,	Nicholas Taylor,	Thomas Screevin,
John Bradshewe,	William Edwards,	Ralph Durbridge,
Randall Richards,	Alexander Head,	William Butterfeild,
George Noble,	Richard Hawkins,	Hugh Hamond

find for the plaintiff and assess damages at 12d and 2d amercement; judgment adjourned.
474:10/12 William Jencks vs John Underill - the jury between parties:

Jerome White,	Francis Collingwood,	Robert Bignill,
William Meatcalfe,	Francis Garter,	Thomas Gee,
William Archer,	Alexander Head,	Phillip James,
Richard Hawkins,	Drewe Gregory,	John Ackley

find for the plaintiff and assess damages at 12d and amercement 2d; judgment adjourned to next court.
Apprenticeship:
507. Richard Skey, son of William Skey yeoman of Oddington, Oxon, recently deceased, binds himself apprentice to William Bradshewe for the term of nine years from 1 November 1611.

(signed by) town clerk.

[f238]

508. View of Frankpledge and Sessions of the Peace, held 21 October 1612, before John Glover mayor, Jerome Kite gent, and Thomas Browne and Thomas Bradshewe gents and JPs. Officers in post.

Jury for the crown:	John Dubber,	Nicholas Taylor,
Jerome White,	John Lowe,	Thomas Screevine,
Thomas Williams,	William Bradshewe,	John Bradshewe,
John Norman,	William Edwards,	Robert Spitle,
John Ackley,	William Hickes senior,	George Noble,
Randall Richards,	Richard Hawkins,	Ralph Durbridge,
Richard Shadd: sworn in.		

[f238v]

Recognisances: 29 July 1612 before William Rayer mayor.

484:2/2 William Ratlife of the university of Oxon', gent., recognisance £40; with Thomas Joyner surety £20.

Under condition that the said William appears in person at this sessions of the peace to make his case and receive judgment: on the action by John Coles for breaking the peace and drawing blood, which is confessed to. Since Ratlife does not appear, therefore Joyner is under recognisance of £40 to appear at the next sessions. Discharged by assent of the mayor.

Thomas Joyner has broken the peace upon John Coles; therefore he is in mercy.

John Coles has broken the peace upon William Ratclife; therefore he is in mercy.

485:7/7 *Recognisances*: taken 4 August 1612 before William Rayer mayor.

Thomas Hanwell of Barton recognisance of £20, with Thomas Hall of Bodicote ('Boddicott'), Oxon surety in £10, on condition that Hanwell appears at this sessions of the peace for breaking the peace on Alice Belcher, to make his case and receive judgment. Hall does not appear; therefore it is returned that recognisance is to be estreated.

509. Forfeit of a weapon: A dagger due to the town which has been left with Mr Rayer by Jenkin Joanes for breaking the peace upon John Fawler and Edward Hickes. Paid out of this to Sturgis for curing Hickes' head - 2s.[94]

510. Election of court officers:

Constables: George Noble and Robert Ducock - sworn in.

Tithingmen: Thomas Gee, William Butterfeild, Richard Browne and William Archer - sworn in.

Tasters: Francis Garter and John Wilkinson - sworn in.

94 See also *WCA*, 23.

[f239]

Portmoot court held 2 October (sic November) 1612...

Actions of debt:

493:4/9 Fawler vs Shurley - executed *venire facias* returned; writ of *habeas corpora* for jury granted.

497:4/6 Gadbury vs Raunson - peremptory day to respond granted.

501:2/7 Fawler vs Harris) the parties put themselves to

Actions of account:) arbitration and court continues

503:2/7 Fawler vs Harris) thereupon under this agreement

504:2/7 Cooke vs Harris) with assent of plaintiffs.

Action of trespass on case:

499:3/6 Screevine vs Harris - peremptory day to respond.

Actions of trespass and assault:

473:11/12 Jencks vs Rea) defendants bring *writ of cerciorari*

474:11/12 Jencks vs Underill) for return in Chancery on the octave of St Martin next, dated 16 October regnal year 46.[95] And the court will advise on the approval thereof.

Actions continuing: **303**:48/53; **444**:16/21; **446**:15/15; **464**:12/17;**465**:12/12; **478**:9/14; **479**:9/14; **483**:8/13.

[f239v]

Actions of debt:

502:2/10 Jarvis vs Stone - peremptory day to respond.

511:1/8 Thomas Willis vs John Cooke - plaintiff declares and copy granted.

512:1/2 Thomas Willis vs John Fawler - similarly.

513:1/1 Giles Coles vs Meriall Taylor widow, administratrix of the goods and chattels of her deceased husband John Taylor - on a plaint of debt on demand of £20 on a bond. Defendant acknowledges the debt through her attorney Edward Rudgate. Therefore court rules that plaintiff should recover the debt and [blank] amercement; and execution is granted against her.

514:1/1 William Rayer vs Merriall Taylor administratrix - plaint of debt on demand for 200 marks similarly; execution granted.

515:1/6 William Rayer vs John Slatter - plaintiff declares and copy granted.

Actions of trespass on case:

505:2/2 Bincks vs Woollam - discharged.

516:1/1 Thomas Poole vs Thomas Trowle - day to declare granted.

Apprenticeship:

517: Edward Whitforde is enrolled apprentice to Thomas Bruce shoemaker for the term of seven years from 21 September last.

(signed by) town clerk.

95 Regnal year 46 must refer to the king's reign as James VI of Scotland, so that the date given is 16 October 1612; see Cheney, 25.

[f240 & 240v] (Blank)

[f241]

Portmoot court held 16 November 1612...

Action of debt:

497:5/6 Gadbury vs Raunson - through his attorney Edward Rudgate the defendant acknowledges the debt; judgment in next court.

Action of trespass on case:

499:4/6 Screevine vs Harris - since defendant does not respond writ of inquiry granted.

Actions of trespass and assault:

473:12/12 Jencks vs Rea) actions remain on consideration
474:12/12 Jencks vs Underill) of the borough recorder.

Actions continuing: **303**:49/53; **444**:17/21; **464**:13/17; **478**:10/14; **479**:10/14; **483**:9/13.

[f241v]

Actions of debt:

502:3/10 Jarvis vs Stone - defendant responds he does not owe in the manner and form of the declaration; therefore *venire facias* for return in next court.
511:2/8 Willis vs Cooke - peremptory day to respond.
512:2/2 Willis vs Fawler - similarly.
515:2/6 Rayer vs Slatter - similarly.

Actions of trespass:

518:1/1 John Phipps vs William Gilbert alias Twinch - discharged.
519:1/1 Richard Reade vs Bartholomew Sharpe - plaintiff declares and copy granted.
493:5/9 John Fawler vs Ralph Shurley -

Action of trespass: (*debt* previously); jury between parties:

Jerome White,	Robert Bignell,	William Bradshewe,
John Bradshewe,	William Edwards,	Francis Garter,
Robert Ducock,	Alexander Head,	Thomas Gee,
William Hickes junior,	Richard Shadd and	Drewe Gregory;

who find for the defendant with judgment adjourned to next court.

Action of trespass on case:

520:1/1 John Fawler vs William Hollymen.

Action of account:

521:1/2 James Allsope vs Randall Richards - plaintiff declares, copy granted; privilege day to defendant.

Actions continuing: **501**:3/7; **503**:3/7; **504**:3/7.

[f242]

Apprenticeship:

522 Edward Longe is enrolled apprentice to John Dubber shoemaker for the term of seven years from the date of his indenture 1 November 1612.
(signed by) town clerk.

[f242v]

Portmoot court held 30 November 1612...

Action of debt:

497:6/6 Gadbury vs Raunson - judgment of [blank] for debt and [blank] amercement; *scire facias* granted.

Actions continuing: **303**:50/53; **444**:18/21; **464**:14/17; **478**:11/14; **479**:11/14; **483**:10/13.

[f243]

Actions of debt:

493:6/9 Fawler vs Shurly - judgment that plaintiff pays defendant [blank] amercement.

502:4/10 Jarvis vs Stone - *venire facias* returned, and *habeas corpora* for next court.

511:3/8 Willis vs Cooke - defendant pleads *per minas*[96] (bond made under threat) and puts himself on the country.

523:1/1 John Salter vs Peter Miles - plaintiff declares, with copy granted. Discharged.

Action of trespass on case:

524:1/2 Thomas Wergo vs Hugh Turferie - plaintiff granted day to declare in next court.

Action of account:

521:2/2 Alsopp vs Richards - second privilege day granted defendant. Discharged.

Actions continuing: **499**:5/6; **501**:4/7; **503**:4/7; **504**:4/7; **515**:3/6.

[f243v]

Portmoot court held 14 December 1612...

Action of debt:

502:5/10 Jarvis vs Stone - writ of *habeas corpora* continues.

Action of account:

504:5/7 Cooke vs Harris -peremptory day to respond granted.

Actions continuing: **303**:51/53; **444**:19/21; **464**:15/17; **478**:12/14; **479**:12/14; **483**:11/13; **499**:6/6; **501**:5/7; **503**:5/7.

[96] In action on a bond a successful plea that it was made under threat ('Per minas') allowed it to be set aside. Ivamy, 153 'Duress', Gilmore, L. 1. 13, 'Bond' 2.

[f244]

Actions of debt:

493:7/9 Fawler vs Shurley - *scire facias* returned against plaintiff and writ of *alias scire facias* granted.

511:4/8 Willis vs Cooke - *venire facias* returned, *habeas corpora* granted.

525:1/13 Thomas Browne vs John Mackereth - defendant delivered on bail; plaintiff appoints Simon James on his behalf and defendant appoints Edmund Rudgate on his behalf. Plaintiff declares and grants defendant leave to imparl until next court.

Action of trespass:

526:1/3 John Symons vs Edward Parsons - defendant delivered on bail; Robert Bignill, Edward Longe and plaintiff appoint on his behalf Simon James, and defendant appoints Edmund Rudgate on his behalf. Plaintiff declares and grants defendant leave to imparl until next court.

Action of trespass on case:

524:2/2 Werge vs Turfery - plaintiff does not bring suit; therefore judgment that defendant should recover [blank] amercement: and *scire facias* against surety of plaintiff.

Action continuing: **515**:4/6.

[f244v]

Actions of debt:

527:1/1 William Bach vs Thomas Bewe - plaintiff declares through his attorney Simon James, and defendant appears through his attorney Edmund Rudgate; day to imparl granted in next court.

528:1/1 John Cooke vs Thomas Bewe - similarly.

529:1/1 John Heath vs Thomas Bewe - similarly.

Actions of trespass on case:

530:1/1 Thomas Gome vs Thomas Bew - similarly.

531:1/7 William White vs Edward Coleman - similarly.

Action of debt:

532:1/1 William Bradshewe vs Randall Richards - discharged.

Action of trespass on case:

533:1/2 Richard Coles vs William Flexney alias Hickes - plaintiff appears through his attorney Edmund Rudgate and requests day to declare in next court; defendant appears through his attorney Simon James.

[f245]

534:1/3 Information. 16 December 1612 before John Glover mayor and Thomas Browne and Thomas Bradshewe justices.

William Todman, a king's keeper in Woodstock Park, says that Robert Dimock, servant to Sir H. Lee baronet, came with others about Michaelmas last at night into Todman's walk in the high park of Woodstock Park and hunted the deer there with greyhounds. He killed a deer and carried it into

Mistress Tustall's assart[97] ('sart') near the park and continued it there until 12 o'clock next day in which time Todman drew (searched for) it unto the said place and found it lying in a bush, and set a man to watch it. And about one o'clock in the afternoon three men, names unknown to him, came with a grey gelding and carried it to Ditchley House. And he says that Dimock consented to the killing of the deer and at that time was either in the park or at the park wall. (mark of) William Todman.
Recognisance: William Todman binds himself in £40 to present his case at the next assizes.

[f245v]

534:2/3 *Examination of Robert Dimock*, at the same court. He denies he was either present at the killing of the deer, or consented thereunto, or was privy to bringing it to Sir H. Lee's house, nor did he at any time see it. Although he knew who did hunt and kill the deer and that it was brought into Lee's house, and heard speeches in the house that there was a deer stolen, and heard Mr Richard Mowlesworth and Mr Bennett Harecourt say they had killed a deer, yet where or how he did not know.

(mark of) Robert Dimock. (signed by) mayor.

534:3/3 *Committal* 19 December 1612:
Thomas Jeames, parson of Wootton and Francis Collingwood each
go surety in £40 and Robert Dimock binds himself in £80 to appear at the next quarter sessions at Oxon'.

[f246]

Portmoot court held 21 December 1612...
Actions continuing: **303**:52/53; **444**:20/21; **464**:16/17; **478**:13/14; **479**:13/14; **483**:12/13; **501**:6/7; **503**:6/7; **504**:6/7; **515**:5/6.

[f246v]

Actions of debt:
493:8/9 Fawler vs Shurley - executed *alias scire facias* against plaintiff's surety returned, execution of action granted.
525:2/13 Browne vs Mackereth - continued by assent of plaintiff.
535:1/29+ John Child gent vs Ralph Shurley - plaintiff declares through his attorney Simon James, with copy; day to imparl granted defendant in next court.
536:1/8 Thomas Browne vs Christopher Hiorne - similarly.
Action of trespass:
526:2/3 Symons vs Parsons - peremptory day to respond.
Actions of trespass on case:
531:2/7 White vs Coleman - plaintiff declares with day to amend in next court.

[97] See *VCH, Oxon* xii, 425.

533:2/2 Coles vs Flexnye - referred to the judgment of aforesaid mayor and Edmund Hiorne.
537:1/16 Stephen Townsend vs Ralph Shurly - plaintiff declares through attorney Simon James, with copy; defendant granted day to imparl in next court.

[f247]

Actions of debt:
502:6/10 John Jarvis vs John Stone - the jury between parties:

Richard Meades,	John Lowe,	John Bradshewe,
William Meatcalfe,	William Edwards,	Robert Ducock,
George Noble,	Robert Spitle,	Richard Hawkins,
Thomas Gee,	William Hickes senior,	Richard Shadd

find for the plaintiff and assess damages of 12d and amercement 2d; with judgment adjourned to next court.
511:5/8 Thomas Willis vs John Cooke - the jury between parties:

Nicholas Taylor,	Robert Bignill,	William Edwards,
Robert Spitle,	Alexander Head,	Richard Hawkins,
Thomas Gee,	William Hickes senior,	William Hickes junior,
Richard Shadd,	John Ackley,	Hugh Hamond

find for the plaintiff and assess damages at ld and amercement 2d; with judgment in next court.

[f247v]

538:1/3 **Examination 22 December 1612 before John Glover mayor, and Thomas Browne and Thomas Bradshewe justices.**
Thomas Basly, butcher of Deddington, Oxon, denies knowing either Nicholas Haynes or Richard Galloway of Hanborough ('Handboughrough'), yet knows Ralph Cox of that place. About three weeks before martlemas last Cox came to his house at Deddington about nine o'clock on a Monday morning and brought him to Deddington bridge between Duns Tew ('Dunstewe') and Deddington where he found two men with two beasts and a bull: one was a big set man with a black head and beard, and the other was a big lubberly (i.e. clumsy) fellow with little hair on his face.
Cox told him that the two men, his neighbours, would sell him the beasts: one being a lean branded heifer, the other a black cow with a white flank, and a little red bull. These they said they brought from a common in Northamptonshire, but he did not know when. As he found the cattle lean and not to his turn (i.e. purpose) he did not ask the price of them, but left them without knowing whether they went with the cattle.

[f248]

He denies stealing or consenting to the stealing of the two beasts or bull, or killing any of them. But he confesses that about a fortnight ago on a Friday Cox brought six wether sheep to Deddington downs, and sent Richard Barrett

of Deddington to fetch him to the downs to buy the sheep. Cox told him he brought them from his brother Burnett out of Northamptonshire, and he thinks they were marked with a 'W'and 'P'. Ahout 10 o'clock that day he went to the downs and bought the six sheep from Cox for 2s6d each, in the presence of Barrett, paying him 3s then and the other 12s a fortnight later to Cox and his wife at Woodstock market.
He denies knowing or persuading himself they were stolen, but now thinks they were. Further Thomas Cox his neighbour and brother of Ralph Cox, told him that about a fortnight before Michaelmas last Ralph had a dozen sheep which Basly should have bought if he had been at home. Of these Ralph drove 11 to the said Burnett and the other he gave to brother Thomas.

(signed by) Thomas Baslie.

[f248v]

538:2/3 *Committal*, 23 December 1612 before John Glover mayor.
Thomas Basley binds himself in £80, with Robert Bignill baker of Woodstock and William Tustian carrier of Deddington each surety in £40, that Basley will appear at the next general gaol delivery held in the aforesaid county and make his case and receive judgment.

539. Corporation moneys.

Remaining with Mr mayor in ready money 56s8d; delivered out of this 20d, remaining 55s.

538:3/3 *Recognisances*:
Robert Bignill delivered to the said Basly and Tustian and to Thomas Cox of Deddington 6d apiece; they severally assumed ('*assumpsit*') under pain of £40 apiece to save Robert Bignill harmless of and from the aforesaid recognisances.
Also the said parties received 6d apiece of Mr. mayor by way of assumption of £10 apiece to deliver Thomas Basly's horse now delivered to him, or 40s in money at the choice of the mayor and commonalty of Woodstock within three days next after the eviction (i.e. legal recovery) of Basley upon the exaction aforesaid or otherwise.

[f249]

Portmoot court held 11 January 1613...

Action of debt:
483:13/13 Dennett vs Shurley - *habeas corpora* granted in next court.
Actions continuing: **303**:53/53; **444**:21/21; **464**:17/17 ; **478**:14/14;**479**:14/14; **501**:7/7; **503**:7/7.

[f249v]

Actions continuing: **515**:6/6; **493**:9/9; **525**:3/13; **526**:3/3.
Actions of debt:
502:7/10 Jarvis vs Stone - the court adjudges plaintiff should recover [blank] debt, and [blank] amercement; scire facias granted against defendant's surety.

511:6/8 Willis vs Cooke - similarly.
535:2/29+ Child vs Shurley - peremptory day to respond.
536:2/8 Browne vs Hiorne - similarly.
Actions of trespass on case:
531:3/7 White vs Coleman - plaintiff completes declaration with copy; day to imparl granted.
537:2/16 Townsend vs Shurley - peremptory day to respond.
Action of account:
504:7/7 Cooke vs Harris - similarly.

[f250]

Actions of debt:
540:1/8 William Hitch vs Richard Coles - plaintiff declares with copy; day to imparl granted.
541:1/1 Ralph Shurley vs Richard Ryly - similarly.
Action of trespass on case:
542:1/1 Ralph Shurley vs Richard Ryly - similarly.

[f250v]

Portmoot court held 22 January 1613[98]
Actions of debt:
502:8/10 Jarvis vs Stone - *alias scire facias* granted.
511:7/8 Willis vs Cooke - similarly.
535:3/29+ Child vs Shurley - defendant does not appear or instruct attorney. Therefore etc..
536:3/8 Browne vs Hiorne - since defendant does not appear therefore judgment that *scire facias* granted.
540:2/8 Hitch vs Coles - second privilege day granted.
Action of trespass on case:
537:3/16 Townsend vs Shurley - defendant does not appear or instruct attorney; therefore writ of inquiry for damages granted.
Actions unspecified:
543:1/24 [blank] Capp vs [blank] Fawler - declaration, day to amend.[99]
544:1/1 Reade vs Coles.
Actions continuing: **525**:4/13; **531**:4/7.

[f251]

Portmoot court held 8 February 1613...
Actions of debt:
502:9/10 Jarvis vs Stone - execution granted against defendant and surety.
511:8/8 Willis vs Cooke - similarly.
536:4/8 Browne vs Hiorne - *alias scire facias* granted.

[98] Date given is a Friday, an error? Month 'February' deleted.
[99] Note also Action **563.**

540:3/8 Hitch vs Coles - final privilege day.
Action of trespass on case:
531:5/7 White vs Coleman - defendant responds and wages law, with copy granted.
Actions unspecified:
543:2/24 Capp vs Fawler - peremptory day to respond.
545:1/2 [blank] Kite vs [blank] Rudgate - day given to declare.[100]
546:1/3 [blank] Meades and [blank]Williams vs [blank] Garter – plaintiffs declare and copy granted.
Actions continuing: **525**:5/13; **535**:4/29+; **537**:4/16.

[f251v]

547:1/2 Examination 31 January 1613 before John Glover mayor and Thomas Browne and Thomas Bradshewe justices.
Ellis Olliver alias Gardner of Hook Norton ('Hoocknorton'), Oxon., was examined whether he was in company with, or consented to hunting with, greyhounds in the king's park at Woodstock, or killing any deer there at night on Christmas eve last. He denies hunting or killing deer there either on that or any other occasion, or hearing any speeches of such things. He also says that John Craddock, late servant to Mr Chadwell, last Christmas day had a pied greyhound which Thomas Varny the keeper there thought in his conscience was the pied dog that killed the deer on Christmas eve at Woodstock. Also the said Craddock flew out of his house when the keepers came to search for him.

(mark of) Ellis Oliver.

547:2/2 Recognisance. Thomas Varny binds himself in £40 to present the case.

[f252]

Portmoot court held 22 February 1613...
Actions of debt:
502:10/10 Jarvis vs Stone - execution of action returned executed.
536:5/8 Browne vs Hiorne - execution of action granted against defendant and his surety.
540:4/8 Hitch vs Coles - peremptory day to respond.
548:1/5 William Jennings vs John Harris - plaintiff declares with day to amend.
549:1/3 Randall Richards vs William Raunson } plaintiff declares, day to amend.
Action of detinue:
550:1/4 Randall Richards vs William Raunson } plaintiff declares, day to amend.
Actions of trespass on case:
531:6/7 White vs Coleman - day given defendant to wage law with four hands.

[100] Note also Action **603.**

551:1/22 Richard Read vs George Stowte - day to make case granted in next court.
Actions unspecified:
543:3/24 Capp vs Fawler - defendant demurrs, and Edmund Ryly for plaintiff mainprises payment of 16s7d to the plaintiff at next court, and then plaintiff is non-suited. Therefore etc.[101]
545:2/2 Kite vs Rudgate - discharged.
Actions continuing: **525**:6/13; **535**:5/29+; **537**:5/16; **546**:2/3.

[f252v]

552:1/3 **Information, 23 February 1613 before John Glover mayor and Thomas Browne JP.**
Margaret Hatten widow of Kidlington, Oxon, says on oath that being in Woodstock market today, Tuesday, she saw one Lewis Floyed come to Richard House of Water Eaton in the pease (pea) market there and viewed him and looked upon his pocket. He put his hand in House's pocket and took out a purse which he carried away about an acre's breadth;[102] but she and House followed him and caused him to be stayed.
Recognisances: She entered recognisance in £40 to give evidence. Richard House recognisance in £40 to prosecute etc., Edward Collier of North Leigh ('Northly') miller, recognisance £40.
552:2/3 *Examination of Lewis Floyde* of Llanfairwaterdine ('Hanver Water deane'), County Salop, tailor.
He says he came from thence about three weeks ago, with his wife, only to sell pedlary ware only in one part. He was married there and his wife was the daughter of John apMorgan, chapman. He says he came from Abingdon ('Abbington') fair yesterday to this market only to sell small wares. He denies taking the purse out of House's pocket according to the information aforesaid.

[f253]

552:3/3 *Information* of the said House.
He says on oath that he brought his purse with a key to it and 8s 4½d in it whereof one piece was a 13½d.[103] When Margaret Hatten told him his purse was gone and who had it, he put his hand in his pocket and found it gone. Presently it was found in the market in the place where Lewis Flyde was taken and held up by one Edward Collier, miller, and being looked into it was found agreeable.

forfeits:	Received of the said Floyd	5sld
	Received of his wife's purse	4s

[101] Some uncertainty here as there are two undecipherable words.
[102] Acre's breadth = 4poles = 22yards.
[103] A silver coin called the mark-piece was current within the united kingdom of James I at the value of 13½ d sterling.

Received 2 purses with 3 keys and a little pair of scissors.
Received a box with divers wares, the key remaining with Mr mayor and the box with George Noble constable.

[f253v]

Portmoot court held 8 March 1613...

Actions of debt:

540:5/8 Hitch vs Coles - attorney not instructed and does not respond for defendant, therefore judgment adjourned to next court.

548:2/5 Jennings vs Harris - copy of declaration granted to defendant.

Action of detinue:

550:2/4 Richards vs Raunson - second privilege day granted.

Unspecified action:

546:3/3 Meades and Williams vs Garter - discharged.

Actions continuing: **525**:7/13; **535**:6/29+; **536**:6/8; **537**:6/16; **543**:4/24; **551**:2/22.

[f254]

Action of trespass:

553:1/10 Edward Coleman vs William White - day to declare in next court.

Actions of trespass on case:

531:7/7 White vs Coleman - defendant wages law with six hands: John Meade, Thomas Gome, John Cave, Robert Hitchman, Thomas Turner and Gregory Boult, and he goes quit.

554:1/10 John Cooke and Joan his wife vs Richard Martine - defendant(sic) declares with day to amend in next court.

Action of detinue:

555:1/3 William Raunson vs Randall Richards - day to declare in next court.

[f254v]

Portmoot court held 22 March 1613...

Actions of debt:

540:6/8 Hitch vs Coles - court rules that plaintiff should recover 17s for debt and [blank] amercement; and *scire facias* granted against defendant's surety.

548:3/5 Jennings vs Harris - peremptory day to respond.

Actions continuing: **525**:8/13; **535**:7/29+; **536**:7/8; **537**:7/16; **549**:2/3; **550**:3/4; **551**:3/22.

[f255]

Action of debt:

556:1/7 Jerome Kite vs Robert Winter - plaintiff requests day to declare in next court.

Actions of trespass:

553:2/10 Coleman vs White - plaintiff declares, with day to amend in next court.

557:1/4 John Cooke vs Richard Martine - similarly.

Actions of trespass on case:
554:2/10 Cooke vs Martine - plaintiffs complete declaration, copy granted.
558:1/5 George Spencer esquire vs Stephen Townsend - day to declare granted plaintiff.
Unspecified action:
543:5/24 Capp vs Fawler - remains as before on payment of amercement.
Action continuing: **555**:2/3.

[f255v]

Portmoot court held 29 March 1613…
Actions of debt:
540:7/8 Hitch vs Coles - *alias scire facias* granted.
548:4/5 Jennings vs Harris - defendant responds by waging law, day given to wage law with six hands.
549:3/3 Richards vs Raunson - discharged.
Actions of detinue:
550:4/4 Richards vs Raunson - discharged.
555:3/3 Raunson vs Richards -– discharged.
Actions continuing: **525**:9/13; **535**:8/29+; **536**:8/8; **537**:8/16; **543**:6/24; **551**:4/22.

[f256]

Actions of debt:
556:2/7 Kyte vs Winter - plaintiff declares; first privilege day to defendant.
559:1/1 John Kinge and Robert Dimock vs John Cooke - referred to arbitration. Discharged.
560:1/18 Robert Hall vs John Wilkinson - declaration with copy.
Actions of trespass:
553:3/10 Coleman vs White - copy of declaration granted.
557:2/4 Cooke vs Martine - plaintiff completes declaration and copy granted.
Actions of trespass on case:
554:3/10 Cooke vs Martine - peremptory day to respond.
561:1/1 John Cooke vs John King - referred to arbitration. Discharged.
562:1/1 Robert Dimock vs John Cooke - similarly.
563:1/19 Maurice Capp and Ann his wife vs John Fawler - day to declare.
Action continuing: **558**:2/5.

[f256v]

564 View of Frankpledge and Sessions of the Peace held 31 March 1613 before John Glover mayor and Jerome Kite, Thomas Browne and Thomas Bradshewe JPs.
Officers: (as before).
Jury for the crown:

John Dubber,	Nicholas Taylor,	Jerome White,
Robert Bignill,	Thomas Screevin,	Thomas Williams,

John Bradshewe,	William Edwards,	George Noble,
Richard Shadd,	Hugh Hamond,	John Norman,
Robert Spitle,	William Raunson,	John Ackley: sworn in.

Affeerers: John Bradshewe, Richard Shadd, John Norman, William Raunson: sworn in.

[f257 & 257v] (Blank)

[f258]

Portmoot court held 12 April 1613…

Action of debt:

540:8/8 Hitch vs Coles - executed *sicut alias scire facias* returned, defendant is committed to sergeant in execution of judgment.

Action of trespass:

557:3/4 Cooke vs Martine - Court will rule on accepting response of foreign plea.[104]

Action of trespass on case:

554:4/10 Cooke vs Martine - defendant pleads a demurrer, and is enjoined by plaintiffs.

Unspecified action:

543:7/24 Capp vs Fawler - continues for amercement.

Actions continuing: **525**:10/13; **535**:9/29+; **537**:9/16; **551**:5/22.

[f258v]

Actions of debt:

560:2/18 Hall vs Wilkinson - peremptory day to respond.

565:1/7 Richard Hawten gent vs Edmund Abbott - plaintiff declares and copy granted.

566:1/1 Robert Ducock vs Edmund Abbott - similarly, with day to amend in next court.

567:1/1 Thomas Williams vs Edmund Abbott - similarly.

568:1/3 Robert Bincks vs Edmund Abbott - similarly.

Action of trespass:

553:4/10 Coleman vs White - peremptory day to respond.

Actions of trespass on case:

563:2/19 Maurice and Ann Capp vs John Fawler - plaintiffs declare with day to amend in next court.

569:1/11 Michael Pulchoe and Ann his wife vs George Barnesey - plaintiffs declare with copy granted.

104 Foreign plea: plea that the action is outside this court's jurisdiction.

Actions continuing: **556**:3/7; **558**:3/5.

[f259]

Actions of debt:
548:5/5 Jennings vs Harris - defendant appears in person and wages law with six hands, namely John Saunders, William Higgins, Edmund Baylies, John Dolton, James Singleton and Robert Joyner; and he goes quit.
570:1/19 Henry Baylies vs Thomas Paynter - plaintiff declares with copy; first privilege day for defendant.
571:1/19 Mary Keene vs Thomas Paynter - similarly.
572:1/19 John Glover vs Thomas Paynter - similarly.
573:1/19 Thomas Browne alderman vs Thomas Paynter - similarly.
574:1/19 Richard Baker vs Thomas Paynter - similarly.
575:1/1 Joseph Harris vs Matthew Parrott - discharged.
576:1/1 William Jennings vs James Singleton - plaintiff declares; defendant personally acknowledges debt of 4s and is committed to sergeant.
577:1/9 William Webb vs Richard Harris - plaintiff declares; defendant responds through his attorney, and court gives him day to wage law with six hands.
Action of trespass:
578:1/10 John Whitton vs Robert Symons - plaintiff declares, with day to amend in next court.

[f259v]

Portmoot court held 26 April 1613…
Actions of trespass:
553:5/10 Coleman vs White - further day to respond.
557:4/4 Cooke vs Martine - defendant in person swears his foreign plea is true; therefore he goes quit.
Action of trespass on case:
554:5/10 Cooke vs Martine - remains on demurrer.
Actions continuing: **525**:11/13; **535**:10/29+; **537**:10/16; **543**:8/24; **551**:6/22; **556**:4/7; **558**:4/5.

[f260]

Actions of debt:
560:3/18 Hall vs Wilkinson - since defendant does not respond judgment adjourned to next court.
565:2/7 Hawten vs Abbott - peremptory day to respond.
570:2/19 Baylies vs Painter- second privilege day granted to defendant.
571:2/19 Keene vs Painter - similarly.
572:2/19 Glover vs Painter - similarly.
573:2/19 Browne vs Painter - similarly.
574:2/19 Baker vs Painter - similarly.
579:1/18 Henry Colesborne vs Thomas Painter - plaintiff declares, first privilege day granted.

580:1/6 William Daby vs George Holloway - plaintiff declares and grants copy.

Action of trespass:

578:2/10 Whitton vs Symons - plaintiff completes declaration and copy granted.

Actions of trespass on case:

563:3/19 Capp and his wife vs Fawler - similarly.

569:2/11 Pulchoe vs Barnesey - peremptory day to respond.

Actions continuing: **568**:2/3; **577**:2/9.

[f260v]

Portmoot court held 10 May 1613...

Action of trespass:

553:6/10 Coleman vs White - further day to respond.

Actions of trespass on case:

537:11/16 Townsend vs Shurley - writ of inquiry into damages granted plaintiff for return in next court.

563:4/19 Capp vs Fawler - defendant pleads a demurrer, with copy for plaintiffs.

Actions continuing: **525**:12/13; **535**:11/29+; **543**:9/24; **551**:7/22; **554**:6/10; **556**:5/7; **558**:5/5; **569**:3/11.

[f261]

Actions of debt:

565:3/7 Hawten vs Abbott - defendant does not appear after three summonses and judgment adjourned to next court.

570:3/19 Baylies vs Painter - final privilege day granted to defendant.

571:3/19 Keene vs Painter - similarly.

572:3/19 Glover vs Painter - similarly.

573:3/19 Browne vs Painter - similarly.

574:3/19 Baker vs Painter - similarly.

579:2/18 Colesborne vs Painter - second privilege day.

580:2/6 Dabie vs Holloway - peremptory day to respond.

Action of trespass:

578:3/10 Whitton vs Symons - similarly.

Action of trespass on case:

581:1/8 John Hiorne vs Esau Brent alias Brunte - day to declare granted in next court.

Actions continuing: **560**:4/18; **568**:3/3; **577**:3/9.

[f261v]

Portmoot court held 17 May 1613...

Action of debt:

525:13/13 Browne vs Mackereth - discharged.

Action of trespass on case:
537:12/16 Townsend vs Shurley - the jury of

Nicholas Taylor,	Thomas Screevin,	Richard Hawkins,
Hugh Hamond,	John Ackley,	Randall Richards,
George Noble,	Richard Browne,	William Butterfeild,
William Archer,	Richard Wright,	Thomas Webb

assess damages at £5:12d. Therefore court awards £5:12d damages and [blank] amercement; and *scire facias* granted against defendant and his surety.
Actions continuing: **535**:12/29+; **543**:10/24; **551**:8/22; **554**:7/10.

[f262]

Actions of debt:
565:4/7 Hawten vs Abbott - judgment grants £4:10s for debt, [blank] amercement, and [blank] damages; *scire facias* against defendant's surety.
570:4/19 Baylies vs Painter - peremptory day to respond granted.
571:4/19 Keene vs Painter - peremptory day to respond granted to defendant.
572:4/19 Glover vs Painter - similarly.
573:4/19 Browne vs Painter - similarly.
574:4/19 Baker vs Painter - similarly.
579:3/18 Colesborne vs Painter - third privilege day granted.
580:3/6 Daby vs Holloway - since defendant does not respond therefore no plea entered.
Actions of trespass:
553:7/10 Coleman vs White - further peremptory day.
578:4/10 Whitton vs Symons - defendant responds not guilty; copy granted.
Actions of trespass on case:
563:5/19 Capp vs Fawler - continues on demurrer.
581:2/8 Hiorne vs Brent - plaintiff puts declaration with day to amend form thereof in next court.
582:1/7 Phillip Sellenger vs Christopher Easte - plaintiff declares, and copy granted.
Actions continuing: **556**:6/7; **560**:5/18; **569**:4/11; **577**:4/9.

[f262v]

583:1/3 **Informations, 29 May 1613 before John Glover mayor, and Jerome Kite and Thomas Browne JPs.**
Elizabeth Smith upon oath says that about 3 weeks since she heard Jane Bradshewe, daughter of alderman Bradshewe, say to widow Coles of Woodstock 'Good day goodwife Coles'; and widow Coles replied 'Why do you say to me good day goodwife Coles, for your father cannot abide me? But it is no matter, he will prosper never the better for it'. (Mark of) Elizabeth Smith.
583:2/3 *Same court, information of Jane Bradshewe on oath.* She says that at the foresaid time goodwife Coles said to her 'Do you call me goodwife Coles: your father cannot abide me, but he prospers never the better, nor will not'.

Since that time (crossed through). And presently after her father fell sick and has ever since languished, and now lieth lame on his limbs and is not able to turn himself in his bed without great help. (Signed by) Jane Brashow.

[f263]

583:3/3 *Same court, same day. Examination of Joyce Coles* widow taken and examined upon suspicion of felony for witchcraft.[105]

[f263v] (Blank)

[f264]

Portmoot court held 31 May 1613...

Actions of debt:

556:7/7 Kite vs Winter - discharged by assent of plaintiff.

565:5/7 Hawten vs Abbott - executed *scire facias* returned and *alias scire facias* granted.

Action of trespass:

553:8/10 Coleman vs White - further peremptory day.

Actions of trespass on case:

537:13/16 Townsend vs Shurley - executed *scire facias* returned and *alias scire facias* granted.

563:6/19 Capp vs Fawler - court will advise on demurrer.

Actions continuing: **535**:13/29+; **543**:11/24; **551**:9/22; **554**:8/10; **569**:5/11.

[f264v]

Actions of debt:

570:5/19 Baylies vs Paynter - defendant responds no debt in the manner and form of the action, and puts himself on country; therefore *venire facias*.

571:5/19 Keene vs Painter - defendant does not respond to three summonses. Judgment adjourned to next court.

572:5/19 Glover vs Painter - similarly.

573:5/19 Browne vs Painter - similarly.

574:5/19 Baker vs Paynter - defendant responds, copy granted.

579:4/18 Colesborne vs Paynter - peremptory day to respond.

584:1/15 Francis Gregory esq., executor of the will of his father John Gregory, deceased vs Paynter - plaintiff declares and copy granted.

580:4/6 Daby vs Holloway - since defendant did not respond in last court, judgment of *scire facias* granted.

585:1/3 Thomas Browne vs William Abbott - declaration with copy.

Action of trespass:

578:5/10 Whitton vs Symons - defendant pleads not guilty and court will advise on trial of action.

105 Thomas Bradshewe died 4 days later on 2 June 1613; MS.Wills Oxon 195:148; 4/3/17. For notes on Coles' imprisonment, and her burial before December 1613, see *WCA*, 46, 47.

Actions of trespass on case:
581:3/8 Hiorne vs Brent - declaration completed with copy.
582:2/7 Sellenger vs Easte - peremptory day to respond.
Actions continuing: **560**:6/18; **577**:5/9.

[f265]

Conveyance:
586:1/4 8 June 1613 before John Glover mayor.
Order: Joan Collingwood widow, John Collingwood and wife Mary that justly etc. they keep the agreement with Richard Pyman concerning six messuages and one close with appurtenances in the borough now separately tenanted by the said Joan, Edward Longe, Elizabeth Bowland widow, William Hickes and William Wheeler. And if they do not do so etc.
And the concord is such that the said Joan, John & Mary acknowledge the said tenements with appurtenances to be the right of the same Richard Pyman as those which Richard has of the gift of the said Joan, John & Mary and remit and quitclaim them for the same Joan, John & Mary and their heirs to the said Richard Pyman and his heirs in perpetuity. And in addition the same Joan, John & Mary concede for themselves and their heirs that they will warrant the said tenements with appurtenances to the said Richard Pyman and his heirs against the said Joan, John & Mary and their heirs in perpetuity. And for this fine etc.[106]
(signed) John Collingwood, mayor and town clerk;
(marks) Joan & Mary Collingwood. First proclamation 19 July 1613.

[f265v]

Portmoot court held 14 June 1613...
Action of debt:
565:6/7 Hawten vs Abbott - executed *alias scire facias* returned and execution of judgment granted.
Actions of trespass on case:
537:14/16 Townsend vs Shurley - similarly.
569:6/11 Pulchoe vs Barnesey - further peremptory day granted.
563:7/19 Capp vs Fawler - continues on advice.
Actions continuing: **535:**14/29+; **543**:12/24; **551**:10/22; **553**:9/10; **554**:9/10.

[f266]

Actions of debt:
570:6/19 Baylies vs Paynter - *venire facias* granted.
571:6/19 Keene vs Painter - judgment to grant execution of action adjourned.
572:6/19 Glover vs Painter - similarly.
573:6/19 Browne vs Painter - similarly.
574:6/19 Baker vs Paynter - plaintiff puts demurrer, day given defendant to imparl.

106 See also *WCA*, 44.

579:5/18 Colesborne vs Paynter - defendant responds no debt in manner and form of action; both parties put themselves on country.
584:2/15 Gregory vs Paynter - second privilege day granted.
580:5/6 Daby vs Holloway - *alias scire facias* granted for return in next court.
585:2/3 Browne vs Abbott - peremptory day to respond granted.
587:1/16+ John Craker vs Robert Winter - plaintiff declares; copy to defendant.
Actions of trespass on case:
581:4/8 Hiorne vs Brente - peremptory day to respond.
582:3/7 Sellenger vs Easte - defendant responds not guilty and both parties put themselves on country; *venire facias* granted.
Actions continuing: **560**:7/18; **577**:6/9; **578**:6/10.

[f266v]

Portmoot court held 28 June 1613...
Actions of debt:
565:7/7 Hawten vs Abbott - remains on execution of judgment as previously; discharged by assent of plaintiff.
570:7/19 Baylies vs Painter - *venire facias* granted in next court.
588:1/4 John Archer vs Robert Bignill - plaintiff declares and defendant requests copy; defendant proffers in this court 6s without amercement, and plaintiff does not accept.
Action of trespass on case:
569:7/11 Pulchoe vs Barnesey - defendant responds not guilty and both parties put themselves on country; *venire facias* granted.
Actions continuing: **535**:15/29+; **537**:15/16; **543**:13/24; **551**:11/22; **553**:10/10; **554**:10/10; **563**:8/19; **578**:7/10.

[f267]

Actions of debt:
571:7/19 Keene vs Painter - remains on execution of judgment.
572:7/19 Glover vs Painter - similarly.
573:7/19 Browne vs Painter - similarly.
574:7/19 Baker vs Paynter - plaintiff submits to imparlance in answer to aforesaid plea; day given to hear judgment in next court on advice of recorder of borough.
579:6/18 Colesborne vs Paynter - executed *venire facias* returned and *habeas corpora* granted.
584:3/15 Gregory vs Paynter - final privilege day granted.
580:6/6 Dabye vs Holloway - executed *alias scire facias* returned and execution of judgment granted against defendant and his surety. Discharged.
585:3/3 Browne vs Abbott - defendant's attorney acknowledges the debt, therefore etc.. Discharged.

589:1/7 Edmund Meese esq. vs Edward Stacy - plaintiff declares, copy to defendant.
Actions of trespass on case:
581:5/8 Hiorne vs Brent - defendant does not respond after three summonses; therefore writ of inquiry for damages granted for return in next court.
582:4/7 Sellenger vs Easte - executed *venire facias* returned and *habeas corpora* granted.
590:1/12 Tobias Brooke vs Robert Bincks - day to declare granted in next court.
Actions continuing: **560**:8/18; **577**:7/9; **587**:2/16+.

[f267v]

Action of trespass and ejectment:
591:1/4 Thomas Rayer vs Alice Barnes widow - plaintiff declares, with day to amend in next court.

[f268]

Portmoot court held 5 July 1613...
Actions of debt:
570:8/19 Baylies vs Paynter - executed *venire facias* returned and *habeas corpora* granted.
574:8/19 Baker vs Paynter - day given for hearing in next court.
579:7/18 Colesborne vs Paynter - continues on *habeas corpora*.
584:4/15 Gregory vs Paynter - since defendant does not respond after three summonses, therefore etc.. Judgment is adjourned to next court.
588:2/4 Archer vs Bignill - second privilege day granted.
Action of trespass on case:
569:8/11 Pulchoe vs Barnesey - continues on *venire facias*.
Actions continuing: **535**:16/29+; **537**:16/16; **543**:14/24; **551**:12/22;**563**:9/19; **571**:8/19; **572**:8/19; **573**:8/19; **577**:8/9; **578**:8/10.

[f268v]

Action of debt:
589:2/7 Meese vs Stacy - peremptory day to respond granted.
Actions of trespass on case:
582:5/7 Sellenger vs Easte - *habeas corpora* renewed.
590:2/12 Brookes vs Bincks - declaration completed, with copy.
Action of trespass and ejectment:
591:2/4 Rayer vs Barnes - peremptory day to respond.
Actions continuing: **560**:9/18; **581**:6/8; **587**:3/16+.

[f269]

Portmoot court held 19 July 1613...
Actions of debt:
588:3/4 Archer vs Bignill - defendant responds and wages law with six hands in next court.

571:9/19 Keene vs Painter - *fieri facias* granted against goods of defendant.
572:9/19 Glover vs Painter - similarly.
573:9/19 Browne vs Painter - similarly.
Actions continuing: **535**:17/29+; **543**:15/24; **551**:13/22; **563**:10/19; **569**:9/11; **578**:9/10.

[f269v]

Actions of debt:
574:9/19 Baker vs Painter - on this appointed day the two parties, through their attorneys, came to read, hear, and understand the aforesaid plea.[107] For himself Thomas Painter previously pleaded the written bonds to have unreasonable conditions,[108] which is seen by this court as a plea insufficient in law to quash and void the said written bonds. Therefore it is adjudged that Richard Baker should recover against Thomas Painter his debts aforesaid and his damages for the action of detaining those debts to him -- With the assent of Richard this court decrees Thomas to be in the wrong, and grants *fieri facias* against his goods.
584:5/15 Gregory vs Painter - court rules plaintiff should recover his debts of [blank], and [blank] fines; and *fieri facias* granted against goods of defendant.
577:9/9 Webb vs Harris, continues - Discharged.
Action of trespass on case:
582:6/7 Sellenger vs Easte - writ of *habeas corpora* renewed.
Actions continuing: **560**:10/18; **581**:7/8; **587**:4/16+; **590**:3/12.

[f270]

Actions of debt:
579:8/18 Henry Colesborne vs Thomas Painter - the jury between them:

Nicholas Taylor,	Jerome White,	Robert Bignill,
John Lowe,	Thomas Screevine,	John Bradshewe,
William Edwards,	Alexander Head,	Richard Hawkins,
Richard Shadd,	Ralph Durbridge,	William Hickes junior,

find for the plaintiff for 50s debt, 3s4d damages and 2d amercement.
589:3/7 Meese vs Stacye - defendant does not appear after three summonses; therefore etc.. Judgment adjourned to next court.
592:1/2 Thomas Slaymaker vs Ralph Durbridge - plaintiff declares, with day to amend in next court.
Action of trespass and ejectment:
591:3/4 Rayer vs Barnes - defendant responds not guilty and puts herself on country.

107 Text reads '. venant... lecto, audito et intellecto pl(ac)ito'.
108 Text reads 'incausacoem' (i.e. 'incassacoem') scripti obligator'.

Conveyance:
586:2/4 First proclamation between Richard Pyman querent and Joan Collingwood widow and John & Mary Collingwood deforciants....

[f270v]

Action of debt:
570:9/19 Henry Baylies vs Thomas Painter - the jury between them:

Richard Meades,	Nicholas Taylor,	Jerome White,
John Bradshewe,	Richard Hawkins,	Richard Shadd,
Hugh Hamond,	John Ackley,	Robert Spitle,
George Noble,	Thomas Bruce,	William Butterfeild

finds for plaintiff for debts of 3s4d, and assesses damages at ld and amercement 2d.
Land claim:
593:At this court William Edwards came in person and made claim to one messuage or tenement and one garden with appurtenances within the borough, now occupied by Alice Barnes widow, as being the right of himself William Edwards.[109]

[f271]

594 Examination 23 July 1613 before John Glover mayor and Thomas Browne JP.
Gilbert alias Robert alias Cupit Bickton vintner of the sign of the Bell, St Margaret's in Westminster says that he and one Christopher Bird vintner, of the same house, came to the George in Woodstock on Wednesday night last and continued there, all day together, on Thursday. That night one William Wheeler, carpenter of Woodstock, offered to strike him with his rule whereupon he drew his rapier. And Wheeler ran upon his rapier and hurt himself in the left thigh about 6 inches in one place before and in another place in the same thigh about 5 inches he was hurt behind; but how Wheeler was hurt he does not know.

[f271v]

Portmoot court held 2 August 1613
Action of debt:
588:4/4 Archer vs Bignill - defendant will wage law with six hands. Discharged by assent of both parties.
Action of trespass on case:
582:7/7 Sellenger vs Easte - defendant produces a royal writ of *habeas corpus* dated 23 June 1613 for return *coram domino rege* at Westminster on the Saturday next after the octave of Michaelmas.
Actions continuing: **535**:18/29+; **543**:16/24; **551**:14/22; **563**:11/19; **569**:10/11; **578**:10/10.

[109] Note also action **591.**

[f272]

Actions of debt:
589:4/7 Meese vs Stacy - court rules plaintiff should recover [blank] for debt and [blank] amercement, with *scire facias* granted.
592:2/2 Slaymaker vs Durbridge - plaintiff completes declaration. Discharged.
Actions continuing: **560**:11/18; **571**:10/19; **572**:10/19; **573**:10/19; **574**:10/19; **581**:8/8; **584**:6/15; **587**:5/16; **590**:4/12; **591**:4/4.
Conveyance:
586:3/4 Second proclamation between Pyman querent and Collingwoods deforciants etc..

[f272v]

Actions of debt:
579:9/18 Colesborne vs Paynter - court rules that plaintiff should recover [blank] debt and [blank] amercement: *fieri facias* granted against defendant's goods.
570:10/19 Baylies vs Paynter - similarly.
595:1/1 Phillip Sellenger vs Christopher Easte - plaintiff declares; discharged.
596:1/2 Abraham Millen vs Edward Stacye - plaintiff declares and copy granted to defendant.

[f273]

Recognisances, 25 July 1613 before John Glover mayor.
597 Robert Sorby vintner of the city of Westminster binds himself in £40.[110] Edward Bassett gent of Dunham, Nottinghamshire, and William Todman park-keeper of Woodstock each binds himself in £20, on condition that the said Robert Sorby appears in person at the next borough sessions to make his case and receive judgment.
598:1/2 Phillip Hawthorne recognisance of £40.
599:1/2 Mary Abbott recognisance of £40.

[f273v]

Portmoot court held 23 August 1613…
Actions of debt:
570:11/19 Baylies vs Painter - *fieri facias* granted against defendant's goods and chattels.
571:11/19 Keene vs Painter - similarly.
572:11/19 Glover vs Painter - similarly.
573:11/19 Browne vs Painter - similarly.
574:11/19 Baker vs Painter - similarly.
579:10/18 Colesborne vs Painter - similarly.
584:7/15 Gregory vs Painter - similarly.

110 Possibly relating to examination **594**, under another alias?

Action of trespass on case:
590:5/12 Brookes vs Bincks - defendant responds *non-assumpsit* to manner and form of the action and puts himself on country; therefore *venire facias* granted.
Actions continuing: **535**:19/29+; **543**:17/24; **551**:15/22; **560**:12/18; **563**:12/19; **569**:11/11; **587**:6/16+.

[f274]

Actions of debt:
589:5/7 Meese vs Stacye - executed *scire facias* returned and *alias scire facias* granted.
596:2/2 Millen vs Stacye - peremptory day for defendant to respond.
600:1/1 Jerome Kite gent vs Thomas Screevin - plaintiff declares with day to amend; first privilege day for defendant.
601:1/19 Francis Poure esq., vs Christopher Easte - plaintiff declares, copy granted.
602:1/1 Robert Pile vs Thomas Screevine - similarly; first privilege day granted.
Conveyance:
586:4/4 Third proclamation between Richard Pyman querent and Joan & John Collingwood deforciants etc..

[f274v]

Portmoot court held 30 August 1613...
Action of debt:
601:2/19 Poure vs Easte - peremptory day to respond.
Action of trespass on case:
551:16/22 Reade vs Stoute - continues. Discharged by assent of plaintiff's attorney.
Actions continuing: **535**:20/29+; **543**:18/24; **560**:13/18; **563**:13/19; **570**:12/19; **571**:12/19; **572**:12/19; **573**:12/19; **574**:12/19; **579**:11/18; **584**:8/15; **587**:7/16+; **589**:6/7; **590**:6/12.

[f275]

Portmoot court held 13 September 1613...[111]
Actions of debt:
601:3/19 Poure vs Easte - defendant does not appear after three solemn summonses and peremptory day. Therefore etc..
603:1/8 Jerome Kyett gent vs Edmund Rudgate - defendant has first privilege day.
Actions continuing: **535**:21/29+; **543**:19/24; **551**:17/22; **560**:14/18; **563**:14/19, **570**:13/19; **571**:13/19; **572**:13/19; **573**:13/19; **574**:13/19; **579**:12/18 **584**:9/15; **587**:8/16+; **589**:7/7; **590**:7/12.

[111] All case entries in this court written in a hand different to the usual one.

[f275v]

Portmoot court held 27 September 1613...

Actions of debt:

560:15/18 Hall vs Wilkinson - court rules that plaintiff should recover [blank] for debt and [blank] amercement; and grants *scire facias* against surety.

603:2/8 Kyte vs Rudgate - second privilege day granted defendant.

Actions of trespass on case:

590:8/12 Brookes vs Bincks - *venire facias* granted.

604:1/5 Salloman Flye & Mary his wife vs Richard Pyman - plaintiffs declare and request day to amend in next court.

Actions continuing: **535**:22/29+; **543**:20/24; **551**:18/22; **563**:15/19; **570**:14/19; **571**:14/19; **572**:14/19; **573**:14/19; **574**:14/19; **579**:13/18; **584**:10/15; **587**:9/16+; **601**:4/19.

[f276]

Actions of debt:

605:1/1 John Glover vs John Butler - discharged.

606:1/1 Francis Gregory esq. vs John George - discharged.

607:1/1 Francis Gregory esq. vs Thomas Parsons - discharged.

608:1/7 William Kinge vs Thomas Baslie - plaintiff declares. copy granted to defendant.

Action of trespass on case:

609:1/4 Nicholas Nickoles vs John Knowles - since plaintiff does not prosecute his plaint court rules he should compensate for the usual amercement.

[f276v]

Portmoot court held 11 October 1613...

Actions of debt:

560.16/18 Hall vs Wilkinson - *alias scire facias* granted against defendant's surety.

603:3/8 Kyte vs Rudgate - final privilege day for defendant.

608:2/7 King vs Basley - peremptory day to respond.

Actions of trespass on case:

590:9/12 Brookes vs Bincks - *habeas corpora* granted.

604:2/5 Flye and his wife vs Pyman - plaintiffs complete declaration, copy to defendant.

609:2/4 Nickoles vs Knowles - *scire facias* granted against plaintiff's surety.

Actions continuing: **535**:23/29+; **543**:21/24; **551**:19/22; **563**:16/19; **570**:15/19; **571**:15/19; **572**:15/19; **573**:15/19; **574**:15/19; **579**:14/18; **584**:11/15; **587**:10/16+; **601**:5/19.

[f277]

Actions of trespass on case:

610:1/1 William Rymill vs William Tustian - sergeant returned a horse (following distraint) valued by William Bradshewe, George Noble, Richard Shad and William Archer at [blank], which is forfeited into the hands of the lord king because he does not appear, to answer the said plea.

611:1/13 Elizabeth Ryly vs Joan Collingwood widow - day to state her case granted to plaintiff.

[f277v]

612 View of Frankpledege and Sessions of the Peace held 20 October 1613 before John Glover mayor, and Jerome Kyte and Thomas Browne JPs.

Officers: William Raunson constable in place of Robert Ducock; Thomas Bruce tithingman in place of Thomas Gee; William Hickes senior taster in place of Francis Garter.

Jury of homage for the crown:

John Dubber,	Richard Meades,	Nicholas. Taylor,
Jerome White,	Robert Bignill,	Thomas Meatcalfe,
John Lowe,	Thomas Screevine,	Thomas Williams,
John Bradshewe,	William Edwards,	George Noble,
John Norman,	William Raunson,	Richard Hawkins,

Randall Richards: sworn in.

Affeerers: John Dubber, Thomas Meatcalfe, John Norman: sworn in.

[f278]

Recognisances.

599:2/2 Recognisance of Mary Abbott. Mary Abbott widow binds herself to appear, on the oath of Elizabeth Busby, under a penalty of £40. Robert Bignill and William Archer as sureties each binds himself in £20. Discharged: 6s5d.

598:2/2 Recognisance of Phillip Hawthorne. Phillip Hawthorne binds himself to appear, on the oath of Gabriel Kelly, under a penalty of £40. Richard Shad and Hugh Hamond sureties each of £20. Discharged.

613:1/1 Recognisance of Thomas Heathon. Thomas Heather binds himself to appear under a penalty of £40 for drawing blood on Thomas Deane. 12d for breach of peace - given to William Bradshewe. Discharged.

614 The names of innholders and victuallers licensed to brew ale and beer in their houses within this borough.

Innholders: John Glover, Henry Bradshewe, Richard Meades.

Victuallers: William Rayer, Thomas Williams, John Dissell, John Ackley,

[f278v]

Nicholas Tayler, William Edwards, Thomas Screevin, Edward Rudgate, William Hickes senior, Hugh Hamond, Thomas Godfery, Jerome White, Thomas Paynter, Ralph Durbridge, Nicholas Glover, Bennett Paynter, Merriall Tayler widow. 16 (sic)

Sessions of the peace adjourned until 8 November next.

[f279 & 279v] (Blank)

[f280]

Portmoot court held 25 October 1613...

Actions of debt:

560:17/18 Hall vs Wilkinson - execution of judgment granted against defendant's surety.

608:3/7 King vs Basly - defendant responds, with copy granted and puts himself on country.

Actions of trespass on case:

604:3/5 Fly vs Pyman - peremptory day to respond.

609:3/4 Nickoles vs Knowles - *alias scire facias* granted against defendant's surety.

Actions continuing: **535**:24/29+; **543**:22/24; **551**:20/22; **563**:17/19; **570**:16/19; **571**:16/19; **572**:16/19; **573**:16/19; **574**:16/19; **579**:15/18; **584**:12/15; **587**:11/16+; **601**:6/19.

[f280v]

Actions of debt:

603:4/8 Kyte vs Rudgate - peremptory day to respond.

615:1/7 John Ball vs John Stone - first privilege day granted.

590:10/12 Tobias Brookes vs Robert Bincks; the jury between parties:

Jerome White,	Thomas Williams,	Robert Bignill,
John Lowe.	John Norman,	Richard Shad,
George Noble,	William Edwards,	William Meatcalfe,
Richard Hawkins,	Randall Richards and	Thomas Webbe sworn in

A special verdict: and judgment of it appears in the court held 14 August 1615.

611:2/13 Ryly vs Collingwood - copy of declaration granted.

Action of account:

616:1/14 Thomas Basly vs Daniel Witham - day to declare granted.

[f281]

Portmoot court held 8 November 1613...

Actions of debt:

560:18/18 Hall vs Wilkinson - judgment is executed against surety and he goes quit.

608:4/7 Kinge vs Basly - defendant through his attorney Edmund Rudgate acknowledges the debt of 14s8d.

Action of trespass on case:

609:4/4 Nickoles vs Knoweles - execution of judgment granted against plaintiff's surety.

Action of account:

616:2/14 Basly vs Witham - plaintiff completes declaration.

Actions continuing: **535**:25/29+; **543**:23/24; **551**:21/22; **563**:18/19; **570-4**:17/19; **579**:16/18; **584**:13/15; **587**:12/16+; **601:**19; **604**:4/5; **611**:3/13.

[f281v]

Actions of debt:
603:5/8 Kite vs Rudgate - defendant in person acknowledges the debt; judgment adjourned.
615:2/7 Ball vs Stone - second privilege day granted.
Action continuing **590**:11/12.

[f282]

Conveyance:
617:1/4 8 November 1613 before John Glover mayor.
Order: Richard Pyman, Joan Collingwood, John Collingwood and Richard Collingwood that they justly etc. keep the agreement with Humphrey Silver concerning one messuage or tenement with appurtenances in Woodstock now in the occupation of William Wheeler. And if they do not do so etc.
And the concord is such that the said Richard Pyman and Joan, John & Richard Collingwood acknowledge the said tenement with appurtenances to be the right of the same Humphrey as those which Humphrey has of the gift of the said Richard Pyman, Joan, John & Richard Collingwood and remit and quitclaim them for the same Richard Pyman, Joan, John, & Richard Collingwood and their heirs to the said Humphrey Silver and his heirs in perpetuity. And in addition the same Richard Pyman, Joan Collingwood, John & Richard Collingwood separately and for their heirs (concede) that they will warrant the said tenement with appurtenances to the said Humphrey Silver and his heirs against their heirs in perpetuity. And by this fine etc.[112]
(signed) Richard Pyman, John & Richard Collingwood; mayor & town clerk.
(mark of) Joan Collingwood.

[f282v]

Portmoot court held 22 November 1613...
Actions of debt:
608:5/7 King vs Basly - *scire facias* granted.
615:3/7 Ball vs Stone - last privilege day granted defendant.
Action of trespass on case:
604:5/5 Fly vs Pyman - discharged.
Action of account:
616:3/14 Basly vs Witham - peremptory day to respond.
Actions continuing: **535**:26/29+; **543**:24/24; **551**:22/22; **563**:19/19; **570-4**:18/19; **579**:17/18; **584**:14/15; **587**:13/16+; **601**:8/19; **611**:4/13.

[112] See also *WCA*, 32, 44.

[f283]

Actions of debt:

603:6/8 Kyte vs Rudgate - judgment granted - *scire facias* granted against defendant's surety.

618:1/1 Henry Triplett vs John Stone - discharged.

619:1/12 Richard Whing vs William Raunson - privilege day granted.

Actions of trespass on case:

620:1/7 William Raunson vs Edward Clark - plaintiff declares. with copy granted to defendant.

621:1/6 William Raunson vs Bartholomew Edging - day given to plaintiff to amend declaration in next court.

Action of detinue:

622:1/4 Elizabeth Ryly vs Nicholas Tayler - plaintiff declares; and first privilege day granted defendant.

Action continuing: **590**:12/12.

Conveyance:

617:2/4 First proclamation between Humphrey Silver querent and Richard Pyman and Joan, John & Richard Collingwood deforciants concerning one messuage or tenement with appurtenances within Woodstock in Oxford Street in the tenure of William Wheeler. Which the same Humphrey has recently purchased and was handed over by the aforesaid Richard Pyman and Joan, John & Richard Collingwood.

[f283v]

Portmoot court held 6 December 1613…

Actions of debt:

603:7/8 Kyte vs Rudgate - *alias scire facias* granted.

608:6/7 King vs Basly - similarly.

615:4/7 Ball vs Stone - peremptory day to respond granted.

619:2/12 Whing vs Raunson - second privilege day granted.

Actions of trespass on case:

620:2/7 Raunson vs Clark - peremptory day to respond.

621:2/6 Raunson vs Edging - plaintiff declares, day to amend in next court.

Action of account:

616:4/14 Basly vs Witham - further peremptory day to respond.

Action of detinue:

622:2/4 Ryly vs Tayler - second privilege day granted to defendant.

Actions continuing: **535**:27/29+; **570-574**:19/19; **579**:18/18; **584**:15/15; **587**:14/16+; **601**:9/19; **611**:5/13.

Conveyance:

617:3/4 Second proclamation between Humphrey Silver querent and Richard Pyman & Joan, John & Richard Collingwood deforciants concerning one messuage etc.

[f284]

Portmoot court held 20 December 1613...

Actions of debt:

603:8/8 Jerome Kyte vs Edmund Rudgate - judgment discharged on payment of the forty marks debt and [blank] amercement.

(Note in margin) He took all the forfeiture of the bond and 40s more.

608:7/7 King vs Basley - execution of judgment granted against defendant's surety

615:5/7 Ball vs Stone - defendant responds, with day to amend.

Actions of trespass on case:

620:3/7 Raunson vs Clarke - defendant pleads a compromise, with a day to amend granted in next court.

621:3/6 Raunson vs Edginge - copy of declaration granted, with peremptory day to respond.

Action of account:

616:5/14 Basly vs Witham - further peremptory day.

Actions continuing: **535**:28/29+; **587**:15/16+; **601**:10/19; **611**:6/13.

[f284v]

Actions of debt:

619:3/12 Whinge vs Raunson - final privilege day granted to defendant.

623:1/1 John King vs John Cook - day to declare granted. Discharged.

624:1/6 William Boddely vs Thomas Norwood - plaintiff declares, copy granted.

625:1/4 William Hickman, clerk vs Thomas Kinge - similarly.

626:1/2 Anthony Crosse vs Matthew Scott - plaintiff declares and defendant does not appear; therefore no plea entered.

627:1/3 John Ball vs John Stone - plaintiff declares, copy granted.

628:1/21 Thomas Browne alderman vs Richard Heath - plaintiff declares, copy granted.

Action of trespass on case:

629:1/3 John Stone vs John Ball - plaintiff declares, day to amend in next court.

Action continuing: **622**:3/4.

Conveyance:

617:4/4 Third proclamation between Humphrey Silver querent and Richard Pyman and others deforciants concerning one messuage aforesaid etc.

[f285]

Apprenticeships 21 December 1613

630: Humphrey Hall the son of Simon Hall put himself apprentice to Robert Spitle for the term of seven years ensuing the date hereof.

631: William Ayers the son of William Ayers of Islip put himself apprentice to William Butterfeild for nine years from this day.

(both signed by) town clerk

[f285v]

Portmoot court held 3 January 1614...

Actions of debt:

615:6/7 Ball vs Stone - *venire facias* granted.

619:4/12 Whing vs Raunson - peremptory day to respond.

624:2/6 Boddely vs Norwood - similarly.

626:2/2 Crosse vs Scott - judgment granted for [blank].

627:2/3 Ball vs Stone - peremtory day to respond.

628:2/21 Browne vs Heath - similarly.

632:1/1 Edward Streete vs Christopher Forty - plaintiff declares; defendant through Edmund Rudgate acknowledges debt of 40s.

633:1/2 William Smith vs Giles Head - plaintiff declares.

634:1/9 Elizabeth Ryly vs Roger Powell - plaintiff makes plaint for debt of 14s; declares, with copy granted.

Actions of trespass on case:

629:2/3 Stone vs Ball - plaintiff declares, copy granted.

635:1/8 Edward Bayles vs Walter Yonge - day to declare granted.

Actions continuing: **535:**29/29+; **587**:16/16+; **601**:11/19; **611**:7/13; **616**:6/14; **620:**4/7; **621**:4/6; **622**:4/4; **625**:2/4.

636:1/2 **Sergeant's arrest:**

Edward Rudgate on oath says that on Saturday last at seven o'clock at night he went into John Stone's shop, the door being open, and arrested him at William Bradshewe's stinte (i.e. restraint). But Stone escaped from him and by sciving with him hurt his, the sergeant's, hand with his knife, and then cried out to shut the door and stab him.

636:2/2 William Raunson says that on Sunday last he heard John Stone speaking about the said arrest say he was sorry that he had not killed them all for he had many enemies.

[f286]

637 Information. 27 September 1613

John Stone affirmed that he heard Christopher Easte of Bletchingdon ('Blechington') about May last upon the highway between Bicester ('Bister') and Chesterton, talking to John Collingridge, John Gibbs a smith of Bletchingdon, himself, and some women. And he said that Phillip Sellenger alias Butcher of Oddington, Mr. Pour's bailiff of Bletchingdon, was a dissembling knave and a false thief, and he would prove them both. First to prove him a dissembling knave was that he denied his master's hand in Islip court. And for proving him a thief he said that he robbed his master Mr.Francis Poure of £14 at one time.

(signed by) John Stone[113]

[113] Possible connections with actions **601, 582** and **595**?

[f286v]

(End-page jottings)

638 8 September 1611

Walnut acres. Buster Feildsman and his brother; Parratt; The Currier's son Durbridge's eldest son

639 Barnes sold to Elizabeth Ryly: Velvet lace sold to goodwife Screevin to lace a petticoat[114]

A pair of stockings sold to Mr Streete may be worth a great deal.

640 Thomas Biggs of Stanton St. John (John's) gent and John Bowden of Marton (i.e. Merton), Oxon yeoman the consideration of £35[115]

[f287]

641 John Eglesbee

John Annison vs Robert Annison; says that the plaintiff was a thief and an arrant thief[116]

642 Simon Smith of Oxon; ?mercer

643 Between George and Parsons[117] (Court fees)

On behalf of plaintiff		*ex p'te q'* [118]
for entering action; & attorney[119]	14d	pro entr' acc' & att';
for declaration & endorsement(s)	4s 9d	pro dec' & all'
for entering confession[120]	8d	pro entr' conf'
for writ of inquiry	4s	pro bre' ad inq'
for serving writ and discharge	6d	pro ser' bill' & exon'
	11s1d	
on behalf of defendant		*ex p'te def'*
for sergeant's fee[121]	3s1d	pro feod' serv'
for court	12d	pro Cur'
for bills (copies)	2d	pro bill'
	5s1d	(signed by) Edmund Hiorne

End of Book WBM 78/2

114 Possibly relating to the thefts of **437.**

115 See WBM B78/3 *ff 5,7 & 8.*

116 See Actions **191** and **217.**

117 See Action **355.**

118 Printed version of text. Interpretation based largely upon GD Gilmore, *Commentaries, L.1/7,* 50 and Glossaries.

119 Warrant of Attorney? See Gilmore, 50.

120 For example of plaintiff paying (4d c.1573) for entering defendant's confession see Bateson, 145.

121 Presumably including function as attorney, see **355**:1/2.

CALENDAR OF WOODSTOCK BOROUGH MUNIMENT WBM 78/3

Minute book of New Woodstock Borough courts
January 1614 to March 1622

[f1]

Portmoot court of our lord King held in the aforesaid borough on the 24th day of January in the eleventh year of the reign of our lord King James by the grace of God, King of England, France and Ireland, defender of the faith and in the forty seventh year of his reign of Scotland Anno domini 1614. Before John Glover, mayor of the aforesaid borough.[1]

Actions of debt:

535:(30/37) Child vs Shurley - case continues.
587:(17/42) Craker vs Winter - case continues.
601:(12/19) Pore vs Este - case continues.
611:(8/12) Ryly vs Collingwood - case continues.
616:(7/15) Basly vs Witham - case continues.
619:(5/12) Whinge vs Raunson - defendant confesses the debt through his attorney, Edmund Rudgate. Judgment to be given in next court.
624:(3/6) Boddely vs Norwood - defendant replies not accountable.
625:(3/4) Hickman vs Kinge - case continues by agreement.
627:(3/3) Ball vs Stone - case discharged by assent of plaintiff.
628:(3/22) Browne vs Heath - defendant does not respond. Therefore etc., and judgment adjourned.
633:(2/2) Smith vs Head - peremptory day to respond. Discharged by assent.
634:(2/12) Ryly vs Powell - defendant does not respond. Therefore etc; and judgment adjourned.

Action of trespass:

629:(3/3) Stone vs Ball - discharged by assent of plaintiff.

Actions of trespass on case:

620:(5/7) Raunson vs Clarke - case continues. (4d owed
621:(5/6) Raunson vs Edginge - case continues. (by plaintiff
635:(2/8) Baylies vs Yonge - plaintiff puts completed declaration.

[1] Following this example of a full heading to a Portmoot court, the rest are abbreviated to the date. Details of the court officers are given in Appendix 1. Case entry numbers follow on directly from main proceedings in WBM B78/2 Calendar.

Action of account:
644:1/16 Edmund Rudgate vs Anthony Deverill - plaintiff puts declaration and copy granted.

[f1v]

Portmoot court held 7 February 1614...
Actions of debt:
619:(6/12) Whinge vs Raunson - judgment given by court that plaintiff should recover both his debt of £8 8s. and 20s.7d costs; *scire facias* granted against defendant's surety.
624:(4/6) Bodely vs Norwood - day to replicate granted to plaintiff.
625:(4/4) Hickman vs Kinge - discharged by agreement with plaintiff.
628:(4/22) Browne vs Heath - judgment is given by court that plaintiff should recover [blank] for his debt and [blank] for costs; *scire facias* granted against surety for said defendant.
634:(3/12) Ryly vs Powell - judgment given by court that plaintiff recover [blank] for his debt and [blank] for costs; *scire facias* granted against surety for said defendant.
Actions of trespass on case:
620:(6/7) Raunson vs Clarke - case continues by assent of both parties.
635:(3/8) Baylies vs Yonge - continues for costs of defendant.
621:(6/6) Raunson vs Edginge - discharged by agreement of plaintiff.
Actions continuing: **535**:(31/37); **587**:(18/42); **601**:(13/19); **611**:(9/12); **616**:(8/15).

[f2]

Action of debt:
646:1/1 John Bowden vs John Dearle (als.Witham) - plaintiff's attorney, Simon Jeames, puts declaration and produces in court an obligation etc. Defendant in person confesses debt specified in aforesaid obligation viz: £12 whence execution is committed by court to sergeant at mace, given that he pay both debt of £12 and 9s 3d costs. Debt and costs paid immediately to plaintiff who declares himself satisfied. Therefore he goes quit.
Action of trespass on case:
645:1/19 Edmund Rudgate vs Anthony Deverill - plaintiff puts declaration and is granted day to amend in next court.
Action of account:
644:2/16 Rudgate vs Deverill - peremptory day granted.

[f2v]

Portmoot court held 21 February 1614...
Actions of debt:
619:(7/12) Whinge vs Raunson - *alias scire facias* granted.
628:(5/22) Browne vs Heath - *alias scire facias* granted.
634:(4/12) Ryley vs Powell - stands upon *scire facias*

648:1/1 William Raunson vs Ferdinand Smith - plaintiff puts declaration and copy granted.
624:(5/6) Boddely vs Norwood - plaintiff puts plea to delay action. Defendant replies and puts himself on judgment of recorder.[2]
616:(9/15) Basley vs Witham - because plaintiff prosecutes (defendant) therefore judgment in respect of costs will be given in next court.
Actions of trespass on case:
620:(7/7) Raunson vs Clark - discharged for defendant.
635:(4/8) Baylies vs Yonge - continues by agreement.
645:2/19 Rudgate vs Deverill - continues by agreement.
647:1/5 Henry Thorneton vs Henry (deleted) Richard Holton (interlined) Howlton - plaintiff puts declaration and day to amend granted.
Action of account:
644:3/16 Rudgate vs Deverill - Continues by agreement.
Actions continuing: **535**:(32/37); **587**:(19/42); **601**:(14/19); **611**:(10/12).

[f3]

Council Meeting 21 February 1614

649 *Memorandum:* At a council held at the (Guild)hall before John Glover, mayor, Thomas Browne, William Rayer and Joseph Harris, aldermen, Edmund Hiorne, town clerk, Simon Jeames gent, Thomas Williams chamberlain, Thomas Meatcalfe, John Dubber, William Meatcalfe, Robert Bignill, John Bradshewe, Richard Shadd, Richard Meades, John Norman, George Noble and Edmund Rudgate:-
Richard Reade was convented for using railing and opprobrious ('approbiose') words to Mr Mayor yesternight in open street, saying that he maintained thieves and rogues in the town and said he lied in his throat and cursed him and all his company and would not submit him etc; therefore it is ordered by said mayor and common council that said Richard Reade shall no longer continue his freedom but is dismissed and disfranchised from his freedom and shall be committed to close prison for the space of three days and pay a fine of 40s and find sureties of his good behaviour hereafter.
Signatures of John Glover, Thomas Browne, William Rayer, Joseph Harris and Edmund Hiorne, town clerk.

[f3v]

Conveyance: 22 February 1614
650:1/4 before John Glover, mayor.
Order: Richard Pyman, Joan Collingwood widow, and John Collingwood that justly etc. they keep the agreement with Thomas Browne concerning 2 messuages with tenements and appurtenances in the aforesaid borough named

[2] Sole example of procedure in these courtbooks.

Mundyes Place and Mainards, now in the occupation of said Joan Collingwood etc.[3]

And the concord is as follows: that the aforesaid Richard Pyman, Joan Collingwood and John Collingwood acknowledge the aforesaid tenement with appurtenances to be the right of Thomas Browne and which the same Thomas Browne has as the gift of aforesaid Richard, Joan and John. And the tenement is remised and quitclaimed for said Richard, Joan and John and their heirs to aforesaid Thomas Browne and his heirs in perpetuity And also the same Richard Pyman, Joan Collingwood and John Collingwood separately concede for themselves and their heirs that they will warrant aforesaid tenement and appurtenances to Thomas Browne and his heirs against themselves and their heirs in perpetuity. And for this fine etc..

(signed by) John Glover mayor, Edmund Hiorne town clerk, Richard Pyman, John Collingwood, (mark of) Joan Collingwood.

[f4]

Portmoot court held 7 March 1614...

Actions of debt:

619:(8/12) Whinge vs Raunson - *alias scire facias* produced and execution granted against defendant and his sureties viz: Robert Bignill and Hugh Hamond.

624:(6/6) Boddely vs Norwood - court wishes to consider.

628:(6/22) Browne vs Heath - *alias scire facias* produced and execution granted against defendant and surety.

634:(5/12) Ryly vs Powell - stands as before.

Actions of trespass on case:

635:(5/8) Baylies vs Yonge - continues by agreement.

645:3/19 Rudgate vs Deverill - plaintiff puts completed declaration and copy granted.

647:2/5 Thorneton vs Houlton - plaintiff puts completed declaration and copy granted.

Action of account:

644:4/16 Rudgate vs Deverill - defendant responds and is granted day to amend in next court

Actions continuing: **535**:(33/37); **587**:(20/42); **601**:(15/19); **611**:(11/12).

[f4v]

Actions of debt:

616:(10/15) Basley vs Witham - judgment granted for costs and *scire facias* granted against Robert Bignill, surety.

651:1/6 Richard Browne vs William Raunson - plaintiff declares and copy granted. Defendant, through Edmund Rudgate, attorney, confesses debt of 31s. and date to pay appointed in next court.

[3] *VCH Oxon,* xii, 350.

Conveyance:
650:2/3 First proclamation between Thomas Browne alderman, querent, and Richard Pyman, Joan Collingwood and John Collingwood, deforciants, for two messuages or tenements with appurtenances in aforesaid borough called Mundyes place and Maynards formerly in occupation of Francis Collingwood deceased etc: And that Thomas Browne lately acquired the same and surrendered to aforesaid Richard Pyman, Joan and John Collingwood

[f5]

Conveyance: 19 March 1614
652:1/4 before John Glover, mayor.
Order: Thomas Bigges and John Bowden[4] that justly etc. they keep the agreement with Bartholomew Edginge concerning one messuage or tenement with appurtenances in the borough aforesaid located in Oxford Street lately under the tenancy of Nicholas Glover etc.[5]
And the concord is as follows that aforesaid Thomas Bigges and John Bowden acknowledge aforesaid tenement with appurtenances to be the right of said Bartholomew Edginge as that which same Bartholomew has of the gift of aforesaid Thomas Bigges and John Bowden And remits and quitclaims it for aforesaid Thomas and John and their heirs to the aforesaid Bartholomew Edginge and his heirs in perpetuity And moreover aforesaid Thomas and John concede for themselves and their heirs that they will warrant said tenement with appurtenances to aforesaid Bartholomew and his heirs against them and all their heirs in perpetuity And for this fine etc:
(signed by) Thomas Bigges (mark of) John Bowden
(signed by) John Glover mayor, and Edmund Hiorne, town clerk.

[f5v]

Portmoot court held 21 March 1614...
Actions of debt:
611:(12/12) Ryly vs Collingwood - discharged by agreement.
616:(11/15) Basly vs Witham - *alias scire facias* against Robert Bignill.
651:2/6 Browne vs Raunson - judgment granted against defendant.
655:1/7 William Bradshewe vs John Stone - plaintiff puts declaration and day to amend granted.
Actions of trespass on case:
645:4/19 Rudgate vs Deverill - defendant responds and plaintiff replicates.
647:3/5 Thorneton vs Howlton - peremptory day to respond.
653:1/4 William Raunson vs John Stone - plaintiff puts declaration and is granted day to amend; copy of declaration granted to defendant.
654:1/7 William Bradshewe vs John Stone - plaintiff puts declaration and day to amend granted.

4 See B78/2, *f.*286v.
5 *WCA,* 49.

Action of account:
644:5/16 Rudgate vs Deverill - defendant responds and plaintiff replicates.
Actions continuing: **535**:(34/37); **587**:(21/42); **601**:(16/19); **619**:(9/12); **628**:(7/22); **634**:(6/12); **635**:(6/8).

[f6]

Conveyances:
650:3/4 Second proclamation between Thomas Browne, alderman, querent and Richard Pyman, Joan Collingwood widow, and John Collingwood deforciants for two messuages etc
652:2/4 First proclamation between Bartholomew Edginge querent and Thomas Bigges and John Bowden deforciants for one messuage or tenement with appurtenances in aforesaid borough in the place called Oxford Street formerly in tenure of Nicholas Glover That same Bartholomew Edginge lately acquired and Thomas Bigges and John Bowden handed over.
[f6v]
Portmoot court held 4 April 1614…
Actions of debt:
616:(12/15) Basly vs Witham - execution granted against Robert Bignill.
651:3/6 Browne vs Raunson - renewal of *scire facias*.
655:2/7 Bradshewe vs Stone - plaintiff puts completed declaration.
Actions of trespass on case:
635:(7/8) Bayles vs Yonge - discharged by agreement.
645:5/19 Rudgate vs Deverill - day granted for rejoinder.
647:4/5 Thorneton vs Holton - defendant demurs in law and joins [issue].
653:2/4 Raunson vs Stone - plaintiff puts completed declaration.
654:2/7 Bradshewe vs Stone - similarly.
Action of account:
644:6/16 Rudgate vs Deverill - day granted for rejoinder.
Conveyance:
650:4/4 Third proclamation between Thomas Browne, alderman, querent and Richard Pyman, Joan Collingwood, widow, and John Collingwood deforciants for two messuages etc..
Actions continuing: **535**:(35/37); **587**:(22/42); **601**:(17/19); **619**:(10/12); **628**:(8/22); **634**:(7/12).

[f7]

Conveyance:
652:3/4 Second proclamation between Bartholomew Edginge querent and Thomas Bigges and John Bowden deforciants for one messuage or tenement with appurtenances in Woodstock aforesaid.
Actions of debt:
656:1/3 John Neele vs Richard Treslowe - plaintiff puts declaration and copy granted.

Actions of trespass on case:
657:1/3 John Ball vs John Stone - plaintiff puts declaration and copy and day to amend granted.
658:1/18 John Ball vs Elizabeth Rylye - similarly.
Action of detinue:
659:1/1 John Jorden vs Richard Meade - action on taking and unjust detention of one horse; discharged by agreement.

[f7v]

Portmoot court held 18 April 1614...
Actions of debt:
616:(13/15) Basly vs Witham - execution granted against Robert Bignill.
651:4/6 Browne vs Raunson - *alias scire facias* returned executed and execution granted against defendant and surety.
655:3/6 Bradshewe vs Stone - peremptory day to respond.
656:2/3 Neele vs Tresloe - peremptory day to respond.
Actions of trespass on case:
635:(8/8) Baylies vs Yonge - action discharged.
645:6/19 Rudgate vs Deverill - parties put themselves on the country;[6] *venire facias* granted.
647:5/5 Thorneton vs Holton - stands as before.
654:3/7 Bradshewe vs Stone - peremptory day to respond.
Action of account:
644:7/16 Rudgate vs Deverill - parties put themselves on the country; *venire facias* granted.
Actions continuing: **535**:(36/37); **587**:(23/42); **601**:(18/19); **619**:(11/12); **628**:(9/22); **634**:(8/12).

[f8]

Actions of trespass on case:
653:3/4 Raunson vs Stone - peremptory day to respond.
657:2/3 Ball vs Stone - plaintiff puts completed declaration .
658:2/18 Ball vs Rylye - plaintiff puts completed declaration and copy granted.
Conveyance:
652:4/4 Third Proclamation between Bartholomew Edginge querent and Thomas Bigges and John Bowden deforciants for one messuage or tenement with appurtenances in Woodstock

[f8v]

View of Frankpledge and Sessions of the Peace held 20th April 1614 before John Glover, mayor, Jerome Kite gent and Thomas Browne gent and alderman of the borough, Justices of the Peace
Officers:
Chamberlains; William Bradshewe and Thomas Williams

6 See Glossary.

Constables; George Noble and William Raunson
Tithingmen; William Archer, William Butterfield, Richard Browne and Thomas Bruce
Ale-tasters; William Hickes senior and John Wilkinson

660: *Jury for the King with homage*

Richard Meade,	John Dubber,	Nicolas Tayler,
Jerome White,	Thomas Screevin,	John Norman,
George Noble,	Hugh Hamond,	Robert Spitle,
John Ackley,	Richard Browne,	Thomas Webb,
Richard Hawkins,	Thomas Heathen.	

Affeerers: John Dubber, Jerome White, John Norman (sworn in).

[f9]

661: *Innholders*

John Glover, alderman	John Ackley
Henry Bradshewe	Nicholas Tayler
Richard Meades	William Edwardes
William Rayer, alderman	Thomas Screevin
Thomas Williams	Edward Rudgate
John Dissell	

Victuallers

William Hickes senior	Ralph Durbridge
Hugh Hamond	Nicholas Glover
Thomas Godfery	Bennett Paynter
Jerome White	Merrial Tayler, widow
Thomas Painter	

[f9v]

Portmoot court held 2 May 1614...

Actions of debt:

616:(14/15) Basley vs Witham - renewal of execution.
651:5/6 Browne vs Raunson - renewal of execution.
655:4/6 Bradshewe vs Stone - [No action recorded by clerk]
656:3/3 Neele vs Tresloe - defendant replies *non est factum* and puts himself on the country; *venire facias* granted.

Actions of trespass on case:

645:7/19 Rudgate vs Deverill - writ of *venire facias* stands.
654:4/7 Bradshewe vs Stone - defendant in person brings writ of *habeas corpus* returnable Thursday next in the month of Easter (dated 12 Feb, 11 Jas. I etc)
657:3/3 Ball vs Stone - stands upon writ of *habeas corpus*.

Action of account:
644:8/16 Rudgate vs Deverill - writ of *venire facias* returned executed and *habeas corpora* granted.
Actions continuing: **535**:(37/37); **587**:(24/42); **601**:(19/19); **619**:(12/12); **628**:(10/22); **634**:(9/12).

[f10]

Actions of trespass on case:
653:4/4 Raunson vs Stone - stands upon writ of *habeas corpus*.
658:3/18 Ball vs Rylye - peremptory day for response granted.
Portmoot court held 16 May 1614...
Actions of debt:
616:(15/15) Basly vs Witham - debt and costs paid on execution against Robert Bignill.
651:6/6 Browne vs Raunson - debt and costs paid; discharged.
Actions of trespass on case:
645:8/19 Rudgate vs Deverill - stands as before.
658:4/18 Ball vs Ryly - defendant demurs in law; copy granted.
Action of account:
644:9/16 Rudgate vs Deverill - *venire facias* continues.
Actions continuing: **587**:(25/42); **628**:(11/22); **634**:(10/12).

[f10v]

Portmoot court held 30 May 1614.
Actions of debt:
662:1/2 Richard Whinge vs William Flexnye - plaintiff puts declaration and copy granted.
663:1/2 Judy Buller, widow, (administratrix of goods and chattels of her husband, William, deceased) vs Richard Buller - plaintiff puts declaration and copy granted to defendant.[7]
664:1/19 Robert Tredwell vs Nicholas Elliott - plaintiff puts declaration and day to amend granted.
Actions of trespass on case:
658:5/18 Ball vs Rylye - plaintiff puts replication and delivers the adjudication of the Recorder.
Action of account:
644:10/16 Rudgate vs Deverill - *venire facias* continues.
Actions continuing: **587**:(26/42); **628**:(12/22); **645**:9/19.
Land recovery:
665: Simon Jeames, gent, by virtue of a royal writ in these words: 'James by the grace of God king of England, Scotland, France and Ireland, defender of the faith; the mayor and community of the borough of New Woodstock

[7] William Buller of Sandford, d.1613 MSS.Wills (Oxon) 106.71; 295/7/41.

greeting, you are commended without delay and according to the custom of the borough that you do full right to Simon Jeames in respect of five messuages, five gardens and two acres of pasture with appurtenances in Woodstock, whereof William Meatcalfe, (*alias* Abraham), is deforcing him. That we may hear no more complaint about this for want of right. Witness myself (the Sovereign) being witness at Westminster on 18th May Jas.I 22 and VI 47'.

Nelson[8] petitioned in the form of a recovery versus William Meatcalfe, (*alias* Abraham), for five messuages, five gardens and two acres of pasture with appurtenances, who vouched to warranty John Whitton who previously vouched Edmund Rudgate who made default. Therefore it is adjudged by the court that said Simon Jeames should recover his seisin concerning the tenements versus the said William Meatcalf.[9] [Marginal note – A recovery for Mr. Meatcalfe]

[f11]

Portmoot court held 6 June 1614 ...

Actions of debt:

662:2/2 Whinge vs Flexnye - defendant responds and puts himself on the country; *venire facias* granted.

663:2/2 Buller vs Buller - action discharged.

664:2/19 Tredwell vs Elliott - completed declaration submitted and copy granted.

Actions of trespass on case:

658:6/18 Ball vs Ryly - court wishes to consider.

666:1/4 William Silverside vs Robert Silverside - plaintiff puts declaration and day to amend granted.

667:1/4 Robert Silverside vs William Silverside - similarly.

Actions continuing: **587**:(27/42); **628**:(13/22); **644**:11/16; **645**:10/19.

[f11v]

Portmoot court held 20 June 1614...

Actions of debt:

664:3/19 Tredwell vs Elliott - peremptory day to respond.

668:1/46 Edmund Hiorne vs Christopher Fortye - day to declare granted to plaintiff in next court.

669:1/10 Jerome Kite vs Jerome White - plaintiff puts declaration.

670:1/11 Jerome Kite vs Randall Richards - similarly.

671:1/1 Jerome Kite vs Richard Hawkins - similarly.

Action of trespass on case:

654:5/7 William Bradshewe vs John Stone - plaintiff brings a King's writ *de prosequendo* dated 6th June 1614. Peremptory day to respond granted to defendant.

[8] The chancery clerk who wrote the writ.

[9] 'Recovery' see Introduction, Some Forms of Action; and Glossary.

Action of account:
644:12/16 Edmund Rudgate vs Anthony Deverill - jury between parties:-

Richard Meade,	Jerome White,	Robert Bignill,
Thomas Screevine,	John Bradshewe,	John Norman,
Richard Shadd,	George Noble,	Will. Hickes, senior,
Will. Hickes, junior,	Thomas Webb,	Randall Richards.

Which jury, on their oaths, find for the defendant etc..
Actions continuing: **587**:(28/42); **628**:(14/22); **645**:11/19; **658**:7/18; **666**:2/14; **667**:2/4.

Breach of the Peace

636:(3/5) William Bradshewe brings action against John Stone - Richard Shad and Thomas Screevin hold bail of £20 each and John Stone £40 to keep the peace and appear at next sessions. (see **702**:(2), **751**:(1))

[f12]

Portmoot court held 4 July 1614.

Actions of debt:
587:(29/42) Craker vs Winter - 6s paid and debt of 5s continues into next court
655:5/6 Bradshewe vs Stone - defendant's attorney reports *non informatus est respondendi*; *nil dicit*; judgment adjourned to next court.
664:4/19 Tredwell vs Elliott - defendant responds and offers £4 in court; but plaintiff's attorney does not accept and plaintiff is granted copy of response.
669:2/10 Kyte vs White - second day of privilege granted.
670:2/11 Kyte vs Richards - similarly.
672:1/15 William Rayer, alderman vs Thomas Williams and John Bradshewe - plaintiff puts declaration and copy is granted to defendants; day of privilege granted.
673:1/1 Justine [?Dormer] ('widow' deleted) vs Thomas Hucwell - plaintiff puts declaration and defendant, committed to custody of sergeant, confesses debt of 14s.

Action of trespass on case:
654:6/7 Bradshewe vs Stone - defendant's attorney reports non informatus est respondendi; nil dicit etc. Writ of inquiry into damages granted.

Actions of account:
644:13/16 Rudgate vs Deverill - court adjudges that defendant should recover his costs of [blank] and *scire facias* is granted against plaintiff's surety
674:1/1 Justine [?Dormer] vs Thomas Hucwell - in similar action to **673**, plaintiff acknowledges receipt of 3s and 6s.
Actions continuing: **628**:(15/22); **645**:12/19; **658**:8/18; **666**:3/4; **667**:3/4.

[f12v]

Action of debt:
668:2/46 Edmund Hiorne vs Christopher Fortye - plaintiff's attorney, Simon Jeames, puts declaration and defendant's attorney, Edmund Rudgate, admits

debt of £12. Therefore court adjudges that plaintiff should recover both his debt and 6s.8d. for costs; *scire facias* granted against defendant's surety.

[f13]

Portmoot court held 18 July 1614...

Actions of debt:

655:6/6 Bradshewe vs Stone - court adjudges that plaintiff should recover both [blank] for debt and [blank] for costs and *scire facias* granted.

664:5/19 Tredwell vs Elliott - day to replicate granted.

668:3/46 Hiorne vs Fourtye - stands in same case as before.

669:3/10 Kyte vs White - continues by agreement. Final day of privilege granted.

670:3/11 Kyte vs Richards - similarly.

672:2/15 Rayer vs Williams and Bradshewe - second day of privilege granted to defendants.

675:1/1 William Tims vs Edward Fox and William Hobcrofte - plaintiff puts declaration; discharged.

Actions of trespass on case:

654:7/7 Bradshewe vs Stone - Sergeant at mace returns executed writ of inquiry into damages and Jury assess for damages £5.3s.4d. and [blank] for costs. Court adjudges plaintiff should recover both damages and costs and *scire facias* granted.

658:9/18 Ball vs Ryly - court wishes to consider.

666:4/4 and **667**:4/4 Silverside vs Silverside – actions discharged.

Action of account:

644:14/16 Rudgate vs Deverill - *alias scire facias* granted.

Action of Qui Tam:

676:1/2 John Taylor of Leafield ('le feilde') in the County of Oxon, yeoman vs Edmund Rudgate - plaintiff lays information on behalf of the king and of himself on a contravention of the statutes.

Actions continuing: **587**:(30/42); **628**:(16/22); **645**:13/19.

[f13v]

Actions of Qui Tam:

677:1/2 John Taylor vs Henry Bradshewe gent } plaintiff
678:1/2 John Taylor vs Robert Bignill } lays
679:1/2 John Taylor vs Thomas Williams } information
on behalf of the king and of himself on a contravention of the statutes.

[f14]

Portmoot court held 1 August 1614

Actions of debt:

664:6/19 Tredwell vs Elliott - plaintiff replicates and is granted day to amend.

668:4/46 Hiorne vs Fortye - stands upon judgment.

669:4/10 Kyte vs White - final day of privilege granted to defendant.

670:4/11 Kyte vs Richards - peremptory day for defendant to respond.
672:3/15 Rayer vs Williams and Bradshewe - final day of privilege granted.
Actions of trespass on case:
658:10/18 Ball vs Ryly - day is granted to defendant in next court for advice upon demurrer.
681:1/13 John Dutton vs Arthur Welbeck - plaintiff puts declaration and copy granted to defendant.
Action of account:
644:15/16 Rudgate vs Deverill - execution of writ granted.
Actions of Qui Tam:
676:2/2, **677**:2/2, **678**:2/2, **679**:2/2, - all actions discharged by agreement of plaintiff.
680:1/2 John Tayler vs Richard Meades - plaintiff lays information on behalf of king and himself on contravention of statutes. Defendant's attorney, Edmund Rudgate, requests court authority to compound; granted.
Actions continuing: **587**:(31/42); **628**:(14/22); **645**:14/19.

[f14v] (Blank)

[f15]

Portmoot court held 15 August 1614...
Actions of debt:
664:7/19 Tredwell vs Elliott - plaintiff produces completed replication and copy granted to defendant.
669:5/10 Kyte vs White - peremptory day to respond granted.
670:5/11 Kyte vs Richards - defendant, through his attorney, Edmund Rudgate, confesses the debt. Therefore judgment adjourned to next court.
Action of account:
644:16/16 Rudgate vs Deverill - plaintiff pays in court 23s.5d. costs under execution of writ; and he goes quit.
Actions continuing: **587**:(32/42); **628**:(18/22); **645**:15/19.

[f15v]

Actions of debt:
668:5/46 Hiorne vs Fortye - stands upon judgment.
686:1/4 Roger Nurth vs Phillipp Symons - plaintiff puts declaration. Defendant does not appear; therefore nil dicit and judgment adjourned.
Actions of trespass on case:
658:11/18 Ball vs Rylye - judgment granted to plaintiff upon advice of the Recorder of the borough and writ of inquiry into damages granted.
681:2/13 Dutton vs Welbeck - peremptory day to respond granted to defendant.
Actions of Qui Tam:
680:2/2 John Tayler vs Richard Meades - discharged by agreement with plaintiff.

682:1/10 John Tayler vs Robert Webb
683:1/10 John Tayler vs John Brookes
684:1/10 John Tayler vs George Stowte[10]
685:1/2 John Tayler vs William Butler
} plaintiff lays information on behalf of king and himself on contravention of the statutes. Defendants granted copy of information.
Action continuing: **672**:4/15.

[f16]

Portmoot court held 29 August 1614...
Actions of debt:
669:6/10 Kyte vs White - defendant, through his attorney Edmund Rudgate, acknowledges the debt etc.
670:6/11 Kyte vs Richards - judgment is given by the court that plaintiff recover both [blank] for debt and [blank] for costs; *scire facias* granted.
Action of trespass on case:
681:3/13 Dutton vs Welbeck - defendant makes 'foreign' plea: i.e. outside the court's jurisdiction.
Actions continuing: **587**:(33/42); **628**:(19/22); **645**:16/19; **664**:8/19; **668**:6/46.

[f16v]

Action of debt:
686:2/4 Nurth vs Symons - judgment given by court that plaintiff should recover both [blank] for debt and [blank] for costs; *scire facias* granted.
Action of trespass on case:
658:12/18 Ball vs Rylye - continues under writ of inquiry into damages.
Actions of Qui Tam:
682:2/10 Tayler vs Webb - plaintiff granted authority to compound.
683:2/10 Tayler vs Brookes - peremptory day to respond.
684:2/10 Tayler vs Stowte - peremptory day to respond.
685:2/2 Tayler vs Butler - defendant's attorney reports *non informatus est ad respondendi*. Therefore *nihil dicit*.
687:1/9 John Tayler vs Thomas Jackman
688:1/9 John Tayler vs Thomas Boult
} plaintiff lays information on contravention of statute.
Information shown and authority to compound granted.
Action continuing: **672**:5/15.

[f17]

Portmoot court held 12 September 1614...[11]
Actions of debt:
669:7/10 Kyte vs White - judgment given by court that plaintiff should recover both [blank] for debt and [blank] for costs; *scire facias* granted.

[10] *WCA*, 50.

[11] Mistakenly titled 'Court Baron'.

670:7/11 Kyte vs Richards - continues under judgment by agreement with plaintiff.
672:6/15 Rayer vs Williams (and Bradshewe) - peremptory day to respond granted.
Actions of trespass on case:
658:13/18 Ball vs Ryly - continues under writ of inquiry into damages
681:4/13 Dutton vs Welbeck - defence puts foreign plea and offers his oath that the plea is true; and because plaintiff's attorney says that the defendant stands a convicted recusant, therefore court wishes to consider upon his oath.[12]
Actions continuing: **587**:(34/42); **628**:(20/22); **645**:17/19; **664**:9/19; **668**:7/46.

[f17v]

Actions of debt:
686:3/4 Nurth vs Symons - *alias scire facias* granted.
689:1/15 Jerome Kyte gent vs Mawriss Capp - plaintiff puts declaration and day to amend granted.
690:1/6 John Warrine vs John Cooke - plaintiff puts declaration; copy granted.
Actions of Qui Tam:
682:3/10 Tayler vs Webb - action adjourned but with permission to agree out of court, until the next court.
683:3/10 Tayler vs Brookes - defendant responds not guilty and puts himself on the country.
684:3/10 Tayler vs Stowte - defendant authorised to compound.
687:2/9 Tayler vs Jackman - defendant does not respond.
688:2/9 Tayler vs Boulte – action adjourned but with permission to agree out of court, until the next court.
691:1/6 John Tayler vs Paul Simon[13] - plaintiff lays information on behalf of king and himself on contravention of statutes. Authorisation granted to defendant to compound.
692:1/8 John Tayler vs John Greene - defendant granted copy of information.

[f18]

Portmoot court held 26 September 1614...
Actions of debt:
669:8/10 Kyte vs White - *alias scire facias* etc.
672:7/15 Rayer vs Williams (and Bradshewe) - defendant confesses the debt through his attorney.
686:4/4 Nurth vs Symons - execution granted against defendant and his surety.
689:2/15 Kyte vs Capp - defendant granted copy of declaration.
690:2/6 Warrine vs Cooke - defendant granted copy of declaration.

[12] Decision on validity of recusant's oath postponed, with action left unresolved.
[13] *WCA*, 50.

Actions of trespass on case:
658:14/18 Ball vs Ryly - continues under writ of inquiry.
681:5/13 Dutton vs Welbeck - court wishes to consider.
Actions continuing: **587**:(35/42); **628**:(21/22); **645**:18/19; **664**:10/19; **668**:8/46; **670**:8/11.

[f18v]

Actions of debt:
695:1/10 Abraham Millen vs Jane Belcher,widow - plaintiff declares and is granted day to amend; defendant granted copy of declaration.
698:1/4 Jerome Kyte vs Thomas Godfery - plaintiff declares; defendant, through Edmund Rudgate his attorney, confesses the debt of £6 16d. Therefore court rules that plaintiff should recover debt and costs.
Action of account:
693:1/2 William Wall vs John Cooke - plaintiff puts declaration and copy granted to defendant.
Action of trespass:
694:1/10 Robert Tredwell vs Nicolas Elliott - day to declare granted.
Actions of Qui Tam:
687:3/9 Tayler vs Jackman - *scire facias* granted against defendant's surety.
691:2/6 Tayler vs Samone - peremptory day to respond.
692:2/8 Tayler vs Greene - peremptory day to respond.
696:1/5 John Tayler vs Abraham Mallen - plaintiff lays information for king and himself on contravention of statutes.
697:1/5 John Tayler vs Thomas White - plaintiff lays information etc and defendant granted copy.
Actions continuing: **682**:4/10; **683**:4/10; **684**:4/10; **688**:3/9.

[f19]

Portmoot court held 3 October 1614...[14]
Actions of debt:
628:(22/22) Browne vs Heath - continues under execution of writ [Memorandum dated 7th May 1616 - Thomas Browne admits himself satisfied with the debt and costs under the writ against Richard Heath. Therefore he goes quit. Discharged].
669:9/10 Kyte vs White - defendant appears in person under *alias scire facias* and is committed in execution of the writ.
672:8/15 Rayer vs Williams (and Bradshewe) judgment given by the court that the plaintiff recover [blank] for debt and [blank] for costs; *scire facias* granted.
689:3/15 Kyte vs Capp - peremptory day for response.
690:3/6 Warrine vs Cooke - peremptory day for response.
695:2/10 Millen vs Belcher - plaintiff places completed declaration and copy granted.

[14] Mistakenly titled 'Court Baron.'

Action of trespass:
694:2/10 Tredwell vs Elliott - copy of declaration granted.
Actions of trespass on case:
658:15/18 Ball vs Rylye - writ of inquiry into damages granted.
681:6/13 Dutton vs Welbeck - court wishes to consider.
Action of account:
693:2/2 Wall vs Cooke - copy of declaration granted.
Actions continuing: **587**:(36/42); **645**:19/19; **664**:11/19; **668**:9/46; **670**:9/11.

[f19v]

Action of debt:
698:2/4 Kyte vs Godfery - judgment given by court that plaintiff recover both debt of £6.16d and costs; *scire facias* granted.
Actions of Qui Tam:
687:4/9 Tayler vs Jackman - *alias scire facias* against defendant's surety.
691:3/6 Tayler vs Samon - defendant's attorney reports non informatus. Therefore *scire facias* granted.
692:3/8 Tayler vs Greene - further peremptory day granted by agreement with plaintiff.
696:2/5 Tayler vs Millen - peremptory day to respond.
697:2/5 Tayler vs White - peremptory day to respond.
Actions continuing: **682**:5/10; **683**:5/10; **684**:5/10; **688**:4/9.

[f20 & 20v] (Blank)

[f21]

View of Frankpledge and Sessions of the Peace held 19 October 1614 before Joseph Harris, mayor and Jerome Kyte and Thomas Browne, Justices of the Peace for the borough.

699 *Jury for the King with homage*:

John Dubber,	Richard Meades,	Nicholas Tayler,
Thomas Screevin,	George Noble,	Thomas Rayer,
William Edwardes,	Hugh Hamond,	Richard Hawkins,
Jerome White,	John Lowe,	John Norman,
Randall Richards,	Thomas Webb,	Thomas Heathen,
Richard Browne,	Thomas Bruce.	

700 *Election of Officers*:
Thomas Rayer and Richard Shad are elected constables and sworn in.
William Archer, William Butterfeild, Richard Browne and Thomas Heathen, are elected tithingmen and sworn in.
William Hickes, senior and John Wilkinson are elected aletasters and sworn in.
Court adjourned to St. Andrew's Day.

[f21v]

701 *Innholders*
John Glover, alderman

Henry Bradshewe, gent
Richard Meades
Victuallers

William Rayer, alderman	William Hickes, senior
Thomas Williams	Hugh Hamonde
John Dissell	Thomas Godferye
John Ackley	Jerome White
Nicholas Tayler	Thomas Paynter
William Edwardes	Bennett Paynter
Thomas Screevine	Nicholas Glover
Edward Rudgate	Merriall Taylor, widow

licence granted to Robert Bignill on recognisance of £10
Sureties Nicholas Tayler William Edwardes each £5
Dorothy Wells, widow - recog: £10
Sureties Thomas Screevin Randall Richards each £5
Affeerers: Thomas Rayer, John Norman, John Lowe, sworn in
Estreats [no entry by clerk]

Sessions of the Peace - Recognisances

Memorandum: 24th May 1614
702:1/2 John Ball vs John Stone
Recognisance taken before John Glover, then mayor of the borough
John Stone £100 John and Ananias Collingwood £80 each
Upon condition that the said John Stone keeps the peace towards John Ball and all people and appears at this sessions of the peace of the borough.
John Stone does not appear therefore recognisances forfeit.

[f22]

Memorandum: 20th June 1614
636:4/5 William Bradshewe brings action against John Stone.
Recognisance taken before John Glover, then mayor etc.,
John Stone £40 Richard Shad and Thomas Screevin £20 each
Upon condition that John Stone keeps the peace against the said William and all the people and appears at this sessions of the peace of the borough.
John Stone does not appear therefore recognisances forfeit.
[Marginal note - Discharged on 2nd May 1615 before Joseph Harris, mayor and Thomas Bradshewe[15]]
Memorandum: 28th September 1614 - before John Glover, then mayor of the borough,
703:1/1Robert Bruce on recognisance of £80 and Thomas Bruce and William Wheeler, his sureties, on recognisance of £40 each.

[15] Thomas Bradshawe died 1613 - Hiorne probably intended to write 'Thomas Browne'.

Upon condition that the said Robert Bruce appeared at this sessions to make his case and receive judgment for and concerning breach of the peace upon William Parsons [Marginal note - The said Robert Bruce appeared and with the assent of William Parsons was discharged in full court].
Memorandum: on the day and year above written:
703a:1/2 the said Robert Bruce before the aforesaid mayor swore that Nicholas Midwinter, shoemaker of the borough, had broken the peace upon Christopher [blank] who had similarly broken the peace upon the said Robert Bruce.
Memorandum: on the day and year above written:
703a:2/2 the said Nicholas Midwinter before the aforesaid mayor; on recognisance of £40 and on recognisance of £40 by his surety, Thomas Webb. Upon condition that the said Nicholas Midwinter appear at this sessions to make his case and receive judgment.
[Marginal note - Discharged by the court and paid 12d for fine and delivered (to) William Bradshewe[16]]

[f22v]

30th August 1615 before Joseph Harris, gent, mayor of this borough.
704:1/3 Elizabeth Parker, wife of Walter Parker - swore on oath as follows:- That she stands in fear of Alexander Head that he will hurt her or her goods and demands the peace of him according to the law.

Elizabeth Parker (her mark)

Recognisance - Alexander Head £20 Edmund Rudgate and William Browne each £10 for keeping the peace and for appearance at the next sessions etc.. [marginal note - recog. d.. 2s]

[f23]

Portmoot court held 17 October 1614...

Action of debt: :
672:9/15 Rayer vs Williams (and Bradshewe) - *scire facias* returned executed and *alias scire facias* granted.
Actions of trespass on case:
658:16/18 Ball vs Ryly - defendant, on return of inquisitions under a writ of inquiry into damages, produces in this court a writ of *habeas corpus* dated 13th October 1614 returnable before King's Bench at Westminster the Saturday next of the octave of St. Martin; and proved etc.
681:7/13 Dutton vs Welbeck - continues under consideration of court.
Actions continuing: **587**:(37/42); **664**:12/19; **668**:10/46; **670**:10/11.

[f23v]

Actions of debt:
669:10/10 Kyte vs White - discharged by agreement with plaintiff.
689:4/15 Kyte vs Capp - defendant responds *non debet modo et forma.*

16 *WCA,* 50.

690:4/6 Warrine vs Cooke - defendant responds *non est factum*; *venire facias* granted.
695:3/10 Millen vs Belcher - peremptory day to respond.
698:3/4 Kyte vs Godfery - *scire facias* returned executed and *alias scire facias* granted.
706:1/24 Thomas Spenser, Knight and Baronet, vs John Tomlins - plaintiff puts declaration, but defendant does not appear, therefore he is in default etc. Judgment will be given in next court.
707:1/6 Thomas Slaymaker vs William Boddely - plaintiff puts declaration and defendant, in person, admits the debt of 9s which he pays in court and immediately seizes back the aforesaid 9s and declares against the said Thomas Slaymaker with a plaint of detinue and for the remainder he requests a copy.
709:1/4 Phillip Hawthorne vs John Collingwood - plaintiff declares and day to amend granted.
710:1/2 Thomas Meatcalfe vs Thomas Screevine - because plaintiff does not prosecute, action goes by default etc.
Action of detinue:
708:1/4 William Boddely vs Thomas Slaymaker - plaint of detinue (see **707** above).
Action of trespass:
694:3/10 Tredwell vs Elliott - stands as before.
Actions of Qui Tam:
682:6/10 Tayler vs Webb - action adjourned but with permission to agree out of court, until the next court.
683:6/10 Tayler vs Brookes - stands awaiting response.
684:6/10 Tayler vs Stowte - action adjourned but with permission to agree out of court, until the next court.
687:5/9 Tayler vs Jackman - *alias scire facias* returned executed.
Action unspecified:
705:1/1 Nicholas Joanes vs John Tomlins - plaintiff declares and immediately, with agreement of plaintiff, court dismisses case.

[f24]

Actions of Qui Tam:
688:5/9 Tayler vs Bowlte - action adjourned but with permission to agree out of court, until the next court etc.
691:4/6 Tayler vs Samone - *scire facias* returned executed and *alias scire facias* granted against defendant's surety.
692:4/8 Tayler vs Greene - defendant responds, through his attorney, Edmund Rudgate, and says that he is not guilty thereof; *venire facias* granted.
696:3/5 Tayler vs Millen - authority to compound granted.
697:3/5 Tayler vs White - authority to compound granted.

711:1/2 John Tayler vs William Danniell - authority granted for defendant to compound with plaintiff.

[f24v]

Portmoot court held 31 October 1614...

Actions of debt:

672:10/15 Rayer vs Williams (and Bradshewe) - *alias scire facias* returned executed and execution granted against defendant and surety.

689:5/15 Kyte vs Capp - parties put themselves on the country and *venire facias* granted.

690:5/6 Warrine vs Cooke - *venire facias* returned executed and *habeas corpora* granted.

695:4/10 Millen vs Belcher - defendant responds and plaintiff replicates and puts himself on the country; *venire facias* granted.

698:4/4 Kyte vs Godfery - *alias scire facias* returned executed and execution granted against the defendant for not less than £6.

[Memorandum - Mr. Kyte is contented to accept £6 at 10s a month, the first payment to begin at the next court; if he make default then execution to be against Godfery only, but not his bail].

Actions of trespass on case:

658:17/18 Ball vs Ryly - stands under writ of *habeas corpus*.

681:8/13 Dutton vs Welbeck - continues under consideration of court.

Actions continuing: **587**:(38/42); **664**:13/19; **668**:11/46; **670**:11/11; **694**:4/10.

[f25]

Actions of debt:

707:2/6 Slaymaker vs Boddely - peremptory day to respond.

709:2/4 Hawthorne vs Collingwood - peremptory day to respond.

Action of trespass:

712:1/2 William Parsons vs Robert Bruce - plaintiff puts declaration and copy granted to defendant.

Action of detinue:

708:2/8 Boddely vs Slaymaker - peremptory day to respond.

Actions of Qui Tam:

682:7/10 Tayler vs Webb - action adjourned but with permission to agree out of court, until the next court.

683:7/10 Tayler vs Brookes - stands awaiting response.

687:6/9 Tayler vs Jackman - execution granted against defendant.

688:6/9 Tayler vs Bowlte - action adjourned but with permission to agree out of court, until the next court.

691:5/6 Tayler vs Samon - *alias scire facias* returned executed and execution granted against defendant, who appeared in person in custody of sergeant.[17]

[17] Sole example of *Qui Tam* defendant in custody in these courtbooks.

692:5/8 Tayler vs Greene - *venire facias* continues.
696:4/5 Tayler vs Millen - action adjourned but with permission to agree out of court, until the next court.
697:4/5 Tayler vs White - action adjourned but with permission to agree out of court, until the next court.
711:2/2 Tayler vs Danniell - discharged by agreement with plaintiff and defendant gives on the part of the king 3s 4d and delivers it to William Bradshewe, chamberlain.[18]
713:1/4 John Tayler vs George Dods - plaintiff puts information and copy granted.
Action unspecified:
714:1/2 Nicholas Elliott vs Ellin Skey, widow - plaintiff puts declaration and copy granted to defendant.
Actions continuing: **684**: 7/10; **706**:2/24; **710**:2/2.

[f25v]

Portmoot court held 14 November 1614...
Actions of debt:
689:6/15 Kyte vs Capp - *venire facias* returned executed and *habeas corpora* granted.
690:6/6 Warrine vs Cooke - discharged by agreement with plaintiff.
695:5/10 Millen vs Belcher - continues under *venire facias*.
709:3/4 Hawthorne vs Collingwood - defendant responds and is given day to wage law with four compurgators in next court.
715:1/4 William Wayte vs Thomas Screevin - plaintiff puts declaration and copy granted to defendant.
716:1/10 Thomas Browne vs William Parrat - day given for plaintiff to state case in next court.
717:1/3 William Parratt vs Henry Ranckle - plaintiff puts declaration and copy granted to defendant.
718:1/3 Thomas Browne vs Richard Lacye - day given for plaintiff to state case in next court.
Action of trespass:
712:2/2 Parsons vs Bruce - discharged by agreement with plaintiff.
Action unspecified:
714:2/2 Elliott vs Skey - continues for plaintiff. Discharged.
Actions continuing: **587**:(39/42); **658**:18/18; **664**:14/19; **668**:12/46; **672**:11/15; **681**:9/13; **694**:5/10; **706**:3/24; **707**:3/6; **708**:3/4.

[f26]

Actions of Qui Tam:
687:7/9 Tayler vs Jackman - execution continues against defendant.

[18] *WCA*, 50.

691:6/6 Tayler vs Samon - discharged; defendant pays 6s. on the part of the king[19] [Marginal note - 6s. delivered to William Bradshewe].
692:6/8 Tayler vs Greene - *habeas corpus* juratorum granted.
696:5/5 Tayler vs Millen - discharged; defendant pays 12d. on the part of the king[20] [Marginal note - 12d delivered to William Bradshewe].
697:5/5 Tayler vs White - discharged; defendant owes nothing to the king or John Tayler.
719:1/2 John Tayler vs Thomas Webb - plaintiff lays information and authority granted to defendant to compound with plaintiff in next court.
Actions continuing: **682**:8/10; **683**:8/10; **684**:8/10; **688**:7/9; **713**:2/4.

[f26v]

Portmoot court held 28 November 1614...

Actions of debt:
689:7/15 Kyte vs Capp - writ of *habeas corpora* continues.
709:4/4 Hawthorne vs Collingwood - defendant wages law with 4 compurgators viz: Simon Jeames gent., Richard Hawkins, William Hickes snr, and Richard Collingwood; therefore he goes quit.
715:2/4 Waite vs Screevin - second day of privilege granted to defendant.
716:2/10 Browne vs Parrate - plaintiff puts completed declaration and copy granted to defendant.
Actions continuing: **587**:(40/42); **664**:15/19; **668**:13/46; **672**:12/15; **681**:10/13; **682**:9/10; **683**:9/10; **684**:9/10; **694**:6/10; **695**:6/10; **706**:4/24; **707**:4/6; **708**:4/4; **717**:2/3; **718**:2/3.

[f27]

Actions of Qui Tam:
720:1/2 John Tayler vs Christopher Hinton - plaintiff lays information and copy granted to defendant.
Action of trespass on case.
721:1/3 Robert Bruce vs Nicholas Midwinter - plaintiff puts declaration and defendant confesses the action; writ of inquiry into damages granted, plaintiff to return it in next court.
Actions continuing: **687**:8/9; **688**:8/9; **692**:7/8; **713**:3/4; **719**:2/2.

[f27v]

Portmoot court held 12 December 1614...

Actions of debt:
707:5/6 Slaymaker vs Boddely - defendant responds with wager of law and is ordered by the court to appear in next court with four compurgators.
715:3/4 Wayte vs Screevin - continues for defendant.
716:3/10 Browne vs Parrate - continues for defendant
717:3/3 Parrat vs Ranckle - discharged for defendant.

[19] *WCA*, 50.
[20] *WCA*, 50.

718:3/3 Browne vs Lacye - discharged for defendant.
Actions of trespass:
694:7/10 Tredwell vs Elliott - copy granted.
723:1/7 John Batt vs John Kerwood - plaintiff puts declaration and day to amend granted.
Action unspecified:
722:1/2 Thomas Jackman vs John Elfrite - plaintiff puts declaration and copy granted to defendant.
Actions continuing: **587**:(41/42); **664**:16/19; **668**:14/46; **672**:13/15; **681**:11/13; **689**:8/15; **695**:7/10; **706**:5/24; **721**:2/3.

[f28]

Actions of debt:
724:1/14 Edmund White vs William Symons - plaintiff's attorney, Simon Jeames, puts declaration; defendant's attorney is Edmund Rudgate; day to imparl is allowed.
Action of trespass on case:
725:1/1 Nicholas Mitchell vs William Muckell } Memorandum
Action of trespass:
726:1/1 William Muckell vs Nicholas Mitchell }
Memorandum: - On this present day about 9 o'clock in the morning, the aforesaid parties by the deliverance of 6d. either to other, submitted themselves to the order of William Rayer and John Glover, aldermen, for the ending of the said two causes and of all other matters between them from the beginning of the world till this day: upon the pain of £10 to be ended before the court, which said arbitrators before the beginning of this court awarded that both these suits shall be no further prosecuted by either of them; and that Muckell shall pay to Mitchell 13s, (which he has paid him), and that Nicholas Mitchell shall have the 10s which is remaining in Mr.Mayor's hands; which shall be in full satisfaction of all matters and trespasses whatsoever between (the parties) until this present day:
(signed by) William Rayer, John Glover, Simon Jeames, Edmund Hiorne and Thomas Rayer.
Actions of Qui Tam:
684:10/10 Tayler vs Stowte - stands as before.[21]
720:2/2 Tayler vs Hinton - day to reply granted.
Actions continuing: **682**:10/10; **683**:10/10; **687**:9/9; **688**:9/9; **692**:8/8; **713**:4/4.

[f28v]

Breach of the Peace:
728:1/2 Memorandum: 12th December 1614 - John Kerwood of Deddington in County of Oxford brings action for the peace against John Batt of the borough aforesaid, to be held in full court:

[21] *WCA*, 50: composition of 3s4d paid.

Recognisance: Before the mayor on the same day and year, John Batt stood on recognisance of £40 on condition that he keep the peace towards the King and all his people but principally towards the said John Kerwood and appear at the next sessions of the peace of this aforesaid borough.
John Dubber and Thomas Bruce each go surety for £20.

[f29]

Portmoot court held 19 December 1614...

Actions of debt:
672:14/15 Rayer vs Williams - renewal of writ.
707:6/6 Slaymaker vs Boddely - defendant takes oath and wages law with four compurgators viz: William Porter, John Mason, Roger Sturgis and John Cotten; therefore he goes quit.
Action of trespass:
694:8/10 Tredwell vs Elliott - peremptory day to respond.
Action unspecified:
722:2/2 Jackman vs Elfrite - defendant responds and wages law with four compurgators viz: Robert Bignill, Richard Shad, William Kynge and William Butterfeild; and he goes quit.
Actions continuing: **587**:(42/42); **664**:17/19; **668**:15/46; **681**:12/13; **689**:9/15; **695**:8/10; **706**:6/24; **715**:4/4; **716**:4/10.

[f29v]

Actions of debt:
724:2/14 White vs Symons - defendant offers a foreign plea, one that he does not (immediately) prove in this court and court wishes to consider before acceptance.
731:1/6 Richard Raves vs Henry Bradshewe, gent - plaintiff puts declaration and copy granted.
732:1/6 William Meatcalfe vs Henry Bradshewe - plaintiff puts declaration and copy granted.
733:1/3 Thomas Browne alderman vs William Abbott - plaintiff puts declaration and defendant granted copy.
Action of trespass on case:
721:3/3 Bruce vs Midwinter - discharged: and Thomas Webb, surety, to pay 12d a week till 10s 6s is paid, the first payment on Sunday next; and if he default then to pay whole amount at John Bruce's house.
Action of trespass:
723:2/7 Batt vs Kerwood - defendant (sic) plaintiff puts declaration and copy granted to defendant.
Action of account:
730:1/4 Edward Abbott vs Robert Symonds - plaintiff puts declaration and copy granted to defendant.

[f30]

Portmoot court held 9 January 1615...

Action of trespass:
694:9/10 Tredwell vs Elliott - defendant responds.
Actions continuing: **664**:18/19; **668**:16/46; **672**:15/15; **681**:13/13; **689**:10/15; **695**:9/10; **706**:7/24.

[f30v]

Actions of debt:
724:3/14 White vs Symons - court wishes to consider.
731:2/6 Raves vs Bradshewe - peremptory day to respond.
732:2/6 Meatcalfe vs Bradshewe - peremptory day to respond.
733:2/3 Browne vs Abbott - peremptory day to respond.
Actions of trespass
723:3/7 Batt vs Kerwood - premptory day to reply.
734:1/3 John Smith vs Richard Young - plaintiff puts declaration and copy granted to defendant.
Action of account:
730:2/4 Abbott vs Symons - peremptory day to respond.
Action continuing: **716**:5/10.

[f31]

Portmoot court held 23 January 1615.

Actions of debt:
664:19/19 Tredwell vs Elliott - Referred to arbitration.[in margin- discharged]
689:11/15 Jerome Keite vs Maurice Cappe - jury between parties in aforesaid case :-

John Lowe,	Robert Bignill,	John Norman,
William Edwardes,	William Butterfeild,	Thomas Gee,
William Archer,	Randall Richards,	Richard Hawkins,
Hugh Hamonde,	William Hickes snr.,	Thomas Bruce.

Which jury, on oath, find for the plaintiff and assess the debt at £4.10s. and costs 2d; judgment adjourned to next court.
Action of trespass:
694:10/10 Tredwell vs Elliott - defendant puts a foreign plea and case referred to arbiters, Thomas Harris and Oliver Smith, gent, in respect of all actions between them to be finished before 25th March next. [in margin - discharged].
Action continuing: **695**:10/10.

[f31v]

Actions of debt:
731:3/6 Richard Raves vs Henry Bradshewe - defendant responds through his attorney, Edmund Rudgate, that he is unable to deny what he owes and offers the plaintiff £10 of the debt. Judgment adjourned to next court.

732:3/6 William Meatcalfe vs Henry Bradshewe - Defendant replies similarly through his attorney, and offers the plaintiff £8 of the debt etc., judgment adjourned to next court.
733:3/3 Browne vs Abbott - discharged.
735:1/1 Thomas Godfery vs John Tayler - plaint of debt of 40s. Sergeant at mace returned that he had seized one horse worth [blank] and forfeited it to the use of the mayor and commonalty of the borough because of no response etc.. and appraised at 53s 4d by William Rayer, Edmund Hiorne, John Dubber and John Woodroofe.
736:1/1 Phillip Dodwell vs Christopher Forty - plaintiff granted day to declare; discharged.
Actions of trespass:
723:4/7 Batt vs Kerwood - defendant responds not guilty, copy granted.
734:2/3 Smith vs Yonge - defendant, through his attorney Edmund Rudgate, confesses his action and writ of inquiry into damages granted.
Action of account:
730:3/4 Abbott vs Symons - defendant pays in court £3.10s. which is delivered to Simon Jeames, plaintiff's attorney, for the use of the plaintiff who requests costs etc.
Actions continuing: **706**:8/24; **716**:6/10; **724**:4/14.

[f32]

Portmoot court held 7 February 1615.
Actions of debt:
689:12/15 Kyte vs Capp - judgment of court is that plaintiff shall recover £4 10s debt and 49s 10d for costs etc., *scire facias* granted against surety for defendant.
731:4/6 Raves vs Bradshewe - judgment of court is that plaintiff shall recover [blank] for debt and [blank] for costs; *scire facias* granted against surety for defendant.
732:4/6 Meatcalfe vs Bradshewe - judgment of court is that plaintiff shall recover £8 for debt and [blank] for costs; *scire facias* granted against surety for defendant.
Actions of trespass:
723:5/7 Bat vs Kerwood - parties aforesaid put themselves on the country and *venire facias* granted.
734:3/3 Smith vs Yonge - judgment of court is that plaintiff recover 3d for damages and 27s 2d for costs etc; payment is made in court and action dismissed.
Action of account:
730:4/4 Abbott vs Symons - Edmund Rudgate, attorney, and surety for defendant, pays 8s 7d for costs; case dismissed.
Actions continuing: **706**:9/24; **716**:7/10.

[f32v]

Actions of debt:
738:1/2 Richard Whinge vs Richard Colesborne - plaintiff puts declaration and copy granted to defendant.
724:5/14 White vs Symons - defendant responds with copy granted to plaintiff.
Action of trespass:
737:1/16 Richard Yonge vs John Smith *alias* Hadden - plaintiff puts declaration and day to amend granted.
739:1/19 William Jenckes vs William Plott - plaintiff puts completed declaration and copy granted to defendant.
Action of trespass on case:
740:1/3 John Leye vs Thomas Meatcalfe - plaintiff puts declaration and is granted day to amend in next court.

[f33]

Portmoot court held 21 February 1615.
Actions of debt:
689:13/15 Kyte vs Capp - *scire facias* returned executed and *alias scire facias* granted.
724:6/14 White vs Symons - copy of response granted plaintiff.
731:5/6 Raves vs Bradshewe - *scire facias* returned executed and *alias scire facias* granted.
732:5/6 Meatcalfe vs Bradshewe - similarly.
738:2/2 Whinge vs Colesborne - defendant appears in person and admits the debt to the plaintiff; he is committed in execution to sergeant at mace.
Actions of trespass:
723:6/7 Batt vs Kerwood - stands under *venire facias.*
737:2/16 Yonge vs Smith - peremptory day to respond granted.
739:2/19 Jenckes vs Plott - peremptory day to respond granted.
Action of trespass on case:
740:2/3 Leye vs Meatcalfe - second day of privilege granted.
Actions continuing: **706**:10/24; **716**:8/10.

[f33v]

Portmoot court held 7 March 1615.
Actions of debt:
689:14/15 Kyte vs Capp - *alias scire facias* returned and execution granted against defendant and his surety.
724:7/14 White vs Symons - peremptory day to reply granted.
731:6/6 Raves vs Bradshewe - plaintiff admits himself satisfied in full court and case is dismissed.
732:6/6 Meatcalfe vs Bradshewe - similarly.
741:1/4 Thomas Meatcalfe vs John Ley - plaintiff puts declaration and copy granted to defendant.

742:1/1 William Durbridge vs Richard Francklyn - dismissed.
Actions of trespass:
737:3/16 Yonge vs Smith - defendant responds and day to amend granted.
739:3/19 Jenckes vs Plott - defendant responds not guilty and court adjudges upon process.
Action of trespass on case:
740:3/3 Ley vs Meatcalfe - plaintiff satisfied; dismissed.
Actions continuing: **706**:11/24; **716**:9/10; **723**:7/7.

[f34]

Portmoot court held 21 March 1615.
Actions of debt:
689:15/15 Kyte vs Capp - Thomas Webb, defendant's surety, had penalty executed against him. [Memorandum - sergeant at mace reports that Mr. Kyte willed him to set the bail at liberty and that he was satisfied.]
716:10/10 Browne vs Parrat - dismissed with agreement of plaintiff and obligation delivered.
724:8/14 White vs Symons - plaintiff replicates that title[22] is not recorded and copy granted to defendant.
741:2/4 Meatcalfe vs Ley - peremptory day to respond.
743:1/3 Anne Leake, widow, vs John Whitton, gent - plaintiff puts declaration and day to amend granted
Actions of trespass:
737:4/16 Yonge vs Smith - defendant pleads not guilty.
739:4/19 Jenckes vs Plott - court wishes to consider on process.
Action continuing: **706**:12/24.

[f34v]

Portmoot court held 3 April 1615.
Actions of debt:
724:9/14 White vs Symons - day for replication appointed.
741:3/4 Meatcalfe vs Ley - defendant responds and arranges to wage law with four compurgators in next court.
743:2/3 Leake vs Whitton - peremptory day for response.
744:1/5 Edmund White vs William Symons - plaintiff puts declaration and copy granted.
Actions of trespass:
737:5/16 Yonge vs Smith - court wishes to consider.
739:5/19 Jencks vs Plott - court wishes to consider.
Action of trespass on case:
745:1/2 William Tayler vs Edmund Surrell - plaintiff puts declaration and copy granted.
Action continuing: **706**:13/24.

[22] See Trice-Martin, 150 'ti-lo' = titulo = to make an entry.

[f35]

Actions of debt:

747:1/1 Anthony Turner vs Thomas Dutton - dismissed for defendant.

748:1/1 Thomas Clemens vs Gabriel Mathewe, gent - dismissed for defendant.

Action of trespass:

746:1/2 George Baker vs Thomas Guye - plaintiff puts declaration and copy granted.

[f35v]

View of Frankpledge and Sessions of the Peace held 5th April 1615 before Joseph Harris, mayor, Jerome Keite and Thomas Browne, gents, Justices for the Peace...

749: *Jury for the King with homage*

John Dubber,	Robert Spitle,	Nicholas Tayler,
Hugo Hamond,	Jerome White,	John Ackley,
John Lowe,	Thomas Webbe,	William Bradshewe,
Thomas Heathen,	George Noble,	Thomas Bruce,
William Edwardes,	William Butterfeild.	

Affeerers : Jerome White, George Noble, William Edwardes - sworn in.

[f36]

750: The names of all the innholders and victuallers which are licenced within the borough :-

Innholders

John Glover, alderman
Henry Bradshewe, gent
Richard Meades

Victuallers

William Rayer, alderman	Hugo Hamond
Thomas Williams	Thomas Godfery
John Dissell	Jerome White
John Ackley	Thomas Paynter
Nicholas Tayler	Bennett Paynter
William Edwardes	Nicholas Glover
Thomas Screevin	Merriall Tayler, widow
Edward Rudgate	Robert Bignill
William Hickes, senior	Dorothy Wells, widow

Sessions of the Peace - Recognisances

636:5/5 John Stone does not appear upon recognisance set at last sessions. Therefore Richard Shad and Thomas Screevin his sureties, upon the oath of William Bradshewe, for keeping the peace etc.

[Marginal note - Recognisance forfeit; dismissed]

702:2/2 John Stone does not appear upon recognisance set at last sessions. Therefore John Collingwood and Ananias Collingwood sureties, upon the oath of John Ball, for the peace etc.
[Marginal note - Recognisance forfeit; dismissed].
754:1/1 Thomas Webbe upon recognisance of £40 that he appear this sessions to make his case and receive judgment. Thomas Screevin and Walter Parker, sureties, each place recognisance of £10 and the said Thomas Webb appears and is dismissed.
[Marginal note - Recognisance of Thomas Webb; dismissed]

[f36v]

755:1/1 Richard Bennet, woolwinder of the borough, on recognisance of his debt to the King of £40 Upon condition that he appear at this sessions to make his case and receive judgment. Nicholas Glover and John Batt, his sureties, separately place recognisance of £20: And the said Richard Bennett appears and, in full court, is discharged.
[Marginal note - Recognisance Richard Bennett; debt 4s.4d]

30 August 1615 before Joseph Harris, gent, mayor

704:2/3 Elizabeth Parker, wife of Walter Parker, brings action for the peace against Alexander Head - Alexander Head's recognisance of £40 Edmund Rudgate and William Browne his sureties for £20 each that Alexander Head shall keep the peace and appear at the next sessions.

Child maintenance:

752:1/3 Richard Meades of the borough, yeoman, on recognisance of his debt to the King of 100 marks of lawful money of England Upon condition that he appears in person at this sessions and then and there make his case and receive judgment. Item: It is ordered by the mayor aforesaid and by Thomas Browne, the King's majesty's Justice of the peace, in open sessions that whereas Elizabeth[23] Robinson who was lately delivered of a base child (being a woman child) within the borough And upon her oath taken before the said mayor and Justice, he the said Richard Meades is the reputed father of the said child: That hereafter he the said Richard Meades shall discharge the town of Woodstock of any charge concerning the keeping of the said base child, and find sufficient sureties before the next sessions to perform this order and likewise shall appear at the next sessions at Woodstock unless he enter security aforesaid before the next sessions: And to stand upon his first Recognisance.
(signed by) Joseph Harris, Thomas Brown

[f37]

Recognisances:

728:2/2 John Batt on recognisance of his debt to the King of £40 Upon condition that he keeps the peace of the King and all his people but principally against John

[23] Later 'Isabell Robins'.

Kerwood of Deddington, upon the oath of the said John Kerwood, and appear at this sessions etc., John Dubber and Thomas Bruce on recognisance of £20 each. Memo: the said John Batt appears in full court and is dismissed upon the aforesaid recognisance and remains at large. [Marginal note - dismissed].

18th September 1615 before Joseph Harris, mayor

756:1/2 Jerome Walford of Hensington, yeoman, on recognisance of £40, Robert Bignill and William Wells sureties for £20 each That Jerome Walford keep the peace and appear at the next sessions.

8th September 1615 before the mayor

757:1/2 John Lowe brings action for the peace vs William Muckell, slater. William Muckell on recognisance of £40 Robert Bignill and John Symons sureties for £20 each. That Muckell keep the peace and appear at the next sessions at Woodstock.

753: **Surveyors of the highway**

Memorandum: Alderman Browne, Alderman Rayer and John Norman were elected surveyors of the highways for the year following

(signed by) Edmund Hiorne.

[f37v]

Portmoot court held 16 April 1615...

Actions of debt:

724:10/14 White vs Symons - defendant's attorney replies *non est informatus replicandi.*; judgment adjourned to next court.

741:4/4 Meatcalfe vs Lea - defendant wages law with four compurgators viz: Christopher Wheeler, William Wheeler, Simon Jeames and Richard Collingwood; therefore he goes quit.

743:3/3 Leake vs Whitton - defendant responds *non est factum*; the plaintiff has died.[24]

744:2/5 White vs Symons - peremptory day to respond granted.

Actions of trespass:

737:6/16 Yonge vs Smith - stands as before.

739:6/19 Jenckes vs Plott - stands as before.

746:2/2 Baker vs Guy - action dismissed for plaintiff.

Action of trespass on case:

745:2/2 Tayler vs Surrell - action dismissed for defendant.

Action continuing: **706**:14/24.

[f38]

Portmoot court held 1 May 1615...

Actions of debt:

724:11/14 White vs Symons - court adjudges plaintiff should recover [blank] for debt and costs.

[24] MSS. Wills (Oxon) 41/2/36.

744:3/5 White vs Symons - defendant responds and plaintiff replicates; *venire facias* granted for return in next court.
Action of trespass:
761:1/5 Robert Symons and Elizabeth, his wife vs Thomas Lowe - plaintiffs declare and day to amend granted.
Actions of trespass on case:
760:1/8 Edward Bulliphant vs Edward Woolly - plaintiff puts declaration and copy granted to defendant.
762:1/1 John Buller vs William Phipps, clerk - plaintiff declares and copy granted.
Actions continuing: **706**:15/24; **737**:7/16; **739**:7/19.

[f38v]

Portmoot court[25] held 15 May 1615...
Actions of debt:
724:12/14 White vs Symons - *scire facias* returned executed and *alias scire facias* granted against defendant's surety.
744:4/5 White vs Symons - *venire facias* returned executed and writ of *habeas corpora* juratorum granted for return in next court.
Action of trespass:
761:2/5 Symons and wife vs Lowe - copy of declaration granted.
Action of trespass on case:
760:2/8 Bulliphant vs Woolly - peremptory day for response.
Actions continuing: **706**:16/24; **737**:8/16; **739**:8/19.

[f39]

Portmoot court held 22 May 1615...
Actions of debt:
634:(11/12) Elizabeth Rylie vs Roger Powell - judgment granted against defendant in Court of 7th February 1614 for 14s for debt and costs and in this court *scire facias* granted against William Raunson and Alexander Head, the defendant's sureties.
724:13/14 White vs Symons - *alias scire facias* returned executed and surety for defendant handed over by the said defendant in execution of this action.
744:5/5 Edmund White vs William Symons - jury between parties:

Jerome White,	Thomas Screevin,	John Lowe,
Richard Shad,	Thomas Rayer,	George Noble,
William Edwardes,	Hugh Hamond,	William Hickes snr,
William Hickes jnr,	Robert Spitle,	Thomas Heathen.

Which jury find for the plaintiff and assess damages of 6d and for expenses and costs 2d; and surety...[unfinished]
763:1/11 Robert Keate vs Richard Meade - plaintiff puts declaration and copy and day of privilege granted to defendant.

[25] 'Baron' crossed through.

764:1/1 Thomas Peesly vs Edward Johnson - plaintiff puts declaration and copy granted to defendant; action dismissed.
Action of trespass:
761:3/5 Symons and wife vs Lowe - peremptory day for response appointed.
Action of trespass on case:
760:3/8 Bulliphant vs Woolly - continues by assent of plaintiff.
Actions continuing: **706**:17/24; **737**:9/16; **739**:9/19.

[f39v]

Portmoot court held 5 June 1615.
Actions of debt:
634(12/12) Ryly vs Powell - sergeant returns *alias scire facias* executed and execution is granted against the defendant, and debt and costs are paid and he goes quit.
724:14/14 White vs Symons - sergeant returns execution, executed and paid in court £20 for debt and 33s.6d. for costs; defendant goes quit.
763:2/11 Keate vs Meade - second day of privilege granted defendant.
Action of trespass:
761:4/5 Symons and wife vs Lowe - defendant responds and date and day to amend and complete in next court granted.
Action of detinue:
765:1/1 William Raunson vs Robert Symons - plaintiff puts declaration and day to amend granted; action dismissed with assent of plaintiff when defendant pays in full court 13s.4d debt and 5s.7d. costs.
Actions continuing: **706**:18/24; **737**:10/16; **739**:10/19; **760**:4/5.

[f40]

Portmoot court held 19 June 1615...
Actions of debt:
763:3/11 Keate vs Meade - last day of privilege granted
769:1/2 Mary Keene vs Thomas Screevin - plaintiff puts declaration and first day of privilege granted to defendant.
766:1/1 Richard Heath vs Michael Pulchoe - plaintiff puts declaration and defendant, remanded in prison, confesses, through his attorney, a debt of 10s and a day to pay is granted at the next court.
Actions of trespass:
761:5/5 Robert Symons and Elizabeth, his wife, vs Thomas Lowe - defendant's attorney brings to court a writ of *habeas corpus* bearing date 14th instant returnable before the Barons of the Exchequer at Westminster on Tuesday 27th of the instant month of June to make case and receive judgment. Witnessed by Laurence Tanfield, knight, at Westminster. And proved etc.
767:1/6 Ambrose Lardner vs Joseph Forde - plaintiff puts declaration and is granted day to amend in next court; defendant's attorney enters plea of not guilty. Court wishes to consider.

Actions of trespass on case:
760:5/8 Bulliphant vs Woolly - because defendant does not respond, judgment is adjourned to next court.
768:1/2 Joseph Forde vs Ambrose Lardner - plaintiff declares and defendant is granted copy.
Actions continuing: **706**:19/24; **737**:11/16; **739**:11/19.

[f40v]

Portmoot court held 3 July 1615...
Actions of debt:
763:4/11 Keate vs Meade - peremptory day to respond granted.
769:2/2 Keene vs Screevin - defendant, in person, confesses to debt; therefore judgment and execution is granted and he remains in hands of sergeant at mace.
Action of trespass:
767:2/6 Lardner vs Ford - court wishes to consider.
Actions of trespass on case:
760:6/8 Bulliphant vs Woolly - writ of inquiry into damages granted to be returned in next court.
768:2/2 Ford vs Lardner - defendant pays £11 for debt, 2s for damages and 6s 8d for costs; therefore he goes quit.
Actions continuing: **706**:20/24; **737**:12/16; **739**:12/19.

[f41]

Portmoot court held 17 July 1615...
Actions of debt:
763:5/11 Keate vs Meade - continues by assent of plaintiff.
771:1/1 Richard Reade vs William Muckell - plaintiff puts declaration and defendant does not appear; judgment adjourned to next court.
772:1/7 Anthony Deverill vs William Edwardes - plaintiff puts declaration and first day of privilege granted defendant.
Actions of trespass on case:
760:7/8 Bulliphant vs Woolly - renewal of aforesaid writ.
770:1/1 John Lowe vs William Muckell - plaintiff puts declaration and defendant does not appear; writ of inquiry into damages granted.
Actions continuing: **706**:21/24; **737**:13/16; **739**:13/19; **767**:3/6.

[f41v]

Portmoot court held 31 July 1615.
Actions of debt:
763:6/11 Keate vs Meade - defendant pleads *per minas* through Edmund Rudgate, his attorney, and immediately plaintiff replicates and puts himself on the country; *venire facias* granted.
772:2/7 Deverill vs Edwardes - second day of privilege granted defendant.

773:1/1 Nicholas Yonge vs William Tredwell - plaintiff declares and defendant pays 13s.8d for debt and 5s.9d for costs etc and he goes quit.
774:1/1 William Back vs William Austine - plaint dismissed.
Action of trespass on case:
760:8/8 Bulliphant vs Woolly - continues under writ of inquiry into damages.
Actions continuing: **706**:22/24; **737**:14/16; **739**:14/19; **767**:4/6.

[f42]

Actions of debt:
775:1/1 John Gearinge and Richard Spencer vs John Hadden - upon demand of two hundred pounds defendant is arrested and remains in custody of sergeant at mace and plaintiffs, through Simon Jeames their attorney, put declaration and bring to court a written obligation; copy of declaration granted defendant.
780:1/16 Rowland Franklyn vs Richard Cale - plaintiff puts declaration and copy granted to defendant.
Actions of trespass:
778:1/4 Dorothy Barratt, widow vs William Fletcher - plaintiff puts declaration and is granted day to amend.
779:1/4 William Fletcher vs Robert Barratt - plaintiff puts declaration and defendant is granted day to amend; defendant instantly responds not guilty and *venire facias* is granted.
Actions of trespass on case:
776:1/4 Henry Brockwell vs Averye Hall, as administrator of the goods and chattels of Edward Hall, his brother, lately deceased - plaintiff puts declaration and defendant is granted copy.[26]
777:1/4 Thomas White vs Averye Hall - plaintiff puts declaration and is granted day to amend.

[f42v]

Portmoot court held 14 August 1615.
Actions of debt:
763:7/11 Keate vs Meade - renewal of *venire facias* in next court, for defendant.
772:3/7 Deverill vs Edwardes - last day of privilege granted defendant in next court.
Actions continuing: **706**:23/24; **737**:15/16; **739**:15/19; **767**:5/6; **776**:2/4.

[f43]

Actions of debt:
780:2/16 Francklyn vs Cale - peremptory day for response.
781:1/19 Richard Heath vs Thomas Williams - plaintiff puts declaration and defendant is granted copy.
Actions of trespass:
778:2/4 Barratt vs Fletcher - copy of declaration granted.

[26] Edward Hall (als.Smith) of Kirtlington d.1612 MSS.Wills (Oxon) 106.62; 297/4/48.

779:2/4 Fletcher vs Barratt - stands as before.
Actions of trespass on case:
777:2/4 Thomas White vs Averye Hall - copy of declaration granted.
782:1/8 Tobias Brookes vs Robert Binckes - court adjudges that said defendant should recover 38s 9d for costs and his expenses by the advice of James Whitlock, Esq., recorder of the borough, and *scire facias* granted against Richard Reade, the plaintiff's surety.

[f43v]

Portmoot court held 28 August 1615.
Actions of debt:
706:24/24 Spenser vs Tomlins - discharged.
763:8/11 Keate vs Meade - renewal of *venire facias*.
772:4/7 Deverill vs Edwardes - peremptory day for response.
780:3/16 Francklyn vs Cale - defendant's attorney reports non informatus. (Therefore 5s. [added later]).
781:2/19 Heath vs Williams - second day of privilege granted.
783:1/3 William Hitche vs John Woodrooffe - plaintiff puts declaration and defendant is granted copy.
Actions of trespass:
737:16/16 Yonge vs Smith - stands as before .
739:16/19 Jencks vs Plott - proceeding for plaintiff if..etc..otherwise..etc..
767:6/6 Lardner vs Ford - stands as before.
778:3/4 Barrat vs Fletcher - peremptory day for response.
Actions of trespass on case:
777:3/4 White vs Averye Hall - peremptory day for response.
782:2/8 Brookes vs Binckes - *alias scire facias* granted against plaintiff's surety to appear here at next court.
Action of account:
784:1/6 Thomas Screevin vs Morgan Jenckins - plaintiff granted day to declare.
Actions continuing: **776**:3/4; **779**:3/4.

[f44]

Portmoot court held 11 September 1615.
Actions of debt:
763:9/11 Keate vs Meade - *venire facias* returned executed and *habeas corpora* granted for return in next court.
772:5/7 Deverill vs Edwardes - defendant pleads *per minas* and *venire facias* is granted.
780:4/16 Francklyn vs Cale - court adjudges plaintiff recover [blank] for debt and [blank] for costs and *scire facias* granted against surety.
781:3/19 Heath vs Williams - last day of privilege granted to defendant.

Actions of trespass:
739:17/19 Jenckes vs Plott - if plaintiff does not proceed, defendant is given leave to bring writ of *venire facias* in next court.
778:4/4 Barratt vs Fletcher - dismissed.
779:4/4 Fletcher vs Barratt - similarly.
Actions of trespass on case:
776:4/4 Brockwell vs Hall - dismissed.
777:4/4 White vs Avery Hall - defendant's attorney reports non est_informatus; writ of inquiry into damages granted for return in next court. [Marginal note - Dismissed for plaintiff].
782:3/8 Brookes vs Binckes - *alias scire facias* returned executed and writ of execution granted against plaintiff and his surety for costs and expenses etc.
Court order for guardianship:
785:1/1 Edmund Rudgate is elected to be guardian of John Robins during his minority.

[f44v]

Actions of debt:
783:2/3 Hitche vs Woodrooffe - defendant's attorney responds that he cannot deny that he owes 44s and for the sum of £14 18s remaining, he asks for leave to bring 4 compurgators to the next court; therefore court decides plaintiff recover aforesaid 44s with costs and *scire facias* is granted.
786:1/10 Edmund Meese vs Richard Heynes - plaintiff puts declaration and defendant is granted copy.
787:1/10 Thomas Gyles vs Richard Heynes - plaintiff granted day to declare.
788:1/4 Richard Webb vs Thomas Rippingall - plaintiff puts declaration and defendant is granted copy.
789:1/2 Richard Greene vs Benjamin Knighte - plaintiff puts declaration and defendant is granted copy.
Action of trespass:
790:1/5 John Whitton, gent vs Robert Symons - defendant has long since pleaded not guilty and *venire facias* was granted; it is ordered by the court that if plaintiff does not wish to prosecute he must appear in next court and defendant then be given licence to bring writ of *venire facias*.
Action of trespass on case:
791:1/1 John Dewe *alias* Sadler vs Phillip Hawthorne - action dismissed.
Action of account:
784:2/6 Screevin vs Ginckins - because plaintiff does not proceed with his action court adjudges defendant can recover costs etc.

[f45]

Court baron of the Royal borough aforesaid held at the Guildhall of the same borough on Monday viz. 15th September 1615 before Joseph Harris, gent, Mayor[27]

Portmoot court held 20th September 1615.

Actions of debt:

772:6/7 Deverill vs Edwardes - sergeant returns *venire facias* executed and *habeas corpora juratorum* issued.

781:4/19 Heath vs Williams - peremptory day for response.

783:3/3 Hitche vs Woodroofe - defendant appears in court under oath with four compurgators viz: William Metcalfe, William Bradshewe, Richard Shad and Richard Hawkins and because plaintiff does not put forward his case therefore defendant goes quit for £14 18s and pays in court 44s and 10s 10d for debt.

786:2/10 Meese vs Heynes - peremptory day for response appointed.

787:2/10 Gyles vs Heynes - similarly.

Action of trespass:

739:18/19 Jenckes vs Plott - plaintiff pays costs and action is dismissed.

Action of trespass on case:

782:4/8 Brookes vs Binckes - renewal of execution against plaintiff.

Action of account:

784:3/6 Screevin vs Ginckins - execution granted against plaintiff for costs.

[f45v]

Actions of debt:

788:2/4 Webb vs Rippingall - peremptory day for response.

789:2/2 Greene vs Knighte - peremptory day for response; action dismissed by assent of plaintiff.

792:1/1 Robert Pile vs George Heath - action dismissed.

793:1/1 Abraham Millen vs Frauncis Cambree - Edward Caple swears that the bull (Latin 'taur..') which was seized was his own property at time of capture.

795:1/1 Christopher Aston vs Edmund Blith - action dismissed in full court.

796:1/1 William Raves, as executor of the will of George Raves, his father, lately deceased[28] v Sampson Hanwell - plaintiff puts declaration and produces in court an Obligation; defendant's attorney, Edmund Rudgate, cannot deny that he owes £20 therefore court decides that plaintiff should recover the £20 debt and costs and execution is granted.

797:1/4 John Haull vs William Page jnr - plaintiff puts declaration and defendant is granted copy.

[27] Above heading wrongly used; title 'Hundred of Wootton with…….' crossed through.

[28] probably George Raves of Duns Tew.

Action of trespass:
790:2/5 Whitton vs Symons - *venire facias* granted defendant with provisions etc..
Action of trespass on case:
794:1/1 Christopher Aston vs Thomas Peesly - action dismissed [case crossed through].

[f46]

Actions of debt:
763:10/11 Robert Keate vs Richard Meades - names of the jurors between the parties :-

Nicholas Tayler,	Jerome White,	Robert Bignil,
John Lowe,	Thomas Rayer,	Richard Shadd,
John Norman,	George Noble,	William Edwardes,
Robert Spitle,	Richard Hawkins ,	William Butterfeild,

which jury say upon oath that they find for the plaintiff and assess 2d for damages and 1d for costs.
780:5/16 Francklyn vs Cale - renewal of *scire facias*.
798:1/1 Henry Triplett vs Henry Abbott - action dismissed for defendant.
Actions of trespass on case:
799:1/2 Richard Browne vs Edmund Ewans - because plaintiff does not bring his case, court adjudges that defendant recover costs.
800:1/2 Richard Browne vs Walter Yonge - as plaintiff does not put his case, court adjudges defendant should recover costs.
801:1/1 Edulph Dingly, gent vs Simon Collier - action dismissed.

[f46v]

Portmoot court held 9 October 1615.
Actions of debt:
772:7/7 Deverill vs Edwardes - dismissed for plaintiff.
781:5/19 Heath vs Williams - defendant's attorney responds non est informatus ad respondendi; judgment adjourned to next court.
786:3/10 Meese vs Heynes- defendant does not respond; judgment adjourned to next court.
787:3/10 Gyles vs Heynes - similarly.
788:3/3 Webb vs Rippingall - defendant pleads *per minas* and plaintiff replicates; *venire facias* granted.
797:2/4 Haule vs Page - peremptory day for response granted.
Actions of trespass:
739:19/19 Jencks vs Plott - dismissed for defendant.
790:3/5 Whitton vs Symons - stands as before.
Actions of trespass on case:
800:2/2 Browne vs Yonge - stands as before.
799:2/2 Browne vs Ewans - similarly.
Actions continuing: **782**:5/8; **784**:4/6.

[f47]

Actions of debt:
763:11/11 Keate vs Meade - dismissed.
780:6/16 Francklyn vs Cale - *alias scire facias* granted.
802:1/11 John Baylies vs Danniel Saunders - plaintiff puts declaration and defendant is granted copy.
803:1/19 Francis Gregory, esquire vs Christopher Aston - plaintiff puts declaration and defendant is granted copy.
804:1/1 Roger Litle vs John Francklyn - plaintiff puts declaration and action dismissed for plaintiff.
Action of trespass:
805:1/1 Richard Yeatman and [blank] his wife vs Christopher Thorneburye - plaintiffs put declaration and defendant is granted copy.

[f47v]

Portmoot court held 23 October 1615.
Actions of debt:
781:6/19 Heath vs Williams - court adjudges that plaintiff should recover [blank] for debt and [blank] for costs and *scire facias* is granted.
786:4/10 Meese vs Heynes - court adjudges that plaintiff should recover [blank] for debt and [blank] for costs and *scire facias* is granted.
787:4/10 Gyles vs Heynes - similarly.
788:4/4 Webb vs Rippingall - *venire facias* returned executed and *habeas corpora* granted; dismissed.
797:3/4 Hall vs Page - defendant does not respond; therefore etc.
Action of account:
784:5/6 Screevin vs Ginckins - [no action listed]
Actions continuing: **782**:6/8; **790**:4/5.

[f48]

Actions of debt:
780:7/16 Francklyn vs Cale - stands as before.
802:2/11 Baylies vs Saunders - peremptory day for response granted.
803:2/19 Gregory vs Aston - peremptory day for response.
808:1/13 Christopher Wheeler vs John Androwes - day to declare granted.

[f48v]

View of Frankpledge and Sessions of the Peace held 25 October 1615 before Joseph Harris, gent, Mayor, Jerome Keite, gent, and Thomas Browne, gent, Justices for the Peace
806: *Jury for the King with Homage*

John Dubber,	Thomas Rayer,	Nicholas Tayler,
William Edwardes,	Jerome White,	Richard Hawkins,
John Lowe,	Thomas Heathen,	John Norman,

Richard Browne,	William Bradshewe,	Thomas Bruce,
George Noble,	William Butterfeild,	William Raunson,
John Ackly.		

[f49]

Sessions of the Peace:

704:3/3 Alexander Head appears upon recognisance and is dismissed with the agreement of Elizabeth Parker.

756:2/2 Jerome Walford appears and is discharged in full court.

757:2/2 William Muckell does not appear; therefore process is granted against him and his sureties.

807:1/1 Christopher Russell of Woodstock Park, yeoman, servant of Edward Bassett, gent, appears upon recognisance and is judged to be discharged by the court. Memo: He submitted himself in full court and was heartily sorry for the disorders he committed against the watchmen and constables and promised never to commit any disorder in Woodstock at any time hereafter.

[f49v]

Portmoot court held 30 October 1615.

Actions of debt:

781:7/19 Heath vs Williams - writ of *scire facias* returned executed and *alias scire facias* granted.

786:5/10 Meese vs Haynes - writ of *scire facias* returned executed and *alias scire facias* granted.

787:5/10 Gyles vs Heynes - similarly.

797:4/4 Hall vs Page - court adjudges that plaintiff should recover both [blank] for debt and [blank] for costs and *scire facias* is granted; dismissed.

802:3/11 Baylies vs Saunders - attorney says defendant responds *per minas* and copy is granted; plaintiff replicates and puts himself on the country and *venire facias* is granted.

Action of trespass:

790:5/5 Whitton vs Symons - stands as before.

Action of account:

784:6/6 Screevin vs Ginckins - [no action listed]

Actions continuing: **780**:8/16; **782**:7/8.

[f50]

Actions of debt:

803:3/19 Gregorye vs Aston - defendant's attorney puts response and immediately plaintiff replicates and puts himself on the country and *venire facias* is granted.

808:2/13 Wheeler vs Androwes - plaintiff puts declaration and day to amend granted in next court.

809:1/3 Thomas Gyles vs Edward Warner - plaint of debt upon demand of £22 and defendant remains in hands of sergeant; plaintiff puts declaration.

[f50v]

Portmoot court held 13 November 1615.

Actions of debt:

781:8/19 Heath vs Williams - *alias scire facias* returned executed and execution granted against defendant and his surety.

782:8/8 Brookes vs Binckes - plaintiff's surety, viz: Richard Reade is held in execution for costs etc and remains in hands of sergeant at mace.

786:6/10 Meese vs Heynes - *alias scire facias* returned executed and writ of execution granted against defendant and his surety.

787:6/10 Gyles vs Heynes - similarly.

802:4/11 Baylies vs Saunders - *venire facias* returned executed and writ of *habeas corpora* granted.

803:4/19 Gregorye vs Aston - similarly.

808:3/13 Wheeler vs Androwes - plaintiff puts completed declaration and defendant is granted copy.

Action continuing: **780**:9/16.

[f51]

Actions of debt:

809:2/3 Gyles vs Warner - continues for defendant.

811:1/8 Salloman Flye vs William Raunson - plaintiff puts declaration and first day of privilege granted defendant.

Action of covenant:

810:1/3 Robert Hopper vs John Phipps - plaintiff requests day to declare in next court which is granted.

[f51v]

Portmoot court held 27 November 1615.

Actions of debt:

781:9/19 Heath vs Williams - renewal of execution.

786:7/10 Meese vs Heynes - renewal of execution.

787:7/10 Gyles vs Haynes - similarly.

802:5/11 Baylies vs Saunders - renewal of *habeas corpora*.

803:5/19 Gregorye vs Aston - similarly.

808:4/13 Wheeler vs Androwes - peremptory day to respond.

809:3/3 Gyles vs Warner - dismissed.

Action of covenant:

810:2/3 Hopper vs Phipps - plaintiff puts declaration and requests day to amend in next court.

Action continuing: **780**:10/16.

[f52]

Actions of debt:

811:2/8 Flye vs Raunson - second day of privilege granted defendant in next court.

812:1/11 Edmund Hiorne vs William Hitchman - plaintiff puts declaration and copy is granted.
813:1/3 James Allsopp and Ann, his wife (executrix of the last will of John Bradshewe her husband, lately deceased[29]) vs William Raunson - plaintiffs put declaration and first day of privilege granted defendant.

[f52v]

Portmoot court held 11 December 1615.
Actions of debt:
808:5/13 Wheeler vs Androwes - defendant responds and *venire facias* is granted.
811:3/8 Flye vs Raunson - last day of privilege granted.
812:2/11 Hiorne vs Hitchman - peremptory day to respond granted.
813:2/3 Allsopp vs Raunson - second day of privilege granted.
Action of covenant:
810:3/3 Hopper vs Phipps - completed declaration placed and action dismissed because plaintiff has died.
Actions continuing: **780**:11/16; **781**:10/19; **786**:8/10; **787**:8/10; **802**:6/11.

[f53]

Actions of debt:
803:6/19 Gregory vs Aston - names of the Jury between the parties :-

Jerome White,	John Lowe,	John Norman,
Richard Shad,	George Noble,	William Edwardes,
Richard Hawkins,	Thomas Heathen,	William Butterfeild,
William Raunson,	William Hickes, snr,	Drewe Gregory,

which jury, under oath, say that the defendant made a written obligation of his own free will and assess for damages 4d and for costs 2d.
814:1/3 Henry White vs Thomas Barnshewe - plaintiff puts declaration and defendant remains in hands of sergeant.
816:1/2 Humphrey Aston vs Robert White - plaintiff puts declaration and defendant is granted copy.
818:1/10 Thomas White vs Arthur Dowson - plaintiff puts declaration and defendant is granted copy.
819:1/3 Averye Hall vs Charles Rickardes - Averye Hall appears as administrator of the goods and chattles of Edward Hall, his brother, lately deceased; day for declaration granted.
820:1/4 Thomas Winchester vs William Whitinge - plaintiff puts declaration and defendant is granted copy.
Actions of trespass on case:
815:1/2 William Ranckle and Elizabeth his wife vs Thomas Clark - plaintiffs put declaration and copy is granted; day to amend appointed.

[29] MSS.Wills (Oxon) 4/3/45.

817:1/4 Edward Anckorne vs Richard Birk - plaintiff puts declaration and day to amend granted.

[f53v]

Portmoot court held 18 December 1615.

Actions of debt:

786:9/10 Meese vs Heynes - Thomas Meatcalfe goes bail for defendant and is held in execution and so it stands.

787:9/10 Gyles vs Heynes - similarly.

808:6/13 Wheeler vs Androwes - *venire facias* returned executed and *habeas corpora* granted.

811:4/8 Flye vs Raunson - peremptory day to respond.

812:3/11 Hiorne vs Hitchman - defendant does not respond therefore judgment is adjourned.

813:3/3 Allsopp vs Raunson - dismissed for defendant.

814:2/3 White vs Barnshewe - defendant remains in hands of sergeant at mace.

Action of trespass on case:

815:2/2 Ranckle vs Clarke - stands as before.

Actions continuing: **780**:12/16; **781**:11/19; **802**:7/11.

[f54]

Actions of debt:

803:7/19 Gregorye vs Aston - the court adjudges that plaintiff should receive [blank] for debt and [blank] for costs and 4d for damages; *scire facias* granted.

816:2/2 Aston vs White - dismissed for plaintiff.

818:2/10 White vs Dowson - peremptory day to respond.

819:2/3 Hall vs Rickardes - plaintiff puts completed declaration and defendant, through Edmund Rudgate, his attorney, responds instantly to wage law with four compurgators. Therefore a day is appointed in next court.

820:2/4 Winchester vs Whitinge - peremptory day to respond.

Action of trespass on case:

817:2/4 Anckorne vs Birk - peremptory day to respond.

[f54v]

Portmoot court held 8 January 1616.

Actions of debt:

780:13/16 Francklyn vs Cale - *alias scire facias* returned executed and execution granted against defendant and his surety.

786:10/10 Meese vs Heynes - Thomas Meatcalfe one of the sureties for defendant, is held in execution and pays debt and costs; therefore defendant goes quit.

787:10/10 Gyles vs Heynes - similarly.

812:4/11 Hiorne vs Hitchman - court adjudges plaintiff should recover both [blank] for debt and [blank] for costs and *scire facias* granted against William Bradshewe, defendant's surety.

Action continuing: **781**:12/19.

[f55]

Actions of debt:
803:8/19 Gregory vs Aston - stands as before.
808:7/13 Christopher Wheeler vs John Androwes - names of jury between parties :-

Nicholas Tayler,	Thomas Rayer,	Robert Spitle,
Jerome White,	William Bradshewe,	John Wilkinson,
John Lowe,	Thomas Heathen,	Alexander Head,
George Noble,	Nicholas Glover,	William Raunson,

who say, under oath, that they find for the plaintiff and assess 25s for debt 2d for damages and 2d for costs; judgment will be given in next court.
811:5/8 Flye vs Raunson - defendant's attorney reports non est informatus ad respondendi.
814:3/3 White vs Barnshewe - dismissed for plaintiff.
818:3/10 White vs Dowson - defendant's attorney reports non est informatus ad respondendi.
819:3/3 Hall vs Rickards - defendant wages law with four compurgators viz: John Meakes, John More, John Hanckes and James Woollington; therefore he goes quit.
820:3/4 Winchester vs Whitinge - continues for defendant.
Action of trespass on case:
817:3/4 Anckorne vs Birk - further licence to imparl, because (defendant) puts foreign plea.

[f55v]

Action of debt:
802:8/11 John Baylies vs Daniel Saunders - names of the jury between parties

Nicholas Tayler,	Richard Shad,	Thomas Bruce,
Jerome White,	George Noble,	William Butterfeild,
John Lowe,	Thomas Rayer,	John Acklye,
William Bradshewe,	William Edwardes,	William Archer.

Which jury, under oath, say they find for the plaintiff and assess £20 for debt and 2d for costs.

[f56]

Portmoot court held 22 January 1616.
Actions of debt:
668:17/46 Edmund Hiorne vs Christopher Fortye - because judgment was returned [reddat] in Portmoot court held 4th July 12 Jas I. Therefore *scire facias* now granted against John Dubber and William Hickes snr, the defendant's sureties.
780:14/16 Francklyn vs Cale - renewal of execution.

811:6/8 Flye vs Raunson - court adjudges plaintiff should recover both [blank] for debt and [blank] for costs; *scire facias* granted.
812:5/11 Hiorne vs Hitchman - *scire facias* returned executed and *alias scire facias* granted.
Action continuing: **781**:13/19.

[f56v]

Actions of debt:
802:9/11 Baylies vs Saunders - court adjudges plaintiff should recover [blank] for debt and [blank] for costs and *scire facias* granted.
803:9/19 Gregory vs Aston - stands under judgment.
808:8/13 Wheeler vs Androwes - court adjudges plaintiff should recover both 25s for debt and 2d for damages with [blank] for costs etc.; *scire facias* granted. Judgment adjourned to next court.
818:4/10 White vs Dowson - court adjudges plaintiff should recover both [blank] for debt and [blank] for costs; *scire facias* granted.
820:4/4 Winchester vs Whitinge - dismissed for defendant.
821:1/3 Robert Abbottes, Doctor of Theology, vs Thomas Screevin - plaintiff puts declaration and defendant, in person, requests day of privilege and this is granted.
Action of trespass on case:
817:4/4 Anckorne vs Birk - defendant, through attorney, enters foreign plea and said defendant in person, swears the plea stands in truth. Therefore he goes quit.

[f57]

Portmoot court held 5 February 1616.
Actions of debt:
668:18/46 Hiorne vs Fortye - *scire facias* returned executed and *alias scire facias* granted against defendant's sureties.
811:7/8 Flye vs Raunson - *scire facias* returned executed and *alias scire facias* granted.
812:6/11 Hiorne vs Hitchman - *alias scire facias* returned executed and execution granted against defendant and his sureties.
818:5/10 White vs Dowson - *scire facias* returned executed and *alias scire facias* granted.
Actions continuing: **780**:15/16; **781**:14/19; **803**:10/19.

[f57v]

Actions of debt:
802:10/11 Baylies vs Saunders - *scire facias* returned executed and *alias scire facias* granted.
808:9/13 Wheeler vs Androwes - continues for defendant.
821:2/3 Abbottes vs Screevin - defendant granted second day of privilege.

823:1/10 William Dunford vs Richard Bentlie - plaintiff puts declaration and copy is granted.

Actions of trespass:

824:1/6 William Morley vs John Arden - plaintiff puts declaration and copy granted.

825:1/6 William Morely vs John Arden - similarly.

826:1/6 John Arden vs William Morley - plaintiff puts declaration, copy granted.

Actions of trespass on case:

822:1/2 Richard Reade vs Thomas Screevin - plaintiff puts declaration and defendant requests first day of privilege which is granted.

828:1/2 Thomas Screevin vs Edward Woolly - day to declare granted.

Action of detinue:

827:1/1 Richard Shadd vs Richard Browne - dismissed.

[f58]

829:1/1 Memorandum: That on 12th of this instant month of February of the year abovesaid - Thomas Screevin brings writ of *habeas corpus* dated at Westminster through Sir Edward Cooke first day of February 13th year abovesaid returnable before Sir John Crook, one of the justices of King's Bench, at his Chambers in Sergeant's Inn situate in Chancery Lane, London, immediately upon receipt of his writ to do and receive etc.... And it is sent by Edmund Rudgate, sergeant, 13th February aforesaid.

[f58v]

Portmoot court held 19 February 1616.

Actions of debt:

668:19/46 Hiorne vs Fourty - said defendant does not appear upon *alias scire facias*. Therefore execution granted against him and his sureties viz: John Dubber and William Hickes snr.

780:16/16 Francklyn vs Cale - action dismissed.

811:8/8 Flye vs Raunson - defendant does not appear upon *alias scire facias*. Therefore execution granted against him and his surety.

812:7/11 Hiorne vs Hitchman - renewal of execution against defendant and William Bradshewe, his surety.

818:6/10 White vs Dowson - defendant does not appear upon *alias scire facias*. Therefore execution granted against him and his sureties.

Action continuing: **781**:15/19.

[f59]

Actions of debt:

802:11/11 Baylies vs Saunders - dismissed after payment of £8 for debt and 39s1d for costs; he goes quit.

808:10/13 Wheeler vs Androwes - court adjudges plaintiff should recover both [25s] for damages and [blank] for costs and *scire facias* granted against surety.

821:3/3 Abbottes vs Screevin - dismissed.
823:2/10 Dunford vs Bentlie - peremptory day to respond.
830:1/8 Thomas Fletcher vs John Glover, alderman - upon demand of £40 plaintiff puts declaration and defendant is granted first day of privilege.
831:1/5 Thomas Fletcher vs John Glover, alderman - similar action upon demand of £20.
Actions of trespass:
824:2/6 Morley vs Arden - defendant granted copy of declaration and peremptory day to respond.
825:2/6 Morley vs Arden - plaintiff puts declaration and requests day to amend in next court.
826:2/6 Arden vs Morley - defendant puts response and copy is granted.
Actions of trespass on case:
822:2/2 Reade vs Screevin - dismissed.
828:2/2 Screevin vs Woolly - dismissed.
Action continuing: **803**:11/19.

[f59v]

Portmoot court held 3 March 1616.
Actions of debt:
808:11/13 Wheeler vs Androwes - *scire facias* returned executed and *alias scire facias* granted.
812:8/11 Hiorne vs Hitchman - renewal of execution.
818:7/10 White vs Dowson - renewal of execution.
823:3/10 Dunford vs Bentlie - Edmund Rudgate, defendant's attorney, reports *non est informatus ad respondendi.*
Actions continuing: **668**:20/46; **781**:16/19; **803**:12/19.

[f60]

Actions of debt:
830:2/8 Fletcher vs Glover - defendant granted second day of privilege.
831:2/5 Fletcher vs Glover - similarly.
Actions of trespass:
824:3/6 Morley vs Arden - continues with the assent of attorney.
825:3/6 Morley vs Arden - similarly.
826:3/6 Arden vs Morley - similarly.

[f60v]

Portmoot court held 18 March 1616...
Actions of debt:
808:12/13 Wheeler vs Androwes - *alias scire facias* returned executed and defendant does not appear; therefore execution granted against him and his surety.
823:4/10 Dunford vs Bently - court adjudges plaintiff should recover both [blank] for debt and [blank] for costs and *scire facias* granted against surety.

Actions continuing: **668**:21/46; **781**:17/19; **803**:13/19; **812**:9/11; **818**:8/10.

[f61]

Actions of debt:
830:3/8 Fletcher vs Glover - last day of privilege granted defendant in next court.
831:3/5 Fletcher vs Glover - similarly.
832:1/5 George Litle vs John Curtis - declaration placed by plaintiff's attorney and copy granted to defendant.
Actions continuing: **824**:4/6; **825**:4/6; **826**:4/6.

[f61v]

Portmoot court held 25 March 1616.

Actions of debt:
808:13/13 Wheeler vs Androwes - case discharged in full court. (In different handwriting 'He pays £4.18s by deduction').
823:5/10 Dunford vs Bently - *alias scire facias* returned executed and *alias scire facias* granted against surety.
830:4/8 Fletcher vs Glover - peremptory day for response granted.
831:4/5 Fletcher vs Glover - similarly.
832:2/5 Litle vs Curtis - similarly.
Actions continuing: **668**:22/46; **781**:18/19; **803**:14/19; **812**:10/11; **818**:9/10; **824**:5/6; **825**:5/6; **826**:5/6.
Marginal note:
833 William Meatcalfe, chamberlain, delivered ['to Richard Shadd, constable' deleted] 2s. which James Jeffs of Oddington paid for breach of the peace on Robert Bruce.[30]

[f62]

View of Frankpledge and Sessions of the Peace held 27 March 1616 before Joseph Harris gent, Mayor, and Jerome Keyte and Thomas Browne gent, Justices of the Peace....

834: *Jury for the King with homage*

John Dubber,	Thomas Williams,	William Raunson,
Richard Meades,	George Noble,	Robert Spitle,
Nicholas Tayler,	Thomas Rayer,	Richard Hawkins,
John Lowe,	William Edwardes,	Thomas Heathen,
John Ackley,	Salloman Flye,	William Hitche.
Affeerers:- John Lowe,	Thomas Rayer,	William Edwards,
Salloman Flye sworn in.		

[f62v]

Sessions of the Peace - Recognisances:
835:1/1 Bennett Paynter appears upon recognisance and no-one brings a case against him. Therefore he is discharged. (marginal note - discharged 6s.5d.).

30 *WCA*, 64.

836:1/1 John Woodrooffe of Old Woodstock, woolman, who owes suit to this court, does not appear; but he is excused by William Meatcalfe.
837:1/1 John Bennet, Guy Beckly and John Deysey, all of Old Woodstock, who owe suit to this court, do not appear at this view of frankpledge. Therefore they are fined.[31]
The court is adjourned to 8 April next.
Victuallers Licences:
838: The names of the victuallers licensed in this sessions. (Victuallers licenced on recognisance of £10 with two sureties of £5 each).

Victuallers:	*Sureties:*
William Rayer	John Dubber, Richard Shad
Thomas Williams	Robert Bignill, William Edwardes
John Ackley	Robert Bignill, Edward Longe
Nicholas Tayler	William Edwards, Jerome White
William Edwardes	Thomas Williams, Richard Shadd
	[f63]
Thomas Screevin	Nicholas Tayler, Richard Shadd
William Hickes, snr.	Nicholas Tayler, William Hickes jnr
Thomas Godfery	Nicholas Glover, William Hickes jnr
Jerome White	Nicholas Tayler, William Butterfeild
Bennett Paynter	Richard Hawkins, William Hickes jnr
Nicholas Glover	Thomas Godfery, William Hickes jnr
Robert Bignill	William Edwardes, Richard Shadd
Edmund Rudgate	Thomas Metcalfe, Richard Shadd
	[f63v]
Elizabeth Hamond	Robert Bignill, John Ackley
Merriall Tayler, widow	Nicholas Tayler, Robert Bignill
Dorothy Wells	Nicholas Tayler, Richard Shadd
William Butterfeild	William Raunson, Robert Bignill
William Raunson	Edward Rudgate, Thomas Screevin
Edward Carden	Thomas Screevin, William Hickes jnr

Estreats: [blank]

[f64] (Blank)
[f64v]

Portmoot court held 8 April 1616.
Actions of debt:
781:19/19 Heath vs Williams - defendant pays debt and costs and is discharged upon payment of £8.11s.2d; he goes quit.
812:11/11 Hiorne vs Hitchman - defendant pays £6 15s and is discharged.

[31] The four men named in **836** and **837** are apparently the sole examples in these proceedings where frankpledge suitors are recorded for non-attendance and fined; and these all from Old Woodstock.

818:10/10 White vs Dowson - defendant pays debt and costs and is discharged.
823:6/10 Dunford vs Bently - *alias scire facias* returned executed and defendant does not appear; therefore execution granted against defendant and his surety.
Actions of trespass:
824:6/6 and **825**:6/6 Morley vs Arden **826**:6/6 Arden vs Morley - cases dismissed by agreement of all parties.
Actions continuing: **668**:23/46; **803**:15/19.

[f65]

Actions of debt:
830:5/8 Fletcher vs Glover - Edmund Rudgate, defendant's attorney, places response *per minas* and copy is granted. Immediately plaintiff replicates, through Simon Jeames, his attorney, and puts himself on the country; *venire facias* is granted.
831:5/5 Fletcher vs Glover - similarly.
832:3/5 Litle vs Curtis - defendant's attorney reports non est informatus ad respondendi. Therefore judgment adjourned to next court.
841:1/29 Thomas Paxon vs Thomas Tapping - plaintiff places declaration and defendant, remaining in custody of sergeant at mace, requests copy.
Action of trespass:
839:1/5 Walter Kinge vs Edward Roberts - plaintiff puts declaration and defendant does not appear; writ of inquiry for damages granted.
Action of trespass on case:
840:1/2 Thomas Rayer vs James Bradshewe, gent - plaintiff requests day to declare in next court. Edmund Rudgate appears for defendant.

[f65v]

Conveyance: 24 April 1616
842:1/4
Order: John Whitton, gent and Hester, his wife that justly etc. he keep the agreement with Thomas Browne, gent, concerning one close of pasture and one granary or dwelling house and appurtenances in Woodstock.[32] And if he does not do so etc...
And the concord is as follows : That the said John and Hester recognise the said close and barn or dwellinghouse with appurtenances to be the right of the said Thomas as those which Thomas has of the gift of John and Hester and remit and quitclaim them for themselves and the heirs of John aforesaid to the said Thomas Browne and his heirs in perpetuity. And in addition the same John and Hester concede for themselves and the heirs of the said John that they will warrant the said close and barn with appurtenances to the said Thomas Browne and his heirs against the said John and Hester and the heirs of John in perpetuity. And for this fine etc...

[32] *WCA*, 64 (i.e. Ned White's Close).

(signed by) John Whitton, Hester Whitton, witnessed by Joseph Harris, mayor, and Edmund Hiorne, town clerk.

[f66]

Warrant of the Peace 30th April 1616.

843: Thomas Rayer, constable, before Joseph Harris gent, mayor makes oath that John Batt of the borough currier about Friday or Saturday last offered to stab him with his knife and swore many oaths, that if he laid hands upon him he would stab him, coming only about him in the execution of his constableship; for he was in very great disorder. Also he swears that he is afraid of the said John Batt, that he will do him some hurt in his body or goods by setting of his house or his father's afire and is in dread of his life of him. And for these causes and also because he stands indicted in the sessions of this borough the 19th October 1614 for being a disorderly man, and one that has made variance and set much strife between neighbours, and disobeyed the King's Majesty's officers of this borough in the execution of their offices, he prays a warrant of the peace and good behaviour against the said Batt

(signed by) Thomas Rayer, witnessed by Joseph Harris, gent, mayor and Edmund Hiorne, town clerk.

[f66v]

Portmoot court held 22 April 1616.

Actions of debt:

823:7/10 Dunford vs Bently - renewal of execution.

830:6/8 Fletcher vs Glover - *venire facias* continues.

832:4/5 Litle vs Curtis - court rules plaintiff should recover debt and costs; *scire facias* granted against defendant's surety.

841:2/29 Paxon vs Tapping - peremptory day for response granted.

Action of trespass:

839:2/5 Kinge vs Roberts - renewal of writ of inquiry.

Action of trespass on case:

840:2/2 Rayer vs Bradshewe - action dismissed.

Actions continuing: **668**:24/46; **803**:16/19.

[f67]

Portmoot court held 6 May 1616.

Actions of debt:

832:5/5 Litle vs Curtis - action discharged.

841:3/29 Paxon vs Tapping - defendant's attorney reports non est informatus ad respondendi. Therefore nihil dicit and judgment adjourned to next court.

844:1/18 Robert Abbotts, Bishop of Salisbury, executor of last will of Anne Leake, widow, lately deceased vs John Whitton, gent - declaration placed by plaintiff's attorney who requests day to amend in next court; defendant attends, represented by Edmund Rudgate, attorney.[33]

[33] MSS. Wills (Oxon) 41/2/36.

Action of trespass:
839:3/5 Kinge vs Roberts - Sergeant at mace reports that jury has assessed 16s for damages and 2d for costs; therefore court rules that plaintiff receive 16s for damages and [blank] for costs; *scire facias* granted against defendant's surety.
Actions continuing: **668**:25/46; **803**:17/19; **823**:8/10; **830**:7/8.

[f67v]

Action of trespass on case:
845:1/4 Robert Sparrocke vs Ralph Loudon [London?] - plaintiff's attorney, Simon Jeames, places declaration and is granted day to amend in next court, defendant attends represented by his attorney, Edmund Rudgate.
Conveyance:
842:2/4 First proclamation between Thomas Browne, alderman, querent and John Whitton and Hester, his wife, deforciants for one close of pasture and one barn or dwelling house with appurtenances in Woodstock; that the same Thomas Browne previously acquired and handed over to the aforesaid John Whitton and Hester his wife.

[f68]

Portmoot court held 13 May 1616.
Actions of debt:
830:8/8 Fletcher vs Glover - discharged with agreement of plaintiff.
841:4/29 Paxon vs Tappinge - continues for plaintiff.
844:2/18 Abbott vs Whitton - copy of declaration granted to defendant.
Action of trespass:
839:4/5 Kinge vs Roberts - *scire facias* returned executed and *alias scire facias* granted against defendant's surety.
Action of trespass on case:
845:2/4 Sparrocke vs Loudon - continues for defendant.
Actions continuing: **668**:26/46; **803**:18/19; **823**:9/10.
Conveyance:
842:3/4 Second proclamation between Thomas Browne, querent and John Whitton and Hester, his wife, deforciants, for one close of pasture with appurtenances in Woodstock.

[f68v]

Portmoot court held 27 May 1619.
Actions of debt:
823:10/10 Dunford vs Bentley - writ renewed; action discharged by agreement of plaintiff.
844:3/18 Abbott vs Whitton - peremptory day to respond.
Action of trespass:
839:5/5 King vs Roberts - executed *alias scire facias* returned and execution granted; action discharged when defendant pays the debt of 48s 3d.
Actions continuing: **668**:27/46 ;**803**:19/19; **841**:5/29; **845**:3/4.

[f69]

Actions of debt:

846:1/9 Thomas Spicer, gent vs William Raunson - Simon Jeames,plaintiff's attorney, puts declaration. Edmund Rudgate, for defendant, requests day for discussion and copy of declaration.

847:1/1 Richard Browne vs Nicholas Hamlen - sergeant at mace returns one gelding, of the goods and chattels of defendant, and because defendant has not appeared on three occasions, therefore his goods are forfeited to the use of the King and appraised at that time by William Meatcalfe, Thomas Rayer and Richard Shadd for 40s. and delivered to Richard Browne through Joseph Harris, mayor for the use of the mayor and commonalty of the borough, upon demand.[34]

Conveyance:

842:4/4 Third proclamation between Thomas Browne, querent and John Whitton and Hester, his wife, deforciants, for one close of pasture with appurtenances in Woodstock.

[f69v]

Conveyance: 14 June 1616

848:1/4

Order: John Whitton gent, and Hester, his wife that justly etc., he keep the agreement with John Hull gent, concerning two messuages or tenements, two curtilages, two orchards and two gardens with appurtenances in Woodstock aforesaid.[35] And if he does not do so etc...

And the concord is as follows: that the said John Whitton and Hester, his wife, recognise the said tenements with appurtenances to be the right of the said John Hull as those which the said John Hull has of the gift of the said John Whitton and Hester, his wife, And remits and quitclaims them for the said John Whitton and his heirs to the said John Hull and his heirs in perpetuity. And in addition, the said John Whitton and Hester his wife concede for themselves and the heirs of the said John Whitton that they will warrant the said tenements with appurtenances to the said John Hull and his heirs against the said John Whitton and Hester his wife and the heirs of the said John Whitton in perpetuity. And for this fine etc...

(signed by) John Whitton, Hester Whitton, Joseph Harris, mayor and Edmund Hiorne, town clerk.

[f70]

Portmoot court held 10 June 1616.

Actions of debt:

844:4/18 Abbott vs Whitton - continues by assent of plaintiff.

846:2/9 Spiser vs Raunson - second day of privilege granted.

[34] *WCA*, 65.

[35] *WCA*, 64.

Actions of trespass on case:
845:4/4 Sparrock vs Loudon - discharged for defendant.
849:1/3 Richard Bowle vs Henry Bowle - plaintiff has not produced his plaint upon three occasions; therefore court rules defendant recover costs and expenses; *scire facias* granted against plaintiff's surety.
Actions continuing: **668**:28/46; **841**:6/29.

[f70v]

Portmoot court held 17 June 1616.[36]
Action of debt:
846:3/9 Spicer vs Raunson - last day of privilege granted.
Action of trespass on case:
849:2/3 Bowle vs Bowle - *alias scire facias* granted.
Conveyance:
848:2/4 First proclamation between John Hull, gent, querent, and John Whitton, gent and Hester, his wife, deforciants, for two messuages, or tenements with appurtenances in Woodstock that the same John Hull recently acquired and remitted for the said John Whitton and Hester, his wife.
Actions continuing: **668**:29/46; **841**:7/29; **844**:5/18.

[f71]

Portmoot court held 1 July 1616.
Action of debt:
846:4/9 Spicer vs Raunson - peremptory day for response.
Action of trespass on case:
849:3/3 Bowle vs Bowle - action discharged.
Conveyance:
848:3/4 Second proclamation between John Hull, gent, querent and John Whitton and Hester, his wife, deforciants for two messuages or tenements with appurtenances in Woodstock
Actions continuing: **668**:30/46; **841**:8/29; **844**:6/18.

[f71v]

The Court of Joseph Harris gent, Mayor of the said Borough, and Clerk of the Market, held on Monday 1st July Anno dmi 1616 Anno.Reg. etc
by virtue of the grant of the King's Majesty's letters patents …
850: *Jury*:

Richard Meades,	Thomas Bruce,	Jerome White,
Thomas Godfery,	Nicholas Taylor (deleted),	William Archer,
John Lowe,	Alexander Head,	Thomas Screevin,
Richard Hawkins,	George Noble,	John Ackly,
William Edwards,	William Hickes, jnr,	Robert Spitle.

[36] 'Baron' crossed through.

851: *Presentments*
The Jury presented the best wheat to be worth 40s per quarter: the second wheat at 36s. per quarter: and the best malt at 24s per quarter: Whereupon the mayor assized the penny white loaf at 8 oz.2dwt (= 8.1 oz.): the penny wheaten (loaf) at 12½ oz: the penny household (loaf) at 17 oz: the barrell of beer at 10s 4d; the kilderkin at 5s 2d; a quart of ale indoors for a penny; and a thirdendall of drink outdoors for a penny.

[f72]

853: A true note of all such weights and measures as were tried and sealed by the said jury the same day, and allowed by the mayor:-
Richard Greene, the miller - one bushel, one half peck and one toll dish
Edward Evans, clerk - one new bushel
Edmund Hiorne, town clerk - one new bushel
Thomas Screevin - one new bushel
Thomas Godfery - two bushels, one peck and one half peck
Richard Meades - one bushel, one peck and one half peck
William Rayer, alderman - two new bushels
George Noble - one new bushel
John Glover, alderman - one half peck
Thomas Williams - one half peck
Jerome White - one half peck
John Lowe - one peck
Anthony Deverell - one peck & one half peck
Robert Spittle - one peck & one half peck
Thomas Heathen - one peck and a quarter
Robert Bignill - one bushel hooped
William Archer - one half peck
Mr Mayor - three ells and two yards
William Metcalfe - two yards
Thomas Rayer - one ell & one yard
by me, (signed) Edmund Hiorne, clerk to the mayor and commonalty of the aforesaid borough.

[f72v] (Blank)

[f73]

Portmoot court held 15 July 1616.
Actions of debt:
846:5/9 Spicer vs Raunson - Edmund Rudgate for defendant acknowledges the debt; court adjudges that plaintiff should recover both £4 10s for debt and [blank] for costs etc; *scire facias* granted.
Actions continuing: **668**:31/46; **841**:9/29; **844**:7/18.

Conveyance:
848:4/4 Third proclamation between John Hull gent, querent, and John Whitton and Hester, his wife, deforciants, for two messuages or tenements with appurtenances in Woodstock. And no-one comes to contest the claim.

[f73v]

Portmoot court held 29 July 1616.
Actions of debt:
846:6/9 Spicer vs Rawnson - sergeant at mace returns *scire facias* against Nicholas Glover and [blank] and *alias scire facias* granted.
854:1/24 Joseph Harris gent, vs Richard Shadd - defendant attends represented by Edmund Rudgate, his attorney, and plaintiff's attorney, Simon Jeames, puts declaration for £4 [and 10s deleted]; copy of declaration and first day of privilege granted.
855:1/4 Thomas Martyn vs John Cox - plaintiff places declaration and defendant does not appear; therefore nil dicit and judgment is adjourned to next court.
Actions continuing: **668**:32/46; **841**:10/29; **844**:8/18.

[f74]

Portmoot court held 12 August 1616.
Actions of debt:
846:7/9 Spiser vs Rawnson - defendant pays debt and costs and goes quit.
854:2/24 Harris vs Shadd - defendant granted second day of privilege.
855:2/4 Martyn vs Cox - court adjudges plaintiff should receive both [blank] for debt and [blank] for costs; *scire facias* granted against defendant's surety.
856:1/3 John Secole vs John Ayers (alias Digger) – Simon Jeames for plaintiff, puts declaration and Edmund Rudgate for defendant requests copy, and a copy of the conditions of the obligation; day for discussion appointed.
Actions of trespass:
857:1/5 James Morton vs William Clement - Simon Jeames for plaintiff puts declaration and a copy is granted; day for discussion appointed.
858:1/5 William Clement vs James Morton - Edmund Rudgate for plaintiff places declaration and a copy is granted; day for discussion appointed.
Actions continuing: **668**:33/46; **841**:11/29; **844**:9/18.

[f74v]

Memorandum: 28 August 1616
846: 8/9 Spicer vs Raunson - Receipt
I, Edward Waterhouse of Whitchurch ('Whichurch') in County of Bucks received of Edmund Hiorne to the use of Thomas Spicer, gent, the sum of:- £4 10s for a debt recovered in Woodstock Court against William Rawnson and 15s 1d for charges. I say received £5 5s by me.

(signed) Edward Waterhous

[f75]

Portmoot court held 26 August 1616.

Actions of debt:

846:9/9 Spicer vs Raunson - discharged.

854:3/24 Harris vs Shadd - last day of privilege granted defendant.

855:3/4 Martyn vs Cox - *scire facias* returned executed and *alias scire facias* granted against defendant's surety.

856:2/3 Secole vs Ayers (als. Digger) - defendant responds *per minas* and plaintiff replicates and puts himself on the country; *venire facias* granted plaintiff.

859:1/1 Yonge vs Browne - Edmund Rudgate, surety, pays debt and costs.

Actions of trespass:

857:2/5 Morton vs Clemente - defendant responds not guilty and puts himself on the country; *venire facias* granted.

858:2/5 Clemente vs Morton - similarly.

Actions continuing: **668**:34/46; **841**:12/29; **844**:10/18.

[f75v]

Portmoot court held 9 September 1616.

Actions of debt:

855:4/4 Martyn vs Cox - defendant pays debt and costs and goes quit.

854:4/24 Harris vs Shadd - peremptory day for response granted.

856:3/3 John Secole vs John Ayers (als.Digger) - sergeant at mace returns executed *venire facias* and defendant's attorney, Edmund Rudgate, in full court, brings writ of *habeas corpus* returnable before King's Bench at Westminster on Thursday after one month after Michaelmas to do and receive etc., dated at Westminster 19th June 14 Jas.I: Copy granted to plaintiff. [Marginal note - *habeas corpus* per Ayers].

860:1/23 John Dubber vs Edmund Rudgate - defendant's surety [blank]; plaintiff's attorney, Simon Jeames, puts declaration and defendant, in person, requests first day of privilege which is granted; copy of declaration granted.

Actions continuing: **668**:35/46; **841**:13/29; **844**:11/18; **857**:3/5; **858**:3/5.

[f76]

Portmoot court held 23 September 1616.

Actions of debt:

854:5/24 Harris vs Shadd - defendant's attorney reports non informatus ad respondendi.

860:2/23 Dubber vs Rudgate - defendant granted second day of privilege.

863:1/1 Thomas Blacknall vs Robert Annison - dismissed.

Action of trespass:

861:1/4 Anne James vs Thomas Androwes - plaintiff's attorney, Simon Jeames, puts declaration and copy granted to to defendant.

Actions of trespass on case:
862:1/3 Christopher Bowman vs John Ford - plaintiff declares and is granted day to amend in next court.
864:1/1 Thomas Boult vs Richard Newton - plaintiff's attorney, Simon Jeames, puts declaration and defendant does not appear; therefore writ of inquiry into damages granted.
Actions continuing: **668**:36/46; **841**:14/29; **844**:12/18; **857**:4/5; **858**:4/5.

865: END OF JOSEPH HARRIS' TIME AS MAYOR

[f76v]

[Marginal note to the effect that the court of 30th September should be entered before this one – but no sitting recorded]

Portmoot court held 14 October 1616.

Actions of debt:
844:13/18 Abbott vs Whitton - further peremptory day to respond.
854:6/24 Harris vs Shadd - court adjudges that plaintiff should recover both £4 for debt and 12s.6d. for costs and *scire facias* is granted against defendant's surety.
860:3/23 Dubber vs Rudgate - peremptory day for response.
Actions continuing: **668**:37/46; **841**:15/29; **857**:5/5; **858**:5/5.

[f77]

Actions of debt:
866:1/8 John Glover, alderman vs Henry Bradshewe, gent - plaintiff's attorney, Simon Jeames, puts declaration; defendant is granted copy and day for discussion appointed.
868:1/7 Richard Whinge vs Thomas Turner - plaintiff's attorney, Simon Jeames, places declaration and defendant, in custody of sergeant at mace, requests copy through his attorney, Edmund Rudgate; day for discussion appointed.
Action of trespass:
861:2/4 James vs Androwes - defendant responds not guilty and puts himself on the country; *venire facias* granted.
Actions of trespass on case:
862:2/3 Bowman vs Ford - plaintiff places completed declaration and copy is granted to defendant.
867:1/17 Robert Binckes vs Henry Bradshewe, gent - plaintiff's attorney, Simon Jeames, places declaration and day to amend is granted.

[f77v]

Breach of the peace: 28 July 1616
869:Katherine Reade brings action against Thomas Browne, alderman, before Joseph Harris, mayor and Jerome Keite J.P.;
Thomas Browne then undertakes bail at £20 penalty to keep the peace against her and all the King's people and to appear at the next sessions of the borough.

[f78]

View of Frankpledge and Sessions of the Peace held 23 October 1616. before William Rayer gent, mayor and before Jerome Kite, gent and Thomas Browne, alderman, Justices of the Peace.

870: *Jury for the King with homage*

Thomas Williams,	Thomas Heathen,	Nicholas Tayler,
Richard Browne,	Jerome White,	Thomas Bruce,
John Lowe,	William Butterfeild,	George Noble,
John Ackly,	William Edwardes,	Edward Carden,
William Raunson,	John Pepper,	Thomas Screevin.

Affeerers - John Lowe William Raunson Richard Browne sworn in.

[f78v]

871 *Licensing of Victuallers:*

Robert Winter admitted to be victualler of the borough in his own house - surety and recognisance £20 John Bruce and Thomas Martyn - separate recognisances of £5 for observing the statute in keeping of victuals.

872 *Election of Officers:*

William Butterfeild and Thomas Heathen are elected constables and sworn in. John Durbridge, John Pepper, William Hickes jnr, and Edward Carden are elected tithingmen and sworn in. Estreats [blank]

[f79 & 79v] (Blank)

[f80]

Portmoot court held 28 October 1616.

Actions of debt:

844:14/18 Abbott vs Whitton - defendant's attorney, Edmund Rudgate, puts response *per minas* and copy is granted to plaintiff who immediately replicates and puts himself on the country; *venire facias* granted.

854:7/24 Harris vs Shadd - fieri facias granted against goods and chattels of defendant.

860:4/23 Dubber vs Rudgate - continues with assent of plaintiff.

866:2/8 Glover vs Bradshewe - peremptory day for response.

Action of trespass:

861:3/4 Jeames vs Androwes - *venire facias* returned executed and *habeas corpora* juratorum granted.

Actions continuing: **668**:38/46; **841**:16/29.

[f80v]

Actions of debt:

868:2/7 Whinge vs Turner - peremptory day for response.

875:1/1 Richard Keene vs Richard Reade - defendant pays into court 17s.9d and 15d. for costs and is discharged.

877:1/3 John Hamond vs Robert Winter - plaintiff puts declaration and copy is granted.

Actions of trespass on case:
862:3/3 Bowman vs Forde - dismissed.
867:2/17 Binckes vs Bradshewe - plaintiff places completed declaration and copy is granted.
873:1/1 Robert Annison vs Thomas Blacknall - dismissed.
874:1/1 Thomas Blacknall vs Robert Annison - dismissed.
876:1/42 James Allsopp vs Richard Coles - plaintiff puts declaration and defendant does not respond.; writ of inquiry into damages granted.

[f81]

Portmoot court held 11 November 1616.
Actions of debt:
844:15/18 Abbott vs Whitton - *venire facias* returned executed and *habeas corpora* juratorum granted.
854:8/24 Harris vs Shadd - fieri facias renewed.
866:3/8 Glover vs Bradshewe - defendant's attorney responds non debet modo et forma and copy is granted. Immediately plaintiff' s attorney puts delay in law; court wishes to consider.
Action of trespass:
861:4/4 James vs Androwes - *habeas corpora* juratorum renewed; defendant's attorney brings writ of privilege returnable before the Court of Common Pleas at Westminster in the quindene of St. Martin dated 7th November of the above year.
Actions continuing: **668**:39/46; **841**:17/29; **860**:5/23.

[f81v]

Actions of debt:
868:3/7 Whinge vs Turner - defendant's attorney, Edmund Rudgate responds *per minas* and plaintiff requests copy; he replicates and puts himself on the country.
877:2/3 Hamond vs Winter - second day of privilege granted defendant.
Action of trespass:
867:3/17 Binckes vs Bradshewe - peremptory day to respond.
Action of trespass on case:
876:2/42 Allsopp vs Coles - continuation of writ of inquiry into damages for next court.

[f82]

Portmoot court held 25 November 1616.
Actions of debt:
844:16/18 Abbott vs Whitton - Edmund Rudgate, defendant's attorney, brings writ of *habeas corpus* bearing date 21st November aforesaid returnable before King's Bench at Westminster on Wednesday next on the eve of the Purification of Blessed Virgin Mary [Marginal note: satisfaction acknowledged in court 10th February 1617]

866:4/8 Glover vs Bradshewe - court adjudges that the plea of the defendant is insufficient in law and his attorney has not been ready to plead on three occasions in this court; therefore it is adjudged that plaintiff should recover both £20 for debt and 20s for costs; *scire facias* granted against defendant's surety.
877:3/3 Hamond vs Winter - discharged.
Actions continuing: **668**:40/46; **841**:18/29; **854**:9/24; **860**:6/23.

[f82v]

Action of debt:
868:4/7 Whinge vs Turner - sergeant at mace returns executed *venire facias* and *habeas corpora* granted.
Actions of trespass on case:
867:4/17 Binckes vs Bradshewe - defendant puts response and copy granted.
876:3/42 Allsopp vs Coles - continues as before.
878:1/9 Richard Deverill vs Thomas Fletcher - plaintiff granted day to declare.
879:1/1 Thomas Crafte vs Thomas Beddall - plaintiff granted day to declare and case dismissed.
880:1/23 Troyleus Butcher vs William Dunford - plaintiff's attorney, Edmund Rudgate, requests day to declare in next court and it is granted; defendant appears represented by Simon Jeames, his attorney.

[f83]

Portmoot court held 9 December 1616.[37]
Actions of debt:
860:7/23 Dubber vs Rudgate - defendant replies non debet modo et forma and *venire facias* granted.
866:5/8 Glover vs Bradshewe - *scire facias* returned executed and *alias scire facias* granted.
Actions of trespass on case:
867:5/17 Binckes vs Bradshewe - defendant responds non assumpsit modo et forma and parties put themselves on the country; *venire facias* granted and court wishes to consider on costs.
878:2/9 Deverill vs Fletcher - because plaintiff does not wish to prosecute therefore court adjudges defendant should recover costs.
880:2/23 Butcher vs Dunford - plaintiff places completed declaration and copy is granted.
Actions continuing: **668**:41/46; **841**:19/29; **854**:10/24; **876**:4/42.

[f83v]

Actions of debt:
868:5/7 Richard Whinge vs Thomas Turner - names of the Jury between the parties :-

John Lowe,	Jerome White,	Richard Shad,

[37] Mistakenly titled 'Court Baron'.

George Noble,	William Edwardes,	Robert Bignill,
William Butterfeild,	Thomas Godfery,	Thomas Gee,
Alexander Head,	William Hickes jnr.,	Edward Carden.

Who say under oath that the defendant made a written obligation of his own free will and not because he was under any threat and assess damages 2d and costs 1d.
881:1/3 John Kirby vs Nicholas Yonge - plaintiff declares and requests day to amend.
882:1/3 John Kirby vs Richard Yonge - similarly.
883:1/3 Thomas Meatcalfe vs Richard Heath - plaintiff puts declaration and copy granted.
884:1/8 Thomas Meatcalfe vs Richard Shadd - plaintiff puts declaration and copy is granted and first day of privilege.
886:1/4 Richard Poure gent vs Leonard Boult – plaintiff places declaration and copy granted.
Actions of trespass on case:
885:1/14 Thomas Joyner vs Thomas Mosse - plaintiff puts declaration and requests day to amend in next court; but defendant does not appear to make response; therefore writ of inquiry into damages issued.
887:1/3 Thomas Sheppard vs Richard Hawle - plaintiff puts declaration and defendant requests copy.

[f84]

Portmoot court held 23 December 1616.
Action of debt:
868:6/7 Whinge vs Turner - court adjudges plaintiff should receive both £30 for debt and 34s.6d. for costs; and defendant is committed into custody of sergeant at mace in execution.
Actions of trespass on case:
867:6/17 Binckes vs Bradshewe - *venire facias* continues.
878:3/9 Deverill vs Fletcher - *scire facias* returned executed.
880:3/23 Butcher vs Dunford - peremptory day to respond.
Actions continuing: **668**:42/46; **841**:20/29; **854**:11/24; **860**:8/23; **876**:5/42.

[f84v]

Actions of debt:
866:6/8 Glover vs Bradshewe - *alias scire facias* returned executed and defendant does not appear; therefore execution granted against defendant and his surety.
881:2/3 Kirby vs Nicholas Yonge - declaration completed and copy granted.
882:2/3 Kirby vs Richard Yonge - similarly.
883:2/3 Metcalfe vs Heathe - peremptory day to respond.
884:2/8 Metcalfe vs Shad - second day of privilege granted.

886:2/4 Poure vs Boult - completed declaration placed.
Actions of trespass on case:
885:2/14 Joyner vs Mosse - renewal of writ to inquire into damages.
887:2/3 Sheppard vs Hall - declaration completed and copy granted.
888:1/11 William Harris vs George Boddy - plaintiff granted day to declare in next court.
Court adjourned until 13 January next

[f85]

Portmoot court held 13 January 1617.
Actions of trespass on case:
867:7/17 Binckes vs Bradshewe - *venire facias* continues and court wishes to consider for allowance of costs under demurrer.
878:4/9 Deverill vs Fletcher - *alias scire facias* returned executed and execution granted against plaintiff's surety.
880:4/23 Butcher vs Dunford - defendant places response and copy granted to plaintiff.
Actions continuing: **668**:43/46; **841**:21/29; **854**:12/24; **860**:9/23; **876**:6/42.

[f85v]

Actions of debt:
866:7/8 Glover vs Bradshewe - writ renewed against defendant and his surety.
868:7/7 Whinge vs Turner - defendant remains in custody of sergeant at mace in execution for £30 debt and 34s.6d costs.
881:3/3 Kirby vs Nicholas Yonge - dismissed for plaintiff.
882:3/3 Kirby vs Richard Yonge - similarly.
883:3/3 Meatcalfe vs Heath - Edmund Rudgate, defendant's attorney, places response *per minas* and plaintiff immediately replicates amd puts himself on country; *venire facias* granted; action dismissed by assent of plaintiff.
884:3/8 Meatcalfe vs Shad - last day of privilege granted.
886:3/4 Poure vs Boult - defendant's attorney, Edmund Rudgate, requests admission in law and is granted day and date to wage law with four compurgators in next court.
Actions of trespass on case:
885:3/14 Joyner vs Mosse - stands as before.
887:3/3 Sheppard vs Hall - dismissed for plaintiff.
888:2/11 William Harris vs George Boddy - plaintiff does not enter his declaration against defendant; therefore court adjudges plaintiff (i.e defendant) should recover [blank] for costs; *scire facias* granted against plaintiff and his surety [Whole clause crossed through and then re-written].

[f86]

Conveyance: 19 January 1617
889:1/4 before William Rayer, mayor

Order: Richard Pyman, Joan Collingwood widow, John Collingwood and Richard Collingwood that justly etc.. they keep agreement with Mary Tame, widow, concerning three messuages or tenements with appurtenances in the borough of Woodstock now in occupation of William Hickes senior and Edward Longe and one close called Spitle Close in Old Woodstock field with appurtenances etc...
And the concord is as follows: that the said Richard Pyman, Joan Collingwood, John Collingwood and Richard Collingwood acknowledge the said tenements and close with appurtenances to be the right of the said Mary Tame as those which the said Mary has of the gift of the said Richard Pyman, Joan Collingwood, John Collingwood and Richard Collingwood And remise and quitclaim them for the said Richard Pyman, Joan, John and Richard Collingwood and their heirs to the said Mary Tame and her heirs in perpetuity. And in addition the same Richard Pyman, Joan, John and Richard Collingwood separately concede for themselves and their heirs that they will warrant the tenements and close with aforesaid with appurtenances to the said Mary Tame and her heirs against themselves separately and their heirs in perpetuity. And for this fine etc...
(signed by) Richard Pyman John Collingwood Richard Collingwood
(mark of) Joan Collingwood and witnessed by William Rayer, mayor and
Edmund Hiorne, town clerk[38]

[f86v]

Portmoot court held 27 January 1617.
Action of debt:
884:4/8 Meatcalfe vs Shadd - day to respond in next court granted.
Actions of trespass on case:
867:8/17 Binckes vs Bradshewe - stands as before.
878:5/9 Deverill vs Fletcher - stands as before.
880:5/23 Butcher vs Dunford - continues.
Actions continuing: **668**:44/46; **841**:22/29; **854**:13/24; **876**:7/42.

[f87]

Actions of debt:
866:8/8 Glover vs Bradshewe - sergeant reports that he holds Robert Bignill in execution of the writ and he remains in custody as surety for the said defendant and execution renewed against defendant and Richard Shadd.
886:4/4 Poure vs Boult - defendant appears in person and wages law with four compurgators viz:- Thomas Meade, Richard Warden, Thomas Stocker and Nicholas Burgen; therefore it is considered that the aforesaid Richard received nothing through his complaint but let him be in mercy for his false claim; and he gives to the defendant a receipt therefore.

[38] *WCA*, 70.

890:1/4 Jerome Keite gent vs William Becon - Simon Jeames appears for plaintiff and Edmund Rudgate for defendant; plaintiff puts declaration and copy is granted.

Action of trespass on case:

888:3/11 Harris vs Boddy - *alias scire facias* granted for costs.

Action continuing: **885**:4/14.

[f87v]

Portmoot court held 10 February 1617.

Action of debt:

668:45/46 Hiorne vs Forty - execution granted.

Apprenticeship:

891: William Seare, son of Robert Seare places himself apprentice to Roger Sturgis, barber, on the second day of this instant month of February for the term of seven years then next ensuing.

Actions continuing: **841**:23/29; **854**:14/24; **876**:8/42; **878**:6/9; **880**:6/23.

[f88]

Actions of debt:

844:17/18 Robert Abbotts, Bishop of Salisbury, as executor of the will of Anne Leake, widow, deceased, vs John Whitton, gent - attorneys for both parties appear and Simon Jeames, for plaintiff, acknowledges satisfaction of the aforesaid debt; therefore defendant is discharged and he goes quit.

884:5/8 Mcatcalfc vs Shadd - Edmund Rudgatc, attorncy for thc said defendant, reports non est informatus ad respondendi.

890:2/4 Keite vs Becon - continues with assent of plaintiff.

Action of trespass on case:

888:4/11 Harris vs Boddy - execution granted against plaintiff and Edmund Rudgate, his surety, for costs.

Conveyance:

889:2/4 First proclamation between Mary Tame, widow, querent, and Richard Pyman, Joan Collingwood, widow, John Collingwood and Richard Collingwood, deforciants, for three messuages or tenements with appurtenances in the borough and for one close called Spitle Close with appurtenances That the same Mary Tame previously acquired and surrendered to the aforesaid Richard Pyman, Joan, John and Richard Collingwood.

Actions continuing: **867**:9/17; **885**:5/14.

[f88v]

Portmoot court held 24 February 1617.

Action of debt:

668:46/46 Hiorne vs Fortye - plaintiff declares himself satisfied with debt and costs and defendant goes quit.

Actions continuing: **841**:24/29; **854**:15/24; **867**:10/17; **876**:9/42; **878**:7/9; **880**:7/23.

[f89]

Actions of debt:

884:6/8 Meatcalfe vs Shadd - court adjudges plaintiff should recover both [blank] for debt and [blank] for costs; *scire facias* issued against defendant and his surety.

890:3/4 Keite vs Becone - defendant in his own person brings writ of cerciorari bearing date at Westminster 5th February Anno regis Jacobi 14 & 50 etc. returnable before the King in Chancery fifteen days after Easter wherever the king may then be.

[Memorandum: William Becone in person tendered in open court 12 pieces of gold, containing £13 4s in discharge of Mr. Keite's debt of £12: Mr. Jeames his attorney said he had warrant to receive it in part of payment of the £24 and his charge, but not in full discharge of the debt: whereupon William Becone put up his gold and then delivered this writ].

Action of trespass on case:

888:5/11 Harris vs Boddy - continues in execution.

Conveyance:

889:3/4 Second proclamation between Mary Tame, widow, querent, and Richard Pyman, Joan, John and Richard Collingwood, deforciants, for three messuages and one close with appurtenances in borough aforesaid.

Action continuing: **885**:6/14.

[f89v]

Actions of debt:

892:1/1 Hugh Fawdery vs Richard Farney - Simon Jeames for plaintiff, declares and Edmund Rudgate for defendant, is granted copy.

894:1/2 Richard Meades vs Richard Coles - Edmund Rudgate, for plaintiff, requests day to declare in next court. Simon Jeames for defendant; first day of privilege granted.

Actions of trespass on case:

893:1/2 Richard Coles vs Richard Meades - Simon Jeames, for plaintiff, places declaration and copy is granted. Edmund Rudgate for defendant is granted first day of privilege.

895:1/4 Robert Bruce vs Morgan Jenckins - Simon Jeames for plaintiff and Edmund Rudgate for defendant; plaintiff puts declaration and requests day to amend in next court.

[f90]

Portmoot court held 10 March 1617.

Action of debt:

884:7/8 Meatcalfe vs Shadd - stands as before, and Edmund Rudgate, surety, pays debt and costs.

Action of trespass on case:

867:11/17 Binckes vs Bradshewe - defendant pays into court 10s for costs, by reason of insufficient response; *venire facias* renewed.

Actions continuing: **841**:25/29; **854**:16/24; **876**:10/42; **878**:8/9; **880**:8/23.

[f90v]

Actions of debt:
890:4/4 Keite vs Becone - stands as before.
894:2/2 Meades vs Coles - dismissed by assent of both parties.
896:1/3 John Cooke vs John Teasler - plaintiff puts completed declaration and defendant does not appear; therefore judgment deferred to next court.
897:1/9 John Batt vs Jerome White - plaintiff puts declaration and copy and day of privilege granted.
Actions of trespass on case:
893:2/2 Coles vs Meades - dismissed by assent of both parties.
895:2/4 Bruce vs Morgan (Jenkins) - plaintiff puts completed declaration and copy granted to defendant.
Conveyance:
889:4/4 Third proclamation between Mary Tame, widow, querent, and Richard Pyman, Joan Collingwood, widow, John and Richard Collingwood, deforciants for three messuages and one close with appurtenances in aforesaid borough.
Actions continuing: **885**:7/14; **888**:6/11.

[f91]

Portmoot court held 24 March 1617.
Actions of debt:
884:8/8 Meatcalfe vs Shadd - defendant pays debt and costs; therefore he goes quit.
Actions of trespass on case:
867:12/17 Binckes vs Bradshewe - sergeant at mace returns executed *venire facias* and writ of *habeas corpora* granted.
878:9/9 Deverill vs Fletcher - stands as before.
Actions continuing: **841**:26/29; **854**:17/24; **876**:11/42; **880**:9/23.

[f91v]

Actions of debt:
896:2/3 Cooke vs Teasler - court adjudges plaintiff may recover £3 10s for debt and [blank] for costs; *scire facias* granted against defendant's surety.
897:2/9 John Batt vs Jerome White - second day of privilege granted defendant.
898:1/1 John Bartlett vs Thomas Head - Simon Jeames for plaintiff and Edmund Rudgate for defendant; declaration placed and copy granted. Dismissed for plaintiff [Marginal note - 'exoneratur' - clause crossed through]
Action of trespass on case:
895:3/4 Bruce vs Morgan (Jenkins) - continues by agreement.
Actions continuing: **885**:8/14; **888**:7/11.

[f92]

Portmoot court held 7 April 1617.

Actions of debt:

896:3/3 Cooke vs Teasler - dismissed with plaintiff's consent.

897:3/9 Batt vs White - last day of privilege granted.

Action of trespass on case:

895:4/4 Bruce vs Morgan (Jenkins) - dismissed for defendant.

Action of account:

899:1/12 William Flye, alderman, vs Thomas Phillipps - Simon Jeames for plaintiff and Edmund Rudgate for defendant; day to declare granted in next court.

Actions continuing: **841**:27/29; **854**:18/24; **876**:12/42; **885**:9/14; **888**:8/11.

[f92v]

Actions of trespass on case:

867:13/17 Robert Binckes vs Henry Bradshewe, gent - names of the Jury between parties :-

Nicholas Tayler,	Richard Meades,	Thomas Williams,
Jerome White,	John Lowe,	George Noble,
William Edwards,	William Butterfield,	William Archer,
John Ackly,	William Hickes, jnr.,	Robert Spitle;

which jury, on their oaths, say that they find for the plaintiff and assess for damages 34s 8d and for costs and expenses 2d.

900:1/10 Robert Spittle vs John Batt - Edmund Rudgate for plaintiff and Simon Jeames for defendant; day to declare granted for next court.

[f93]

Portmoot court held 14 April 1617.

Action of debt:

897:4/9 Batt vs White - peremptory day to respond.

Actions of trespass on case:

867:14/17 Binckes vs Bradshewe - court adjudges that plaintiff should recover 34s 8d for his damages and 46s 3d for costs and his expenses and execution is granted against the goods and chattels of Thomas Bradshewe gent, deceased, father of the aforesaid defendant.[39]

900:2/12 Spittle vs Batt - plaintiff places declaration and requests day to amend in next court.

Action of account:

899:2/12 Flye vs Phillipps - plaintiff places declaration and copy is granted.

Actions continuing: **841**:28/29; **854**:19/24; **876**:13/42; **885**:10/14; **888**:9/11.

[39] MSS.Wills (Oxon) 4/3/17 Thomas Bradshawe d.1613.

[f93v]

View of Frankpledge and Sessions of the Peace held 16 April 1617 before William Rayer gent, mayor and before Jerome Keite gent and Thomas Browne gent, Justices of the Peace

901: *Jury for the King with homage*

John Dubber,	William Edwardes,	Richard Meades,
William Raunson,	Nicholas Tayler,	Robert Spitle,
Jerome White,	Thomas Heathen,	John Lowe,
John Acklye,	Thomas Williams,	John Durbridge,
Thomas Screevin,	Edward Carden,	George Noble.

902: [Affeerers] Nicholas Tayler, John Lowe, William Edwards, Thomas Heathen, George Noble sworn in. Estreats – blank.
[No action recorded by Clerk].

[f94]

Portmoot court held 28 April 1617.

Actions of debt:

841:29/29 Paxon vs Tappinge - action dismissed.

897:5/9 Batt vs White - defendant's attorney reports *non est informatus ad respondendi.*

Actions of trespass on case:

867:15/17 Binckes vs Bradshewe - renewal of execution.

900:3/12 Spittle vs Batt - plaintiff puts completed declaration.

Actions of account:

899:3/12 Flye vs Phillipps - peremptory day to respond.

903:1/1 John Batt vs Edmund Rudgate - [no action listed].

Apprenticeship:

904: Richard Wells, son of John Wells of the borough of Woodstock, tailor, binds himself apprentice to Thomas Williams of the borough, baker, for the term of seven years from the 25th day of March last past: by Indenture made between them dated 25th March 1617; it is clear and apparent.

Actions continuing: **854**:20/24; **860**:10/23; **876**:14/42; **885**:11/14; **888**:10/11.

[f94v]

Portmoot court held 12 May 1617.

Actions of debt:

897:6/9 Batt vs White - court adjudges that the plaintiff should recover both [blank] for debt and [blank] for costs and *scire facias* is granted.

905:1/22 John Duncombe gent vs Arthur Dowson - plaintiff's attorney, Simon Jeames, puts declaration and is granted day to amend; defendant appears, represented by his attorney, Edmund Rudgate.

906:1/16 Richard Hanwell vs Arthur Dowson - plaintiff's attorney, Simon Jeames, puts declaration; copies of declaration and condition of the obligation granted. Edmund Rudgate appears for defendant.

Action of trespass on case:
900:4/10 Spittle vs Batt - defendant demurs in court and plaintiff replicates and stands on the consideration of the court.
Action of account:
899:4/12 Flye vs Phillipps - peremptory day to respond.
Actions continuing: **854**:21/24; **867**:16/17; **876**:15/42; **885**:12/14; **888**:11/11.

[f95]

Actions of debt:
907:1/16 John Cooke vs Walter Horne - plaintiff's attorney, Simon Jeames, puts declaration and is granted day to amend; defendant appears represented by his attorney, Edmund Rudgate.
908:1/12 Anne Holdeing, widow vs Edmund Rudgate - plaintiff's attorney, Simon Jeames, puts declaration and first day of privilege is granted.
909:1/3 Ema Deane vs William Bache - plaintiff's attorney, Simon Jeames, puts declaration and requests day to amend; defendant appears, through his attorney, Edmund Rudgate.
Action continuing: **860**:11/23.

[f95v]

Portmoot court held 26 May 1617.
Actions of debt:
897:7/9 Batt vs White - *alias scire facias* granted.
905:2/22 Duncombe vs Dowson - peremptory day for response.
906:2/16 Hanwell vs Dowson - similarly.
Actions of trespass on case:
867:17/17 Binckes vs Bradshewe - plaintiff's attorney, Simon Jeames, declares him to be satisfied with damages and costs; therefore he goes quit.
900:5/10 Spitle vs Batt - court wishes to consider.
910:1/21 Ethelbert Widdowes vs Arthur Dowson - plaintiff's attorney, Simon Jeames, puts declaration and requests day to amend and defendant is represented by Edmund Rudgate
Actions continuing: **854**:22/24; **876**:16/42; **885**:13/14.

[f96]

Actions of debt:
908:2/12 Holdeing vs Rudgate - second day of privilege.
909:2/3 Ema Deane vs William Bache - continues by equal agreement.
911:1/3 Richard Trubshewe vs Frauncis Billinge - plaintiff's attorney, Simon Jeames, declares and copy is granted.
912:1/17 Thomas Gyles vs Walter Yonge - plaintiff's attorney, Simon Jeames, requests day to declare; defendant represented by Edmund Rudgate.

Action of account:
899:5/12 Flye vs Phillipps - defendant places response and plaintiff is granted copy, he immediately demurs and copy then granted to defendant who immediately replicates and requests the advice of the court; plaintiff makes similar request; therefore the court wishes to consider for the next hearing.
Actions continuing: **860**:12/23; **907**:2/16.

[f96v]

Portmoot court held 2 June 1617.
Actions of debt:
897:8/9 Batt vs White - *alias scire facias* returned executed and execution granted.
905:3/22 Duncombe vs Dowson - defendant responds *per minas* and copy is granted; plaintiff replicates and puts himself on the country; *venire facias* granted.
906:3/16 Hanwell vs Dowson - continues for both parties.
908:3/12 Holden vs Rudgate - last day of privilege granted.
909:3/3 Deane vs Bache - dismissed for defendant.
913:1/18 Richard Tyms vs Arthur Dowson - plaintiff's attorney, Simon Jeames, puts declaration; copy granted to defendant who is represented by his attorney, Edmund Rudgate.
Action of trespass on case:
910:2/21 Widdowes vs Dowson - peremptory day to respond.
Actions continuing: **854**:23/24; **876**:17/42; **885**:14/14; **907**:3/16.
[f97]
Action of debt:
912:2/17 Gyles vs Yonge - defendant (sic) places declaration and requests day to amend in next court.
Action of trespass on case:
900:6/10 Spitle vs Batt - stands as before.
Action of account:
899:6/12 Flye vs Phillipps - court wishes to consider.
Actions continuing: **860**:13/23; **880**:10/23; **911**:2/3.

[f97v]

Portmoot court held 16 June 1617.
Actions of debt:
854:24/24 Harris vs Shad - stands as before.
897:9/9 Batt vs White - defendant pays £5 2s 8d for debt and costs. Discharged.
905:4/22 Duncombe vs Dowson - stands as before.
908:4/12 Holden vs Rudgate - peremptory day to respond.
911:3/3 Trubshewe vs Billinge - dismissed.
912:3/17 Gyles vs Yonge - copy of declaration granted.

913:2/18 Tyms vs Dowson - peremptory day to respond.
Action of account:
899:7/12 Flye vs Phillipps - stands as before.
Actions continuing: **860**:14/23; **876**:18/42; **880**:11/23; **900**:7/10; **906**:4/16; **907**:4/16; **910**:3/21.

[f98]

Portmoot court held last day of June 1617.
Actions of debt:
905:5/22 Duncombe vs Dowson - *venire facias* returned executed and *habeas corpora juratorum* granted.
907:5/16 Cooke vs Horne - peremptory day to respond.
908:5/12 Holden vs Rudgate - defendant, in person, responds *per minas* and copy is granted to plaintiff who immediately replicates and puts himself on the country; *venire facias* granted.
913:3/18 Tymes vs Dowson - defendant does not appear to make response and judgment is adjourned to next court.
Actions continuing: **860**:15/23; **876**:19/42; **880**:12/23; **899**:8/12; **906**:5/16; **910**:4/21.

[f98v]

Actions of debt:
912:4/17 Gyles vs Yonge - defendant responds *nil debet (per patriam)* and copy is granted.[40]
914:1/4 William Meatcalfe vs Thomas Williams - plaintiff's attorney, Simon Jeames, places declaration and copy and first day of privilege is granted.
915:1/8 James Allsopp vs Edmund Rudgate - plaintiff places declaration and copy and first day of privilege granted.
Action of trespass on case:
916:1/2 Jerome White vs John Batt - dismissed by plaintiff.
Action continuing: **900**:8/10.

[f99]

Portmoot court held 14 July 1617.
Actions of debt:
907:6/16 Cooke vs Horne - defendant does not appear after three calls, therefore judgment is adjourned.
908:6/12 Holden vs Rudgate - *habeas corpus juratorum* granted.
913:4/18 Tyms vs Dowson - court adjudges plaintiff should recover both £20 debt and 25s.10d for costs and execution is committed to Edmund Rudgate, sergeant.
Actions continuing: **860**:16/23; **876**:20/42; **880**:13/23; **906**:6/16; **910**:5/21.

[40] Plea to traverse a declaration in debt by verdict of a jury (Gilmore,L.1.13, Glossary).

[f99v]

Actions of debt:

905:6/22 John Duncombe vs Arthur Dowson - names of the jury between parties :-

Richard Meades,	Nicholas Tayler,	Jerome White,
John Lowe,	Thomas Screevin,	George Noble,
Robert Bignill,	William Edwardes,	William Butterfeild,
William Hickes, jnr,	Edward Carden,	Thomas Heathen.

Which jury, under oath, find for the plaintiff and assess 2d. for damages and 1d for costs.

912:5/17 Gyles vs Yonge - parties put themselves on the country and *venire facias* is granted.

914:2/4 Meatcalfe vs Williams - second day of privilege granted defendant.

915:2/8 Allsopp vs Rudgate - second day of privilege granted.

Action of trespass on case:

916:2/2 White vs Batt - action discharged.

Actions continuing: **899**:9/12; **900**:9/10.

[f100]

Clause written and then crossed through *see* **921**

[f100v]

Portmoot court held 28 July 1617.

Actions of debt:

905:7/22 Duncombe vs Dowson - court adjudges plaintiff should recover [blank] for debt and [blank] for costs and defendant is entrusted to pay.

907:7/16 Cooke vs Horne - court adjudges plaintiff should recover [blank] for debt and [blank] for costs; *scire facias* granted.

913:5/18 Tyms vs Dowson - stands in execution.

Actions continuing: **860**:17/23; **876**:21/42; **880**:14/23; **906**:7/16; **910**:6/21.

[f101]

Actions of debt:

912:6/17 Gyles vs Yonge - *venire facias* returned executed and *habeas corpora* juratorum granted.

914:3/4 Meatcalfe vs Williams - last day of privilege granted defendant for next court.

915:3/8 Allsopp vs Rudgate - last day of privilege granted to defendant for next court.

918:1/1 John Crony vs Ralph Turner als. Stockes - day to declare granted.

Action of trespass on case:

900:10/10 Robert Spitle vs John Batt - defendant produces in court a writ returnable before Court of Common Pleas at Westminster on Thursday next in the octave of St. Michael. Witness - H. Montagu at Westminster 9 July Anno Reg 15 and 50 James I & VI

Action of account:
899:10/12 Flye vs Phillipps - on the advice of the recorder of the borough it is adjudged by the court that the defendant cannot wage law (i.e.agree to produce compurgators) where the receipt is laid by the hands of another and that the defendant is to account at the next court.

[f101v]

Actions of debt:
908:7/12 Anne Holdinge, widow, vs Edmund Rudgate - jury between parties

Nicholas Tayler,	Jerome White,	John Lowe,
Thomas Screevin,	George Noble,	Robert Spitle,
Robert Bignill,	William Edwardes,	William Butterfield,
William Hickes, jnr.,	John Durbridge,	Thomas Heathen.

Which jury find for plaintiff and assess 2d for damages and 1d for costs; judgment adjourned to next court.
920:1/1 Thomas Browne vs William Austine - action dismissed.
Action of trespass:
919:1/6 William Whiting vs William Seely - plaintiff's attorney, Simon Jeames, puts declaration and defendant is granted copy; day for discussion appointed.
Property claim:
921:1/1 Margery Fletcher, widow, who was the wife of Henry Fletcher, ironmonger of this borough, lately deceased;[41] appears through Simon Jeames, her attorney, and claims against Thomas Browne, alderman of the borough, for three parts of seven messuages with appurtenances in Woodstock now in the several tenure of the said Thomas Browne:
[Note by Edmund Hiorne - Mr. Browne's records are all written in paper rem(aining) with my precedents ('presidents') and Mr. Browne has it in parchment under Mr. Mayor's seal].

[f102] [blank]

[f102v]

Portmoot court held 11 August 1617.
Actions of debt:
905:8/22 Duncombe vs Dowson - stands under execution.
907:8/16 Cooke vs Horne - *scire facias* granted.
908:8/12 Holdinge vs Rudgate - judgment adjourned.
912:7/17 Gyles vs Yonge - *habeas corpora* continues.
914:4/4 Meatcalfe vs Williams - discharged.
915:4/8 Allsopp vs Rudgate - peremptory day to respond.
922:1/5 Jerome Keite, gent vs John Yonge - plaintiff's attorney, Simon Jeames, puts declaration and is granted day to amend; defendant's attorney is Edmund Rudgate.

[41] MSS.Wills (Oxon) 187:344.

Action of trespass:
919:2/6 Whitinge vs Seelye - peremptory day to respond.
Action of account:
899:11/12 Flye vs Phillipps - process granted against defendant to produce an account.
Actions continuing: **860**:18/23; **876**:22/42; **880**:15/23; **906**:8/16; **910**:7/21; **913**:6/18.

[f103]

Portmoot court held 25 August 1617.
Actions of debt:
907:9/16 Cooke vs Horne - *alias scire facias* granted.
915:5/8 Allsopp vs Rudgate - defendant responds *non debet modo et forma* and puts himself on the country; *venire facias* granted.
Action of trespass:
919:3/6 Whitinge vs Seely - defendant's attorney, Edmund Rudgate, puts response and plaintiff is granted copy, and immediately replicates and copy is granted; he puts himself on the country. [Memo: The said parties by the delivery of 6d apiece either to other by way of assumption upon the pain of £20 apiece, have referred all matters between them from the beginning of the world until this day to John Perry of Ascott and Thomas Silvester of Burford to be set down in writing under their hands and seals before the sixth of September next].
Action of account:
899:12/12 Flye vs Phillipps - action discharged.
Actions continuing: **860**:19/23; **876**:23/42; **880**:16/23; **905**:9/22; **906**:9/16; **910**:8/21; **912**:8/17; **913**:7/18.

[f103v]

Actions of debt:
922:2/5 Keite vs Yonge - defendant granted copy of declaration.
923:1/2 Katherine Brente, widow vs Christian Brente, widow - Edmund Rudgate, sergeant at mace of the borough, reports that he, on 19th August, captured within the town, two geldings valued at [blank] and plaintiff's attorney, Simon Jeames, puts declaration and defendant's attorney, Edmund Rudgate, requests copy and day for discussion.
Action continuing: **908**:9/12.

[f104]

Portmoot court held 1 September 1617.
Actions of debt:
907:10/16 Cooke vs Horne - *alias scire facias* returned executed and writ of execution granted against defendant and his surety.
915:6/8 Allsopp vs Rudgate - *venire facias* continues.
922:3/5 Keite vs Yonge - peremptory day to respond.

923:2/2 Brent vs Brente - action discharged.
Action of trespass:
919:4/6 Whiting vs Seely - continues by equal agreement.
Action of trespass on case:
924:1/5 John Glover vs John Webster - plaintiff puts declaration and defendant does not appear; writ of inquiry into damages granted.
Actions continuing: **860**:20/23; **876**:24/42; **880**:17/23; **905**:10/22; **906**:10/16; **908**:10/12; **910**:9/21; **912**:9/17; **913**:8/18.

[f104v]

Breach of the Peace:
925:1/1 12th September 1617 - John Hutchins appears before William Rayer, mayor of the borough, and demands the peace against Thomas Screevin; therefore warrant to keep the peace granted against the said Thomas (see also **928**).

[f105]

Portmoot court held 15 September 1617.
Action of debt:
907:11/16 Cooke vs Horne - renewal of writ of execution.
Action of trespass:
919:5/6 Whitinge vs Seely - sergeant at mace returns executed *venire facias* and writ of *habeas corpus* granted.
Actions continuing: **860**:21/23; **876**:25/42; **880**:18/23; **905**:11/22; **906**:11/16; **908**:11/12; **910**:10/21; **912**:10/17; **913**:9/18; **915**:7/8.

[f105v]

Actions of debt:
922:4/5 Keite vs Yonge - defendant responds and wages law with four compurgators in next court.
928:1/8 John Hutchins vs Thomas Screevin - plaintiff's attorney, Simon Jeames, puts declaration and is granted day to amend; defendant's attorney, Edmund Rudgate, requests copy and first day of privilege.
Actions of trespass on case:
924:2/5 Glover vs Webster - renewal of writ of inquiry into damages.
926:1/6 Jerome White vs John Batt, senior - plaintiff's attorney, Edmund Rudgate, puts declaration but requests day in next court according to the form of the judgment and defendant's attorney, Simon Jeames, requests day for discussion and first day of privilege.
Action of account:
927:1/6 Jerome White vs John Batt, senior - similar action to action **926**.

[f106]

Portmoot court held 29 September 1617.
Actions of debt:
908:12/12 Holdinge vs Rudgate - judgment adjourned.

915:8/8 Allsopp vs Rudgate - *venire facias* continues.
Actions continuing: **860**:22/23; **876**:26/42; **880**:19/23; **905**:12/22; **906**:12/16; **907**:12/16; **910**:11/21; **912**:11/17; **913**:10/18.

[f106v]

Actions of debt:
922:5/5 Keite vs Yonge - defendant appears in person to wage law with four supporters vizt: Richard Goddard, [Maurice] Mannett, Boyse, Ores and John Henberry and he is discharged and goes quit.
928:2/8 Hutchins vs Screevin - plaintiff puts completed declaration and defendant is granted copy with second day of privilege.
Action of trespass:
919:6/6 Whitinge vs Seely - Names of the jury between parties [none listed]- defendant in person brings writ of privilege dated at Westminster 9th July Anno reg. 15 Jas. I etc, returnable before Court of Common Pleas at Westminster on Thursday next on the eve of All Souls – Brownlowe.[42]
Actions of trespass on case:
924:3/5 Glover vs Webster - continues for defendant.
926:2/6 White vs Batt - second day of privilege.
Action of account:
927:2/6 White vs Batt - second day of privilege.

[f107]

Actions of debt:
930:1/2 Richard Browne vs John Bonde - plaintiff's attorney, Simon Jeames, puts declaration and requests day to amend; Edmund Rudgate is defence attorney.
931:1/3 William Ranckle vs William Wacklyn - plaintiff's attorney, Simon Jeames, puts declaration and day to amend granted; defendant does not respond.
934:1/4 John Merrell vs Anthony Wenman, gent - plaintiff's attorney, Simon Jeames, puts declaration; Edmund Rudgate, for defendant, is granted copy.
Action of trespass:
933:1/2 John Knapp vs William Wakelyn - plaintiff's attorney, Simon Jeames, puts declaration; defendant does not respond and writ of inquiry into damages granted.
Actions of trespass on case:
929:1/2 Henry Triplett vs Thomas Shilton - plaintiff's attorney, Simon Jeames, puts declaration and requests day to amend. Edmund Rudgate is defence attorney.
932:1/2 William Wacklyn vs William Ranckle - because plaintiff does not wish to prosecute the court adjudges defendant should recover costs etc.

[42] Brownlowe – a Westminster court officer or clerk.

[f107v]

Actions of trespass:

936:1/1 and **937**:1/1 John Wyly vs John Yonge - actions discharged.

940:1/2 Christopher Bowman vs Anthony Warde - plaintiff's attorney, Edmund Rudgate, puts declaration and defendant's attorney, Simon Jeames, is granted copy.

941:1/2 Anthony Warde vs Christopher Bowman - plaintiff's attorney, Simon Jeames, puts declaration and defendant's attorney, Edmund Rudgate, is granted copy.

Action of trespass on case:

938:1/8 Thomas Fletcher vs Richard Reade - plaintiff's attorney, Edmund Rudgate, requests day to declare in next court; defence attorney Simon Jeames.

Action of account:

935:1/1 Nicholas Yonge vs John Wyly - action discharged.

Action of detinue:

939:1/8 Thomas Fletcher vs Richard Reade - plaintiff's attorney, Edmund Rudgate, requests day to declare in next court; defence attorney Simon Jeames.

[f108]

Action of debt:

931:2/3 Ranckle vs Wakelyn - 11 October 1617 - William Wakelyn,on his release from prison at Mr. Ranckles suit, confessed and acknowledged himself satisfied of all [reckonings], debts, accounts, trespasses and demands whatsoever due to him from William Ranckle from the beginning of the world until this day: This was done before me; signed Edmund Hiorne, Stephen Horne, Richard Waklyn and Jerome White, sergeant.

(mark of) William Waklyn

Marginal note:

943: paid Mr.mayor all his fees.

[f108v]

Portmoot court held 13 October 1617.

Action of debt:

860:23/23 Dubber vs Rudgate - stands as before.

Action of trespass on case:

926:3/6 White vs Batt - last day of privilege.

Action of account:

927:3/6 White vs Batt - last day of privilege.

Actions continuing: **876**:27/42; **880**:20/23; **905**:13/22; **906**:13/16; **907**:13/16; **910**:12/21; **924**:4/5.

[f109]

Actions of debt:

928:3/8 Hutchins vs Screevin - last day of privilege granted defendant.

930:2/2 Browne vs Bond - action dismissed.

931:3/3 Wakelyn vs Ranckle - action dismissed.

934:2/4 Merrell vs Wenman - defendant's attorney, Jerome White cannot deny the debt because the same (defendant) owes the aforesaid plaintiff £30 in declaration afore-mentioned; therefore court adjudges plaintiff recover both £30 for debt and [blank] for costs; *scire facias* granted.

944:1/3 Richard Webb vs Christopher Saunders - upon demand of £36 plaintiff's attorney, Simon Jeames, puts declaration and Jerome White, for defendant, states in this court that he cannot deny the debt because the same (defendant) owes plaintiff the aforementioned £36 detailed in declaration; therefore court adjudges plaintiff recover both £36 for debt and [blank] for costs; *scire facias* granted.

Actions of trespass:

933:2/2 Knapp vs Wakelyn - action dismissed.

940:2/2 Bowman vs Warde - action dismissed.

941:2/2 Warde vs Bowman - similarly

Actions of trespass on case:

929:2/2 Triplett vs Shilton - plaintiff puts completed declaration and copy is granted; defendant pays in full court £5 6s 8d for debt and 8s 4d for costs and is discharged.

932:2/2 Wakelyn vs Ranckle - action dismissed.

938:2/8 Thomas Fletcher vs Richard Reade - continues with agreement of both parties.

Action of detinue:

939:2/8 Fletcher vs Reade - continues with agreement of both parties

[f109v]

Actions of debt:

912:12/17 Thomas Gyles vs Walter Yonge - Names of Jury between parties :-

Nicholas Tayler,	William Butterfeild,	Thomas Screevin,
Thomas Gee,	Thomas Rayer,	John Bruce,
Robert Spitle,	Edward Carden,	Robert Bignill,
John Durbridge,	William Edwardes,	Richard Reade.

Which jury say, under oath, that they find for plaintiff and that defendant owes for debt £9 15s and assess damages at 2d and costs at 1d. Judgment adjourned to next court.

945:1/1 Thomas Heady vs John Lea - plaintiff's attorney, Simon Jeames, puts declaration and Jerome White, for defendant, requests copy.

946:1/4 Jerome Nashe, gent vs Richard Meades - plaintiff's attorney, Simon Jeames, puts declaration but defendant does not appear to respond. Judgment adjourned to next court.

Apprenticeship:

947:Memorandum: John Woodrooffe, son of John Woodrooffe of Old Woodstock, places himself apprentice with George Barnsley of the borough, joiner, for the term of seven years from the feast of St. Michael the Archangel next ensuing. signed Edmund Hiorne

Marginal note:
942: Paid Mr.mayor.

[f110]

View of Frankpledge and Sessions of the Peace held 22 October 1617 before William Rayer, mayor; Thomas Browne and Jerome Keite, Justices and Edmund Hiorne, clerk to the council.

950: *Jury for the King with homage*

John Dubber,	Thomas Bruce,	Nicholas Tayler,
John Ackly,	John Lowe,	John Durbridge,
Thomas Williams,	John Pepper,	Thomas Rayer,
Thomas Lowe,	William Edwardes,	Richard Reade,
Robert Spitle,	Thomas Martyn,	Thomas Heathen,
George Barnsly.		

Affeerers: John Lowe, Robert Spitle, Thomas Martyn sworn in

Estreats: [no entry]

[f110v]

Memorandum:
752:2/3 Isabel Robins[43] brings Elizabeth her daughter (aged 3 years at Our lady day next or thereabouts), being her base child by Richard Meades of this borough which she has heretofore sworn on oath: It is therefore ordered by the mayor and Justices in open sessions that the said Richarde Meades shall hereafter pay 12d a week for the keeping of the child for the term of 5 years from the date hereof if the said child shall live so long: and if there shall be found cause after the said time, that the said child shall be kept by the said Meades that then he shall stand to such further order as the said mayor and Justices of the said borough for the time being shall appoint: And also it is ordered that the said Richard Meades shall find sufficient sureties to perform his order if he do or shall refuse to pay the said 12d a week for the keeping of the said child according to the true intent of the said order: Also it is ordered in this open sessions, that the said Isabel Robbins shall in like manner pay 8d a week towards the keeping of the said base child; and that if she make default of payment thereof then she will be committed to the common goal unless she shall find sufficient sureties to perform this order according to the true intent and meaning of the statute in that case made and provided
(signed by) William Rayer mayor, Thomas Browne

[f111]

Portmoot court held 27 October 1617.

Actions of debt:
928:4/8 Hutchins vs Screevin - peremptory day to respond.

[43] previously 'Elizabeth Robinson'.

934:3/4 Merrell vs Wenman - *alias scire facias* granted.
944:2/3 Webb vs Saunders - *alias scire facias* granted.
Actions of trespass on case:
924:5/5 Glover vs Webster - action dismissed.
926:4/6 White vs Batt - peremptory day to respond.
938:3/8 Fletcher vs Reade - continues by equal agreement.
Action of account:
927:4/6 White vs Batt - peremptory day to respond.
Action of detinue:
939:3/8 Fletcher vs Reade - continues by equal agreement.
Actions continuing: **876**:28/42; **880**:21/23; **905**:14/22; **906**:14/16; **907**:14/16; **910**:13/21.

[f111v]

Actions of debt:
912:13/17 Gyles vs Yonge - court adjudges plaintiff recover £9 15s for debt and [blank] for costs etc; *scire facias* granted.
946:2/4 Nashe vs Meades - court adjudges plaintiff recover [blank] for debt and [blank] for costs; *scire facias* granted.
954:1/14 Thomas Browne, alderman vs Thomas Screevin - plaintiff's attorney, Simon Jeames, puts declaration and Jerome White, for defendant, is granted copy.
955:1/8 Thomas Meatcalfe vs Leonard Boult - plaintiff's attorney, Simon Jeames, puts declaration and Jerome White, for defendant, is granted copy.
Actions of trespass and assault:
952:1/3 Thomas Trevinor vs Phillip Johnson - plaintiff's attorney, Simon Jeames, puts declaration and Jerome White, for defendant, is granted copy.
953:1/3 Phillip Johnson vs Thomas Trevinor - similar action to **952** Jerome White for plaintiff and Simon Jeames for defendant.
Apprenticeships
956: Memorandum that Anthony Lambard places himself apprentice to Robert Bignill of the borough, baker, for the term of seven years from the feast of St. Michael last past. [Marginal note - Enrolled Anthony Lambard]

[f112]

948: Memorandum that William Hickes, son of John Hickes of Milton in the County of Oxon, yeoman, places himself apprentice with John Glover, baker and alderman of the borough for the term of seven years from the feast of St. Michael the Archangel last past.
949: Memorandum that Henry Hickes, son of the said John Hickes of Milton, aforesaid, places himself apprentice with Robert Bignill of this borough, baker, for the term of seven years from the feast of St. Michael the Archangel last past. by me (signed) Edmund Hiorne, town clerk

[f112v]

Portmoot court held 10 November 1617.

Action of trespass on case:

926:5/6 White vs Bat - defendant produces writ of *habeas corpus* dated 31 November abovesaid returnable before King's Bench at Westminster on Tuesday next of the quindene of St. Martin.

Action of account:

927:5/6 White vs Bat - similarly.

Actions continuing: **876**:29/42; **880**:22/23; **905**:15/22; **906**:15/16 **907**:15/16; **910**:14/21; **913**:11/18.

[f113]

Actions of debt:

912:14/17 Gyles vs Yonge - *scire facias* returned executed and *alias scire facias* granted.

928:5/8 Hutchins vs Screevin - defendant responds non retinuisset and puts himself on the country; *venire facias* granted.

934:4/4 Merrell vs Wenman - *alias scire facias* returned executed and execution granted against defendant and surety; action dismissed by agreement of plaintiff who acknowledges satisfaction.

939:4/8 Fletcher vs Reade - because plaintiff does not wish to prosecute, court adjudges he should recover costs etc.

944:3/3 Webb vs Saunders - dismissed for plaintiff.

946:3/4 Nashe vs Meades - *scire facias* returned executed and *alias scire facias* granted.

954:2/14 Browne vs Screevin - second day of privilege granted.

955:2/8 Meatcalfe vs Boult - continues for defendant.

957:1/2 Robert Watson vs Richard Gilkes - plaintiff's attorney, Simon Jeames, requests day to declare. Jerome White is attorney for defendant.

Action of trespass on case:

938:4/8 Fletcher vs Reade - because plaintiff does not wish to prosecute, court adjudges he should recover costs.

Actions of trespass and assault:

952:2/3 Trevinor vs Johnson - peremptory day to respond.

953:2/3 Johnson vs Trevinor - similarly.

[f113v]

Portmoot court held 23 November 1617.

Actions of debt:

907:16/16 Cooke vs Horne - sergeant at mace pays into court £3 6s 10d in full satisfaction of the execution.

928:6/8 Hutchins vs Screevin - *venire facias* continues.

Actions continuing: **876**:30/42; **880**:23/23; **905**:16/22; **906**:16/16 **910**:15/21; **913**:12/18.

[f114]

Actions of debt:

912:15/17 Gyles vs Yonge - defendant committed to sergeant in execution of the action.

939:5/8 Fletcher vs Reade - court adjudges plaintiff recover [blank] for costs etc.

946:4/4 Nashe vs Meades - stands as before.

954:3/14 Browne vs Screevin - last day of privilege granted defendant.

955:3/8 Meatcalfe vs Bolte - continues for plaintiff.

957:2/2 Watson vs Gilkes - action dismissed.

Action of trespass on case:

938:5/8 Fletcher vs Reade - court adjudges plaintiff recover [blank] for costs etc.

Actions of trespass and assault:

952:3/3 Trevinor vs Johnson - action dismissed by agreement of both parties.

953:3/3 Johnson vs Trevinor - similarly.

[f114v]

Portmoot court held 8 December 1617.

Actions of debt:

912:16/17 Gyles vs Yonge - remains under execution.

928:7/8 Hutchins vs Screevin - sergeant returns executed *venire facias* and *habeas corpora* granted.

939:6/8 Fletcher vs Reade - *alias scire facias* granted against plaintiff's surety.

954:4/14 Thomas Browne vs Thomas Screevin - defendant appears in person and in full court says that he cannot deny the aforesaid debt of £12 specified in the declaration; therefore court adjudges that plaintiff recover both debt of £12 and 10s 4d for costs; *scire facias* granted.

[Marginal note - Memorandum 27 Nov 1618 the said Thomas Browne expressed himself satisfied with aforesaid £12 10s 4d and goes quit and the judgment is closed].

955:4/8 Meatcalfe vs Bolte - defendant responds *per minas* and plaintiff replicates and puts himself on the country; *venire facias* granted for return in next court.

Action of trespass on case:

938:6/8 Fletcher vs Reade - *alias scire facias* granted against plaintiff's surety.

Actions continuing: **876**:31/42; **905**:17/22; **910**:16/21; **913**:13/18.

[f115]

Actions of debt:

958:1/7 Anne Holding, widow vs Thomas Screevin - plaintiff's attorney, Simon Jeames, puts declaration and defendant's attorney, Jerome White, requests copy and day of privilege.

960:1/10 Robert Maye vs William Hutt - plaintiff's attorney, Simon Jeames, puts declaration and Jerome White, defendant's attorney requests copy and day to amend in next court granted.
961:1/10 Robert Maye vs William Hutt - similar action to **960.**
962:1/7 John Lumbard vs William Fly, alderman - [No action recorded].
Action of detinue:
959:1/2 Thomas Screevin vs John Hutchins - plaintiff's attorney, Jerome White, puts declaration and Simon Jeames, for defendant, is granted copy.
Action of trespass on case:
963:1/1 Richard Carter vs Henry Croker, gent - plaintiff's attorney, Simon Jeames, puts declaration and Jerome White, for defendant cannot deny the debt of 40s.owed to the plaintiff which is paid in full satisfaction of the aforesaid debt; therefore he goes quit.
[Marginal note - ? 7d to me].

[f115v]

Portmoot court held 22 December 1617.
Actions of debt:
912:17/17 Gyles vs Yonge - stands as before; dismissed.
928:8/8 Hutchins vs Screevin - dismissed.
955:5/8 Meatcalfe vs Bolte - *venire facias* returned executed and *habeas corpora* granted.
Action of trespass on case:
938:7/8 Fletcher vs Reade - *alias scire facias* granted against surety for non-prosecution by plaintiff, which is returned executed: and plaintiff pays 22s for costs for the two actions [**938** and **939**] and is discharged.
Action of detinue:
939:7/8 Fletcher vs Reade - [See action **938**]
Actions continuing: **876**:32/42; **905**:18/22; **910**:17/21; **913**:14/18.

[f116]

Actions of debt:
954:5/14 Browne vs Screevin - remains under judgment.
958:2/7 Holding vs Screevin - second day of privilege.
960:2/10 May vs Hutt - plaintiff puts completed declaration and copy granted.
961:2/10 May vs Hutt - similarly.
965:1/1 Richard Reade vs John Wyly - plaintiff's attorney, Simon Jeames, puts declaration and Jerome White, for defendant, requests copy; day to amend granted.
Action of trespass on case:
964:1/6 Richard Reade vs John Wyly - plaintiff's attorney, Simon Jeames, puts declaration. Jerome White, for defendant, requests copy; day to amend granted.

Action of detinue:
959:2/2 Screevin vs Hutchins - action dismissed.
Apprenticeship
966: Memorandum: Francis Bennett, son of Richard Bennett of Woodstock, woolman, places himself apprentice with William Archer of the aforesaid borough, tailor, for the term of ten years at 25th March 1618. Dated 22 December 1617. (signed) Edmund Hiorne, town clerk
[Marginal note - Entered indenture of apprenticeship]

[f116v]

Portmoot court held 12 January 1618.
Actions of debt:
955:6/8 Metcalfe vs Bolt - stands as before.
958:3/7 Holding vs Screevin - last day of privilege.
960:3/10 May vs Hutt - defendant puts response and day to amend granted.
961:3/10 May vs Hutt - similarly.
Actions of trespass on case and detinue:
938:8/8 and **939**:8/8 Fletcher vs Reade - both actions dismissed at previous sitting.
Actions continuing: **876**:33/42; **905**:19/22; **910**:18/21; **913**:15/18; **954**:6/14.

[f117]

Action of debt:
967:1/3 William Ayleworth, gent vs Edward Woolly - plaintiff's attorney, Simon Jeames, puts declaration and Jerome White, for defendant, requests copy.
Action of trespass on case:
964:2/6 Reade vs Wyly - court wishes to consider for next sitting.

[f117v]

Portmoot court held 26 January 1618.
Actions of debt:
955:7/8 Meatcalfe vs Bolt - *habeas corpora* granted.
958:4/7 Holding vs Screevin - defendant's attorney puts response and says that the aforesaid writing was not made by him and puts himself on the country; plaintiff does likewise; *venire facias* granted.
960:4/10 May vs Hutt - defendant puts completed response and copy is granted. plaintiff immediately places demurrer in law.
961:4/10 May vs Hutt - similarly.
Actions continuing: **876**:34/42; **905**:20/22; **910**:19/21; **913**:16/18 ; **954**:7/14.

[f118]

Actions of debt:
962:2/7 John Lumber vs William Flye, alderman - plaintiff's attorney is Simon Jeames and defendant's attorney is Jerome White, against the aforesaid John

Lumber, and plaintiff declares and defendant requests copy; day for discussion at next court and first day of privilege are granted.
967:2/3 Ayleworth vs Woolly - peremptory day to respond.
Actions of trespass on case:
964:3/6 Reade vs Wilye - court considers further for next session.
968:1/1 John Bartlett vs John Lawrence - action dismissed.

[f118v]

Portmoot court held 9 February 1618.
Actions of debt:
955:8/8 Metcalfe vs Bolt - dismissed.
958:5/7 Holden vs Screevin - *venire facias* returned executed and *habeas corpora* granted.
960:5/10 May vs Hutt - peremptory day for rejoinder to be discussed in next court.
961:5/10 May vs Hutt - similarly.
962:3/7 Lumbard vs Flye - second day of privilege.
Action of trespass on case:
964:4/6 Reade vs Wyly - stands as before.
Actions continuing: **876**:35/42; **905**:21/22; **910**:20/21; **913**:17/18 ; **954**:8/14.

[f119]

Actions of debt:
967:3/3 Ayleworth vs Woolly - defence attorney puts response and copy is granted, plaintiff immediately replicates, and puts himself on the country; *venire facias* granted.
969:1/9 John Batt jnr vs Thomas Meatcalfe - plaintiff's attorney, Simon Jeames, declares and is granted day to amend; defendant's attorney, Jerome White, puts the case to the suit of the said John Batt jnr.
970:1/7 Thomas Meatcalfe vs John Batt jnr - plaintiff's attorney, Jerome White, declares and is granted day to amend; defendant's attorney, Simon Jeames, puts the case to the suit of the said plaintiff.
Action of trespass on case:
926:6/6 Jerome White vs John Batt - plaintiff brings *writ of procedendo* bearing date at Westminster 26 January 1618 and the defendant, as before, is represented by Simon Jeames, his attorney; who, to the plaint of trespass on case, puts response of demurrer in law; and plaintiff immediately replicates and rejoins and requests advice of court.
Action of account:
927:6/6 Jerome White vs John Batt - similar response to action **926** and attorney says plaintiff has not recovered the aforesaid 55s and the account must be rendered accordingly; Jerome White in his own person requests copy.

Memorandum:
971: Jerome White, sergeant, died the 18th of February 1618 and Thomas Heathen was chosen in his place.[44]

[f119v]

Portmoot court held 23 February 1618.
Actions of debt:
905:22/22 Duncombe vs Dowson - stands in execution.
913:18/18 Tyms vs Dowson - similarly.
958:6/7 Holden vs Screevin - renewal of *habeas corpora*.
962:4/7 Lumbard vs Flye - last day of privilege granted.
Action of trespass on case:
910:21/21 Widdowes vs Dowson - continuing.
Actions continuing: **876**:36/42; **954**:9/14.

[f120]

Actions of debt:
960:6/10 Maye vs Hutt - defendant's attorney, Thomas Heathen, puts his replication upon the plea of the plaintiff and requests the judgment of the court; and court first considers before giving judgment.
961:6/10 Maye vs Hutt - similarly.
970:2/7 Thomas Meatcalfe vs John Batt jnr - continues with agreement of plaintiff.
969:2/9 John Batt jnr vs Thomas Meatcalfe - continues with agreement of defendant.
Action continuing: **964**:5/6.

[f120v]

Portmoot court held 9 March 1618.
Action of debt:
960:7/10 Robert Maye vs William Hutt -
On this day both Robert and the said William come (appear) here through their attorneys. Whereupon, after the said plea had been seen and understood by the mayor it seemed to the king's (court) that the said plea pleaded above by the said William Hutt is not sufficient in law to preclude the said Robert from his said action. It is therefore adjudged that the said Robert Maye recover his said debt against the said William Hutt and his damages by reason of the detention of the debt as adjudged by the court here to the said Robert by his assent and the said William is to be amerced.
Action continuing: **876**:37/42.

[f121]

Actions of debt:
961:7/10 Robert Maye vs William Hutt - similar action to **960**; amount of debt 45s. [blank] for damages.

[44] *WCA*, 71.

958:7/7 Holden vs Screevin - dismissed for plaintiff.
962:5/7 Lumbarde vs Flye - peremptory day to respond.
964:6/6 Reade vs Wily - stands as before.
970:3/7 Meatcalfe vs Batt - second day of privilege and copy granted.
969:3/9 Batt vs Metcalfe - similarly.
Action continuing: **954**:10/14.

[f121v]

Actions of debt:
972:1/1 George Webb vs Mathew Scott - plaintiff's attorney, Simon Jeames, declares and defendant's attorney, Thomas Heathen, requests copy of declaration.
973:1/1 Thomas Webb vs Mathew Scott - similarly.

[f122]

Portmoot court held 23 March 1618.
Actions of debt:
960:8/10 May vs Hutt - *scire facias* returned executed and *alias scire facias* granted.
961:8/10 May vs Hutt - similarly.
962:6/7 Lumbard vs Fly - defendant, in person, says that he cannot deny his debt to the plaintiff; therefore court adjudges that plaintiff recover both [blank] for debt and [blank] for costs etc.
[Marginal note -Memorandum: The plaintiff promised to accept £3 in satisfaction of this judgment, if it is paid at or before the 26th of May next].
970:4/7 Meatcalfe vs Batt - last day of privilege granted.
969:4/9 Batt vs Meatcalfe - similarly.
974:1/28 Martin May vs Robert May - plaintiff's attorney, Thomas Heathen, requests day to declare and defendant's attorney is Simon Jeames.
Actions continuing: **876**:38/42; **954**:11/14.

[f122v]

Portmoot court held 30 March 1618.
Actions of debt:
960:9/10 May vs Hutt - *alias scire facias* returned executed.
961:9/10 May vs Hutt - similarly.
970:5/7 Meatcalfe vs Batt - peremptory day to respond granted in next court.
969:5/9 Batt vs Meatcalfe - peremptory day to respond.
Action continuing: **876**:39/42.

[f123]

Actions of debt:
962:7/7 Lumbard vs Flye - discharged.
974:2/28 Maye vs Maye - plaintiff's attorney puts declaration and requests day to amend the form in next court.

977:1/1 Christopher Brewer vs John Roffe - plaintiff's attorney, Thomas Heathen, requests day to declare; defendant's attorney is Simon Jeames.
Action of trespass:
975:1/5 John Osbaldeston, gent vs Simon Hall - plaintiff's attorney, Simon Jeames, requests day to declare in next court; Thomas Heathen for defendant.
Actions of trespass on case:
976:1/1 John Roffe vs Christopher Brewer - plaintiff's attorney, Simon Jeames, declares and requests day to amend the form; Thomas Heathen for defendant.
978:1/2 John Mosly vs Thomas Williams - plaintiff's attorney, Thomas Heathen, is granted day to declare. Simon Jeames for defendant.
Action continuing: **954**:12/14.

[f123v]

Portmoot court held 13 April 1618.
Actions of debt:
954:13/14 Browne vs Screevin - [No action recorded]
960:10/10 May vs Hutt - stands as before.
961:10/10 May vs Hutt - similarly.
970:6/7 Meatcalfe vs Batt - defendant responds by waging law with four compurgators in next court.
969:6/9 Batt vs Metcalfe - defendant responds non retinuisset and puts himself on the country; *venire facias* granted.
974:3/28 May vs May - defendant's attorney puts completed declaration and copy is granted.
Action of trespass:
975:2/5 Osbaston vs Hall - plaintiff puts declaration and copy granted.
Action of trespass on case:
978:2/2 Mosly vs Williams - discharged.
Action continuing: **876**:40/42.

[f124]

View of Frankpledge and Sessions of the Peace held 13 April 1618 before William Rayer, gent, mayor of the borough and Jerome Keite, gent and Thomas Browne, gent, Justices of the Peace.
979: *Jury for the King with Homage*:

John Dubber,	William Archer,	Nicholas Tayler,
John Ackly,	John Lowe,	Thomas Lowe,
Thomas Williams,	Richard Reade,	William Edwardes,
Thomas Martyn,	George Noble,	Thomas Godfery,
Robert Spitle,	William Hickes, jnr.,	Richard Browne.

Affeerers: John Lowe, Thomas Williams, Thomas Martyn sworn in.

[f124v]

980: *Names of victuallers allowed at this Sessions*

Thomas Heathen -	recognisance £10
Richard Reade	Edward Longe £5 each
William Archer -	recognisance £10
Richard Browne	William Butterfeild £5 each
William Hickes jnr. -	recognisance £10
Thomas Godfrey	Edward Carden £5 each
John Tassell -	recognisance £10
William Edwardes	Thomas Williams £5 each
John Durbridge -	recognisance £10
Nicolas Tayler	John Pepper £5 each

981: *Election of officers*

John Pepper is elected constable in place of Thomas Heathen
John Tassell is elected tithingman in place of John Pepper
Supervisors (of the highways) Nicholas Tayler, Thomas Williams

[f125]

Portmoot court held 27 April 1618.

Actions of debt:

954:14/14 Browne vs Screevin - renewal of execution.

969:7/9 Batt vs Meatcalfe - *venire facias* returned executed and *habeas corpora* granted for return in next court.

970:7/7 Meatcalfe vs Batt - defendant in person wages law with Richard Newell, William Browne, John Doa and Thomas Gee; therefore he goes quit.

974:4/28 Maye vs Maye - defendant responds, copy granted.

Action of trespass:

975:3/5 Osbaston vs Hall - defendant responds and copy granted; parties put themselves on the country and *venire facias* is granted.

Action continuing: **876**:41/42.

[f125v]

Action of trespass:

983:1/3 George Burgine and Mary his wife vs Thomas Orpwood – plaintiffs' attorney, Simon Jeames, declares and Thomas Heathen, for defendant, requests copy

note - Burgins charge is	12s 5d	
paid hereof	5s 11d	7s. 10d
remainder unpaid		
Orpwoods charge	16d	
		13s 9d

Action of trespass on case:

982:1/1 John Charlett, clerk vs John Symons - plaintiff declares and George Noble, surety, pays costs.

[f126]

Portmoot court held 11 May 1618.

Actions of debt:

969:8/9 Batt vs Metcalfe - defendant brings writ of *corpus cum causa* returnable before King's Bench at Westminster on Friday next on the quindene of Holy Trinity dated at Westminster 28th April abovesaid.

974:5/28 May vs May - day to replicate granted.

984:1/1 William Ayleworth, gent vs Edward Woolly - dismissed.

Actions of trespass:

975:4/5 Osbaston vs Hall - stands as before.

983:2/3 Burgine vs Orpwood - peremptory day to respond.

Action of trespass on case:

876:42/42 Allsopp vs Coles - continuing.

Marginal note: (crossed through)

985: 15s.6d. I owe to Thomas Heathen [...] 7s paid.

[f126v]

Portmoot court held 18 May 1618.

Actions of debt:

969:9/9 Bat vs Meatcalfe - stands as before.

974:6/28 May vs May - parties put themselves on the country; *venire facias* granted.

986:1/1 Thomas Williams vs William Raunson - [no action noted]

Actions of trespass:

975:5/5 Osbaston vs Hall - continues for costs.

983:3/3 Burgine vs Orpwood - defendant does not respond therefore writ of inquiry as to damages granted; and defendant says on Tuesday next he will pay costs for plaintiff of 12s 5d and costs for defendant of 16d, in total 13s 9d and he is discharged with agreement of plaintiff.

[f127]

Actions of debt:

987:1/3 John Marriatt vs John Curtis - plaintiff's attorney, Simon Jeames, declares and defendant is in custody of sergeant; his attorney, Thomas Heathen, requests copy of declaration.

988:1/3 Francis Knight vs John Curtis - similarly.

989:1/3 William (?Punn) vs John Curtis - similarly.

993:1/1 Thomas Browne vs Robert Winter - discharged.

995:1/1 Richard Bruce vs Thomas Gee - discharged.

Actions of trespass:

994:1/1 Thomas Stone vs Nicholas Edmunds - discharged through Thomas Heathen.

Actions of trespass on case:

990:1/3 Thomas Martine vs John Curtis - plaintiff's attorney, Simon Jeames, declares and requests day to amend the form; Thomas Heathen for defendant.

991:1/1 Thomas Mosse vs Richard Buller - discharged through Simon Jeames.
992:1/1 Richard Buller vs Thomas Mosse - similarly.

[f127v]

Portmoot court held 1 June 1618.
Actions of debt:
974:7/28 May vs May - stands as before.
987:2/3 Marriat vs Curtis - peremptory day to respond granted .
988:2/3 Knighte vs Curtis - similarly.
989:2/3 (?Punn) vs Curtis - similarly.
996:1/2 Thomas Winchester vs John Curtis - plaintiff's attorney, Simon Jeames, declares and defendant appears through Thomas Heathen; copy granted.
997:1/5 Richard Browne vs John Brookes - plaintiff's attorney, Thomas Heathen, declares and requests day to amend the form in next court. Defendant's attorney is Simon Jeames.
Action of trespass on case:
990:2/3 Martine vs Curtis - plaintiff's attorney puts completed declaration and defendant is granted copy.

[f128]

Apprenticeship:
998: Memorandum dated 13 June 1618 - John Patterick, son of William Patterick of the city of London, glover, places himself apprentice to Thomas Heathen, chandler, for the term of seven years at the Feast of Epiphany last past.

(signed) Edmund Hiorne, town clerk

[f128v]

Portmoot court dated 15 June 1618.
Actions of debt:
987:3/3 Marriat vs Curtis - defendant, through his attorney, pleads *per minas* and plaintiff responds by putting himself on the country; *venire facias* granted.
988:3/3 Knight vs Curtis - similarly.
989:3/3 (?Punn) vs Curtis - similarly.
996:2/2 Winchester vs Curtis - similarly (crossed out).
Action of trespass on case:
990:3/3 Martine vs Curtis - defendant pleads *non assumpsit modo et forma* and puts himself on the country; *venire facias* granted.
Action continuing: **974**:8/28.

[f129]

Actions of debt:
997:2/5 Browne vs Brookes - plaintiff puts completed declaration and copy is granted.

1002:1/6 William Pope, knight and baronet vs William Collier - plaintiff's attorney, Simon Jeames, puts declaration and is granted day to amend; defendant's attorney, Thomas Heathen, requests copy.

Actions of account:

1000:1/1 William Greene vs Thomas Bruce - discharged.

1001:1/1 William Greene vs Robert Bruce - discharged.

Action of detinue:

999:1/1 John Hutchins vs William Edwardes - discharged.

[f129v]

Actions of debt:

1003:1/6 William Pope, knight and baronet vs William Collier - plaintiff's attorney, Simon Jeames, puts declaration and is granted day to amend; defendant's attorney, Thomas Heathen, requests copy.

1004:1/4 Thomas Mowlder vs William Collier - plaintiff's attorney, Simon Jeames, declares and defendant's attorney, Thomas Heathen, requests copy.

1005:1/8 Henry Churchill vs William Hickes junior - plaintiff's attorney, Simon Jeames, declares and defendant's attorney, Thomas Heathen, requests copy and first day of privilege.

Apprenticeship:

1006: Memorandum: That Thomas Castell, son of William Castell of Wootton in the County of Oxon, yeoman, places himself apprentice with Brian Steevens of the aforesaid borough, tailor, at 13th November last past until the end of seven years next following.

(signed) Edmund Hiorne, town clerk

[f130]

Portmoot court held 29 June 1618.

Actions of debt:

997:3/5 Browne vs Brookes - peremptory day to respond.

1002:2/6 Pope (knight) vs Collier - peremptory day to respond.

1003:2/6 Pope (knight) vs Collier - similarly

1004:2/4 Mowlder vs Collier - peremptory day to respond.

1005:2/8 Churchill vs Hickes - second day of privilege.

Marginal note:

1007: Made even with Mr. mayor and with Thomas Heathen.

Action continuing: **974**:9/28.

[f130v]

Portmoot court held 6 July 1618.

Actions of debt:

997:4/5 Browne vs Brookes - defendant responds by waging law with four compurgators in next court and offers in court 24s 6d parcel of the aforesaid debt but plaintiff's attorney delays acceptance etc., copy response granted.

1002:3/6 Pope vs Collier - defendant's attorney responds *non debet modo et forma* and puts himself on the country; *venire facias* granted.
1003:3/6 Pope vs Collier - similarly.
1004:3/4 Mowlder vs Collier - defendant's attorney responds *per minas* and copy is granted to plaintiff who replicates and puts himself on the country; *venire facias* granted.
1005:3/8 Churchill vs Hickes - defendant does not respond on three occasions.
Action continuing: **974**:10/28.

[f131]

Actions of debt:
1008:1/5 John Whitton, gent vs Rawlen Croshawe gent.
1009:1/5 John Cupper, gent vs Rawly Croshawe gent.
1010:1/5 Nicholas Tilman vs Raughlen Crowshawe gent.
[No action listed in above three cases]
Arrest:
1011: Croshewe was arrested 8th July 1618.

[f131v]

Portmoot court held 20 July 1618.
Actions of debt:
997:5/5 Browne vs Brooks - defendant appears in person to wage law with four compurgators viz: John Bruce, George Webb, Thomas Richardson and Robert Bruce; therefore he goes quit and plaintiff is granted peremptory day to replicate for the aforesaid 24s 6d granted to him. Dismissed.
1002:4/6 Pope vs Collier - sergeant returns executed *venire facias* and writ of *habeas corpora* juratorum is granted.
1003:4/6 Pope vs Collier - similarly.
1004:4/4 Mowlder vs Collier - similarly; discharged.
Action continuing: **974**:11/28.

[f132]

Actions of debt:
1005:4/8 Churchill vs Hickes - court adjudges plaintiff should recover both [blank] for debt and [blank] for costs; *scire facias* granted.
1008:2/5 John Whitton, gent vs Rawlen Croshawe, gent - plaintiff's attorney, Simon Jeames, declares and Thomas Heathen, for defendant, requests copy.
1009:2/5 John Cupper, gent vs Rawly Croshawe, gent - Simon Jeames, for plaintiff, declares and Thomas Heathen, for defendant, requests copy.
1010:2/5 Nicholas Tilman vs Raughlen Crowshawe, gent - Simon Jeames, for plaintiff, declares and Thomas Heathen, for defendant, requests copy.
Memorandum:
1012: Made even with Mr. mayor and Thomas Heathen.

[f132v]

Portmoot court held 3 August 1618.

Actions of debt:

1002:5/6 Pope vs Collier - continues for defendant with assent of plaintiff.

1003:5/6 Pope vs Collier - similarly.

1005:5/8 Churchill vs Hickes - sergeant returns executed *scire facias* and *alias scire facias* granted.

Action continuing: **974**:12/28.

[f133]

Actions of debt:

1008:3/5 Whitton vs Crosshewe - defendant granted peremptory day to respond in next court.

1009:3/5 Cupper vs Crosshewe - similarly.

1010:3/5 Tillman vs Crosshewe - similarly.

1013:1/3 Robert Russell vs Rawlen Crosshawe, gent - Simon Jeames, for plaintiff, declares and Thomas Heathen, for defendant, requests copy.

Actions of trespass on case:

1014:1/4 Edward Townsend vs Ambrose Lardner - Simon Jeames, for plaintiff, requests day to declare in next court. Thomas Heathen appears for defendant.

1015:1/6 Ambrose Lardner vs Edward Townsend - Simon Jeames, for plaintiff, requests day to declare in next court. Thomas Heathen appears for defendant.

1016:1/15 Henry Alberte vs Anthony Fyndall, gent - Simon Jeames, for plaintiff, requests day to declare in next court. Thomas Heathen appears for defendant.

[f133v]

Actions of debt:

1018:1/7 William Meatcalfe vs George Poure, gent - Simon Jeames, for plaintiff, declares and Thomas Heathen, for defendant, requests copy.

1019:1/1 John Gadbury gent, vs William Teaser - Simon Jeames, for plaintiff, declares and Thomas Heathen, for defendant, requests copy. [Dismissed and case crossed through].

1020:1/4 Edward Goodiar, executor of the last will and testament of Edmund Meese Esq. deceased[45] vs Dodulphus Lunand *alias* Lunden - Simon Jeames, for plaintiff, declares and Thomas Heathen, for defendant, requests copy.

Guardianship

1021: 1/1 To this court comes Ralph (Rodulphus) Bradshewe, (aged seven years or thereabouts) only son and heir of William Bradshewe, mercer of this town, recently deceased, in person, and chooses Ralph Clement of Bicester ('Burcester'), Oxon, tanner, to be his guardian and have custody of himself,

[45] Possibly of Grays Inn, Middlesex. Owned property in Swalcliffe. Ox.Arch. Dash.VI/72 1607.

the said Ralph, and his lands and [tenements] in the said borough (during his minority) and according to the custom of the said borough. Admitted.[46]

[f134]

Portmoot court held 17 August 1618.

Actions of debt:

1002:6/6 Pope vs Collier - continues.

1003:6/6 Pope vs Collier - continues.

1005:6/8 Churchill vs Hickes - *alias scire facias* returned executed and execution granted against defendant and surety.

1008:4/5 Whitton vs Crosshewe - defendant responds to the charge and plaintiff replicates and puts himself on the country; plaintiff (sic defendant) likewise and *venire facias* granted.

Action continuing: **974**:13/28.

[f134v]

Actions of debt:

1009:4/5 Coupper vs Crosshewe - defendant responds *per minas* and plaintiff is granted copy and immediately replicates and puts himself on the country; *venire facias* granted.

1010:4/5 Tillman vs Crosshewe - similarly.

1013:2/3 Russell vs Crosshewe - defendant's attorney responds non debet modo et forma; *venire facias* granted.

Actions of trespass on case:

1014:2/4 Townsend vs Lardner - plaintiff declares and requests day to amend in next court.

1015:2/6 Lardner vs Townsend - similarly.

[f135]

Actions of debt:

1018:2/7 Meatcalfe vs Poure - defendant granted peremptory day to respond in next court.

1020:2/4 Goodiar vs London *alias* Lunden - peremptory day to respond granted.

1022:1/17 William Blith and Richard Gresbrooke vs William Shawe - plaintiffs' attorney, Simon Jeames, declares and defendant does not respond; therefore nil dicit.

Actions of trespass on case:

1016:2/15 Alberte vs Fyndall - plaintiff puts completed declaration and copy is granted.

1017:1/14 Anthony Fyndall vs Henry Alberte - Thomas Heathen, for plaintiff, declares and requests day to amend in next court. Simon Jeames appears for defendant.

[46] See Introduction – guardianship, MSS. Wills (Oxon) 4/4/17.

Memorandum
1023: Made even with Mr. mayor and Thomas Heathen.

[f135v]

Actions of debt:
1025:1/8 Richard Hanwell vs Ellen Rudgate, widow - plaintiff's attorney, Simon Jeames, declares and defendant's attorney is Thomas Heathen.First day of privilege granted.
1026:1/1 Thomas Lowe vs William Hickes junior - [No action noted].
Actions of trespass on case:
1024:1/14 Thomas Harris, gent vs William Cumpton - plaintiff's attorney, Simon Jeames, puts declaration and Thomas Heathen, for defendant, is granted copy.
Memorandum
1027: Made even with Mr. mayor and Thomas Heathen.

[f136]

Portmoot court held 31 August 1618.
Actions of debt:
1005:7/8 Churchill vs Hickes - sergeant reports that he is holding William Hickes in execution of writ.
1008:5/5 Whitton vs Crosshewe
1009:5/5 Cooper vs the same
1010:5/5 Tillman vs the same
1013:3/3 Russell vs the same
} Sergeant returns *venire facias* executed; and immediately Edulphus Dingly, gent, brings a writ of privilege for the aforesaid defendant returnable before Henry Hobart, knight and baronet, Chief Justice of the King's Bench at his chambers situate in the parish of St. Bartholomew the Great in London immediately upon receipt of this writ. Testified by H. Hobart at Westminster 25th June 16 Jas.I. abovesaid and allowed in this Court.
Action continuing: **974**:14/28.

[f136v]

Actions of debt:
1018:3/7 Meatcalfe vs Poure - defendant does not respond; therefore judgment adjourned to next court.
1020:3/4 Goodiar vs London - defendant's attorney responds *per minas* and plaintiff requests copy and immediately replicates and puts himself on the country, defendant similarly; *venire facias* granted.
1022:2/17 Blith & Gresbrooke vs Shawe - continues for plaintiffs.
1025:2/8 Hanwell vs Rudgate - second day of privilege granted.
Actions of trespass on case:
1014:3/4 Townsend vs Lardner - defendant granted copy of declaration.
1015:3/6 Lardner vs Townsend - plaintiff does not wish to proceed; therefore judgment adjourned to next court for costs.

1016:3/15 Albert vs Fyndall - continues by equal agreement.
1017:2/14 Fyndall vs Alberte - similarly.
1024:2/14 Harris vs Cumpton - peremptory day to respond granted.

[f137]

Actions of debt:
1022:3/17 Blithe & Gresbrooke vs Shawe - continues for plaintiffs as before.
1028:1/13 Edward Goodiar vs Ethelbert Sharpe - Simon Jeames, for plaintiff, declares and defendant does not appear to respond.
1029:1/1 Thomas Lowe vs William Hickes jnr., plaintiff declares and defendant responds; first day of privilege granted. [clause later deleted]

[f137v]

Portmoot court held 14 September 1618.
Actions of debt:
1005:8/8 Churchill vs Hickes - discharged by assent of plaintiff.
Actions of trespass on case:
1014:4/4 Townsend vs Lardner - discharged for defendant with assent of plaintiff.
1015:4/6 Lardner vs Townsend - continues for plaintiff.
Actions continuing: **974**:15/28; **1016**:4/15; **1017**:3/14.

[f138]

Actions of debt:
1018:4/7 Meatcalfe vs Poure - court adjudges that plaintiff should recover both [blank] for debt and [blank] for costs; *scire facias* granted against defendant's surety.
1020:4/4 Goodiar vs London - dismissed by assent of plaintiff.
1025:3/8 Hanwell vs Rudgate - last day of privilege granted.
1028:2/13 Goodiar vs Sharpe - court adjudges plaintiff should recover both [blank] for debt and [blank] for costs; *scire facias* granted.
1029:1/7 William Rayer vs Robert Bignill - Simon Jeames, for plaintiff, declares and Thomas Heathen, for defendant, requests day for discussion. First day of privilege granted.
Action of trespass on case:
1024:3/14 Harris vs Cumpton - defendant, through attorney, replies non assumpsit modo et forma and parties put themselves on the country; *venire facias* granted.
Action continuing: **1022**:4/17.

[f138v]

Portmoot court held 28 September 1618.
Actions of debt:
1018:5/7 Meatcalfe vs Poure - *scire facias* returned executed and *alias scire facias* granted.
1028:3/13 Goodiar vs Sharpe - stands as before.

1029:2/7 Rayer vs Bignill - second day of privilege granted.
Actions of trespass on case:
1015:5/6 Lardner vs Townsend - continues for defendant.
1024:4/14 Harris vs Cumpton - *venire facias* returned executed and writ of *habeas corpora juratorum* granted.
Actions continuing: **974**:16/28; **1016**:5/15; **1017**:4/14.

[f139]

Actions of debt:
1022:5/17 Blith and Gresbrooke vs Shawe - continues.
1025:4/8 Hanwell vs Rudgate - peremptory day to respond.
1032:1/1 John Bolter and Elizabeth his wife vs William Flexnye - Simon Jeames, for plaintiffs, declares and Thomas Heathen, for defendant requests copy.
1033:1/7 John Davis vs Sericum Edkins - plaintiff's attorney, Simon Jeames, puts declaration and defendant does not appear to respond; therefore nil dicit.
Action of trespass on case:
1031:1/14 Robert Hopkins vs William Allen - plaintiff's attorney, Simon Jeames, requests day to state his case. Defendant's attorney is Thomas Heathen.
Action of trespass and assault:
1030:1/7 William Busby vs Richard Key - plaintiff's attorney, Simon Jeames, states his case and defendant's attorney, Thomas Heathen, requests copy of declaration.

[f139v]

Actions of debt:
1034:1/3 Henry Cornish vs William Harris - sergeant at mace reports that he has seized two cows of defendant which are in his custody And John Wheate of Ducklington ('Ducklynton') claims the aforesaid (cows) are his goods and properly belong to him. And Robert Harris, brother of the defendant, says that the goods and chattels aforesaid are rightfully the goods and chattels of the said John Wheate.
Marginal note: it appears upon their evidence that the property is not certain to belong to the said Wheate; Therefore defendant must pay at the first Court.
1035:1/1 John Salter vs Edward Dudson - plaintiff's attorney, Simon Jeames, puts declaration; and Thomas Heathen, for defendant, requests copy.
Action of trespass:
1037:1/1 Thomas Screevin vs Richard Hawkins - [No action entered].
Action of trespass and assault:
1036:1/5 Richard Hawkins and Anne his wife vs Thomas Screevin - plaintiffs' attorney, Simon Jeames, puts declaration and defendant does not respond; therefore writ of inquiry into damages granted.
Action continuing: **1024**:5/14.

[f140]

Portmoot court held 5 October 1618.

Actions of debt:

1018:6/7 Meatcalfe vs Poure - *alias scire facias* returned executed, and execution granted against defendant and surety.

1029:3/7 Rayer vs Bignill - last day of privilege granted.

Actions of trespass on case:

1015:6/6 Lardner vs Townsend - continues for defendant; discharged.

Actions continuing: **974**:17/28; **1016**:6/15; **1017**:5/14; **1022**:6/17; **1028**:4/13.

[f140v]

Actions of debt:

1025:5/8 Hanwell vs Rudgate - defendant does not respond therefore judgment adjourned to next court.

1033:2/7 Davis vs Edkins - judgment of court is that plaintiff should recover both [blank] for debt and [blank] for costs and *scire facias* granted.

1034:2/3 Cornish vs Harris - defendant, solemnly demanded on second day to respond to plaintiff, and he does not appear.

1038:1/1 Thomas Tolly vs Elizabeth Hurste - plaintiff's attorney, Simon Jeames, declares and in this court (action) is dismissed by assent of plaintiff.

Actions of trespass on case:

1031:2/14 Hopkins vs Allen - plaintiff puts declaration and seeks day to amend in next court.

Actions of trespass and assault:

1030:2/7 Busby vs Keye - peremptory day to respond.

1036:2/5 Hawkins vs Screevin - renewal of writ of inquiry into damages.

Action continuing: **1024**:6/14.

END OF YEAR OF WILLIAM RAYER AS MAYOR OF THE BOROUGH

[f141]

15th October 1618

WILLIAM FLYE TAKES OFFICE AS MAYOR OF THE BOROUGH

Portmoot court held 19 October 1618.

Actions continuing: **974**:18/28; **1016**:7/15; **1017**:6/14.

[f141v]

Actions of debt:

1018:7/7 Meatcalfe vs Poure - [No action recorded].

1025:6/8 Hanwell vs Rudgate - judgment of court is that plaintiff recover both [blank] for debt and [blank] for costs and *scire facias* granted.

1029:4/7 Rayer vs Bignill - peremptory day to respond granted.

1033:3/7 Davis vs Edkins - *alias scire facias* granted.

1034:3/3 Cornishe vs Harris - defendant solemnly charged for not responding upon three occasions; therefore the aforesaid chattels are forfeit. Therefore court orders that the chattels are appraised by three men of the borough and that the chattels are delivered to the plaintiff, valued at £4 10s by William Rayer, alderman, John Gadbury, Edmund Hiorne and William Metcalfe and delivered to Thomas Hewes of Tew ('Tewe') to the use of the plaintiff.
Action of trespass on case:
1031:3/14 Hopkins vs Allen - completed declaration placed and copy granted.
Actions of trespass and assault:
1030:3/7 Busby vs Key - defendant responds through attorney and plaintiff replicates and puts himself on the country; *venire facias* granted.
1036:3/5 Hawkins vs Screevin - renewal of writ of inquiry into damages.
Actions continuing: **1022**:7/17; **1028**:5/13.

[f142]

Actions of debt:
1040:1/2 Peter Slatter vs Richard Bantinge - plaintiff's attorney, Thomas Heathen, seeks day to declare and defendant's attorney, Simon Jeames, offers in court 33s.4d and requests day to wage law.
1041:1/1 Mauriss Merrick, gent vs Richard Martine - plaintiff's attorney, Simon Jeames, requests day to state case and defendant's attorney is Thomas Heathen.
1042:1/1 William Rayer vs Thomas Martin - action discharged.
Action continuing: **1024**:7/14.

[f142v]

View of Frankpledge and Sessions of the Peace held 21 October 1618 before William Flye, mayor and Jerome Keite and Thomas Browne, gents, Justices of the Peace for the borough.

1043: *Jury for the King and Homage*

John Dubber,	William Archer,	Richard Meades,
Thomas Lowe,	Thomas Williams,	Robert Bruce,
George Noble,	Richard Reade,	Robert Spitle,
Richard Hawkins,	Richard Browne,	Bryan Steephens,
John Acklye,	Thomas Martine.	

Affeerers: Thomas Martyn, Thomas Williams, George Noble, Robert Spitle sworn in.

[f143]

1044: *Election of Officers*:
William Edwardes and Richard Browne are elected constables and sworn in.
John Durbridge, William Hickes, Bryan Steephens and John Dissell are elected tithingmen and sworn in.
Francis Garter and John Wilkinson are elected ale-tasters.

Memorandum:
1045: Estreats of this court amounted to £8 17s 10d and were delivered to William Edwardes, constable 17 December 1618

(signed by) Edmund Hiorne, town clerk

[f143v]

Portmoot court held 2 November 1619.

Action of debt:
1029:5/7 Rayer vs Bignill - defendant does not reply, therefore nil dicit and judgment postponed to next court.
Action of trespass and assault:
1030:4/7 Busby vs Key - *venire facias* returned executed and *habeas corpora* granted.
Actions continuing: **974**:19/28; **1016**:8/15; **1017**:7/14; **1022**:8/17; **1028**:6/13.

[f144]

Actions of debt:
1025:7/8 Hanwell vs Rudgate - *alias scire facias* granted.
1033:4/7 Davis vs Edkins - execution granted.
1040:2/2 Slatter vs Banting - discharged.
1046:1/8 Walter Wilkins, gent vs William Hickes, junior - plaintiff's attorney, Simon Jeames, states his case and defendant neither responds nor appears, therefore nil dicit.
1047:1/2 Alice Bradshewe, widow vs William Raunson - Simon Jeames, for plaintiff, declares and Thomas Heathen, for defendant. requests copy and first day of privilege.
1048:1/10 Thomas Bird, gent vs Robert Winter - Simon Jeames, for plaintiff, declares and Thomas Heathen, for defendant, requests copy and first day of privilege.
Actions of trespass on case:
1031:4/14 Hopkins vs Allen - peremptory day granted.
Action of trespass and assault:
1036:4/5 Hawkins vs Screevin - judgment of court is that plaintiff recover both 20s damages and [blank] for costs; *scire facias* granted.
Action continuing: **1024**:8/14.

[f144v]

Portmoot court held 16 November 1618.

Action of trespass and assault:
1030:5/7 William Busby vs Richard Key - Names of jury between parties:-

John Norman,	William Edwardes,	George Noble,
Robert Spitle,	Richard Browne,	John Ackly,
Thomas Martin,	William Archer,	Robert Bruce,
Richard Reade,	William Hickes, jnr.,	Edward Carden.

Plaintiff does not bring suit and judgment etc adjourned.

Actions continuing: **974**:20/28; **1016**:9/15; **1017**:8/14.

[f145]

Actions of debt:
1025:8/8 Hanwell vs Rudgate - execution granted.
1029:6/7 Rayer vs Bignill - court adjudges that plaintiff should recover both [blank] for debt and [blank] for costs; *scire facias* granted.
1033:5/7 Davis vs Edkins - renewal of execution.
1046:2/8 Wilkins vs Hickes - continues for plaintiff.
1047:2/2 Bradshewe vs Raunson - Mistris Raunson, surety, pays debt and costs.
1048:2/10 Bird vs Winter - second day of privilege granted.
Action of trespass on case:
1031:5/14 Hopkins vs Allen - defendant does not respond; therefore etc. writ of inquiry into damages etc.
Action of trespass and assault:
1036:5/5 Hawkins vs Screevin - discharged etc. and John Glover, surety, pays 48s.2d.
Actions continuing: **1022**:9/17; **1024**:9/14; **1028**:7/13.

[f145v]

Actions of debt:
1049:1/1 Alexander Harris vs John Hedge - discharged.
1050:1/1 John Hedge vs Alexander Harris - discharged.

[f146]

Portmoot court held 30 November 1618.
Actions of debt:
1029:7/7 Rayer vs Bignill - stands upon judgment.
1048:3/10 Bird vs Winter - last day of privilege granted.
Action of trespass and assault:
1030:6/7 Busby vs Key - discharged.
Actions continuing: **974**:21/28; **1016**:10/15; **1017**:9/14; **1022**:10/17; **1024**: 10/14; **1028**:8/13; **1033**:6/7; **1046**:3/8.

[f146v]

Actions of debt:
1051:1/6 William Bedwell vs William Allen - on plea of debt of 55s, plaintiff's attorney, Simon Jeames, states his case; defendant's attorney, Thomas Heathen, seeks allowance of aforesaid writ and it is allowed.
1052:1/5 Thomas Bagwell vs William Allen - on plea of debt of 13s, plaintiff's attorney, Simon Jeames requests day to declare and Thomas Heathen for defendant requests etc.. in order to complete; and it is allowed.
Action of trespass on case:
1031:6/14 Robert Hopkins vs William Allen - sergeant at mace returns executed writ of inquiry into damages and jury assess damages at £7 23d; and

defendant's attorney brings a writ of privilege returnable before the Court of Common Pleas at Westminster on Monday next of the octave of Hilary next. Testified by H.Hobart 28th November - Brownlowe.[47]
[marginal note - writ of privilege for W.Allen: allowed]
Apprenticeship:
1053: John Staynoe, son of Nicholas Staynoe, places himself apprentice to Brian Steephens, tailor, for term of seven years from first day of this month of November. As by an indenture made between them bearing date 1st November abovesaid as is clearly shown. [marginal note - Entry. John Staynoe]

[f147]

Portmoot court held 14 December 1618.
Actions of debt:
1028:9/13 Goodiar vs Sharpe - executed writ of *scire facias* returned and *alias scire facias* granted.
1033:7/7 Davis vs Edkins - discharged.
1048:4/10 Bird vs Winter - peremptory day to respond.
1051:2/6 Bedwell vs Allen - stands as before.
1052:2/5 Bagwell vs Allen - stands as before.
Action of trespass on case:
1031:7/14 Hopkins vs Allen - stands as before.
Action of trespass and assault:
1030:7/7 Busby vs Key - discharged.
Actions continuing: **974**:22/28; **1016**:11/15; **1017**:10/14; **1022**:11/17; **1024**: 11/14; **1046**:4/8.

[f147v]

Actions of debt:
1054:1/1 Richard Heath vs John Teasler - plaintiff's attorney, Simon Jeames, declares and Thomas Heathen for defendant requests copy; discharged.
1055:1/1 George Webb vs John Teasler - similarly; discharged.

[f148]

Portmoot court held 21 December 1618.
Actions of debt:
1028:10/13 Goodiar vs Sharpe - *alias scire facias* returned executed. Writ of execution granted against defendant and his surety.
1046:5/8 Wilkins vs Hickes - court adjudges that plaintiff recover both debt of 22s and [blank] for costs; *scire facias* granted.
1048:5/10 Bird vs Winter - defendant does not respond, therefore judgment will be given in next court.
1051:3/6 Bedwell vs Allen - stands under writ of privilege.
1052:3/5 Bagwell vs Allen - similarly.

[47] Brownlowe – a Westminster court officer or clerk.

Action of trespass on case:
1031:8/14 Hopkins vs Allen - stands under writ of privilege.
Actions continuing: **974**:23/28; **1016**:12/15; **1017**:11/14; **1022**:12/17; **1024**: 12/14.
Breach of the peace:
1056: Thomas Heathen, sergeant, makes oath as follows:- viz: that on Tuesday night last he arrested Jerome Walford at the suit of Richard Bently and required Robert Banting and John Bignill then present to aid him, but they would not aid him whereby the prisoner escaped from him, out of Robert Bignill's house and Walford wounded the sergeant: Therefore court adjudges that the said Robert Banting and John Bignill each be fined 40s and [improsecut.. durant.. £10]

[f148v]

Portmoot court held 11 January 1619.
Actions of debt:
1028:11/13 Goodiar vs Sharpe - renewal of execution.
1046:6/8 Wilkins vs Hickes - *scire facias* returned executed and *alias scire facias* granted.
Actions continuing: **974**:24/28; **1016**:13/15; **1017**:12/14; **1022**:13/17; **1031**: 9/14; **1051**:4/6; **1052**:4/5.

[f149]

Actions of debt:
1048:6/10 Bird vs Winter - judgment of court is that plaintiff should recover £10 debt and [blank] for costs; *scire facias* granted against defendant's surety.
1058:1/2 Edmund Blith vs John Berriman - plaintiff's attorney, Simon Jeames states his case and asks day for amendment; and Thomas Heathen, for defendant, requests copy of declaration.
Actions of trespass on case:
1057:1/16 Tobias Thomas vs Robert Binckes - plaintiff's attorney, Thomas Heathen, requests day to declare in next court. Simon Jeames is defendant's attorney.
1059:1/6 Edward Bulliphant vs Francis Barnsdall *alias* Barnslee - plaintiff, represented by attorney, Simon Jeames, states his case and requests day to amend and defendant's attorney, Thomas Heathen, requests copy of declaration.
Action continuing: **1024**:13/14.

[f149v]

Action of trespass:
1060:1/3 Richard Smith and Anne his wife vs William Bullock - Simon Jeames, plaintiffs' attorney, states the case and requests day to amend and defendant's attorney, Thomas Heathen requests copy.

Action of trespass on case:
1061:1/3 Robert Whiting vs William Bullock - plaintiff's attorney, Simon Jeames, states case and asks for day to amend. Thomas Heathen, for defendant, requests copy.

[f150]

Portmoot court held 25 January 1619.
Action of debt:
1046:7/8 Wilkins vs Hickes, jnr. - sergeant at mace returns executed *alias scire facias* and execution granted against defendant and his surety.
Actions continuing: **974**:25/28; **1016**:14/15; **1017**:13/14; **1022**:14/17.

[f150v]

Actions of debt:
1048:7/10 Bird vs Winter - stands as before.
1058:2/2 Blith vs Berryman - discharged through Thomas Heathen.
1052:5/5 Bagwell vs Allen - stands as before.
Action of trespass:
1060:2/3 Smith vs Bullock - plaintiff puts completed declaration and copy granted.
Actions of trespass on case:
1024:14/14 Harris vs Cumpton - discharged.
1057:2/16 Toms vs Binckes - plaintiff's attorney puts completed declaration and copy granted.
1059:2/6 Bulliphant vs Barnsdall - peremptory day.
1061:2/3 Whiting vs Bullock - plaintiff puts completed declaration and copy granted; discharged.
Actions continuing: **1028**:12/13; **1031**:10/14; **1051**:5/6.

[f151]

Actions of trespass and trespass on case:
1060:3/3 and **1061**:3/3 - Memorandum:25 January 1619
Robert Whiting and William Bullock by the delivery of 6d. either to other did assure and promise under the pain of £40 to stand to the award of Edmund Hiorne for the ending of all controversies and suits and all other matters duties and demands between them from the beginning of the world until this day: So that the same award be made and made known to them at or before the 8th of February next following. Also Robert Whiting upon the aforesaid acceptance of 6d from William Bullock assures and promises that Richard Smith and Ann his wife shall also stand to the award of the said Edmund Hiorne for all matters between them and William Bullock until this day So as the award be made as aforesaid And also the said William Bullock likewise assures and promises Also it was and is meant that this award shall bind Robert Whiting, Richard Smith and Ann his wife and the said William Bullock, to stand to

such award as shall be made concerning Richard Johnson, brother in law to William Bullock.
3rd February 1619 I, Edmund Hiorne do award that William Bullock shall pay to Robert Whiting 8s 10d in full satisfaction of all matters between them until this day; which he paid before me: Also I award that the said Bullock shall seal a bill to pay Richard Smith 15s on the 11th of May next in full satisfaction of all matters between them: which he did in my presence. Also that all matters between the said Whiting, Smith and Richard Johnson, shall be ended till this day. (signed by) Simon Jeames Edmund Hiorne.

[f151v]

Portmoot court held 8 February 1619.

Actions of debt:
1028:13/13 Goodiar vs Sharpe - discharged upon execution.
1046:8/8 Wilkins vs Hickes - discharged upon execution.
Actions of trespass on case:
1016:15/15 Albert vs Fyndall - stands as before.
1017:14/14 Fyndall vs Alberte - stands as before.
1057:3/16 Toms vs Binckes - peremptory day to respond.
1059:3/6 Bulliphant vs Barnsdall - continues for plaintiff: and Joan Davis widow, by adjudgment this court, at her request surety will pay debt and costs in next court.
Actions continuing: **974**:26/28; **1022**:15/17; **1048**:8/10.

[f152]

Actions of debt:
1063:1/1 William Archer vs John Poynes [knight] - sergeant at mace reports on the seizure of one horse (in English 'a sorrel nagg') worth 40s which is in his custody; and plaintiff, through his attorney Thomas Heathen, requests day to state his case. (marginal note - it is void). [Action then crossed out].
1064:1/1 Edmund Hiorne vs Richard Lock - plaintiff's attorney, Simon Jeames, states his case and defendant remains in his custody. Thomas Heathen appears for defendant.
Actions of trespass on case:
1031:11/14 Hopkins vs Allen - plaintiff's attorney brings writ de procedendo testified by H. Hobart at Westminster 23rd January 16 Jas.I.; court adjudges plaintiff should recover both £7 23d for his damages with 48s 8d for costs. *scire facias* granted against surety for defendant.
1062:1/5 Richard Warde vs Richard Jeames - plaintiff, by his attorney, Simon Jeames, requests day to declare. Thomas Heathen for defendant.

[f152v]

Action of debt:
1051:6/6 Bedwell vs Allen - stands as before.

Portmoot court held 22 February 1619.
Actions of trespass on case:
1031:12/14 Hopkins vs Allen - *scire facias* returned executed and *alias scire facias* granted against defendant's surety.
1057:4/16 Toms vs Binckes - defendant puts response, namely of demurrer, and plaintiff's attorney requests copy.
1059:4/6 Bulliphant vs Barnsdall - continues for plaintiff.
1062:2/5 Warde vs Jeames - plaintiff puts declaration and day to amend granted.
Actions continuing: **974**:27/28; **1022**:16/17; **1048**:9/10.

[f153]

Portmoot court held 8 March 1619.
Actions of debt:
974:28/28 May vs May - stands as before.
1022:17/17 Blith and Gresbrock vs Shawe - stands as before.
Actions of trespass on case:
1031:13/14 Hopkins vs Allen - *alias scire facias* returned executed and defendant does not appear; therefore execution granted against defendant and his surety.
1057:5/16 Toms vs Binckes - plaintiff, through his attorney, joins the demurrer and seeks consideration of court.
1062:3/5 Warde vs Jeames - continues for plaintiff.
Actions continuing: **1048**:10/10; **1059**:5/6.

[f153v]

Actions of debt:
1065:1/5 Anne Holdinge, widow vs Thomas Screevin - plaintiff's attorney, Simon Jeames, states the case and defendant seeks copy and first day of privilege.
1066:1/6 Jerome Kyte, gent vs John Cooke - plaintiff's attorney, Simon Jeames, states his case and copy granted.
1067:1/6 William Meatcalfe vs John Cooke - similarly.
1068:1/1 Thomas Wilkshere vs Nicholas Shorter - plaintiff declares, through Simon Jeames, and defendant does not respond; therefore *nil dicit* etc.

[f154]

Portmoot court held 22 March 1619.[48]
Actions of debt:
1065:2/5 Holdinge vs Screevin - second day of privilege.
1066:2/6 Kyte vs Cooke - peremptory day.
1067:2/6 Meatcalfe vs Cooke - peremptory day.

48 'Baron' crossed through.

Action of trespass:
1069:1/2 Clement Tutchine, administratrix of goods and chattels of Richard Tutchine deceased[49] vs Christopher Forty - plaintiff's attorney, Simon Jeames, declares and is granted day to amend in next court. Thomas Heathen appears for defendant; discharged through Thomas Heathen.
Actions of trespass on case:
1057:6/16 Toms vs Binckes - day and date for parties aforesaid in next court; court wishes to consider.
1059:6/6 Bulliphant vs Barnsdall - continues.
1062:4/5 Ward vs Jeames - plaintiff puts completed declaration and copy is granted.

[f154v]

Action of trespass:
1070:1/2 Tutchine vs Forty - plaintiff's attorney, Simon Jeames, declares and is granted day to amend in next court. Thomas Heathen appears for defendant; discharged through Thomas Heathen.
Portmoot court held 5 April 1619.
Actions of debt:
1066:3/6 Keite vs Cooke - defendant does not respond; therefore *nihil dicit.*
1067:3/6 Meatcalfe vs Cooke - similarly.
Actions of trespass:
1069:2/2 Tutchine vs Forty - discharged for defendant.
1070:2/2 Tutchine vs Forty - similarly.

[f155]

Actions of debt:
1065:3/5 Holden vs Screevin - last day of privilege granted.
1071:1/3 William Clementes vs Edward Chamberlyn - plaintiff's attorney, Simon Jeames, declares and defendant's attorney, Thomas Heathen, requests copy.
Actions of trespass on case:
1057:7/16 Toms vs Binckes - court wishes to consider for next sitting.
1062:5/5 Warde vs Jeames - discharged for plaintiff.
Apprenticeship:
1072: Memorandum - John Woodrooffe the son of John Woodrooffe of Old Woodstock in the County of Oxon did put himself apprentice to Robert Busby of this borough, tailor, for the term of seven years from the 11th day of March last past by me (signed) Edmund Hiorne Clerk of the borough council

[f155v] & [f156] (Blank)

[49] Richard Tutchine of Kidlington d.1618 MSS.Wills (Oxon) 106.109; 300/4/13.

[f156v]

View of Frankpledge and Sessions of the Peace held 7 April 1619 before William Flye gent, mayor and Jerome Keite gent and Thomas Browne gent, Justices of the Peace for the borough.

1073: *Jury for the King with Homage*

Henry Bradshewe,	Thomas Bruce,	Thomas Williams,
William Archer,	John Norman,	John Durbridge,
George Noble,	Robert Bruce,	John Ackly,
Richard Hawkins,	Thomas Martyn,	Brian Steephens,
William Raunson,	Robert Busby,	Bartholomew Love.

Affeerers: Thomas Williams, John Norman, Thomas Martin (sworn in).

[f157]

1074: *Election of officers*:
Henry Bradshewe and Thomas Martyn are elected constables and sworn.
John Norman and Bartholomew Love elected supervisors (of the highways).
Sessions of the Peace adjourned until 19th instant month April 1619

1075: *Victuallers licenced:*
The names of the victuallers allowed, and which entered recognisance this sessions according to the King's Majesty's proclamation made at Newmarket ('New Markett') the 19th January in the 16th year of the King's Majesty's reign etc..1618 to continue till 6th April 1620.

Thomas Williams £10
    Robert Bignill and Thomas Heathen each £5
William Edwardes £10
    Thomas Heathen and William Raunson each £5
Thomas Godfery £10
    Anthony Deverill and Edward Longe each £5
Bennett Paynter £10
    John Durbridge and William Archer each £5

[f157v]

Robert Bignill £10
    Thomas Williams and William Raunson each £5
Thomas Heathen £10
    Thomas Williams and William Edwardes each £5
Elizabeth Hamond, widow £10
    Edward Carden and William Browne each £5
Merriall Tayler, widow £10
    John Collingwood and Robert Bignill each £5
Dorothy Wells, widow £10
    John Collingwood and Edward Longe each £5
John Durbridge £10
    Bennett Paynter and Edward Carden each £5

John Tassill £10
Bennett Paynter and William Edwardes £5 each
Alice White, widow £10
John Collingwood and Robert Bignill each £5
Nicholas Tayler £10
John Glover, alderman, and Bennett Paynter each £5
William Raunson £10
Anthony Deverill and Robert Bignill each £5

[f158]

William Archer £10
William Butterfield and Bennett Paynter each £5
Robert Winter £10
Thomas Martyn and Richard Browne each £5
William Rayer, Alderman £10
Thomas Rayer and John Dubber each £5
Joan Glover £10
Anthony Deverill and John Collingwood each £5

Imprisonment of unlicenced victuallers:

1076: Thomas Screevin, William Butterfeild and Edward Carden are committed to Mr. Bradshewe to be committed to prison for 3 days for victualling without licence (signed by) Jerom Keyt Thomas Browne Edmund Hiorne
(mark of) William Flye, mayor

[f158v]

Portmoot court held 19 April 1619.[50]

Actions of debt:

1066:4/6 Keite vs Cooke - court adjudges plaintiff recover both 55s for debt and [blank] for costs; *scire facias* granted.

1067:4/6 Meatcalfe vs Cooke - court adjudges plaintiff should recover both 26s.8d for debt and [blank] for costs; *scire facias* granted.

[f159]

Actions of debt:

1065:4/5 Holden vs Screevin - peremptory day to respond.

1071:2/3 Clementes vs Chamberlyn - peremptory day to respond.

Action continuing: **1057**:8/16.

[f159v]

Portmoot court held 3 May 1619.[51]

Actions of debt:

1065:5/5 Holden vs Screevin - discharged for defendant.

1066:5/6 Kyte vs Cooke - *scire facias* returned executed and *alias scire facias* granted.

[50] 'Baron' crossed through.

[51] 'Baron' crossed through.

1067:5/6 Meatcalfe vs Cooke - similarly.
1071:3/3 Clementes vs Chamberlyn - discharged for defendant.
Action continuing: **1057**:9/16.

[f160]

Portmoot court held 10 May 1619.

Actions of debt:
1066:6/6 Kyte vs Cooke - *alias scire facias* returned executed and execution granted.
1067:6/6 Meatcalfe vs Cooke - similarly.
Action of trespass on case:
1031:14/14 Hopkins vs Allen - William Edwardes, surety for defendant, pays damages and costs of £9 10s 7d and is discharged.
Action continuing: **1057**:10/16.
Apprenticeship:
1077: Memorandum: Peter White, the son of Jerome White, deceased, places himself apprentice to Richard Phillipps, weaver from first day of this instant month of May for the term of seven years in succession.

by me (signed) Edmund Hiorne

[f160v]

Portmoot court held 24 May 1619.

Action of debt:
1078:1/1 Richard Clark vs Thomas Martin - plaintiff's attorney, Simon Jeames, declares; defendant's attorney, Thomas Heathen, granted copy of declaration.
Action continuing: **1057**:11/16.
1080: [marginal note - Made even with Mr mayor, the sergeant and the crier.

[f161]

1081:**Portmoot court** of 7 June 1619 adjourned until 21 June by William Flye, mayor.
1082:**Portmoot court** of 21 June 1619 adjourned until 5 July by William Flye, mayor.
1083:**Portmoot court** of 5 July 1619 adjourned until 19 July by William Flye, mayor.

[f161v]

Portmoot court held 2 August 1619.

Action of trespass on case:
1084:1/5 William Willis vs Martin Willis - plaintiff's attorney, Simon Jeames, declares and requests day to amend in next court; defendant's attorney, Thomas Heathen, requests day for discussion.
Action continuing: **1057**:12/16.

[f162]

Action of debt:
1088:1/1 Richard Mylles vs Edward Jacobb - plaintiff's attorney, Simon Jeames, declares and defendant appears in person; discharged.

Actions of trespass on case:
1085:1/8 Martin Willis vs William Willis - plaintiff's attorney, Thomas Heathen, requests day to declare in next court and defendant's attorney, Simon Jeames, requests day for discussion.
1086:1/1 William Willis vs Justin Symons - Simon Jeames, for plaintiff, puts declaration and requests day to amend in next court; defendant's attorney, Thomas Heathen, requests day to imparl: discharged.
1087:1/5 Justin Symons vs Martin Willis - Simon Symons (sic) Jeames, plaintiff's attorney, puts declaration and requests day to amend in next court. Thomas Heathen, for defendant, requests day to imparl.
Action of trespass and assault:
1089:1/1 Simon Jeames vs Richard Bently - plaintiff requests day to declare in next court and Thomas Heathen, for defendant, requests day for discussion; discharged.

[f162v]

Portmoot court held 16 August 1619.
Action of trespass on case:
1084:2/5 William Willis vs Martin Willis - plaintiff's attorney places completed declaration and defendant's attorney requests copy.
Action continuing: **1057**:13/16.

[f163]

Actions of trespass on case:
1085:2/8 Martin Willis vs William Willis - plaintiff's attorney places declaration and requests day to amend the form in next court.
1087:2/5 Justin Symons vs Martin Willis - plaintiff puts declaration and requests day to amend the form in next court.

Breaches of the Peace:
19 August 1619
1090a:1/5 Katherine Coles, the wife of Richard Coles brings action for the peace against Richard Richard (sic) Reade etc - John [Manning] saw him beat her on Monday last with a bull's pizzle ('peesell')[52] at Morgan's gate 16 August 1619.
29 August 1619
1090b:1/1 Richard Reade used many railing speeches against Mr. Browne unto his face in the open street in the presence of many people viz: Richard Coles, William Raunson and widow Browne. The words were that Mr. Browne was 'a forsworne man in his office'
30 August 1619 before William Flye, gent, mayor:-

[52] pizzle – a penis: that of a bull used as a flogging instrument; Chambers & Shorter O.E.D.

1090a:2/5 Richard Reade places surety of £40 with William Raunson, woolman, and Robert Busby, tailor, £20 each That Richard Reade keeps the peace against Katherine Coles aforesaid and all the King's people, and appears in person at the next session of the peace of the aforesaid borough.

[f163v]

Portmoot court held 30 August 1619.

Action of debt:

1091:1/18 John Jennings vs Edulphe Dinglie - plaintiff's attorney, Simon Jeames, puts declaration and Thomas Heathen, for defendant, requests copy and day for discussion.

Actions of trespass on case:

1084:3/5 William Willis vs Martin Willis - defendant's attorney responds_non assumpsit modo et forma; and *venire facias* granted.

1085:3/8 Martin Willis vs William Willis - plaintiff puts completed declaration and defendant granted copy.

1087:3/5 Justin Symons vs Martin Willis - similarly.

Action continuing: **1057**:14/16.

[f164]

3 August 1619 before William Flye, gent, mayor:

1092:1/3 Richard Reade brings action for the peace vs Richard Coles viz:- that he is in great danger of his life by him because he has used many threatening speeches against him.

1093:1/3 Katherine Reade brings action for the peace vs Katherine Coles, the wife of Richard Coles, viz:- that she is in great danger of her life by reason of the many threatening speeches which the said Katherine Coles has spoken to her and of her; and desires sureties of the peace against her.

6 September 1619 before William Flye, gent, mayor -

1092:2/3 Richard Coles - recognisance £40

Richard Browne and Robert Bignill - £20 each

Upon condition that Richard Coles shall keep the peace against Richard Reade and all the King's people and shall appear at the next sessions at Woodstock.

1093:2/3 Richard Coles - recognisance £40

Richard Browne and Robert Bignill - £20 each

Upon condition that Katherine Coles shall keep the peace against Katherine Reade and all the King's leige people; And that she shall personally appear at the next sessions of the peace within the borough of Woodstock and not to depart thence without licence.[53]

(signed) Edmund Hiorne, town clerk

[53] Solitary courtbook record of borough confinement control by licence.

[f164v]

Portmoot court held 13 September 1619.

Action of debt:

1091:2/18 John Jennings vs Edulphe Dingly - peremptory day for response granted.

Actions of trespass on case:

1084:4/5 William Willis vs Martin Willis - sergeant at mace returns *venire facias* executed and writ of *habeas corpus* granted.

1085:4/8 Martin Willis vs William Willis - defendant's attorney responds *non assumpsit modo et forma* and puts him on the country; plaintiff takes similar action; *venire facias* granted.

Marginal note:

[fee of this account debited 2s 10d]

1087:4/5 Justin Symons vs Martin Willis - peremptory day for response granted.

Action continuing: **1057**:15/16.

[f165]

Action of debt:

1097:1/4 Thomas Williams vs John Batt - plaintiff's attorney, Thomas Heathen, declares and defendant's attorney, Simon Jeames, requests copy.

Actions of trespass on case:

1095:1/4 Richard Reade vs Richard Coles - Simon Jeames, for plaintiff, puts declaration and requests day to amend in next court and Thomas Heathen, for defendant, requests copy.

1096:1/4 Richard Coles vs Richard Reade - plaintiff's attorney, Thomas Heathen, requests day to declare in next court. Simon Jeames appears for defendant.

Action of trespass and assault:

1094:1/4 Richard Coles and Katherine, his wife, vs Richard Reade – plaintiffs' attorney, Thomas Heathen, puts declaration and defendant's attorney, Simon Jeames, is granted copy.

Marginal note:

1098: Made even till this court with Mr. mayor, Thomas Heathen and Longe.

[f165v]

Portmoot court held 27 September 1619.

Action of debt:

1091:3/18 Jennings vs Dingly - defendant puts response *per minas* and defendant is granted copy and plaintiff immediately replicates and puts himself on the country; defendant takes similar action and *venire facias* is granted.

Actions of trespass on case:

1057:16/16 Toms vs Binckes - court wishes to consider.

1084:5/5 William Willis vs Martin Willis - defendant brings writ of *habeas corpus* returnable before King's Bench at Westminster on Saturday next of the

month of St. Michael: Dated 16th June 1619. Heath and Shute.[54] (marginal note - Writ of *habeas corpus* for Willis).
1087:5/5 Justin Symons vs Martin Willis - similarly.
1085:5/8 Martin Willis vs William Willis - *venire facias* renewed for plaintiff.
1095:2/4 Reade vs Coles - continues with assent of both parties.
1096:2/4 Coles vs Reade - similarly.
Action of trespass and assault:
1094:2/4 Coles vs Reade - similarly.

[f166]

Actions of debt:
1097:2/4 Williams vs Batt - peremptory day to respond granted.
1099:1/2 Thomas Burgis vs Richard Greeneway - Simon Jeames, for plaintiff, declares and Thomas Heathen, for defendant, requests copy.
1102:1/4 Alice Tyms vs Thomas Sodon - Simon Jeames, for plaintiff, declares and Thomas Heathen, for defendant, requests copy.
1103:1/3 Henry Cornish vs Richard Tymes - Simon Jeames, for plaintiff, declares and Thomas Heathen, for defendant, requests copy.
Action of trespass:
1101:1/2 William Butterfeild vs William Eden - plaintiff's attorney, Simon Jeames, puts declaration and Thomas Heathen, for defendant, requests copy.
Action of trespass and assault:
1100:1/2 Thomas Huggins vs Thomas Morly - Simon Jeames, for plaintiff, puts declaration and Thomas Heathen, for defendant, requests copy.

[f166v]

Portmoot court held 11 October 1619.
Actions of debt:
1091:4/18 Jennings vs Dingly - *alias venire facias* renewed.
1097:3/4 Williams vs Batt - defendant responds; copy granted.
1099:2/2 Burgis vs Greeneway - dismissed through Simon Jeames.
Action of trespass:
1101:2/2 Butterfeild vs Eden - dismissed through Simon Jeames.
Actions of trespass on case:
1085:6/8 Martin Willis vs William Willis - *habeas corpora* granted.
1095:3/4 Reade vs Coles - peremptory day to respond granted.
1096:3/4 Coles vs Reade - plaintiff does not wish to prosecute; therefore judgment as to costs granted.
Actions of trespass and assault:
1094:3/4 Coles vs Reade - peremptory day to respond granted.
1100:2/2 Huggins vs Morly - dismissed through Thomas Heathen.

[54] Heath and Shute probably officers or clerks of Westminster courts.

[f167]

Actions of debt:

1102:2/4 Tyms vs Sodon - peremptory day to respond granted.

1103:2/3 Cornish vs Tyms - peremptory day to respond granted.

1104:1/2 Richard Meades vs Nicholas Mitchell - plaintiff's attorney, Simon Jeames, declares and defendant appears, through Thomas Heathen and requests copy.

Apprenticeship:

1105: Memorandum: Joseph Fletcher, the son of Henry Fletcher, of the city of London, barber chirurgion, puts himself apprentice to Richard Reade of this borough, butcher, for the term of eight years from the 29th day of September last past. (signed) Edmund Hiorne, clerk to the borough aforesaid.

[f167v]

Portmoot court held 25 October 1619.

Actions of debt:

1091:5/18 Jennings vs Dingly - continues for plaintiff.

1097:4/4 Williams vs Batt - charged by plaintiff and debt settled.

1102:3/4 Tyms vs Sodon - continues for defendant.

1103:3/3 Cornish vs Tyms - defendant pleads *per minas* and copy is granted. Plaintiff replicates and puts himself on the country; *venire facias* granted.

1104:2/2 Meades vs Mitchell - discharged through Thomas Heathen.

Actions of trespass on case:

1085:7/8 Martin Willis vs William Willis - renewal of writ of *habeas corpus*.

1095:4/4 Reade vs Coles - discharged and paid.

1096:4/4 Coles vs Reade - similarly.

Action of trespass and assault:

1094:4/4 Coles vs Reade - discharged and paid.

[f168]

Action of debt:

1106:1/2 Philip Johnson vs Thomas Symons - plaintiff's attorney, Simon Jeames, declares and defendant's attorney, Thomas Heathen, requests copy and day for discussion. Dismissed.

[f168v]

View of Frankpledge and Sessions of the Peace held 27 October 1619 before William Flye, mayor, and Jerome Kyte and Thomas Browne, Justices of the Peace.

Election of officers:

Henry Whiteside, Robert Busby, Robert Bruce and Richard Plumpton are elected tithingmen and sworn in.

[f169]

1107: *Jury for the King with homage*

John Dubber,	William Archer,	Thomas Williams,
Thomas Godfery,	John Norman,	John Ackley,

Thomas Screevin,	Bryan Steephens,	George Noble,
Robert Busby,	William Raunson,	Richard Plumpton,
William Edwardes,	Thomas Woodward,	Bennett Paynter,
Henry Whiteside,	Richard Browne.	

Affeerers: John Norman, George Noble, Bennett Paynter (sworn in).

Sessions of the Peace: Recognisances:

1108:1/1 John Tidmarch of Newent ('Newont') in County of Gloucester, yeoman, recognisance under penalty of £40 appears at this sessions and by agreement of the court is discharged.

1090a:3/5 Richard Reade, under recognisance of £40 and William Raunson and Robert Busby put recognisance of £20 each that he will appear at this sessions. And he does not appear and therefore it is forfeit.

1092:3/3 Richard Coles under recognisance of £40 and Richard Browne and Robert Bignill put recognisance of £20 each that Richard Coles will appear at this sessions. And he does appear and [di feodi] ? half fee.

1093:3/3 Richard Coles under recognisance of £40 and Richard Browne and Robert Bignill put recognisance of £20 each that Katherine Coles will appear at this sessions. And she does appear and [di feodi] ? half fee.

[f169v]

Memorandum:

752:3/3 For that Isabel Harbert,[55] the wife of Thomas Harbert of St Peter le Bailey ('St. Peeters on the Bailly'), Oxford, slatter, has complained that Richard Meades has not kept her base child according to the order set down by the Justices of Woodstock aforesaid: It is now ordered in this sessions that the said Richard Meades shall keep the said child And that the said Isabel shall pay all such arrears as she is yet behind of the payment of 8d a week according to the first order And that hereafter she shall pay 8d. a week towards the keeping of the said child until it is fit to be put to service: If she or he refuse to perform this order then they shall be comitted to the common gaol according to the first order. (sign of) William Flye, mayor (signed) Jerome Keyt, Thomas Brown, JPs, Edmund Hiorne, town clerk.

[f170]

Portmoot court held 8 November 1619.

Actions of debt:

1102:4/4 Tyms vs Soddon - dismissed through Thomas Heathen.

1106:2/2 Johnson vs Symons - dismissed.

Action of trespass on case:

1085:8/8 Martin Willis vs William Willis - Names of the jury between parties:-

Thomas Williams,	John Norman,	William Raunson,
Robert Bignill,	Robert Spittle,	Bennett Paynter,
Richard Browne,	Thomas Godfery,	John Ackly,

[55] Formerly Isabell Robins, also Elizabeth Robinson.

Alexander Head, Bryan Steephens, Robert Busby;
which jury, under oath, say that they find for the plaintiff and assess for damages 20s.6d and for costs 2d.
Action continuing: **1091**:6/18.

[f170v]

10 November 1619 before William Flye, mayor

Recognisances:
1113:1/2 Christopher Smith, baker, recognisance of £40
Bryan Steephens and John Durman, recognisance of £20 each
On condition that Christopher Smith appear at the next sessions of this borough and in the meantime be of good behaviour and keep the King's Majesty's peace.[56]
1114:1/2 Richard Phillipps, weaver, recognisance of £40
William Raunson, Bennett Paynter, recognisance of £20 each
On condition that Richard Phillipps shall appear at the next sessions of this borough and in the mean time be of good behaviour and keep the King's Majesty's peace.

(signed) Edmund Hiorne[57]

[f171]

Portmoot court held 22 November 1619.

Action of debt:
1115:1/9 Thomas Meatcalfe vs John Cooke - Simon Jeames, for plaintiff, puts declaration and Thomas Heathen, for defendant, is granted copy.
Actions of trespass on case:
1116:1/12 William Archer vs Thomas Heady - plaintiff's attorney, Simon Jeames, places declaration and has day to amend the form in next court and Thomas Heathen appears for defendant.
1117:1/6 Bryan Steephens vs Thomas Heady - Simon Jeames, for plaintiff, puts declaration and has day to amend the form in next court and Thomas Heathen represents defendant.
Action continuing: **1091**:7/18.

[f171v]

Portmoot court held 6 December 1619.

Action of debt:
1115:2/9 Meatcalfe vs Cooke - peremptory day to respond.
Actions of trespass on case:
1116:2/12 Archer vs Headye - plaintiff puts completed declaration and copy granted.
1117:2/6 Steephens vs Headye - similarly.
Action continuing: **1091**:8/18.

[56] *WCA*, 81.
[57] *WCA*, 81.

1118: (Note - Made even with Mr. mayor and Thomas Heathen till this 7th of December 1619).

[f172]

Claim:

1119: 7th December 1619 - William Fawdery the son of Richard Fawdery of Cleveley ('Cleevely') claims one stray colt of black colour and 2 years old now in the hands of Bennett Paynter, constable, to be the proper colt of the said Richard Fawdery, and which he bred and is appraised at 40s: The said William Fawdery promises to pay 40s or redeliver the said colt to the mayor and commonalty of Woodstock if he shall be proved to be any other man's colt within a year and a day next following the date hereof:[58] Under £40 penalty at the handing over (to the claimant).

Confirmed: Edmund Hiorne (signed by) William Fawdry

[f172v]

Portmoot court held 20 December 1619.

Actions of debt:

1115:3/9 Meatcalfe vs Cooke - defendant does not respond upon three occasions.

1120:1/4 Anthony Ives vs William Raunson - plaintiff's attorney, Simon Jeames, requests day to declare in next court and defendant's attorney, Thomas Heathen, requests first day of privilege.

1121:1/7 Robert Binckes vs George Heath - Simon Jeames, for plaintiff, declares and Thomas Heathen, for defendant, requests copy.

Actions of trespass on case:

1116:3/12 Archer vs Headye - peremptory day to respond.

1117:3/6 Steephens vs Headye - defendant responds not guilty and puts himself on the country and plaintiff requests copy of response and does likewise; *venire facias* granted.

Action continuing: **1091**:9/18.

[f173]

Portmoot court held 10 January 1620.

Actions of debt:

1115:4/9 Meatcalfe vs Cooke - court adjudges plaintiff should recover both [blank] for debt and [blank] for costs; *scire facias* granted.

1120:2/4 Ives vs Raunson - Simon Jeames, for plaintiff, declares and Thomas Heathen, for defendant, is granted copy and second day of privilege.

1121:2/7 Robert Binckes vs George Heath - defendant does not respond.; therefore *nil dicit.*

1122:1/2 Margaret Trewman, widow vs Nicholas Blunt - Simon Jeames, for plaintiff, declares and Thomas Heathen, for defendant, is granted copy.

[58] 'A year and a day': standard interval representing a complete year with certainty (Ivamy, 509).

Actions of trespass on case:
1116:4/12 Archer vs Heady - defendant responds with rejoinder in law and copy is granted to plaintiff who immediately replicates and requests consideration of court.
1117:4/6 Steephens vs Heady - *venire facias* continues for plaintiff.
Action continuing: **1091**:10/18.

[f173v]

Actions of debt:
1123:1/1 John Goldsmith vs Thomas Keene - plaintiff's attorney, Simon Jeames, declares and defendant appears in person and offers 20s; court adjudges that plaintiff should recover both said 20s for debt and [blank] for costs and this is put into execution.
1124:1/1 James Platt vs Thomas Keene - plaintiff declares and defendant offers debt of 4s.1d.; therefore court adjudges that plaintiff should recover the said 4s for debt and [blank] for costs and this is put in execution by the sergeant at mace.

[f174]

Portmoot court held 24 January 1620.

Actions of debt:
1115:5/9 Meatcalfe vs Cooke - *alias scire facias* granted.
1120:3/4 Ives vs Raunson - last day of privilege granted.
1121:3/7 Binckes vs Heath - stands as before for plaintiff.
1122:2/2 Trewman vs Blunt - defendant brings writ of privilege returnable before Court of Common Pleas at Westminster on Friday next on eve of the feast of Purification, February 2nd, dated at Westminster 29th November Anno 17 & 53 Jas.I Brownlowe;[59] Copy granted plaintiff and writ allowed.
Actions of trespass on case:
1116:5/12 Archer vs Heady - stands as before.
1117:5/6 Steephens vs Heady - similarly.
Action continuing: **1091**:11/18.

[f174v]

Portmoot court held 7 February 1620.

Actions of debt:
1115:6/9 Meatcalfe vs Cooke - sicut *alias scire facias* returned executed and execution granted.
1120:4/4 Ives vs Raunson - dismissed for plaintiff.
Action of trespass on case:
1117:6/6 Steephens vs Heady - continues for plaintiff.
Actions continuing: **1091**:12/18; **1116**:6/12; **1121**:4/7.

[59] Brownlowe: a Westminster court officer or clerk.

[f175]

Portmoot court held 21 February 1620.

Actions of debt:

1115:7/9 Meatcalfe vs Cooke - renewal of execution.

1121:5/7 Binckes vs Heath - court adjudges that plaintiff should recover both 35s. for debt and [blank] for costs; *scire facias* granted.

Action of trespass on case:

1116:7/12 Archer vs Heady - court wishes to consider.

Action continuing: **1091**:13/18.

[f175v]

Flesh in Lent and Assize of bread and beer 1st March 1620.

Memorandum: At a meeting at the Guildhall of the said borough before William Flye gent, mayor, Jerome Kyte and Thomas Browne the King's Majesty's Justices of the Peace within the said borough; the several parties hereunder written were sworn on a Jury to inquire concerning the killing, dressing and eating of flesh within this borough in this time of Lent or on fish days appointed by the law to be hereafter strictly observed by all sorts of people: As by His Majesty's proclamation given at Royston the 14th day of November last may appear :-

1125: *Jury named:*

Henry Whiteside,	Richard Reade,	John Norman,
John Doa,	Richard Browne,	Thomas Gee,
John Batt, snr.,	Thomas Godferye,	William Archer,
Frauncis Garter,	Thomas Woodward,	William Butterfeild,
Edward Hull,	John Tassill,	Bryan Steephens.

[f176]

The aforesaid Jury under oath find that Richard Coles has killed flesh; therefore he is in mercy.

And that Robert Phillipps, slatter, dressed and ate bacon in his house; therefore he is in mercy.

1st March 1620.

1126: An assize of bread, ale and beer set down by Mr. Flye, mayor :-

The penny white loaf to weigh 1oz.4dwt. (= 11.2 oz.)

The penny wheaten loaf to weigh 16½oz.4dwt. (= 16.7 oz.)

The penny household loaf to weigh 28oz.4dwt.(= 28.2 oz.)

The barrell of beer at 10s.

The kilderkin of beer at 5s.

A quart of ale within doors for a 1d.

Two quarts of small drink for a 1d. By me Edmund Hiorne - clerk to the court

[f176v] (Blank)

[f177]

Portmoot court held 6 March 1620.

Action of debt:

1121:6/7 Binckes vs Heath - *scire facias* returned executed and *alias scire facias* granted.

Actions continuing: **1091**:14/18; **1115**:8/9; **1116**:8/12.

[f177v]

Portmoot court held 20 March 1620.

Actions of debt:

1115:9/9 Meatcalfe vs Cooke - discharged.

1121:7/7 Binckes vs Heath - stands as before.

1127:1/1 William Meatcalfe, alderman vs Thomas Heathen - plaint of debt of £3; plaintiff's attorney, Simon Jeames, declares and defendant requests copy. Discharged.

1128:1/1 Robert Russell vs Edward Hollyday - plaintiff's attorney, Simon Jeames, states his case; and so it stands.

Actions continuing: **1091**:15/18; **1116**:9/12.

[f178]

Portmoot court held 27 March 1620.

Action of debt:

1130:1/10 Thomas Turner vs William Turner - plaintiff's attorney, Simon Jeames, declares and has day to amend the form in next court. Thomas Heathen, defendant's attorney, requests copy.

Action of trespass:

1129:1/2 John Batt senior vs John Ball - plaintiff's attorney, Simon Jeames, declares and Thomas Heathen, for defendant, requests copy. And defendant, through his attorney, acknowledges the action; therefore writ of inquiry into damages granted.

Actions continuing: **1091**:16/18 ; **1116**:10/12.

[f178v]

Action of trespass on case:

1131:1/1 Richard Jennings vs Andrew Homes - plaintiff's attorney, Simon Jeames declares and defendant's attorney, Thomas Heathen, requests copy; day to amend declaration is granted and action discharged.

Action of trespass and assault:

1132:1/2 Robert Bruce vs Simon Maunder - Simon Jeames, plaintiff's attorney, narrates and defendant's attorney, Thomas Heathen, requests copy.

Memorandum: [written and then crossed through]

Thomas Heathen owes me (debet mihi) - 2s and 10s more that I paid to Mr. Abram.[60]

[60] Probably William Metcalfe, alias Abraham; see **1127**:1/1.

[f179]

Portmoot court held 10 April 1620.

Actions of debt:

1130:2/10 Turner vs Turner - defendant does not respond; therefore etc..

1133:1/9 William Brounckloe, gent vs John Norman - plaintiff's attorney, Simon Jeames, requests day to declare in next court; defendant represented by Thomas Heathen, has first day of privilege.

1134:1/9 Ann Holden, widow vs Thomas Williams - plaintiff's attorney, Simon Jeames, declares and defendant's attorney, Thomas Heathen requests copy and first day of privilege.

Action of trespass:

1129:2/2 Batt vs Ball - discharged by Simon Jeames on delivery of 4d.

Action of trespass and assault:

1132:2/2 Bruce vs Mawnder - dismissed.

Actions continuing: **1091**:17/18; **1116**:11/12.

[f179v] (Blank)

[f180]

View of Frankpledge and Sessions of the Peace held 12 April 1620 before William Flye, gent, mayor, with Jerome Kyte and Thomas Browne, gents, Justices of the Peace for the borough.

[f180v]

1135: *Jury for the king with homage*

John Dubber,	Robert Bignill,	John Norman,
Thomas Screevin,	William Edwardes,	Richard Browne,
Thomas Woodward,	Bennett Painter,	Henry Whiteside,
Thomas Godferye,	Robert Bruce,	Christopher Smith,
Richard Phillipps,	John Tassell.	

Affeerers: John Norman, Henry Whiteside, Bennett Paynter sworn in.

Sessions of the Peace:

Recognisances:

1090a:4/5 Richard Reade did not appear at the last sessions upon recognisance of £40. Therefore it is forfeit.

Memorandum: Richard Coles' debt not discharged in last sessions 8s.10d. (see **1092**, **1093**).

[f181]

1113:2/2 Christopher Smith, baker, 10 November 1619 recognises his debt [to the King] £40 and Bryan Steephens and John Durman his sureties separately place recognisance of £20 Upon condition that Christopher Smith appear in this sessions. He is fined by the court 5s. and discharged.[61]

(In margin - 12d delivered [to] Thomas Rayer)

[61] *WCA*, 81.

1114:2/2 Richard Phillipps, weaver, 10 November 1619 recognises his debt [to the King] of £40 and William Raunson and Bennett Painter his sureties separately place recognisance of £20 upon condition that Richard Phillipps appear in this sessions. He is fined 5s. and discharged.[62]
(In margin - 12d delivered [to] Thomas Rayer)
1136:1/2 John Busby of Woodstock, tailor, recognisance of £40 and Robert Busby, tailor, his surety for £20. Upon condition the said John Busby appear at this sessions. (Marginal note - John Busby recognisance £40 and Robert Busby recognisance £20 that John appears at the next sessions).
Robert Busby's debt adjudged at 4s. and 3s.4d.
1136a:1/4+ John Pulchoe of Woodstock, slater, recognisance of £20 and Richard Phillipps his surety for £20 upon condition that John Pulchoe appear at this sessions.

[f181v]

1137: The names of all the victuallers which were licensed within the said borough until the 6th of this instant month of April and which were new licensed at this sessions until the 6th April 1621 according to his Majesty's proclamation made at Newmarket ('Newmarkett') 19th January 1619

Thomas Rayer £10	John Dubber, Christopher Smith each £5
William Edwardes £10	Robert Bignill, Bennett Paynter each £5
Thomas Godfery £10	John Doa, Anthony Deverill each £5
Bennett Painter £10	John Durbridge, William Edwardes each £5

[f182]

Robert Bignill £10	Thomas Williams, William Edwardes each £5
Thomas Heathen £10	Thomas Williams, Edward Longe each £5
John Durbridge £10	Bennett Painter, John Tassill each £5
John Tassell £10	Henry Whiteside, John Durbridge each £5
William Archer - discharged	
Margaret Raunson, widow £10	
	Robert Bignill, William Edwardes each £5

[f182v]

Elizabeth Hamond, widow £10	
	Richard Brown, John Tassill each £5
Merriall Tayler, widow £10	Robert Bignill, John Doa each £5
Thomas Williams £10	Robert Bignill, Thomas Heathen each £5
Alice White, widow – discharged	
Joan Glover, widow - discharged	
Nicholas Tayler £10	Robert Bignill, Bennett Paynter each £5
Henry Whiteside £10	John Tassill, Anthony Deverill each £5

[In margin - 8 March 1620 licensed by Mr. Flye, mayor, and Mr. Kyte]

62 *WCA*, 81.

[f183]

14th April 1620

1138:1/4 Priscilla Barnaby upon her oath charged Anthony Crowdson, slater, with the begetting her with child on Combe Wake ('Coombe') day last.[63]

1139: *Victuallers imprisoned:*

Memorandum: At this sessions Thomas Screevin, William Butterfeild, William Hickes, snr., William Bradshewe, William Rayer and widow Carden being presented for victualling without licence were appointed to be committed to prison for 3 days and to pay 20s fine and to find sureties not to victual without licence according to the Statute[64] by me Edmund Hiorne,

clerk to the mayor and Commonalty

Fine:

1140: Memorandum - 12d delivered to Thomas Rayer, chamberlain, as taken from Edward Silver for a fine for refusing to aid the constable to attach (arrest) Pulchoe.[65] (signed) Edmund Hiorne

1141: *Victuallers licenced:*

28 April 1620 - before William Flye, mayor and Thomas Browne, Justice William Butterfeild recognisance £10, Bennett Painter, William Bradshewe each £5 - licensed a victualler till the 6th of April 1621.

William Butterfeild paid for his fine of 20s… 5s and remained 3 days in prison which 5s. was paid to Mr.Rayer.

William Bradshewe and widow Carden paid for a fine 5s. apiece= 10s[66] Edmund Hiorne delivered to Mr.Rayer.

[f183v]

Portmoot court held 24 April 1620.

Actions of debt:

1091:18/18 Jennings vs Dingly - discharged.

1130:3/10 Turner vs Turner - judgment granted.

1133:2/9 Brounckloe vs Norman - plaintiff's attorney declares and has day to amend form in next court, and second day of privilege.

1134:2/9 Holden vs Williams - second day of privilege granted defendant in next court.

1143:1/6 Jerome Kite, gent vs Thomas Screevin - Simon Jeames, plaintiff's attorney, puts declaration. Thomas Heathen, for defendant, requests first day of privilege.

Action of trespass on case:

1116:12/12 Archer vs Heady - court considering on action.

63 Combe Wake Day, 29 August 1619 *VCH Oxon* xii, 81.

64 *WCA*, 79.

65 *WCA*, 81.

66 *WCA*, 81.

[f184]

Portmoot court held 8 May 1620.

Actions of debt:

1130:4/10 Turner vs Turner - writ of *scire facias* granted against surety.

1133:3/9 Brounckloe vs Norman - plaintiff's attorney puts completed declaration and copy is granted.

1134:3/9 Holden vs Williams - last day of privilege granted defendant.

1143:2/6 Kyte vs Screevin - continues on behalf of plaintiff.

1144:1/1 Thomas Meatcalfe vs Robert Busbye - dismissed.

1145:1/2 Thomas Rayer vs Richard Meades - plaintiff's attorney, Simon Jeames, declares and Richard Meades does not appear; therefore judgment will be given in next court. [In margin - 12d due].

[f184v]

Breach of the Peace 9 May 1620... before Thomas Browne, gent..

1146:1/3+ Richard Meades vs William Munday of the city of Oxford, butcher - that he is in danger of his life by reason of threatening speeches which he used against him and he desires sureties of the peace.

Richard Meades' recognisance to be processed at next sessions at Woodstock.

William Munday - recognisance £20

Richard Browne, butcher and Richard Eedens of Oxon, butcher - each £10

Upon condition that William Mondy shall keep the peace against Richard Meades and all the King's people and appear at the next sessions at Woodstock then and there etc. (signed) Edmund Hiorne

[f185]

Portmoot court held 22 May 1620.

Actions of debt:

1130:5/10 Turner vs Turner - *alias scire facias* granted.

1133:4/9 Brunckloe vs Norman - peremptory day to respond.

1134:4/9 Holden vs Williams - peremptory day for response granted defendant.

1143:3/6 Keyte vs Screevin - continues for plaintiff for costs.

1145:2/2 Rayer vs Meades - discharged. 12d due to me from defendant.

1147:1/4 John Aingell vs William Flexny - upon demand for £24 plaintiff's attorney, Simon James, declares; defendant does not appear, therefore *nil dicit.*

1148:1/4 John Aingell vs William Flexny - upon demand of £40; similarly.

[f185v]

Actions of debt:

1149:1/1 John Goffe vs Anthony Crowdson - defendant does not respond; therefore *nil dicit*. Action dismissed.

1150:1/21 Thomas Harris, gent vs William Hickes junior - debt of 6s.4d. Plaintiff's attorney, Simon Jeames, declares and defendant's attorney, Thomas Heathen, requests copy and first day of privilege.

1151:1/2 Thomas Browne, alderman, vs Richard Meades - Simon Jeames, plaintiff's attorney, declares and defendant does not appear; therefore *nil dicit.*

[f186]

Breach of the Peace 26 May 1620... before William Flye, mayor..

1152:1/2 Edward Shawe, Clerk, on recognisance of £20 to appear at the next sessions.

[f186v]

Portmoot court held 29 May 1620.

Actions of debt:

1130:6/10 Turner vs Turner - *alias scire facias* granted against defendant's surety.

1133:5/9 Brownckloe vs Norman - defendant's attorney places response and has day to amend the form in next court.

1134:5/9 Holden vs Williams - defendant replies *per minas* and plaintiff replicates and puts herself on the country; *venire facias* granted.

1143:4/6 Keite vs Screevin - continues on behalf of plaintiff for costs.

[f187]

Actions of debt:

1147:2/4 Aingell vs Flexnie - court adjudges that plaintiff should recover both £24 for debt and 31s. for costs; *scire facias* granted against defendant's surety. [According to etc]

1148:2/4 Aingell vs Flexnie - court adjudges plaintiff recover both £40 for debt and 41s.8d. for costs; *scire facias* granted against defendant's surety. [According to etc.]

1150:2/21 Harris vs Hickes - second day of privilege granted.

1151:2/2 Thomas Browne, alderman vs Richard Meades - court adjudges plaintiff should recover both £8 for debt and [blank] for costs; *scire facias* granted.

1153:1/1 Thomas Martin vs John Buller - upon demand of £30, plaintiff's attorney, Simon Jeames, declares and defendant is discharged by assent of plaintiff.

Action of trespass on case:

1154:1/3 Richard Plumpton vs Edward Shawe, clerk - plaintiff's attorney, Simon Jeames, declares and defendant's attorney, Thomas Heathen, requests copy.

[f187v] (Blank)

[f188]

Portmoot court held 12 June 1620.

Actions of debt:

1130:7/10 Turner vs Turner - *alias scire facias* returned executed and execution granted against defendant and his surety.

1133:6/9 Browncklowe vs Norman - defendant puts response and plaintiff requests copy and immediately seeks delay in law; copy granted to defendant.
1134:6/9 Holden vs Williams - *venire facias* returned executed and writ of *habeas corpora* granted.
1143:5/6 Keite vs Screevin - defendant does not respond.
1147:3/4 Aingell vs Flexnye - *scire facias* returned executed and *alias scire facias* granted.
1148:3/4 Aingell vs Flexnye - similarly.

[f188v]

Actions of debt:
1150:3/21 Harris vs Hickes - last day of privilege granted.
1155:1/2 John Glover, alderman vs Richard Bently - plaintiff's attorney, Simon Jeames, declares and defendant's attorney, Thomas Heathen, requests copy.
Action of trespass on case:
1154:2/3 Plumpton vs Shawe - continues by assent of both parties.

[f189]

Portmoot court held 26 June 1620.
Actions of debt:
1130:8/10 Turner vs Turner - renewal of execution.
1133:7/9 Browncklowe vs Norman - court considering.
1134:7/9 Holden vs Williams - Jury between parties:-

John Norman,	Robert Spitle,	William Edwardes,
Bennett Painter,	Thomas Woodward,	Henry Whiteside,
Alexander Head,	John Ackly,	Richard Reade,
Bryan Steephens,	Christopher Smith,	John Durman.

Which jury, under oath, say that the defendant made the aforementioned writing of his own free will and assess damages of 2d and for costs 2d. Judgment will be given in next court.

[f189v]

Actions of debt:
1143:6/6 Keite vs Screevin - court adjudges plaintiff should recover [blank] for debt and [blank] for costs. (Marginal note - 11s 5d costs [I bated the 5d]).
1147:4/4 Aingell vs Flexnye - *alias scire facias* returned executed and execution granted against defendant and surety.
1148:4/4 Aingell vs Flexnye - similarly; discharged.
1150:4/21 Harris vs Hickes - peremptory day to respond granted.
1155:2/2 Glover vs Bentlye - discharged by Thomas Heathen.
Action of trespass on case:
1154:3/3 Plumpton vs Shawe - discharged by Thomas Heathen.

Memorandum:
1156: The Portmoot Court was adjourned the 10th day of July 1620 by William Flye, mayor.

[f190]

Portmoot court held 24 July 1620.
Actions of debt:
1134:8/9 Holden vs Williams - judgment adjourned to next court.
1150:5/21 Harris vs Hickes - defendant does not respond.
Action of trespass:
1157:1/8 Edward Clarke vs Nicholas Yonge - plaintiff's attorney, Simon Jeames, declares and has day to amend the form. Defendant's attorney, Thomas Heathen, requests copy.
Actions continuing: **1130**:9/10; **1133**:8/9.

[f190v]

Actions of debt:
1159:1/2 Thomas Cottmore vs Edward Hames - Simon Jeames, plaintiff's attorney, declares and Thomas Heathen, for defendant, requests copy.
1160:1/5 Margery Androwes, widow vs Edward Hames - similarly.
1162:1/1 Edward Wilde vs Thomas Rogers - plaintiff's attorney, Simon Jeames, puts declaration.
Actions of trespass on case:
1158:1/1 Ralph Stockdall vs William Kinge - plaintiff's attorney, Simon Jeames, puts declaration.
1161:1/1 Edward Hames vs Thomas Cottmore - defendant's attorney is Simon Jeames; plaintiff does not attend to state his case; therefore court decides defendant should recover costs.

[f191]

Action of debt:
1163:1/2 Richard Fletcher vs George Armestronge - plaintiff's attorney, Simon Jeames, declares. Sergeant at mace reports that he has seized one horse, the goods and chattels of the defendant, (which remains in his custody) valued at [blank]; defendant's attorney, Thomas Heathen, requests day for discussion and copy of declaration.

[f191v]

Portmoot court held 7 August 1620.
Actions of debt:
1130:10/10 Turner vs Turner - renewal of execution.
1133:9/9 Browncklowe vs Norman - court wishes to consider.
1134:9/9 Holden vs Williams - action discharged.
1150:6/21 Harris vs Hickes - court adjudges plaintiff should recover both 6s 4d for debt and [blank] for costs; *scire facias* granted.

Action of trespass:
1157:2/8 Clarke vs Yonge - defendant granted peremptory day for response.

[f192]

Actions of debt:
1159:2/2 Cottmore vs Hames - defendant granted peremptory day for response.
1160:2/5 Androwes vs Hames - similarly.
1163:2/2 Fletcher vs Armestronge - peremptory day to respond granted. Discharged for plaintiff by Simon Jeames.
1165:1/32 Edmund Hiorne vs Nicholas Tayler - plaintiff's attorney, Simon Jeames, states his case and defendant's attorney, Thomas Heathen, requests copy and first day of privilege.
Action of trespass on case:
1166:1/27 Nathaniell Miller vs Joan Glover, widow - plaintiff's attorney, Simon Jeames, states his case and defendant's attorney, Thomas Heathen, requests copy and first day of privilege; day to amend declaration granted.
Action of account:
1164:1/1 Gray Bridges, Lord Shandoes, vs Richard Fletcher - plaintiff's attorney, Thomas Heathen, declares and defendants's attorney, Simon Jeames, requests copy.

[f192v]

Actions of debt:
1169:1/31 Edmund Hiorne vs Alexander Head - plaintiff's attorney, Simon Jeames, puts declaration and defendant appearing in full court, does not respond; judgment is adjourned to next court.
1170:1/2 Simon Jeames vs William Jennings - plaintiff places declaration, defendant acknowledges debt of 10s 4d and so it stands.
Action of trespass:
1168:1/1 John Norman vs Humphrey Hamond - Simon Jeames, for plaintiff, declares and Thomas Heathen, for defendant, requests copy of declaration.
Action of trespass and assault:
1167:1/1 John Norman vs Humfrey Hamond - Simon Jeames, plaintiff's attorney, declares and defendant's attorney, Thomas Heathen, requests copy.

[f193]

Portmoot court held 21 August 1620.
Actions of debt:
1150:7/21 Harris vs Hickes - *alias scire facias* granted.
1160:3/5 Androwes vs Hames - defendant does not appear upon three occasions; therefore judgment will be given in next court.
1165:2/32 Hiorne vs Tayler - defendant granted second day of privilege.
1169:2/31 Hiorne vs Headd - judgment will be given in next court by assent of plaintiff.

Action of trespass:

1157:3/8 Clarke vs Yonge - defendant puts his response and says he is not guilty. Copy of declaration granted plaintiff who puts himself on the country; *venire facias* granted.

Action of trespass on case:

1166:2/27 Miller vs Glover - plaintiff puts completed declaration. Defendantis granted copy and second day of privilege.

[f193v]

Actions of debt:

1170:2/2 Jeames vs Jennings - judgment adjourned to next court by assent of plaintiff.

1174:1/2 Gowin Champnies, gent vs Richard Meades - plaintiff's attorney, Simon Jeames, declares and has day to amend the form; defendant's attorney, Thomas Heathen, requests copy of declaration and first day of privilege.

Action of trespass:

1172:1/5 Richard Bently vs Thomas Rymill - Thomas Heathen, plaintiff's attorney, declares and Simon Jeames for defendant, requests copy and immediately, in full court, says that he is not guilty, copy will be given in next court, and puts himself on the country; *venire facias* granted.

Action of trespass on case:

1171:1/1 Thomas Meatcalfe vs William Parrat - plaintiff's attorney, Simon James, declares and Thomas Heathen, for defendant, requests copy.; discharged. Note - plaintiff delivers 5s 5d to me (mihi.).

Action of detinue:

1173:1/17 Richard Bently vs Thomas Rymill - plaintiff's attorney puts declaration and Simon Jeames, for defendant, requests copy of declaration; and immediately defendant puts response and says that the chattels were always his free chattels. Copy granted plaintiff.

[f194]

Actions of debt:

1175:1/3 William Hobcrafte vs Walter Beesly - sergeant reports the capture of one gelding, valued at 13s 4d and plaintiff's attorney, Simon Jeames, places declaration. Defendant does not appear; therefore the gelding is forfeit and seizure is granted; appraised by Henry Whiteside and Nicholas Yonge.

1176:1/2 Nicholas Mitchell vs Richard Meades - Simon Jeames, plaintiff's attorney, declares and Thomas Heathen, for defendant, requests copy and first day of privilege.

[f194v]

Portmoot court held 4 September 1620.

Actions of debt:

1150:8/21 Harris vs Hickes - *alias scire facias* returned executed and execution granted.

1160:4/5 Androwes vs Hames - defendant pays into court 29s. for debt and [blank] costs and is discharged. And immediately Edward Hames brings an action of account for 25s. against Margery Androwes and the said silver coins [denarrius] are held in court in the hands of Edmund Hiorne and the said Hames, by Simon Jeames, his attorney, declares and has day to amend the form. Mr. Harris bail for Hames. [In margin - 6d debt]
Action of trespass:
1157:4/8 Clarke vs Yonge - renewal of *venire facias*.

[f195]

Actions of debt:
1165:3/32 Hiorne vs Tayler - last day of privilege granted.
1169:3/31 Hiorne vs Head - stands as before under judgment.
1174:2/2 Champnies vs Meades - continues by equal assent. [Note - the defendant died].
1175:2/3 Hobcrafte vs Beesly - stands as before.
1176:2/2 Mitchell vs Meades - continues by equal assent [The defendant is dead][67]
1178:1/4 John Glover, alderman vs Joan Glover, widow, administratrix of the goods and chattels of Nicholas Glover her husband lately deceased.[68] - Upon demand of £10 Simon Jeames, plaintiff's attorney, puts declaration; and Thomas Heathen, for defendant, requests copy and says that she acknowledges the debt to the said John Glover. Therefore court adjudges the aforesaid John should recover both £10 for debt and [blank] for costs and execution is granted against the goods and chattels which belonged to the said Nicholas at the time of his death.
Action of trespass:
1172:2/5 Bently vs Rymill - renewal of *venire facias*.
Action of trespass on case:
1166:3/27 Miller vs Glover - last day of privilege granted.
Action of detinue:
1173:2/17 Bently vs Rymill - plaintiff replicates and defendant requests copy.

[f195v]

Portmoot court held 18 September 1620.
Actions of debt:
1150:9/21 Harris vs Hickes - *alias* execution granted.
1160:5/5 Androwes vs Hames - copy of declaration granted.
1165:4/32 Hiorne vs Tayler - peremptory day to respond granted.
1169:4/31 Hiorne vs Head - court adjudges that plaintiff recover both 40s for debt and [blank] for costs; *scire facias* granted against defendant's surety.

[67] MSS.Wills (Oxon) 44/1/70.
[68] MSS.Wills (Oxon) 80/1/30 (Admin.Bond).

Action of trespass on case:
1166:4/27 Miller vs Glover - peremptory day to respond granted.
Action continuing: **1157**:5/8.

[f196]

Actions of debt:
1175:3/3 Hobcrafte vs Beesly - stands as before. [Memorandum - the horse was delivered to the plaintiff at 16s. price and he paid all charges].
1178:2/4 Glover vs Glover - renewal of execution.
Action of trespass:
1172:3/5 Bently vs Rymill - renewal of *venire facias*.
Action of detinue:
1173:3/17 Bently vs Rymill - defendant puts rejoinder and plaintiff is granted copy.

[f196v]

Portmoot court held 25 September 1620.
Actions of debt:
1150:10/21 Harris vs Hickes - renewal of execution.
1165:5/32 Hiorne vs Tayler - continues by assent of plaintiff.
Action of trespass:
1157:6/8 Clarke vs Yonge - continuation of *venire facias*.
Action of trespass on case:
1166:5/27 Miller vs Glover - defendant responds and says that her husband, in his lifetime, non assumpsit modo et forma; therefore parties put themselves on the country and *venire facias* is granted.

[f197]

Actions of debt:
1169:5/31 Hiorne vs Head - *alias scire facias* renewed.
1178:3/4 Glover vs Glover - renewal of execution.
1181:1/2 Thomas Rayer vs Thomas Allen - sergeant returns one cloak valued at 30s, that Alice Finmore, wife of John Finmore of Northbrook ('Northbrock')[69] claims is her goods and makes an oath in full court that this is true; therefore the cloak is delivered to her. (It is ordered that she makes further process).
Action of trespass:
1172:4/5 Bently vs Rymill - renewal of *venire facias* and proviso granted to defendant. If etc..
Actions of trespass on case:
1179:1/2 Lewis Bownie, clerk vs Robert Wattson, gent - plaintiff's attorney, Simon Jeames, requests day to declare and defendant, represented by Thomas Heathen, appears in person and has copy of declaration.

[69] Northbrook in Kirtlington, Oxon.

1180:1/1 Anthony Amsden vs John Key - sergeant returns that he has seized one horse worth 26s 8d appraised by Henry Whiteside, Richard Bently and William Richardson. Plaintiff declares and defendant does not appear; therefore the aforesaid horse is delivered to George Watkins for the use of the said Anthony Amsden.
Action of detinue:
1173:4/17 Bently vs Rymill - plaintiff rebuts and puts himself on the country; *venire facias* granted.

[f197v]

Action of debt:
1183:1/2 Thomas Tully vs [blank] Williams - plaintiff is represented by Simon Jeames, his attorney, and the defendant, in person, states he cannot deny that he owes the plaintiff the debt of 10s; therefore judgment is granted and he is committed in execution.
Actions of trespass on case:
1182:1/16 Richard Manninge and Anne, his wife, vs Thomas Allibone and Katherine, his wife - sergeant at mace reports that he holds the said Katherine. Plaintiffs' attorney, Simon Jeames, declares; and Katherine's attorney, Thomas Heathen, requests copy of declaration and process continues against the said Thomas Allibone.
1184:1/1 Robert Busby vs Edward Woolly - action discharged.

[f198]

Portmoot court held 2 October 1620.
Actions of debt:
1169:6/31 Hiorne vs Head - *alias scire facias* renewed.
Action of trespass:
1157:7/8 Clarke vs Yonge - *venire facias* returned executed and writ of *habeas corpora* granted.
Actions of trespass on case:
1166:6/27 Miller vs Glover - renewal of *venire facias*.
Actions continuing: **1150**:11/21; **1165**:6/32.

[f198v]

Action of trespass:
1172:5/5 Bently vs Rymill - plaintiff pays defendant 9s 9d and is discharged.
Action of detinue:
1173:5/17 Bently vs Rymill - sergeant returns *venire facias* executed and writ of *habeas corpora* granted.
Action of debt:
1178:4/4 John Glover vs Joan Glover, widow - Thomas Heathen, sergeant at mace, returns that by virtue of the precept of *fieri facias* he is directed to make levy of the goods and chattels which were owned by Nicholas Glover, lately

deceased, now in the hands of Joan Glover, his widow and administratrix of all the goods and chattels which were his at the time of his death viz:-
'Imprimis:- one table with a frame, one old cupboard, one joined chair, seven joined stools, three old cushions, certain wearing aparrel, one coverlet ('keeverlid'), one joined bedstead, one bolster, one coverlet, one boarded bedstead, one pair of tables, a little wheel, one flockbed, one bolster, one pillow, one coverlet, one bedstead, one little pallett, two coffers, one feather bed; six pair of old coarse sheets, one table cloth, two napkins, six platters, one saucer, two salt cellars, one pewter candlestick, one quart pot, two pint pots, one maltmill ('mawltemill'), one little furnace ('furnesse') kettle, one little kettle ('keetle') one pair of andirons, one paire of pothangers, one gridiron, one dripping pan, one paire of bellows,

[f199]

one posnet, one skimmer ('skeemer)', one spit, one chafing dish, two old tubs, one pair of pot hangers, one yielding vat ('yeelevate'), one barrell, two kinderkins, two keevers, one cooler ('cowle'), one pail, one bushel, with other lumber one woollen wheel, and the posts and sleepers of the hovel' to the value of £8.10s. and *fieri facias* renewed for recovery.
1181:2/2 Rayer vs Allen - discharged by assent of plaintiff.
1183:2/2 Tully vs Williams - discharged by sergeant.
1185:1/1 William Martin vs John Seman - plaintiff's attorney, Simon Jeames, declares and action is discharged by assent of plaintiff.
[Memorandum - I gave all the fees of the court].
Actions of trespass on case:
1179:2/2 Bownie vs Wattson - discharged by plaintiff.
1182:2/16 Richard Manning, and Anne, his wife vs Thomas Allibone and Katherine, his wife - sergeant reports that he has custody of Thomas and Katherine Allibone. Simon Jeames, plaintiffs' attorney, states their case and Thomas Heathen, for the defendants, requests copy of declaration.
Memorandum:
1186: After this court was discharged, John Glover, alderman, was sworn mayor of this borough for the year following - by me Edmund Hiorne, town clerk.

[f199v]

Apprenticeship:
1187: Memorandum: Lawrence Millen, son of William Millen of Cleveley ('Cleevely'), Oxon, places himself apprentice to Robert Spitle from the Feast of St.Michael last for the term of seven years then next ensuing the 12th October 1620 - by me Edmund Hiorne, town clerk.

The time of John Glover, mayor of the borough.

30th October 1620 - before John Glover, mayor

Child maintenance:

1138:2/4 Anthony Crowdson - recognisance of £20
Under condition to pay 6d a week for one year towards the maintenance of Prissilla Barnaby's base child: and afterwards to stand to such further order as he shall be enjoined unto.

[f200]

Portmoot court held 16 October 1620.

Action of trespass:

1157:8/8 Edward Clarke vs Nicholas Yonge - Names of the jury between the parties:- [none named] - plaintiff in his own person retracts complaint and the action is discharged.

[f200v]

Actions of debt:

1169:7/31 Hiorne vs Head - continues under execution.

1189:1/2 John May vs Robert Maye - plaintiff's attorney, Simon Jeames, puts declaration and defendant, in custody of sergeant at mace, requests copy through his attorney, Thomas Heathen.

1190:1/2 William Buckley vs William Hickes - Simon Jeames, plaintiff's attorney, declares and Thomas Heathen, defendant's attorney, requests copy.

Actions of trespass on case:

1166:7/27 Miller vs Glover - referred to arbitration of John Glover, mayor and Edmund Hiorne, to be ended before 22nd December next.

1182:3/16 Manninge vs Allibone - defendants respond through Thomas Heathen, their attorney, and say they are not guilty; *venire facias* granted.

Action of detinue:

1173:6/17 Bently vs Rymill - Renewal of writ of *habeas corpora* in next court.

Actions continuing: **1150**:12/21; **1165**:7/32.

[f201] (Blank)

[f201v]

View of Frankpledge and Sessions of the Peace held 25 October 1620 before John Glover, gent, mayor and Jerome Keite, gent, two of the Justices of the borough.

[f202]

1191: *Jury for the king with homage*:

Thomas Williams,	Robert Bignill,	John Norman,
William Edwardes,	Thomas Bruce,	Thomas Woodward,
Bennett Painter,	Henry Whiteside,	Thomas Godfery,
John Ackly,	John Pepper,	Robert Bruce,
John Durman,	Richard Phillipps,	John Durbridge.

Affeerers: John Norman, Thomas Woodward, Henry Whiteside sworn in.

Sessions of the Peace

Recognisances:

1136:2/2 John Busby in last sessions on recognisance of £40 and Robert Busby £20 Upon condition that John Busby appear at this sessions: Memorandum - The said John Busby, by order of the court was released from his recognisance and [of 4s 5d deleted] r (received?) 4s 3d.

1136a:2/4+ John Pulchoe continues under recognisance until this sessions: Richard Phillipps his surety.

Memorandum: Process is awarded against John Pulchoe for his not appearing upon his recognisance and the recognisance is forfeit.

1090a:5/5 Richard Reade continues under recognisance placed at sessions of 27 October 1619.

[Memorandum: it is ordered by the court that he shall be released of the recognisance paying his fees - r (received?) 4s 4d.. ..discharged].

[f202v]

9th May 1620 before Thomas Browne:

1146:2/3+ William Munday of city of Oxford, butcher, on recognisance of £20 - Richard Browne and Richard Edens of Oxon butchers, separately on recognisance £10. That William Monday appear at this sessions and keep the peace against Richard Meades:

Memorandum: the said William Monday did not appear therefore it was ordered by the court that process be made against the said Monday and his bail: upon the forfeiture of his recognisance.

1152:2/2 Edward Shawe, clerk, on recognisance of £20 before William Fly, mayor, 26th May 1620 Upon condition that he appear at this sessions.

Memorandum: it is ordered by the court that he shall be committed to prison during Mr. mayor's pleasure, and to pay his fees.

7th June 1620 before Thomas Browne

1192a:1/2+ Francis Pyman recognisance of £40 with Richard Reade and John Pepper separately recognisance of £20.

Upon condition that Francis Pyman appear at this sessions and keep the peace. Memorandum: ordered by court that he shall be discharged on paying his fees.

[f203]

1192b:1/1 John Bignill recognisance of £40 with Robert Bignill on recognisance of £20 Upon condition that John Bignill appear at this sessions. Memorandum: ordered by court that he shall be released on paying his fees.

Child Maintenance:

1138:3/4 Anthony Crowdson on recognisance of £40 with Bennett Painter and John Batt junior, on separate recognisances of £20.

Upon condition that Anthony Crowdson appears at this sessions and submits to the order of the court. Item: the said party appeared and is committed to prison

till he find sureties to perform the order that he shall be enjoined unto viz: that he shall pay 8d a week for 10 years till Margaret Crowdson be 11 years old
1192c:1/1 Richard Plumpton on recognisance of £40 with Edward Hull on recognisance of £20 Upon condition that Richard Plumpton appear at this sessions. Memorandum: it is ordered by the court that he shall be discharged of his recognisance paying his fees; and to pay 5s fine or five days imprisonment.
1193: Marginal note - 5s paid to Edward Hull to be paid to the chamberlains.[70]

[f203v]

Portmoot court held 30 October 1620.

Actions of debt:
1189:2/2 May vs May - discharged on behalf of plaintiff.
1190:2/2 Buckly vs Hickes - discharged.
1194:1/1 Edmund Hiorne vs Thomas Fletcher - upon demand of £20 plaintiff's attorney, Simon Jeames, declares and defendant, in custody of sergeant at mace, appears personally in full court, and through his attorney, Thomas Heathen, requests copy.
Actions of trespass on case:
1166:8/27 Miller vs Glover - stands as before.
1182:4/16 Manning vs Allibone - continues by equal assent.
Action of detinue:
1173:7/17 Bently vs Rymill - renewal of *habeas corpora*.
Actions continuing: **1150**:13/21; **1165**:8/32; **1169**:8/31.

[f204]

Portmoot court held 13 November 1620.

Action of detinue:
1173:8/17 Richard Bently vs Thomas Rymill - Names of the jury between parties:

Thomas Williams,	Robert Bignill,	John Norman,
Robert Spittle,	William Edwardes,	Thomas Godfery,
Alexander Head,	John Pepper,	John Durbridge,
John Durman,	Robert Bruce,	Bennett Painter.

Which jury under oath say that they find for the plaintiff and assess for damages 4s and for costs 2d and as for restoration of chattels they find for plaintiff and assess for damages 2d and for costs 1d. Judgment will be given in next court. [Marginal note - Rymill had warrant for 1 witness (12d)].
Actions continuing: **1150**:14/21; **1165**:9/32; **1166**:9/27; **1169**:9/31; **1182**:5/16.

[f204v]

Action of trespass and assault:
1195:1/19 Thomas Burgin vs Thomas Rymill - plaintiff's attorney, Thomas Heathen, states his case and defendant's attorney, Simon Jeames, requests copy of declaration.

[70] *WCA*, 83.

[f205]

Portmoot court held 27 November 1620.

Action of trespass and assault:

1195:2/19 Burgin vs Rymill - peremptory day to respond.

Action of detinue:

1173:9/17 Bently vs Rymill - judgment adjourned to next court.

Actions continuing: **1150**:15/21; **165**:10/32; **1166**:10/27; **1169**:10/31; **1182**:6/16.

[f205v]

Portmoot court held 11 December 1620.

Action of trespass and assault:

1195:3/19 Burgin vs Rymill - defendant's attorney puts response and has day to amend in next court.

Actions continuing: **1150**:16/21; **1165**:11/32; **1166**:11/27; **1169**:11/31.

Apprenticeship:

1196: James Paine, son of Henry Paine of Steeple Aston in County of Oxon, yeoman, puts himself apprentice to John Sea of Woodstock, joiner, for the term of seven years as from the feast of St.Michael last past - by me Edmund Hiorne - clerk to the council. [marginal note - enrolment of apprentice].

[f206]

Actions of debt:

1198:1/1 Edward Burcott vs Robert Rogers - discharged.

1200:1/1 John Manning vs Christopher Hiorne *alias* Jarnes - plaintiff's attorney, Simon Jeames, puts declaration and defendant appears in person and acknowledges the debt; and he is committed in execution.

Action of trespass on case:

1197:1/1 Jane Whickers, widow vs Ferdinand Smith - plaintiff's attorney, Simon Jeames, declares and requests day to amend the form in next court. Defendant appears, represented by Thomas Heathen, and requests copy.

Action of detinue:

1173:10/17 Bently vs Rymill – judgment to be given in next court; in as much as...

Action unspecified:

1199:1/10 Richard Lorde vs Humphrey Lewes, gent - plaintiff's attorney, Simon Jeames, requests day to declare and Thomas Heathen appears for the defendant and requests copy

Action continuing: **1182**:7/16.

[f206v]

Portmoot court held 18 December 1620.

Action of trespass and assault:

1195:4/19 Burgin vs Rymill - stands as before.

Action of detinue:
1173:11/17 Bently vs Rymill - court adjudges plaintiff should recover both [blank] for his damages and [blank] for costs; and *scire facias* is granted.
Actions continuing: **1150**:17/21; **1165**:12/32; **1166**:12/27; **1169**:12/31; **1182**: 8/16.

[f207]

Action of debt:
1201:1/1 Thomas Yonge vs Hugo Steephenson of Weston - Simon Jeames, for the plaintiff, declares and Thomas Rayer, surety, pays the fee; and Thomas Heathen is paid 4d for the discharge. [Marginal note - these fees Mr. Jeames must pay].
Action unspecified:
1199:2/10 Lorde vs Lewes - declaration placed and day granted to amend the form in next court.
Memorandum:
1202: Mr. Jeames owes for 2 bills - Burgen & Rymill and Bently & Rymill .. 4d.

[f207v]

Portmoot court held 10 January 1621.
Action of trespass and assault:
1195:5/19 Burgin vs Rymill - continues at request of plaintiff.
Actions continuing: **1150**:18/21; **1165**:13/32; **1166**:13/27; **1169**:13/31; **1182**: 9/16.

[f208]

Action of debt:
1204:1/1 Thomas Stiles vs Richard Phillipps - plaintiff's attorney, Simon Jeames, declares and Thomas Heathen, defence attorney, requests copy and first day of privilege. [marginal note - discharged without fee - and whole clause crossed through].
Action of detinue:
1173:12/17 Bently vs Rymill - *scire facias* renewed and Mr mayor, ['Simon Jeames' interlined] surety pays costs and damages.
Action unspecified:
1199:3/10 Lord vs Lewes - stands as before.
Action of account:
1203:1/2 John Poure, gent vs Anthony Crowdson - plaintiff's attorney, Simon Jeames, declares and defendant's attorney, Thomas Heathen, requests copy.

[f208v]

Portmoot court held 22 January 1621.
Action of trespass and assault:
1195:6/19 Burgin vs Rymill - continues at request of plaintiff and court wishes to consider upon his plea.

Action of detinue:
1173:13/17 Bently vs Rymill - 40s paid and action stands to be resolved.
Action of account:
1203:2/2 Poure vs Crowdson - discharged through Simon Jeames and fee [feodi].
Action unspecified:
1199:4/10 Lord vs Lewes - plaintiff puts completed declaration and copy granted.
Actions continuing: **1150**:19/21; **1165**:14/32; **1166**:14/27; **1169**:14/31; **1182**:10/16.

[f209]

Action of trespass and assault:
1205:1/2 John Archer vs Richard Ackly - plaintiff's attorney, Simon Jeames, puts declaration and defendant remains in custody of the sergeant; defendant personally requests copy of declaration and on hearing the judgment, acknowledges the action. Writ of inquiry into damages granted.

[f209v]

Portmoot court held 5 February 1621.
Actions of trespass and assault:
1195:7/19 Burgin vs Rymill - continues on behalf of plaintiff.
1205:2/2 Archer vs Ackly - renewal of writ of inquiry into damages.
Action of detinue:
1173:14/17 Bently vs Rymill - stands as before.
Action of account:
1206:1/5 William Wells vs John Parker - plaintiff's attorney, Simon Jeames, requests day to declare and Thomas Heathen represents defendant.
Action unspecified:
1199:5/10 Lorde vs Lewes - peremptory day to respond granted.
Actions continuing: **1150**:20/21; **1165**:15/32; **1166**:15/27; **1169**:15/31; **1182**:11/16.

[f210]

Breach of the Peace 7 February 1621..before John Glover, Mayor
1207:1/3 Ellinor Batson swears that Robert Phillipps of Woodstock did say in her presence, and in the presence of John Kirbye's son, that rather than the goodwife White should dwell in John Kirbye's house that she has taken of the said Kirby in Woodstock, he would burn the said house. Also he is charged with using of threatening speeches against the officers when they came to execute their offices. And he is charged with buying of stolen wood which was taken and found in his house and given to the poor.
7th February 1621 before the mayor
1207:2/3 Robert Phillipps on recognisance of £200
Robert Bignill, Thomas Screevin, Richard Phillipps - these several parties acknowledged severally to the King's use £100

That Robert Phillipps shall be of good behaviour towards the King's Majesty and all his leige people and shall appear at the next sessions of the peace to be held at Woodstock to answer to such matters as shall be objected against him

(signed) Edmund Hiorne

1207:3/3 Memorandum 28 April 1621 - the said Robert Phillipps at the request of John Kirby, and upon his submission and acknowledgment of the aforesaid offences, he was by John Glover, gent, mayor of the said borough discharged of his recognisance aforesaid: And for his fine for his abuse to the officers and for buying of unlawful wood, he is fined at 2s.6d. to the use of the poor.

(signed) John Glover, mayor

[marginal note - fine 2s.6d. paid to Bennett Paynter][71]

[f210v]

Flesh in Lent.. 30 January 1621.

1208: *Memorandum*: At a meeting at the guildhall of the aforesaid borough before John Glover gent, mayor of the said borough and Jerome Keite gent, the King's Majesty's justice of the peace within the said borough the several parties hereunder written were sworn on a jury to inquire, concerning the killing, dressing, and eating of flesh within this borough in this time of Lent or on fish days appointed by the law to be hereafter strictly observed by all sorts of people As by His Majesty's proclamation given at his palace of Westminster the 30th day of January 1621 may appear

Thomas Williams,	William Edwardes,	William Butterfeild,
Thomas Godfery,	John Doa,	Francis Pyman,
Christopher Smith,	Richard Phillipps,	William Richardson,
John Tassill,	Richard Skey,	Thomas Warde,
Robert Busby,	John Durbridge	

- which jury present in form following:

That Richard Coles, butcher, has dressed flesh in the time of lent against the form of the Statute: therefore he is fined 3s.4d.

That Thomas Williams, Thomas Godfery, Thomas Warde, Richard Phillipps, Frauncis Pyman and Robert Busby did dress and eat flesh in their several houses in the time of this lent: 'But for that they were sick or else their wives' childing,' their fines by Mr. mayor were spared.

(signed by) Edmund Hiorne and John Glover, mayor

[f211] (Blank)

[f211v]

1209: **Recognisances** taken at the guildhall before John Glover, gent, mayor and Jerome Kite gent, the King's Majesty's justice of the peace within the said borough, the **17th day of February 1621** by virtue of the King's Majesty's

[71] *WCA*, 82.

proclamation dated at Westminster the 30th of January last concerning the restraint of killing, dressing and eating of flesh in Lent or on fish days appointed by the law to be hereafter strictly observed by all sorts of people as follows :-

John Glover gent, innholder £10
Nicholas Paynter, Bennett Paintereach £5
Thomas Williams, innholder £10
Thomas Heathen, William Edwardes each £5
Robert Parker, innholder £10
Bennett Paynter, Thomas Warde each £5
Thomas Rayer, vintner £10
Thomas Woodward, Richard Skey each £5

[f212]

John Norman, butcher £10
Thomas Heathen, Thomas Godfery each £5
Richard Browne, butcher £10
John Dubber, Bennett Paynter each £5
(held before John Glover, mayor)
Richard Reade, butcher£10
John Doa, John Durbridge each £5
Thomas Rayer, victualler £10
Thomas Woodward, Richard Skey each £5
Thomas Williams, victualler (discharged)
William Edwardes, victualler £10
Thomas Williams, Bennett Painter each £5
Bennett Paynter, victualler, £10
William Edwardes, Henry Whiteside each £5

[f212v]

Thomas Godfery, victualler £10
Henry Whiteside, William Lyddam each £5
Robert Bignill, victualler £10
Henry Whiteside, Bennett Painter each £5
Thomas Heathen, victualler£10
William Butterfeild, Thomas Williams each £5
John Durbridge, victualler £10
Thomas Warde, Richard Reade each £5
Margaret Raunson, victualler £10
William Butterfeild, Edward Longe each £5
John Tassill, victualler £10
William Butterfeild, Henry Whiteside each £5
Elizabeth Hamond, widow, victualler £10
Henry Whiteside, Bennett Painter each £5

[f213]

Merriall Tayler widow, victualler, £10,

Thomas Godfery, John Tassill each £5

Nicholas Tayler, victualler £10

Henry Whiteside, Bennett Painter each £5

Henry Whiteside, victualler£10

Bennett Painter, Thomas Godfery each £5

William Butterfeild, victualler,£10,

John Tassill, John Doa each £5

[f213v]

Portmoot court held 19 February 1621.

Action of debt:

1150:21/21 Harris vs Hickes - Thomas Heathen pays 6s 4d and 20s and action is discharged.

Action of account:

1206:2/5 Wells vs Parker - plaintiff puts completed declaration and defendant is granted copy.

Action unspecified:

1199:6/10 Lorde vs Lewes - defendant brings writ of privilege bearing date 12th February returnable before the Court of Common Pleas at Westminster on the Saturday next of the quindene of Easter next. Browncklowe and Warberton;[72] copy granted.

Actions continuing: **1165**:16/32; **1166**:16/27; **1169**:16/31; **1173**:15/17; **1182**: 12/16; **1195**:8/19.

[f214]

Apprenticeship:

1210: 5th March 1621 Nicholas Coles, son of Richard Coles of the borough, butcher, places himself apprentice to Richard Browne of the borough, butcher for the term of seven years from the 20th February 1621. [marginal note - enrolment of apprentice].

[f214v]

Victuallers recognisances 26th February 1621:

1211: Before John Glover, gent, mayor and Jerome Keite the Justices,

Thomas Warde £20 Bennett Painter, Robert Parker each £10 (paid 20s 0d; 2s to me) That Robert Warde shall not victual or sell ale or beer within any house in this borough unless he be licensed.

Christopher Smith £20 Henry Whiteside, Richard Reade each £10 (paid 20s 0d; 2s). Upon condition aforesaid.

Edward Longe £20 Henry Whiteside, Robert Bruce each £10 (paid 20s, fined 2s). Upon condition aforesaid.

Bonds to be made to save harmless.

[72] Browncklowe and Warberton, Westminster court clerks.

[f215] (Blank)
[f215v]

Portmoot court held 5 March 1621.

Action of debt:

1212:1/1 William Ayers vs Thomas Keene - plaintiff's attorney, Simon Jeames, declares and defendant's attorney, Thomas Heathen, requests copy. [Discharged for defendant].

Action of account:

1206:3/5 Wells vs Parker - defendant responds and copy is granted; parties put themselves on the country and *venire facias* is granted.

Action unspecified:

1199:7/10 Lord vs Lewes - stands as before under writ.

Actions continuing: **1165**:17/32; **1166**:17/27; **1169**:17/31; **1173**:16/17; **1182**: 13/16; **1195**:9/19.

[f216]

Portmoot court held 19 March 1621.

Action of detinue:

1173:17/17 Bently vs Rymill - stands as before.

Action of account:

1206:4/5 Wells vs Parker - discharged by plaintiff.

Actions continuing: **1165**:18/32; **1166**:18/27; **1169**:18/31; **1182**:14/16; **1195**: 10/19; **1199**:8/10.

[f216v]

The examination of Alice White of Woodstock, widow, taken before John Glover gent, mayor the 30th of March 1621.

1213: The said examinate says that a tall man of a high colour and brownish hair (now in Oxon gaol as she hears) of late has been at her house several times and but one night at a time and spent money in her house, but had not wherewith to pay her: And because he owed her about 3s 4d. for diet, he pawned to her a table cloth, a sheet, and two aprons ('apernes'); which Mr. Lodwick Bowine of Barton claims were stolen from his hedge about twelve-tide last:[73] which goods were found in this examinate's possession: But she denies that she suspected him to be a lewd man, or that he had unlawfully come by them, but believed that he was a very honest man for that he said he was a widower and sold them for want of money only.

(the mark of) Alice White

[f217]

Portmoot court held 9 April 1621.

Action of trespass on case:

1214:1/8 Thomas Winter vs Thomas Haddock - plaintiff's attorney, Simon Jeames, requests day to state his case in next court. Thomas Heathen appears for defendant.

[73] Twelve-tide: the season of Epiphany, 6 January.

Action of account:
1206:5/5 Wells vs Parker - discharged; plaintiff is paid debt and costs.
Actions continuing: **1165**:19/32; **1166**:19/27; **1169**:19/31; **1182**:15/16; **1195**: 11/19; **1199**:9/10.

[f217v]

Actions of debt:
1217:1/1 George Cowurde, gent vs Richard Tasker - plaintiff's attorney, Simon Jeames, puts declaration and Thomas Heathen, for defendant, requests copy. [marginal note - discharged - and clause crossed out].
1218:1/1 William Loggon, gent vs Richard Tasker - plaintiff declares through his attorney, Simon Jeames and defendant's attorney, Thomas Heathen, requests copy. [marginal note 'discharged' and clause crossed out].
Actions of trespass on case:
1215:1/1 William Ayers and Anne his wife vs Richard Holloway - plaintiff's attorney, Simon Jeames, requests day to state his case and Thomas Heathen appears for defendant. [marginal note - discharged by plaintiff].
1216:1/10 Thomas Roberts vs Richard Tasker - plaintiff's attorney, Simon Jeames, declares and has day to amend in next court. Thomas Heathen for defendant.

[f218]

View of Frankpledge and Sessions of the Peace held 18th April 1621... before John Glover, gent, mayor [rest of heading crossed out]
[Marginal note - For that Mr. Kyte would not come to the hall this day , therefore the Leet only was held and not the Sessions of the Peace].
1219: *Jury for the King with homage*

John Dubber,	Robert Bruce,	Thomas Williams,
Bennett Paynter,	John Norman,	Henry Whiteside,
William Edwards,	Richard Reade,	Thomas Woodward,
John Durbridge,	Thomas Bruce,	Thomas Warde.

Affeerers: John Norman, Thomas Woodward, Thomas Warde sworn in.

[f218v]

1220: *Recognisances:*
John Pulchoe - continues (see **1136a**)
William Monday - continues (see **1146**)
Francis Pyman - continues (see **1192a**)
Anthony Crowdson - continues (see **1138**)
1207:2/2 Robert Phillipps on recognisance of £200 appears at this sessions; action continues.
1136a:3/4+ John Pulchoe on recognisance of £20 appears at this sessions; William Rayer, his surety, recog. £10.

[f219]

1221: *Victuallers licensed:*

The names of all the victuallers licensed according to the form of the Statute and not according to the King's Majesty's proclamation [clause crossed out].
[Memorandum: for that these sessions were not kept at the leet, therefore they were not bound] .
[List of victuallers afterwards crossed out] :-

Thomas Rayer,	William Edwardes,	Bennett Painter,
Thomas Godfery,	Robert Bignill,	Thomas Heathen,
John Durbridge,	Margaret Raunson,	John Tassill,
	[f219v]	
Elizabeth Hamond, widow	Merriall Tayler, widow	
Henry Whiteside,	Nicholas Tayler,	William Butterfeild.

[f220]

Portmoot court held 23 April 1621.
Actions of trespass on case:
1182:16/16 Manning vs Allibone - discharged on behalf of defendant.
1214:2/8 Winter vs Haddock - plaintiff's attorney puts completed declaration and defendant's attorney requests copy.
1216:2/10 Roberts vs Tasker - plaintiff's attorney declares and defendant's attorney requests copy.
Action unspecified:
1199:10/10 Lord vs Lewis - stands as before.
Actions continuing: **1165**:20/32; **1166**:20/27; **1169**:20/31; **1195**:12/19.

[f220v]

Breach of the peace: 23 April 1621 before John Glover, gent, mayor.
1222:1/2 William Richards swears in form following; viz:
That Thomas Peeterson has given many threatening speeches against him and (said) that he would pull his shop to pieces and that he would be even with him: whereby he is persuaded in his conscience that he is in danger of his life of him and desires that he may be bound to the peace and also to his good behaviour for he is continually drunk and uses railing speeches against diverse men in Woodstock. (signed) William Richards
28 April 1621
1222:2/2 The said Thomas Peeterson at the request of Edward Kilby and Robert Pyle, and upon his own submission and promise never hereafter to offend William Richards in the like kind; he was by John Glover, gent, mayor of the said borough discharged of his recognisance aforesaid. And for his fine he is taxed at 12d which was paid to the constables.
(signed) John Glover, mayor
Fine 12d paid to Bennet Paynter [Marginal note - delivered to me 7s.5d]

[f221]

Sessions of the Peace held 23rd April 1621 before John Glover, mayor.

Memorandum: Mr. Kyte refused to sit with Mr. mayor therefore this sessions was not kept nor the victuallers bound:

1223: *Recognisances*:

(**1136a**) John Pulchoe, (**1146**) William Monday, (**1192a**) Francis Pyman, (**1138**) Anthony Crowdson, (**1207**) Robert Phillipps, (**1136a**) John Pulchoe, (**1222**) Thomas Peeterson.

[f221v]

1224: *Victuallers licensed:* The names of the victuallers licensed according to the form of the statute; which licences are to continue until the 6th of April next coming and no longer:

Thomas Rayer,	William Edwardes,	Bennett Paynter,
Thomas Godferye,	Robert Bignill,	Thomas Heathen,
John Durbridge,	Margaret Raunson,	John Tassill,
Elizabeth Hamond, widow,		

[f222]

Merriall Tayler, widow	Henry Whiteside,	Nicholas Tayler,
William Butterfeild,	Thomas Warde,	Joan Glover,
widow Carden,	William Bradshewe,	widow White.

These persons are thought fit to be licensed and to enter recognisance to be victuallers for one whole year from this day, viz: 9th May 1621.

(signed) James Whitelocke, recorder (signed) John Glover, mayor

[f222v]

1225: *The condition of the Recognisance:*

The Condition of this Recognisance is such:- Whereas Thomas Rayer, victualler, is admitted and allowed by the mayor and Justices of the Peace within this borough to keep a common alehouse, or tipling house, and to use common selling of ale, or beer, only within the now house of him the said Thomas Rayer (and not elsewhere) situate within the Borough of New Woodstock aforesaid until the Sixth day of April next coming and no longer: If therefore the said Thomas Rayer during such time as he shall keep such common alehouse there, shall not suffer any unlawful play, at the tables, dice, cards, tennis, bowls, cloche ('Closh'), quoits ('Coytes'), logetts, or other unlawful games, to be used in his said house, or in his garden, orchard, or other his ground or place. Nor dress or cause or suffer to be dressed any flesh to be eaten upon any day forbidden by the law or Statute of this Realm: Nor wittingly and willingly admit or receive into his said house or any part thereof, any person notoriously defamed of or for theft incontenancy or drunkenness: Or that shall be beforehand notified to him the said Thomas Rayer, by the officers of the said borough for the time being, to be an unmeet person, to be received into a common alehouse: Nor keep or lodge there any strange......

[f223]

person (above the space of one day and one night together) without notice thereof first given to the officers of the said borough And finally if the said Thomas Rayer during all the time that he shall keep common selling of ale or beer in the said house shall and will there use and maintain good order and rule. That then this present Recognisance etc. Or else etc.. by me

(signed) Edmund Hiorne

We think it fit that this form of Recognisance for licences for the victuallers be followed : 9 May 1621 (signed) John Glover, mayor

(signed) James Whitelocke, Recorder

[f223v]

Portmoot court held 7 May 1621.

Actions of trespass on case:

1214:3/8 Winter vs Haddock - defendant's attorney, Thomas Heathen, responds non assumpsit modo et forma; therefore *venire facias* granted.

1216:3/10 Roberts vs Tasker - peremptory day for response granted.

Actions continuing: **1165**:21/32; **1166**:21/27; **1169**:21/31; **1195**:13/19.

[f224]

Portmoot court held 14 May 1621.

Action of debt:

1169:22/31 Hiorne vs Head - renewal of levy.

Actions of trespass on case:

1214:4/8 Winter vs Haddock - renewal of *venire facias.*

1216:4/10 Roberts vs Tasker - defendant does not respond upon three occasions; writ of inquiry into damages granted.

Actions continuing: **1165**:22/32; **1166**:22/27; **1195**:14/19.

Adjournment:

1226: The Court of 28th May 1621 was adjourned until 11th June 1621

(signed) Edmund Hiorne

[f224v]

Recognisances dated 17 May 1621.

1227: The true note of such Recognisances as John Glover, gent, mayor of the said Borough did take at his own house the 17th day of May 1621 of all such victuallers as were licensed by him and Sir James Whitlock, knight, Chief Justice of Chester and recorder of the said borough under the conditions above specified under both their hands, as follows :-

Thomas Rayer £10	Thomas Woodward £5	Ric.Collingwood 12d
William Edwardes £10	Bennett Painter £5	Nicholas Tayler 12d
Bennett Painter £10	Henry Whiteside £5	Thomas Warde 12d
Thomas Godfery £10	Henry Whiteside £5	Thomas Heathen 12d
Robert Bignill £10	Bennett Painter £5	Will. Edwardes 12d
	[f225]	
Thomas Heathen £10	Henry Whiteside £5	Thomas Godfery 12d

John Durbridge £10	Anthony Deverill £5	James Nickoles
Margaret Raunson £10	Thomas Heathen £5	Edward Longe 12d
John Tassill £10	Bennett Painter £5	Will. Edwardes 12d
Elizabeth Hamond, wid.£10	Bennett Painter £5	Henry Whiteside 12d
Merriall Tayler, wid. £10	Thomas Godfery £5	Henry Whiteside 12d
Henry Whiteside £10	Thomas Godfery £5	Thomas Heathen 2s
	[f225v]	
Nicholas Tayler £10	Bennett Painter £5	Thomas Warde 12d
William Butterfeild £10	Henry Whiteside £5	Thomas Warde 12d
Thomas Warde £10	Bennett Painter £5	Henry Whiteside 12d
Joan Glover, widow £10	Anthony Deverill £5	Francis Pyman 12d
Anne Carden, widow £10	John Durbridge £5	Nicholas Tayler 12d
William Bradshewe not licensed		
Alice White, widow £10	Bennett Painter £5	Edward Longe 12d

All these 18 persons above written did acknowledge their several recognisances 17th May 1621.. before me (signed) John Glover, mayor

(signed) Edmund Hiorne, town clerk

[f226]

Portmoot court held 11 June 1621.

Action of debt:

1229:1/9 William Baylies and Walter Baylies vs William Hitche - William and Walter Baylies, as executors of the will of Roger Baylies, their late father, lately deceased, bring plaint of debt against William Hitche - plaintiffs' attorney, Simon Jeames, requests day to declare in next court. Thomas Heathen appears for defendant.[74]

Actions of trespass on case:

1214:5/8 Winter vs Haddock - *venire facias* returned executed and *habeas corpora* granted.

1216:5/10 Roberts vs Tasker - writ of inquiry into damages granted.

Action of account:

1228:1/9 Thomas Browne, gent vs Thomas Browne, woolman - Thomas Browne, gent, as executor of the last will of Thomas Browne, his late father, recently deceased, brings plea of account against Thomas Browne, woolman. Plaintiff's attorney, Simon Jeames, requests day to declare in next court. Defendant represented by Thomas Heathen.[75]

Actions continuing: **1165**:23/32; **1166**:23/27; **1169**:23/31; **1195**:15/19.

Election of officers:

1230: Edward Hull and John Saye are elected to be tithingmen and sworn in.

[74] MSS. Wills (Oxon) 196.175d. Roger Bayles, glover, of Bicester d.1616.

[75] P.C.C. Wills PRO Prob. 11/137.

[f226v]

Portmoot court held 25 June 1621 .

Action of trespass on case:

1214:6/8 Thomas Winter vs Thomas Haddock - Jury between parties :-

Nicholas Tayler,	John Norman,	Robert Spitle,
Bennett Paynter,	Richard Browne,	Thomas Bruce,
Thomas Woodward,	Robert Bruce,	Richard Reade,
Alexander Head,	Thomas Godfery,	Richard Phillipps.

Which jury, under oath, find for the plaintiff and assess for damages 53s 4d and for costs etc. 2d. And judgment is deferred to next court.

Action of trespass and assault:

1195:16/19 Burgin vs Rymill - stands upon costs of plaintiff.

Actions continuing: **1165**:24/32; **1166**:24/27; **1169**:24/31.

[f227]

Actions of debt:

1229:2/9 Baylies & Baylies vs Hitche - plaintiffs put declaration and defendant's attorney, Thomas Heathen, requests copy.

1231:1/2 John Tyrer vs Edward Silver - plaintiff's attorney, Thomas Heathen, declares and has day to amend the form in next court. Simon Jeames, for defendant, requests copy.

Action of trespass on case:

1216:6/10 Thomas Roberts vs Richard Tasker - sergeant at mace reports that jury assess for damages, 46s 8d and for costs 1d; therefore court adjudges that plaintiff should recover both 46s 8d for damages and [blank] for costs and his expenses; *scire facias* granted.

Action of account:

1228:2/9 Browne vs Browne - plaintiff puts declaration and requests day to amend the form in next court; defendant's attorney, Thomas Heathen, requests copy.

[f227v]

Conveyance: 27th June 1621

1232:1/4

Order: Henry Standard that justly etc., he keeps the agreement with Thomas Woodward concerning three messuages and three gardens with appurtenances in borough [of Woodstock] now in the seperate occupancies of Matthew [?Tombs], Alice Shadd, Richard Claridge, widow Wright and Elizabeth Gelly.[76]

And the concord is as follows: that the aforesaid Henry Standard acknowledges the said messuages, gardens and appurtenances aforesaid to be the right of the said Thomas Woodward and that the same Thomas has as the gift of the aforesaid Henry Standard. And the property is remised and quitclaimed for the said Henry Standard and his heirs to the aforesaid Thomas Woodward and his

[76] *VCH Oxon* xii, 348 (now 6 Market Place, Woodstock).

heirs in perpetuity And also the same Henry Standard concedes for himself and his heirs that he will warrant the aforesaid property to Thomas Woodward and his heirs against himself the said Henry Standard and his heirs in perpetuity. And for this fine etc... (signed) Henrie Standard
(signed) John Glover, mayor and Edmund Hiorne, town clerk

[f228]

Portmoot court held 9 July 1621.

Action of debt:
1229:3/9 Baylies and Bayles vs Hitche - peremptory day for response granted to defendant.
Action of trespass on case:
1214:7/8 Winter vs Haddock - court adjudges that plaintiff should recover 53s.4d for damages and [blank] for his costs etc; *scire facias* granted.
Action of trespass and assault:
1195:17/19 Burgin vs Rymill - stands for costs etc.
Action of account:
1228:3/9 Browne vs Browne - plaintiff puts completed declaration and defendant requests copy.
Actions continuing: **1165**:25/32; **1166**:25/27; **1169**:25/31.

[f228v]

Action of debt:
1231:2/2 Tyrer vs Silver - continues on behalf of defendant; discharged.
Actions of trespass on case:
1216:7/10 Roberts vs Tasker - sergeant at mace returns executed *scire facias* and *alias scire facias* is granted.
1214:8/8 Winter vs Haddock - *alias scire facias* granted.
1233:1/7 Michael Collins vs John Writington - plaintiff's attorney, Simon Jeames, puts declaration and defendant's attorney, Thomas Heathen, requests copy.
Conveyance:
1232:2/4 First proclamation between Thomas Woodward, querent and Henry Standard gent, deforciant, for three messuages and three gardens with appurtenances in Woodstock that the said Thomas Woodward recently acquired and remitted for the said Henry Standard.

[f229]

Portmoot court held 23 July 1621.

Action of debt:
1229:4/9 Baylies and Baylies vs William Hitche - defendant responds and requests day in next court to wage law with four compurgators; copy of response granted.
Actions of trespass on case:
1166:26/27 Miller vs Glover - continues in status quo as before.

1216:8/10 Roberts vs Tasker - sergeant at mace returns executed writ of *alias scire facias* and writ of execution granted against defendant and his surety.
1233:2/7 Collins vs Wrightington - peremptory day for response granted in next court.
Action of trespass and assault:
1195:18/19 Burgin vs Miller (sic Rymill) - continues on behalf of plaintiff for costs only.
Action of account:
1228:4/9 Browne vs Browne - defendant requests peremptory day to respond in next court.
Actions continuing: **1165**:26/32; **1169**:26/31.
Conveyance:
1232:3/4 Second proclamation between Thomas Woodwarde querent and Henry Standard deforciant, for three messuages and three gardens with appurtenances in Woodstock.

[f229v]

Action of debt:
1234:1/9 William Morton vs Richard Gilkes - plaintiff's attorney, Simon Jeames, places declaration and defendant's attorney, Thomas Heathen, requests copy.

[f230]

Portmoot court held 6 August 1621.
Action of debt:
1229:5/9 Baylies and Baylies vs William Hitche - defendant brings writ of privilege dated 20th June 19 James I, returnable before Court of Common Pleas at Westminster on Wednesday next in three weeks of St. Michael next following, and proved in this court.
Action of trespass on case:
1166:27/27 Miller vs Glover - continues in status quo as before.
Action of trespass and assault:
1195:19/19 Burgin vs Rymill - continues on behalf of plaintiff for costs only.
Action of account:
1228:5/9 Browne vs Browne - defendant brings writ of *habeas corpus* bearing date at Westminster on 15th day of June 19 James I etc and returnable at Westminster on Friday next of the quindene of St.Michael and proved. And copy of judgment granted.
Actions continuing: **1165**:27/32; **1169**:27/31.

[f230v]

Actions of debt:
1234:2/9 Morton vs Gilkes - peremptory day to respond.
1235:1/16 William Pope, knight and baronet vs John Hollins, gent - plaintiff's

attorney, Simon Jeames, declares and requests day to amend in next court. Thomas Heathen appears for defendant.

Actions of trespass on case:

1216 9/10 Roberts vs Tasker - sergeant at mace reports that execution is made and that in his hands is silver (English plate) to the value of £5 and day and date is given for sergeant to come to next court. [crossed out – 'which said money one Thomas Gyles raised upon a bond and declared in court and Mr. Jones appeared for Thomas Roberts and prayed a copy of the declaration and oyer of the condition and a day of imparlance'].

1233:3/7 Collins vs Wrightington - defendant's attorney puts response of not guilty and copy of response granted.

Action of trespass and assault:

1236:1/3 Hugh Hardway and Richard Fyndall - plaintiff's attorney, Thomas Heathen, puts declaration and defendant appears and his attorney, Simon Jeames, requests copy.

Conveyance:

1232:4/4 Third proclamation between Thomas Woodward, querent and Henry Standard, deforciant for three messuages and three gardens with appurtenances in Woodstock.

[f231]

The Court of John Glover, mayor of the borough and Clerk of the Market with Joseph Harris and William Meatcalfe, aldermen, and assistants elected and sworn to join with him held Monday 20 August 1621.

1237: *Jurors*:-

Thomas Williams,	Thomas Woodward,	William Edwardes,
Thomas Godferye,	Richard Browne,	John Acklye,
Henry Bradshewe,	John Durbridge,	Thomas Bruce,
John Sea,	Robert Bruce,	William Butterfeild.

1238: *Presentments of Jury*

The Jury aforesaid present that the best wheat is worth a quarter. 32s.
And that the second wheat is worth by the quarter. 29s 4d.
And that the best malt is worth by the quarter. 13s 4d.
And that the second malt is worth by the quarter...12s.

[f231v]

1239: *Mayor's Assizes*

The mayor aforesaid, with the consent of the said assistants do give and set down the several Assizes following, commanding them to be observed and kept within the said borough... viz:

The penny white loaf drawn from the fine cockett[77] to weigh 10¼oz.1dwt.
(= 10.3 oz.)

[77] See Glossary and Introduction.

The penny wheaten loaf to weigh 15¾oz.1dwt. (= 15.8 oz.)
The penny household loaf to weigh 21oz.2dwt. (= 21.1 oz.)
A barrell of the best beer not to be sold for above 8s 8d.
The kilderkin of the best beer not to be sold for above 4s 4d.
Every victualler to sell (within his house) an ale quart of the best beer or ale for 1d and to sell two quarts of small drink for 1d.
The butchers not to sell their tallow for above the stone 3s 2d.
The chandlers not to sell their candles for above the pound [no figure]
(signed by) John Glover mayor Joseph Harris William Meatcalfe

[f232] (Blank)

[f232v]

Portmoot court held 20 August 1621.

Actions of debt:

1234:3/9 Morton vs Gilkes - continues by consent of both parties.

1235:2/16 Pope vs Hollins - plaintiff's attorney puts completed declaration and defendant's attorney requests copy and has day for discussion in next court. And the same day and date are told to the plaintiff here.

Action of trespass on case:

1233: 4/7 Collins vs Wrightington - parties put themselves on the country; *venire facias* granted.

Actions continuing: **1165**:28/32; **1169**:28/31.

[f233]

Actions of debt:

1241:1/3 Rowland, Bishop of Bristol and William Bostock, gent vs William Cotes senior - [Marginal note - £300 debt] - plaintiffs' attorney, Simon Jeames, puts declaration and requests day to amend the format in next court. Thomas Heathen appears for defendant and requests copy.

1242:1/3 William Bostock, gent vs William Cotes senior - [Marginal note -£20 debt] - plaintiff's attorney, Simon Jeames, places declaration and requests day to amend in next court. Thomas Heathen, defendant's attorney, requests copy.

Action of trespass on case:

1240:1/3 Rowland, Bishop of Bristol and William Bostock, gent vs William Cotes senior - [In margin - £600 damages] - plaintiffs' attorney, Simon Jeames, puts declaration and requests day to amend in next court. Thomas Heathen, for defendant, requests copy.

Action of trespass and assault:

1236:2/3 Hardway vs Fyndall - continues.

[f233v]

Action of debt:

1243:1/3 William Bostock, gent vs William Cotes senior - [Marginal note - £5 debt] - plaintiff's attorney, Simon Jeames, puts declaration and requests day to amend in next court; defendant's attorney, Thomas Heathen, requests copy.

Actions of trespass on case:

1216:10/10 Roberts vs Tasker - sergeant at mace pays in court £4 6s 11d to the use of the plaintiff; and immediately a certain Thomas Gyles takes the said £4 6s 11d; and, through his attorney Thomas Heathen, places declaration. And the said Thomas Roberts, through his attorney Simon Jeames, requests copy of the declaration and oyer of condition, and a day for discussion of the matter is appointed for next court.

1244:1/3 William Bostock, gent vs William Coates senior - [Marginal note - 20 marks damages]- plaintiff's attorney, Simon Jeames, puts declaration and requests day to amend in next court. Thomas Heathen, for defendant, requests copy.

1245:1/3 William Bostock, gent vs William Coates senior - [Marginal note - 20s damages] - similarly.

[f234]

Portmoot court held 3 September 1621.

Actions of debt:

1234:4/9 Morton vs Gilkes - said defendant does not appear upon three occasions; therefore, etc..

1235:3/16 Pope vs Hollins - peremptory day for response in next court.

Action of trespass on case:

1233:5/7 Collins vs Writington - sergeant returns executed *venire facias* and writ of *habeas corpora* granted.

Action of trespass and assault:

1236:3/3 Hardway vs Fyndall - continues by assent of both parties.

Actions continuing: **1165**:29/32; **1169**:29/31.

[f234v]

Actions of debt:

1241:2/3 Rowland, Bishop of Bristol and William Bostock, gent vs William Coates snr - plaintiffs' attorney puts completed declaration and defendant's attorney requests copy; day to imparl appointed.

1242:2/3 William Bostock vs William Coates - similarly.

1243:2/3 William Bostock vs William Coates - similarly.

Actions of trespass on case:

1240:2/3 Rowland, Bishop of Bristol and William Bostock, gent vs William Coates snr - plaintiffs' attorney puts completed declaration and defendant requests copy; day to imparl appointed.

1244:2/3 William Bostock vs William Coates - plaintiff's attorney places completed declaration and defendant's attorney requests copy; day to imparl appointed.

1245:2/3 William Bostock vs William Coates - similarly.

1246:1/2 Ambrose Lardner vs Justin Pavye - plaintiff's attorney, Thomas Heathen, declares and requests day to amend the form in next court. Simon Jeames, defendant's attorney, requests copy.

[f235]

Portmoot court held 17 September 1621.
Actions of debt:
1234:5/9 Morton vs Gilkes - court adjudges plaintiff should recover £10 for debt and [blank] for costs; *scire facias* granted against surety.
1235:4/16 Pope vs Hollins - defendant's attorney places response and requests wager of law; day and date appointed in next court for four compurgators; plaintiff granted copy of response.
1241:3/3 Bishop of Bristol and William Bostock vs William Cotes - [No action noted].
Actions of trespass on case:
1233:6/7 Collins vs Writington - renewal of *habeas corpora.*
[Marginal note - 6s10d due defendant for costs]
1240:3/3 Bishop of Bristol and William Bostock vs William Coates - [No action noted].
Actions continuing: **1165**:30/32; **1169**:30/31.

[f235v]

Actions of debt:
1242:3/3 Bostock vs Coates - [No action noted].
1243:3/3 Bostock vs Coates - [No action noted].
1247:1/1 John Tyro vs Humfrey Silver - dismissed on behalf of defendant.
Actions of trespass on case:
1244:3/3 Bostock vs Coates - [No action noted].
1245:3/3 Bostock vs Coates - [No action noted].
1246:2/2 Lardner vs Pavye - continues by assent of both parties; dismissed.
Memorandum:
1240/41/42/43/44/45: William Cotes senior brings writ of *habeas corpus* dated 20th June 19 James I returnable at Westminster on Tuesday next of the octave of St. Michael; plaintiffs granted copy.

[f236]

Breach of the Peace dated 19 September 1621...before John Glover, mayor
1248:1/2 Richard Yeate, butcher, was committed to prison for beating Richard Reade and breaking his head yesternight and for beating Bennett Painter's wife and Reade's wife at Painter's house.
Richard Reade recognisance £20 to give evidence against Richard Yeate at the next sessions - Richard Yeate recognisance £40 to appear at the next sessions held at Woodstock to answer etc., John Dubber and Bennett Painter each place surety for £20.

[f236v]

Portmoot court held 1 October 1621.

Actions of debt:

1165:31/32 Hiorne vs Tayler - stands as before.

1169:31/31 Hiorne vs Head - renewal of execution.

Action of trespass on case:

1233:7/7 Collins vs Writington - Names of the jury between parties:-

Nicholas Tayler,	William Edwardes,	Bennett Paynter,
Richard Browne,	Thomas Woodward,	Thomas Godfery,
Robert Bruce,	William Butterfeild,	John Durbridge,
John Acklie,	John Durman,	William Richards.

Which jury, under oath, said:- [Memorandum - the Jury was withdrawn; matter referred to the ending of Mr. mayor and Mr. Harris upon the deliverance of 6d either to other under penalty of £20 to be ended by next Court].

[f237]

Actions of debt:

1234:6/9 Morton vs Gilkes - sergeant returns executed *scire facias* and *alias scire facias* granted.

1235:5/16 Pope vs Hollins - defendant appears in person with four supporters to wage law; and at the same time plaintiff places demurrer;[78] copy granted.

Actions of trespass on case:

1249:1/9 Matthew Reeve vs John Ball - plaintiff's attorney, Simon Jeames, puts declaration and requests day to amend the form; defendant's attorney, Thomas Heathen, requests copy.

1250:1/10 Edward Mallins vs William Fawderye - plaintiff's attorney, Simon Jeames, narrates declaration and defendant's attorney, Thomas Heathen, requests copy.

Action of covenant:

1251:1/2 Richard Fletcher vs Richard Hinde - plaintiff's attorney, Simon Jeames, narrates declaration and defendant's attorney, Thomas Heathen, requests copy.

[f237v]

Actions of debt:

1252:1/8 Humphrey Hamond vs Richard Reade - plaintiff's attorney, Simon Jeames, narrates declaration and defendant's attorney, Thomas Heathen, requests copy; first day of privilege granted.

1253:1/2 Thomas Rayer vs Richard Coles - plaintiff appears as executor of the last will and testament of his father, William Rayer, lately deceased.[79] Plaintiff's attorney, Simon Jeames, narrates declaration and defendant, in

[78] Although the court had agreed to wager of law at the previous sitting, they allow the demurrer to stand: the defendant may have decided to change his ground.

[79] P.C.C. Wills PRO Prob. 11/134 f.75.

custody of Thomas Heathen, sergeant at mace, personally requests day of privilege.

1254:1/10 Anthony Deverill vs Richard Bentlie - plaintiff's attorney, Simon Jeames, narrates declaration and defendant's attorney, Thomas Heathen, requests copy.

[f238]

Portmoot court held 15 October 1621.

Actions of debt:

1165:32/32 Hiorne vs Tayler - stands as before.

1234:7/9 Morton vs Gilkes - *alias scire facias* returned executed and execution granted against defendant and surety.

1235:6/16 Pope vs Hollins - defendant enjoins with plea of demurrer and copy is granted to plaintiff.

1255:1/3 Thomas Rayer vs Joan Meade, widow - plaintiff's attorney, Simon Jeames, narrates and defendant appears by Thomas Heathen, her attorney, and requests copy.

Actions of trespass on case:

1249:2/9 Reeve vs Ball - peremptory day granted.

1250:2/10 Malins vs Fawdery - peremptory day granted.

[f238v]

Actions of debt:

1252:2/8 Hamond vs Reade - second day of privilege granted.

1253:2/2 Rayer vs Coles - second day of privilege granted.

1254:2/10 Deverill vs Richard Bently - peremptory day granted.

1256:1/1 William Bradshewe vs [blank] Morris - [Memorandum: The plaintiff paid Mr. [Jeames] 43s.11d for costs of defendant].

1257:1/11 Alice Luckett vs Thomas Warde - plaintiff's attorney, Simon Jeames, narrates and defendant's attorney, Thomas Heathen, requests copy.

1258:1/1 Joan Heard, widow vs George Frauncis - plaintiff's attorney, Simon Jeames, narrates and has day to amend; defendant's attorney, Thomas Heathen, requests copy.

1259:1/1 Robert Bignill vs George Francis - plaintiff's attorney, Simon Jeames, places declaration and the said defendant appears in person and acknowledges the debt of £3.3s.4d., and the Court adjudges that plaintiff should recover the aforesaid debt and [blank] for costs.

Action of covenant:

1251:2/2 Fletcher vs Hinde - peremptory day granted.

[f239]

View of Frankpledge and Sessions of the Peace held 24 October 1621 before John Glover gent, mayor, Jerome Keite, gent, and alderman Joseph Harris, gent, three Justices of the Peace for the borough.

1260: *Jury for the King with homage*:

Thomas Williams,	Bennett Painter,	John Norman,
Henry Whiteside,	William Edwardes,	Thomas Godfery,
William Raunson,	Richard Reade,	Thomas Woodward,
Edward Hull,	Thomas Bruce,	John Durbridge,
Robert Bruce,	Bartholomew Love,	William Hitche.

Affeerers: John Norman, William Raunson, Thomas Woodward sworn in.

[f239v]

Sessions of the Peace

Recognisances:

1136a:4/4+ John Pulchroe - process continues.

1146:3/3+ William Munday - process continues.

1192a:2/2+ Francis Pyman - process continues and he is committed to custody of the sergeant.

1248:2/2 Richard Yeate - on recognisance of £40. He appears and is discharged etc.

Marginal note:

2s paid to the chamberlains delivered to Thomas Rayer.

Child maintenance:

1138:4/4 process continues against Anthony Crowdson and he is committed to prison.

Election of officers:

1262: Bennett Painter and Thomas Woodward elected constables and sworn in; Edward Hull, John Say, John Durman, Christopher Smith elected tithingmen and sworn in.

Francis Garter and John Doa elected ale-tasters. Estr[eats: no entry].

[f240]

Portmoot court held 29 October 1621.

Actions of debt:

1234:8/9 Morton vs Gilkes - sergeant at mace reports he is holding Bennett Painter and John Doa in execution.

1235:7/16 Pope vs Hollins - said parties enjoin in demurrer; court wishes to consider for next sitting.

Action of trespass on case:

1249:3/9 Reeve vs Ball - defendant's attorney responds that he is not guilty in any way of the aforesaid transgression; therefore parties put themselves on the country; *venire facias* granted.

[f240v]

Actions of debt:

1252:3/8 Hamond vs Reade - last day of privilege granted.

1254:3/10 Deverill vs Bently - defendant's attorney says that he does not owe the debt of 30s.8d to the plaintiff in the manner and form claimed; and he puts himself on the country; *venire facias* granted.

1255:2/3 Rayer vs Meade - peremptory day granted.
1257:2/11 Luckett vs Warde - second day of privilege granted.
Action of trespass on case:
1250:3/10 Malins vs Fawdery - defendant's attorney responds non assumpsit. He puts himself on the country and *venire facias* is granted.
Apprenticeship:
1263: John Hiorne junior places himself apprentice to Robert Spittle of Woodstock, smith and farrier, for the term of seven years from 29th September 1621. (marginal note - enrolment)

[f241]

Portmoot court held 12 November 1621.
Actions of debt:
1234:9/9 Morton vs Gilkes - [No action recorded].
1235:8/16 Pope vs Hollins - court to consider further.
Actions of trespass on case:
1249:4/9 Reeve vs Ball - *venire facias* returned executed and *habeas corpora* granted.
1250:4/10 Malins vs Fawdery - *venire facias* returned executed and *habeas corpora* granted.

[f241v]

Actions of debt:
1252:4/8 Hamond vs Reade - peremptory day granted.
1254:4/10 Deverill vs Bently - *venire facias* returned executed and *habeas corpora* granted.
1255:3/3 Rayer vs Meades - defendant does not respond.
[Marginal note - dismissed on behalf of plaintiff].
1257:3/11 Luckett vs Warde - last day of privilege.
Action of trespass:
1264:1/7 Matthew Parratt vs Henry Triplett - plaintiff's attorney, Thomas Heathen, places declaration and requests day to discuss in next Court. Simon Jeames appears for defendant.

[f242]

Portmoot court held 26 November 1621.
Actions of debt:
1252:5/8 Hamond vs Reade - continues by assent of plaintiff.
1257:4/11 Luckett vs Warde - defendant's attorney, Thomas Heathen, places response and plaintiff's attorney requests copy.
Action continuing: **1235**: 9/16.

[f242v]

Action of debt:
1254:5/10 Anthony Deverill vs Richard Bently - Names of the jury between parties:-

Nicholas Tayler, Thomas Williams, John Norman,

William Raunson,	Bennett Painter,	Robert Bruce,
Thomas Woodward,	Alexander Head,	Thomas Godfery,
Richard Reade,	John Dissell,	John Durman.

Which jury, under oath, say they find for the plaintiff and adjudge the defendant owes the plaintiff 30s 8d and assess for damages 4d and for costs 2d. Judgment adjourned to next court.

Action of trespass:

1264:2/7 Parratt vs Triplett - plaintiff's attorney puts declaration and defendant's attorney requests copy.

Actions of trespass on case:

1249:5/9 Matthew Reeve vs John Ball - Names of the jury between parties:-

Nicholas Tayler,	Thomas Williams,	Thomas Screvin,
William Edwardes,	William Raunson,	Bennett Painter,
Robert Bruce,	Thomas Woodward,	Thomas Godfery,
Alexander Head,	John Dissell,	John Durman.

Which jury, under oath, say that they find for the plaintiff and assess damages 3s 4d and for costs 2d. Judgment adjourned to next court.

1250:5/10 Edward Malins vs William Fawdery - Names of the jury between parties:-

Nicholas Tayler,	William Butterfeild,	Thomas Godfery,
Alexander Head,	John Durbridge,	Richard Reade,
Bryan Steephens,	Christopher Smith,	John Dissell,
John Durman,	William Richardson,	Edward Hull.

Which jury, under oath, say they find for the plaintiff and assess for damages £6 12s and for costs 2d. Judgment adjourned to next court.

[f243]

Market Court and Assize held 1 December 1621 before John Glover, gent, mayor and assisted by aldermen Joseph Harris and William Meatcalfe.

1265: *Presentments*

Jury - [no names entered] Which Jury, under oath, present in form following:-
That the best wheat by the quarter ...
That the second wheat by the quarter...
That the best malt by the quarter...
That the second malt by the quarter... [no prices entered].

[f243v]

1266: *Assize*

Mayor and assistants aforesaid give and set down the several assizes following, commanding they be observed and kept within the said borough :-
The penny white loaf drawn from the fine cockett[80] to weigh 9oz.
The penny wheaten loaf to weigh... 14oz.

[80] See Glossary and Introduction.

The penny household loaf to weigh ... 18oz.
The brewer not to sell a barrell of his best beer for above ...9s 4d.
and not to sell a kilderkin of his best beer above 4s 8d.
Every victualler to sell an ale quart of the best ale and beer for a penny and two quarters of small drink for 1d.
(signed by) John Glover, mayor Joseph Harris, William Meatcalfe, Edmund Hiorne, town clerk.

[f244]

Portmoot court held 10 December 1621.

Actions of debt:

1252:6/8 Hamond vs Reade - defendant does not appear upon three occasions; therefore judgment will be given in next court.

1257:5/11 Luckett vs Warde - copy of response granted.

Action of trespass:

1264:3/7 Parratt vs Triplett - defendant's attorney, Simon Jeames, places response and plaintiff requests copy.

Action continuing: **1235**:10/16.

[f244v]

Actions of debt:

1229:6/9 Walter Baylies and William Baylies vs William Hitche – defendants (i.e. plaintiffs) deliver writ of procedendo bearing date 28 November 1621; defendant's attorney, Thomas Heathen, requests copy of the writ and court considers the process of judgment for next court because defendant then seeks process to wage law .

1254:6/10 Deverell vs Bently - court adjudges plaintiff should recover 30s 8d for debt and 44s for costs; *scire facias* granted. [note - last day of March 1622 the particular bill of costs was delivered to Mr. Lenthall, recorder, at Mr.mayor's house].[81]

Actions of trespass on case:

1249:6/9 Reeve vs Ball - court adjudges plaintiff should recover [blank] for debt and [blank] for costs; *scire facias* granted.

1250:6/10 Malins vs Fawdery - similarly.

Action of account:

1228:6/9 Thomas Browne, gent vs Thomas Browne - defendant's attorney, Thomas Heathen, previously produced a writ of *habeas corpus* bearing date 22 November 1621 returnable before the King at Westminster on Saturday after the octave of Hilary. And because plaintiff has a writ de procedendo in the same plea and produces this in court, the court wishes to consider whether to allow this writ by the next sitting.

[81] First reference to Recorder William Lenthall in this court.

[f245]

Portmoot court held 24 December 1621.

Action of debt:

1252:7/8 Hamond vs Reade - defendant pays into court 35s.4d and judgment is adjourned to next sitting.

Action continuing: **1235**:11/16.

[f245v]

Actions of debt:

1229:7/9 Baylies (and Baylies) vs Hitche - defendant does not appear upon wager of law; therefore judgment will be given at next sitting.

1254:7/10 Deverill vs Bentley - *scire facias* returned executed and *alias scire facias* granted.

1257:6/11 Luckett vs Warde - stands as before for plaintiff.

Action of trespass:

1264:4/7 Parratt vs Triplett - proviso that if plaintiff is unwilling to proceed at the next court then defendant can be granted writ of *venire facias*.

Actions of trespass on case:

1249:7/9 Reeve vs Ball - *scire facias* returned executed and *alias scire facias* granted.

1250:7/10 Malins vs Fawdery - *scire facias* returned executed and *alias scire facias* granted.

1267:1/1 Simon Jeames vs Richard Reade - plaintiff personally makes declaration and is granted day to amend the form.

Action of account:

1228:7/9 Browne vs Browne - aforesaid writ allowed.

[f246]

Portmoot court held 7 January 1622.

Action of debt:

1252:8/8 Hamond vs Reade - stands as before. [in margin -dismissed]

Action of trespass:

1264:5/7 Parrat vs Triplett - discontinued by direction of William Lenthall esquire, recorder for the borough, because plaint cannot be tried in this court.

Actions continuing: **1235**:12/16; **1257**:7/11.

[f246v]

Actions of debt:

1229:8/9 Baylies (and Baylies) vs Hitche - said defendant produces writ of *habeas corpus* issued on 28 November 1621 returnable at Westminster on Wednesday next of the quindene of Hilary.

1254:8/10 Deverill vs Bently - sergeant returns *alias scire facias* executed and execution granted against defendant and his surety.

Actions of trespass on case:
1249:8/9 Reeve vs Ball - sergeant returns *alias scire facias* executed and execution granted against defendant and his surety.
1250:8/10 Malins vs Fawdery - similarly.
Action of account:
1228:8/9 Browne vs Browne - stands as before.

[f247]

Portmoot court held 21 January 1622.
Actions of debt:
1257:8/11 Luckett vs Warde - plaintiff's attorney places demurrer upon response of defendant who requests copy.
Action of trespass:
1264:6/7 Parrat vs Triplett - judgment upon rights of defendant will be given in next court.
Action of trespass on case:
1249:9/9 Reeve vs Ball - sergeant pays 3s 4d. for damages and 35s 1d for costs and defendant is discharged.
Action continuing: **1235**:13/16.

[f247v]

Actions of debt:
1229:9/9 Baylies (and Baylies) vs Hitche - stands as before.
1254:9/10 Deverill vs Bentlie - sergeant at mace returns '25 owing of plate'[82] and day for them to come is granted.
1268:1/4 Thomas Meatcalfe vs Thomas Peart - plaintiff's attorney, Simon Jeames, puts declaration and has day to amend form etc. Defendant's attorney, Thomas Heathen, requests copy.
Actions of trespass on case:
1250:9/10 Malins vs Fawdery - sergeant pays damages and costs into court and defendant is discharged.
1269:1/4 William Hickes jnr. vs Michael Cubige - plaintiff's attorney, Simon Jeames, puts declaration and has day to amend the form; defendant's attorney, Thomas Heathen, requests copy.
Action of account:
1228:9/9 Browne vs Browne - stands as before.

[f248]

Portmoot court held 4 February 1622.
Actions of debt:
1235:14/16 Pope vs Hollins - court considering further for next court.
1257:9/11 Luckett vs Warde - copy of demurrer granted to defendant.

82 '25 owing of plate': commonly coins.

Action of trespass:
1264:7/7 Parrat vs Triplett - stands as before.
Action of trespass on case:
1250:10/10 Malins vs Fawderye - discharged.

[f248v]

Actions of debt:
1254:10/10 Deverill vs Bently - sergeant at mace pays debt, damages and costs; and defendant goes quit.
1268:2/4 Meatcalfe vs Peart - plaintiff places completed declaration and defendant is granted copy.
1270:1/3 John Hobbs vs Edward Silver - plaintiff's attorney, Simon Jeames, puts declaration and defendant's attorney, Thomas Heathen, requests copy.
1271:1/2 Richard Jeffs vs William Hitche - plaintiff's attorney, Simon Jeames, puts declaration and defendant's attorney, Thomas Heathen, requests copy.
Action of trespass on case:
1269:2/4 Hickes vs Cubbidge - plaintiff puts completed declaration and defendant is granted copy. (marginal note - revoked 15th February 1622)

[f249]

Portmoot court held 18 February 1622.
Actions of debt:
1235:15/16 Pope vs Hollins - court wishes to consider.
1257:10/11 Luckett vs Warde - peremptory day to enjoin on demurrer.
1268:3/4 Meatcalfe vs Pearte - peremptory day to respond.

[f249v]

Actions of debt:
1270:2/3 Hobbs vs Silver - peremptory day to respond granted defendant in next court.
1271:2/2 Jeffs vs Hitche - discharged by plaintiff; acknowledging the fee.
Actions of trespass on case:
1269:3/4 Hickes vs Cubbidge - peremptory day to respond granted defendant in next court.
1272:1/2 William Browne and Ellin Browne vs John Norman - William Browne and Ellin Browne, *alias* Robins, wife of the aforesaid William, and administratrix of all and singular the goods etc of Michael Nurse, her brother, which were never administered. Action for damages of £120. Plaintiffs' attorney, Simon Jeames seeks day to narrate in next court and defendant's attorney, Thomas Heathen, requests day to imparl.[83]
1273:1/2 Richard Francklyn vs John Chewe - plaintiff's attorney, Thomas Heathen, requests day to narrate in next court; defendant's attorney, Simon Jeames, requests day to imparl.

83 MSS.Wills (Oxon) 89/1/16 and 17.

[f250]

Action of debt:
1275:1/1 Jerome Keite vs Richard Bently - plaintiff's attorney, Simon Jeames, declares and defendant's attorney, Thomas Heathen, requests copy of court's judgment and has day for discussion in next court. [Marginal note - discharged by Heathen].
Action of trespass on case:
1274:1/2 Edward Silver vs John Hobbs - plaintiff's attorney, Thomas Heathen, requests day to declare in next court and defendant's attorney, Simon Jeames, has day for discussion.

[f250v]

Flesh in Lent
1276: The names of the taverners, innholders, victuallers, butchers and keepers of ordinary tables inhabiting within the borough of New Woodstock which were bound by recognisance from killing, dressing and eating of flesh in Lent or on fish days appointed by the law according to His Majesty's proclamation bearing date the fourth day of February in the nineteenth year of the King's Majesty's reign that now is etc: Taken at the guildhall of the said borough the second day of March etc. 1622 before John Glover, gent, mayor, Jerome Kyte and Joseph Harris, aldermen, two of the King's Majesty's justices of the peace for the said borough as follows etc.. by Edmund Hiorne town clerk etc..

[f251]

The form of the Recognisance
1277: The condition of this recognisance is such that if the above named Thomas Rayer, do not nor any other of his family household or servants do at any time this Lent season or on other fish days prohibited by the laws and statutes of this realm of England to be observed and kept as fasting days: directly or indirectly dress or cause or suffer to be dressed any flesh in or about his house or houses, whereof he has charge or government to the intent thereto spend utter or sell the same But do only observe and keep the laws and Statutes of this realm in that case provided And do also perform and keep all such articles directions and orders as are set down in His Majesty's proclamation bearing date the fourth day of February Anno 1622 That then the said recognisance to be void and of no effect or else to stand in full force and virtue
By Edmund Hiorne, town clerk of the borough.

[f251v]

The names of the innholders, taverners, victuallers, and butchers which were licensed the 2 of March 1622 according to the said Proclamation:
1278: *Innholders*:

John Glover £10 Thomas Williams Robert Parker £10	£102s6d	Bennett Painter, Nicholas Tayler £5 each Bennett Paynter, Thomas Heathen £5 each

1279: *Vintner*:

Thomas Rayer £10	Robert Spitle, Henry Whiteside £5 each

1280: *Butchers*:

John Norman £10	Thomas Godfery, Richard Reade £5 each
Richard Browne £10	John Dubber, Bennett Paynter £5 each
Richard Coles £10	Alexander Head, Robert Busby £5 each
Jerome Longe £10	Robert Spitle, Edward Hull £5 each
Richard Reade £10	Thomas Godfery, John Norman £5 each

[f252]

1281: The names of the victuallers licensed which entered recognisance the day and year aforesaid:

Thomas Rayer £10	Henry Whiteside, Robert Spitle £5 each
William Edwardes £10	Nicholas Tayler, John Tassill £5 each
Bennett Paynter £10	Thomas Williams , Nicholas Tayler £5 each
Thomas Godfery £10	John Norman, Richard Reade £5 each
Robert Bignill £10	John Dubber, Bennett Paynter £5 each
[in margin - 6d]	
Thomas Heathen £10	Thomas Williams, Bennett Painter £5 each
John Durbridge £10	Christopher Smith, John Pepper £5 each
Margaret Raunson £10	Edward Hull, John Tassill £5 each

[f252v]

John Tassill £10	William Edwardes, Nicholas Tayler £5 each
Elizabeth Hamond £10	Henry Whiteside, John Seare £5 each
Merriall Tayler £10	Nicholas Tayler, Henry Whiteside £5 each
Henry Whiteside £10	William Butterfeild,Christopher Smith £5 each
Nicholas Tayler £10	William Edwardes, John Tassill £5 each
William Butterfeild £10	Henry Whiteside, John Seare £5 each
Joane Glover £10	Christopher Smith, John Tassill £5 each
Anne Carden £10	Edward Longe, John Grainger £5 each
Anne White £10	Edward Longe , Francis Pyman £5 each

[f253]

Market Court 2nd March 1622.

The court of John Glover gent, mayor of the said borough and clerk of the market with Joseph Harris and William Meatcalfe aldermen, assistants elected and sworn to join with him held on Saturday 2nd March 1622.

1282: *Jury*

William Edwardes,	John Grainger,	Henry Whiteside,
John Durbridge,	Robert Bruce,	John Doa,
Christopher Smith,	Edward Longe,	Bennett Paynter,
Thomas Godfery,	Thomas Woodward,	Edward Hull.

1283: *Presentments*

The jury, under oath, present in form following :-

That a quarter of the best wheat is worth 41s 4d
That a quarter of the second wheat is worth 37s 4d
That a quarter of the best malt is worth 21s 4d
That a quarter of the second malt is worth 20s attested by Edmund Hiorne, town clerk.

[f253v]

1284: *Assize*
The mayor and assistants give the assize following :-
The penny white loaf to weigh 7oz.3dwt. (= 7.15 oz.)
The penny wheaten to weigh 12oz.4dwt. (= 12.2 oz.)
The penny household to weigh 16oz.1dwt. (=16.05oz.)[84]
The barrell of the strongest beer and ale at 10s
The kilderkin of beer at 5s.
An ale quart of the best beer and ale for 1d
Two quarts of small drink for a penny 1d.
(signed by) John Glover, mayor, Joseph Harris, William Meatcalfe
Edmund Hiorne, town clerk.

[f254]

Flesh in Lent 2 March 1622.
Memorandum At a meeting at the guildhall of the aforesaid Borough before John Glover gent, mayor, and Joseph Harris gent, the King's Majesty's justices of the peace within the said borough the several parties hereunder written were sworn on a jury to enquire concerning the killing dressing and eating of flesh within this borough in this Lent time and on fish days appointed by the law to be strictly observed by all sorts of people As by His Majesty's proclamation given at Newmarket ('New markett') the fourth day of February last may appear.
1285: *Jury*

William Edwardes,	John Durbridge,	Henry Whiteside,
John Tassill,	John Pepper,	John Sea,
Edward Hull,	Thomas Godfery,	John Grainger,
William Seare,	William Butterfeild,	Richard Reade,
Christopher Smith.		

Who present that all is well. Edmund Hiorne, town clerk.

[f254v]

[Following sentence written and then crossed through]
Memorandum: 'it is ordered that no players hereafter but the Kings, princes.'[85]

84 These bread prices are notably higher than in Woodstock in the dearth year 1608, at similar grain prices.
85 Possibly a cancelled memo. relieving Lenten observance for royal players?

[f255]

Portmoot court held 4 March 1622.

Actions of debt:

1235:(16/16+) Pope vs Hollins - court wishes to consider.

1257:(11/11+) Luckett vs Warde - defendant places response and enjoins demurrer.

1268:4/4 Meatcalfe vs Pearte - discharged.

Action of trespass on case:

1269:4/4 Hickes vs Cubbidge - defendant brings writ of cerciorari dated 12 February 1622 returnable before the King in Chancery in quindene of Easter next. Plaintiff requests copy of writ; court wishes to consider upon allowance.

[f255v]

Actions of debt:

1270:(3/3+) Hobbs vs Silver - defendant responds non debet modo et forma and *venire facias* is granted.

Actions of trespass on case:

1272:(2/2+) Browne vs Norman - plaintiff puts declaration and requests day to amend the form in next court; first day of privilege granted to defendant.

1273:(2/2+) Francklyn vs Chewe - plaintiff puts declaration and requests day to amend the form in next court.

1274:(2/2+) Silver vs Hobbs - similarly.

1286:1/1 John Batt senior vs [blank] Jurden - discharged on behalf of plaintiff.

ENDPAPERS (i)[86]

[f256]

Undated

1287: The Freeman's oath of Woodstock

In Consideration of the Freedom of this Town granted unto you, ye shall from henceforth be obedient and attendant unto the Mayor and Aldermen and their officers in executing of their Offices, and to your power ye shall stick to the liberties, customs, and freedoms, of the same Borough of old time lawfully used, and by the King's progenitors granted, And by no means be assenting to the breach of any of them; And to be a quiet man amongst your neighbours always ready to do good and profitable things amongst them : And to pay your duties to God, and the King, and their officers, at the lawful summons and request of the Ministers thereto appointed, without grudging, from time to time, So help you God, and as you believe the contents of the book

86 See end of Introduction, xli.

ENDPAPERS (ii)

[f256v]

16th August 1619 In the time of William Fly gent, mayor of the borough

1288: The names of the mayor, aldermen and common council of the said borough appointed to be called and to sit in council as they are hereunder written:

The names of the common council

1. William Flye, mayor
2. Thomas Browne, alderman
3. John Glover, alderman
4. Joseph Harris, alderman
5. William Meatcalfe, alderman
6. Edmund Hiorne, town clerk
7. Simon Jeames gent
8. Thomas Rayer, chamberlain
9. John Dubber
10. Richard Meades
11. Nicholas Tayler
12. Robert Bignill
13. Thomas Williams
14. Thomas Meatcalfe
15. John Norman
16. Thomas Screevin
17. George Noble
18. William Rawnson
19. Robert Spittle
20. William Edwardes
21. Thomas Heathen
22. Henry Bradshewe
23. Bennett Painter
24. Richard Browne
25. Thomas Bruce

[f257]

Freemen not of the common council

John Dissell senr.
William Butterfeild
John Wilkinson
Francis Garter
Thomas Godferye
Thomas Gee
John Batt senr
John Batt Jnr
Alexander Head
John Pepper
John Durbridge
William Browne
John Doa
John Acklye
Roger Sturgis
William Hickes senior
William Hickes junior
Richard Reade
Robert Busbye
Christopher Smith
John Dissell Jnr
Richard Phillipps
John Grainger
Humfry Silver
William Richardson als.Lyddam
John Sea
Edward Hull
John Durman
Richard Plumpton
Richard Skaye
William Whitinge
Thomas Woodward
Henry Whiteside
Richard Coles
Robert Bruce
John Prise, Bryan Steephens

[f257v] (Blank)
[f258] (Blank)
[f258v]

ENDPAPERS (iii)
Borough of New Woodstock, Oxon

Sir Thomas Spencer knight and baronet, a Freeman and High Steward of this borough

1289: The names of the common council and of the Freemen and Inhabitants of this borough taken the 11th day of November 14 James I and VI 1616 in the time of William Rayer mayor of the aforesaid borough

Freemen of the common council viz:
William Rayer, alderman, mayor
Thomas Browne, alderman.
William Flye, alderman
John Glover, alderman
Joseph Harris, alderman.
Edmund Hiorne, town clerk
Simon Jeames, gent
William Meatcalfe)
John Norman) chamberlains
John Dubber
Thomas Williams
Richard Meades
Nicholas Taylor
Jerome White
Robert Bignill
Thomas Meatcalfe
John Lowe
Thomas Screevin
Richard Shadd
Edmund Rudgate, sergeant
George Noble
Thomas Rayer
William Edwardes
William Raunson
Robert Spitle

Freemen viz:

Richard Wrighte
John Dissell
John Wilkinson
William Butterfield
Richard Lowe
Francis Garter
Thomas Godferye
Thomas Gee
John Batt, senr
William Archer
Alexander Head
Robert Winter
Thomas Paynter
Bennett Paynter
John Ackley
William Hickes, senr
William Hickes, jnr
John Bruce
Thomas Bruce
Edward Carden
John Durbridge
John Pepper
Richard Hawkins
Richard Browne

[f259]

Freemen viz:
William Browne
Thomas Heathen
John Doa
Richard Reade
Nicholas Glover
John Price
Robert Spitle [crossed out]
Richard Coles
Bryan Steephens
Thomas Martyn
William Lyddam (als Richardes)
Francis Pyman
Robert Bruce
Thomas Lowe
John Batt, jnr
George Barnesley
Gyles Hooper

Foreign Freemen viz:

Humfry Fitzharberte gent

Henry Ladbrock
Phillip Jeames
Robert Bruce

Inhabitants of the said Borough which are not Freemen viz:
Jerome Keite gent
John Gadburye gent
Henry Bradshewe gent
William Holloway gent
Richard Pryvate
John Symons
William Porter
Anthony Deverill
John Mason
John Seely

[f259v] (Blank)
[f260] (Blank)
[f260v] (Blank)

ENDPAPERS (iv)

Three Woodstock dwelling feoffments of the 14th/15th centuries.

1290: A feoffment dated at Woodstock 4 June 30 Edward I (1302): Simon Jeffs of Woodstock sold to Robert of Bladon and his wife Joan that corner messuage with curtilage and a plot of vacant land with all its appurtenances everywhere, which messuage and curtilage are situated between the tenement formerly belonging to the said Walter of Bladon to the west and the said vacant plot to the east in Woodstock. And the said vacant plot of land between the king's highway leading to Oxford to the east and the said corner messuage and curtilage to the west in Woodstock and contains in width at the north end ten feet and at the other end to the south sixteen feet and in length from the upper part of the front of the said messuage to the end of the said curtilage.[87]
1291: A feoffment dated at Woodstock on the feast of St. Laurence in the ninth regnal year of king Edward, the fourth after the Conquest (10 August 1469): Walter Dennet of Woodstock sold to Richard Tayler *alias* Fyssher one parcel of my toft at the end of the town of Woodstock, which parcel lies between my toft to the east on one side and the tenement of the said Richard to the west on the other and contains in width thirteen feet by the highway and extends in length from the king's highway to the garden of the said Richard as it is enclosed by walls.[88]
1292: A feoffment dated 26 May in the tenth regnal year of king Henry the fourth after the Conquest (1409): John Dyer of Woodstock gave Richard Tayler who married my daughter Joan sixteen feet of my land, that is a small plot from my tenement extending in length from the wall of my house called 'le Spence' to my well on the said plot to the South and in width four feet from the window of the said house called 'le Spence' to the small plot of the said Richard to the East'.

[87] See *VCH*, xii, 336.
[88] See *VCH*, xii, 345, 359.

APPENDIX 1

List of Officers at Portmoot and Frankpledge Courts

These lists detail the changes recorded in the officers attending the court meetings :-
M = Mayor; Ch = Chamberlain; Co = Constable; Ti = Tithingmen
A-T = Aletasters

WBM B78/2

Portmoot

21 Dec.1607;	M:	William Meatcalfe	
	Ch:	William Rayer, John Glover	
	Co:	Edmund Rudgate, Thomas Williams	
	Ti:	Joseph Harris, John Lowe, Robert Seare, Richard Hawkins	
	A-T:	Ralph Durbridge, John Wilkinson	
	Sergeant: Henry Rudgate		
18 Jan.1608;	M:	Alderman Thomas Browne for William Meatcalfe	

Frankpledge

13 Apr.1608;	Ti:	John Bradshewe for John Lowe

Portmoot

3 Oct.1608;	M:	Thomas Bradshewe
31 Oct.1608;	Ti:	Francis Garter, Richard Hawkins, Thomas Martyn, William Kinge
12 Dec.1608;	no presiding JP named	
19 Dec.1608;	Ch:	Richard Meade for William Rayer
6 Feb.1609;	no presiding JP named	

Frankpledge

19 Oct.1609;	Co:	replaced by Joseph Harris and Thomas Meatcalfe
	Ti:	Robert Spitle, John Norman, William Bradshewe and Thomas Martyn
	A-T:	William King, Richard Shadd, Edmund Rudgate (deleted)

Portmoot

5 Mar.1610;	no presiding JP named	
16 Apr.1610;	A-T:	Francis Garter for William Kinge
13 Aug.1610;	Ti:	William Meatcalfe for Thomas Martyn
1 Oct. 1610;	M:	John Raunson elected Mayor

Frankpledge			
17 Oct.1610;	Co:	William Meatcalfe, William Bradshewe elected	
	Ti:	John Norman, John Doa, George Noble, Robert Ducock elected	
	A-T:	Richard Shad, John Doe	
Portmoot			
7 Jan.1611;	no presiding JP named		
	Ch:	Joseph Harris, Thomas Meatcalfe	
4 Feb.1611;	M:	William Rayer	
Frankpledge			
17 Apr.1611;	Thomas Williams, William Edwards elected Surveyors		
Portmoot			
26 Aug.1611;	no presiding JP named		
Frankpledge			
7 Oct.1611;	Co:	John Bradshewe, John Norman	
	Ti:	Robert Ducock, George Noble, Randall Richards and Richard Reade	
	A-T:	Richard Shad, Edward Longe	
Portmoot			
6 Apr.1612;	no officers other than mayor listed		
10 May 1612 (Sunday)	no officers other than mayor listed		
19 Oct.1612;	M:	John Glover	
	Sergeant:	Edmund Rudgate	
Frankpledge			
21 Oct.1612;	Co:	George Noble, Robert Ducock	
	Ti:	Thomas Gee, William Butterfeild, Richard Browne, William Archer	
	A-T:	Francis Garter, John Wilkinson	
Portmoot			
21 Dec.1612;	Ch:	William Bradshewe for Thomas Meatcalfe	
Frankpledge			
20 Oct.1613;	Co:	William Raunson for Robert Ducock	
	Ti:	Thomas Bruce for Thomas Gee	
	A-T:	William Hickes [senior] for Francis Garter	
Portmoot			
3 Jan.1614;	no officers other than mayor listed		

On five occasions (12 Dec.1608, 6 Feb.1609, 5 Mar.1610, 7 Jan. 1610/1 and 26 Aug. 1611), neither the mayor, nor another alderman, was recorded as the presiding JP at the Portmoot court. Presumably a JP did sit on those days, or at least an officer such as the town clerk or the sergeant must have helped in conducting proceedings. Conversely, on three sittings (6 Apr. and 10 May 1612, 3 Jan.1614) no officers other than the mayor are listed.

Periodically the lists of Portmoot officers have sums of money superscribed over individual names: sums are commonly 6d-12d, occasionally 2s6d or 3s4d, and exceptionally 20s against Richard Browne on 22 Nov.1613 following a succession of smaller sums. These moneys, which often occur in runs, may presumably refer to fines for misdemeanours such as absences from court.

WBM B78/3

Portmoot		
24 Jan.1614;	M:	John Glover
	Ch:	William Bradshewe, Thomas Williams
	Co:	George Noble, William Raunson
	Ti:	William Archer, William Butterfeild, Richard Browne, Thomas Bruce
	A-T:	John Wilkinson, William Hickes [sen]
Frankpledge		
20 Apr 1614;	M:	John Glover,
	JPs:	Jerome Kite, gent. Alderman Thomas Browne
Portmoot		
28 Jul.1614;	Co:	Thomas Screevin for William Raunson
Frankpledge		
19 Oct.1614;	M:	Joseph Harris
	Co:	Thomas Rayer, Richard Shadd for George Noble and Thomas Screevin
	Ti:	Thomas Heathen for Thomas Bruce
Portmoot		
9 Jan. 1615;	Ch:	William Meatcalfe for William Bradshewe
Frankpledge		
5 Apr.1615;	Alderman Thomas Browne and John Norman elected Surveyors of Highways	
Portmoot		
8 Jan.1616;	Ch:	John Norman for Thomas Williams
Frankpledge		
27 Mar.1616;	A-T:	William Hickes [jun] for William Hickes [sen]
Portmoot		
14 Oct.1616;	M:	William Rayer
	Co:	William Butterfeild for Thomas Heathen
	Ti:	John Durbridge, John Pepper, William Hickes [jun], Edward Carden

Frankpledge		
16 Apr.1617;	A-Ts not listed as present	
Portmoot		
13 Oct.1617;	Sergeant: Jerome White	
Portmoot		
22 Dec.1617;	Ch:	Thomas Rayer for John Norman
Portmoot		
18 Feb.1618;	Sergeant: Thomas Heathen	
Frankpledge		
13 Apr.1618;	Co:	John Pepper for Thomas Heathen
	Ti:	John Tassell for John Pepper
	Supervisors:	Nicholas Tayler, Thomas Williams
Portmoot		
19 Oct.1618;	M:	William Flye
Frankpledge		
21 Oct.1618;	Co:	William Edwardes, Richard Brown
	Ti:	Bryan Stevens, John Dissell [junior]
	A-T:	Francis Garter for William Hickes [junior]
Portmoot		
25 Jan.1619;	no presiding JP named	
Frankpledge		
7 Apr. 1619;	Co:	Henry Bradshewe, gent and Thomas Martyn elected
	Supervisors:	John Norman and Bartholomew Love elected
Portmoot		
16 Aug.1619;	Co:	William Raunson for Thomas Martyn
	Ti:	Robert Busby for William Hickes [junior]
Frankpledge		
27 Oct. 1619;	Co:	Bennett Painter for Henry Bradshewe
	Ti:	Henry Whiteside, Robert Bruce and Richard Plumpton elected
Portmoot		
24 Jan. 1620;	Ch:	George Noble for William Meatcalfe
21 Feb.1620;	Co:	Thomas Bruce for William Raunson
	Ti:	William Richardson [als.Lyddam] for Robert Busby. Richard Plumpton deleted.
27 Mar.1620;	Co:	Henry Whiteside for Thomas Bruce
	Ti:	Robert Busby for Henry Whiteside
Frankpledge		
12 Apr.1620;	Ti:	Richard Phillips for Richard Plumpton

Portmoot

16 Oct 1620; M: John Glover

Frankpledge

25 Oct.1620; Only two JPs presiding (M: John Glover and Jerome Kite gent)

18 and 28 Apr.1621; Jerome Kite JP refused to attend. Court held over (see Introduction)

Portmoot

7 and 14 May 1621; Ti: Three only named. (William Richardson not listed).

11 June 1621; Mayor presiding, list of officers missing.

Portmoot

23 Jul.1621;	Ti:	Edward Hull, John Say, Robert Bruce, Richard Phillips
20 Aug.1621;	Ti:	Thomas Warde for Richard Phillips

Frankpledge

24 Oct.1621;	JPs:	Jerome Kite and Alderman Joseph Harris
	Co:	Thomas Woodward for Henry Whiteside
	Ti:	John Durman, Christopher Smith for Robert Bruce and Thomas Warde
	A-T:	John Doa for John Wilkinson.

The officers attending Portmoot and Frankpledge courts are listed in full throughout B78/3 with only two exceptions (16 Apr.1617 and 25 Jan. 1618 – see above). On these occasions the missing names may be simply an oversight by the clerk.

After just one entry (12d for Richard Browne on 7 Feb. 1614) Hiorne ceased the practice of superscribing small sums over his lists of officers attending court. Presumably he used another document or system for these notes.

In general the officers of the court seem to change more frequently as the years progress and it is possible to detect the 'promotion' of some individuals from the lower to higher positions. Notably one or both of the constables was replaced on five occasions between April 1619 and March 1620 and a similar pattern of changes of tithingmen occurred during the same year.

APPENDIX 2

Portmoot Actions commenced in WBM B78/3 and unresolved at March 1622
[all on *f 255* and *255v* and indicated thus: - **1235**:(16/16+)]

1235: Pope vs Hollins
1257: Luckett vs Warde
1270: Hobbs vs Silver
1272: Browne vs Norman
1273: Franklyn vs Chewe
1274: Silver vs Hobbs

INDEX OF PERSONS

Reference is made only to the first appearances in cases, which can then be followed by case numbers in bold, e.g. **167**:1/11, 2/11 etc.; references on consecutive pages are run together; there may be more than one entry for a name on any page.

References to: Introduction pages are in roman numerals.
Ordinary numbers refer to text pages, not to folios.

Standard abbreviations have been used for Christian names.

Abbreviations: ald., alderman; appr., apprentice; bkr., baker; bart., baronet; blksm., blacksmith; bro., brother; butch., butcher; carp., carpenter; chamb., chamberlain; chandl., chandler; chapm., chapman; clk., clerk; cloth., clothier; cordw., cordwainer; counc., councillor; ct., court; d., died; dau., daughter; fam., family; frmn., freeman; husb., husbandman; innk., innkeeper; ironm., ironmonger; join., joiner; jun., junior; kt., knight; lab., labourer; m., married; sawy., sawyer; sen., senior; serg., sergeant-at-mace; shep., shepherd; shoem., shoemaker; s., son; svt., servant; tail., tailor; tan., tanner; vctlr., victualler; vint., vintner; Westm., Westminster; w., wife; wid., widow; W., Woodstock; yeo., yeoman.

Abbott
Edm., 121, 169
Edw., 213
Hen., 228
Isabel, w., of Jn., 131, 133, 138
Jn., W., non-frmn., sawy., 30, 48, 73, 94, 131, 138
Mary, w., of Thos., 138, 155, 179
Thos., W., frmn., sawy., vctlr., 4, 10, 27, 28, 29, 38, 48, 73, 84, 96, 128, 136, 138, 141, 155
Will., of Bladon, xxii, 70, 77, 79, 117, 144, 149, 173, 213
Abbott(e)s
Robt., Bishop of Salisb., 235, 241
Abraham (Abram)
(als. Me(a)tcalf(e)), Thos., 99
(als. Me(a)tcalf(e)), Will., jun., W., 198, 313
Ackl(e)y (Acklie)
Jn., jun., 131
Jn., W., frmn., vctlr., 4, 7, 10, 27, 28, 29, 38, 39, 48, 63, 68, 73, 83, 84, 95, 96, 103, 107, 110, 113, 114, 128, 129, 141, 144, 145, 146, 155, 156, 162, 169, 172, 178, 182, 196, 206, 218, 230, 234, 238, 239, 244, 249, 258, 259, 270, 279, 291, 292, 300, 307, 308, 319, 327, 345, 349, 363, 364
Ric., 332
Ad(d)ams
Simon, shoem., 105, 107
Walt., 58
Addison
Robt., butch., 5
Aingell. *See also* Ayngell
Jn., 317
Alberte (Albett, Albott)
Hen., xxii, 51, 66, 67, 70, 72, 285, 286
Allen
Robt., 113
Thos., 324
Will., 289, 293
Allibone
Kath., w., of Thos., 325
Thos., 325
Allsope (Allsopp)
Ann, (wid., of Jn. Bradshewe, (d. 1613)), w., of Jas., 232
Jas., 158, 232, 250, 262

Altoffe
Will., 63
Amsden
Anth., 325
Anckorne
Edw., 233
Androwes
Jn., 229
Margery, wid., 320
Thos., 247
Annison
Jn., 61, 68, 188
Robt., 61, 68, 188, 247, 250
Anstell (als. Austen)
Ric., 57
apMorgan
Jn., chapm., 166
Arabella
the Lady, 111
Archer
Clement, W., appr., 112
Jn., W., svt., 24, 30, 128, 151, 153, 175, 332
Robt., W., tail., 131
Will., W., frmn., tail., vctlr., 29, 115, 128, 129, 155, 156, 172, 182, 196, 205, 214, 234, 244, 245, 258, 275, 279, 280, 291, 292, 297, 300, 301, 307, 309, 312, 315, 364, 368, 369
Arden
Jn., 236
Armestronge
Geo., 320
Arthure
Jas., of Eynsham, yeo., 103
Ascole (Ashcole)
Jn., of Hanborough, 103, 110
Ashley
Sir Francis, recorder of Dorchester, Dorset, xxxv
Ashpole (Ashpoole)
--., 1
a boy, 93
Jn., W., non-frmn., 25, 30, 37
wid., W., vctlr., 93, 97, 106
Aston
Chris., 227, 228, 229
Humph., 232
Austen (Austine)
Will., 102, 116, 224, 264, *See also* Anstell
Ayers
(als. Digger), Jn., 246
Anne, w., of Will., (Islip), 337
Will., of Islip, 186, 336, 337
Will., s., of Will., (Islip), 186
Ayleworth
Thos., gent., 1
Will., gent., 275, 281
Ayngell. *See also* Aingell
Geo., of Evesham, Worcs., join., 16
Aynger (Ainger)
Thos., 82

Bache (Back)
Will., 160, 224, 260
Bagge
Edw., 105
Bagott
Walt., JP., of Blithfield, Staffs., 104
Bagwell
Mr., of Oxford, gaoler, 13
Thos., 293
Baker
Geo., 218
Jn., of Witney, cloth., 24
Ric., 170
Will., 22
Ball
Dorothy, w., of Will, 42
Jn., 183, 186, 189, 195, 206, 219, 313, 349
Will., W., counc., ironm., (d. 1615), 29, 34, 39, 42, 50, 64, 108, 109, 110
Banting(e)
Ric., Old W., tan., 291
Robt., s., of Ric., Old W., 295
Barnaby
Priscilla, W., 36, 316, 327
Barnes
Alice, wid., 176, 178
Ann, w., of Ric., xxxiv, 99, 100, 131, 133
Edw., W., 23, 29, 73
Jn., s., of Ric. & Ann, tail., xxxiii, xxxiv, 98, 107, 130, 133, 138, 188
Ric., W., non-frmn., 30, 99, 101, 133

Barnesey (Barnsey)
Geo., W., frmn., join., 169
Barneshawe (-shewe)
children, 6
Hen., xxvii, 6, 11
Thos., 232
Barnesly (Barnesley, Barnsly)
Geo., 269, 270, 365
Barnsdall (als. Barnslee)
Fras., 295
Barraclewe
Ric., of York, carrier, 13
Barrett (Barratt)
Dorothy, wid., 224
Jn., 38
Jn., of Weston-on-the-Green, yeo., 146
Owen, of Weston-on-the-Green, (d. by 1612), 146
Ric., of Deddington, 163
Robt., 224
Barrie (Barry, Bery)
Vincent, 111
Bartlett
Jn., 257, 276
Basly (Basley, Baslie)
Thos., of Deddington, butch., xxii, xxvi, xxxvi, 81, 92, 94, 162, 181, 183, 189
Bassett
Edw., gent., of Dunham, Notts., 179
Edw., gent., of Woodstock park, 230
Batson
Ellinor, 332
Batt
--., 1
Jn., (described 'jun'), W., frmn., xxi, 276, 328, 363, 365
Jn., (described 'sen'), W., 266, 312, 313, 361, 363, 364
Jn., W., frmn., currier, xxi, xxv, 1, 8, 19, 29, 212, 219, 241, 257, 258, 259, 262, 305
Battman
Jn., of Clifton-upon-Dunsmore, Warks., 56
Ric., bro. of Jn., 56
Bayles (Baylies)
Edm., 170
Edw., 187, 189
Hen., 170
Jn., 229
Ric., 85, 86
Roger, (d. by 1621), 341
Walt., s. of Roger, 341
Will., s. of Roger, 341
Beacham (Beecham)
--., of Nottingham, 14
Thos., of Bromley, Kent, horse-dealer, 13
Beck
Robt., 42
Beckly(e)
Guy, Old W., non-frmn., 30, 239
Becon(e)
Will., 255
Bed(d)all
Thos., 111, 251
Bedwell
Will., 293
Beedle
Geo., W., shoem., svt., 24
Beesly
Walt., 322
Belcher
Alice, W., 81, 150, 156
Jane, wid., 204
Robt., s. of Alice, W., appr., 70, 81
Thos., 66
Will., 102
Bellingham
Thos., 7
Bellsire
Thos., 30
Bennet(t)
--., w. of Humph., 90
Alice, w. of Geo., xxxvi, 118
Fras., s. of Ric., W., appr., 275
Geo., of Hanlinge, Worcs., lab., xxxvi, 118
Humph., of Bladon, 37, 90
Jn., Old W., non-frmn., 30, 239
Ric., W., woolwinder, 219, 275
Bently (Bentley, Bentlie)
--., of Cutteslowe mill, (his man), 131
Ric., W., 236, 295, 303, 319, 322, 325, 350, 358

Benwell
Will., of Littlemore, 143
Berriman
Jn., 295
Berry. *See* Barrie
Bewe
Thos., 160
Bickerstaffe
Will., 49
Bicks (Bicke)
Ric., of Great Tew, vctlr, 54
Bickton
Gilbert, als. Robt., als. Cupit, The Bell, St.Margaret's, Westm. vint., 178
Bigg(e)s
Thos., gent., of Stanton St. John, 188, 193
Bignill (Bignell)
Eliz., w. of Robt., 120
Jn., 295, 328
Robt., W., counc., bkr., vctlr., 3, 4, 7, 9, 11, 27, 29, 34, 35, 38, 41, 42, 45, 46, 50, 52, 61, 62, 64, 65, 67, 74, 77, 83, 84, 87, 102, 103, 110, 118, 120, 121, 129, 137, 141, 145, 147, 153, 155, 158, 160, 162, 163, 168, 175, 177, 182, 183, 191, 199, 200, 206, 213, 214, 218, 220, 228, 239, 245, 252, 254, 263, 264, 269, 271, 288, 300, 301, 304, 308, 314, 315, 327, 328, 329, 332, 334, 338, 339, 340, 350, 359, 363, 364
Billinge
Fras., 260
Billins
Andrew, of London, scrivener, 12
Bincks (Binckes, Bynks)
Robt., of Bladon, xxii, 70, 73, 140, 169, 176, 225, 248, 295, 310
Thos., 155
Bird(e)
Chris., The Bell, St.Margaret's, Westm., vint., 178
Jn., 67
Thos., gent., 292
Birk
Ric., 233
Bishop
Mary, of Oxford, xxxv, 16
Blackman
Simon, 39
Blacknall
Thos., 247, 250
Blake
Thos., 121
Blay
Martin, of Littlemore, yeo., 142
Blith (Blithe, Blyth)
Edm., 227, 295
Thos., W., counc., (d. by 1613), 4, 29, 36, 42, 45, 50, 61, 68, 74, 83, 102, 118, 144
Will., 286
Blunt
Nic., 310
Boddely (Bodely)
Will., W., cutler, 87, 88, 93, 186, 189, 208
Boddy(e)
Geo., 253
Jn., W., non-frmn., 30
Bolter
Eliz., w. of Jn., 289
Jn., 289
Bonde
Jn., 267
Borman
Will., 44
Bostock
Will., gent., xxiii, 346, 347
Boult(e)
Greg., 167
Leonard, 252, 271
Thos., 202, 248
Bowden
Jn., of Merton, yeo., 188, 190, 193
Bowine
Lodwick, of Barton, 336
Bowland
Eliz., wid., W., non-frmn., 30, 174
Bowle
Hen., 244
Ric., 244
Bowman
Chris., W., non-frmn., 30, 248, 268
Rog., 153

Bown
Fras., of County Radnor, 58
Bownie
Lewis, clk., 324
Boyse
(Horace?), 267
Bradborne
Will., 37, 61, 78, 92
Bradford(e)
Thos., of Ludlow, Salop., sawy., xxxv, 43
Bradforth
Brian, 66
Bradshewe (Bradshawe)
--., w. of Will., (mercer), 130
Alice, wid., 292
Ann (Allsopp), wid. of Jn., 232
Hen., gent., W., counc., innk., 182, 196, 200, 206, 213, 218, 248, 300, 345, 363, 365, 370
Jane, dau. of Thos., 172
Jas., s. of Thos., 240
Jn., W., counc., mercer, (d. 1613), 9, 18, 19, 21, 26, 29, 30, 34, 45, 50, 53, 57, 61, 63, 65, 67, 74, 77, 83, 84, 95, 98, 102, 107, 110, 113, 114, 115, 118, 119, 120, 121, 126, 141, 142, 153, 155, 156, 158, 162, 169, 177, 178, 182, 191, 199, 232, 367, 368
Mr., 301
Ralph, s. of Will., (mercer), xxix, 285
Ric., 99
Thos., gent., W., ald., JP., innk., (d. 1613), xxxii, xxxvii, xxxviii, 5, 6, 8, 10, 12, 16, 22, 23, 24, 25, 26, 28, 29, 34, 35, 36, 37, 38, 39, 41, 42, 43, 46, 47, 48, 50, 51, 52, 53, 54, 58, 59, 61, 63, 66, 70, 73, 74, 76, 77, 81, 82, 83, 84, 91, 92, 95, 96, 102, 103, 110, 111, 112, 113, 114, 118, 120, 129, 130, 131, 138, 139, 141, 147, 150, 156, 160, 162, 165, 168, 172, 258, 367
wid., (Joan) mother of Will., & Jn., (mercers) W., non-frmn., (d. by 1616), 30, 100
Will., s. of Thos., W., counc., vctlr., 93, 316, 339, 341, 350
Will., W., counc., mercer, (d. 1616), xvi, xxxiii, xxxiv, 3, 29, 30, 34, 36, 39, 45, 50, 57, 61, 63, 74, 83, 84, 97, 102, 107, 111, 114, 118, 129, 130, 141, 144, 148, 155, 156, 158, 160, 182, 187, 193, 195, 199, 207, 210, 211, 218, 227, 230, 234, 236, 285, 367, 368, 369
Brangwin(e)
--., 79
Fras., 66
Brent(e)
(als. Brunte), Esau, 171
Christian, wid., 265
Kath., wid., 265
Brewer
Chris., 279
Bridges
Gray, Lord Chandos (Shandoes), xxvi, xxxv, 321
Will., of Oxford, lab., 43
Brockwell
Hen., 224
Brod
Anth., of Broadway, Worcs., 16
Brooke(s) (Brokes)
Jn., 202, 282
Tobias, 176, 225
Will., of Eynsham, 47
Brooman
Jn., of Littlemore, (d. 1612), xxxi, 142
Will., bro. of Jn., of Littlemore, yeo., 143
Brotherton
Will., 8
Brown(e)
(als. Robins), Ellin, w. of Will., 357
--., 247
Edm., 58, 62
Edw., of Eynsham, bkr., xxiii, 99, 102, 107, 117
Hen., kt., of Kiddington, 140
Jn., W., non-frmn., 30
Mr., 303
Ric., W., counc., butch., 54, 58, 62, 156, 172, 192, 196, 205, 228, 230, 236, 243, 249, 267, 279, 280, 282, 291, 292, 301, 304, 308, 312, 314,

Ric., W. (cont.), 315, 317, 334, 335, 342, 345, 349, 359, 363, 364, 368, 369, 370, 371
Thos., gent., W., ald., JP., (d. 1620), xx, xxvii, xxxii, xxxiv, 1, 3, 5, 7, 8, 10, 11, 12, 15, 16, 20, 22, 23, 24, 25, 26, 28, 30, 34, 35, 36, 38, 39, 41, 42, 43, 46, 47, 50, 52, 53, 54, 59, 61, 63, 64, 70, 73, 74, 77, 82, 83, 84, 86, 90, 91, 92, 93, 95, 97, 102, 103, 105, 108, 110, 111, 113, 114, 118, 120, 124, 129, 130, 138, 139, 141, 144, 156, 160, 161, 162, 165, 166, 168, 170, 172, 173, 178, 182, 186, 191, 195, 204, 205, 206, 210, 213, 218, 219, 220, 229, 238, 240, 248, 249, 259, 264, 270, 271, 279, 281, 291, 300, 301, 307, 308, 312, 314, 316, 317, 318, 328, 341, 363, 364, 367, 369
Thos., jun., gent., Rector of Bladon, 341
Thos., woolman, 341
Will., W., frmn., 107, 207, 219, 280, 300, 357, 363, 365
wid., 303

Brownelowe (Brownckloe, Brounckloe)
Will., gent., 314
--., clk., at Westm., 267, 294, 311, 335

Bruce
Geo., 62
Jn., W., frmn., shoem., 15, 24, 29, 36, 38, 66, 249, 269, 284, 364
Ric., 281
Robt., jun., 53
Robt., W., frmn., shoem., 24, 29, 36, 38, 62, 99, 107, 206, 209, 211, 238, 256, 283, 284, 291, 292, 300, 307, 313, 314, 327, 329, 335, 337, 342, 345, 349, 351, 353, 359, 363, 365, 370, 371
Thos., W., counc., shoem., 29, 128, 129, 157, 178, 182, 196, 205, 206, 213, 214, 218, 220, 230, 234, 244, 249, 270, 283, 300, 327, 337, 342, 345, 351, 363, 364, 368, 369, 370

Buckley
Will., 327

Buller
Jn., 221, 318
Judy, wid. of Will., 197
Ric., 197, 282
Will., (d. by 1614), 8, 197

Bulliphant
Edw., 221, 295

Bullock
Will., 295, 296

Burcott
Edw., 330

Burgen (Burgin, Burgine)
Geo., 280
Mary, w. of Geo., 280
Nic., 254
Thos., 329

Burgis
Thos., 306

Burnett
--., of Northants., 163

Busby(e)
Edw., (W., barber?), 153
Eliz., 182
Hugh, of Sandford St.Martin, vctlr., 76
Jn., W., tail., 315
Ric., 8, 63, 126
Robt., W., frmn., tail., 299, 300, 304, 307, 308, 309, 315, 317, 325, 333, 359, 363, 370
Will., 289

Butcher (Boutcher)
Hen., 67
Robt., 53
Thos., 73
Troylus, of Combe, 66, 251

Butler
Edm., gent, 58, 62
Jn., 181
Will., 202

Butterfeild
Will., W., frmn., tail., xxxiii, 29, 93, 98, 103, 128, 136, 138, 145, 153, 155, 156, 172, 178, 186, 196, 205, 213, 214, 218, 228, 230, 232, 234, 239, 249, 252, 258, 263, 264, 269, 280, 301, 306, 312, 316, 333, 334, 335, 338, 339, 341, 345, 349, 353, 359, 360, 363, 364, 368, 369

Cale
Ric., 224
Callcott
Walt., 109
Cambree
Fras., 227
Camden
Edw., 113
Caple
Edw., (als. Jn.), 113, 118, 227
Mr., of Caple, Herefs., 125
Capp
Ann, w. of Maurice, 168
Maurice, 164, 168, 203
Carden
Anne, wid. of Edw., W., vctlr., 316, 339, 341, 359
Edw., W., frmn., vctlr., (d. 1619), 239, 249, 252, 259, 263, 269, 280, 292, 300, 301, 364, 369
Carpenter
Edw., 19
Carter
Geo., 140
Hugh, 113
Ric., 274
Thos., (of Wootton?), 108
Cartright
Jn., 108
Cashworth
Thos., of Edenbridge, Kent, tan., 58
Castell
Thos., s. of Will., appr., 283
Will., of Wootton, yeo., 38, 119, 283
Catesby
Isabel, dau. of Marg., W., svt., 7
Marg., of Great Tew, 7
Cave
Jn., 167
Chadwell
Mr., 165
Chamberlain (-laine,-layn,-lyn)
Edw., 299
Helen, w. of Robt., 51
Robt., W., 6, 51
Thos., (of Wootton?), 109
Champnies
Gowin, gent., 322
Chandos, Lord, *see* Bridges
Charles
--., w. of Jn., xx
Jn., xx, 86
Charlett
Jn., clk., 280
Charman
Jn., 77, 151
Chaundler
Jonas, of Watford, Herts., horsescorcer, 129
Cherry
Alice, w. of Robt., 129
Jn., of Ledwell, 54
Ric., of Cassington, yeo., 40, 47
Robt., of Cassington, xxiii, 126, 129
Chesterman
Jas., of Oxford, 95
Chettwine
Will., kt., JP., Staffs., 104
Chewe
Jn., 357
Child
Jn., gent., 161, 189
Churchill
Hen., 283
Claridge
Ric., W., 342
Clark(e)
Edw., of Bicester, glover, 24, 112, 185, 189, 320
Ric., 302
Thos., 232
Will., W., appr., 113
Cleevely
Jn., 102
Clement(e) (Clements, Clemens)
Ralph, of Bicester, tan., xxix, 285
Thos., 218
Will., 246, 299
Coates (Cotes)
Will., sen., xxiii, 346, 347
Cobbett
Jn., (of Marston?), 60, 72, 79
Cole
Magdalen, 126
Colegrove
Will., of Bladon, 72

Coleman
Edw., 160, 167
Coles
--., 164
Giles, W., non-frmn., 30, 157
Jn., W., 150
Joyce, wid., W., (d. 1613), xxxii, 173
Kath., w. of Ric., 303, 304, 305
Nic., s. of Ric., W., appr., 335
Ric., W., frmn., butch., xxi, 4, 22, 30, 73, 74, 128, 160, 164, 250, 256, 303, 304, 305, 312, 314, 333, 335, 349, 359, 363, 365
Colesborne
Hen., 170
Ric., (of Bladon?), 93, 216
Collett
Ric., 152
Collier (Collyer, Colliar)
Edw., of North Leigh, miller, 166
Jas., of Harborough, Leics., shoem., 105
Phil., 9, 36, 50
Simon, W., non-frmn., 9, 25, 30, 34, 36, 37, 102, 126, 228
Will., 283
Collingwood
--., 189
Ananias, s. of Fras., 206, 219
fam., xxvii
Fras., W., counc., woolman, (d. 1613), xxi, xxvii, 9, 26, 29, 34, 35, 36, 39, 42, 50, 58, 60, 64, 65, 68, 74, 102, 103, 110, 118, 128, 129, 141, 149, 155, 161, 193
Jn., s. of Fras.,, 36, 174, 184, 191, 206, 208, 219, 254, 300, 301
Joan, wid. of Fras., xxvii, 174, 182, 184, 191, 254
Mary, w. of Jn., 174
Ric., s. of Fras., 99, 184, 211, 220, 254, 340
Collinridge
Jn., 187
Collins
Mich., 343
Combes (Coombs)
Jn., W., non-frmn., 29, 81
Cook(e)
Edw., kt., of Westm., 236
Jn., of Begbroke, xxii, 70, 72, 78, 132, 139, 155, 157, 160, 167, 168, 186, 203, 204, 257, 260, 298, 309
Joan, w. of Jn., 132, 167
Cooper
Ann, W., svt., 98
Jn., W., non-frmn., 30
Cornish(e)
Hen., of Chipping Norton, 289, 306
Thos., (of Witney?), 40
Cotten
Jn., 213
Cottmore
Thos., 320
Cowurde
Geo., gent., 337
Cox
Jn., 246
Ralph, of Hanborough, 162
Thos., bro. of Ralph., of Deddington, 163
Craddock
Jn., 165
Crafte
Thos., 251
Craker
Jn., 86, 175, 189
Crok(e)
Jn., kt., JP., Bucks., 23
Croker
Hen., gent., 274
Crony(e)
Jn., xxv, 106, 263
Crook(e) Crooks
John, kt., King's Justice, 84, 92, 236
Crosly
Mris., 76
Crosse
Anth., 186
Crosshawe(-ewe) (Croshawe(-ewe), Crowshawe)
Edm., gent., 113
Raughlen (Rawlen, Rawly), 284, 285
Crowdson
Anth., W., slater, 316, 317, 327, 331
Margaret, dau. of Anth. & Prisc. Barnaby, 329

Crutchl(e)y
Geoff., 67
Cubige (Cubbidge)
Mich., 356
Culpep(p)er
Walter, esq., JP., xv, 35
Cumpton
Will., 287
Cundall
Eliz., W., svt., 132
Cupper
Jn., gent., 284
Curtis
Jn., 238, 281, 282

Daby(e) (Dabie)
Will., 171
Dalby(e)
Jn., 113
Damery(e) (Damerie)
Alice, w. of Anth., 115
Anth., of Bladon, 86, 115, 140
fam., of Bladon, masons, xxvii
Danforde
Robt., of Shipston-on-Stour, Warks., vctlr., 104
Danniell
Jn., of London, tallow chandl., 22
Will., 209
Daunter
Abraham, W., weaver, (d. 1604), xxvii
Joan, wid. of Abraham, xxvii, 143
Davi(e)s
(als. Butcher), Jn., 26
Humph., 126
Jn., 289
Joan, wid., 297
Daysey (Deysey)
Jn., Old W., non-frmn., 30, 239
Deane
Emma, 260
Thos., 182
Dearle. *See* Witham
Debanck
(als. Johnson), Robt., xxxvi, 55
Hen., bro. of Robt., of Droitwich, Worcs., 55
Thos., tail., 135
Decon
--., wid., of Evesham, 16
Dennet(t)
fam., xli
Mich., 149
Walt., W., 366
Dennis
Donhowe, 24
Deverill (Deverell)
Anth., W., non-frmn., 190, 223, 245, 300, 301, 315, 341, 350, 365
Ric., 251
Dewe
(als. Sadler), Jn., 226
Will., 108
Dey(e)
Geo., s. of Jn., 2
Jn., (d. by 1608), 2
Thos., 67
Digger. *See* Ayers
Dimock
Robt., of Ditchley, svt., to Sir Henry Lee, xxxvi, 160, 168
Dingl(e)y (Dinglie)
Edulph(e), gent., W., (d. 1622), 228, 304
Dison
Robt., of Inkberrow, Worcs., yeo., 108
Will., of Inkberrow, Worcs., yeo., 108
Dissell (Dissill)
Jas., W., frmn., 15, 29, 45, 63, 66, 68, 74
Jn., jun., W., frmn., 363, 370
Jn., W., frmn., innk., 3, 4, 10, 29, 30, 34, 48, 53, 96, 110, 114, 128, 129, 141, 182, 196, 206, 218, 291, 353, 363, 364
Doa (Doe)
Jn., W., frmn., xxiii, 29, 62, 83, 84, 99, 102, 107, 109, 110, 280, 312, 315, 333, 334, 335, 351, 359, 363, 365, 368, 371
Mary, w. of Jn., 107
Ric., W., non-frmn., 30
Dod(s)
Geo., 210
Mr., of Holborn, London, 55
Dodwell
Phil., 215

Dol(e)man
(his charity), xl
Mr., 23, 25
Dolefyn
Will., of Adlestrop, Glos., 16
Dolton
Jn., 170
Doren
Jn., kt., JP., Bucks., 23
Dormer
Justine, 199
Dowson
Arth., 232, 259, 260, 261
Drewe (Gregory?)
--., 1
Drinkwater
Jn., 126, 129
Dubber
Jn., W., counc., shoem., 9, 11, 15, 29, 30, 34, 35, 36, 37, 38, 41, 61, 63, 83, 95, 110, 113, 115, 141, 156, 159, 168, 182, 191, 196, 205, 213, 215, 218, 220, 229, 234, 238, 239, 247, 259, 270, 279, 291, 301, 307, 314, 315, 334, 337, 348, 359, 363, 364
Ducock
Robt., W., frmn., 29, 83, 95, 103, 110, 112, 113, 115, 120, 121, 129, 144, 156, 158, 162, 169, 182, 368
Dudson
Edw., 289
Duncombe
Jn., gent., 259
Dunford(e)
Will., W., non-frmn., xxvii, 44, 60, 66, 124, 236, 251
Durbridge
--., 27, 188
Jn., W., frmn., vctlr., 249, 259, 264, 269, 270, 280, 291, 300, 315, 327, 329, 333, 334, 337, 338, 339, 341, 345, 349, 351, 353, 359, 360, 363, 364, 369
Ralph, W., frmn., vctlr., (d. 1614), 7, 10, 26, 28, 29, 35, 39, 46, 48, 50, 58, 84, 95, 96, 107, 114, 118, 129, 141, 142, 144, 153, 155, 156, 177, 182, 196, 367
Will., 76, 79, 217
Durdon
Thos., 120
Durman
Jn., W., frmn., 309, 314, 319, 327, 329, 349, 351, 353, 363, 371
Durran(d)
Ric., of London, player, 43
Thos., of Stratton Audley, Oxon, 35
Dutton
Jn., 201
Thos., 218
Dyer
Jn., W., (1409), 366

East(e) (Este)
Chris., of Bletchingdon, xxii, 44, 79, 172, 179, 180, 187, 189
Eden(s) (Eedens)
Ric., of Oxford, butch., 317
Will., 306
Edging(e)
(als. Love), Barth., W., non-frmn., glover, 30, 46, 78, 185, 193, 300, 351, 370
--., 189
Edkins (Edgkins)
Jn., 109
Sericum, 289
Edmunds
Nic., 281
Edward(e)s
Will., svt., to Edw., Painter of Woodstock park, 93
Will., W., counc., vctlr., 3, 5, 7, 9, 10, 26, 27, 28, 29, 30, 34, 36, 37, 38, 39, 41, 42, 45, 48, 50, 53, 63, 67, 72, 73, 74, 83, 84, 92, 95, 96, 103, 107, 110, 113, 114, 115, 118, 121, 129, 141, 144, 145, 147, 153, 155, 156, 158, 162, 169, 177, 178, 182, 183, 196, 205, 206, 214, 218, 221, 223, 228, 229, 232, 234, 238, 239, 244, 249, 252, 258, 259, 263, 264, 269, 270, 279, 280, 283, 291, 292, 300, 301, 308, 314, 315, 319, 327, 329, 333, 334, 337, 338, 339, 340, 341, 345, 349, 351, 353, 359, 360, 363, 364, 368, 370

Eglesbee
Jn., 106, 188
Elfrite
Jn., 212
Elliott
Jn., of Deddington, 118
Nic., 92, 197, 204, 210
Evans
Edm., of Edenbridge, Kent, gardener, 58
Edw., W., clk., (Rector of Woodstock), 245
Will., bro. of Edm., (of Lymm?), Cheshire, 58
Every (E(a)verie)
Thos., of Begbroke, 107
Ewans
Edm., 228

Farney
Ric., 256
Farrer
Jn., of Oxford, innk., 43
Fawdery(e)
Hugh, 151, 256
Ric., of Cleveley, 310
Will., 349
Will., s. of Ric., 310
Fawler
Jn., of Hanborough, xxii, 153, 155, 156, 157, 158, 164, 168
Feilding
Will., kt., of Newnham, Warks., 148
Feildsman
Buster, 188
Fidler
Edm., 128, 139
Edw., 109
Fras., 144
Finmore
Alice, w. of Jn., 324
Jn., of Northbrook, 324
Fitzharbert(e)
Humph., gent., of Begbroke, foreign frmn., xxii, 85, 94, 118, 365
Flem(m)ing(e)
children of Eliz., xxvii
Eliz., wid., W., non-frmn., xxvii, 30, 51, 97
Geo., s. of Eliz., 97
Jn., s. of Eliz., 97
Fletcher
Hen., of London, barb.surg., 307
Hen., W., counc., ironm., (d. 1595), 264
Jos., s. of Hen., (London), W., appr., 307
Margery, wid. of Hen., W., non-frmn., 30, 264
Ric., 320, 321, 349
Thos., (of Bladon?), 237, 251, 268, 329
Will., 224
Flexny(e) (Flexney, Flexnie)
(als. Hickes), Will., 160
Hen., of Stanton Harcourt, 119
Will., 197, 289, 317
Floyd(e) (Floyed)
Lewis, of Salop., tail., 166
Fly(e)
Ann, w. of Will., 122
Jn., 131
Mary, w. of Salloman, 124, 181
Mr., xxxviii
Salloman, s. of Will., W., non-frmn., xxi, xxvi, xxvii, 30, 77, 122, 124, 128, 181, 231, 238
Will., W., ald., 29, 35, 42, 82, 94, 110, 122, 124, 258, 274, 290, 291, 300, 301, 302, 303, 304, 307, 308, 309, 312, 314, 315, 316, 320, 328, 363, 364, 370
Ford(e)
Jn., 248
Jos., 222, 223
Forest
--., 1
Forty (Fortie)
Chris., of Sandford St. Martin, 78, 187, 198, 215, 299
Fowler
Ric., of Great Barrington, Glos., 59
Fox
Edw., 200
Kath., W., svt., 99
Francis (Frauncis)
Geo., 350
shepherd to Mr.Gregorie, 137

Franklyn (Francklyn)
Hen., 68
Jn., 229
Ric., 217, 357
Rowland, 224
Frewen
Jn., of Littlemore, 143
Fryer
Will., 92
Fyndall
Anth., gent., 285, 286
Ric., 345

Gadbury(e)
Jn., gent., W., non-frmn., 7, 29, 81, 145, 146, 285, 291, 365
Mr., 39
Will., gent., 70, 153
Galloway
Ric., of Hanborough, 162
Garter
--., 165
Fras., W., frmn., 4, 5, 7, 15, 26, 29, 30, 36, 37, 41, 45, 46, 48, 50, 53, 61, 63, 73, 74, 78, 141, 144, 145, 153, 155, 156, 158, 182, 291, 312, 351, 363, 364, 367, 368, 370
Gaskine
Dorothy, 114
Gearing(e)
Jn., 224
Thos., 111
Gee
Thos., W., frmn., 23, 29, 48, 73, 120, 128, 145, 155, 156, 158, 162, 182, 214, 252, 269, 280, 281, 312, 363, 364, 368
Gelly
Eliz., W., 342
Georg(e)
--., 188
Jn., of Ledwell, blksm., xxxiii, 54, 181
Mich., 106
Nic., 60
'the winder', 107
Gibbs
Jn., of Bletchingdon, blksm., 187
Jn., W., non-frmn., 30
Lettice, wid., W., 92
Gibson
Thos., 21
Gilberd (Gilbert)
(als. Twinch), Will., 158
Jn., W., non-frmn., 30
Giles. *See* Gyles
Gilke(s)
Ric., 272, 344
Will., W., non-frmn., 30
Glover
Jn., gent., W., ald., innk., xxxiv, 10, 11, 12, 24, 27, 28, 29, 34, 35, 38, 41, 42, 43, 46, 48, 61, 74, 96, 102, 105, 110, 114, 128, 141, 152, 156, 160, 162, 165, 166, 168, 170, 172, 174, 178, 179, 181, 182, 184, 189, 191, 193, 195, 196, 205, 206, 212, 218, 237, 245, 248, 266, 271, 293, 301, 319, 323, 326, 327, 332, 333, 334, 335, 336, 337, 338, 339, 340, 341, 345, 346, 348, 350, 353, 358, 359, 360, 363, 364, 367, 368, 369, 371
Joan, wid. of Nic., W., vctlr., 301, 315, 321, 323, 339, 341, 359
Nic., W., frmn., vctlr., (d. 1620), 7, 9, 10, 23, 28, 30, 34, 36, 39, 73, 84, 96, 114, 141, 142, 182, 193, 196, 206, 218, 219, 234, 239, 246, 323, 365
Goddard
Ric., 267
Godfery(e)
-., 27
Thos., W., frmn., glover, vctlr., 4, 10, 24, 28, 29, 34, 39, 46, 47, 48, 84, 96, 110, 114, 141, 182, 196, 204, 206, 215, 218, 239, 244, 245, 252, 279, 280, 300, 307, 308, 312, 314, 315, 327, 329, 333, 334, 335, 338, 339, 340, 341, 342, 345, 349, 351, 353, 359, 360, 363, 364
Godwine
Anth., of Wookey, Som., 8
Will., of Wookey, Som., yeo., 8
Goffe
Jn., 317
Goldsmith
Jn., 311

Gome
Thos., 160, 167
Goode
Justin, 83
Goodiar
Edw., 285, 288
Goodwin
Fras., kt., JP., Bucks., 23
Grainger
Jn., 359, 360, 363
Greene
Jn., 11, 203
Ric., 226
Ric., Old W., miller, 245
Will., 283
Greeneway
Ric., 306
Gregory(e) (Gregorie)
--., 1
Drewe, W., frmn., cutler, 10, 29, 70, 112, 122, 124, 129, 137, 155, 158, 232
Fras., esq., s. of Jn., (dec'd), of Hordley, xxiii, 173, 181, 229
Jn., gent., of Hordley, (d. April 1613), xxii, 12, 60, 63, 70, 72, 136, 173
Gresbrooke
Ric., 286
Griffine
Joan, wid., of Britwell, Oxon, 28
Grigson
Ric., clk., 57, 58
Grove
Thos., xxvii, 1
Guy(e)
Thos., 113, 218
Gyles (Giles)
Jn., 23
Thos., 226, 230, 260, 345
wid., W., 126

Hadden (Haden, Haddon)
(als. Smith), Jn., 216
Jn., 78, 224
Miles, 108
Haddock
Thos., 336
Hall
Avery, bro. of Edw., 224, 232
Edw., (d. 1615), 224, 232
Edw., of Bicester, brazier, 68, 119
Humph., s. of Simon, appr., 186
Jn., 92
Robt., 168
Simon, 186, 279
Thos., of Bodicote, 156
Hames
Edw., 320
Hamlen
Nic., 243
Hamond(e)
--., W., vctlr., 27
Eliz., wid. of Hugh, W., vctlr., 239, 300, 315, 334, 338, 339, 341, 359
Hugh, W., frmn., vctlr., (d. 1615), 4, 10, 28, 29, 30, 38, 39, 48, 50, 61, 73, 74, 83, 84, 95, 96, 107, 110, 113, 114, 115, 118, 122, 128, 129, 131, 140, 141, 155, 162, 169, 172, 178, 182, 196, 205, 206, 214, 218, 221
Humph., Old W., xxii, 53, 57, 61, 66, 74, 85, 140, 321, 349
Jn., W., non-frmn., 30, 249
Hampshire
Mris., ---., of Eynsham, 47
Hanckes
Jn., 234
Hanwell
Ric., 259, 287
Sampson, 227
Thos., of Barton, 150, 156
Harbert
formerly Robins(on), Isabel, w. of Thos., 308
Thos., of St.Peter le Bailey, Oxford, slater, 308
Hardway
Hugh, 345
Harecourt
Bennett, 161
Harper
Eliz.,wid. of Thos., 21, 108
Thos., of Gosford, Kidlington, (d. by 1608), 21, 108

Harris
--., of St.Thos., Oxford, vctlr., 13
Alex., 293
Edw., 39
Jas., of Great Barrington, Glos., 59
Jn., 22, 140, 165
Jos., W., ald., JP., innk., xxxiv, 3, 11, 15, 23, 26, 27, 28, 29, 36, 37, 38, 41, 42, 45, 50, 61, 64, 65, 67, 71, 81, 82, 89, 97, 102, 110, 120, 143, 170, 191, 205, 206, 207, 218, 219, 220, 227, 229, 238, 241, 243, 244, 246, 248, 323, 345, 346, 349, 350, 353, 358, 359, 360, 363, 364, 367, 368, 369, 371
Marg., wid. of Thos., (sen)., of Charlbury, 106
Ric., 170
Ric., clk., 78
Robt., bro. of Will., 289
Thos., gent., 57, 94, 287, 317
Thos., gent., arbiter, 214
Thos., jun., s. of Thos., & Marg., of Charbury, 106
Thos., sen., of Charlbury, 106
Will., xxii, xxv, xxvii, xxviii, 7, 44, 57, 61, 67, 69, 72, 73, 78, 94, 154, 155, 253, 289
Harton
Phil., of Bread street, London, chapm., 22
Hasle
Jn.(i), 19, 52
Jn.(ii), 77
Joan, wid. of Jn.(i), 52
Hastey
Will., 7
Hastings
Mr. --., of Towcester, Northants., mercer, 43
Hatten
Marg., wid., of Kidlington, xxiii, 149, 166
Haull
Jn., 227
Hawkins
Anne, w. of Ric., 143, 150, 289
Ric., W., frmn., weaver, 4, 5, 7, 9, 26, 29, 30, 37, 38, 48, 52, 65, 73, 102, 118, 128, 129, 143, 147, 150, 155, 156, 162, 172, 177, 178, 182, 183, 196, 198, 205, 211, 214, 227, 228, 229, 232, 238, 239, 244, 289, 291, 300, 364, 367
Hawle
Ric., 252
Hawten
Ric., gent., 169
Hawthorne
Phil., W., non-frmn., lab., 23, 30, 36, 37, 39, 179, 208, 226
Haynchoe
Will., 140
Haynes. *See also* Heynes
Nic., of Hanborough, 162
Hayward
Edw., of London, 12
Head(d) (Hed(d))
--., 189
Alex., W., frmn., 3, 9, 15, 21, 29, 30, 36, 38, 41, 45, 50, 53, 63, 65, 67, 95, 103, 107, 113, 114, 115, 118, 121, 129, 155, 158, 162, 177, 207, 219, 221, 234, 244, 252, 309, 319, 321, 329, 342, 353, 359, 363, 364
Giles, 187
Thos., 257
Heady(e)
Thos., 269, 309
Heard
Joan, wid., 350
Hearles
Mich., W., (d. by 1611), 121
Ric., s. of Mich., W., appr., 121
Hearne
Will., 40
Heath
--., (clk., at Westm.), 306
Frances, w. of Robt., 7
Geo., W., non-frmn., 30, 227, 310
Jn., W., counc., xxi, 3, 8, 9, 11, 25, 27, 28, 29, 30, 35, 36, 38, 39, 41, 42, 44, 50, 52, 53, 61, 63, 67, 74, 77, 78, 83, 84, 87, 88, 102, 103, 109, 118, 121, 125, 141

Heath (cont.)
Ric., W., glover, xxi, 8, 12, 49, 61, 78, 83, 87, 90, 121, 186, 204, 222, 224, 252, 294
Robt., W., 7, 14
Will., 21, 30, 35
Heathen
Thos., W., counc., serg., attorney, (*passim* from 1618), chandl.,vctlr., xvi, 78, 182, 196, 205, 218, 221, 229, 232, 234, 238, 245, 249, 259, 263, 264, 270, 277, 278, 279, 280, 281, 282, 283, 284, 287, 295, 300, 305, 310, 313, 315, 325, 334, 335, 338, 339, 340, 341, 358, 359, 363, 365, 369, 370
Hedge(s)
Humph., 77
Jn., 293
Heming
--., cornbuyer, 124
Henberry
Jn., 267
Henworth
Chris., svt., to John Throckmorton esq., 5
Hewbande (als. Hibbotts)
Thos., gent., of Inkberrow, Worcs., 17
Hewes
Thos., of Tew, 291
Hewett (Huet(t))
Jn., 82
Heynes
--., 30
Jn., 77
Ric., 66, 226
Hiat(e)
Eliz., w. of Robt., 113
Jn., of Hordley, miller, 39
Robt., 113
Hibbotts. *See* Hewbande
Hick(e)s
Edw., 156
Hen., s. of Jn., (Milton), W., appr., 271
Jn., 46
Jn., of Milton, yeo., 271
Will., (unspec.,), 291, 327
Will., jun., W., frmn., 4, 15, 19, 29, 30, 45, 48, 63, 68, 69, 78, 96, 101, 115, 118, 128, 129, 158, 162, 177, 199, 221, 239, 244, 249, 252, 258, 263, 264, 279, 280, 283, 287, 288, 292, 317, 356, 363, 364, 369, 370
Will., of Standlake, lab., xxxvi, 46
Will., s. of Jn., (Milton), W., appr., 271
Will., sen., W., frmn., vctlr., 10, 27, 28, 29, 38, 39, 45, 48, 53, 57, 61, 68, 73, 74, 78, 84, 92, 96, 101, 107, 114, 129, 141, 144, 145, 153, 156, 162, 174, 182, 196, 199, 205, 206, 211, 214, 218, 221, 232, 234, 239, 254, 316, 363, 364, 368, 369
Hickman
Will., clk., 186
Higgins
Will., 170
Hinde
Ric., 349
Hinnett
Jn., of Tew, 7
Hinny(e)
Ellen, w. of Thos., 9
Thos., of Begbroke, 9
Hinton
Chris., 211
Hiorne
--., 1
Edm., gent., W., town clk., xiii, xiv, xviii, xxi, xxii, xxvi, xxvii, xxx, xxxiii, xli, 1, 3, 11, 24, 34, 35, 39, 41, 42, 50, 60, 61, 67, 72, 86, 92, 97, 102, 115, 140, 144, 150, 191, 198, 212, 215, 232, 245, 246, 264, 270, 291, 296, 297, 301, 308, 321, 323, 327, 329, 360, 363, 364
as clerk of court, xiii, xx, xxxii, 25, 90, 91, 312
Edm., sen., father of Edm.(town clk.), of Great Tew, xxii, 52
Jn., 77, 113, 171
Jn., jun., W., appr., 352
Hiorne (als. Jarnes)
Chris., 161, 330
Hitch(e)
Will., W., non-frmn., 30, 146, 164, 225, 238, 341, 351, 357

Hitchman
Robt., 167
Will., 232
Hobart
Hen., kt.& bt., Chief Justice, Kings Bench, London, 287, 294
Hobbs
Jn., 357, 358
Hobcrafte (Hobcrofte)
Will., 200, 322
Hobson
Will., Mr., of Wootton Underwood, Bucks., minister, 23
Hodges
Barth., of Leafield, lab., 59
Jn., 86
Will., of Leafield, lab., 59
Hold(e)ing(e), Holden
Anne, wid., 260, 273, 298, 314
Hollins
Jn., gent., 344
Hollis
Eadie, wid., W., non-frmn., 20, 29
Walt., W., svt., xxxiv, 97, 107, 132
Holloway(e)
Dorothy, wid., 102
Felix, W., non-frmn., 30
Geo., 171
Ric., 337
Will., gent., W., non-frmn., 30, 97, 122, 124, 365
Hollyday
Edw., 313
Hollyman
Will., 158
Homes
Andrew, W., 313
Will., W., non-frmn., 29
Hooper
Gyles, W., frmn., 365
Hopkins
Robt., 289
Hopper
Robt., 231
Horne
--., 130
Ric., 119
Stephen, 268
Walt., 260
Horskins
Ric., 61, 81
Horsman. *See* Knevett
Houlebrock (Howlebrock)
Alex., gent, 68
Houlton (Howlton)
Hen., 121
Ric., 126, 191
House
Ric., of Water Eaton, 166
Howell(s)
Davy, of Westm., embroiderer, 54
Walt., of Winchcombe, Glos., butch., xxxvi, 54
Hucwell
Thos., 199
Huet(t). *See also* Hewett
Robt., 58, 62
Huggins
Thos., 306
Hull
Edw., W., frmn., 312, 329, 341, 351, 353, 359, 360, 363, 371
Jn., gent., W., 243
Ralph, W., non-frmn., (d. 1610), 29
Humphries
Thos., of Farmington, Glos., 10
Tustian, of Hanborough, 44, 116
Will., s. of Thos., W., appr., 10
Hun(n)iborne
Isabel, 42
Hunslowe
Anth., of Thrupp, shep., 12
Hunte
Jn., 140
Hursle
Jn., 116
Hurste
Eliz., 290
Hutchins
Jn., 266, 274, 283
Hutt
Will., 274

Inglishe
Will., W., shoem., 25

Ingrome (Ingram, Ingraham)
Ric., 40, 42, 91
Issard
Jn., of Gloucester, 130
Ives
Anth., 310
Iveto
Thos., 35

Jackman
Thos., 202, 212
Jackson
Thos., W., non-frmn., 30, 51
Jacobb
Edw., 302
Jarnes
(als. Hiorne), Chris., 161, 330
Andrew, W., frmn., xxi, 2, 7, 19, 29, 37, 48, 52, 68, 109, 125
Ric., W., frmn., 4, 15, 29, 53, 57, 68, 70
widow, W., non-frmn., 30
Jarratt (Jarrard, Jarret(t))
Austen, of Campden, Glos., 108
Jellian, w. of Jn., 146
Jn., of Weston-on-the-Green, yeo., 146
Thos., of Cherrington, Warks., lab., xxxvi, 59
Jarvis
Jn., 155
Jeames (James)
--., 151
Anne, 247
Arth., of Wootton, yeo., 24
Geo., of Evesham, Worcs., 16
Mr., 331
Phil., W., frmn., (foreign frmn., by 1616), 29, 141, 150, 153, 155, 365
Ric., 297
Robt., 93
Simon, gent., W., counc., schoolm., attorney (*passim* B78/3), xvi, xxi, xxvii, xxx, 14, 29, 35, 41, 42, 74, 102, 110, 145, 191, 197, 211, 212, 220, 297, 303, 321, 331, 355, 363, 364
Thos., parson of Wootton, 161
Jeff(e)s
fam., xli
Jas., of Oddington, 238
Ric., 357
Simon, W., (1302), 366
Will., of Bladon, xxiii, 37, 90
Jenck(e)s
Will., gent., of Yarnton, 145, 146, 216
Jenckins (als. Morgan)
Morgan, W.,, 225, 256
Jennings
Jn., 304
Ric., 313
Will., 165, 170, 321
Jepson
Jn., of Warsop, Notts., innk., 12
Joan
w. of Robt., of Bladon (1302), 366
Johnson
Edw., 222
Hen., W., non-frmn., 29
Phil., 271, 307
Ric., 297
Robt., see also Debanck, 55
Jones (Joanes)
Jenkin, 156
Mr., 345
Nic., 208
Jorden (Jordon, Jurden)
--., 361
Clement, of Banbury, 22
Jn., 195
Joyner
Robt., 170
Thos., W., frmn., bkr., 29, 70, 107, 156, 252
Judge
Hercules, of Stonesfield, 100
Thos., W., non-frmn., 30

Keate
Robt., 221
Keene
Mary, W., 170, 222
Ric., 249
Thos., 311, 336
Keite. *See* Kyte

Kelly
Gabriel, 182
Kempe
Bridget, w. of Edw., 127
Edw., of Hampton Poyle, 127
Kent(e)
Jn., 38, 39, 53
Jn., sen., 57
Thos., 58
Kerbie. *See* Kirby
Kerke
Mr., 38
Kerkwood
Thos., 102
Kerle (Kerld)
Jn., esq., JP., of Much Marcle, Herefords., 124
Kerwood
Jn., of Deddington, 212, 220
Key(e)
Jn., 325
Ric., 289
Keyte. *See* Kyte
Kilby
Edw., 338
King(e) (Kynge)
Jn., 168, 186
Thos., of Heyford Bridge, 12, 186
Walter, 240
Will., W., frmn., shoem., xxviii, 11, 25, 29, 37, 53, 61, 67, 69, 181, 213, 320, 367
Kinget
Nic., of Lambeth, attorney, 59
Kirby (Kirbie, Kirbye)
--., s. of Jn., 332
Jn., W., xxvii, 115, 122, 125, 252, 332
Kite. *See* Kyte
Knapp
Jn., 267
Jn., of Oxford, saddler, 25, 37
Knevett
(als. Horsman), Ric., 44
Knight(e)
Benjamin, 226
Fras., 281
Knotsford
Mr., 93
Knott
Will., of Littlemore, yeo., 142
Knowles
Jn., 181
Kyte (Keite, Kite, Keyte, Kyett)
--., 165
Jer., esq., W., non-frmn., JP., lawyer, maltster, xxi, xxxiv, 195, 198, 203, 204, 205, 218, 229, 238, 248, 249, 255, 259, 264, 270, 279, 291, 298, 300, 301, 307, 308, 312, 314, 315, 316, 327, 333, 335, 337, 339, 350, 358, 365, 369, 371

Lacye
Ric., 210
Ladbrock (Ledbrock, -broke)
Hen., W., frmn., currier, (later foreign frmn.), 29, 42, 365
Lambard (Lumbard, Lumber)
Anth., W., appr., 271
Jn., 274
Lardner
Ambrose, 222, 223, 285, 348
Laude (?Lande)
Ric., 39
Laughton
Robt., 67
Lawrence
Jn., 276
Lea (Ley, Leye)
Jn., 216, 269
Leake
Anne, wid., W., non-frmn., (d. 1613), xxi, 29, 38, 51, 110, 144, 149, 217, 241
Lee
Hen., kt., & bt., Ditchley, 160
Ric., kt., MP., (deceased), xvi, 41
Legg(e)
Rog., of Enstone, butch., 17, 114
Leighe
Thos., 108
Lenthall
Will., esq., recorder, xv, 354, 355
Lewes
Humph., gent., 330
Lillie (Lyllie, Lylly)
--., 120

Lillie (Lyllie, Lylly) (cont.)
Jn., 93
Litle
Geo., 238
Rog., 229
Littleford
Mr., of The Bull's Head, Nottingham, vctlr., 14
Lock
Ric., 297
Loggon
Will., gent., 6, 40, 60, 337
Longe
Edw., ?s.of Edw., W., appr., 159
Edw., W., frmn., clk. of church, ct. crier, shoem., xvi, 27, 28, 29, 35, 43, 46, 82, 84, 115, 121, 142, 160, 174, 239, 254, 280, 300, 305, 315, 334, 335, 341, 359, 368
Jer., W., butch., 359
Jerome, s. of Edw., W., appr., 121
Longworth
Ralph, 72
Lorde
Ric., 330
Love. *See* Edging
Lowe
Jn., W., counc., (d. 1618), 5, 9, 11, 26, 29, 30, 34, 35, 36, 38, 41, 42, 45, 50, 63, 64, 66, 74, 77, 83, 84, 95, 102, 103, 110, 113, 114, 118, 121, 129, 141, 144, 155, 156, 162, 177, 182, 183, 205, 206, 214, 218, 220, 221, 223, 228, 229, 232, 234, 238, 244, 245, 249, 251, 258, 259, 263, 264, 270, 279, 364, 367
Ric., W., frmn., 29, 133, 364
Thos., W., frmn., 221, 270, 279, 287, 288, 291, 365
Winifred, dau. of Ric., 133
Lucas
Jn., W., non-frmn., 30
Ralph, W., svt., bkr., 137
Luckett
Alice, 350
Ludnam
Nic., W., non-frmn., 30
Lunand (als. Lunden, London)
Ralph, 242, 285
Lyddam. *See* Richardson
Lynn
widow, W., non-frmn., 30

Mackereth
Jn., 160
Mallins
Edw., 349
Man(n)ing(e)
Anne, w. of Ric., 325
Jn., 303, 330
Ric., of Begbroke, xxii, 57, 94, 118, 325
Mannett
(Maurice?), 267
March
Robt., W., non-frmn., 30
Marriatt
Jn., 281
Marshowe
Jas., of Oxford, aqua-vite man, 76
Robt., bro. of Jas., 76
Martin(e) (Martyn)
Mr., 123
Ric., 291
Ric., gent., of Eynsham, 103, 167
Thos., W., frmn., 5, 7, 29, 37, 45, 48, 50, 61, 63, 65, 246, 249, 270, 279, 281, 291, 292, 300, 301, 302, 318, 365, 367, 370
Will., 108, 326
Mason
Giles, W., 107
Jas., W., svt., shoem.,, 37
Jn., W., non-frmn., 29, 81, 213, 365
Masse
Leonard, 8
Mathew(e) (Mathews)
Gabriel, gent., 218
Hugh, of Churchill, 59
Maud
Kit, of Islip, 130
Maulthouse
Robt., 74
Maunde (Mawnde)
Anth., W., clk., 1, 81
Geo., of Bicester, yeo., 24

Maunder
Simon, 313
Maurice
Thos., 101, 102
Mawkins
Will., W., 23
May(e)
Jn., 327
Martin, 278
Robt., 21, 108, 121, 274, 278, 327
Will., 146
Maynard
widow, W., non-frmn., 29
Mayne
Jn., of South Leigh, 59
Mayor and Commonalty, 125
Me(a)tcalf(e)
(als. Abraham), Will., 198, 313
Thos., s. of Will (sen)., W., woollendraper, xxi, 1, 29, 49, 50, 61, 64, 65, 67, 70, 78, 89, 99, 106, 110, 111, 117, 147, 182, 191, 208, 216, 233, 239, 252, 271, 276, 309, 317, 322, 356, 363, 364, 367, 368
Will., jun., s. of Will., W., ald., woollendraper, 1, 9, 29, 36, 38, 41, 45, 50, 52, 53, 63, 65, 66, 67, 77, 83, 91, 107, 110, 114, 118, 121, 129, 141, 155, 162, 183, 191, 213, 227, 238, 239, 243, 245, 262, 285, 291, 298, 313, 345, 346, 353, 359, 360, 363, 364, 367, 368, 369, 370
Will., sen., W., ald., (d. 1608), xvi, xxvii, 1, 3
Meacock
Simon, 74
Meade(s)
--., 165
Anth., of London, (born Swerford), svt., sawy., 152
Jn., 117, 167
Joan, wid. of Ric., 350
Ric., W., innk., yeo., (d. 1620), 3, 9, 10, 11, 29, 34, 37, 41, 42, 48, 71, 82, 84, 96, 114, 120, 128, 131, 141, 162, 178, 182, 191, 195, 196, 199, 201, 205, 206, 218, 219, 221, 238, 244, 245, 256, 258, 259, 263, 269, 270, 291, 307, 308, 317, 318, 322, 363, 364, 367
Thos., 254
Meadowes
widow, W., non-frmn., 30
Meakes
Jn., 234
Meares
Robt., of Warks., pedlar, 71
Medhopp
Stephen, xxiii, 125
Meese
Edm., esq., 176, 226, 285
Mercer
Anth., of Deddington, vctlr., 119
Merrall (Merrell)
Jn., 267
Jn., of Cheltenham, Glos., bkr., 10
Merrick
Maurice, gent., 291
Mettam
Thos., kt., London, 13
Midwinter
Nic., W., shoem., 207, 211
Miles
Peter, 159
Millen(s)
Abraham, of Cleveley, 47, 83, 179, 204, 227
Lawrence, s. of Will., appr., 326
Will., of Cleveley, 326
Miller
Nathaniel, 321
Minchine (Mincham)
Jn., 93
Jn., of Lambeth, London, svt. to Nic. Kinget, 59
Will., 57
Mitchell
Nic., W., 212, 307, 322
Montagu
H., clk., at Westm., 263
Moore (More)
Humph., of Beamhurst, Staffs., husb., xxxvi, 103
Jn., 234
Marg., mother of Humph., 103
widow, W., non-frmn., 30

Morcam (Morcombe)
Mr., of Allerton, Notts., 111
Mris., 111
Morgan. *See* Jenckins
--., 303
Thos., of Merton College, Oxford, scholar, 143
Morley (Morely, Morly)
Thos., 306
Will., 236
Morris
--., 350
Morton
(als. Hassam), Nic., 63
Jas., 246
Will., 344
Mosley (Mosly(e), Moslie)
Fras., of Attercliffe, Yorks., cutler, 70
Jn., 279
Jn., of Broad Campden, Glos., 108
Mosse
Mr., (Royal) clerk of market, xl
Thos., 252, 282
Mowlden
Ric., grain supplier, 38
Mowlder
Thos., 283
Mowlesworth
Ric., of Ditchley House, 161
Muckell
Will., W., slater, 133, 212, 220, 223
Mudd
Robt., 74
Munck
--., gent., 120
Jn., W., 4
widow, W., non-frmn., 30, 98, 136
Munday
Will., of Oxford, butch., 317
Mylles
Ric., 302

Nash(e) (Nasshe)
Hen., 41
Jerome, gent., Old W., 11, 38, 152, 269
his shepherd, 100
Needler
Mr., of Farthingstone, 43
Thos., 2
Neele
Jn., 194
Nelson
--., chancery clk., 198
Newall (Newell)
Ric., W., non-frmn., 30, 37, 280
Newberrye
Mr., (of Shipton-on-Cherwell?), grain supplier, 38
Newinton
Chris., gent., of Offenham, Worcs., 16
Newman
Jn., 44, 139
Newton
Chris., shoem., 105
Ric., 248
Nicholes (Nickoles)
Jas., W., bkr., 341
Nic., 181
Ric., W., blksm., 107, 112
Noble
Anth., W., non-frmn., clk., (d. 1613), xxv, 19, 29, 34, 38, 110
Geo., s. of Anth., W., counc., cooper, xxvi, xxviii, 29, 30, 67, 83, 89, 110, 115, 129, 141, 145, 155, 156, 162, 167, 169, 172, 178, 182, 183, 191, 196, 199, 205, 218, 221, 228, 230, 232, 234, 238, 244, 245, 249, 252, 258, 259, 263, 264, 279, 280, 291, 292, 300, 308, 363, 364, 368, 369, 370
Mr., 34
Nath., s. of Anth., W., 51, 70
Nolton
Hen., of Lenton, Notts., horsescorcer, 14
Norman
Jn., W., counc., butch., 30, 61, 83, 95, 97, 99, 103, 110, 115, 121, 156, 169, 182, 183, 191, 196, 199, 205, 206, 214, 220, 228, 229, 232, 292, 300, 307, 308, 312, 314, 319, 321, 327, 329, 334, 337, 342, 351, 352, 357, 359, 363, 364, 367, 368, 369, 370

Norwood
Benedict, W., non-frmn., 30, 73
Thos., W., non-frmn., 30, 85, 186
Nurs(s)e
Ann, wid. of Mich., W., 72
Mich., W., counc., butch., (d. 1609), 9, 26, 27, 28, 29, 30, 34, 35, 36, 37, 39, 41, 45, 48, 50, 53, 61, 63, 65, 72, 357
widow (Margery), W., non-frmn., (d. 1607), 30
Nurth
Rog., 201
Will., 6

Ockly
Ric., xxv, 40, 45
Olliver
(als. Gardner), Ellis, of Hook Norton, xxxvi, 165
Olyverte
Mr., of London, 22
Oram(e)
Ric., 101
Orpwood
Thos., 280
Osbaldeston
Jn., gent., 279
Ovmine
Chas., clk., 108

Page
Will., jun., 227
Paine (Payne)
--., w. of Robt., 86
Hen., of Steeple Aston, yeo., 330
Jas., s. of Henry, W., appr., 330
Jn., 66, 78
Robt., of Cassington, xx, xxii, 63, 76, 79, 86
Painter (Paynter)
--., 173
--., w. of Bennett, 348
Bennett, W., counc., vctlr., 9, 10, 29, 36, 38, 52, 84, 87, 96, 99, 105, 122, 142, 182, 196, 206, 218, 238, 239, 300, 301, 308, 309, 310, 314, 315, 316, 319, 327, 328, 329, 333, 334, 335, 337, 338, 339, 340, 341, 342, 348, 349, 351, 353, 358, 359, 363, 364, 370
Edw., of Woodstock park, keeper, 93
Mary, w. of Thos., xxvi, 86, 87, 125
Nic., 334
Thos., W., frmn., vctlr., (d. 1619), xxi, xxvi, 5, 11, 29, 35, 64, 84, 86, 87, 96, 110, 111, 113, 114, 125, 139, 142, 170, 182, 196, 206, 218, 364
Pangborne
Clive, of Charlton-on-Otmoor, yeo., 127
Will., 83
Parker
Eliz., w. of Walt., 207, 219
Giles, of Great Tew, butch., 17
Jn., W., non-frmn., 30, 86, 115, 332
Ric., of Wells, Som., vctlr., 8
Robt., W., innk., 334, 335, 358
Walt., W., non-frmn., 30, 94, 110, 120, 207, 219
Parran
Robt., 44
Parrate (Parratt,-ett,-ott)
--., 'the currier's son', 188
Matt., 53, 170, 352
Will., 210, 322
Parrishe
Fowck, of Bicester, carrier, 24
Parryn
Hen., kt, JP., of Nottingham, 14
Parsons
--., 188
Edw., 160
Hen., 106
Jn., 8
Thos., 181
Will., 207, 209
Patterick
Jn., s. of Will., W., appr., 282
Will., of city of London, glover, 282
Pavye
Justin, 348
Paxon
Thos., 240
Paxton
Edm., 152
Payne. *See* Paine
Paynter. *See* Painter

Pearce
Paul, W., svt., shoem., 24
Pearson
Thos., 81
Peart(e)
Jn., of Bicester, 25
Thos., 356
Peat
Mr., of London, 22
Peesly
Thos., 222, 228
Peeters
Ric., W., non-frmn., (also woolman of London, (d. 1610)), 30
Peeterson
Thos., 338
Penn
Thos., xxv, 26, 40, 45
Pepper
Jn., W., frmn., 249, 270, 280, 327, 328, 329, 359, 360, 363, 364, 369, 370
Perkins
Thos., of Dunstable, Beds., upholsterer, 71
Perry
Jn., of Ascott-under-Wychwood, 265
Peton
Ric., 26
Pettybone
Walt., 105
Phillip(p)s
Jn., W., frmn., glover, (d. 1608), 94
Mary, wid. of John, W., non-frmn., xxvii, 30, 86, 94
Ric., W., frmn., weaver, 302, 309, 314, 315, 327, 331, 332, 333, 342, 363, 370, 371
Robt., W., slater, 312, 332
Thos., 258
Will., W., non-frmn., 30
Phillippson
Thos., of Akeley, Bucks., xxxvi, 70
Phipps
--., s. of Robt.,, 59
fam., xxxvi
Jn., 231
Jn., of Ledwell, 59, 158
Robt., of Aynho-on-the-hill, 59
Will., bro. of Jn., of Oxford, 59
Will., clk., 221
Piggott
Chris., kt., JP., Bucks., 23
Pile (Pyle)
Robt., 180, 227, 338
Pimm. *See* Punn
Platt
Jas., 311
Plot(t)
Will., 22, 216
Plumpton
Ric., W., frmn., 307, 308, 318, 329, 363, 370
Polly
Jn., of Oxford, musician, 61, 62
Poole
Thos., 157
Ursula, W., svt., 131
Pope
Will., kt., & bt., 283, 344
Porter
Mr., of Buckingham, innk., 43
Will., W., non-frmn., chapm., (d. 1622), 4, 19, 20, 22, 29, 110, 140, 213, 365
Potter
Isaac, kt., JP., Kent, 58
Pour(e) (Pore, Poore, Power)
Fras., esq., of Bletchingdon, 132, 180
Daniel, his svt., 132
Geo., gent., 285
Jn., gent., 331
Ric., gent., 252
Robt., of Derbyshire, 54
Powell
Amy, widow, W., 4
Jn., W., frmn., 25, 29, 68, 73, 74
Rog., 111, 187
Powlton
Jn., 105
Poynes
Jn., kt., 297
Price (Prise)
--., of Smithfield, London, alehousekeeper, 54
Barnaby, s. of Jn., (Cumnor), 28
Hen., W., non-frmn., chapm., 5, 22, 30, 36, 70, 71, 97, 126, 145

Price (Prise)(cont.)
Jn., of Cumnor, sieve-maker, 28
Jn., W., frmn., 30, 363, 365
Prince
Edw., 8
Priste
Thos., sen., of Fencott, yeo., 127
Pritchett
Lewis, of Llantilio Crossenny, Wales, 54
Prydy
Jn., W., non-frmn., 139
Pryvate
Ric., 29, 95, 365
Pufford
Will., 109
Pulch(r)oe (Pulcrowe)
Ann, w. of Mich., 107, 169
Jn., W., slater, 315, 316
Mich., W., non-frmn., 30, 169, 222
Punn (?Pimm)
Will., 281
Pyman
Fras., W., frmn., 328, 333, 341, 359, 365
Ric., 174, 181, 184, 191, 254

Quench
--., Standlake, 47

Ranckle
Eliz., w. of Will, 232
Hen., 210
Will., 232, 267
Rat(c)life
Will., gent., of Oxford Univ., xxv, 150
Rathbone
Marg., wid., W., non-frmn., 30, 98
Raunson, 29
--., 189
Jn., W., ald., glover, (d. 1611), xvi, xxx, 11, 15, 26, 30, 34, 35, 36, 37, 39, 41, 42, 45, 50, 53, 61, 63, 67, 74, 77, 82, 83, 86, 87, 89, 91, 125, 367
Marg., wid. of Jn., W., vctlr., 125, 315, 334, 338, 339, 341, 359
Mris., 110, 293
Will., W., counc., woolman, vctlr., xx, xxi, xxiii, 9, 29, 36, 37, 52, 68, 78, 81, 125, 144, 153, 165, 167, 169, 182, 185, 187, 191, 192, 193, 196, 221, 222, 230, 231, 232, 234, 238, 239, 243, 246, 249, 259, 281, 292, 300, 301, 303, 304, 308, 309, 310, 315, 351, 353, 363, 364, 368, 369, 370
Raves
Geo., (of Duns Tew?) (d. 1614), 227
Ric., 213
Will., s. of Geo., 227
Rawlins (Raulins)
Thos., gent., W., town clk., to 1607, counc., xiv, 29, 35, 86, 95
Rayer
Jn., 116
Simon, 107
Thos., s. of Will., W., innk., vint., 7, 14, 22, 29, 176, 205, 206, 212, 221, 228, 229, 234, 238, 240, 241, 243, 245, 269, 270, 301, 315, 316, 317, 324, 331, 334, 338, 339, 340, 349, 350, 351, 358, 359, 363, 364, 369, 370
Will., W., ald., innk., (d. 1619), xxi, xxvi, 2, 5, 6, 7, 8, 10, 12, 14, 20, 23, 25, 29, 34, 35, 38, 41, 42, 48, 64, 82, 86, 87, 88, 91, 92, 93, 95, 96, 97, 102, 103, 105, 110, 111, 113, 114, 115, 118, 119, 120, 124, 128, 129, 130, 138, 139, 141, 142, 145, 146, 147, 152, 155, 156, 157, 182, 191, 196, 199, 206, 212, 215, 218, 220, 239, 245, 249, 259, 266, 270, 279, 288, 290, 291, 301, 349, 364, 367, 368, 369
Will., W., non-frmn., vctlr., 29, 316, 337
Rea
Thos., gent, of Severn Stoke, Worcs., 145, 146
Reade
Kath., w. of Ric., xxi, 248, 304, 348
Ric., W., frmn., butch., xxi, 54, 107, 115, 149, 158, 164, 166, 191, 223, 225, 236, 249, 268, 269, 270, 274, 279, 280, 291, 292, 303, 304, 305, 307, 312, 314, 319, 328, 334, 335, 337, 342, 348, 349, 351, 353, 355, 359, 363, 365, 368

Redgate. *See* Rudgate
Redhead
Justinian, 8
Reeve
Matthew, 349
Reynolds (Raynolds)
Nic., 77, 113
Richards
--., w. of Randall, 132
Randall, W., frmn., xxi, xxv, 29, 62, 68, 110, 113, 115, 118, 126, 128, 132, 140, 141, 144, 146, 153, 155, 156, 158, 160, 165, 167, 172, 182, 183, 198, 199, 205, 206, 214, 368
Richards (Richardson)
(als. Lyddam), Will., W., frmn., 29, 36, 52, 325, 333, 338, 349, 353, 363, 370, 371
Thos., 284
Will., of Kettering, Northants., 55
Rickardes
Chas., 232
Right. *See* Wright
Rippingall
Thos., 226
Riste
Thos., of Leafield, 59
Robert
of Bladon (1302), 366
Roberts
Bennett, 22
Edw., (als. Will.), xxii, 44, 107, 108, 240
Thos., 337
Robins
(als.Browne), Ellin, w. of Will., W., 357
(als.Robinson), Eliz., dau. of Isabel (als.Eliz.), 219, 270
(als.Robinson), Isabel (als.Eliz.) W., (m. Thos. Harbert of Oxford), 219, 270
Jn., W., (a minor), xxix, 226
Robinson
Abel, manservant, 105
Geo., 57, 58
Jn., 30
Roffe
Jn., 279
Rogers
--., 'Sir', priest, of Welford, Warks., 17
Ric., W., appr., 43
Robt., 330
Thos., 320
Rooke
Thos., 61, 113, 140
Rose
Fras., 93, 109
Robt., of Deddington, ironm., 87, 88
Rowden
Jn., W., silkweaver, 43
Thos., 57
Rowland
--., of Gloucester, 7
Bishop of Bristol, xxiii, 346
Ric., of Hanborough, 59
Rowleright
Hen., 66
Rudgate (Redgate)
--., 165
Edm./Edw./Ned., W., serg., attorney (*passim*), shoem., (d. 1618), xvi, xxix, 3, 5, 9, 25, 26, 27, 28, 29, 37, 38, 41, 48, 50, 53, 58, 61, 62, 63, 74, 83, 84, 95, 96, 99, 107, 110, 113, 114, 115, 118, 120, 122, 124, 128, 129, 135, 141, 145, 152, 157, 158, 160, 180, 182, 187, 189, 190, 191, 192, 196, 198, 199, 200, 206, 207, 218, 219, 226, 236, 239, 247, 250, 256, 259, 260, 262, 265, 364, 367, 368
Ellen, wid. of Edm., 287
Hen., W., serg., attorney (*passim*), shoem., (d. 1613), xvi, xxx, xxxi, 1, 8, 10, 11, 14, 19, 27, 28, 29, 34, 35, 39, 41, 42, 48, 49, 52, 56, 60, 61, 62, 63, 78, 82, 84, 90, 91, 92, 95, 96, 102, 106, 110, 111, 114, 125, 141, 367
Russell
Anth., 40
Chris., of Woodstock park, yeo., 230
Mr., of Smithfield, London, toll-keeper, 14
Ric., 49
Robt., 285, 313

Ryly(e) (Ryley)
Edm., 166
Eliz., wid. of Jn., W., xxi, 131, 144, 182, 185, 187, 188, 195
Jn., W., frmn., (d. 1610), 5, 6, 10, 29, 48, 64, 74, 77
Ric., 164
Will., W., ald., (d. 1609), 28
Rymill
Thos., 322, 329
Will., 182
Ryves
Geo., W., town clk., from 1663, xiv

Sadler. *See* Dewe
Salter
Jn., 159, 289
Sambridge
Mr., of Evesham, 104
Samon(e) Symon
Paul, 203
Samwell
Thos., gent., W., xxvii, 1
Sansom(e) (Sanson)
--., chapman, 74
Jn., 37
Saunders
Ambrose, 101
Chris., 269
Daniel, 229
Edw., of Much Marcle, Herefs. butch., 124
Grace, w. of Thos., 107
Jn., 153, 170
Ralph, xxv, 49
Thos., 107, 120
Savidge
Isabel (married Jas.Smith), of London, 12
Say(e)
Jn., W., 341, 351, 371
Scasborowe (Skasborowe)
Eliz., W., 132
Scott
--., 149
Matthew, 186, 278
Screevin(e)
--., w. of Thos., 131
'goodwife', 188
Thos., W., counc., glazier, vctlr., xxi, 4, 5, 7, 8, 9, 10, 11, 15, 23, 27, 28, 29, 36, 39, 41, 42, 45, 46, 50, 61, 65, 67, 72, 74, 75, 84, 95, 96, 102, 103, 110, 113, 114, 121, 129, 131, 141, 142, 144, 153, 154, 155, 156, 168, 172, 177, 180, 182, 196, 199, 205, 206, 208, 210, 218, 219, 221, 222, 225, 235, 236, 239, 244, 245, 249, 259, 263, 264, 266, 269, 271, 273, 274, 289, 298, 301, 308, 314, 316, 332, 353, 363, 364, 369
Sea(re)
--., 1
Jn., W., frmn., join., 330, 345, 359, 360, 363
Robt., W., frmn., cordw., (d. 1609), 3, 6, 7, 11, 15, 26, 29, 37, 38, 255, 367
Will., s. of Robt., W., appr., 255, 360
Secole
Jn., 246
Seely(e)
Jn., W., non-frmn., 29, 365
Will., 264
Sellenger
(als. Butcher), Phil., of Oddington, 172, 179, 187
Seman
Jn., 326
Shad(d)
--., w. of Ric., 131
Alice, wid. of Ric., W., 342
Anth., W., non-frmn., 30
Ric., W., counc., chandl., (d. 1617), 9, 29, 30, 35, 38, 41, 45, 50, 61, 63, 68, 74, 78, 83, 84, 87, 103, 107, 110, 113, 115, 121, 131, 141, 145, 156, 158, 162, 169, 177, 178, 182, 183, 191, 199, 205, 206, 213, 218, 221, 227, 228, 232, 234, 236, 238, 239, 243, 246, 251, 252, 254, 364, 367, 368, 369
Sharpe
Barth., 158
Chris., of Murcott, yeo., 127
Ethelbert, 288

Shawe
Edw., clk., 318
Jn., 108
Will., 286
Shaylord(e)
Jn., 109
Sheppard
Hen., of Sutton, Herefords., 124
Jn., 106
Thos., 252
Shilton
Thos., 267
Shirt(e) (Shurte)
Edw., of Charlton-on-Otmoor, yeo., 127
Rog., 8
Shorter
Nic., 298
Shurl(e)y (Shurlie)
Ralph, xxii, 109, 111, 139, 144, 149, 153, 161, 162, 164, 189
Shute
--., (clk., at Westm.), 306
Silliard
Nic., esq., JP., Kent, 58
Silver
Edw., W.., ironm., 316, 342, 357, 358
Humph., W., frmn., xxvii, 79, 184, 348, 363
Silverside
Fras., of Charlton-on-Otmoor, 121
Robt., 40, 198
Will., 198
Silvester
Thos., of Burford, arbiter, 265
Sims
Hen., 112
Singleton
Jas., 170
Skaye (Skey)
Ellin, wid., 210
Ric., s. of Will., W., appr., 155
Ric., W., frmn., 333, 334, 363
Thos., 19
Will., of Oddington, yeo., 155
Slatter
Jn., 157
Peter, 291
Slaymaker
Thos., 177, 208
Smith
(als. Hadden), Jn., 216
--., w. of Jerome., 137
Anne, w. of Ric., 295
Chris., W., frmn., bkr., 309, 314, 315, 319, 333, 335, 351, 353, 359, 360, 363, 371
Eliz., W., svt., 172
Ferdinand, 191, 330
Isabel, w. of Jas., xxxv, 12
Jas., of London, glover, xxxv, 12
Jerome, of Hanborough, 137
Jn., gent., of London and Leyton, Essex, 16
Mr Doctor, commissary, Bucks., 70
Mr., (owner of horse), Glos., 108
Mr., of Morton-in-Marsh, 104
Oliver, gent.,arbiter, 214
Peter, of Holden, Yorks., 13
Ric., 295
Simon, of Oxford, mercer, 188
Thos., W., non-frmn., 19, 30
widow, W., non-frmn., 16, 30
Will., 187
Sodon
Thos., 306
Sorby
Robt., of City of Westm., vint., 179
Sparrocke
Robt., 242
Spencer (Spenser)
Geo., esq., 168
Ric., 224
Sir Thos., kt & bart., High Steward, xv, 208, 364
Spicer
Thos., gent., 243, 246
Spit(t)le
Bridget, wid., W., non-frmn., 30, 64, 110
Robt., W., counc., blksm., farrier, 30, 61, 112, 130, 156, 162, 169, 178, 186, 196, 218, 221, 228, 234, 238, 244, 245, 258, 259, 264, 269, 270, 279, 291, 292, 308, 319, 326, 329, 342, 352, 359, 363, 364, 365, 367

Springall
Will., 8
Stacy(e) (Stacey)
Edw., 70, 92, 176, 179
Standard
Hen., gent., W., 342
Stanhopp
Nic., of Aldenham, Herts., horsescorcer, 129
Stayner (Staynoe)
Jn., s. of Nic., W., appr., 294
Nic., W., non-frmn., 30, 294
Ste(e)phens (Ste(e)vens)
Bryan, W., frmn., tail., 29, 81, 106, 128, 283, 291, 294, 300, 308, 309, 312, 314, 319, 353, 363, 365, 370
Ste(e)phenson (Stevenson)
Hugo, of Weston., 331
Mr., 135
Walt., of Stanton Harcourt, 119
Steere
Jn., 74
Ric., 74
Stiles
Hen., 109
Thos., 331
Stockdall
Ralph, 320
Will., of Ashby-de-la-Zouch, Leics., yeo., 147
Stocker
Thos., 254
Stocklie
Mich., 112
Stockman
Ric., 125
Stone
Jn., W., frmn., shopk., xxi, 29, 155, 183, 185, 186, 187, 189, 193, 195, 199, 206, 218
Thos., 281
Stowt(e) (Stoute)
Geo., 59, 166, 202
Streete(r)
--., 139
Edw., 187
Mr., 188
Ric., 101, 128, 144
Sturgis
Rog., W., frmn., barber-surg., 3, 9, 15, 29, 45, 50, 67, 74, 78, 83, 84, 95, 107, 129, 130, 140, 153, 156, 213, 255, 363
Stutter
Ric., of Hanborough, yeo., xxii, xxiii, 60, 61, 63, 66, 68, 70, 72, 79
Surrell
Edm., 217
Sutton
Thos., 153
Swaffame
Joan, of Greenwich, 58
Symon. *See* Samon(e)
Symon(d)s
Eliz., w. of Robt., 221
Jn., (W., non-frmn.,) of Bladon, carp., xxi, 5, 20, 29, 37, 78, 149, 160, 220, 280, 365
Justin, 303
Phil., 201
Robt., jun., s. of Robt., 5
Robt., of Hensington, xxiii, 5, 7, 90, 94, 170, 213, 221, 222, 226
Thos., 307
Will., 121, 140, 212, 217

Tame
Mary, wid. of Ralph, 254
Ralph, W., svt., 130
Tanfield
Lawrence, kt., recorder, xv, 3, 91, 222
Tanner
widow, W., non-frmn., 29
Taper
Jasper, of Aldenham, Herts., horse-dealer, xxxvi, 129
Tapping(e)
Thos., 240
Tasker
Ric., 337
Tassell (Tassill)
Jn., W., vctlr., 280, 301, 312, 314, 315, 333, 334, 335, 338, 339, 341, 359, 360, 370
Taylor (Tayler)
(als. Fyssher), Ric., 366
--., 25

Taylor (Tayler) (cont.)
Ann, dau. of Nic., 131
fam., xli
Jn., clk., 7, 14
Jn., of Leafield, yeo., xxii, xxviii, 200, 201, 202, 203, 204, 209, 210, 211, 215
Jn., W., counc., woolman, (d. 1612), 7, 10, 14, 28, 29, 30, 34, 39, 84, 96, 110, 114, 142, 155, 157
Merriall, wid. of Jn., (woolman), W., vctlr., xxi, 7, 155, 157, 182, 196, 206, 218, 239, 300, 315, 335, 338, 339, 341, 359
Nic., W., counc., tail., vctlr., 7, 10, 11, 27, 28, 29, 35, 38, 41, 42, 48, 50, 74, 76, 77, 83, 84, 95, 96, 102, 113, 114, 115, 118, 121, 131, 141, 142, 144, 155, 156, 162, 168, 172, 177, 178, 182, 185, 196, 205, 206, 218, 228, 229, 234, 238, 239, 244, 249, 258, 259, 263, 264, 269, 270, 279, 280, 301, 315, 321, 335, 338, 339, 340, 341, 342, 349, 352, 353, 358, 359, 363, 364, 370
Ric., 5, 366
Will., 217
Teaser
Will., 285
Teasler
Jn., 257, 294
Temple
Ric., 140
Thomas. *See* Toms
Thorneburye
Chris., 229
Thorneton
Hen., 191
Throckmorton
Geo., kt. & JP of Bucks, 23
Jn., esq., 5
Tidmarch
Jn., of Newent, Glos., yeo., 308
Tilman
Nic., 284
Timms. *See* Tym(e)s
Todman
Will., of Woodstock park, keeper, 1, 8, 137, 160, 179
Tolly (Tully)
Thos., 290, 325
Tombs
Matthew, 342
Tomlins (Tomlyns)
Jn., W., non-frmn., 30, 73, 208
Tompson
Jn., of St.Giles, London, sawy., 152
Toms
(als. Thomas), Tobias, 295
Chris., 92
Towe
widow, W., 6
Townsend
Edw., 285
Fras., 60
Stephen, 162, 168
Thos., 72
Tredwell
Hen., 94
Robt., 155, 197, 204
Will., 224
Trenton (Trentham)
Thos., of Deddington, shoem., 118
Treslowe
Ric., 194
Trevinor
Thos., 271
Trewman
Marg., widow, 310
Triplett
'goodman', of Oxford, 111
Hen., 5, 78, 88, 185, 228, 267, 352
Trowle
Thos., 157
Trubshawe (-shewe)
Ric., 146, 260
Turferie (Turfery)
Hugh, 153, 159
Turner
(als. Stockes), Ralph, 263
Anth., 218
Thos., 153, 167, 248, 313
Will., 313
Will., Queen's groom, 25
Turpin
Will., kt., (his son), 148

Turtle
(als. Glover), Jn., 9, 10
Marg., mother of Jn., W., 9, 10
Turton
Thos., 108
Tustall
Mris., 161
Tustian
Will., of Deddington, carrier, 163, 182
Tutchine
Clement, wid. of Ric., 299
Ric., of Kidlington, (d. 1618), 299
Will., of Tackley, grain supplier, 38
Tym(e)s (Tim(m)s)
Alice, 306
Hen., 35, 40
Jn., 40, 42, 139
Ric., 91, 261, 306
Will., 200
Tyrer (Tyro)
Jn., 342, 348

Underill
Jn., of Severn Stoke, Worcs., yeo., 145, 146
Ursula
(surname unknown), 58

Vardam
Jn., W., non-frmn., 23, 30, 102, 107
Vaughan (Vahan)
Fras., of Presteigne, Co. Radnor, 58
Verny (Varney,-nie,-ny,-nye)
(als.Waringe) Thos., park-keeper, 109, 165

Wacklyn (Wakelyn, Waklyn)
Ric., 268
Will., 267
Walford
Jerome, of Hensington, yeo., 220, 295
Will., 62
Walker
--., his wife, of Wootton., 138
Abner, s. of Robt., 89
Robt., W., cordw., (d. 1607), 89
Thos., s. of Robt., 89
Tim., s. of Robt., W., frmn., 11, 29
Wall(e)
Will., 127, 204
Wallwine
--., esq., JP of Much Marcle, Herefords., 124
Walter
of Bladon (1302), 366
Warberton
--., clk., at Westm., 335
Warde
--., of Tysoe, Warks., 104
Anth., 268
Ric., 297
Robt., W., 335
Thos., W., frmn., vctlr., 333, 334, 335, 337, 339, 340, 341, 350, 371
Warden
Ric., 254
Warner
Edw., 230
Warr(e)
Edw., of Tackley, grain supplier, 39
Warren (Warrine)
fam., of Bladon, masons, xxvii
Jn., 70, 139, 203
Ric., of Bladon, 87, 122
Ursula, w. of Ric., 122
Waste
Christian, wid. of Jas., 42
Jas., (d. 1609), 42
Wat(t)son
Mris., of Offenham, Worcs., vctlr., 16
Robt., gent., 272, 324
Waterhouse
Edw., of Whitchurch, Bucks., 246
Watkins
Geo., 325
Wayte
Will., 210
Webb(e)
Geo., 278, 284, 294
Ric., 226, 269
Robt., 202
Thos., W., svt., 99, 172, 183, 196, 199, 205, 207, 211, 213, 217, 218, 219, 278
Will., 170
Webster
Jn., 266

Weedon
Chris., 72, 140
Welbeck
Arth., 201
Wellman
Thos., 107
Wells
Dorothy, wid. of Will., W., vctlr., 206, 218, 239, 300
Jn., W., tail., 259
Ric., s. of Jn., W., appr., 259
Thos., of Farthinghoe, Northants., upholsterer, 119
Will., jun.?, 220, 332
Will., W., frmn., vctlr., (d. by 1613), 29, 84, 96
Wenman
Anth., gent., 267
Wergo (Werge)
Thos., 159
Weswod?
Ric., W., non-frmn., 29
Wheate
Jn., of Ducklington, 289
Wheeler
--., w. of Will., 132
Chris., 220, 229
Will., W., carp., 92, 132, 174, 178, 184, 206, 220
Whickers
Jane, wid., 330
Whing(e)
Ric., xxii, 1, 19, 21, 63, 185, 197, 216, 248
Whit(t)field (Whit(t)feild)
Will., 58, 113
White
Alice, wid. of Jerome, W., vctlr., 301, 315, 336, 339, 341, 359
Edm., 212, 217
Edw., 49
'goodwife', 332
Hen., 232
Jerome, W., serg., attorney, shoem., vctlr., (d. 1618), xvi, 3, 7, 9, 10, 11, 26, 29, 30, 34, 35, 38, 39, 41, 42, 45, 48, 50, 53, 61, 73, 74, 77, 83, 84, 95, 96, 103, 107, 108, 110, 113, 114, 115, 118, 121, 128, 129, 141, 142, 144, 145, 153, 155, 156, 158, 168, 177, 178, 182, 183, 196, 198, 199, 205, 206, 218, 221, 228, 229, 232, 234, 239, 244, 245, 249, 251, 257, 258, 259, 262, 263, 264, 266, 268, 269, 271, 272, 273, 274, 275, 276, 277, 302, 364
Joan, 40
Mich., W., 23
Peter, s. of Jerome, W., appr., 302
Robt., 232
Thos., 111, 204, 224, 232
Will., 160, 167
Whitelock(e) (Whitlock(e))
Jas., kt., recorder, xv, xvi, xxx, 3, 23, 41, 50, 58, 91, 116, 138, 139, 225, 339, 340
Whiteside
Hen., W., frmn., shoem., vctlr., 307, 308, 312, 314, 315, 319, 322, 325, 327, 334, 335, 337, 338, 339, 340, 341, 351, 359, 360, 363, 370, 371
Whitforde
Edw., W., appr., 157
Whiting(e)
Robt., 296
Will., W., frmn., 232, 264, 363
Whitton
(als. Darling(e)), Jn., s. of Geo., xxiii, xxvii, 4, 20, 66, 78, 81, 170, 198, 217, 226, 240, 241, 243, 284
Geo., esq., of Woodstock park (d. 1606), 20, 66
Hen., gent., W., 4, 81
Hester, w. of Jn., xxvii, 240, 243
Mr., 38, 82, 93
Whorde
Dorothy, wid. W., (d. 1617), 66
Widdowes
Ethelbert, 260
Wierman
--., 1
Wiggins
Jn., 105
Wilde
Edw., 320
Wilkins
Walt., gent., 292

Wilkinson
Jn., W. frmn., 3, 29, 48, 53, 73, 156, 168, 196, 205, 234, 291, 363, 364, 367, 368, 369, 371
Wilkshere
Thos., 298
Williams
--., 165, 325
--., w. of Jn., Market Harborough, 119
Griffin, of Banbury, ostler, 22
Jn., of Market Harborough, Leics., 119
Thos., W., counc., innk., bkr., 7, 9, 10, 11, 12, 23, 26, 29, 34, 35, 37, 38, 41, 42, 45, 46, 48, 50, 58, 61, 65, 67, 74, 83, 84, 95, 96, 98, 102, 103, 110, 113, 114, 115, 118, 129, 141, 153, 156, 168, 169, 182, 183, 191, 195, 196, 199, 200, 206, 218, 224, 238, 239, 245, 249, 258, 259, 262, 270, 279, 280, 281, 291, 300, 305, 307, 308, 314, 315, 327, 329, 333, 334, 337, 345, 351, 352, 353, 358, 359, 363, 364, 367, 368, 369, 370
Williamson
Thos., of Clandon, Surrey, yeo., 111
Willis
Martin, 302, 303
Thos., 139, 157
Will., 302, 303
Wilse
Ann, wid., mother of Jas., 124
Jas., of Much Marcle, Herefords., butch., 124
Winchester
Thos., 232, 282
Winter
Robt., W., frmn., vctlr., 6, 29, 167, 175, 189, 249, 281, 292, 301, 364
Thos., 336
Wise
Thos., 101
Will., xxii, 39, 78, 79, 83
Witham
(als.Dearle) Jn., 190
Daniel, xxvi, 183
Withe
Fras., gent., of Leyton, Essex, svt., horse dealer, xxxv, 16
Wood(d)
Fras., 42
Woodbridge
--., 79
Will., grain supplier, 39
Woodroof(f)e (Woodrough)
Jn., Old W., woolman, 30, 37, 41, 215, 225, 239, 269, 299
Jn., s. of Jn., W., appr., 269, 299
Woodward
Thos., W., frmn., 308, 312, 314, 319, 327, 334, 337, 340, 342, 345, 349, 351, 353, 359, 363, 371
Woollam
Jn., 155
Woollington
Jas., 234
Woolly
Edw., 221, 236, 275, 281, 325
Wright(e) (Write, Right)
Jas., of Bledington, Glos., 130
Mr., of Oxford, goldsmith, 25, 28
Mr., of Smithfield bar, innk., 111
Ric., of Clapton, 124
Ric., W., counc., 11, 19, 29, 30, 61, 74, 81, 83, 139, 172, 364
widow, W., 342
Writington (Wrightington)
Jn., 343
Writon
Ric., 81
Wyly (Wilye)
Jn., 268, 274

Yeate
Ric., butch., 348
Yeatman
--., w. of Ric., 229
Ric., 229
Yonge
--., 247
Jn., W., frmn., 264, 268
Nic., W., 146, 224, 252, 268, 320, 322
Ric., 216, 252
Thos., 331
Walt., 187, 228, 260

INDEX OF PLACES

Oxfordshire places are indexed without the county identification but other places are identified by the counties to which they belonged before the local government reorganization of 1974.

Abergavenny (Mon.), 54
Abingdon ('Abbington') (Berks.)
  fair, 166
Adderbury, 119
Adlestrop (Glos.), 16
Akeley ('Ackly') (Bucks.), 70, 75
Alcester ('Auster') (Warks.)
  Avon Bridge, 103
  market, 103
Aldenham (Herts.) ('Alnam in Com. Hatford'), 129, 130
Allerton (Notts.), 111
Allym (?Lymm) (Chesh.), 58
Ascott (under Wychwood), 265
Ashby-de-la-Zouch ('Asbie de la zouch') (Leics.), 147
Attercliffe ('Aterclife') (Yorks.), 71, 75
Aynho ('Aynow')-on-the-hill (Northants.), 55, 59

Banbury ('Bandbury'), xxx, 22, 104, 130
  market, 104
Barton, 98, 156, 336
Basford ('Baseforth','Basonworth') (Notts.), 14
Bath ('Bathe') The, 148
Beamhurst ('Beamehurst') (Staffs.), 103
Bedfordshire, 71, 75
Begbroke, xxii, 9, 132
Berkshire, xvii, 28, 166
Bicester ('Bissiter' 'Bister' 'Burcester'), xxix, xxxvi, 24, 58, 98, 99, 112, 118, 119, 187, 285
  fair, 98
  market, xxxvi, 104
Birmingham ('Broomecham'), 71, 103
  market, 71
Bladon, xxii, xxiii, xxiv, xxvii, xxxiv, 49, 366
Bledington (Glos.), 130
Bletchingdon ('Blechington'), xxii, xxiv, 187
Blithfield ('Blifild') (Staffs.), 104
Bodicote ('Boddicott'), 156
Bourton-on-the-Hill (Glos.), 16
Bristol ('Bristowe'), xxiii, 148, 346
Britwell, 28
Broad Campden ('Broade Camden') (Glos.), 108
Broadway (Worcs.), xxxv, 16
  Green Dragon Inn, 16
  Hill, 16
Bromley (Kent), 13
Buckingham, xxxvi, 43, 71
  Bell inn, 43
Buckinghamshire, xxxiii, 12, 23, 43, 58, 70, 75, 100, 246
Burford, xxx, 59, 265
  market, 46

Caen, University, France, xiii
Campsfield, 12, 136
Cassington, xx, xxii, xxiii, 47
  West Mead, 47
Charlbury, 76, 106
Charlton-on-Otmoor ('Charleton'), 127
Cheltenham (Glos.), 10
Cherrington (Warks.), 59
Cheshire, 58
Chester, 340
Chesterton, 187
Chipping Norton, 8, 16, 104
  Chapel-on-the-Heath, 17
  Hart inn, 104
  market, 104
  Swan Inn, 8, 17
Churchill, 59
Clandon (Surrey), 111

Clapton (Glos.?), 124
Cleeve (?Prior) (Worcs.), 16
Cleveley ('Cleevely' 'Clifly'), xxxi, 47, 310, 326
field, 47
Clifford (Leics.), 13
Clifton-upon-Dunsmore (Warks.), 56
Combe ('Coombe'), 316
Cornwall, 8
Cotswolds, xxxvi
Coventry (Warks.), 71
Cowley, 142, 143
Cumnor (Berks.), 28
Cutteslowe ('Cutislow')
mill, 131

Dedbone tower, 47
Deddington, xxii, xxvi, xxxvi, 13, 76, 95, 104, 118, 119, 162, 163, 212, 220
alehouse, Anthony Mercer's, 119
bridge, xxxvii, 162
downs, 162
fair, xxxvi, 118, 119
Derbyshire, xxxvi, 54
Ditchley, xxxvi
House, 161
Dorchester, (Dorset), xxxv
Droitwich (Worcs.), 55
Ducklington ('Ducklynton'), 289
Dunham (Notts.), 179
Dunstable (Beds.), 71, 75

Edenbridge ('Eatonbridge') (Kent), 58
Enstone, xxxvi, 16, 17, 104, 130
market, 130
Talbot ('Tabut') inn, 17
Essex, xxxv, 16
Evesham ('Eysham') (Worcs.), xxxv, 16, 17, 104
Hart inn, 104
market, 104
Eynsham ('Ensham'), xxii, xxiii, xxxiii, xxxvi, 43, 46, 47, 99, 103
Broadclose, 46, 47

Farmington (Glos.), 10
Farthinghoe ('Farthingoe') (Northants.), 118, 119
Farthingstone (Northants.), 43
Fencott, 127
France, xiii

Gloucester, 7, 130
Gloucestershire, 10, 16, 28, 54, 59, 104, 108, 124, 130, 308
Great Barrington (Glos.), 59
Greenwich ('Greenewich') (Kent), 58

Hampton Meade, 25
Hanborough ('Handborowe' 'Handboughrough'), xxii, 59, 110, 137, 162
Hanley or Hanbury ('Hanlinge') (Worcs.), 118
Harborough ('Harborowe') (Leics.). *See* Market Harborough
Helmdon ('Helmeden') (Northants.), 43
Hensington, xxiii, xxiv, xxvii, 220
Herefordshire, xxxiii, 124
Hertfordshire ('Com. Hatford'), xxxvi, xxxviii, 129, 130, 312
Heyford ('Hayford'), 104
Bridge (ad pontem) (Lower Heyford), 12
inn, 104
Holden ('Howden'), (Yorks.), 13
Hook Norton ('Hoocknorton'), xxxvi, 165
alehouse, 104

Inkberrow ('Inckbourough' 'Inckborrough') (Worcs.), 17, 108
Islip ('Islipp'), xxxvi, 130, 186, 187

Kegworth (Leics.), 13
Kent, xxxiii, 12, 13, 58
Kettering (Northants.), 55
Kidlington, 166
Kirtlington, xxiv, 111

Lambeth ('Lambarte ') (Surrey), 59
Lancashire, xxxii
Leafield ('Le Feild'), xxii, xxviii, 59, 200
common, 59
Ledwell, 54, 56, 59
Leicestershire, 13, 105, 119, 147
Lenton (Notts.), 14

Leyton (Essex), 16
Lichfield ('Litchfeild') (Staffs.), 103
  Hart inn, 103
Littlemore ('Litlemore'), xxxi, 142, 145
Llanfairwaterdine ('Hanver Water deane') (Salop.), 166
Llantilio Crossenny ('Landilo Cresselle') (Mon.), 54
London, xxxi, xxxii, xxxv, xxxvi, 12, 13, 16, 43, 148, 152
  Bread Street ('Bredstreet'), 22
  Carter Lane, Bell inn, 54
  Chancery, 157
  city of, 282, 307
  Cripplegate, St.Giles without, 12
  Drury ('Drewery') Lane, 13
  Holborn ('Howborne')
    Plover inn, 55
    Three Cups inn, 13
  Lambeth, 59
  Ludgate Hill, Cross Keys inn, 22
  Old Bailey, Roebuck Inn, 16
  Sergeant's Inn, Chancery Lane, 236
  Smithfield, 14, 148
    Pye Corner, 54
  Smithfield bar, The Castle inn, 111
  St. Bartholomew the Great parish, 287
  St. Giles, 152
  Strand, 12
    White Hart inn, 148
  Westminster, xix, xxiii, xxix, xxxviii, 60, 70, 90, 105, 107, 108, 111, 120, 145, 178, 179, 198, 207, 222, 236, 247, 250, 256, 263, 267, 272, 276, 281, 287, 294, 297, 305, 311, 334, 335, 344, 348, 354, 355
    King's Street, 54
    palace of, 333
    St.Margaret's, Bell inn, 178
Loudon, (Cornwall) (?Lewdown, (Devon)), 8
  Red Cock inn, 8
Ludlow (Salop.), xxxv, 43

Market Harborough ('Markett Harborowe') ('Warks.') (i.e. Leics.), 119
Merton ('Marton'), 188
Midlands, xxxvi
Milton, xxxi, 271
Monmouthshire, 54
Moreton-in-Marsh ('Morton Hinmost') (Glos.), 104
Much Marcle ('Mitch Markle') (Herefords.), 124, 125
  Hind inn, 124
Murcott, 127

Newent, ('Newont'), (Glos.), 308
Newmarket, ('New markett' 'Newmarkett') (Suffolk), xxxviii, 300, 315, 360
Newnham ('Newnam') (Warks.), 148
Normandy, (France), xiii
North Leigh ('Northly'), 166
North Staffordshire, xxxvi
Northamptonshire, xxxvii, 43, 55, 59, 104, 118, 119, 163
Northbrook, ('Northbrock'), 324
Nottingham, xxxiii, 13, 14
  Bull's Head inn, 14
Nottinghamshire, 12, 13, 14, 111, 179

Oddington, 155, 187, 238
Offenham (Worcs.), xxxv, 16, 17
  alehouse, 16, 17
Otmoor, xxix, xxxi
Oxford, xiii, xv, xxxii, xxxv, xxxvi, 13, 16, 25, 47, 56, 59, 76, 92, 98, 111, 148
  city of, 43, 61, 76, 317, 328
  gaol, xxxiii, xxxv, xxxvi, 13, 336
  highway, 366
  Holywell, 76
  market, 47
  Merton ('Martyn') College, 143
  New Inn, 43
  St.Peter le Bailey, ('St.Peeters on the Bailly') parish, 308
  St.Thomas parish, 13
  university, xxv, 150, 156
Oxfordshire, North, xxxvi

Pershore ('Parshewe') (Worcs.), 104
  Bull inn, 104
Presteigne ('Presteene') (Radnor.), 58

Radnorshire ('Com. Ladnock'), 58
Royston, (Herts.), xxxviii, 312

Saintbury ('Sayntbury') (Glos.), 16
Salisbury, (Wilts.), 241, 255
Sandford, 76
  Hugh Busby's alehouse, 76
Sandford (St.Martin), 55
Severn ('Seaverne') Stoke (Worcs.), 145
Sheffield (Yorks.), 71
Shipston-on-Stour ('Shipson') (Worcs.), 104
  market, 104
  Swan inn, 104
Shropshire (Salop.), xxxv, 43, 166
Somerset, 8
South Leigh, 59
South Wales, xxxvi
Staffordshire, xxxiii, xxxvi, 103, 104
Standlake, xxxvi, 46, 47
Stanton Harcourt ('Stannton Harecout'), 119
Stanton St. John('s'), 188
Staunton (Glos.), 54
Steeple Aston, xxxi, 330
Stonesfield ('Stonsfeild'), 100
Stowe (Bucks.), 58
  Hartshorn inn, 58
Stow-on-the-Wold (Glos.), 28
Stratford-upon-Avon (Warks.), 103, 104, 124
  market, 103
  Swan inn, 103
Stratton Audley, 35
Suffolk, xxxviii, 315, 360
Surrey, 59, 111
Sussex, xxxv
Sutton (Herefords.), 124
Swerford ('Swarford'), 152

Tackley, 39
Tanworth ('Tannworth') (Warks.), 55
Tew ('Tewe'), 7, 291
  Duns Tew ('Dunstewe'), 55, 162
  Great (Magna), 7, 17, 52
    Ric.Bicks' alehouse, 54
Thrupp, 12
Towcester (Northants.), 43
Troyes, France, xiii
Tysoe ('Ticoe') (Northants.), 104

Virginia, America, 55

Warsop ('Worsopp') (Notts.), 12, 13, 14
  inn, 12
Warwick, 71, 103
  New Inn, 103
Warwickshire, xxxvi, 17, 55, 59, 71, 103, 104, 119, 124, 148
Water Eaton, 166
Watford ('Wattford') (Herts.), 129
Welford (Warks.), 17
Wells, (Somerset), 8
  Three Horseloaves inn, 8
Weston-on-the-Green, xxiv, 146, 331
Whitchurch ('Whichurch') (Bucks.), 246
Wiltshire, 241, 255
Winchcombe (Glos.), xxxvi, 54
Windsor, New, (Berks.), xvii
Witney, xxx, 24
Woodstock Park, xxxvi, 93, 160, 165, 230
  Hensgrove, 93
  high park, 160
  wall, 161
Woodstock, New, xvi, xxxvi, 230, 243, 366
  alehouses
    Henry Rudgate's, 27
    Nich.Glover's, 23
    widow Ashpole's, 106
  bays, the, 95
  Blackhall Lane, 51
  borough of, 197, 342, 362
  Bull inn, 22, 25
  Chantry House, xxvi, 89
  church, 35, 89
  Common Green, the, 4
  Coop(er)yware Street, 82
  Cross, The High, 100, 134, 152
  Crowe's Lane, 110
  fair, xxxvi, 55, 93, 114, 130
  George Inn, 71, 178
  Guildhall, xvii, 3, 35, 61, 102, 191, 226, 312, 333, 358, 360
  Hogmarket Street, 4
  Holloway, the, xxvii, 6, 11, 51

Woodstock, New (cont.)
Horsemarket Street, 82
John Bruce's house, 213
John Kirbye's house, 332
'king's highway', xli
Le Poole, 136
'le Spence', 366
Mainards, 192
malthouse, Jerome Kyte's, 95
manor, xiv
market, xl, 63, 76, 96, 104, 163, 166
Mr. Whitton's close, 82
Munck's mead, 136
Mundyes Place, 192
Oxford Road, xli
Oxford Street, 7, 185, 193
pease market, 166
Petty John's Lane, 4, 20
Pigeon-house garden, 82
prison, 2, 24, 191, 222
Rose Inn, 12
stocks, xxxiv, 107
town clerk's house, 92
whipping post, 101
Woodstock, Old, xviii, 152, 239, 269, 299
field, 254
Jerome Nash's close, 152
Spitle Close, 254
Wookey, (Somerset), 8
Wootton, xxii, xxiii, 24, 119, 125, 138, 283
Hordley, xviii, xxii, xxiii
Mill, 39
Hundred, xviii, xxiii
parson, 161
Wootton Underwood (Bucks.), 23
Worcester, xxxvi, 104
market, xxxvi
Worcestershire, xxxv, xxxvi, 16, 17, 55, 104, 108, 118, 145
Wycombe ('Wyckham'), (Bucks.), 12

Yarnton ('Yearneton'), 145
York, xxxv, 12, 13, 14
Wainegate, 13
Yorkshire, 13, 71, 75

INDEX OF SUBJECTS

Specific trades and occupations are grouped under the entry 'trades'; court and borough officers are grouped under 'officers'; references to other courts are collected under 'courts'; in the Portmoot the various plaints are grouped under 'actions' and the types of process under 'procedure' including a section on forms of writ.

abatement, plea in, 153
abduction, plaint of, xx, 86
access, to property, 123
acknowledgement, of plaint, 174, 183, 184, 187, 188
acre's breadth, 166
actions (Portmoot)
  account, xviii, xxv, xxix, xliii, 19, 45, 155, 158, 183, 190, 199, 204, 213, 225, 258, 259, 266, 268, 283, 321, 323, 331, 332, 341
  against (clerk of court and) Commonalty, xx, 25, 90
  common recovery, xix, xxvi, xxvii, xliv, 1, 14, 110, 197
  covenant, 231, 349
  debt, xxv, *See* text *passim*
    on stated demand, 224, 230, 237, 269, 317, 323, 329, 346, 347
    under threat (*per minas*), xlvii, 159, 223, 225, 228, 230, 240, 247, 249, 250, 253, 261, 262, 273, 282, 284, 286, 287, 305, 307, 318
  detainer, 121
  detinue, xviii, xxvi, xxix, xliv, 49, 72, 79, 150, 165, 167, 185, 195, 208, 222, 236, 268, 274, 283, 322
  dower, xix, xxvi, xxvii, 86, 94
  ejectment, xix, xxii, xxvi, xxvii, xxix, xliv, 73, 94, 176
  land claim, 178
  Qui Tam, xviii, xxii, xxv, xxviii, xlvi, xlviii, 7, 44, 57, 67, 69, 200, 201, 202, 203, 204, 205, 208, 209, 210, 211
  slander, xxxiv, 49
  trespass, xviii, *See* text *passim*
  trespass on case, xviii, *See* text *passim*
    non-payment, 88
  unspecified, xix, 79, 164, 165, 208, 210, 212, 330
  waste, xxii, l, 116, 118
administrator(-trix), xxi, xliii, 2, 72, 106, 155, 157, 197, 224, 232, 299, 323, 326, 357
advice
  of jury, 51
  of Portmoot, 18, 21, 105, 106, 153, 157, 173
  of recorder, xv, 54, 96, 175, 191, 197, 201, 225, 264, 355
affeerers, xliii, 9, 37, 61, 74, 83, 115, 169, 182, 196, 206, 218, 238, 249, 259, 270, 279, 291, 300, 308, 314, 327, 337, 351
ale
  assize of, xxxi, xxxix, 15, 30, 31, 32, 63, 140, 245, 312, 345, 353, 354, 360, *See also* assize of bread and ale
  brewing rate, xxxix, 15, 38
  -tasters, xvi, *See* officers of borough and courts
ale-draper, xliii, 147
alehouses. *See* victuallers
alienation of property
  wife's, xxvi, 86
allegiance
  oath of, 82, 83
appraisers, 182, 215, 243, 291, 310, 322, 325
apprentices(-ships), xxxi, 43, 81, 98, 100, 112, 113, 121, 137, 155, 157, 159, 186, 255, 259, 269, 271, 275, 282, 283, 294, 299, 302, 307, 326, 330, 335, 352
  bakers, rules of, xxxi, 31
  runaway, xxxiv, 10

arbitration. *See under* procedures
(Portmoot)
order on, 96
Arches. *See also* courts
Court of, 12
arrears, 18, 25, 36, 308
arrest, custody, prison. (civil) *see under* procedure (Portmoot)
arrest, custody, prison (criminal), 5, 13, 16, 23, 24, 37, 69, 95, 97, 107, 111, 187, 295, 351
assart ('sart'), 161
assault, xviii, *See* breaches of the peace
assize of bread and ale, xxxix, 15, 30, 31, 34, 63, 140, 345, 353, 360
assizes. *See under* courts
assumpsit, xxix, xliii, 22, 95, 108, 163
attorneys
costs of, 188
non-instruction of (*non sum informatus*), xxx, 164, 167, 199, 202, 205, 225, 226, 228, 234, 237, 240, 241, 247, 255, 259
of Lambeth, 59
Portmoot, xvi, xx, xxi, xxx
Westminster Courts, xxiii, 198, 263, 267, 294, 306, 311, 335

bacon (Lent), 312
bail, delivered on, 84, 160
bailiff(s)
at Oxford, 16
of land (Bletchingdon), 187
of Wootton Hundred, 125
bakers. *See* trades and occupations
assize, 31, 32, 33, 63
grain usage in dearth, xxviii, xxxix, 38
barley, usage in dearth, 38
barns, 1, 14, 110, 123, 240
base-child, xxxiv, xxxviii, xliii, 9, 36, 58, 219, 270, 308, 316, 327
bays, xliii, 95
beating, 303, 348
bible, 55
bill a veva (notice of inspection), 96
bill of costs, 354
bills (money), 22, 36
bishop
of Bristol, xxiii, 346
of Salisbury, 241, 255
blown, xliii, 33
bonds
made under threat (*per minas)*, xlvii, 159
with unreasonable conditions, 177
bonds (money), xviii, xxv, 3, 12, 22, 45, 53, 65, 88, 114, 118, 146, 148, 157, 177, 186, 345
borough
bylaws, xiv, xxxi, 96
census, xxvii, xxxix
charters, xvii, xxxii, 26
constitution, xvi
customs, xxix
officers. *See under* officers, borough
actions against, 90
orders, xxxi, 191, 226, 270, 328
records, xiii
box, shop-, 131
breaches of the peace, xiii, xxxi, xxxiii, xxxv, xxxvi, 5, 22, 24, 25, 26, 37, 39, 52, 53, 77, 84, 87, 93, 95, 107, 119, 142, 143, 156, 182, 199, 206, 207, 212, 218, 219, 220, 238, 241, 248, 266, 295, 303, 304, 317, 318, 328, 332, 338, 348
bread. *See* assize of bread and ale
baking rates at dearth, 38
cheat, xliii, 31
cocket, xliii, 345, 353
brewers. *See* assize of bread and ale
assize rules, 15, 31, 63, 354
at dearth, xxxix, 38
brewhouse, common, 138
burgage plots, 4, 6, 7, 11, 51, 66, 81, 89, 97, 115, 143
burgesses. *See* Parliament
(freemen-burgesses. *See* freemen and commonalty)
butchers. *See* trades *and* Lent, flesh in
assize rules, 31, 47, 64, 358
licence, 48, 334, 359
bylaws, xxxi, 96

cadman, 137

calf-skins, 25
candles, xliii, xlix
  assize of, 31, 33, 64, 346
cast (vomit), 147
census of the borough, xxvii, xxxix, 28, 29
chandlers. *See under* trades
  assize. *See under* candles
charity, xv, xxvii, xxxviii, xl, 6, *See also* Doleman's charity
child maintenance, xxxiv, xxxviii, 9, 10, 36, 58, 219, 270, 308, 327, 328
childing ('childing' wives), 333
clerk of the church, 35
clerk of the court. *See* officers of the borough
clerk of the market. *See* officers of the borough
  Royal, xxxviii, xl
clerks, 3, 7, 11, 14, 58, 78, 108, 110, 186, 221, 245, 280, 318, 324, 328
  of Bucks., 23
  of Warks., 17
closes, 81, 152, 174, 240, 254
commissioner ('commissary') of Bucks., 70
commodity prices, xxxviii, *See* assize of bread and ale
common council, xv, 9, 25, 28, 35, 91, 93, 102, 191
common law process, xviii
commonalty of Woodstock, xv, xvii, xx, xxiii, 91, 125, 163, 215, 243, 310, *See also* freemen of Woodstock
communion gift, 99
compounding, xxviii, xliv, 67, 69, 201, 202, 203, 208, 211
compurgators, xxix, xliv, *See* procedure (Portmoot); trial by wager of law
concord (compromise), 79, 80, 186
confiscations. *See* forfeits
considerations, 188, *See also assumpsit*
constables. *See* officers of borough and courts
  of Deddington, 118, 119
consumption, food in dearth, 38
contempt of court, 25
convented, 191
conveyances (final concords), xiv, xvii, xix, xxvi, 1, 4, 6, 7, 11, 20, 51, 66, 81, 86, 87, 97, 115, 122, 124, 125, 143, 146, 150, 174, 184, 191, 193, 240, 243, 253, 342
  land use, xxvii
  none objects, 154
  wife's alienation of property by, xxvi, 86, 87
copulation, unlawful, xxxiv, xxxviii, 92
coram justiciarii Domini Regis, xliv, 60, *See* courts, Westminster, Common Pleas
coram nobis and *coram dominum rege*, xliv, *See* courts, Westminster, King's Bench
coroner's court, xxxi, 142
corporation, Woodstock
  business, xiv, xxxi, xl, 95, 102, 138, 188
  land, xl, 25, 95, 102
  moneys, xl, 75, 163
costs, court, 188
counterfeiter of letters, xxxiv, xxxvi, 59
country, put oneself on (*ponit se super patriam*), xliv, *See* procedures (Portmoot), trial by jury
court books, xiii
court days, xvi
courts
  Arches, court of, 12
  Banbury, xxx
  baron, court, xviii, 226
  Burford, xxx
  Cowley, court leet, 142
  Dorset, quarter sessions and assizes, xxxv
  East Sussex, quarter sessions, xxxv
  Inns of Court, 236
  Islip, 187
  Oxford (Oxon')
    assizes
      attendances, xv, xxxii, *See* officers; mayor and town clerk
      cases, indictments, xxxiii, xxxiv, 13, 16, 17, 24, 59, 103, 136, 148, 161, 163
    gaol delivery, general. *See as* main item
    Oxford town sessions, xxxiii, 16
    quarter sessions, Oxfordshire, xxxiii, xxxv, 24, 43, 56, 136, 161

courts (cont.)
Oxford University, Vice-Chancellor's court, xxv, 150
Westminster, xix, xx, xxiii, xxix
Barons of the Exchequer, xxviii, 222
Chancery, xxv, 157, 247, 256, 361
Common Pleas, xx, xxiii, 60, 250, 263, 267, 294, 311, 335, 344
King's Bench, xxiii, 18, 70, 71, 90, 105, 108, 111, 120, 145, 147, 178, 207, 236, 247, 256, 272, 281, 287, 305, 354
unspecified courts, xx, xxiii, xxvi, 68, 78, 79, 107, 117
Witney, xxx
Wootton Hundred, xviii
cows, 72, 289
craw fishing, 99
crimes, major, xxxii, *See* Oxon' assizes and sessions
curtilages, 97, 243
custody. *See* arrest
custom of the borough, xxix, 62, 150, 286, 362
custom of the court (Portmoot), 80
cut-purse, 13

dagger-strike, 5, 99, 108, 156
dancing, night-time, xxxvii, 10
dearth, grain survey, xxviii, xxxvii, xxxix, 38
death
cases of, xxxi, xxxii, 142, 173
mayoral, in office, xvi, 3, 91
penalty, xxxiii, xxxv, xxxvi, 56
settlement, 86
under threat of, xxxiii, 25, 35, 103, 107, 143, 187, 207, 241, 304, 317, 338
debt. *See* actions (Portmoot)
on demand, 157, 224, 230, 237, 269, 317, 323, 329, 346
deeds
settlement, 86
deeds (*scripti obligator*), 68, 118, 177, *See* bonds
deer, xxxiii, xxxvi, 160, 165
defaults. *See* procedure (Portmoot)
deforciants, xliv, *See* conveyances
depositions of criminal examinations, xxxii, xxxv, *See* examinations
dereliction of duty, borough officers, xxxiv, 92, 107
detinue. *See* actions (Portmoot)
diet, 92
discharge of victuallers, xxxvii, *See* licensing, victuallers
disorder, xxxiii, 5, 23, 107, 120
display of stolen goods, 100
disseisin, xxvii
distraint, 23
Doleman's charity, xl, 23, 25
dower, action of. *See* actions (Portmoot)
draw to, 161
drunkenness, xxxiii, 99, 108, 142, 338, 339, *See also* disorder

ejectment, xxvi, xliv, *See* actions (Portmoot)
elections, xvi
freemen, xvi, 11, 42
MP. *See* Parliament
officers of borough and courts, 115, 156, 205, 220, 249, 280, 291, 300, 307, 341, 351, *See* as main item
to Common Council, 35, 93
ell, xliv, 34, 97, 110, 118, 119, 245, *See also* weights and measures
encroachments, xxxi, 95, and *see* mounds
escape from custody, 58, 62, 75, 187
esquire, 229, 285, 355
estreats, xxxi, 9, 37, 156, 292
eviction (legal recovery), 163
examinations
criminal, xiv, xv, xxxii, 5, 7, 8, 10, 12, 16, 22, 23, 24, 25, 28, 37, 43, 46, 54, 58, 59, 61, 71, 76, 92, 97, 103, 108, 111, 118, 119, 124, 129, 130, 136, 137, 143, 147, 152, 161, 162, 165, 166, 173, 178, 328, 332, 336
depositions, xxxii
summary, xxxii
travellers', xxxv
vagrants', xxxv, 152
private, xxvi, 86, 87

executor(-trix), 21, 52, 106, 108, 125, 173, 227, 232, 241, 285, 341, 349
extension of borough sessions and leet, 96

fairing, xlv, 98
fairs, xxxii, xxxiii, xxxiv, xxxvi, 55, 93, 108, 114, 130, *and see* Abingdon, Bicester and Deddington
fathers, reputed, xxxiv, xxxviii, xliii, 9, 36, 58, 219, 316
felons' goods. *See* forfeits *and* punishments
fields (Old Woodstock), 254
final concords (fines). *See* conveyances
fines (penalties). *See* punishments *and* sessions, borough court
fish days (Lent), 312, 333, 334, 358
flaxen cloth, 97
flaying, 47
foot-clothes, xlv, 147
forfeits
  by defendant for non-appearance, 182
  of bail, 36, 206, 218, 219, 230, 239, 308, 314, 328
  of bond, 186
  of felon's goods, 6, 8, 43, 58, 71, 119, 156, 163, 166, 188, 324, 332
  of livestock, 215, 243, 291, 322
  of sureties, 62, 75
  of weapon, 156
frame, wooden, 95
frankpledge, view of, xxxi, 8, 50, 61, 74, 83, 95, 115, 141, 156, 168, 182, 195, 205, 218, 229, 238, 249, 259, 270, 279, 291, 300, 307, 314, 327, 337, 350
freemen-burgesses (commonalty), xv, xvi
  census, xxxix, 28, 29
  disfranchisement, 191
  elections, xvi, 11, 42
  lists, 363, 364, 365
furlong, xlv, 47
fustian, 55

galloon, xlv, 134
games, 26, 138, 339
gaol. *See also* arrest *and* prison
  delivery, general, xxxv, 24, 43, 47, 56, 59, 103, 119, 136, 137, 163
  Oxford, xxxiii, xxxv, 13, 43, 336
  threat, 97
gaoler of Oxford, 13
garbell ('garbol'), xlv, 32
gardens, 1, 14, 20, 82, 97, 102, 110, 122, 124, 178, 198, 243, 339, 342
gawne, xlv, 118
gelding, 148, 150, 161, 243, 265, 322
gentlemen. *See* texts *passim*
  arrested, 230, 284
  in conveyances, 240, 243, 343
  innholders, 196, 206, 218, 334
  litigants, 197, 200, 213, 217, 218, 226, 228, 241, 243, 246, 248, 252, 255, 259, 264, 267, 269, 274, 275, 279, 281, 284, 285, 287, 291, 292, 298, 314, 316, 317, 322, 324, 330, 331, 337, 341, 344, 346
gold, 256
goods and chattels, 2, 5, 18, 26, 27, 72, 106, 155, 157, 197, 224, 232, 243, 249, 258, 289, 299, 320, 323, 357, *See also* administrator(-trix)
goods of defendant. *See* writ of *fieri facias*
grain
  dearth. *See under* dearth
  suppliers, 38
  see also assize of bread and ale
granary, 240
greyhounds, hunting with, xxxvi, 160, 165
groats, 103
guardianship, xxix, 226, 285
guildhall, xvii, 3, 35, 91, *and see* B78/3 text *passim*
gurgeons, xlv, 137

habere facias seisinam, xlv, *See* procedure (Portmoot) - writs
half-seal of University of Oxford, xxv, 150
hay, 12, 136, 137
  -mow, xlv, 97
headings for court sittings, xviii
heir, nearest, 146
high cross, 100, 134, 152
hoggerel, xlv, 104
holland ('hallan'), xlv, 119, 132, 134
horseloaves, xlv, 31

horses, 43, 54, 108, 136, 150, 161
  assault on, 108
  confiscated, 56, 163, 215, 243, 322
  -scorcers, xxxv, xxxvi, xlv, 12, 13, 14, 129
  theft. *See under* thefts
  -thieves, xxxiii, xxxv, xxxvi
  valued, 215, 243, 310, 322
hundred bailiff (Wootton), 125
hunting, felonies with greyhounds, xxxvi, 160, 165
husbandman, 103

imprisoning, private, 86
information, xlv
  on criminal offences, xxxii, 12, 39, 56, 70, 87, 93, 97, 99, 103, 105, 112, 120, 160, 166, 172, 187
  on penal statutes. *see Qui Tam under* actions (Portmoot)
informer, paid, xxxiii, 56
inns, 10, 12, 23, 25, 71, 178, *See* Broadway, Buckingham, Chipping Norton, Enstone, Evesham, Hook Norton, Heyford, Lichfield, London, Loudon, Moreton-in-Marsh, Much Marcle, Nottingham, Oxford, Pershore, Shipston-on-Stour, Stowe, Stratford-upon-Avon, Warsop, Warwick, Wells
  minister's stay at, 23
inquest, xxxi, 142
inquiry, writ of. *See* procedure (Portmoot)
inspection, notice of (leet jurors), 10, 95

jakes, xlvi, 47
judge (Sir Jn.Crooke), 84, 92
juries, xix, xxix, xxx, xxxi, xxxii, xxxvii, xxxviii, xxxix
  flesh in Lent, 4, 47, 73, 128, 312, 333, 360
  for clerk of market, 15, 63, 110, 244, 345, 353, 359
  for coroner (signatures), 145
  frankpledge/sessions, xxxi, xxxii, 9, 36, 50, 61, 74, 83, 95, 113, 115, 141, 156, 168, 182, 196, 205, 218, 229, 238, 249, 259, 270, 279, 291, 300, 307, 314, 327, 337, 350
  licensing assize, 312, 316, 333, 359, 360
    drafted from sessions offenders, xxxvii, 62
  Portmoot, xix, 3, 7, 26, 41, 45, 50, 53, 65, 67, 68, 74, 77, 103, 114, 118, 121, 123, 129, 144, 153, 155, 158, 162, 172, 177, 178, 183, 199, 214, 221, 228, 232, 234, 251, 258, 263, 264, 269, 292, 308, 319, 327, 329, 342, 349, 352, 353
Justices of the peace
  external, xxxiii
    Bucks., 23, 70
    Chester (Chief Justice), 340
    Great Tew, 52
    Herefords., 125
    Kent, 58
    Notts., 13
    Oxford (Culpeper), 35
    Staffs., 104
    Westminster (Chief) Justice at King's Bench, 236, 287
  Woodstock, xv, xxxi, xxxii, xxxiv, xxxvii, *See* main text *passim*

keys, 55, 97, 166
killing of flesh. *See* Lent, flesh in
  cattle, 162
  deer, 160, 165
  sheep, 46
king's abode, 25
knights (and baronets), 208, 222, 236, 283, 287, 297, 340, 344

land claim, 178
land transfers. *See* conveyances (final concords)
land, common recovery. *See* actions (Portmoot)
lawn, xlvi, 98, 135
leases. *See* corporation land
leet court, xiii, xxxi, 8, 37, 95, 96, 337
  Cowley, 142
  presentments, xxxi, 9, 95
Lent, flesh in, xxxviii, 4, 47, 73, 93, 128, 312, 333, 358, 360

letters, xxxiv, xxxvi, 13, 59, 91, 125
letters, patent, 110, 244
levy, 108, 325
licensing
butchers, 48, 334, 359
goldsmith, Oxford, 25
marriage, xxxv, 12, 17
unlicensed selling, 25, 97
victualling, xxxvii, 10, 28, 48, 62, 84, 96, 114, 141, 182, 206, 218, 239, 249, 280, 300, 315, 316, 335, 340, 359
conditions of licence, 26, 339
discharge, xxxvii, 10, 62, 84, 97, 139
exemplary licence, xxxvii, 26, 339
fees and sureties, xxxvii, 10, 27
for poverty relief, 84
full record, 26
National covenant, xxxvii, 26
Privy Council Order, xxxvii
unlicensed victualling, 97
literacy, xvi, xxx, xxxi, 86
litigants (Portmoot), provenance of, xx
freemen, xx, 28, 29
non-freemen, xxi, 29, 30
outsiders ('others'), xxii, xxiv
loaves. *See* assize of bread and ale
lockram, xlvi, 133
lodging houses, 76, 105, 131, 147
Lord Chandos, xxvi, xxxv, 43, 321
Lords of the Council, 13
lovers and friends, 88

Magdalen Day fair, 55, 108, 114
magistrates. *See* Justices of the peace
maintenance order, child, xxxiv, 9, 58, 219, 270, 308, 328
malt
assize conditions, 34
holdings and usage in dearth, 38
prices, xxxix, *See* assize of bread and ale
malthouse, 95
market stalls, 96
markets. *See also* clerk of the market
others. *See* Alcester, Banbury, Bicester, Birmingham, Burford, Chipping Norton, Enstone, Evesham, Oxford, Shipston-on-Stour, Stratford-upon-Avon, Worcester
Woodstock, xxxii, xxxiv, xxxix, 59, 76, 98, 104, 130, 163, 166
marks (coinage), 2, 54, 86, 157, 186, 219, 347
marks on animals, 56, 71, 103, 162, 163
marriage, xxvi, xxxv, 12, 17, 28, 100, 122, 166, *and see* licensing
contract in, 92
maslin, 38
measures. *See* weights and measures
medley, xlvi, 70
mercer's shop, xxxiii, xxxiv, 97, 130
messengers, 13, 124
messuages, xxvi, xlvi, 1, 6, 7, 11, 14, 66, 86, 87, 89, 94, 97, 110, 115, 122, 124, 125, 143, 146, 150, 174, 178, 184, 191, 193, 198, 240, 243, 254, 264, 340, 342, 366
mezled ('mozled'), xlvi, 33
mills
Cutteslowe, 131
Hordley, 39
minister, of Bucks, 23
minors, xxix, 226, 286
misdemeanours, various, xxxii, *See* breach of peace
moneys, 23, 58, 103, 148, 323, 336, *see also* bonds, and *see under* theft
deposit, xxxvi, 104
notable sums in Portmoot actions, xxi, xxii, xxiii, 6, 18, 21, 36, 45, 54, 69, 72, 86, 101, 125, 129, 140, 146, 153, 157, 172, 186, 224, 346
mounds, xlvi, 10, 102, 123
musicians, 61, 120

neat, xlvi, 34
neglect of duty (borough officers), xxxiv, 58, 62, 92, 107, 187
new building, the (Woodstock), 100
noble (coinage), 108
oaths
examination under, xxxiv, 13, 23, 43, 70, 93, 100
freeman's, xvi, xxxix, 362
of allegiance, 82, 83
of mayoralty, xv, 35
of recusant, 203

oaths (cont.)
  of sergeant-at-mace, 295
  of sureties, 182
obligation (written), 217, 224, 227, 232, 246, 252, 259, 319
officers of borough and courts, xiv
  aldermen, xv, xvi, xix, *See* main text *passim*
  aletasters, xvi, 61, 196, 205, 291, 351, 367
  chamberlains, xvi, 6, 8, 12, 23, 25, 43, 67, 75, 97, 114, 182, 195, 210, 238, 316, 329, 351, 363, 364, 367
  clerk of the church, xvi, 35
  clerk of the court (Portmoot), xiv, xx, 90, 91
  clerk of the market. *See* assize of bread and ale
  constables, xvi, 9, 24, 35, 37, 58, 61, 71, 83, 107, 111, 119, 120, 139, 152, 156, 167, 196, 205, 230, 238, 241, 249, 280, 291, 300, 310, 316, 338, 351, 367, 371
    escape from, xxxiv, 58
    money and estreats, 37, 292
  coroner, xxxi, 142
  criers of the court, xvi, 35, 82, 302
  elections, xvi, *See* this main item *and* under various officers
  high steward, xv, 364
  Justices of the peace. *See* as main item
  mayor, xv, 363, 364, 367
    accosted, 13
    appointment/election, xvi, 3, 35, 82, 91, 152, 290, 367
    at assizes, xxxii, xxxix
    death in office, xvi, 3, 91
    oath of office, 35
  mayor and common council, 25
  mayor and commonalty, 125
    consent of, 95
    judgment by, 19, 191
  recorder, xv, 3, 158, 175, 191, 197, 201, 225, 340, 354, 355
    attendance, xv, 23, 41, 50, 54, 58, 84, 89, 91, 96, 116, 138, 139, 339, 340
    signature, 139, 339
  sergeant-at-mace, xvi, xxx, 152, *See* procedures (Portmoot), *passim*
    dereliction of duty, 92
  surveyors of the highways, xxxi, 95, 220
  tithingmen, xvi, xxxi, 37, 61, 83, 97, 99, 115, 156, 196, 205, 249, 280, 291, 307, 341, 351, 367
  town clerk, xiv, xviii, *passim*
    at assizes, xxxii
    salary, xv
  watchmen, xxxiv, 23, 93, 107, 147, 230
orchards, 122, 124, 243, 339
order(s)
  by recorder on arbitration, 96
  corporation, xvi, xxxi, 97, 138
Orders, Book of, xxxix
Osnaburg, xlvii, 132, 133
overplus, xlvii, 137
oyer of condition, xlvii, 345, 347

parchment, xiii, 264
Parliament, borough member, xv, xvi, 41
parson, of Wootton, 161
passport, xlvii, 43
pasture, 14, 110, 198, 240
patent, letters (for clerk of market), 15, 30, 110, 244
pawning, 148
pedlary ware, 166
per minas, xlvii, *See* actions (Portmoot), debt
piping (and dancing), xxxvii, 10
pistol, charged, 55
players, Lord Chandos, xxxv, 43
points ('poynts'), 130
ponit se super patriam, xlvii, *See* procedure (Portmoot): country, put oneself on, *See* procedure (Portmoot): country, put oneself on
poverty, victual licence relief, 84
preacher, 23
presentments (leet), xxxi, 9, 95, 96, 245, 345
priest, 17, 71
prison, xvi, xxxii, xxxiii, 2, 24, 25, 37, 95, 191, 222, 301, 316, 328, *See also* arrest *and* gaol
  on acquittal, 37, 268
privilege day, xvii, xlvii, *See* Portmoot *passim*

Privy Council, xxxvii, 26
procedendo, writ of. *See* procedures - writs
procedures (Frankpledge), xxxi
procedures (Portmoot), xviii
abandoned plaint, 80
abatement, plea in, 153
arbitration, xix, 88, 96, 114, 120, 129, 157, 168, 212, 214, 265, 296, 327, 349
order on, 96
arrest, custody (execution), 11, 21, 50, 67, 85, 140, 169
attachment, *capias*, arrest (summons), 2, 19, 35, 42, 67, 72, 82, 83, 86, 125, 140, 154, 160, 170, 199, 209, 223, 224, 230, 231, 232, 240, 248, 252, 254, 273, 281, 284, 287, 297, 325, 327, 329, 332, 350, 351
bail, delivered on, 84, 160
bar, 49
common law process, xviii
compounding, xxix, 67, 69, 201, 202, 203, 208, 211
concord (compromise), 79, 80, 186
continuances, xix
country, put oneself on the *(ponit se super patriam)*, xxx, xliv, 2, 40, 41, 42, 52, 56, 62, 64, 65, 68, 69, 76, 77, 79, 81, 85, 88, 94, 101, 106, 111, 116, 117, 121, 127, 139, 140, 148, 150, 152, 159, 173, 175, 177, 180, 183, 195, 196, 198, 203, 209, 215, 223, 230, 240, 247, 248, 249, 250, 251, 253, 261, 262, 263, 265, 272, 273, 275, 276, 279, 280, 281, 282, 284, 286, 287, 288, 291, 305, 307, 310, 318, 322, 324, 325, 336, 346, 351, *See also* trial by jury - below
custom of the borough, 150
defaults, xix, 5, 19, 24, 41, 65, 89, 101, 107, 112, 117, 123, 140, 151, 152, 154, 158, 160, 164, 167, 171, 172, 176, 177, 181, 208, 320, *See* below 'not respond'
demurrer, xliv, 42, 44, 80, 81, 85, 114, 166, 169, 171, 174, 194, 197, 253, 260, 261, 275, 276, 350, 356
denies the deed, 52, 65, 88, 112, 116
execution of actions, xix, xx
fiat executio, xlv, 68, 71, 72
file, cases remaining on, 9, 111, 115
foreign plea, xlv, 18, 50, 80, 169, 202, 213, 214, 234
ignorance of procedure, 81
imparlance, xix, 46, 57, 164, 174, 234, 345, 347
innocent of charge, 75
insufficient in law, 177, 251, 256, 277
judgments, xix, *passim*
jury calls. *See* juries, Portmoot *and* procedures 'country' *and* 'trial by jury'
manner and form (*modo et forma*), xlvi, 140, 150, 158, 175, 180, 207
nihil dicit, xlvi, 72, 85, 101, 152, 172, 186, 199, 201, 202, 241, 246, 286, 289, 292, 298, 299, 310, 317, 318
non assumpsit, xlvi, 42, 76, 140, 150, 180, 251, 282, 288, 304, 305, 324, 340, 352
non cul (not guilty), xlvi, 81, 111, 117, 140, 147, 154, 172, 175, 177, 203, 208, 215, 217, 222, 224, 226, 247, 248, 310, 322, 327, 345, 351
non debet, xlvi, 158, 173, 175, 207, 250, 251, 262, 265, 284, 286, 351, 361
non declaration, 112, 117
non est factum, xlvii, 65, 88, 112, 116, 151, 196, 208, 220
non informatus respondendi, xlvii, *See* attorneys, non instruction
non prosecution, 46, 89, 91, 101, 140, 149, 160, 181, 208, 226, 228, 244, 251, 253, 267, 272, 274, 287, 306, 320, 355
non retinuisset, xlvii, 272, 279
nonsuit, 91, 94, 160
not respond, 57, 80, 101, 107, 112, 123, 151, 152, 153, 154, 158, 164, 167, 170, 171, 172, 173, 176, 177, 182, 189, 201, 203, 208, 223, 228, 229, 233, 236, 237, 240, 246, 247, 250, 252, 257, 262, 266, 267, 269, 281, 286, 287, 288, 289, 290, 292, 293, 294, 298, 299, 310, 314, 317, 319, 320, 321, 352

plea for mercy, 105
pleading, xviii
quit, defendant goes, 4, 18, 25, 42, 49, 74, 86, 140, 167, 170, 183, 190, 201, 204, 211, 213, 220, 222, 223, 224, 227, 233, 234, 235, 236, 239, 246, 247, 255, 257, 260, 267, 273, 274, 280, 284, 357
read, hear and understand, 177
rebuttal, 325
recovery, illegal ('rescue'), xlviii, 125
rejoinder, xlviii, 22, 77, 85, 194, 276, 311, 324, 350
release, xlviii, 49, 68, 88, 149
replication, xlviii, 41, 76, 78, 85, 106, 116, 117, 118, 120, 152, 190, 194, 197, 200, 209, 217, 221, 223, 228, 230, 240, 247, 249, 250, 253, 260, 261, 262, 265, 273, 276, 277, 281, 284, 286, 287, 291, 305, 307, 311, 318, 323
rescue, xlviii, 125
retraction, 327
silentia (silence), 57
special title to, 89
special verdict, xlix, 105, 115, 183
surname unknown, 153
surrejoinder (?), 85
three summonses, 1, 5, 15, 22, 53, 57, 60, 63, 65, 68, 69, 70, 72, 85, 90, 101, 112, 171, 173, 176, 177, 180, 243, 244, 251, 284, 291, 310, 321, 340, 347, 354
trial by jury, xix, xxix, *See* above 'country' *and* juries, Portmoot
trial by wager of law, xxix, xlix, 46, 73, 126, 127, 139, 165, 168, 170, 178, 210, 211, 213, 217, 233, 254, 266, 279, 283, 291, 343, 348
umpirage, 129, 162, *See also* above 'arbitration'
  judgment of mayor and clerk of court, 162
Writs of
  capias, xliii, 150
  certiorari, xxv, xliii, 157, 256, 361
  corpus cum causa, xxiii, xliv, 68, 281
  error, xxiii, xliv, 18, 108, 116, 147
  execution (royal), xliv, 19, 91
  fieri facias, xlv, 18, 177, 179, 249, 325
  habeas corpora (juratorum), xlv, *see* juries, Portmoot, passim
  habeas corpus, xlv, passim
    removal to central courts, xxiii, 196, 197, 222, 236, 247, 250, 266, 272, 305, 344, 348, 355, *and see* courts, Westminster
  habere facias seisinam, xlv, 2, 14, 123
  inquiry, xlvi, 56, 73, 78, 80, 106, 107, 116, 123, 146, 152, 158, 164, 171, 176, 188, 199, 201, 211, 215, 223, 224, 226, 240, 248, 250, 266, 267, 281, 289, 293, 313, 332, 340, 341
  privilege, xxv, xlvii, 60, 107, 250, 267, 287, 294, 295, 311, 335, 344
  procedendo, xlvii, 3, 124, 276, 354
  scire facias, xix, xlviii, 1, 4, 6, 15, 18, 21, 28, 44, 46, 49, 54, 57, 65, 66, 67, 68, 72, 73, 78, 90, 92, 113, 117, 121, 146, 151, 153, 154, 159, 160, 163, 164, 167, 172, 173, 179, 181, 184, 185, B78/3 *passim*
  venire facias, xlix, *passim - see* juries, Portmoot
procedures (Sessions of the Peace), xxxii
proclamation
  discharge of prisoners by, 16
proclamation by King, xxxviii, 300, 312, 315, 333, 358, 360
proclamation(s). *See* conveyances
prosecution of crime, xxxiii, *passim* B78/2
provenance of Portmoot litigants, xxii, *See* litigants (Portmoot)
prunes, 134
punishments
  capital, xxxii, xxxiii, 56
  confiscation of property or money, xxxiv, 6, 8, 12, 58, 71, 119, 156, 163, 167

fines, xxxiv, 6, 9, 22, 37, 93, 99, 101, 114, 142, 182, 191, 207, 239, 295, 314, 316, 333, 338
prison, xvi, xxxii, 24, 37, 43, 95, 191, 268, 316, 328, 348, 351, *See* arrest, criminal
stocks, xxxiv, 23, 100, 107
whipping, xxxiv, 24, 100, 101, 134, 152
putgally, xlvii, 138

Qui Tam, xviii, xxviii, xlviii, *See* actions, Portmoot
quorum, for court of record, xv

racking, xlviii, 24, 71
railing words, 191, 303, 338
rash, xlviii, 43
recognisance. *See* B78/2 *passim*
essoins, 239
for Lent, 334, 358
for non-appearance, 206, 218, 230, 239, 308, 314, 328
to keep peace, 199, 206, 207, 213, 233, 248
victuallers, 339
recusant, 203
rejoinder. *See* procedures (Portmoot)
release. *See* procedures (Portmoot)
rentals (corporation), xl, 25, 102, 138
replication. *See* procedures (Portmoot)
rescue. *See* procedures (Portmoot)
rings, 13, 28, 98
rogues, xlviii, 43, 58, 191, *See also* vagrants

safeguard, xlviii, 13
say, xlviii, 131, 137
scholars of Oxford, xxv, 142, 150
schoolmaster, xvi, 35, *See* Simon James (Jeames)
scire facias. *See* procedures (Portmoot) - writs
scorce, xlix, 16, *See* horse-scorcers
score (paces), 142
scotch hallan, 119
seals
alehouse licences, 28
half-, of Oxford University, xxv, 150
of a bond, 148
of measures, 32, 33, 34, 35, 64, 110, 245
of sheriff of County Oxon', 125
seisin, 1, 14, 123, 198
sergeant-at-mace, xvi, xxix, xxx, xxxiv, *See* **officers** of borough and courts *and* Henry and Edmund Rudgate - Portmoot *passim*
death, 277
election, 277
seizure of livestock, 56, 215, 265, 289, 297, 320, 322, 325
wounded, 187, 295
sessions court (Woodstock), xxxii, 8, 36, 50, 62, 74, 83, 95, 113, 141, 156, 168, 182, 183, 195, 205, 218, 229, 238, 248, 259, 270, 279, 291, 300, 307, 314, 337, 339, 350
adjourned, 183, 300, 338
cancelled, 339
settlement deed, xlix, 86
settlement of theft case, 101
sheep
-dealing, xxxvi, 12, 46, 59, 100, 103
-droving, xxxvi, 103
stealing. *See* thefts
sheriff, seal of, xxiii, 125
shop board, xlix, 131
shops, xxxiii, 122, 130, 187, 338
sickness, 173, 333
signatures, xiv, xvi, xxx, 55, 59, 134, 135, 143, 145, 187, 191, 192, 212, 219, 220, 241, 246, 268, 270, 271, 275, 282, 292, 297, 299, 301, 302, 304, 307, 308, 309, 310, 317, 333, 338, 339, 340, 341, 346, *and see* main texts, conveyances
silver plate, 345
sister-in-law (step-sister), 119
skittles, 138
skiving, xlix, 187
slander, xxxiv, 49
sow, 101
stables, 24, 99, 123
stalls, market, 96
startups (boots), 33
stint, 187
stone (stallion), 12, 108

stone (weights), xxxviii, 31, 64, 110, 346
supervisors, 280, 300, 370
surcingle, 71
surgeon, 103, 156, *See* trades and occupations
survey of grain dearth, xxviii, xxxix, 38
suture, 98
sweet powder, 98

tallet, xlix, 97
tallow, assize, xxxviii, 31, 33, 64, 346
tammy, xlix, 135
tanning, assize regulations, 33
tasters. *See* **officers** of borough - aletasters
tenements. *See* messuages
thefts
- cabbage plants, 76
- canvas, 134
- cattle, xxxiii, 72, 162
- cloak, xxxvi, 24, 37, 43, 70
- cloth and clothing, xxxiii, 7, 8, 13, 24, 43, 55, 58, 70, 71, 97, 111, 118, 130, 135, 152
- cut-purse, xxxv, 12, 13
- deer, xxxiii, xxxvi, 160, 165
- display of stolen goods, 100
- flaying sheep, 47
- food, 137
- fruit, 134
- hay, 12, 136, 137
- hooking, xxxvi, xlv, 70
- horses, xxxiii, xxxv, xxxvi, 12, 16, 24, 55, 58, 71, 130, 148, 163, 310
  - -gear, 13, 17, 55, 58, 71, 111
  - theft tools, xxxvi, 55
- kettle, 118
- lace, xxxiii, xxxiv, 130, 135, 137, 148
- meal and flour, 138
- money, xxxiii, 7, 13, 43, 98, 105, 118, 130, 138, 166, 187
- oats, 136
- picklock keys, 55
- pickpocket, 166
- purses, xxxv, 98, 166
- ribanding, xlviii, 130
- sheep, xxxiii, 59, 125, 163
- sheepskins, xxxvi, 46
- silk, 55, 130
- smallwares, 100
- wood and thorns, 93

Theology, Dr.of, 235
theve, xlix, 59, 104
third holding (widow's dower), xxvii, 94, 122, 123
thirdendall, xlix, 31, 32, 141
thirteen-and-a-half pence piece (?), 166
threat of
- arson, 241, 332
- bodily harm, 241
- death, 207, 241, 304, 317, 338

threat, bond made under (*per minas*), xlvii, 159
threatening words, 14, 25, 120, 147, 187, 241, 303, 304, 317, 332, 338
three summons. *See* procedures (Portmoot)
tippling house, 339, *See* alehouse/ victuallers
tithingmen. *See* officers of borough and courts
tokens of love, 98, 99
toll dish, 33, 245
toll-book, 14, 55, 71, 104, 148
- non-use *passim* in horse, sheep and cattle dealing, 12

town clerk, xiv, *See* officers of borough and courts
- office, 92, 123

trades and occupations
- alehouse-keeper, xxxvii, xxxviii, 26, 27, 76, 106, 138, *See also* victualler
  - of Deddington, 119
  - of Great Tew, 54
  - of Offenham, xxxv, 16
  - of Sandford (St.Martin), 55, 76
  - of Smithfield, London, 54
  - of St.Thomas, Oxford, 13
  - unlicensed, 96
- aqua-vitae man, 76
- baker, xxxi, xxxix, 10, 15, 31, 34, 38, 63, 70, 98, 137, 163, 259, 271, 309
  - 'foreign' bakers, 32
  - of Cheltenham, 10
  - of Eynsham, xxiii, 99
- barber (chirurgion)
  - of London, 307

trades and occupations (cont.)
barber, 130, 255
bottle maker, of Bicester, 99
brazier, of Bicester, 118
brewer, xxxix, 15, 31, 33, 138, *See also* assize of ale
at dearth, xxxix, 38
butcher, xxi, xxxi, xxxviii, 5, 31, 33, 48, 121, 307, 317, 333, 334, 335, 346, 348, 358
of Deddington, xxii, xxvi, xxxvi, 162
of Enstone, 17
of Great Tew, 17
of Kirtlington, 111
of Much Marcle, Herefs., 124
of Oxford, 317
of Winchcombe, Glos., 54
cadman, 137
carpenter, 5, 92, 178
carrier
of Bicester, 24
of Clifford, Leics., 13
of Deddington, 163
of York, 13
carter, 12
chandler, xliii, 33, 64, 282, 346
of London, 22
chapman, 22, 71, 74, 75, 166
of London, 22
clothier
of Witney, 24
cloth-trader
of London, 22
corn-buyer
of Herefs., 124
currier, 33, 42, 188, 241
cutler, 70, 93, 112, 137
of Sheffield, 71
draper, 97
embroiderer
Westminster, 54
farrier, 352
gardener
of Kent, 58
glover, xxi, xxxvi, 12, 46, 47, 94, 112
of Bicester, 24
of London, 12, 282
of Oxford, 47
goldsmith, 25
groom, 24
horse-scorcer, xlv
of Herts., xxxvi, 129
of Kent, 12, 13
of Notts., 12
innholder, xxxii, xxxvii, xxxix, 10, 12, 33, 37, 48, 62, 96, 114, 120, 141, 182, 196, 205, 218, 334, 358
ironmonger, 264
of Deddington, 87
joiner, xxxi, 269, 330
of Evesham, 16
labourer, 23, 59
of Leafield, 59
of Notts., 14
of Oxford, 43
of Standlake, 46
of Warks., 59
of Worcs., 118
mercer, xvi, xxxiii, xxxiv, 61, 97, 130, 285
of Oxford, 188
of Tanworth, Warks., 55
of Towcester, Northants., 43
miller, 33, 166, 245
of Cutteslowe, 131
of Hordley, 39
of Northleigh, 166
musician, 120
of Oxford, 61
ostler, 33, 131
of Banbury, 22
of the Strand, London, 148
park-keeper, 93, 137, 160, 165, 179
pedlar, 166
of Warks., 71
players, Lord Chandos, xxxv, 43
porter, king's, 25
saddler, of Oxford, 25
sawyer, 134
of Ludlow, 43
of St.Giles, London, 152
scrivener, 12
servant, 7, 10, 16, 22, 24, 37, 43, 59, 93, 97, 98, 99, 101, 105, 131, 132, 133, 135, 137, 149, 152, 160, 165, 230, 358

trades and occupations (cont.)
sheep-dealer, of Staffs., xxxvi, 103
shepherd, 100, 136, 137
of Thrupp, 12
shoemaker, xxxi, 10, 11, 24, 25, 33, 37, 105, 107, 121, 157, 159, 207
assize regulations, 33
of Deddington, 118
of Leics., 105
shopkeeper, 130, 187
sieve-maker ('sivier'), 28
silk-weaver, 43
slater, 220, 308, 312, 315, 316
smith, xxxi, 55, 112, 352
of Bletchingdon, 187
of Ledwell, 54, 56
surgeon, 103, 156, 307
tailor, xxxi, 43, 81, 98, 103, 130, 131, 135, 136, 259, 275, 283, 294, 299, 304, 315
of Salop., 166
tallow chandler, of London, 22
tanner, 33
of Bicester, 285
of Glos., 16
of Kent, 58
taverner, 358, See also innholders in main index
traveller, 8
upholsterer
of Dunstable, Beds., 71
of Farthinghoe, 118
victualler, xxxvii, xxxix, 10, 27, 28, 33, 48, 62, 84, 96, 105, 107, 114, 139, 141, 182, 196, 206, 218, 239, 249, 280, 300, 315, 334, 346, 358
of Helmdon, 43
of Moreton-in-Marsh, 104
of Much Marcle, Herefs., 124
of Warks., 103
vintners, 334, 359
of Westminster, 178, 179
weaver, xxvii, 5, 302, 315
woolman, 7, 39, 239, 275, 304, 341
woolwinder, 107, 219
trades, statutes controlling, xxxvii, xxxix, 31
travellers, xxii, xxxv, *See* B78/2 *passim*
tree preservation, 102
twelve-tide, 336

umpirage, 129, 162, *See also* procedures (Portmoot) - arbitration
unlawful games, 26, 339
unlicensed selling, 25
unlicensed victualling, 97, 316

vagrants, xxxv, 152, *See also* rogues
venire facias, xlix, *See* procedures, writs
verbal abuse, 120, 147, 172, *See also* slander
victualling. *See* trades, victuallers *and* licensing, victualling *and* assize of bread and ale
assize regulations, 31, 32, 34
at Sandford, 55
conditions in borough, 138
of Great Tew, 54
of Hook Norton, 104
signpost, 139
view (inspection by jury), 10, 95
vouchers (common recovery), 1, 14, 55, 110, 181, 197

wager of law, xxix, *See* procedures (Portmoot) - trial by wager of law
wake day (Combe), 316
walls, building, 95
walnut acres, 188
warrant of County Oxon', 125
waste, l, *See* actions (Portmoot)
watchmen, xxxiv, 23, 93, 107, 147, 230
water (river) flow, 95
weapons, xxxiv, xxxvi
bill (watchman's), 23
bodkin, 55
broadsword, 55
dagger, forfeited, xxxiv, 156
dagger-strike, 5, 99, 108, 156
knife, 187
pistol, charged, 55
rapier, 178
sanguined, 148
rule, 178
staff, 143
stone-pots, 26, 107
swords, 12, 55, 58, 108, 120

weights and measures, xxxviii, 31, 32, 33, 34, 64, 110, 245
wheat prices, xxxix, *See* assize of bread and ale *and* grain
whipping. *See* punishments
widows, xxi, xxiii, xxvii, 4, 6, 7, 14, 16, 20, 28, 29, 30, 38, 42, 51, 52, 64, 66, 72, 86, 92, 93, 94, 97, 98, 99, 106, 108, 124, 126, 131, 136, 149, 155, 157, 166, 172, 173, 176, 182, 196, 199, 204, 206, 210, 217, 218, 224, 239, 241, 254, 260, 264, 265, 273, 287, 292, 297, 298, 300, 303, 310, 314, 315, 316, 320, 321, 323, 330, 331, 336, 338, 339, 341, 342, 350
  in conveyances, xxvii, 97, 174, 184, 191, 254
wife's property, xxvi, 86, 87
wills and testaments, 2, 21, 52, 94, 106, 108, 125, 146, 173, 227, 232, 241, 285, 341, 349
witchcraft, xxxii, 173
woodlands, 1, 14, 110
wool and yarn, 80, 89
writs. *See* procedures (Portmoot)
wrought, 'wrote' (worked), l, 47, 99, 124, 137
yards (fields), 25
yeomen
  of Bicester, 24
  of Cassington, 47
  of Charlton-on-Otmoor, 127
  of Clandon, Surrey, 111
  of Eynsham, 103
  of Fencott, 127
  of Great Tew, 52
  of Hanborough, 60
  of Hensington, 220
  of Inkberrow, Worcs., 108
  of Leafield, xxii, 200
  of Leics., 147
  of Littlemore, 142, 143
  of Merton, 188
  of Milton, Oxon., 271
  of Murcott, 127
  of Newent, Glos., 308
  of Oddington, 155
  of Severn Stoke, Worcs., 145
  of Steeple Aston, 330
  of Weston-on-the-Green, 146
  of Woodstock, 219
  of Woodstock park, 230
  of Wookey, Somerset, 8
  of Wootton, 24, 283